ESTABLISHING JUSTICE
IN MIDDLE AMERICA

ESTABLISHING JUSTICE

IN MIDDLE AMERICA

*A History of
the United States Court of Appeals
for the Eighth Circuit*

JEFFREY BRANDON MORRIS

FOREWORD BY WILLIAM H. WEBSTER

PUBLISHED FOR THE HISTORICAL SOCIETY OF
THE UNITED STATES COURTS IN THE EIGHTH CIRCUIT

University of Minnesota Press
Minneapolis
London

Published by the University of Minnesota Press
111 Third Avenue South, Suite 290
Minneapolis, MN 55401-2520
http://www.upress.umn.edu

LIBRARY OF CONGRESS CATALOGING-IN-PUBLICATION DATA

Morris, Jeffrey Brandon, 1941–
    Establishing justice in Middle America : a history of the United States
Court of Appeals for the Eighth Circuit / Jeffrey Brandon Morris.
        p.   cm.
    "Published for the Historical Society of the United States Courts
in the Eighth Circuit."
    Includes bibliographical references and index.
    ISBN: 978-0-8166-4816-0 (hc : alk. paper)
    ISBN-10: 0-8166-4816-6 (hc : alk. paper)
    1. United States. Court of Appeals (8th Circuit)-History. I. Title.
    KF87528th .M67 2007
    347.73'2409-dc22

                                                          2007023934

Printed in the United States of America on acid-free paper

The University of Minnesota is an equal-opportunity educator and employer.

15 14 13 12 11 10 09 08 07   10 9 8 7 6 5 4 3 2 1

CONTENTS

* * * * * * *

William H. Webster

Much has been written about the history and workings of the U.S. Supreme Court and the justices who have served there. It may come as a surprise to some that in the exercise of its certiorari powers, the Supreme Court annually hears less than 2 percent of the appeals from the cases decided in the circuit courts of this country. Thus, in a real sense, these thirteen circuits are the courts of last resort for some 98 percent of the cases in the federal system.

Yet, outside the legal profession, relatively little is known of our circuit courts, how they are composed, how cases are decided, and their impressive history. One is more apt to read in the press or hear in the media that "a federal appeals court sitting in St. Louis has held that . . ." Very little information that might enlighten the general public is included about the diverse backgrounds of the judges or the history of the circuits.

This is, I might add, how most circuit judges like it. They work in their individual chambers throughout the circuit and collectively, when cases are argued before them, and communicate with each other by today's most modern means. Their opinions are signed and published, as in the Supreme Court, but with far greater anonymity and much more media focus on the outcome rather than the author.

In this history of the Eighth Circuit Court, professor Jeffrey Brandon Morris has undertaken to record how federal justice came to Middle America, tracing its development from the earliest days following the Louisiana Purchase and the pathway to the West set by Meriwether Lewis and William Clark, who started their long journey at St. Louis on May 14, 1804. It is a fascinating story and deserves to be told.

In its earliest stages, the Eighth Circuit covered approximately one-third of continental America—a gigantic territory. As trial courts were established in various parts of this "empire," a series of arrangements for hearing appeals was established. Justices of the Supreme Court were detailed to hear appeals in each circuit with the participation of district judges from the circuit. Traveling from place to place by horseback, trains, and riverboats, these forerunners of the modern judicial system covered thousands of miles each year on circuit. The cases were fewer than those heard today, but the distances were larger. These justices and judges must have come from hardy stock.

By 1929, the westernmost states had gravitated into what is now the Tenth Circuit, and the states east of the Mississippi River had been added to the Seventh Circuit. What remained—seven states in all—was still a vast and diverse area stretching from North Dakota, at the Canadian border, to Arkansas in the Deep South. Its judges were selected by the president from states within the circuit. As the workload increased, additional judges were added. When I joined the Eighth Circuit in 1973, there were eight active judges and three senior judges; today there are eleven active judges and ten senior judges. They bring a rich mixture of cultural, educational, and legal backgrounds to the work of the court.

Today the Eighth Circuit courtrooms, chambers, and administrative offices occupy the top floors of the Thomas Eagleton Federal Courthouse in St. Louis, Missouri, the largest federal courthouse in the United States. My chambers were in the old federal courthouse, across the street from the new Thomas Eagleton building. The old courthouse was built in the 1930s following many years during which the court had been housed in the old federal post office building. It was rugged and handsome, in the art deco style, with benches and counsel tables designed to reflect the same architecture. I had served in that building from 1960 to 1961 as U.S. Attorney and from 1971 to 1973 as judge of the U.S. District Court for the Eastern District of Missouri. I continued on as circuit judge until 1978, when I was appointed director of the Federal Bureau of Investigation and moved to Washington, D.C.

I recall attending my first judicial conference of the Eighth Circuit in 1960. Before that time, only judges were invited, and this time the conference was opened to U.S. Attorneys in the circuit (who were allowed to sit around the walls of the conference room, but not to talk). Today members of the bar are invited and participate in meaningful ways.

In 1970 I was approached by Chief Judge Marion C. Matthes, who expressed his concern that young people were losing confidence in our justice system; some had taken to the streets and burned ROTC buildings. He urged me to think about a career on the bench, and I did. Those were great years for me.

For the bicentennial celebration in 1976, we sat in many places outside the normal St. Louis–St. Paul axis. We sat in courtrooms in Des Moines, Kansas City, Little Rock, and at the University of South Dakota. But the most memorable session for me was the session in the "Old Courthouse" in St. Louis (now a museum) in the room where the Dred Scott case was heard so long ago. A seal of the Eighth Circuit was commissioned that showed the states in the circuit sheltered under an eagle's wing. A copy of the seal has hung in my office for almost three decades.

Some of my warmest memories involve the judges whom I knew and with whom I served on the Eighth Circuit. When I was U.S. Attorney, the Chief Judge was Harvey M. Johnsen, a wise and well-organized bachelor who reserved Saturdays for vacuum cleaning and dusting. Just as I was a new U.S. Attorney, the newest circuit judge was Harry Blackmun. He and Dottie were very solicitous of me and became warm friends for the next four decades. My mentor was Chief Judge Marion C. Matthes, better known to his friends as Charlie. He was an experienced jurist and a wise and kindly man. I went to the Eighth Circuit when Judge Matthes took senior status, and it was largely due to his encouragement that I reluctantly agreed to leave the court five years later to take on the responsibilities of director of the Federal Bureau of Investigation. Judge Donald Ross, a hero of World War II, likewise encouraged me. Judge Roy Stephenson, another war hero, was a friend from U.S. Attorney days who moved up the ranks in Iowa to district judge and then to the circuit. He was a strong and stable force on the court, and I deeply regret his tragic end.

Chief Judge J. Pat Mchaffy, who swore me in, had been Chief Judge only a year but brought a unique understanding of the workings of government. Chief Judge Floyd Gibson, a fellow Missourian, had a fine judicial temperament that made him an able leader. Besides, we were both fellow farmers on the side. Judge Myron Bright and I had some tough cases together, including the famous Reserve Mining case. His unfailing good humor, whether on the bench or on the tennis court, always brought us through.

I had watched Judge Smith Henley, from Arkansas, as a masterful district judge, and it was a pleasure to serve with him on the Court of Appeals. Judge Donald Lay, from Nebraska, who had had a brilliant career as a trial lawyer, joined the court quite young in 1966 and later served as Chief Judge for more than twelve years. He continued to serve as a senior judge along with my former colleagues Judge Bright and, until their recent retirements, Judges Ross and Heaney. Both Judges Ross and Heaney had been leaders in their respective political parties before "taking the veil," and both cheered from the sidelines with great good humor. Judge Bright continued to teach courses on trial procedure and evidence at St. Louis University, and Judge Heaney recently took time to chronicle the desegregation disputes in the St. Louis school district in a compelling book, *Unending Struggle: The Long Road to an Equal Education in St. Louis.*

I had the pleasure of sitting with two other senior judges, former Chief Judge Charles J. Vogel and former Chief Judge Martin D. Van Oosterhout. Judge Vogel was always gracious, even when we disagreed. Judge Van Oosterhout, who looked like one of the Dutch masters on the famous cigar box, handled reversal by the Supreme Court with much greater equanimity than some of us who were more restive in reversal. We were also fortunate to have the services of retired Supreme Court Justice Tom Clark from time to time, and it was refreshing and enlightening to have judges from the district courts of our circuit participate (as I once did) as members of the panel.

It has been my privilege to know all of the Supreme Court justices for the past thirty years. They were, and are, great justices and warm human beings. Equally so are the judges who have served on our outstanding Eighth Circuit and with whom I was honored to serve and share a common dedication to the cause of justice.

This is a history of the U.S. Court of Appeals for the Eighth Circuit that begins with the earliest federal court in one of the states of the circuit and continues until the end of 2001. As with my histories of the federal courts of the Second and District of Columbia Circuits, this book attempts to cover all important facets of the court—the judges who have served, its major decisions, and the administration of the court—while placing the court within the history of the region and nation. Such histories of courts other than the Supreme Court of the United States are few in number, but the price paid is that no one judge, decision, or administrative development can be treated exhaustively.

Because of the emphasis that scholars and other observers have placed on the Supreme Court, a national court specializing in constitutional law and in the interpretation of federal statutes, the significance of the important roles performed by the tier of courts just beneath it has largely been overlooked. These roles run from simply adjudicating disputes, acting as a buffer between the federal district courts and the Supreme Court so that it will not be overwhelmed with cases, to supervising the federal district courts as well as acting as a balance wheel in the federal system, both enforcing centralizing national policies and acting as a brake on centralizing tendencies by reflecting the concerns of states and localities.

This book describes and analyzes the ways that the Court of Appeals for the Eighth Circuit has made itself useful in the growth of the Midwest, by settling disputes over land, facilitating the growth of the region's infrastructure, helping to unleash the creative energies of a market economy, deciding cases spurred by attempts to have and regulate development, as well as by maintaining an atmosphere of constitutionalism, permitting the United States to make the transition from a decentralized to a centralized nation and from a relatively laissez-faire nation to a welfare state.

The reader will see how the circuit's two great rivers, its rich farmland and valuable resources—its forests and minerals—as well as the different cultures of its states have affected not only its economic development but also the work of its federal courts. The work of the circuit's courts has also been impacted by changes in transportation, communications, and production, as well as by political change.

The major geophysical characteristics of the Eighth Circuit at the time it was settled by people of European descent are described in the Introduction. Chapter 1 is devoted to the work of the federal courts before the creation of the U.S. Court of Appeals for the Eighth Circuit in 1891. Federal courts embodied the mixture of centralization, regionalism, state centeredness, and localism that characterizes the American federal system. In the period before 1891, the federal courts were primarily centralizers enforcing federal laws and Supreme Court decisions. Where Native Americans were concerned, the courts demonstrated, at least periodically, more sensitivity to the rights of the indigenous peoples than did most other governmental offices. The most politically sensitive cases of the period, however, involved enforcing bond liabilities of municipalities (especially in Iowa), as well as enforcing constitutional barriers to local expenditure of tax monies to attract and assist businesses. Cases involving the regulation of railroads and grain storage facilities attracted national attention.

During the period covered by chapter 2—from the creation of the Court of Appeals in 1891 to the division of the Eighth Circuit in 1929—the major function expected of the court was to divert the stream of federal appeals away from the Supreme Court. Successful in that task, the Court of Appeals for the Eighth Circuit also dealt with important public policy cases in the areas of antitrust, railroad rate regulation, labor-management conflicts, and the "radical" program of the Nonpartisan League. The Court of Appeals also dealt with perennial staples of federal law—patent and trademark, taxation, and federal criminal law, including prosecutions for political corruption. The court strongly supported antitrust prosecutions, restrained state regulation of railroads, supported the federal policy of assimilation of Native Americans, and, during World War I, was unusually sensitive to individual rights.

During the years covered by chapter 3 (1919–1959), the United States was transformed into a centralized welfare state and superpower. During this period, the lower federal courts including the Eighth Circuit increasingly applied centralizing policies generated by laws passed by Congress and Supreme Court decisions. The Court of Appeals contributed to the growing centralization by oversight of federal administrative agencies and the federal system of revenue collection, as well as a greater number of prosecutions for violating an increasing number of federal criminal laws. But at the same time that the court was overseeing the powers wielded by the federal government during the Great Depression and World War II, it dealt with distinctive regional problems and issues, including litigation connected with Mississippi River flood control projects and cases involving farming and Native Americans.

Chapter 4 portrays the Eighth Circuit between 1956 and 1969, when federal judges were asked with increasing frequency to wield judicial power to redress inequality in American society. The Court of Appeals handled explosive school desegregation cases and highly controversial cases involving legislative redistricting, the rights of criminal defendants, and the First Amendment. But if the court staunchly followed the nationalizing decisions of the Supreme Court in civil rights cases, in reapportionment cases the judges sitting on three-judge district courts were sensitive to local interests and political realities. During this period, the Court of Appeals moved from a court slightly to the right of center to one that could be described as moderately progressive.

During the 1970s, the period covered in chapter 5, the court confronted a docket shaped in many ways by the activism of the Supreme Court and Congress between 1961 and 1973 with a membership more committed to actively protecting individual liberty than it had been in the past. Not only did the court continue as a strong friend to civil rights, but it was particularly sympathetic to gender discrimination claims and cases involving the rights of students, and it supported the judicial supervision of the Arkansas prison system. Also during this period the court began to hear cases involving statutes (often from Minnesota or Missouri) restricting abortion. Throughout the 1970s, the cases that gave a regional flavor to the docket involved the environment and Native American militancy, the most visible cases of which derived from a violent confrontation between the American Indian Movement (AIM) and the FBI at the site of the 1891 Wounded Knee massacre.

The most significant characteristic of the work of the Court of Appeals during the 1980s, the period covered by chapter 6, was the strong intellectual differences between judges newly appointed by President Ronald Reagan and the more senior judges. These differences were evidenced by the number of en banc proceedings overturning decisions made by panels of the court, as well as the large number of dissents from the denial of rehearing en banc. The docket of the court continued to include a large number of value-laden cases in areas such as abortion and school desegregation (including major cases from St. Louis and Kansas City). For the first time in the court's history, it heard a considerable number of church-state cases. There were also a number of difficult cases involving bankruptcy, capital punishment, and federalism. Regional cases of note involved farm bankruptcies, Native Americans, and water diversion and irrigation projects.

The final chapter covers the last years of the twentieth century and the first year of the new century. The court continued to face important abortion, capital, desegregation, and Native American cases, although litigation involving President Bill Clinton had the greatest visibility. There were also important criminal cases involving drugs, sentencings, political corruption, and capital punishment. In cases involving preemption of state law by federal legislation and the Dormant Commerce Clause, the Court of Appeals continued to take positions that supported federal authority and opposed state parochialism. It also heard a rich variety of cases involving the environment. As it had been throughout its history, the Court of Appeals was rightfully obedient to the Supreme Court, remained sensitive to the norm of collegiality, and maintained high professional standards.

One of my major reasons for undertaking the history of the U.S. Court of Appeals for the Eighth Circuit was that it offered the opportunity to study a court whose jurisdiction encompassed a very different part of the United States from the courts I had previously written of, which were in the Second and District of Columbia Circuits. Beyond that, it offered the opportunity to become acquainted with a region I had not known save for its two largest cities. Two extended trips west permitted me to visit six of the Eighth Circuit's seven states. It was a privilege to travel the length of Nebraska, to canoe in the Boundary Waters Canoe Area Wilderness, to visit the richly wooded hills of Eastern Iowa, to work within sight of the Gateway Arch, and to see North Dakota's Red River Valley. Wherever possible, I stopped to visit or at least see the sites of notable Eighth Circuit cases, from the (now abandoned) plant of Reserve

Mining on the shore of Lake Superior, to South Dakota's Oahe Dam, to Samuel Freeman Miller's home in Keokuk, Iowa.

The major purpose of these trips was to interview the judges of the Court of Appeals, and I was able to speak with fifteen members of the court: Richard S. Arnold, C. Arlen Beam, Pasco Bowman, Myron H. Bright, George G. Fagg, David R. Hansen, Gerald W. Heaney, John D. Kelly, Donald P. Lay, James B. Loken, Frank J. Magill, Michael J. Melloy, William J. Riley, Donald R. Ross, and Roger L. Wollman. I spoke with all but two in their home chambers. Each was generous with his time, and each was forthcoming. I was unable to speak with one member of the court whom I tried to see during my trips but we faced unavoidable scheduling conflicts. I had hoped to see the remaining judges on a third trip but was unable to make that trip.

On my travels I also spoke with several district judges: Bruce Van Sickle of the District of North Dakota, John B. Jones of the District of South Dakota, Warren Urbom of the District of Nebraska, Edward J. McManus of the Northern District of Iowa, and Ronald E. Longstaff of the Southern District of Iowa, as well as Magistrate Judge Richard W. Peterson of the Southern District of Iowa, author of works on the district courts of Iowa. I was also able to speak with Ardell Tharaldson, author of a book on the history of the District of North Dakota; Peggy Tesla, author of a book on South Dakota district judges; Professor John Wunder, who is working on a history of the District Court for the District of Nebraska; and Professors R. Alton Lee and Robert Vogel, who are both very knowledgeable on aspects of the work of the federal courts in the Eighth Circuit. June L. Boadwine, former circuit executive of the Eighth Circuit, not only submitted to an interview but offered materials and guidance. To all of my interviewees, my deep appreciation for the time you gave me, and for your hospitality and information.

I also acknowledge with appreciation the assistance of Millie Adams, circuit executive for the Eighth Circuit, and her office; Beth M. Mobley, associate director of the Touro Law School library; and Roger K. Newman, a distinguished scholar, who for thirty years has generously shared with me findings from his indefatigable digging in archives and interviews.

A special acknowledgment should be made to the late Gerald T. Dunne, an important scholar, who was the original and admirable choice to write this history. When his health made it impossible for him to continue, he shared his materials and great good spirits and stories with me.

It is a particular honor to have the Foreword to this book written by one of the most distinguished public servants of my lifetime, William Webster, former director of both the FBI and the CIA as well as U.S. Attorney, district judge, and judge of the U.S. Court of Appeals for the Eighth Circuit.

Judges Pasco Bowman and Morris S. Arnold of the Court of Appeals supported this project in a variety of ways for which I am very grateful.

In this lengthy undertaking, I was blessed by the oversight of Judge Gerald W. Heaney of the Court of Appeals and Thomas H. Boyd, former president of the Historical Society of the United States Courts in the Eighth Circuit, both of whom are published legal scholars in their own right. Judge Heaney could not have done anything more to make this history a reality. One of the joys of this project—achieved in St. Louis, New York, and Duluth—was the opportunity to hear him speak about his experiences in World War II and in Minnesota politics.

Tom Boyd was responsible for the logistics of this undertaking, which were dispatched impeccably. Beyond that, he added considerable intellectual strength and judgment by his readings of the manuscript. His enthusiasm for this project, his steadiness, reliability, and unfailing courtesy are greatly valued.

A writing project of so many years is kept afloat by a loving family, and so it is appropriate here to state how very much my wife, Dona, and my (grown-up) children, David and Deborah, mean to me.

ACKNOWLEDGMENTS

★ ★ ★ ★ ★ ★ ★

The Court of Appeals Branch of the Historical Society of the United States Courts in the Eighth Circuit is grateful to Professor Jeffrey B. Morris for his diligence and hard work in preparing this history of the United States Court of Appeals for the Eighth Circuit. His painstaking research has resulted in a wonderful book, which stands as a testament to his skills as one of the country's finest legal historians.

We also acknowledge and thank the Honorable William H. Webster for contributing the Foreword to this work.

We wish to acknowledge all the judges, both past and present, of the United States Court of Appeals for the Eighth Circuit, and we extend particular thanks to the Honorable Gerald W. Heaney, the Honorable Pasco Bowman, and the Honorable Morris S. Arnold for their tireless efforts in support of this project.

Finally, we are deeply grateful and indebted to the following individuals, law firms, bar organizations, and federal courts who have provided critical and generous support for this project:

June L. Boadwine
Elizabeth R. Boyd
Thomas H. Boyd
Briggs and Morgan, PA
Dickinson Mackaman Tyler & Hagen, PC
Dorsey & Whitney LLP
Eighth Circuit Bar Association
Faegre & Benson LLP
Lincoln Inne
Maslon Edelman Borman & Brand, LLP
Minnesota Chapter of the Federal Bar Association

ACKNOWLEDGMENTS

Nyemaster Goode West Hansell & O'Brien PC
Robins Kaplan Miller & Ciresi LLP
Rider Bennett, LLP
United States Court of Appeals for the Eighth Circuit
United States District Court for the Eastern District of Arkansas
United States District Court for the Northern District of Iowa
United States District Court for the Southern District of Iowa
United States District Court for the District of Nebraska
Vogel Law Firm
Winthrop & Weinstine, PA

We hope the reader will be satisfied with the end product, and we again thank Professor Morris, the judges, and all the others listed here for their contributions in making this book a reality.

Thomas H. Boyd
President, Court of Appeals Branch
Historical Society of the United States Courts in the Eighth Circuit

Middle America during the Nineteenth Century

*T*he land that would become the Eighth Circuit was barely settled by Europeans when the U.S. Constitution was adopted. Not for a century would all the states that today constitute the Eighth Circuit be sufficiently settled to be admitted to the American Union.

Common elements unite large parts of the Eighth Circuit and distinguish it from other parts of the United States. Two great rivers flow through or by each of the states, shaping their land and determining the course of exploration and settlement, as well as economic growth. A great inland water system linking a third of the North American continent drains this region.

This land felt vast to its settlers, and indeed it was. Largely lacking in forests and mountains, much of it was grassland stretching from horizon to horizon, ruled by weather of elemental violence—extremes of hot and cold, savage thunderstorms, blinding blizzards, hailstorms, and tornadoes. In addition to the Mississippi and the Missouri rivers, great railroad routes would traverse it as well. Much of the farmland was rich beyond compare, and where the soil was not fertile, there was room for grazing cattle and sheep. Underneath the topsoil lay valuable deposits of iron, lead, and gold.

Nature did not, of course, treat each of the region's seven states alike, and the differences among them were of no small importance to the legal issues that would be generated there.[1] The most significant features of Minnesota that determined the course of its settlement and economic growth were its great forests, extensive beds of iron, and large number of waterways. In Iowa, the extraordinarily rich soil and relative freedom from brutal weather permitted corn to mature in abundance. Rapid settlement was made possible by the absence of physical barriers, while the great rivers that marked the state's eastern and western borders facilitated the marketing of its products.

Much of Nebraska's soil—at least in its eastern section—was as deep and rich as that of Iowa, but Nebraska shared with North Dakota and South Dakota a harsh climate, cyclical droughts, and, in the west, light rainfall, all of which contributed to making Nebraska's agriculture less prosperous. However, a ribbon of rivers flowing eastward did provide fertile, irrigated soil, while the valley of the River Platte, running the length of the state, acted as a spinal cord for transportation and became a natural highway to the west.

Missouri, the meeting place of three great rivers, had a climate that, with its different terrains—prairie rich soil, alluvial plains, and highlands—made it possible to cultivate nearly every crop (save citrus fruits) grown in the continental United States. Two-thirds covered with forests at the time of its settlement, Missouri contained significant deposits of lead, zinc, and iron.

Arkansas, the southernmost state of the Eighth Circuit, was made up of coastal plains, the mountains of the Ozarks, and the hot and swamplike Mississippi Delta, which was particularly fit for growing. Different cultures would flourish in each of the state's sections. Like Missouri, the settlement of Arkansas would be fostered by the broad river flowing across it, which made it easy to reach the interior.[2]

Development and Settlement from the Louisiana Purchase until 1862

Exploration, Early Trade, and Transportation

Before the Louisiana Purchase, the area of the Eighth Circuit was the land of the largely nomadic Native Americans, buffalo, prairie dog, and pronghorn, intermittently visited after 1500 by Spanish conquistadors, French and British fur traders, and French missionaries. Almost all those lands became American territory through the Louisiana Purchase.[3] At the time of the purchase, there were only a sprinkling of Europeans living in this vast area, almost none of them American citizens. The process of American development began with the explorer; then came the fur trader, the prospector, and the farmer. Forts were built to protect traders, settlers, and wagon trains, for some of these states would also become highways to more desirable areas still farther west. Before the Civil War, the most important factors affecting development of the region were explorers, river transportation, cheap land, and relations with the Native Americans.

The first Americans who "rode" the Eighth Circuit, Meriwether Lewis and William Clark, began their journey at St. Louis, the city that holds the present seat of the Court of Appeals for the Eighth Circuit, on May 14, 1804, shortly after ceremonies marking the formal transfer of Upper Louisiana to the United States. The party of explorers crossed Missouri from east to west and entered present-day Nebraska through its southwestern corner. Encountering Native Americans for the first time at Council Bluffs, the voyagers detoured briefly into Iowa to bury one of their number, who had died of natural causes. Lewis and Clark traveled through present-day South Dakota, entering North Dakota in mid-October 1804. There they would spend 212 days, more time than in any other state, wintering with the friendly Mandan Indians, where the Missouri and the Knife rivers met. On their return journey of a voyage that took two years, four months, and covered 7,689 miles, the party passed through all the states of the present Eighth Circuit save Iowa and Minnesota.[4]

Even before Lewis and Clark returned, commercial exploitation of the region by white Americans had begun. On their outward journey, the explorers had met no fewer than eight parties of traders coming downstream. Foreseeing the need to protect fur traders, the government commissioned Zebulon Pike, who in 1805 made an expedition by keelboat to scout sites for military posts. Pike reached what later would become St. Paul. In 1817, Major Stephen H. Long selected the sites of Fort Smith (Arkansas) and Fort St. Anthony (the Twin Cities) to be the southern and northern ends of the government's line of defense along the western frontier. In 1819 Fort Atkinson was established at Council Bluffs, a few miles north of present-day Omaha. During the decade before the Civil War, fur trading and logging were important areas of commerce.

The states and territories of the Eighth Circuit played an important role in western expansion. St. Louis became a major center for the outfitting of expeditions west, while Nebraska City, Omaha, Independence, and St. Josephs (Missouri) were important points of embarkation for settlers crossing the plains. Before rails spanned the continent, half a million or more used the Platte Valley of Nebraska as the overland route to Utah and the states bordering on the Pacific, stopping at trading posts and way stations.

Thriving commerce would have been impossible without developments in transportation. In the beginning, it was the two great rivers that both united and divided the circuit. The Mississippi and Missouri Rivers, especially the Missouri, which flowed through or by five of the states, were full of snags and sandbars, uprooted trees, swirls and whirlpools. Making their way up the Missouri by keelboat, Lewis and Clark could cover only fifteen to twenty miles on a good day.[5]

The first steamboat, the *Independence,* described as "a huge serpent, black and scaly," and "a monster of the deep," ascended the Missouri in 1817.[6] By 1831, the practicality of steamboating on the Upper Missouri had been established, although the northern section of the river could not be used during the winter. Voyages were no sure thing. More than four hundred vessels were sunk or damaged due to boiler explosions and as a result of collisions with the Missouri's floating trees, ice, and snags. Nevertheless, although the all-time record for a steamboat on the Missouri was only thirteen miles per hour, the steamboat was many times faster than the keelboat and piragua, and its capacity to haul freight was much greater.

Thus the steamboat stimulated commerce, created new markets, and spurred the development of commercial centers. By 1850, some three thousand steamboats carrying nearly one million tons of freight tied up annually at the St. Louis levee. So long as the steamboat was dominant, commerce and communications went north to south rather than east to west, and all the river towns depended to some degree on St. Louis, the leading city in the West. Its port received goods from the northern Rockies and Great Plains via the Missouri; from the northern prairies and Illinois via the Mississippi; and from as far away as the Appalachians via the Ohio River.[7]

In the first part of the nineteenth century, roads lagged behind water as a means of transportation. Indeed, the Mississippi, a great nautical highway, proved a major barrier to road travel. The construction of bridges across the river was delayed because of the bitter opposition of steamboat companies and ferry operators. Nevertheless, a company like the Western Stage Company, which operated throughout Iowa, Missouri, eastern Nebraska, and Wisconsin in midcentury, owned 600 coaches, 3,000 horses, and employed 1,500 persons.[8] Although road travel improved significantly in a generation, by the end of the Civil War, a stage-coach in the Platte Valley could go only ten miles an hour, while a few years later, it took a passenger riding the 653 miles from Atchison, near Kansas City, to Denver, four and one-half days.[9]

Settlement of the Land, "Removal" of Native Americans, and Statehood

Settlement required available land and the settlers' confidence that they would be secure from attack by Native Americans. This appeared to depend in large measure on resolution of the "Indian problem," a problem that, of course, was solved on terms satisfactory to people of European descent. The questions of title to land and issues involving relations with Native Americans would lead to important litigation in the Eighth Circuit throughout its history.

As a result of the Louisiana Purchase or of Indian cessions, much of Arkansas, Missouri, Iowa, and Minnesota was at some point owned by the United States. When the U.S. government first considered what to do with the lands newly acquired by the Louisiana Purchase, it envisioned a great plan of organized growth, which, while often circumvented, would nevertheless be of continual significance. Government land was systematically and comprehensively surveyed using physical descriptions that were given scientifically, rather than by the old English system of metes and bounds, in which property description depended on physical objects such as trees or creeks. In this process, old French and Spanish land titles were "regularized," a process not free of fraud, forgery, and favoritism. Moreover, much land would be sold to speculators, and a great deal went to squatters.

The first public land sales in Missouri took place in 1818 and became the model that would generally be used for sales of public land in the region. Federal law provided that tracts no smaller than 160 acres be sold by bid, with a minimum price of two dollars per acre.[10] Though it had been only sparsely populated by people of European origin at the time of the Louisiana Purchase, Missouri was rapidly settled by pioneers from Kentucky and Tennessee, as well as from Virginia and North Carolina, giving the potential state a significant southern and slave population.

However, the U.S. government was unable to fully control westward expansion. Thousands of families, for example, headed west to Arkansas, picked out choice sites, and erected crude cabins. If at first these squatters lived in a "legal no-man's-land," Congress would pass a series of preemption laws giving those living on the land the first choice of purchasing it.[11]

In Iowa, thousands of settlers arrived in the southeastern part of what became the state before the area was officially opened for settlement and ahead of the surveying and sales. The Preemption Act of 1841 essentially recognized the squatters by permitting them to purchase "their land" at $1.25 per acre. Other land in Iowa was purchased outright from the federal government, and still other land was acquired by redeeming land warrants given to soldiers for their service. In Minnesota, squatters were benefited by the Preemption Act of 1854, which permitted them to buy unsurveyed land.[12]

For Americans of European background to acquire more land and greater security, it appeared that the Native American had to be "removed." While the details of the removal differed from state to state, in essentials it did not. The press of settlement, microbes, malnutrition, negotiation, and war all played a part. In Missouri, tribes that were weak and helpless at the time white Americans entered the area were pushed aside easily. Others were bought off after the War of 1812, agreeing to exchange lands in Missouri for ones farther west in present-day Kansas and Oklahoma. By 1837, the Native American had been removed from Missouri. The fourteen thousand Cherokee, Choctaw, and Quapaw in Arkansas were easily removed, but their relocation to land directly west of the state (which would ultimately become part of the state of Oklahoma) would form a barrier to trade and westward expansion that would thwart development. In Iowa, Indian land cession was largely accomplished without violence, although there was the so-called Black Hawk War of 1831–32, in which Abraham Lincoln saw action. Cession of the southern half of Minnesota by the Sioux in 1851 led to massive settlement in that state. Pressed against the wall, the Santee Sioux struck back, but as a result of armed conflicts in 1858 and 1862, the number of Native Americans in Minnesota was greatly reduced.[13]

By the end of the Civil War, the lush eastern part of what would be the Eighth Circuit had been settled—at least those areas that were well watered and timbered and favored by good soil. The settlers swiftly reestablished the essentials of the life they had left behind—churches, schools, newspapers. Statehood was achieved by Missouri, Arkansas, Iowa, and Minnesota. The formal process was essentially the same from state to state. A territory was first organized, and the major officials (including the territorial judges, who served for terms of years) responsible for its administration were appointed by the president. Then, after the population reached a certain threshold, a territorial legislature could be elected and a nonvoting delegate seated in the U.S. Congress. Finally, after the population reached a higher threshold, the territory could apply for statehood. Statehood meant, of course, full equality with other states and full participation in the life of the nation, though not, as will be seen, treatment in exactly the same way where the federal court system was concerned. The price that had to be paid for statehood was local assumption of the cost of paying for local officials.

Statehood was not, however, automatic but occurred at the end of a highly political process. Missouri was the first of the states of the modern Eighth Circuit to achieve statehood, doing so in 1820, but not until the congressional debate over its admission had brought home to the nation the divisiveness of slavery. Under the Missouri Compromise, one free state (Maine) was admitted to the Union; one slave state (Missouri) was admitted; and slavery was banned in all the territory acquired through the Louisiana Purchase north of Missouri's southern border. As a result, Arkansas was the only other state in the modern Eighth Circuit to have had slavery. Indeed, in the political maneuvering that preceded the adoption of the Missouri Compromise, the House of Representatives rejected by only two votes an amendment that would have banned importation of slaves into the Arkansas Territory and required ultimate emancipation. Nevertheless, Arkansas was admitted to the Union as a slave state in 1837, paired with Michigan.

Iowa's admission, too, hung on the slavery issue. After 1830, the territory of Iowa embraced most of Minnesota and part of the Dakotas. Northerners sought Iowa's admission as a small state, which would leave open the possibility that several more free states could be carved from the Iowa Territory. Southerners wanted Iowa admitted as a large state, but they lost the battle. Iowa was admitted to the Union in 1846 as a relatively small state.

After both Iowa and Wisconsin (1848) were admitted to the Union, Congress created the Minnesota Territory, which included the land from the Mississippi to the Missouri River north of Iowa. Settlement surged in southeastern Minnesota after the land cession by the Sioux in 1858. Admission came rapidly, although delayed briefly because of the divisive battle over whether Kansas would be admitted as a free or slave state, a battle that poisoned American politics.

Thus, when in 1862 a circuit that greatly resembled what would become the Eighth Circuit was created, four states were charter members: Missouri, Iowa, Minnesota, and Kansas. Commerce in the area, dependent on waterways, thrived. Many river ports (most notably St. Louis) were centers for trade and for the outfitting of expeditions west. In those four states, the "Indian problem" had largely been solved. The potential of the area for agriculture was being realized. And yet, as rural as the region was, it had already been affected by the market revolution that was transforming the United States from a relatively simple preindustrial society into an increasingly complex, modern economy.[14]

The Eighth Circuit from 1862 to 1890

Land, Native Americans, Settlement

For the United States as a whole, the period from 1862 to 1890 was an era of cascading vitality. Making use of abundant raw materials and rich soil and developing a superb system of transportation, America surged forward, fueled by a seemingly endless flow of immigrants and a people driven by a spirit of enterprise and optimism. No small contribution to these extraordinary achievements was made in the Eighth Circuit, where an agricultural miracle was reaped, turning the United States into the world's largest bread basket. The states on the prairies and Great Plains became integrated into a huge common market, drawn together by the telegraph, the telephone, and, most importantly, by railroads. A century after Alexander Hamilton had enjoined his fellow countrymen to "think continentally," the frontier was closed on the Great Plains at the end of this period, concurrently with the addition of North and South Dakota (as well as Wyoming) to the Eighth Circuit.

At the center of the economies of the states of the Eighth Circuit was land. Four great laws enacted during the Civil War brought new settlers to the prairies and facilitated the populating of the Great Plains. The Homestead Act of May 20, 1862, offered homesteads of 160 acres free after five years of settlement or for sale at $1.25 per acre after six months of settlement.[15] The Morrill Act of July 2, 1862, granted to each state loyal to the Union 30,000 acres of government land for each member of Congress for the purpose of endowing at least one agricultural college in each state. Finally, in laws passed in 1862 and 1864, Congress authorized the construction of a transcontinental railroad and provided its financing by making available to the companies constructing it twenty alternating sections per mile of public domain in the states, forty in the territories. By 1871 the United States had given away 129 million acres, three times the size of New England. Much of the land acquired as a result of these enactments went to settlers rather than speculators.[16]

Standing in the way of the settlement of this land by the millions who would come from Europe and the eastern United States were the Indians of the Great Plains. The removal of Native Americans from the eastern part of the circuit and Nebraska had been relatively peaceful. Weakened by disease and dissipation caused by the white man, the Quapaw, Otoes and Osage, Sac and Meskwaki, Omaha, and Pawnee had been forced to cede their land. But the Sioux would not go so easily.

The wagon trails west, traffic on the Missouri River, discovery of gold in Montana, railroads, and the creation of the Dakota Territory stimulated white migration over the plains and into the hunting ground of the Hunkpapas and Northern Sioux. Hemmed in by ever-tightening bands of ranches, farms, and other settlements, the Sioux resisted. Fighting for their land and way of life, they negotiated aggressively and fought hard. At first, the Sioux were limited to a vast reservation encompassing all of present-day South Dakota and much of North Dakota, but pressures from settlers influenced the federal government to attempt to force all the Indians from the open range onto smaller reservations, where they would be wards of the United States. The last of the great confrontations between white and Native American took place on the Great Plains. With the massacre at Pine Ridge in 1890, a century of Native American collaboration, resistance, and dissolution ended with subjugation and forced acculturation. Within the Eighth Circuit, there would be several large reservations in South Dakota, one shared by both Dakotas, and smaller reservations in Nebraska, Minnesota, and Iowa and on the Missouri-Nebraska border. Shocked by defeat, deprived of their land, weakened by disease, badgered by missionaries, reduced to dependency on government handouts, most of the Indians of the plains sunk into destitution.[17]

The states of the Eighth Circuit grew rapidly in population between 1862 and 1890. Although Missouri was the site of some of the most bitter fighting of the Civil War, it became the nation's fifth largest state, as its population increased by more than 83 percent during the 1860s to 1.7 million people. By 1890, 2.7 million people lived in Missouri. In neighboring Iowa, the population grew from 675,000 in 1860 to 1,912,000 in

1890. Although immigration to Minnesota had slowed during the 1860s because of the Sioux uprising, it still grew from 172,000 to 440,000. Among its settlers were a large number of Scandinavians seeking cheap land, religious freedom, and the absence of class distinctions. Even in Arkansas, on the losing side during the Civil War, with a debt-ridden one-crop economy, profligate government spending during Reconstruction, and widespread political corruption in the 1880s, population climbed from 435,000 in 1860 to 1,128,000 in 1890.[18]

The population of Nebraska, created as a territory and not open for settlement until 1854, surged after the Homestead Act. Over four million acres were distributed under the act between 1863 and 1873.[19] Many of the purchasers were from Iowa, Illinois, and Pennsylvania. Although county government did not extend much beyond seventy-five miles west of the Missouri, Nebraska's population was large enough (80,000) for statehood by the end of the Civil War, but that would be briefly held up by Reconstruction politics. So that Radical Republicans in the Congress could demonstrate that the Congress could impose conditions either when state making or in letting states back into the Union, Nebraska was required to remove from its proposed state constitution a clause limiting the franchise to free white males. Nevertheless, Nebraska's statehood was proclaimed on March 1, 1867, and it became part of the Eighth Circuit a few weeks later.[20] Statehood and railroads would transform Nebraska from the place Americans traveled through, to a land of settled farmers. The state's population grew to 1,063,000 in 1890.

Kansas and Colorado

In 1862 Missouri, Iowa, and Minnesota were placed in a circuit that was renumbered the eighth in 1866. Arkansas was added at that time;[21] Nebraska the following year. The other two states which would become permanent members of the Eighth Circuit, North and South Dakota, placed in the circuit in 1889, are discussed in the following chapter. Seven other states would temporarily be part of the circuit: Wisconsin (1863–66), Kansas (1862–1929), Colorado (1876–1929), Wyoming (1890–1929), Utah (1896–1929), Oklahoma (1907–29), and New Mexico (1912–29). Kansas and Colorado in particular were the sites of important federal jurisprudence between 1862 and 1890, so a brief discussion of their settlement is appropriate.

Kansas was admitted to the Union as a free state on January 29, 1861, after the violent struggle following passage of the Kansas-Nebraska Act (1854) over whether it was to be a slave or a free state. After the Civil War, Kansas developed a strong economy, based on wheat growing, ranching, manufacturing, and the production of oil and natural gas.[22] The third circuit judge of the Eighth Circuit, David J. Brewer, was appointed in 1884 while he was a member of the Kansas Supreme Court.

While eastern and central Colorado had been acquired by the Louisiana Purchase, the western part of the state was part of the spoils of the Mexican War. The discovery of gold in 1858 near present-day Denver led to the settlement of what became the Colorado Territory, created by Congress in 1861 out of the Kansas, Nebraska, Utah, and New Mexico territories. Although armed conflict with Native Americans followed, ranches and farms sprang up along the streams of Colorado in the early years of the territory. After it attained statehood in 1876, silver mining brought great wealth.[23] A rich economy based on mining, farming, ranching, and manufacturing generated difficult legal questions involving water rights, railroads, and the 1872 federal mining law.

Railroads

No single factor was more important to the development of the states of the Eighth Circuit than the railroad, which closed distances, opened new territories to settlement, brought settlers, greatly increased the market for the sale of crops, made possible the creation of farm-related industries, created a profound demand for labor, and lured much business away from the river towns. While doing all of this, the railroads corrupted politics and became the most important source of litigation in the Eighth Circuit, spawning great legal issues over bridge construction, passenger and freight rates, as well as personal injury cases.[24]

The immense capital required for the construction of railroads came from national and state governments, towns, and private individuals—through land grants and the issuing of bonds. It was the attempted repudiation of bond obligations by municipalities that brought about the most controversial litigation in the circuit courts of the Eighth Circuit between 1862 and 1890.

Relatively little railway building went on in the states of the Eighth Circuit before the end of the Civil War, although the Chicago and Rock Island Railroad reached Iowa in 1854, making it possible to go from Rock Island to New York in forty-two hours.[25] Although Iowa would come to have more railroad mileage than any state in the Union, in 1860 there were only 655 miles of track in the state.[26] At the beginning of the Civil War, only one railroad in Missouri, the Hannibal and St. Joseph, had completed its 810-mile line. The only railroad line in Arkansas on which much progress had been made before the outbreak of war was the Memphis and Little Rock line, which, although badly damaged by Mississippi River floods of 1857, proved to be a first step in the economic domination of Memphis over eastern Arkansas.[27] The first railroad did not come to Minnesota until 1862.

Railroad construction surged after the Civil War. By 1870, approximately 1,200 miles of rail had been laid in Missouri. The construction of the great Eads Bridge over the Mississippi tied Missouri into the emerging national railroad network. Within five years of Minnesota's first line, there was a connection to Chicago and the East. After track was laid from St. Paul to Duluth in 1870, what had been a bone-crunching weeklong stagecoach ride took but a single day. Arkansas was somewhat of an exception because the "boodling" of state officials and the "peculations" of outsider officials kept the operating and construction companies strapped for funds. Only 256 miles of track were laid in Arkansas before 1870. By 1880, that number had risen to 859, and by 1890 to 2,200.[28]

The great impetus for railroad growth in Iowa (as in Nebraska) was the transcontinental railroad. The eastern terminus of the Union Pacific would be Council Bluffs. By 1870, there were four railroads running across Iowa, and the state was crossed by 2,683 railroad miles. The completion of the Chicago–Sioux City connection in 1868 began the recentering of the upper Missouri trade from Saint Louis to Chicago. The bridge connecting Iowa with the Union Pacific at Council Bluffs was not built until 1873, but by 1880, Iowa officials were boasting that no one in the state lived more than twenty-five miles from a railroad station.[29]

Nearly one-sixth of Nebraska was given away to railroad companies to finance construction. East of the Mississippi, the railroad had to take account of towns, but on the northern Great Plains, it was the railroad that determined their placement. As the railroad crews moved across the land, movable cities of "pimps and prostitutes, saloon keepers and gamblers, lawmen and criminals followed." In time, families became more numerous; towns grew; schoolhouses, churches, and grist mills appeared. Rail mileage continued to surge in Nebraska after the transcontinental railroad was completed, climbing from 1,900 in 1880 to 5,100 in 1890.[30]

By 1873 five railroads would span the West. The eastern terminus of four of them was in the Eighth Circuit: the Great Northern (completed in 1883, its terminus in the Twin Cities); the Union Pacific/ Central Pacific (1869/1873, Omaha/Council Bluffs); the Great Northern (Duluth); Atchison, Topeka and Santa Fe (1881, Topeka). Nebraska, Iowa, Minnesota, and Missouri were thus joined with lands to the west as well as with eastern markets. The Mississippi River, once a dominant highway, had become a mere feeder for railroads.[31]

Farming and Other Commerce

The primary business of the Eighth Circuit was farming, leaving its inhabitants dependent on the weather and on outsiders to transport, store, and buy their crops. The climate was suitable enough for the "world's breadbasket" but could be particularly harsh on the plains, where, during the 1870s, there was a prolonged drought, vicious dust storms, and plagues of locusts. A little more than a decade later, during the winter of 1887–88, there were extremely low temperatures and blizzards of extraordinary magnitude. There were also farm depressions; one began in 1868 and lasted for much of the 1870s, and during the 1880s the price of wheat declined dramatically throughout the world.

Nevertheless, it is possible to overstate the plight of the farmer in the Eighth Circuit during this period. New (or newly made available) inventions and their improvements, such as the horse-drawn corn planter, the riding straddle row cultivator, the heavy gang plow, and McCormick's reaper greatly increased farm productivity, as did the introduction of drought-resistant forage crops and techniques of dry farming. Crop yields nearly tripled in the quarter century after the Homestead Act, and farmers also profited from cheaper manufactured goods and higher land values.[32]

But if it appears a century later that the lot of the farmer was improving between 1862 and 1890, generally it did not appear so to the farmers of the Eighth Circuit at the time. Experiencing high interest rates, inadequate credit, monopolistic marketing, and high prices for farm machinery and other necessities, farmers felt exploited by eastern moneyed interests, railroads, and grain elevators. With lives and fortunes held hostage, westerners saw their states as colonies of a not very benevolent imperium. Such agricultural discontent would bring about the Granger laws, the constitutionality of which would be argued in the courts of the circuit.[33]

The growth of railroads did stimulate the growth of new industries—cattle ranching in Kansas and Nebraska, stockyards in St. Louis and Kansas City, meatpacking in Iowa, flour milling in Minneapolis. Other agriculturally related industries developed in the region, such as the manufacture of agricultural implements in Iowa. Nebraska experienced a sevenfold growth of manufacturing in the 1880s. The Twin Cities, Kansas City, and Omaha became large centers of commerce similar to St. Louis, now in decline. Though smaller, Duluth became an important commercial center as a result of its proximity to the Mesabi Range and location on Lake Superior. Iron in Minnesota, silver in Colorado, and lead and zinc in Missouri contributed to the region's economy from beneath the ground.

During the nineteenth century, the major characteristics of the states of the Eighth Circuit that affected its work were both the region's expanse and isolation and the factors that diminished its isolation and linked it to the rest of the Union: rivers, steamboats, and particularly railroads; a complex systems of land titles; a Native American population, seen as a barrier to settlement and growth; and the region's volatile agricultural economy which, although it was slowly being diversified, nevertheless left a residue of deep resentment against the banks and industries of the eastern United States, as well as against the railroad corporations.

CHAPTER 1

"An Empire in Itself"

The Eighth Circuit before 1891

*T*he first Eighth Circuit state to be admitted to the federal judicial system, Missouri, was made a judicial district in 1822 with a district judge who exercised circuit court jurisdiction. The state would not become a full-fledged part of the lower federal court system until 1837. The first circuit resembling the modern Eighth Circuit, numbered the Ninth, was created in 1862 and included Iowa, Missouri, Illinois, and Kansas. By 1867 there was an Eighth Circuit, which included those four states plus Nebraska. Colorado would be added in 1876, the Dakotas and Wyoming in 1889–90.

Between 1862 and 1890, the federal courts of the Eighth Circuit helped to expedite the settlement of the West by settling disputes over land and commerce, facilitating the growth of the region's infrastructure, helped unleash the creative energies of a market economy, enforced federal law, and handled, with greater sensitivity than most, official government cases involving Native Americans.

The Role of the Federal Court System and Establishment of the Eighth Circuit

One of the earliest achievements of the first congressional session under the U.S. Constitution was the establishment of a federal court system. Many participants at the Constitutional Convention believed that a federal court system was necessary to adjudicate disputes between states, create a common body of law to govern maritime commerce, protect out-of-state litigants from the prejudice of local juries, and enforce treaty obligations and federal law. Nevertheless the Constitution specifically provided for one Supreme Court and left it to Congress to "from time to time ordain and establish . . . inferior courts." During the struggle over ratification of the Constitution, considerable concern was expressed about the problems that a strong federal court system might cause: unnecessary expenses, hardships for litigants and witnesses, and the risk that federal courts might ultimately absorb the courts of the states.[1]

In the end, the first Congress created a specialized court system limited in reach. Three tiers of courts were established, staffed by two tiers of judges. State lines were followed in establishing the lowest tier—the district courts. District courts were established in each of the existing eleven states, one judge to a district. No district crossed a state border. The district judges were to be residents of their districts, and the custom would shortly evolve of state politicians (particularly members of the U.S. Senate of the president's party) playing a central role in the judges' selection. Each district court was required to employ the procedures of the state courts of the state in which they were located.

Initially the district courts were expected primarily to be admiralty tribunals. They were given exclusive jurisdiction over admiralty and maritime cases, as well as over most customs matters and minor federal crimes. The district courts were given concurrent jurisdiction with state courts over suits brought at common law by the United States, where the amount involved was over $100.

The intermediate tier of courts, the circuit courts, also essentially followed state lines. At first, three circuits were created for the regions of a nation whose states were all located east of the Appalachians. While each circuit—the East, the Middle, and the South—encompassed several states, the circuit courts were to hold two terms annually in each district (the district corresponding to the district of the district court) and were to be composed of two justices of the U.S. Supreme Court and the district judge from the particular district. Within a few years, the law was modified to permit the circuit court to be composed of one Supreme Court justice and one district judge.

The circuit courts were given both appellate and trial functions. They were authorized to review the district courts by writ of error in civil cases in which the matter in controversy exceeded $50 and to review on appeal final decrees in admiralty cases in which the matter in controversy exceeded $300. However, their trial functions were more important. The circuit courts were the federal courts of general trial jurisdiction. The circuit courts were given exclusive jurisdiction over serious federal crimes, and concurrent jurisdiction with the state courts over cases where the United States brought suit for an amount above $500, as well as in controversies between citizens of different states where the amount in question was above $500. The First Judiciary Act also provided for removal to federal court, before trial, of certain types of private civil litigation begun in state court, including actions where the defendant was an alien or a citizen of another state and the amount was over $500, as well as over certain land title actions.

Congress had not attempted through the First Judiciary Act to give the full range of jurisdiction possible for the federal courts, nor had it attempted to remove the federal court system from state influence. The district courts were locally based, and the circuit courts were organized on a local basis. Exclusive federal jurisdiction was severely circumscribed, while in most matters, state courts retained concurrent jurisdiction with the lower federal courts. Regional, state, and local influences competed with national ones.[2]

Although members of Congress viewed what they had created by the First Judiciary Act as an experiment, fully expecting that it would soon have to be modified, much of what they created lasted for a century, and some endures to this day.[3] Not until 1875 was federal jurisdiction greatly expanded. The appellate functions of the circuit courts would survive until 1891, when the courts of appeals were created, while the circuit courts themselves lasted until 1911. A three-tiered federal court system remains with us today.

More than inertia has been involved in the perpetuation of the structure of the federal courts. National courts, organized on state and regional lines and staffed according to national and state interests, embodied the mixture of centralization, regionalism, state centeredness, and localism that characterizes the American federal system. Furthermore, the First Judiciary Act reinforced the judicial independence established by the Constitution by failing to provide a mechanism to review the manner in which lower federal court judges administered their caseload. No central administration of the judicial branch was established. No minister of justice, no home office, not even a chief justice, could command the decentralized lower courts. The only control of federal judges would come through appellate reversals for errors of law and through impeachment.[4]

Perhaps the most important function of the circuit courts during the early years of the Republic was that they brought the federal government visibly to the people. Adapting an English tradition that was hundreds of years old to the needs of the new national government, the circuit courts became important agents of political socialization, employing grand jury charges as lectures on the meaning of the new Constitution. On the other hand, the judicial system established by the First Judiciary Act brought great hardships on justices, judges, lawyers, litigants, witnesses, and jurors. In the early years of the Republic, travel was expensive, difficult, unreliable, and disliked—by Supreme Court justices and the average litigant as well.

Although the three-tiered system of the First Judiciary Act would survive without major change for over a century,[5] it had to be adapted to a nation that would expand from the Appalachians to the Pacific. Indeed, one of the benefits of statehood for most states was to leave behind their territorial courts, all too often staffed by politicians unable to find a sinecure elsewhere (Iowa, with a distinguished territorial judiciary, was a notable exception). The expansion of the federal judiciary was accomplished in a number of ways: by adding to the number of states in a circuit; by expanding the number of circuits and appointment of Supreme Court justices to ride those circuits; and by creating district judgeships in states newly admitted to the Union and authorizing those judges to hold the local circuit court themselves. Since the jurisdiction of the federal courts was continually increased and the U.S. population also increased while litigiousness rarely declined, Congress was also frequently required to resort to ad hoc expedients, such as the creation of more than one district in a state, as well as altering the terms and places of court sessions. Not a session of Congress passed without some such legislation.

The states that would make up the modern Eighth Circuit were admitted to the federal judicial system through one or another of these expedients. Soon after Missouri was admitted to the Union, it was made a judicial district with a district judge who exercised circuit court jurisdiction.[6] That also happened with Arkansas.[7] Westerners felt that they were not being treated equally, and complained. As Senator John H. Eaton of Tennessee (then in the West) put it in 1825: "The Western country had not had a fair dealing on the subject, and, until they should be placed on the same footing with the other States of this Union, as respected their Judiciary, they would never cease to complain and to ask redress."[8] Finally, in 1837, Missouri and Arkansas received treatment equal to the other states. By the Act of March 3, 1837, Congress added two members to the Supreme Court and divided the United States into nine circuits.[9] Missouri was placed in the Eighth Circuit with Tennessee and Kentucky, while Arkansas, admitted to the Union less than a year before, was placed in the Ninth Circuit.[10] That this legislation did not prove to be a panacea for either the state or the circuit is suggested by Justice John McKinley's report to Congress the year after its passage. McKinley, who had traveled ten thousand miles the previous year to attend the terms of the Supreme Court and those of the circuit courts for Alabama, Louisiana, and Mississippi, wrote: "I have never yet been at Little Rock, the place of holding the court in Arkansas; but from the best information I can obtain, it could not be conveniently approached in the spring of the year, except by water, and by that route, the distance would be greatly increased."[11]

The steady growth of the business of the Supreme Court, the admission of new states to the Union, three vacancies on the Supreme Court, and the effects of the Civil War led Congress to reconfigure the circuits in 1862. Both Iowa (admitted to the Union in 1846) and Minnesota (admitted in 1858) were, at the time, outside the circuit system, as were Florida, Texas, Wisconsin, California, Oregon, and Kansas. Shrewd politics during consideration of the circuit bill netted a seat on the Supreme Court for Iowa's Samuel Freeman Miller. The astute lobbying of Senator James W. Grimes and Representative James F. Wilson ensured that Iowa would not be placed in a circuit where Miller would encounter direct competition with other leading aspirants for the High Court, especially Orville H. Browning and David Davis of Illinois and Secretary of the Interior Caleb B. Smith of Indiana. Iowa's legislature passed a resolution on March 10, 1862, urging its congressional delegation to battle for a suitable circuit and petition Congress to grant its wishes. To separate Iowa from Illinois and Indiana, there was a call for a trans-Mississippi circuit. It was argued that the commerce and trade of Iowa, Minnesota, Missouri, and Kansas were connected by the Mississippi and Missouri rivers; that the four states had similar codes of practice; that they were "all more or less affected by the old Spanish and French [land] grants"; and that territories that would ultimately receive statehood could be added conveniently to a circuit of those four states.[12] And so, by the Act of July 15, 1862, a new Ninth Circuit was created.[13]

During the rest of the decade, Congress tinkered with the circuit courts. Among the smaller modifications pertinent to this study, Wisconsin (which in 1862 had been placed in the Eighth Circuit with Michigan and Illinois) was placed in the Ninth Circuit in 1863,[14] but when following the Civil War the readmission of the Southern states required yet another reordering of the circuits, Wisconsin in 1866 was placed in the Seventh Circuit (with Indiana and Illinois) and Arkansas in a renumbered Eighth Circuit, which also contained Iowa, Missouri, Kansas, and Minnesota.[15] Less than a year later, Nebraska, which had in the meantime been admitted to the Union, was added to the Eighth Circuit.[16] The next three territories to be admitted as states—Colorado (August 1, 1876), North and South Dakota (November 2, 1889), and Wyoming (July 10, 1890)—were all added to the Eighth Circuit. Indeed, all states newly admitted to the Union between 1866 and 1929 were assigned to either the Eighth Circuit or the Ninth. Thus, by the time of the Circuit Court of Appeals Act of 1891, the Eighth Circuit was spoken of as "an empire in itself" because of its vast and varied area.[17]

In 1869 Congress took a major step toward reorganizing the federal judicial system. Relieving the overburdened Supreme Court was the major goal. To reduce the attendance of the justices on circuit to a single term every two years, nine circuit judgeships—one for each circuit—were created by the Act of April 10, 1869.[18] The circuit court could be held by the circuit justice, the circuit judge, or a district judge; any two were empowered to sit as a panel. While this reform did not achieve its major purpose, it proved useful in enabling the circuit courts to deal with the increase in the volume of cases they would confront after the federal courts were given the full range of federal jurisdiction in 1875.

During the years between passage of the Act of April 10, 1869, and of the Circuit Court of Appeals Act of March 3, 1891,[19] the circuit justice for the Eighth Circuit, Samuel F. Miller, rode circuit in the spring and summer, generally convening half of the circuit courts. In 1877, for example, Miller embarked on his circuit on May 6. He held a term in Des Moines during the last two weeks of May, at Leavenworth and St. Paul for ten days each in June, and in Denver from July 3 to 15.[20] The work could be fatiguing for a sixty-year-old man. Miller wrote in 1879 that, after sitting for six weeks in very hot weather, hearing "heavy mining and railroad cases in which every move of the court involved millions of dollars, and the personal feelings of clients invaded the court room too visibly in the ill concealed temper of their lawyers," he had developed "a shaky hand, an interrupted pulse, and strong evidences of heart trouble," and was "coming very near [to] breaking down."[21]

Because of the great increase in the volume of business—the number of cases in the circuit increased tenfold during the ten years John F. Dillon was circuit judge (1869–79)[22]—much of the work of the circuit court came to be handled by district judges.[23] However, at times the circuit justice, circuit judge, and district judge might each be holding court in neighboring rooms.[24] Most of the circuit business was trial, not appeal. The range of cases could be vast. Riding circuit in the 1880s, Judge David J. Brewer heard patent, trademark, and copyright cases; cases involving railroad lands, pensions, and federal elections; litigation brought by, against, or about Native Americans and foreign corporations; and conflicts over state boundaries. Criminal cases were relatively few, save in the Circuit Court for the Western District of Arkansas, which embraced the lawless Indian Territory.[25]

The Judges

Samuel F. Miller

Samuel Freeman Miller, the man whose potential appointment as circuit justice shaped the contours of the Eighth Circuit, was a jurist of great ability and considerable force of personality. Besides wielding considerable influence on the U.S. Supreme Court between 1862 and 1890, Miller was a conscientious circuit justice, who maintained close relations with the judges in the Eighth Circuit, and a superb trial judge.

Miller was born on April 5, 1816, in Richmond, Kentucky, which was located in the bluegrass country in the central part of the state. Raised on a farm, Miller earned an M.D. from Transylvania University in Lexington, then practiced medicine in a town of two hundred in the Cumberland Mountains in southern Kentucky. Bored and frustrated with medicine, Miller educated himself in the law and in 1847 was admitted to the county bar. Believing in gradual manumission, Miller saw no future for himself in a state where pro-slavery sentiment was growing. In 1850 he moved to Keokuk in southeastern Iowa, a thriving city of three thousand, located where deepwater navigation of the Mississippi became possible.

The Iowa to which Miller moved was developing rapidly. Settlement had begun less than twenty years before. Free of physical barriers and Native Americans, with all its rich land suitable for either agriculture or livestock grazing, with great rivers on its borders and smaller rivers cutting through the state, settlement exploded. Iowa was opened, organized, and attained statehood in less than a single generation. By 1870, forty years after it was open to settlement, all parts of Iowa had been settled.

Most of Iowa's settlers came from Pennsylvania, Indiana, and Ohio, bringing the institutions and values of New England to the state—a belief in education for learning and moral guidance, the Protestant work ethic, utilitarianism, and a strong impulse toward social reform.[26] Though some settlers came from the South, the impulse Iowans had toward social reform included an abhorrence of slavery, although they did not eschew racism. Indeed, in 1851, the Iowa legislature passed a law, never put into effect, that barred free blacks from coming into the state.[27]

So, in moving to Keokuk, Miller had settled in an important commercial center, where his fellow members of the bar included George W. McCrary and Henry C. Caldwell, later both to be circuit judges for the Eighth Circuit. Miller would also find in Iowa fertile soil for his Whig political beliefs in public education, federal involvement in internal improvements, and unrestricted immigration. The tensions caused by the Kansas-Nebraska Act propelled the antislave Miller into the Republican Party, which quickly took root in Iowa. By 1860, Miller was one of the leading political figures in Iowa. Although in the following year he was defeated by the popular incumbent, Samuel Kirkwood, when he sought the Republican nomination for governor, Miller would soon be rewarded by his party with a seat on the U.S. Supreme Court. On that appointment, a not entirely unbiased hometown newspaper wrote that Miller was "the model of the beau ideal Western Lawyer and Western Judge and his advent to the bench cannot fail to create a sensation even in that fossilized circle of venerated antiquities which constitutes the Bench of the Supreme Court of the United States."[28]

It is unlikely that Miller created a sensation when he reached the High Court, but he would go on to a career of great distinction, holding his own with colleagues of the caliber of Stephen J. Field and Joseph Bradley. In twenty-eight years, Miller wrote 616 majority opinions for the Supreme Court, as well as 169 dissents. More statesman than lawyer, Miller was an able judge, but not a scholar, caring more "about what was needed than what courts earlier had decided, more about the logic of events than the logic of law."[29]

Where constitutional cases were concerned, Miller was a workhorse and left an enduring mark on the law. He was part of the bare majority upholding the exercise of executive power in the *Prize* cases.[30] Miller's approach to cases involving Reconstruction was one of judicial restraint. His construction of the Fourteenth Amendment in the *Slaughterhouse* cases limited its reach, reflecting the view that the Civil War had not made any radical change in the relationship between the federal government and the states but had been fought principally to protect the rights of the freedmen (a promise that took ninety years to keep).[31] Sharing some of the agrarian radicalism of his adopted state, Miller would, as circuit justice, confront the dilemma of having to implement decisions of the Supreme Court enforcing municipal bond obligations—decisions with which he was unsympathetic—even to having to place local officials in jail for contempt. Sharing some of Iowa's agrarian radicalism, Miller considered the bond-holding class selfish and conniving, believing that their "only object in life seems to be [to] have their golden egg, shell meat and although they destroy the goose from which they know it must come if it come at all."[32]

As circuit judge for the Eighth Circuit, Miller worked hard and maintained close relations with the circuit and district judges (although he constantly angled for the appointment to the Supreme Court of his brother-in-law, William P. Ballinger, over the Eighth Circuit judges John Forrest Dillon and Henry C. Caldwell). Miller seems to have been a first-rate trial judge—industrious, fast on his feet in ruling on motions, disposing of court business with dispatch. He avoided hung juries and controlled the lawyers in his courtroom. While generally retaining the respect of attorneys, Miller could be so intolerant of genteel sophistication, garrulity, and legal mumbo-jumbo that one attorney stated that he did not care to go into his courtroom to be "stamped upon by that hippopotamus."[33]

A vigorous man of indomitable will, six feet tall and weighing over two hundred pounds, Miller was a "westerner" who, as one biographer wrote, "liked to ride a horse, dance a jig, sing a song," "a laughing, living, hating, feeling man with the fire of youth and the courage of the warrior."[34] Easy and natural of manner, Miller's kindly smile inspired adoration from the pages of the Supreme Court. Never wealthy, Miller died intestate; his cash assets—the balance due on his salary, money from the sale of his law books, and what could be gleaned from publication of his law school lectures—barely met the bills that were due. On Miller's death, his casket was taken by rail to Burlington, Iowa, and thence to Keokuk, where the buildings in the downtown were draped in black. There his body laid in state in the courtroom, where throngs came to pay their respects.[35]

John Forrest Dillon (1869–79)

The first circuit judge for the Eighth Circuit, John F. Dillon, was, as practitioner, professor, scholar, and judge of both state and federal courts, one of the most influential shapers of nineteenth-century constitutional law. Dillon was born in upstate New York in 1831 but moved with his family to Davenport, Iowa, in 1838. His early life was marked by hardship and poverty. Like Miller a physician before he was an attorney, Dillon's career as a doctor was cut short by a hernia, which made it difficult for him to continue the horseback riding that was required to practice medicine on the frontier. Dillon was admitted to the bar in 1852 and shortly thereafter became county attorney. In 1858 he was elected judge of Iowa's Seventh Judicial District. Six years later, he was elected to the Iowa Supreme Court and became its chief justice in 1867. President Ulysses S. Grant appointed Dillon the first circuit judge for the Eighth Circuit, and Dillon took up his duties on December 22, 1869.

Serving as circuit judge for the Eighth Circuit was no sinecure. Dillon held terms in each district, requiring about ten thousand miles of travel each year. Yet he was able to teach medical jurisprudence at the University of Iowa, found and edit for one year the *Central Law Journal* and write three treatises: the 808-page *Treatise on the Law of Municipal Corporations* (first published in 1872); a 138-page book, *Removal of Causes from State Courts to Federal Courts* (1875); and a sixty-three-page work, *The Law of Municipal Bonds* (1876).

Dillon's treatise, which remedied the almost total lack of accumulated knowledge about municipal corporations, as well as a work by Thomas A. Cooley,[36] would be the sources most cited by judges, attorneys, and delegates to constitutional conventions seeking to limit what cities might do under delegated police powers and taxing power.[37] Certain passages from Dillon's book became standard citations for the restrictions on the taxing and spending powers of states and local governments. They supplied the bar with numerous constitutional principles on which to restrict the powers of legislative bodies and popularized within the profession principles encompassing laissez-faire policies desired by much of the emerging business class. Dillon's treatise stressed the constitutional constraints on municipal bond repudiation and fostered the notion of an interventionist judiciary resisting political pressures.

Meanwhile, from the bench, Dillon began to articulate principles that would ultimately be employed by businesses seeking freedom from government regulation. The first such, which became known as "Dillon's Rule," was the principle that municipal corporations were "mere tenants at will of the legislature," which could create, destroy, abridge, or control them."[38] His second principle was that taxation had to be for a public purpose. If that concept is more properly credited to Cooley, Dillon added to it his weight as judge and treatise writer. Dillon wrote the opinion in *Hanson v. Vernon,* in which the Iowa Supreme Court held invalid a statute that authorized counties and cities to levy taxes for the purpose of subsidizing private railroad corporations.[39] The courts were, Dillon wrote, not at liberty to strike down laws on the ground that they conflicted with judicial notions of natural rights and sound public policy. However, the court held that because the tax had appropriated private property for private purposes (to assist railroads, which were private corporations organized for the profit of their investors), it was not in the nature of a law. Furthermore, the citizens affected by the statute had been deprived of their property without due process of law.[40] While the Iowa Supreme Court would overturn its own decision a year later,[41] the public-purpose maxim would gain widespread approval after 1870 as state legislatures and state constitutional conventions considered enacting restrictions on the functions of cities, their debt ceilings, and tax structures.[42]

When Dillon resigned from the circuit court in 1879, he was probably the best-known lower federal court judge in the nation. He moved to New York and became perhaps the nation's leading railroad attorney, living until 1914. Within a dozen years, Dillon the attorney and scholar would urge a philosophy of constitutional conservatism and a standard of judicial review not far from that of the most outspoken advocates of laissez-faire.[43] But that was later. As shall be seen in discussion of the *Granger* cases, Dillon the circuit judge had been far more flexible.

George Washington McCrary (1879–84)

George Washington McCrary, who served with distinction in the legislative and executive branches of the federal government, succeeded Dillon as circuit judge. McCrary was born near Evansville, Indiana, in 1835. He moved with his family when he was two years old to Van Buren County, Iowa, then the "edge of the frontier." Reading law in the office of John W. Rankin and Samuel F. Miller, McCrary was admitted to the bar and became active in politics as a Republican, serving in the state legislature from 1858 to 1861.

From 1869 to 1877, McCrary was an influential member of Congress. He served on the committee that investigated the Credit Mobilier scandal. McCrary took the lead in fighting for reform of the federal judiciary by sponsoring a bill, which passed the House of Representatives, aimed at correcting the two great problems in judicial administration of the time—lack of speedy justice in the courts of first instance, and lack of reasonable and prompt review. The bill, which never emerged from the Senate Judiciary Committee, would, among other things, have established an intermediate appellate court in each circuit.[44]

McCrary also played a leading role in the crisis over the presidential election of 1876, making an important contribution to the formation of the Electoral Commission and participating in its proceedings. When Rutherford B. Hayes became president as the result of the decision of the commission, he appointed McCrary secretary of war. In that position, McCrary was responsible for withdrawing federal troops from the "carpetbagger" governments of South Carolina and Louisiana and for dispatching federal troops during the great railroad strike of 1877.

McCrary's old mentor and friend Samuel F. Miller strongly recommended McCrary as Dillon's replacement in 1879. An able jurist, McCrary edited for publication five volumes of decisions of the circuit courts of the Eighth Circuit for the years 1873 to 1883.[45]

McCrary, like Dillon, succumbed to the blandishments of railroads, resigning his judgeship in 1884 to practice law in Kansas City and serve as counsel to the Atchison, Topeka and Santa Fe. McCrary died in St. Josephs, Missouri, in 1890 and is buried in Keokuk.[46]

David J. Brewer (1884–89)

David J. Brewer, the third circuit judge of the Eighth Circuit, would, after six years in the position, be elevated to the Supreme Court. At one time, Brewer was considered one of the great justices of the Supreme Court by observers as astute as Felix Frankfurter and Jerome Frank, but his reputation has slipped considerably. Yet his most recent biographer concludes that Brewer went beyond the dictates of the legal formalism of his time to establish a more pragmatic jurisprudence, one better suited to addressing the multitude of problems created by the rapid and unsettling changes of his own time.[47]

The son of a missionary, Brewer was born on June 20, 1837, in the ancient Greek city of Smyrna (now Izmir, Turkey). His mother, Emilia A.

Field, was the sister of Justice Stephen J. Field, David Dudley Field (the great codifier of law), and Cyrus W. Field, developer of the transatlantic cable. Brewer grew up in New England and graduated from Yale. He then read law with David Dudley Field, attended Albany Law School, and was admitted to the New York bar. After an unsuccessful attempt at prospecting for gold on Pike's Peak, Brewer settled and practiced law in Leavenworth, Kansas, a river town and a center for overland freight and staging. In 1861, Brewer was appointed commissioner of the U.S. Circuit Court for the District of Kansas, which brought in a few extra dollars in fees for preparing warrants and other routine paperwork.[48] Then, beginning in 1862, in swift succession Brewer was elected to serve as a county probate and criminal court judge, as a state district judge, and as county attorney. In 1870 he was elected to the Kansas Supreme Court.

As a member of the Kansas Supreme Court for fourteen years, Brewer was a workhorse—writing some four hundred opinions within three years of ascending the bench. On that court, Brewer's decisions in railroad liability cases often went against the railroad, and he supported state and local taxing power over railroad property. He wrote opinions holding unconstitutional laws allowing counties and localities to purchase stock in railroad companies, and paying for stock by local bond issues.[49] The use of public monies for private purposes always disturbed Brewer. In cases involving women's rights, Brewer was unusually progressive for his time, but in a dissent he voted to uphold racially segregated schools.[50] Brewer also dissented in *State v. Mugler*,[51] arguing that the state's prohibition on the manufacturing of intoxicating liquors was unconstitutional as a taking of private property for public use without compensation. He came to the same opinion as a circuit judge.[52] The U.S. Supreme Court ultimately sustained his position in the *Mugler* case.

Brewer, recommended for the circuit judgeship when Dillon resigned, was passed over for McCrary but received the position in 1884 from President Chester Alan Arthur, who chose Brewer over former Kansas attorney general A. L.Williams.

A candidate for elevation to the Supreme Court in 1889, Brewer wrote a letter to a friend in support of Judge Henry B. Brown of the U.S. District Court in Michigan. President Benjamin Harrison reportedly was so impressed by Brewer's generosity that he chose him for the position over Brown.[53] Brewer was confirmed by a vote of 52–11 over opposition from prohibitionists, the Kansas State Grange, the senators from North and South Dakota (their noses out of joint because Brewer had appointed Kansas and Nebraska men as clerks of court in the Dakotas), as well as from senators from Arkansas, who were critical of Brewer for having convicted some of their constituents for using "harsh language to a colored man."[54]

In his twenty-year career on the Supreme Court, Brewer replaced his uncle Stephen J. Field as the Court's preeminent judicial conservative. Brewer was enough of a legal formalist to often be against legislative action and against regulation while being a staunch defender of judicial review. His constitutional views on property may be suggested by his dissent in *Brass v. North Dakota*, a case in which the Supreme Court sustained by a 5–4 vote a North Dakota law regulating maximum charges by grain elevators. Brewer concluded: "I can only say that it seems to me that the country is rapidly traveling the road which leads to the point where all freedom of contract and conduct will be lost."[55]

Few justices have come close to the number of speeches, writings, and interviews covering controversial and public topics as Brewer. He decried attacks on property through taxation, eminent domain, and the use of the policy power. Yet he also denounced the evils of big business, found "much of good" in labor unions, and supported the forfeit of all property to the government at death. Brewer also attacked the shameful treatment of African Americans, Native Americans, and Chinese in the United States. He was a supporter of women's rights, even predicting a female president. An anti-imperialist and antimilitarist, Brewer was a strong supporter of an international court of arbitration. He served with Chief Justice Melville Weston Fuller on the international tribunal that arbitrated the conflict between Venezuela and Great Britain over the disputed boundary between Venezuela and British Guiana. Coauthor of a treatise in international law,[56] Brewer presided at the 1904 International Congress of Lawyers and Judges in St. Louis.

Jurisprudence

Before turning to the actual jurisprudence of the circuit courts of the Eight Circuit during the years between 1862 and 1890, it would be wise to pause and consider the role that the federal courts played during this period in the development of national law.

Although the lower federal courts continued to be limited and specialized courts throughout this period (by far the greater share of important lawmaking continued to be the work of state courts), their importance had greatly increased. In 1862 the jurisdiction of the lower federal courts had primarily encompassed admiralty and maritime matters and suits brought under certain federal laws—especially patent, copyright, and bankruptcy, but also including a large number of miscellaneous statutes—as well as acting as a forum for lawsuits between citizens of different states.

As a result of Civil War and Reconstruction, Congress greatly extended federal jurisdiction by providing in many instances for removal of cases from state courts, as well as by granting the federal courts federal question jurisdiction concurrent with state courts in all matters exceeding $500. The result over time was to transform the federal courts from "restricted tribunals of fair dealings between citizens of different states . . . [to] become the primary and powerful reliances for vindicating every right given by the Constitution, the laws and treaties of the United States."[57] But such a transformation did not truly occur in the federal courts as the role of the federal government and the federal courts remained limited. Most of the "governing" occurring in the United States during this period was performed by states and localities. Thus the dockets of the lower federal courts of the Eighth Circuit from 1862 to 1890 were largely made up of the "classic" federal staples—bankruptcy, patent, copyright—cases resulting from the relatively small number of federal criminal and revenue laws, a few new areas of federal jurisdiction (such as trademark), and diversity of citizenship cases.

Throughout American history, the lower federal courts have generally performed at least four functions.[58] First, like almost all courts, they settle disputes between some combination of persons, governments, and corporations. Second, the courts offer a forum for the enforcement of such centralizing policies as the collection of federal taxes or the protection of interstate commerce. The lower federal courts have proved much more likely than the state courts to protect out-of-state commercial interests from state legislatures. Third, the federal courts have also acted as a brake on centralizing tendencies. For example, from 1862 to 1890, living and working in their communities, the circuit and district judges (and even the circuit justice) had a firsthand understanding of the problems of their region, an understanding that often made them sensitive to state and local concerns in such important cases as those involving the enforcement of municipal bond obligations. Finally, in their role as appellate courts, the circuit courts (before 1891) and the courts of appeals (after 1891) have acted as a buffer between the district courts and the Supreme Court, providing a place for correction of substantial errors made in the conduct of trials and making the work of trial judges more uniform. This freed the justices of the Supreme Court (who, in any event, were overwhelmed with cases) from some routine appellate review.

Between 1862 and 1890, the major characteristics of the region that affected the docket of the circuit courts of the Eighth Circuit were disputes over land, the agricultural economy, the channels and instrumentalities of interstate commerce (in particular, rivers, steamships, and railroads), the Native American population, and the attempts of states and localities both to lure development and regulate its engines.

The circuit courts of the Eighth Circuit were very much part of the development of the region. Those courts would, sometimes unconsciously, expedite the settlement of the West by resolving disputes over land; by resolving patent cases to help make available to farmers farm implements and machinery, sometimes (but not always) at a lower cost than otherwise would have been the case; and by facilitating the growth of the region's infrastructure by enforcing Supreme Court decisions that protected the holders of bonds issued to promote railroads, and allowing railroads a favored position in cases involving bankruptcy, labor strife, and personal injuries. The circuit courts also helped to unleash the creative energies of a market economy by permitting capital to be mustered and private property protected and by playing a role in keeping local taxes low.

The federal circuit courts of the Eighth Circuit also acted as a kind of balance wheel, both enforcing centralizing policies and acting as a brake on centralizing tendencies. Generally, the courts were centralizers, enforcing federal laws and Supreme Court decisions. The courts enforced federal laws, including those involving revenues and crime, but spoke with a Western voice in some highly charged cases, evincing their sympathy for localities in their disputes with railroads and for state police powers used for oversight of railroads and grain elevators. Finally, the federal courts of the Eighth Circuit performed a special role in cases involving Native Americans—one that was more sensitive to the zigs and zags of the policies of the national government than settlers pressing west, and therefore demonstrating, at least periodically, more sensitivity to the rights of Native Americans than did most other government officials.

Disputes over Land

The federal courts were often used to settle contests over land titles, as the forum for equity actions to construe deeds, for actions to compel specific performance of contracts to convey real estate, and for suits to determine ownership of property affected by the meandering courses of rivers and streams. Considerable litigation over land in the West was inevitable given the potential wealth involved, the history of Spanish and French control of the area, and because all too often the desire for rapid settlement prevailed over careful surveying.

Perhaps the most complex suit in the Eighth Circuit involving title to land arose over the Maxwell Land Grant, a "tract almost an empire in size," located in a "region of the country unoccupied, little known and deemed of but trifling value."[59] At issue were millions of acres in New Mexico and Colorado—land involving mountain peaks, extensive plateaus, slopes, mesas, and traveled passes. The Maxwell Land Grant Company claimed title against the claims of squatters, cattlemen, mining interests, and the federal government. Three Maxwell cases came before Circuit Judge Brewer in the Circuit Court for the District of Colorado in the 1880s. Brewer ruled for the Maxwell interests each time.[60]

Many cases involved Iowa land. One of the most difficult series of cases involved grants made by the state pursuant to a federal law enacted in 1846 to fund improvements for navigation on the Des Moines River, which were to be made by the Des Moines Navigation and Railroad Company. Alternating sections of public lands in strips five miles wide on each side of the river were granted to the Iowa Territory to be used for funding the improvements. The matter was complicated by land grants to four railroads, which ran across the disputed navigation grants. The State of Iowa, the navigation company, and the railroads all made conveyances of land to settlers. Conflicting opinions, decisions, and administration by both the federal and the state governments produced chaos affecting more than a million acres of potentially rich farmland. A series of cases generated by these disputes arose in the Eighth Circuit and reached the U.S. Supreme Court. Ultimately, those who owned land based on the original grant won in court, but Congress then paid over a million dollars in claims to those who lost land.[61] There was also much litigation over 1.2 million acres of Iowa land that was set aside to make swampland accessible.[62]

Cases Involving Waterways and Their Traffic

Cases involving the rivers in the circuit arose in its courts. Some involved steamboats that had sunk, for sandbars, snags, ice, and logjams took a fierce toll. Such cases often required all sorts of exasperating continuances because witnesses were scattered throughout the nation's river systems.[63]

More important cases involved conflicts between nautical and rail interests. In 1859, Judge James M. Love of the District of Iowa ordered removal of the part of the first railroad bridge across the Mississippi, the Rock Island–Davenport Bridge, that lay on Iowa's side of the river, holding the bridge to be a serious obstruction to water commerce amounting to a nuisance. Love was reversed by the Supreme Court three years later. The effect of the High Court's decision was to assist the budding railroad aspirations of Chicago over the established river interests of St. Louis.[64]

In October 1864 an injunction was obtained from Love against the building of a railroad drawbridge across the Mississippi at Clinton, Iowa. Justice Miller overturned an order committing the builders for defiance of the injunction, and the bridge was completed in 1865. Nevertheless, with litigation pending to declare the bridge a hazard and an illegal obstruction to traffic on a navigable stream, its builders sought legislation from Congress authorizing the bridge. When Congress eventually acted, the circuit court was left with the questions as to whether the statute was unconstitutional either because Congress lacked the constitutional power to authorize the bridge or because its law improperly prescribed a rule to decide a pending case.

The decision of the Circuit Court for the District of Iowa (Justice Miller and Judge Love) left no doubt about their view of the significance of railroads to interstate commerce. The Chicago and North Western Railroad was to use the bridge at Clinton to reach Council Bluffs, where it would make contact (by ferry across the Missouri) with the Union Pacific. In a little more than two years, the Union Pacific would connect with the Central Pacific to complete the transcontinental railroad. After holding that the statute had not deprived the court of jurisdiction, the circuit court upheld the statute. Miller called the Clinton Bridge part of "an unbroken road from the Atlantic Ocean to the Missouri River" and a vital link in the east–west rail network. He observed further that the railroad had become as important as the steamboat, that rails were being connected for "the great highway of our Union." Miller thought that, in 1867 as in 1787, federal control was necessary to protect commerce among the states from local barriers. He had "no doubt of the right of Congress to prescribe all needful and proper regulations for the conduct of the immense traffic." The following year, the Supreme Court affirmed, finding the case so easy that it rendered its decision twelve days after oral argument.[65]

Cases Affecting Farming

Several important patent cases in the Eighth Circuit made important inventions available to farmers, often at much lower prices. Among the most important cases were those involving the drive well, the harvester, and barbed wire. Drive wells (wells constructed not by digging but by driving steel tubing into the ground) were widespread in Iowa after the Civil War. A patent for the method had been obtained by Col. Nelson Green in 1868, after the drive well had come into wide use. Farmers in four Iowa counties organized to combat the threat of wholesale suits brought by Green and his allies. The Circuit Court for the Southern District of Iowa held the patent invalid by a vote of 2–1. The verdict was estimated to have saved Iowa farmers as much as two million dollars.[66]

The harvester cases were brought by William Deering against the Winona Harvester Works and the McCormick Harvesting Machine Company. Among the devices involved were the "knotter," by which a cord is held around a bundle of grain; a combination of toothed arms, slotted recovery platform, and fixed spring arms for compacting the grain; a mechanism for compressing the bundle of grain just before tying; and a mechanism for raising and fastening the grain platform. In the lawsuits brought by Deering in the Circuit Court for the District of Minnesota, Deering was successful against the Winona Company in the contest over the knotter patents. But Deering did not prevail in the suit against McCormick for the combination of tooth arms, slotted recovery platform, and fixed spring.[67]

Perhaps no invention was more important to the settlement of the Great Plains than barbed wire because it worked out to be an excellent substitute for timber in fencing. The advent of barbed wire forced the cattleman to patronize the railroad, made stock farming, rather than ranching, the dominant occupation of the plains, and ultimately brought about the disappearance of the open free range.

In 1873, J. F. Glidden, a De Kalb, Illinois, farmer, braided two strands of wire together and placed pointed metal bars in between the two strands. At first, his application for the patent was disallowed, but in 1874 it was granted, although by no means was Glidden's the only patent for barbed wire. While Judge Brewer's decision in the Circuit Court for the District of Iowa in 1885 sustaining the Glidden patent for barbed wire was neither the first nor the last lawsuit involving that invention, it proved to be of critical importance to the Glidden interests, which would achieve virtual monopoly control of the barbed wire market.[68]

Brewer, who detested patent cases, stated that his decision in *Washburn & Moen Manufacturing Co. v. Grinnel Wire Co.*, which upheld the Glidden patent against the argument that it was something more than the coiling of wires, was one of the hardest cases he ever had to try. "It is also true that the entire combination . . . is a very simple thing," Brewer wrote, "but, simple though it is, Mr. Glidden first introduced it to the world; and . . . it has been found of value in the uses of the world, it would seem as though he should be entitled to the benefit of the value of that which he has contributed." Even if each element separately were contained in earlier barbed wires, stated Brewer, "it is unquestionably new . . . and the product of invention." Though not conclusive, "it is a fair matter of consideration" that "of all the structures and devices this has been the one that has met the want of the public."[69]

Cases involving farm foreclosures have often occurred in the Eighth Circuit, especially where legislatures have attempted to extend the time for mortgage repayments. In *Singer Manuf'g Co. v. McCollock*, decided by Judge Caldwell in the Circuit Court for the Eastern District of Arkansas in 1884, at issue was an 1875 state statute that appeared to give the mortgagor twelve months to redeem the mortgaged premises after foreclosure had been made under the decree of the state chancery courts. Judge Caldwell construed the statute as not applying to past sales of land under decrees of chancery courts, but permitting redemption from sales under decrees of foreclosure rendered since the act became law.[70]

Other Federal Staples

While the most important work of the circuit courts of the Eighth Circuit during this period in dealing with the staples of federal jurisdiction was in the area of patent law, contributions of consequence also occurred in the areas of bankruptcy, trademark, tax, and federal criminal cases.

There were many cases brought under the 1867 Bankruptcy Act.[71] There were also important questions involving trademarks. After the Supreme Court held the 1870 federal trademark law unconstitutional in 1879,[72] Judge McCrary held the following year in a Colorado case involving a trademark for a brand of beer that even though there was no trademark law on the books, the trademark at issue was good because for centuries trademarks had been recognized as property under the common law.[73] Congress reenacted the trademark statute in 1881 under its commerce power, and it was upheld. Nevertheless, in an indictment for violation of an 1876 statute imposing penalties for trespass upon rights obtained by trademark registration, Judge Brewer held that the 1876 law had fallen with the 1870 law and had not been "vivified or given operative force by the act of 1881."[74]

Although not as frequently as later would be the case, the circuit courts interpreted federal revenue statutes in suits brought to enforce them. Their work may be suggested by three cases that were decided by the Circuit Court for the District of Iowa and appealed to the U.S. Supreme Court. In *Henderson's Tobacco,* the circuit court held in a prosecution for making false and fraudulent records to avoid paying the excise tax on tobacco that certain provisions of the tax laws had been repealed by implication by a later statute. The Supreme Court, however, construed the effect of the repeal differently, reversing and remanding for further proceedings against those accused of tax fraud.[75] In *United States v. Glab,* the Supreme Court upheld the district and circuit courts for Iowa, which had ruled for the taxpayer in a case involving a tax for carrying on the business of a brewer. The courts held that where a partnership dissolved during the taxable year, the succeeding partner could carry out his business without paying a second tax.[76] In *Dobbins's v. United States,* the circuit court was upheld in a civil forfeiture action. The United States had seized the land on which a distillery had been maintained because the distillery owner was keeping books fraudulently. The Supreme Court held that even where the owner of the land was ignorant of illegal activities, in an action in rem the government was entitled to the verdict. If the owner of the property permitted his land to be used for a distillery, the law placed him "on the same footing as if he were the distiller."[77]

While criminal prosecutions were generally not a major part of the business of the federal courts (excluding the territorial courts) during this period, the circuit and district courts did, however, have jurisdiction over offenses such as violation of the revenue laws, illegal cutting of timber, and fraudulent use of federal lands, as well as postal offenses such as stealing money from letters.[78]

The Eighth Circuit was the jurisdiction for many of the prosecutions for political corruption in the foremost scandal of the Gilded Age, the evasion of internal revenue taxes by distillers connected with the "Whisky Ring," a scandal that reached into the White House. Over 230 persons were indicted in the Eastern District of Missouri. About one hundred pleaded guilty; twenty were tried and convicted; a dozen fled the country. The most notorious defendant, however, General Orville E. Babcock, President Grant's private secretary, was acquitted after a trial in St. Louis. Grant considered testifying in person but instead gave a deposition in Babcock's favor.[79]

There was no appellate review in criminal cases in the federal court system, except by certificate of division of opinion by lower court judges (and only then upon a specific question of law) until 1879, when Congress provided for appeal by writ of error from the district courts to the circuit courts.[80] Passage of a statute in 1889, which gave a right of appeal to the Supreme Court in a criminal case where the defendant had been sentenced to death, was, in important measure, the result of the conduct of one of the district judges in the Eighth Circuit, the notorious "hanging judge" Isaac Parker of the Western District of Arkansas.[81]

Parker, only thirty-six years old, became a district judge in 1875 and served until his death in 1896. When Parker came to Fort Smith in 1875, it was a town of three thousand without paved streets, sidewalks, public schools, or a decent hotel.[82] The District Court for the Western District of Arkansas had jurisdiction not only over cases in that state but also over those arising in what was known as the Indian Territory, the area that became the state of Oklahoma. That jurisdiction was vast—174,000 acres of long-grass pastures, creek bottoms, lonely ranches, and raw prairie towns. The only courts within the Indian Territory were Indian courts, and their jurisdiction was confined to members of the various Indian tribes. Seven-eighths of Parker's caseload came from a place "infected" with outlaws and desperadoes, where the Daltons and Belle Starr and many other notorious bandits preyed, robbing railroads, stealing horses, and rustling cattle, a jurisdiction where killing was an everyday occurrence.[83]

A historian has written that "administrative efficiency in the savage tradition is a salient characteristic of the federal judiciary in Oklahoma."[84]

So it may have been with Parker and the Indian Territory. Unaccountable via appeal, Parker tried cases from homicides and rapes to illegal grazing of cattle and bigamy. He became known worldwide for his hangings. In a little more than two decades, of the 164 men found guilty of murder (more than 300 were tried), 160 were sentenced to death, of whom 79 were hanged, while 4 others died while awaiting sentence or were shot trying to escape.

While it is true that Parker could be a partisan judge, coaching government witnesses and bullying those called by the defense, he probably did not deserve the series of rebukes given him by the Supreme Court. From 1889 to 1896, Parker was reversed thirty-seven out of fifty times by the high court, which found Parker's charges inaccurate, prolix, and prejudicial and held that he often decided cases on points not raised by the attorneys. Justice Brewer often stood alone in support of Parker in the Supreme Court.[85] Parker's power began to ebb in 1889, when Congress passed statutes providing for appeal to the Supreme Court in capital cases and abolishing the circuit court powers of the Western District of Arkansas.

There was another side to this unusual judge. Parker was an able administrator who brought order to a corrupt and chaotic jurisdiction. He was honest and remarkably hardworking, deciding 1,500 civil and 12,000 criminal cases in just over twenty years.[86] Although there were many hangings, only three lynchings occurred on Parker's watch.[87] He granted habeas corpus in cases where courts lacked jurisdiction; sought "to do equal and exact justice to Indians," who memorialized him as "one of their staunchest friends and one of the ablest and most consistent defenders of their rights under the Treaties with the United States";[88] and took a hard line against the "Boomers," white settlers in southern Kansas who periodically launched land-grabbing expeditions in what they wanted to become Oklahoma. To head off such predatory whites, Parker ruled in 1891 that the Arkansas Valley Railroad Company Bridge could not be opened for pedestrians and wagon traffic from Fort Smith into the Indian Territory. Here, too, he would be reversed.[89]

Cases Involving Native Americans

The years from 1862 to 1890 marked the final subjugation of the Native Americans on the Great Plains and the beginning of attempts at assimilation. Since that time, important cases involving Native Americans have become a regular feature of the work of the Eighth Circuit. Three decisions arising from the geographical area of the Eighth Circuit (one was from the Dakota Territory) are particularly worthy of mention.

The first, *United States ex rel Standing Bear v. Crook*, was one of the few major victories for Native Americans in courts of the United States during the late nineteenth century.[90] In 1858 the Ponca tribe relinquished almost all the land it owned or claimed in Nebraska except for a small reserve along the Niobrara River, which was promised to them permanently, along with a commitment by the United States to protect them. But through a bureaucratic error, Ponca lands were given to the Sioux a decade later. Instead of restoring the land or protecting the Ponca from Sioux harassment, Congress gave a small indemnity to the tribe. Then, during the full flush of revenge following Custer's defeat at Little Bighorn, the Ponca were included in a list of northern tribes exiled to the Indian Territory.

The forced removal from their historic land had a profound effect on the Ponca. Within a year, one-third of the tribe had died, and most of the remainder had taken ill. In 1879, Standing Bear, the Ponca chief, returned to Nebraska with a group of followers to bury the remains of his sons. The Ponca were arrested and brought back to Fort Omaha to be returned to the Indian Territory.

News stories written by a Omaha journalist dramatized the plight of the Indians and led two Omaha lawyers, Andrew J. Poppleton (chief attorney for the Union Pacific) and John L. Webster, to offer their services to the Ponca. With the tacit agreement of General George Crook, whose company of soldiers had arrested and was holding the Indians, habeas corpus was sought from Nebraska's federal district judge, Elmer S. Dundy. A rugged frontiersman, Dundy was reached by messenger while he was out hunting bear.

Obeying the writ, General Crook brought the Ponca into court on April 8, 1879, and produced the military orders under which he had acted. The U.S. District Attorney argued that the Indians were "not persons within the meaning of the law," while Webster and Poppleton countered that Standing Bear and any other Indian had the right to separate himself from his tribe and live under the protection of U.S. laws like any other citizen. Given permission to speak, Standing Bear called on the Almighty to "send a good spirit to brood over you, my brothers, to move you to help me." "Take pity on me," cried Standing Bear, "and help me to save the lives of the women and children."

Beginning his opinion, Judge Dundy stated that "during the fifteen years in which I have been engaged in administering the laws of my country, I have never been called upon to hear or decide a case that appealed so strongly to my sympathy."[91] Dundy then ruled for the Ponca. He held that an Indian is a "person" within the meaning of the laws of the United States and therefore had the right to sue out a writ of habeas corpus; that no rightful authority existed for removing the Native Americans by force to the Indian territory; and that the Indians possessed the inherent right of expatriation and the "inalienable right to 'life, liberty, and the pursuit of happiness.'" Then he ordered the Indians discharged from custody. It is said that when Judge Dundy concluded the proceedings, the audience in the courtroom rose to its feet and "such a shout went up as was never heard in a courtroom."[92] At the May 1879 term of the circuit court, Justice Miller refused to hear an appeal by the United States because "the Indians who had petitioned for the writ of habeas corpus were not present, having been released by the order of Dundy, District Judge, and no security for their appearance had been taken."[93] Standing Bear would live out his life in northeastern Nebraska. President Rutherford B. Hayes appointed a commission that worked out an arrangement where one-quarter of the Ponca returned to Nebraska and were allotted land along the Niobrara, while the rest remained in the Indian Territory.

The resolution of "Crow Dog's case" would have an enormous long-run impact on the use of U.S. courts for the prosecution of crimes allegedly committed by Native Americans against other Native Americans. In a case of apparent first impression, three years after the Ponca case, a Brule Sioux named Kan-Gi-Shun-Ca (or Crow Dog) was convicted in the First Judicial Court of the Dakota Territory of the murder of Spotted Tail, chief of the Brule Sioux band. The Supreme Court of the Dakota Territory affirmed, holding that even though the act of Congress extending the Crimes Act to Indian Country excepted crimes by Indians against Indians within tribal jurisdiction, U.S. jurisdiction had been conferred by a treaty that Spotted Tail himself had signed.[94]

Crow Dog then petitioned for habeas corpus in the U.S. Supreme Court. A unanimous Court ruled that the federal courts had no criminal jurisdiction in such a case. The High Court saw the case as one in which law,

> by argument and inference only, is sought to be extended over aliens
> and strangers; over the members of a community separated by race,
> by tradition, by the instincts of a free though savage life, from the

authority and power which seeks to impose upon him the restraints of an external and unknown code, and to subject to the responsibilities of civil conduct, according to rules and penalties of which they could have no previous warning; which judges them by a standard made by others and not for them, which takes no account of the conditions which should except them from its exactions, and makes no allowance for their inability to understand it.[95]

In response to *Ex Parte Crow Dog,* Congress extended the jurisdiction of U.S. courts over major crimes committed on reservations, thus further weakening tribal organization.[96]

In 1884, the year after the Supreme Court decided the *Crow Dog* case, an important case involving Indian civil rights arose in the courts of the Eighth Circuit. John Elk claimed that he had severed his relation to his former tribe, and that as a U.S. citizen, he was entitled to vote in a local election. Living, working, and paying taxes in Omaha, Elk, represented by Poppleton and Webster, brought suit against Charles Wilkins, the voting registrar in Omaha's fifth ward, who had refused to register Elk or to let him vote. In the Circuit Court for the District of Nebraska, Judge Dundy was joined by Circuit Judge McCrary.

The circuit court ruled against Elk, and the Supreme Court affirmed by a vote of seven to two. It took the High Court twelve pages to rule that Indians were not citizens of the United States if they had not been subject to the jurisdiction of the United States at the time of their birth or had not been naturalized by procedure according to treaty. Justice John Marshall Harlan, who had dissented alone the year before in the *Civil Rights* case and who would dissent alone twelve years later in *Plessy v. Ferguson,*[97] was joined in dissent this time by Justice William Woods. Harlan argued that the Fourteenth Amendment had been intended to confer national citizenship on persons of the "Indian race." Harlan concluded that as a result of the decision, "There is still in this country a despised and rejected class of persons, with no nationality whatever; who . . . are yet not members of any political community nor entitled to any of the rights, privileges, or immunities of citizens of the United States."[98]

State and Local Involvement with Business

The enormous industrial boom that followed the Civil War spawned efforts by governments throughout the nation to spur economic development and to regulate existing businesses. In the region of the Eighth

Circuit where development was occurring rapidly, railroad lines and grain elevators were essential but were also visible targets for vulnerable westerners confronting extreme fluctuations of farm prices coupled with high fixed (or growing) charges for storage and transportation, which appeared to be the result of the abuse of economic power. There resulted a series of conflicts between farmers and big business, farm and town, East and West, even state and federal courts. Thus the courts of the Eighth Circuit found themselves in the middle of a number of important constitutional controversies. The most important of these involved attempts to repudiate municipal bond obligations, to lure businesses to municipalities through the expenditure of taxpayer monies, to regulate railroads and grain elevators, and to protect railroads from strikes and the consequences of insolvency. Judges demonstrated a new assertiveness in resolving these conflicts.

MUNICIPAL BONDS   Beginning in the 1850s, railroad promoters, playing one community off against another, received many millions of dollars in land grants and property-tax-supported bonds as incentives to construct railroad lines. Iowa, lying astride the path from Chicago to the west and south, received much of the early wooing. All too often, these enormous grants failed to achieve the objectives for which the money was raised. As railroad construction lagged, disenchantment set in, and state courts, reversing previous judgments, often held that the legislatures had lacked the power to have authorized municipalities to issue such bonds.

Many millions of dollars and the credit of U.S. governments in European financial markets were at stake as states and localities sought to avoid their bond liabilities. The Supreme Court, which, as Judge Dillon wrote, "set a face of flint against repudiation,"[99] refused to follow state court decisions based on interpretations of state constitutions and state laws that denied the validity of state railroad bonds. Exercising unrestrained independence in matters of "general jurisprudence," the High Court formulated its own commercial law on the subject, attempting to discourage every form of attempted repudiation of debt while enforcing the obligation of bonds.

Over three decades, the Supreme Court heard approximately three hundred municipal bond cases. Fifty of these were from Missouri, and twenty-five each came from Kansas and Iowa. This line of cases placed federal courts in Iowa and later Missouri into conflict with state courts. Even in the Dakota Territory, the territorial court held Yankton County bonds invalid, and the U.S. Supreme Court reversed. The circuit justice, Samuel Miller, did not agree with most of these decisions and was placed in the unenviable position of having to hold court in his home state of Iowa to enforce them.[100]

The battle may be said to have begun in 1862, when the Iowa Supreme Court held that as a matter of state constitutional law, principal and interest on municipal bonds could not be paid for out of property taxes.[101] However, when the same issue arose the next year in diversity actions in the federal courts, the U.S. Supreme Court held in *Gelpcke v. Dubuque* that those courts need not be bound by the latest Iowa Supreme Court decision but rather ought to apply Iowa law as it was when the bonds had been issued.[102] One week after the *Gelpcke* decision, the Supreme Court held that if municipal bonds had been validly issued, they were negotiable and, in the hands of a bona fide purchaser, were proof against fraud or illegality.[103] Relying on concepts of common law, natural law, and the Contract Clause, the Supreme Court served notice that it was not prepared to follow the "oscillations" of state courts in such a vital area.

Justice Miller fought hard against this trend within the Supreme Court. In *Butz v. City of Muscatine*,[104] for example, a bondholder had sought mandamus against city officials to force them to levy a tax "sufficient" to pay off a judgment with interest and costs. However, under the city charter, the maximum assessment the council was able to levy was 1 percent of assessed value. The Supreme Court reversed the Circuit Court, which had followed the Iowa Supreme Court. The High Court said that to follow those decisions would be to "abdicate performance of a solemn duty" because it would take away a remedy that was in force at the time the bonds were issued and would thus impair the obligations of contracts.[105] In dissent, Miller (joined by Chief Justice Salmon P. Chase) called the decision "an entire and unqualified overthrow of the rule imposed by Congress and uniformly acted on by this court up to the year 1863, that the decisions of the state courts must govern in the construction of state statutes."[106]

As various communities defied the authority of the federal courts, Miller and the Iowa Circuit Court had to give way and apply *Gelpcke* and its progeny. Miller did so, but at times slowly and without enthusiasm, delaying those seeking their monies several years.[107]

The climax came in a case in which the Iowa courts had perpetually enjoined county officers from issuing a tax to give effect to a judgment received by a foreign bondholder. The U.S. Supreme Court responded by holding that state process could not bar mandamus and directed the circuit court to grant the writ.[108] In May 1869, Miller held on circuit that city and county officials who failed to obey a court order to levy taxes to pay bonds would be placed in the custody of the marshal of the circuit court until they agreed to obey. He held in another case that county supervisors would be released on bail if they agreed to obey the mandate of the court. The supervisors did.[109]

After the officials of Washington County (just south of Iowa City), attempting to comply with the federal court order, were arrested for contempt of a state court order enjoining the tax, Judge James M. Love directed the U.S. District Attorney to bring habeas corpus proceedings in the Circuit Court. The writ was executed. The county supervisors were discharged from state custody. The tax was then levied.[110] Judge Dillon, also an Iowan, went further and held, in a case involving Lee County in southeast Iowa, that his court could direct the marshal to collect the tax at once.[111] The municipalities finally began to give in late in the summer of 1870, when Miller, writing a public letter at the request of influential citizens, urged that the matter be settled, and President Grant indicated that he would not hesitate to use force.[112]

In the 1870s the scene shifted to Missouri. There federal and state courts rendered conflicting decisions in cases involving railroads, and mass meetings were held to determine how to evade the federal decisions. Arnold Krekel, judge of the U.S. District Court for the Western District of Missouri, imprisoned local officials for failing to raise tax money to pay municipal bond obligations in full. The Missouri State Democratic Party Convention went so far as to adopt a plank that stated that the jurisdiction of the federal judiciary, as it was then being exercised, was "unwise and hurtful to the true interests of the people." Once again, the U.S. Supreme Court prevailed.[113]

There was also prolonged litigation over Minnesota's liability for the bonds it had issued to the St. Paul and Sioux City Railroad.[114] The major exception to the trend occurred over the validity of Arkansas Civil War bonds. The Circuit Court for the Eastern District of Arkansas certified the issue to the U.S. Supreme Court via a division of opinion. The Supreme Court then held that the consideration for the note was void as being against public policy, the U.S. Constitution, and the president's proclamation, as well as under the principles of public law.[115]

That this bitter conflict between state and federal courts (and between the federal courts and Iowa politicians and citizens) took a toll
on Miller is undeniable. He wrote in 1878: "It is the most painful matter
connected with my judicial life that I am compelled to take part in a
farce whose result is invariably the same, namely to give more to those
who have already, and to take away from those who have little, the little
that they have."[116]

"TAXATION FOR A PUBLIC PURPOSE" At the same time that municipalities were being ordered to pay off their bond obligations, the federal courts were limiting their power to repeat such errors. The courts
of the Eighth Circuit imposed federal constitutional barriers to local
expenditure of tax monies to attract and assist businesses. In the development of this doctrine limiting municipal expenditures to those for
a "public purpose"—a doctrine that ultimately won the approbation of
the Supreme Court—John F. Dillon, as state chief justice, circuit judge,
and treatise writer, exercised an enormous influence on developments
throughout the nation.

Once again, Iowa was at the forefront of legal developments. At the
same time that the citizens of Iowa were defying federal court decisions
to repudiate municipal debt, the Iowa legislature passed a law authorizing municipalities to assist a railroad by levying a tax not to exceed
5 percent of the assessed valuation of property. In 1869, in the case of
Hanson v. Vernon,[117] the Iowa Supreme Court (Chief Justice Dillon writing) held that law unconstitutional on the ground that taxation could
only be for a public purpose.

Shortly after Dillon left the Iowa Supreme Court, that court overruled *Hanson v. Vernon*. Dillon, now circuit judge, chose to uphold the
new state court decision that permitted governmental units to levy
taxes for outright rail subsidies. To do otherwise, Dillon thought, would
create "intolerable mischief that would flow from the consequent confusion of rights."[118] Concurrently, Dillon and Judge Dundy certified a
division of opinion to the U.S. Supreme Court in a case dealing with a
Nebraska statute authorizing county commissioners to issue $105,000
in bonds to any railroad that would secure to Nebraska City a direct
connection to the East. The commissioners were authorized to act without the need for approval by a referendum, as had otherwise been provided by state law. The Supreme Court sustained the statute 5–3. Miller
dissented without opinion.[119]

Then came two important cases from Kansas involving the use of $2 million of bonds that had been issued to encourage private enterprises, such as manufacturing companies and hotels, to settle in Kansas municipalities. In *Commercial Nat'l Bank v. Iola*,[120] the City of Iola had adopted an ordinance authorizing $50,000 in bonds to be issued for the erection of buildings to be used by a company manufacturing bridges, plows, and stoves. The ordinance had been approved by referendum before the state statute authorizing the activity was enacted. Dillon, following the Kansas Supreme Court, held that a legislature could not compel or coerce citizens to aid in the establishment of purely private enterprises just because they incidentally might promote the general good of the community. "Taxation," wrote Dillon, "is a mode of raising revenue for public purposes. When it is prostituted to objects in no way connected with the public interest or welfare, it ceases to be taxation and becomes plunder." Taxation to aid railroads, Dillon wrote, had already gone to the "verge of legislative authority," and bonds to aid a bridge factory were "void from the beginning."[121]

Citizens' Sav. Ass'n v. Topeka involved $100,000 in bonds donated by the City of Topeka and authorized by the state of Kansas to aid in the establishment of an iron bridge and iron works company.[122] Dillon, writing for the Circuit Court for the District of Kansas and following his decision in *Iola,* held the municipal bond issue unconstitutional. The bonds were held to be devoid of legal obligation on the ground that the state legislature lacked the power to authorize the city to issue them.

The U.S. Supreme Court affirmed both decisions in an opinion by Justice Miller in the *Topeka* case. Miller, citing in part to Dillon's Law of Municipal Corporations, held that such statutes were void for two reasons: (1) because the taxes necessary to pay the bonds would, if collected, constitute the transfer of property to individuals to aid in projects not for public use, and (2) because the legislature lacked the authority to pass such a statute. As a result of the decision in the *Topeka* case, it became a settled proposition of American constitutional law for generations that aid to private business enterprises (excepting railroads) was not a public purpose for which state legislatures could exercise monetary and spending powers.[123]

THE GRANGER CASES Just after the height of the conflict between the federal courts and Iowa officials over municipal bond repudiations and contemporaneous with the "taxation for a public purpose" cases, the Granger cases arose. Agricultural discontent has been a deep-seated characteristic in the Eighth Circuit. Between 1862 and 1890, with farm prices low, interest rates high, and rail rates inconsistent, farmer anger was manifested in a variety of ways—defaults on municipal bonds, support for Greenback currency, the growth of interest groups such as the National Farmers Alliance and of political parties such as the People's Party and the Greenback Party. Farmers viewed state governmental efforts to attract railroads as the result of wholesale bribery of the legislature. In Iowa, for example, when the legislature in 1868 authorized towns to vote taxes not to exceed 5 percent of taxable property, the taxes were to be given to the railroads as a gift.[124] In Missouri, to complete the lines left unfinished at the beginning of the Civil War, the state paid the price of cancellation of the $25 million the company owed the state.[125] Certainly, farmers whose livelihood depended on railroads and grain elevators could not be expected to warm to these rich and powerful corporations, which, moving in secret ways, influenced public officials and sought freight rates designed to earn a rich return on fictitious capitalization.[126]

The most effective effort to regulate railroads and grain storage facilities was the Granger laws of the 1870s. Oliver Kelly had begun the Grange in 1867. Local groups spread swiftly. There were 2,000 in Missouri and 1,999 in Iowa.[127] The movement was also strong in Kansas, Nebraska, and Minnesota. The result in four of the states—Minnesota, Iowa, Wisconsin, and Illinois—was the passage of laws prescribing maximum railroad rates for freight and passengers (and for storing grain) by direct legislation or through delegation to commission. Discriminatory rates were proscribed.

At the time of the passage of the Granger laws, the assertion of a general power of state legislatures to regulate railroads had never been successfully challenged in any U.S. court. Nevertheless, the railroad corporations, bolstered by advisory opinions from well-known attorneys, put their faith in the courts.[128] The earliest Granger law, passed by Minnesota in 1871, fixed rates, created a railroad commissioner to report violations of the law, and provided a fine of $100 per violation or forfeiture of the railroad's charter. The railroads did not comply directly with the terms of the law, although they did reduce charges. In proceedings brought against the Winona and St. Paul Railroad by Minnesota's attorney general in 1873, the Minnesota Supreme Court upheld the law. In the circuit court, Judges Dillon and Rensselaer R. Nelson declined to instruct the receiver of another railroad to disregard or obey the law without there being full argument or an authoritative decision else-where.[129]

In 1874 Iowa enacted a law classifying railroads on the basis of gross earnings per mile and used that as a basis to fix passenger and freight rates. The governor of the state was authorized to prosecute any action brought for a violation of the law, if requested by an aggrieved person supported by twenty taxpayers.[130] While most of the railroads in Iowa complied with the state law, the Chicago, Burlington and Quincy Railroad, an Illinois corporation with a perpetual lease of the Burlington and Missouri River Railroad (an Iowa corporation, which held a major east–west trunk line making connections with Chicago and Nebraska), refused to comply with the law. After consultation with the other Iowa trunk lines, the CB&Q brought suit in the Circuit Court for the District of Iowa, attacking the statute on federal Commerce Clause and Contract Clause, as well as on state constitutional, grounds. The railroad did not contend that it could be free of all governmental restrictions on rates but strongly opposed rates directly prescribed by the legislature.

The CB&Q's motion for an injunction was argued before Justice Miller and Judge Dillon in Davenport early in 1875. On March 18, the circuit court upheld the law in an opinion written by Judge Dillon. The railroad's charter was construed in favor of the public. The state's right to regulate commerce within the state was upheld. The right of public supervision and control of the railroad was held to arise from the fact that it was a highway built for the convenience of the public, and there-fore it was "in part public and in part private."[131]

The railroad appealed to the U.S. Supreme Court, where the Iowa case was joined with the two from Minnesota and five from Wisconsin and Illinois. The Granger cases thus presented a major constitutional challenge to legislative control of rates. In the Supreme Court, the CB&Q attorneys argued that property was more than a tangible physi-cal substance, that it should be thought of as an asset that could rise and fall in value. Thus, by setting a maximum rate for the railroad's services, Iowa had deprived the company of property without due pro-cess of law.[132]

The Supreme Court announced its decisions in the Granger cases on March 1, 1877, more than a half decade after the first suits were filed, sixteen months after the lead Minnesota case was argued, and thir-teen months after the Iowa case was argued. All the statutes before the

Court in the Granger cases were upheld. Probably chosen by the Court as the lead case because it presented an issue of a regulation free from Commerce Clause and Contract Clause issues,[133] *Munn v. Illinois* involved an Illinois law that had created a Railroad and Warehouse Commission, empowered to investigate costs, receipts, earnings, and indebtedness of railroads and prevent abuse of the monopoly of grain elevator rates for the storage of grain in Chicago.

In an opinion written by Chief Justice Waite, the Supreme Court upheld the Illinois statute in *Munn*,[134] consciously deferring to the policy judgments of the legislature. The Court held that property rights were not absolute and that the state police power was broad. It held further that when private property is devoted to a public use, it is subject to public regulation for the public good. Railroads and grain elevators were held to be "affected by the public interest." In a concession that did not seem important at the time, Chief Justice Waite indicated that under some circumstances a regulatory statute might be so arbitrary as to be unconstitutional under the Due Process Clause. But that was for another day. Justice Field, joined by Justice Strong, strongly dissented, stating that the majority's opinion in *Munn v. Illinois* was "subversive of the rights of property."

In *Chicago, Burlington & Quincy R.R. v. Iowa*, Dillon was completely upheld. The Supreme Court held that the legislature's power over rates was complete, that no contract rights had been impaired, and that the law did not apply to interstate commerce. Chief Justice Waite wrote that railroads are "engaged in a public employment affecting the public interest and, under . . . *Munn* . . . subject to legislative control as to rates of fare and freight."[135]

Ironically, by the time the Supreme Court decided the Granger cases, many of the Granger laws had already been weakened or repealed. This was because some railroads had made reforms, many railroads were in dire financial straits, and the laws appeared to be slowing the growth of railroads. Nor can the cajolery, threats, bribery, and newspaper manipulation by the railroads be ignored. In Iowa, on March 23, 1878, four years to the day of the enactment of the Granger law, the governor signed a law that repealed the earlier law and created a railroad commission to investigate complaints and examine books. The commission was to report its findings to the legislature and recommend prosecution in the civil courts, if need be.[136] Although *Munn* seemed to be a barrier to prevent invalidation or even the cabining of legislative power to regulate prices and place ceilings on them, its authority would soon be eroded—a story left for the next chapter.

RAILROAD BANKRUPTCY AND RECEIVERSHIPS   Even apart from the cases involving bond issues and rate regulation cases, railroad cases constituted an important part of the business of the circuit courts of the Eighth Circuit. There were cases involving the taxation of railroads, cases arising out of injuries to railroad employees, attempts by the federal government to reclaim unsold portions of land grants to railroads, and battles over the consolidation of railroads. One of the most important of these was the battle between James J. Hill and James P. Farley over the St. Paul, Minneapolis and Manitoba Railroad Co. and the St. Paul and Pacific Railway Company, a battle fought in state courts as well as the Circuit Court for the District of Minnesota. Hill's syndicate acquired the St. Paul and Pacific, and Farley, at one point its receiver, sought some of the spoils. For over fourteen years the battle raged, reaching the U.S. Supreme Court twice. In the end, Hill was the winner in a decision by Circuit Justice Brewer, which was upheld by the Supreme Court.[137]

There were many railroad bankruptcy cases as a result of over-construction, heavy indebtedness, and hard times. Foreclosures were often unavoidable, and as a result the courts were asked to resolve issues as to the nature and disposition of railroad mortgage proceeds and the priority of claims, including the priority of mechanics' liens over mortgage lien rights.[138]

Solicitude for the rights of business as well as growing judicial activism can be seen in the development of the railroad receivership. On the eve of Reconstruction, receivership and railroad reorganization had become staples of the business of the lower federal courts. However, it was not until the repeal of the federal bankruptcy law in 1878 that federal judges, who had the recognized authority of chancellors in equity, began to accept petitions from railroads in difficulty (subject to varying state bankruptcy laws) and appointed receivers, not to wind up the business but to continue it. The Supreme Court gave its imprimatur to railroad receiverships in 1881.[139]

Railroads were businesses essential to the survival of the West, and their insolvency "rendered necessary the exercise of large and modified control" over the railroads by the courts.[140] Railroad receiverships produced an enormous increase in the work of the federal courts. The receivers appointed by the court paid for labor and improvements, and the court was ultimately responsible for the performance of duties that included negotiation among the antagonistic interests of mortgagees, unsecured creditors, material men, laborers, and stockholders.

For the railroad, receivership brought pronounced advantages. The courts ordinarily appointed company officers as receivers. A railroad in federal receivership was freed of the control of state railroad commissions, and receiverships were often used to protect the existing railroad system from heavy indebtedness and labor unrest. Railroad receivers thus might have a freer hand in bankruptcy than otherwise. As Justice Miller explained in his dissent in *Barton v. Barbour*:

> The receiver generally takes the property out of the hands of the owner, operates the road in his own way, with an occasional suggestion from the court, which he recognizes as a sort of partner in the business; sometimes, though very rarely, pays some money on the debts of the corporation, but quite as often adds to them, and injures prior creditors by creating new and superior liens on the property pledged to them.[141]

Judge Henry Clay Caldwell of the Eastern District of Arkansas (and later circuit judge) sought to redress some of the inequity by conditioning receiverships on the terms that claims for labor and materials should be paid ahead of the mortgages,[142] a position, though cautiously and within narrower limits, that was adopted by the Supreme Court.[143] On the other hand, Judge Brewer thought that Caldwell's approach thoroughly destroyed the sanctity of contract obligations of the mortgages.[144]

The receivership was easily perverted during times of labor strife. During the widespread railroad strikes of 1877, federal judges with railroads in receivership made "virtuoso use of the contempt power."[145] During the strikes of 1885–86, judges issued writs of assistance and bench warrants and instituted contempt proceedings against workers.

The most important cases involving labor troubles in the Eighth Circuit during this period involved the Wabash, St. Louis and Pacific Railway. During a labor dispute in 1885 while the railroad was in receivership, workers blocked its tracks and otherwise prevented the use of railway engines and freight cars in the railroad yards. More particularly, strikers were accused of spiking and blocking the tracks, drawing water from the engines, inciting employees to quit work, and making threats aimed at nonstriking employees. Judge Brewer held in *In re Doolittle* that striking was legal, but interference with the operation of a railway in federal receivership and with the rights of other employees was not.[146]

Brewer gave the strikers before him sixty days in jail and assessed costs, which was far too lenient for the colleague sitting with him, Samuel Treat of the Eastern District of Missouri.[147]

First organized as a recognizable circuit in 1862, the Eighth Circuit came to encompass a huge geographic area. Organized to do the tasks imposed on the federal courts by the Constitution and Congress, the courts of the Eighth Circuit helped integrate a large part of the continent into a unified nation while providing a forum to protect property from transient majorities. The circuit courts of the Eighth Circuit made themselves useful in a variety of ways—by settling disputes over land and mining claims, employing federal law to protect patents and trademarks, settling cases involving the region's great river and rail highways, applying federal criminal law, and from time to time attempting to dole out some justice for Native Americans, seeing that little was offered by other federal officials. The most important constitutional conflicts of the early years of the circuit were spawned by western attempts to lure development and to regulate the great corporations that contributed to that development, cases in which tensions between East and West were often not far from the surface. The circuit justice and circuit judges were able, and three of them, Samuel Miller, John F. Dillon, and David J. Brewer, made major contributions to national law.

A new era was coming—one in which the area of the Eighth Circuit would be greatly enlarged and a tier of federal intermediate appellate courts would be created to relieve the U.S. Supreme Court of more routine controversies. The courts of the Eighth Circuit would come to perform an important role in that era as the reach of federal jurisdiction was enlarged to include the exercise of federal police power, regulation of monopoly, the application of sedition laws during wartime, and Prohibition.

CHAPTER 2

★ ★ ★ ★ ★ ★ ★

The Early Years

1891–1929

Reaching from New Mexico's mountainous Hidalgo County backing into Mexico, to Angle Inlet beside Lake of the Woods jutting into Canada, in the early years of the twentieth century the Eighth Circuit sprawled across the central United States. Farthest east was Dorena, Missouri, almost touching Kentucky. Out west the jurisdiction went as far as Wendover, perched on Utah's Great Salt Lake Desert.

This circuit of great size was a by-product of admission to statehood of six states between 1889 and 1912: North and South Dakota (1889), Wyoming (1890), Utah (1896), Oklahoma (1907), and New Mexico (1912). At the time, although the land area was large, the Eighth Circuit was administratively manageable because the population of many of its states was sparse and federal jurisdiction was still limited. However, as population increased and federal jurisdiction rapidly grew, size eventually became a deterrent to efficient administration. The solution, enacted in 1929, was the division of the circuit, largely on an east–west basis. Three states of the Great Plains (North and South Dakota and Nebraska) and four of the Mississippi Valley (Minnesota, Iowa, Missouri, and Arkansas) would remain in the Eighth Circuit. The remaining six states (Kansas, Colorado, Wyoming, Utah, Oklahoma, and New Mexico) would constitute a newly created Court of Appeals for the Tenth Circuit.

State and Regional Developments

The New States

Of the new additions, North and South Dakota, which remained in the circuit, deserve particular mention. Sharing an extremely harsh climate, the Dakotas came into the Union as sparsely populated agricultural states, though much of their land was ill suited for farming. Remote from important centers of population, industry, and political decision making, each state was unusually dependent on railroads, grain elevators, and financial institutions in states to their east and resented it.[1] That resentment was harnessed to bring about a period of Progressive reform and then, as a result of the efforts of the relatively short-lived Nonpartisan League, a sort of state socialism that in North Dakota produced a state mill, state bank, and state hail insurance, and in South Dakota a state cement plant. In these years, the states shared a political culture of clean if rambunctious politics, an unusual blend of radical proscriptions and conservative prescriptions.[2]

During the years when Oklahoma would be a part of the Eighth Circuit, the state generated a number of important cases involving Native Americans or petroleum or a combination of both. The eastern part (or "Indian Territory") of what is now the state of Oklahoma largely belonged to the "Five Civilized Tribes" (Cherokee, Chickasaw, Choctaw, Creek, and Seminole) until the twentieth century. The central part of the state, which included Oklahoma's Panhandle, only opened for settlement to non-Native Americans in 1889, was established as the Territory of Oklahoma by Congress in 1890. Pressed by interests seeking to settle the Indian Territory, pressures that greatly increased when petroleum was discovered, Congress in 1893 created the Dawes Commission with a mandate to bargain for land and achieve the dissolution of the Indian nations. Those aims were achieved so well that, by 1905, whites had come to outnumber Native Americans by five to one in the Indian Territory. Congress refused in 1905 to admit to the Union the Indian Territory alone but in 1907 admitted the "Twin Territories" together as the state of Oklahoma. For over two decades, the U.S. District Courts for the Eastern and Western District of Oklahoma[3] would be important sources of appeals to the Court of Appeals for the Eighth Circuit.[4]

Neither Wyoming nor Utah nor New Mexico made a contribution to the work of the Court of Appeals comparable to that of Oklahoma.

Wyoming, with a population of 63,000 when admitted to the Union, did give the Court of Appeals (and U.S. Supreme Court) one important judge, Willis Van Devanter. Its rich oil deposits would generate several important cases over private exploitation of federal land. Although Utah's territorial courts had been the forum for bitterly fought litigation brought about by federal attempts to suppress Mormonism, those legal conflicts were largely in the past when Utah entered the Union in 1896. While Utah was in the Eighth Circuit, the most important cases it sent the Court of Appeals involved mining. New Mexico, admitted to the Union in 1912 with a population of 330,000 (almost 100,000 more than Utah's when admitted), produced few cases for the Court of Appeals, the most interesting of which involved land claims and Native Americans.

Regional Developments

The eastern part of the Eighth Circuit was far ahead of the western part in settlement, although its rate of population increase slowed. Minnesota, for example, grew only from 1.3 million to 1.6 million. Arkansas was an exception. In spite of a large outmigration of African Americans, the state grew from 1.1 million to 1.9 million. The rate of population increase in the more newly admitted states was more rapid: North Dakota from 191,000 to 681,000; South Dakota from 350,000 to 693,000. The most dramatic increase of all was registered by Oklahoma. The Sooner State increased from 259,000 in 1890 to 2.4 million in 1920.[5] In the eastern part of the circuit there was also a considerable migration from farm to town or city. By 1929, Missouri's rural population had become a minority. Here, too, Arkansas was an exception. In 1930, 80 percent of its population still lived in rural areas.[6]

Agriculture remained the dominant sector of the state economies. The introduction of new crops (or new strains of old crops), successful irrigation, and soil conservation greatly increased productivity. Enactment of the Newlands Act in 1902 initiated important government irrigation projects.[7] However, the agricultural economy is cyclical, and during this period there were two extreme farm depressions—in the 1890s and the 1920s. In the 1920s, for example, the wholesale price index, which had risen during the war from 100 (1914) to 211 (1920), dropped to 121 (1921) and for the rest of the decade would not exceed 149. The purchase price of wheat per bushel declined from $2.02 (1919) to $.82 (1921).[8] Real estate values in South Dakota declined 58 percent between 1920 and

1930. Between 1921 and 1932, there were 34,419 farm foreclosures in the state, 19.6 percent of farm acreage on the assessment rolls.[9]

Fortunately, the economies of many of the states of the Eighth Circuit continued to diversify. Agriculturally related industry became increasingly important to the economy. Minnesota, for example, had great sawmills and produced cereal, pasta, and farm machinery.[10] Iowa had a meatpacking industry. Farm implements such as John Deere tractors were also manufactured in Iowa, as were butter, flour, and pearl buttons.[11]

Nonagriculturally related manufacturing also grew. Between 1890 and 1910, capital invested in manufacturing in Nebraska nearly tripled to almost one billion dollars.[12] Iowa manufactured Schaeffer pens, Collins radios, and Maytag dishwashers. By the end of this period, Missouri ranked tenth in the nation in the total value of its manufactured products.[13]

Mining became increasingly important to the economic success of the circuit. Extraction of iron from Minnesota's Mesabi Range began in the 1890s. From that source would come a large part of the steel that built the United States in the twentieth century. Petroleum was discovered in Oklahoma, Kansas, Colorado, New Mexico, and Wyoming. There was even a boom in Arkansas with the discovery of the El Dorado field in 1921. Gold was mined in Colorado, potash in New Mexico, and coal and copper in Utah. Vigorous and diversified commerce yielded new opportunities for litigation in the federal courts.

During these years, political protest movements affected the fabric of life in the circuit. Farmer discontent was a constant, regardless of prosperity or depression—the result, no doubt, of the difficulties of farm life and farmers' dependence on others for marketing their commodities and for purchasing necessaries and luxuries. Westerners often felt that they were bearing the brunt of the cost of the expansion of industry and the accumulation of capital.[14]

The first of these movements, the Populist Party, created in 1890, was a response to the economic problems of the late 1880s—deflation and depression, high railroad rates, and low wheat prices.[15] Pitting farmers and miners against the "moneyed classes," the Populists had immediate, if short-term, successes in Nebraska, Minnesota, South Dakota, and Kansas and among whites in the South. The principal yield for the federal courts from the Populist movement was a new surge of railroad regulation, which generated important constitutional litigation.

The Populist movement had largely been confined to the Midwest and South. The Progressive movement impacted a much wider area and affected local, state, regional, and national politics. The impact of Progressivism on the courts of the Eighth Circuit occurred through the prosecutions brought in federal courts against big-city party machines and the passage of state police regulations, particularly those enforcing Prohibition, which from time to time generated constitutional litigation.[16]

The third wave of reform politics resulted in the Nonpartisan League, created by Arthur C. Townley in North Dakota in 1915. Even at its height, the Nonpartisan League was limited to the north central states. The Nonpartisan League seemed, for a time, to offer more substantive change than the Progressives, who sought, first of all, to "clean up" politics. Townley, however, pushed for creation of state-run institutions to assist farmers directly in their battles against private banking, marketing, and transportation interests.[17] In 1916, the Nonpartisan League swept to victory in North Dakota. In a few legislative sessions, not only were the state bank, mill, and hail insurance created, but the Nonpartisan League may fairly be credited with the adoption of a better system for grading grain, a state grain elevator association, an inheritance tax, a minimum-wage law for women, and a state highway system. Poised for regional success at the time of America's entry into World War I, the league fell victim to the mass conformity and antiradicalism that followed. By 1920, the league had ceased to be a factor in the politics of any state except North Dakota and, possibly, Minnesota. Even in a short time, however, the league's leaders and program became involved in prosecutions under the Espionage and Sedition Acts, bankruptcy proceedings, and suits challenging the constitutionality of the league's program.[18]

During this period, the Eighth Circuit would become less remote, less isolated, and less unique than it had been as a result of developments in transportation and communications and the effects of World War I. The extraordinary social effects of the automobile on society were felt during these years. The acceptance of the automobile, which produced so much change, was astonishingly rapid. In Missouri, for example, the number of vehicles in the state increased from 16,400 (1911) to 297,000 (1920) to 762,000 (1930).[19] The automobile brought the isolated farmer to town and city, reducing the pressures of small-town life and diminishing the political importance of the railroads. The manufacture of cars, the construction of roads, and the use of trucks for freight increased marketing opportunities for producers of both agricultural and industrial goods.

One further development that resulted from the automobile was a growing tourist industry, soon to become important in the circuit.[20]

While the railroad continued to be the primary carrier of freight, railroad rates dropped as a result of competition from trucking and later from the airplane. There would be new waves of state rate regulation, which generated major constitutional decisions by the courts of the Eighth Circuit and received Supreme Court review. Cases involving federal regulation of railroads would reach the dockets of the district courts during the first decade of the twentieth century.

The telephone (which began to be widely used in these years), radio, and motion pictures also made life on the plains and in the mountains less remote. By 1930, people living in small towns and even many on farms had become integrated into a national system of news and entertainment that altered social mores and political attitudes. Such changes in communications and transportation meant that national and international events impacted more directly (or were felt to impact more directly) on the region's economy and cultural life. For the first time in American history, there were expectations that the federal government should really govern. On the national scene, a series of laws were passed, the handiwork of the Progressives, which greatly increased and diversified the work of the federal courts. These included laws regulating railroads, laws protecting consumers, laws aimed at unfair business practices, and federal criminal laws aimed at "immoral acts" such as drinking, prostitution, and the taking of narcotics.

America's involvement in World War I had profound effects. The war brought about a frenzy of superpatriotism and intolerance everywhere in the nation, aimed first at German Americans, then at radical groups. In the Eighth Circuit as elsewhere, civil liberties were threatened by government and the mob.

In spite of centripetal forces between 1891 and 1929, the Eighth Circuit remained distinctive. The vastness of the circuit, coupled with the still strong constitutional position of the states in the federal Union, made possible the local variations that continued to give such richness of texture (for good and bad) to American life. Political cultures varied from state to state—the result of different economies, different histories, and different ethnic backgrounds. Life in each of the states had distinctive features, and that distinctiveness may be discerned in the work of their federal courts. Searching the docket of the Court of Appeals, one sees the economic potential of the Mesabi Range, the rancorous relations between North Dakota's farmers and the large economic institutions of the Twin Cities, the poisonous labor-management conflicts of Colorado's mines, the effects of virulent racism on Arkansas life, the unique history of Oklahoma's Indian Territory, and the exceptional difficulties of accurately determining land titles in New Mexico. Unfortunately, space does not permit discussion of each. Litigation spawned by distinctive features of life in different parts of the circuit found its way into the federal courts and ultimately colored the docket of the Court of Appeals.

Two important minorities remained outside the mainstream of regional and nation life: Native Americans and African Americans. During these years, the only states in the Eighth Circuit with sizable African American populations were Arkansas, Missouri, Oklahoma, and Kansas. Each of those states had some kind of formalized segregation. Race relations were at their most primitive in Arkansas. There the failure of Populism to ameliorate economic hardships was followed immediately by increased racism.[21] Arkansas's first Jim Crow law, a separate coach act, was passed in 1891. As the result of the adoption in 1893 of a literacy test, later followed by a poll tax and a white primary law, the 1894 elections in Arkansas would be the last for some time in which significant numbers of blacks would vote. Between 1889 and 1918, there were 214 lynchings in Arkansas, placing the state sixth in the nation.[22] When President Theodore Roosevelt visited Little Rock, Governor Jefferson Davis, who in 1900 had become the first major party candidate in the state to appeal openly to racial prejudice, welcomed the president in a speech that praised lynching as sound public policy.[23] African Americans began moving north from Arkansas in the 1890s. After the Elaine riot of 1919, one of the bloodiest black-white encounters in American history (probably more than one hundred blacks were killed, and five whites), the rate of black outmigration accelerated. Those who remained had to learn a dehumanizing servility.[24]

Not all grave racial problems took place in the South, in states with formal segregation, or in states with a large African American population. In 1919, Omaha, the largest city in a state with only 13,000 African Americans in a total population of almost 1.3 million, had a horrible antiblack riot. Not only was an alleged black rapist lynched by beating, hanging, and burning, but the city's white mayor, who sought to halt the mob, barely escaped being lynched himself. It took eight hundred federal and state troops to restore order after the city's downtown was pillaged and a courthouse burned.[25] On the whole, however, race relations were not an important issue for whites who lived north of Missouri's northern border during these years, although in the years after World War I there was some Ku Klux Klan activity in Nebraska, South Dakota, and Colorado.[26]

Creation of the Circuit Courts of Appeals

The Court of Appeals for the Eighth Circuit was one of nine created by the Circuit Court of Appeals Act of March 3, 1891 (otherwise known as the Evarts Act),[27] a milestone of judicial reform. The growth of the United States since the end of the Civil War—in settled land area, population, economy, and infrastructure—pressed hard on the federal court system, especially on the Supreme Court, where some litigants were waiting as long as four years for a decision. In their turn, the lower federal courts also faced crowded dockets, the result of the enormous economic expansion that had followed the end of the Civil War. Not only could the justices of the Supreme Court no longer make a significant contribution to the work of the circuit courts, but even the circuit judges were unable to sit in all their districts in a given year. The result was that the circuit courts often became tribunals of one—the district judge. When that occurred, not only was the regional balance intended by the framers of the First Judiciary Act missing, but the district judge might be hearing appeals from his own decisions.

The Evarts Act was a compromise between the commercial and nationalistic interests of the East and the concerns of the Populist South and Midwest, which feared the extension of federal power. In 1891, Congress created a new tier of courts, the circuit courts of appeals, which were given appellate jurisdiction over both the circuit and district courts. Each of the nine circuit courts of appeals was composed of two circuit judges, save the Second Circuit, which was given three. Appeals were ordinarily heard by a panel of two circuit judges and one district judge, a quorum being two. Congress bowed to tradition by preserving the circuit courts for the time being, but those courts were shorn of their appellate jurisdiction and became, for the most part, indistinguishable in actual operation from the district courts. Occasionally, members of the circuit courts of appeals presided over important cases in the circuit courts, such as those involving the constitutionality of state railroad rates; and in a few areas, most notably antitrust, the duty of court of appeals judges to sit was imposed by statute. Although in the Evarts

Act, Congress had left open the possibility of continued circuit riding by the justices, after 1891 this rarely occurred. The circuit courts were finally abolished in 1911.

The main purpose of the creation of the circuit courts of appeals was achieved by diverting the stream of federal appeals away from the Supreme Court. Direct appeals to the U.S. Supreme Court continued in what would ordinarily be the most important cases—cases involving interpretation of the Constitution or treaties that arose either in federal or state court. The jurisdiction of the Supreme Court over criminal appeals was increased. But the new courts of appeals became responsible for the bulk of federal appeals. It was intended that the decisions of the courts of appeals be final in more routine cases, such as diversity, patent, revenue, and admiralty, subject only to discretionary Supreme Court review via the writ of certiorari. Under the new act, when courts of appeals were confronted with novel issues of law that they believed required resolution by the Supreme Court, they were authorized to certify the case to the Court for resolution of those particular questions. For its part, when cases were certified to the Supreme Court, the justices had discretion to answer the certificates, call for the whole record from the court of appeals and decide the entire case, or turn down the certification.

The Circuit Court of Appeals Act worked. The courts of appeals took over the function of oversight of the district courts, freeing the Supreme Court from routine cases. The docket of the Supreme Court was substantially relieved for many years. Increasingly, the Supreme Court became a public law court making public policy.

The creation of the courts of appeals did more than give the Supreme Court desperately needed assistance. It made it possible for the federal courts to keep up with rising number of cases which arose from the broadened role of the federal government during the Progressive era. In a little more than two decades, Congress passed the Interstate Commerce Commission Act (1887), the Sherman Antitrust Act (1890), the Elkins and Hepburn Acts regulating railroads (1903; 1906), and the Clayton and Federal Trade Commission Acts (1914), aimed at unfair business practices. Additionally, there were regulatory statutes to protect the consumer, such as the Pure Food and Drug and Meat Inspection Acts (1906). Federal criminal jurisdiction was greatly broadened by passage of laws aimed at white slavery, narcotics, and liquor. Because of this rapid increase in federal jurisdiction, the lower federal courts during this period were being transformed from courts dealing primarily with diversity cases, a few federal specialties, such as admiralty, bankruptcy, trademark, and several other classes of cases, into courts with a heavy public law docket, requiring the interpretation of federal statutes, the application of federal criminal laws, and the oversight of administrative agencies.

The courts of appeals succeeded so well that by passage of the law known as the Judge's Bill or the Judiciary Act of 1925,[28] there was difficulty in greatly enlarging the Supreme Court's discretionary jurisdiction. Under that law, the classes of appeals that the Supreme Court was required to hear were largely reduced to cases growing out of the antitrust and interstate commerce laws, suits to enjoin the enforcement of state statutes and the actions of state officials, and writs of error brought by the United States in criminal cases.

Judicial Administration in the Eighth Circuit

The Court of Appeals for the Eighth Circuit met for the first time on June 16, 1891, in St. Louis. Circuit Justice David Brewer and Circuit Judge Henry Clay Caldwell, who had succeeded Brewer as circuit judge in 1890, were in attendance. When the court heard its first case on October 12, 1891, Judge Caldwell presided. He was joined by two district judges, Amos Thayer of the Eastern District of Missouri and Moses Hallett of the District of Colorado. Walter Sanborn, who had been appointed to the second judgeship provided by the act, took his seat on the bench in the spring of 1892.

The Eighth Circuit Court of Appeals was busy from the beginning. In 1892 it disposed of 120 cases, 30 percent of the cases of all nine courts of appeals.[29] In 1893, the court disposed of 145 cases out of a nationwide total of 684. Congress responded by creating a third judgeship in 1894, to which Amos Madden Thayer was appointed.[30] However, six years later, in 1900, the Eighth Circuit disposed of 191 cases (compared with 917 for all nine circuits). In 1903 Congress added still another judgeship.[31] During the first decade of extensive government regulation, the number of cases heard in the Eighth Circuit climbed from 147 (1904) to 241 (1910). By its second decade, in addition to the frequent sittings in St. Louis, the Court of Appeals was meeting once a year in St. Paul and Denver. From 1891 to 1919, the Eighth Circuit was often the busiest court of appeals.

During the second decade of the twentieth century, the caseload of the Court of Appeals was erratic. In 1911, the court decided 335 cases; in 1913, only 104; in 1915, 284. When Congress abolished the U.S. Commerce Court in 1913, Judge John Emmett Carland, who had been the U.S. district judge for South Dakota before being named to the commerce court, was assigned to the circuit. The position lapsed with his death.

The docket pressed harder in the 1920s. The Court of Appeals led the circuits in dispositions in 1923 (322) and 1927 (492), and its backlog grew. Congress added two more judgeships in 1925, but there was a net gain of only one because of the death of Carland.[32] By the middle of the 1920s, there was a growing feeling that rather than the creation of another one or two judgeships, more radical surgery was in order. While the caseload per authorized judgeship did not by itself justify division of the circuit, there were other reasons for doing so. First, district judges were being worked too heavily—40 percent of the decisions of the Court of Appeals were being written by district judges.[33] Second, because of the circuit's geographic size, judges spent too much time traveling from their homes to the place of sitting. Third, it was argued that it was becoming increasingly difficult to keep the case law of the Eighth Circuit consistent because of the number of court of appeals judges, the use of district judges, the number of cases, and geographical distance.

The problems of the Eighth Circuit during the 1920s were not unique. Prohibition and growing federal regulation were trying the resources of most of the federal courts. However, the problem seemed more serious in the Eighth Circuit than elsewhere. In 1927, a subcommittee of the American Bar Association recommended attacking the problems of the federal judiciary on a national basis. It suggested redrawing the lines of every circuit, adding an additional circuit, and creating a number of additional judgeships. This holistic solution encountered a fusillade of criticism. As earlier and later warriors in the trenches of federal judicial reform have to their misfortune learned (often belatedly), when remapping the federal circuits is proposed, lawyers, judges, and politicians develop sudden, extraordinary circuit loyalty. Inextricable connections are found to justify keeping New York with Vermont in the Second Circuit, for example, or Tennessee with Michigan in the Sixth Circuit. As a result, Congress in the twentieth century has found it virtually impossible to undo the handiwork of the nineteenth-century Congresses. The ABA subcommittee was sharply criticized for recommendations that moved states into different circuits, for ending the link between the number of circuits and the number of justices, and for proposing that New York State be made a circuit of its own.

In the midst of all the criticism of the subcommittee proposals, it was possible to discern considerable support, including that from the unusually influential chief justice, William Howard Taft, for dividing the Eighth Circuit. Following a suggestion of Justice Van Devanter, Representative Maurice Thatcher of Kentucky introduced a bill in 1928 that would have divided the Eighth Circuit on an east-west axis, creating a northern and a southern circuit. Such a division made sense from the standpoint of travel because the major railroad lines ran east to west. The ABA established a committee of Eighth Circuit attorneys to consider the issue.

The division of the Eighth Circuit occurred with extraordinary speed for any legislative action, but miraculously rapid for reform in judicial administration. Only three obstacles had to be overcome. Senior Judge Kimbrough Stone would not admit that the Eighth Circuit had any kind of backlog problem. The judges had to be convinced that dividing the circuit would not preclude immediately creating additional judgeships. Finally, there was the sensitive problem of determining which state would go into which circuit. It was the willingness of Congress to create additional judgeships that made the division of the circuit a reality. Although Kimbrough Stone bristled at the notion that anyone would believe his circuit was "even one case behind in its docket," he would get behind division so long as additional judgeships were created.[34]

All the members of the Court of Appeals signified their support for division by putting forth their own plan. Their proposal was for three circuits, each rotating around a seat of the court. The St. Louis circuit would have consisted of Missouri, Kansas, and Arkansas; the St. Paul circuit of Minnesota, Iowa, Nebraska, and the Dakotas; the Denver circuit of Colorado, Wyoming, Utah, New Mexico, and Oklahoma. This plan had the virtue of interfering little with the present seats of the court and would have left room for future growth, but it commanded no support outside the court. While the plan itself went nowhere, it demonstrated that the members of the court were not adamantly opposed to division.

The plan that gained widespread support was put forward in H.R. 13567, introduced by Representative Walter H. Newton of Minnesota in May 1928. Newton proposed to divide the court into eastern and western circuits. In this way, agricultural and manufacturing litigation would cluster in the eastern circuit, and mining and irrigation cases in the western. The two sitting judges from the western part—Lewis of Colorado and Cotterall of Oklahoma—were to join the new circuit, which was also to receive two new judgeships. The reorganized Eighth Circuit would be constituted by four sitting judges (Stone, Kenyon, Booth, and Van Valkenburgh) and receive one new judgeship.

The Newton bill sped through the Congress. By the close of the third day of congressional hearings (January 11, 1929), all the Court of Appeals judges, sixteen district judges from the circuit, the American Bar Association, and eight state bar associations had endorsed the bill. The House passed the bill unanimously on February 11, 1929. As the valuable support of the chairman of the Senate Committee on the Judiciary, George W. Norris, had been ensured by the expedient of adding Omaha to the places the revised Eighth Circuit could sit, the Senate passed the House bill on February 23 with only a single amendment—Kansas City was also to be made a seat of the new court, the U.S. Court of Appeals for the Tenth Circuit. The House agreed to the Senate amendment on February 25. President Coolidge signed the bill into law on February 28, 1929.[35] With a bare minimum of political posturing, acrimony, and other causes of delay, the Eighth Circuit was divided.

The Judges

Fourteen men served as judges of the U.S. Court of Appeals for the Eighth Circuit between 1891 and 1929. Although none of their names are household words, several were judges of considerable distinction. Missouri had the largest number of appointees—four. From 1925 on, the bench included two judges from Missouri. There was at least one Minnesotan on the court throughout the entire period, and two sat together in the last years. An Iowa seat on the court may be said to have begun with the appointment of Walter I. Smith in 1911. When Smith died in 1922, he was succeeded by William Kenyon. No other state had more than one appointee to the court, and four—North Dakota, Nebraska, Utah, and New Mexico—had none.

Half of the judges were elevated to the Court of Appeals from the federal district bench, and one, John E. Carland, had also served as a district judge, but he was assigned to the Eighth Circuit from the short-lived Commerce Court. Four of the appointees had served on state courts. Three had served as U.S. Attorneys and two others—Van Devanter and Kenyon—had important legal experience with the federal government.

All but Arba Van Valkenburgh had run for office or held high party office, but none held high state office, and only two had served in the Congress. As all the presidents who made appointments were Republicans save Cleveland and Wilson, only a few Democrats were appointed, although both Theodore Roosevelt and Calvin Coolidge crossed party lines once with appointments.

Benjamin Harrison's Appointments

The fourth circuit judge and the first senior judge of the Court of Appeals for the Eighth Circuit, Henry Clay Caldwell (1890–1903), had, like the circuit, roots in both the North and the South. Born in Virginia, Caldwell grew up on a farm in Iowa. He read law in Keosauqua with the firm of Wright and Knapp, with whom he practiced after being admitted to the bar in 1851. An early supporter of the Republican Party, Caldwell was elected to the Iowa House of Representatives and quickly became chairman of its judiciary committee.

When the Civil War broke out, Caldwell joined the Third Iowa Cavalry with the rank of major. He saw action in the lower Mississippi Valley and led the advance column that took Little Rock. Leaving the army with the rank of colonel, Caldwell sought, and with the support of Samuel F. Miller received, the appointment as district judge from Arkansas. Although Arkansas had two judicial districts at the time, only one federal judge was provided by Congress until 1871.[36]

A so-called carpetbagger, Caldwell cautiously made his way through the minefield of Reconstruction. He was called on to enforce laws confiscating the property of Confederates and contracts that had arisen from the purchase and sale of slaves. Cases involving enforcement of the Fourteenth Amendment and elections also came before him. Yet during Reconstruction, Caldwell was reversed by the Supreme Court only once—in a case where he had refused to enforce a promissory note in payment for the sale of a slave.[37]

Very popular in the South and well respected in the North, Caldwell was under consideration as early as 1869 for a seat on the Supreme Court. Justice Miller was a strong advocate—he called Caldwell "the ablest District Judge that is in my circuit and equal to any I believe in the United States." Miller added that Caldwell "has all the elements of an able judge, and will be if appointed as pure, and as impartial as it is in the nature of man to be."[38] Caldwell would be considered for the Supreme

Court by presidents Hayes, Cleveland, and Benjamin Harrison. He was also mentioned as both a possible Republican and a possible Democratic candidate for vice president.[39]

The judge was a tall man, standing over six feet with a large head and broad forehead. He wore a beard that, the older he got, the longer it grew, so that by the time of his retirement, he "had the appearance of a trapper or mountain man."[40]

A judge who did not avoid extrajudicial activities, Caldwell led the fight in the state for married women's individual property rights and was a supporter of women's suffrage. He wrote the Arkansas homestead law and prepared the act that permitted debtors to try suits to vacate usurious mortgages without initially having to pay the first lender the principal and interest of the loan. He also urged that the state prohibit all encumbrances on the homestead and limit the mortgaging of crops.

As a judge, Caldwell saw the law "as an active vehicle of substantive justice." He possessed a "homespun populist philosophy" coupled with "an extreme sense of fairness."[41] Caldwell's reputation for standing up to the railroads and their principal bondholders developed as a result of his approach to railroad receiverships discussed in the last chapter. He required that parties requesting the appointment of a receiver for a railroad agree to permit the receiver to pay preferentially all future claims of supplies in cash and allow the receiver to be sued at law in state courts, especially for torts that the railroad had committed.

Appointed circuit judge at the age of fifty-seven over Walter Sanborn and Amos Thayer, Caldwell seemed reluctant to leave home and "live the life of a 'tramp' wandering all over the vast territory that made up the Eighth Judicial Circuit."[42] His burden, however, was relieved quite considerably by passage of the Circuit Court of Appeals Act shortly thereafter. During twelve years on the Court of Appeals, Caldwell wrote 306 opinions for the court, thirty dissents, and one concurring opinion. With his health declining, Caldwell tendered his resignation on June 2, 1903, after thirty-nine years on the bench. He died twelve years later.[43]

Benjamin Harrison's second appointee, Walter Henry Sanborn (1892–1928), was among the most able judges to have sat on the Court of Appeals for the Eighth Circuit. Sanborn was born on October 19, 1845, in Epson, New Hampshire, "in the same farm house that was the birthplace of his father, grandfather and great grandfather."[44] After graduating from Dartmouth College as valedictorian of his class, Sanborn taught school for three years and served as principal of the Milford High School before moving in 1870 to St. Paul. Sanborn studied law in New Hampshire in the law office of Bainbridge Wadleigh, later U.S. senator, and in Minnesota with his uncle John B. Sanborn. John Sanborn had been a general in the Civil War. After the war, he served on the Peace Commission created to negotiate with Native American tribes. "Black Whiskers" Sanborn was one of the few commissioners the Native Americans trusted.[45]

After being admitted to the Minnesota bar, Walter Sanborn practiced law with his uncle. In two decades of practice, Sanborn was involved in more than four thousand cases.[46] While he was practicing law, Sanborn was a member of the St. Paul City Council and Republican county chairman. Active in the Minnesota State Bar Association, Sanborn was elected its President in 1890. The first Minnesotan to be appointed to the federal bench since 1858, Sanborn took his seat on May 2, 1892 and remained on the Court of Appeals until his death in 1928. With a commanding presence, piercing eyes, Van Dyke beard, and barrel chest, Sanborn was a dominating figure in conference and open court.[47] In his distinguished thirty-six year career, Sanborn wrote 1,300 opinions. Perhaps his most important came in the antitrust prosecution of Standard Oil.

Sanborn and his Eighth Circuit colleagues, William C. Hook and Willis Van Devanter, were rivals for appointment to the Supreme Court, which seems to have strained relations for a time at least between Sanborn and Van Devanter.[48] Theodore Roosevelt worried about the breadth of Sanborn's views regarding the Commerce Clause in 1906 when he chose William Moody. Taft passed over Sanborn in 1910 because of age, fixing on Van Devanter.[49]

Sanborn remained on the court until his death in 1928. At the memorial proceedings, his colleagues wrote of Sanborn: "His opinions are masterpieces in legal literature, containing no subterfuge, leaving no opposing contention unanswered, showing upon their face the wide scope of his investigation, the thoroughness of his study, and the soundness of his reasoning."[50] Four years after Walter Sanborn's death, his cousin John B. Sanborn Jr., then U.S. district judge for the District of Minnesota, was elevated to the Court of Appeals. He would serve until 1964 with great distinction.[51]

Grover Cleveland's Appointment

To fill the seat created by Congress in 1894, President Grover Cleveland appointed Amos Madden Thayer (1894–1905), then district judge for the Eastern District of Missouri. Born in Mina in upstate New York, Thayer graduated from Hamilton College, served as an officer in the Union army, and read law with his uncle. Thayer practiced law in St. Louis from 1868 to 1876, when he was elected judge of the state circuit court. Cleveland appointed him district judge in 1887. As district judge, Thayer frequently sat with Judges Caldwell and Sanborn, who thought highly of him, as did Justice Brewer. Thayer's opinions suggest a willingness to adjust legal doctrines to the needs of society. In 1890, Thayer began teaching at the Washington University School of Law. He compiled a book, *Jurisdiction of the Federal Courts* (1895), and also authored *A Synopsis of the Law of Contracts*. His most notable opinion came in the *Northern Securities* case, upholding the United States.[52]

Theodore Roosevelt's Appointments

The most notable, although not the most able, judge of the Court of Appeals for the Eighth Circuit during this period, Willis Van Devanter (1903–10), succeeded David Brewer on the Supreme Court. Born in Marion, Indiana, Van Devanter received his law degree from the University of Cincinnati Law School, then practiced law for three years in Indiana before moving to Cheyenne in 1884.

Van Devanter came to Wyoming when it was booming and became a prominent attorney, representing big cattle, railroad, and land interests. He practiced throughout the large state, traveling by stagecoach and horseback, and was as comfortable in handling cattle-rustling cases as in representing the Union Pacific Railroad. Active in Republican politics and a close ally of the territorial governor Francis E. Warren, to whom he was confidant, counsel, and political manager, Van Devanter served as a commissioner to revise the statutes of Wyoming, as city attorney for Cheyenne, Republican leader of the territorial legislature, and Republican state chairman. In 1889, at the age of thirty, Van Devanter became Chief Justice of the Territorial Court and, for a short time, the first Chief Justice of the state before he resigned to return to private practice.

Although his state judicial career was brief, Van Devanter had ambitions for a federal judgeship, seeking appointment to the Eighth Circuit in 1891, as well as to other judicial positions.[53] Francis Warren began serving in the U.S. Senate in 1890. Warren became Van Devanter's man in Washington as Van Devanter was Warren's man in Wyoming.

However, in 1897 Van Devanter moved to Washington himself, seizing the opportunity to become assistant attorney general in the Department of the Interior. There he deepened his expertise in the laws governing public lands, riparian rights, mining, and Native Americans (arguing the landmark case of *Lone Wolf v. Hitchcock*,[54] which recognized near-absolute plenary congressional power over Indian affairs) that would later make him invaluable on the Eighth Circuit and also proved useful on the Supreme Court.

In 1903 Theodore Roosevelt appointed Van Devanter to the newly created seat on the Eighth Circuit. As a member of the Court of Appeals, Van Devanter was a sound judge, a good technician who held his own on a strong bench. At this point, he did not demonstrate the judicial conservatism that would characterize the latter part of his career on the Supreme Court. In the two most important cases on which he sat, Van Devanter ruled for the United States in the Northern Securities and Standard Oil antitrust cases. He applied federal statutes regulating railroads sympathetically, although he "was generally a hard man to get a judgment for the plaintiff from" in a negligence case."[55] While serving on the Court of Appeals, Van Devanter presided over several dozen major circuit court cases, including antitrust prosecutions, railroad rate cases, and trials for political corruption. Although he was not as productive an opinion writer as some of his colleagues, at this time he did not suffer from the pen paralysis that afflicted him on the U.S. Supreme Court.

Although Van Devanter loved the West—at one point hunting grizzly bears in the Bighorn Mountains with Buffalo Bill—his eyes were on Washington. His effective mentor, Francis Warren, was working for his interests, as were a growing number of Washington friends. A serious candidate for secretary of the treasury in 1909, Van Devanter was nominated to the Supreme Court the following year.

Van Devanter was only able to deliver 346 majority opinions in twenty-six years on the Supreme Court. In his final years, he averaged just three opinions a term. Yet his colleagues thought him invaluable. In the conference of justices, Van Devanter was a star. The Court relied on him in difficult and arcane matters—jurisdictional disputes, as well as cases involving land, Indians, water rights, and admiralty law. He was a trusted adviser to Chief Justices White and Taft, a constructive critic of his colleagues' opinions, and a consensus builder. Although in his last years on the Court Van Devanter was strongly anti–New Deal, his retirement in May 1937 helped defuse the court-packing crisis by giving Franklin D. Roosevelt an immediate appointment to the High Court. Thereafter Van Devanter served as a judge in the Southern District of New York, trying complex criminal cases. He died in 1941 at the age of eighty-one.[56]

Roosevelt's second appointee, William C. Hook (1903–21) almost received the Supreme Court appointment that went to Van Devanter. President William McKinley named Hook to the District Court for the District of Kansas in 1899. With a reputation as an "antitruster," Hook was elevated to the Court of Appeals in 1903. He turned out to be an unusually able judge with good judgment, sound judicial temperament, and the ability to write opinions that read well today. A leading candidate to succeed Justice Brewer in 1910, Hook was passed over because of the assiduous lobbying for Van Devanter and because President Taft may have feared that a Hook appointment would be seen as giving in to Republican insurgents. He had strong support for appointment the following year, but this time he lost out to Mahlon Pitney, partially because of the claims of the Third Circuit to a seat on the Court, but also because he was branded unfairly as being pro-railroad and antiblack. What was written at his death remains true: that few men have come "so near to being appointed to the Supreme Bench and not be, as Judge Hook, and that on two occasions."[57]

Elmer B. Adams (1905–16) succeeded Thayer in 1905. Adams served as judge of the Missouri Circuit Court from 1879 to 1885, practiced law for a decade, and was appointed by Grover Cleveland to succeed Thayer as judge of the Eastern District of Missouri. Theodore Roosevelt elevated Adams, a Democrat, to the Court of Appeals.[58]

William Taft's Appointments

William Howard Taft made two appointments to the Court of Appeals. The first, Walter I. Smith (1911–22), was a member of the U.S. House of Representatives from Iowa at the time of his appointment in 1911.[59] The second, John E. Carland (1913–22), was actually appointed by Taft to the ill-fated Commerce Court in 1911.[60] After the demise of that court in 1913, Carland, the U.S. district judge for South Dakota from 1896 to 1911, was continued as a member of the Court of Appeals for the Eighth Circuit.[61] However, after Carland's death in 1922, the position ceased to exist.

Woodrow Wilson's Appointment

Woodrow Wilson made only one appointment to the Court of Appeals, but it was long lasting. Kimbrough Stone served on the court from 1917 until 1958 and was its senior judge for nineteen years (1928–47). The son of Wilbur Stone, a governor of Missouri and U.S. senator, Kimbrough Stone will be discussed at greater length in the following chapter.[62]

Warren Harding's Appointments

President Harding made two appointments to the Court of Appeals. Robert E. Lewis (1921–29) had been an unsuccessful candidate for Congress and for governor of Missouri, before moving to Colorado, where he was elected to a state judgeship. Lewis served on the U.S. District Court for the District of Colorado from 1906 to 1921. When the circuit was divided in 1929, Lewis became the first senior judge of the Tenth Circuit.[63]

Harding's second appointment to the Court of Appeals, William Squire Kenyon (1922–33), had been a state judge but was much better known as a member of the U.S. Senate from Iowa between 1911 and 1922. Kenyon was a leading Progressive, who cosponsored the Clayton, Federal Trade Commission, and Child Labor Acts. His most important legislative work, though, may well have been the creation of the bipartisan "farm bloc" in 1921, which produced a string of legislative successes including the Packing and Stockyards Control Law, regulation of the grain exchanges and futures trading in grain, and the Fordney-McCumber Tariff. Because he offered Kenyon a seat on the Court of Appeals, Harding was accused of attempting to seriously weaken the farm bloc. In 1924, Kenyon received 172 votes for the vice presidential nomination of the Republican Party. He was also seriously considered for the Supreme Court vacancy in 1930 that was filled by Owen Roberts.[64]

Calvin Coolidge's Appointments

Calvin Coolidge made three appointments to the Court of Appeals. The first, William Franklin Booth (1925–32), had been U.S. district judge for the District of Minnesota. As part of the political horse-trading connected with passage of the 1925 Judiciary Act, Booth, a Democrat who had the support of Chief Justice Taft and Justice Van Devanter, was nominated to the Court of Appeals by Coolidge.[65]

Coolidge's second appointee was Arba Van Valkenburgh (1925–33). As U.S. Attorney for the Western District of Missouri, Van Valkenburgh had aggressively prosecuted railroads for paying rebates. As U.S. district judge for the Western District of Missouri, Van Valkenburgh was perhaps best known for his harsh rulings in cases growing out of the First World War.[66]

John H. Cotterall (1928–29), Coolidge's third appointee, had served less than a year on the Court of Appeals when the circuit was divided and he was transferred to the Tenth Circuit. Cotterall had been one of the Sooners who entered Oklahoma on April 22, 1889, the day nearly two million acres were opened for settlement. Cotterall served as judge of the Western District of Oklahoma from 1907 until his appointment to the Court of Appeals in 1928. He would serve as judge of the Court of Appeals for the Tenth Circuit until 1933.[67]

Two District Judges

During this period, panels of the Court of Appeals were ordinarily made up of two courts of appeals judges and one district judge. Thus the participation of district judges was very much a part of the life of the Court of Appeals. During this period, there were two exceptional district judges who made major contributions to the law of the Eighth Circuit both at the trial and at the appellate level: Charles Fremont Amidon and Jacob Trieber. Amidon, judge of the U.S. District Court for the District of North Dakota from 1897 to 1928, wrote more than 150 opinions for the Court of Appeals and was a quintessential Progressive with a dynamic view of the law and a broad view of national power. Sympathetic to the rights of labor, Amidon was one of the handful of federal judges who, during and just after World War I, resisted intolerance and xenophobia and protected civil liberties.[68] Trieber, the first Jewish federal district court judge, and a very liberal one to boot, was judge of the Eastern District of Arkansas from 1900 to 1927. From 1913 until his death, Trieber heard more than 350 Court of Appeals cases, writing opinions in more than two-thirds. In cases involving racial civil rights, Trieber was generations ahead of his time.[69]

Jurisprudence

In the early years of the courts of appeals, much of the work was far from glamorous. The courts' reason for existence was to free the Supreme Court from relatively routine appellate review, and so it was that the "great cases" continued to go to the Supreme Court: whether the Constitution followed the flag, whether the federal income tax was constitutional, whether state maximum-hours laws violated the right to contract. At first, when important, novel questions arose before the courts of appeals, they were certified to the Supreme Court.

Nevertheless, important issues of public policy did come before the judges of the Court of Appeals for the Eighth Circuit between 1891 and 1929. If relatively few of them occurred in the federal staples of the years before 1890, enactment of the Sherman Antitrust Act, as well as of legislation during the Progressive era, greatly enriched what came before the Courts of Appeals—statutes requiring interpretation, regulators requiring oversight.

The major sources of important jurisprudence for the Eighth Circuit Court of Appeals continued to be disputes over land, railroad cases, and cases involving Native Americans, although there were a few important cases involving farming. A new regional specialty was cases spawned by the radical politics of the northern part of the circuit—cases involving the Nonpartisan League. The impact of national developments may be seen not only in the cases involving the Sherman Act and Progressive legislation but also in prosecutions during World War I under the Sedition and Espionage Acts. Space precludes more than a brief discussion of the jurisprudence generated by labor-management conflicts and mineral leasing rights. Two significant racial civil rights cases from this period are discussed later in chapter 4. On the whole, the Court of Appeals strongly supported antitrust prosecutions, restrained state regulation of railroads, supported the federal policy of assimilation for Native Americans, and was notably sensitive to individual rights during World War I.

Disputes over Land, Including Mining

There continued to be much litigation over land. Litigation related to the Homestead Laws and the Timber Laws persisted. There were also suits over federal laws that provided for the allocation of land to railroads and over land granted to states at the time they were admitted to the Union. Many suits were brought by the United States to quiet (i.e., make secure) title to land in the public domain. Important litigation growing out of land allocated to Native Americans is discussed in a separate section later in this chapter.

There were two land cases of far more than technical interest, both over petroleum-bearing land in Wyoming. In 1897, Congress had opened public land, chiefly valuable for petroleum and mineral deposits, to exploration and purchase by U.S. citizens. Shortly thereafter, concern grew that the oil deposits were being depleted too rapidly. William Howard Taft, surely among the least imperial of presidents, withdrew three million areas of public land without express statutory authority to do so. Congress then passed a law on the subject, but the law neither ratified nor overruled Taft's proclamation.

The Midwest Oil case involved an action by the United States to recover some of the land Taft had withdrawn in Natrona County that was still being exploited and to obtain an accounting for fifty thousand barrels of oil that allegedly had been illegally extracted. John A. Riner, Wyoming's federal district judge, upheld the company's claim. Anticipating that the case would be appealed because of the significance of the issue and the value of the land, Riner wrote an opinion, a little over a page long, that held that, in the absence of a statute, the president lacked the authority to act on his own.[70]

The United States appealed. The role of the Court of Appeals proved to be that of a conduit, certifying questions to the Supreme Court, which then directed that the entire record be sent up. The Supreme Court reversed the district court by a vote of five to three.[71]

Midwest Oil would come to stand for an important proposition in constitutional interpretation—that long-standing usage may generate a presumption on behalf of the legitimacy of governmental action. Since the nation's early history, presidents had been withdrawing land, which Congress by general statute had thrown open to American citizens. Justice Joseph R. Lamar, who wrote the opinion for the Supreme Court, thought that such a presumption was entitled to some weight. Government was, Lamar wrote, "a practical affair intended for practical men ... Officers, law-makers and citizens naturally adjust themselves to any long-continued action of the Executive Department—on the presumption that unauthorized acts would not have been allowed to be so often repeated as to crystallize into a regular practice."[72] In dissent, Justice William R. Day argued that the grant of constitutional authority to the executive, as to other departments of the government, "ought not to be amplified by judicial decision."[73] Midwest Oil would become a precedent trotted out by latter-day presidents to defend sweeping uses of executive power.[74]

The second case, *United States v. Mammoth Oil Co.*[75] involved some of the same Wyoming land that Taft had withdrawn from private development in 1909. In 1920, by statute, Congress gave the secretary of the navy power to meet the problem of conserving certain oil reserves on this land, making it clear that it was of vital importance that the oil reserves not be drained away for private benefit, for it would be insurance if the navy needed oil in an emergency. Shortly after Warren Harding took office in 1921, he signed an executive order transferring those reserves to the custody of the Interior Department. Secretary of the Interior Albert B. Fall then, secretly and without competitive bidding, leased Reserve No. 3, the Teapot Dome reserve in Natrona County, to Harry F. Sinclair's Mammoth Oil Company. Later it would be discovered that Fall had received $260,000 in Liberty Bonds from Sinclair.[76]

When the Teapot Dome scandal broke after the death of President Harding, Congress, by joint resolution, called for the federal government to take legal action to have the public lands whose resources had been purloined returned, and to void the leases and rescind the contracts that authorized Mammoth Oil to take the petroleum.[77] The United States went into the District Court in Wyoming to have the lease and contract canceled, arguing that they had been secured fraudulently, as a result of a conspiracy between Fall and Sinclair. Although the defense contended that no criminal conduct had been involved, neither Sinclair nor Fall testified at the trial. Although their not doing so was protected by the privilege against self-incrimination, it was highly suspect in what was an action in equity rather than a criminal prosecution. Nevertheless, Judge T. Blake Kennedy held that both the lease and agreement had been authorized by the special act of Congress and that there had been neither fraud nor conspiracy connected with the lease and contract.[78] Kennedy was harshly criticized for his decision, which probably cost him elevation to the Court of Appeals.[79]

The Court of Appeals, former Senator Kenyon writing, agreed that the lease and contract had been authorized by the act of Congress, but reversed, holding that the lease and contract had been secured fraudulently. The court was clearly persuaded by the silence and evasions of many of those connected with the affair. For example, Kenyon asked rhetorically about Sinclair:

> Why is silence the only reply of Sinclair, a man of large business affairs, to the charge of bribing an official of his government? . . . It would seem that men of standing in the business world when accused of being bribers, would be quick to resent the charge, and eager to furnish all information possible that might remove such stain upon their reputations.[80]

Kenyon noted that "a court of equity [still] has the right to draw reasonable and proper inferences from all the circumstances in the case" and concluded that a "trail of deceit, falsehood, subterfuge, bad faith and corruption" ran through the transactions incident to and surrounding the making of the lease, which should not receive the approval of the courts.[81] *Mammoth Oil* was remanded to Judge Kennedy with instructions that he enter a decree canceling the lease and contract, enjoining the appellees from further trespassing, and providing for an accounting for the value of the oil taken. The Supreme Court held that Kennedy had been wrong about both aspects of the case: the lease and contract had not been authorized by act of Congress and therefore were void; the facts and circumstances required a finding that "Fall and Sinclair, contrary to the Government's policy for the conservation of oil reserves for the Navy and in disregard of law, conspired to procure for the Mammoth Company all the products of the reserve."[82]

In the nineteenth century, the Eighth Circuit had handled much litigation over the Federal Mining Law of 1872.[83] In a case spawned in Utah, *United States v. Sweet*,[84] the Supreme Court settled the principle that, under the 1873 Coal Land Act, the federal government retains the rights to minerals underneath land it has granted to the states. Congress punctuated the decision with a statute, the Mineral Leasing Act of February 25, 1920, which mandated that coal-bearing substrata remains forever with the federal government and may be worked only under federal lease.[85] The *Sweet* decision and the statute have become the cornerstone of American land law, a precedent for national ownership of mineral lands.[86]

Finally, the United States also emerged the victor in a series of prosecutions brought during Theodore Roosevelt's presidency against the owners of some of Nebraska's largest ranches to deter the fencing of government land and other illegal practices used to increase landholding. When the two owners of the enormous Spade ranch, Bartlett Richards and Will G. Comstock, were prosecuted for fencing in their land, they were able to cop a plea and received a slap on the wrist from

Judge William H. Munger—a $939 fine plus six hours in the custody of the U.S. Marshal—after the U.S. Attorney recommended a light sentence. Roosevelt was furious. He discharged the U.S. Attorney and U.S. Marshal and apparently said that he regretted that he could not discharge the judge. The new U.S. Attorney, Charles A. Goss, secured indictments against twenty-six ranchers (including Richards and Comstock) for conspiracy in securing fraudulent land titles. This time a different judge, Thomas C. Munger, fined Richards and Comstock $1,500 each and sent them to prison for one year.[87] So much land was reopened that a great influx of homesteaders occurred.

Antitrust Cases

Some of the most important work performed by the judges of the Circuit Court of Appeals occurred in the area of antitrust law, which, at the turn of the century, was among the most visible and contentious areas of law, invested by both legal commentators and the general public with an importance far transcending its real potential. The judges of the Court of Appeals for the Eighth Circuit, sitting as circuit court judges,[88] decided two of the most eagerly awaited antitrust decisions in the early history of the Sherman Act—the *Northern Securities* and *Standard Oil* decisions.

The Act of July 2, 1890, or Sherman Antitrust Act, had two principal sections.[89] The first made illegal every contract, combination in the form of trust, or conspiracy in restraint of trade. The second section prohibited monopolies or combinations or conspiracies to monopolize any part of trade or commerce. While there were difficult questions as to how wide or deep the Sherman Act might sweep, the law was not applied vigorously in its early years. It took over a decade until the administration of Theodore Roosevelt began serious enforcement. By that time, the Supreme Court had damaged the act by its holding in the 1895 *E. C. Knight* case that the act could not constitutionally reach manufacturing because "manufacturing" was not "commerce" and therefore did not come within the Commerce power.[90] However, in three decisions handed down in the waning years of the century, the Supreme Court held that several prosecutions for rate fixing were not barred by the Commerce Clause or by the doctrine of "liberty of contract.[91]

Public expectations that the Sherman Act could effectively counter the enormous enterprises of the time grew during Roosevelt's presidency. The first real test of the act during that presidency occurred when the United States sued in the Eighth Circuit to break up the holding company that controlled the two most important railroads in the West.

The Northern Securities Company was the handiwork of James J. Hill, Edward H. Harriman, and J. P. Morgan. Incorporated in New Jersey, the holding company acquired the stock of two enormous railroads, the Northern Pacific and Great Northern, which ran across the northwestern states from the Great Lakes to the Pacific coast. The two lines were competitors on parts of, but by no means all, their routes. The holding company also included the Chicago, Burlington and Quincy Railroad, which gave the two trunk lines a feeder into Chicago.

After the state of Minnesota unsuccessfully attempted to attack the holding company,[92] the U.S. Department of Justice brought suit under the Sherman Act in the Circuit Court for the District of Minnesota. The four judges of the Court of Appeals—Caldwell, Thayer, Sanborn, and Van Devanter—made up the court that tried the case. The court, with Thayer writing, gave the United States a clear victory. Although the holding company had been incorporated in New Jersey and stock transactions were within the province of the states, the court nevertheless had no problem finding the requisite interstate commerce. Interstate commerce was "affected" because the holding company "destroyed every motive for competition" between "natural competitors for business by pooling the earnings of the two roads for the common benefit of the stockholders of both companies." Because the relationship between the two companies had the potential to establish unreasonable restraints of trade, a Sherman Act violation had been made out.[93]

A very closely divided Supreme Court affirmed the result the Circuit Court had reached in *Northern Securities,* but took a much narrower view of the Sherman Act. Justice John Marshall Harlan wrote for four justices of the majority and had no problem finding ample national power to prevent the destruction of competition among railroad lines. Those four justices, though, were opposed by four others, who took a much more limited view. Justice Oliver Wendell Holmes thought the Sherman Act only prohibited practices that kept people from entering a trade or business. Justice White was concerned that if every stock transaction or change of ownership involving a business operation was held to be interstate commerce by the virtue of its impact on competition, then there would be virtually no limit to the scope of congressional power. Justice Brewer held the swing vote, and while he ruled for the United States on the particular facts of the case, he essentially agreed with the dissenters about the scope of the Sherman Act.[94] *Northern Securities* gave a boost to Sherman Act enforcement but left the reach of the law unclear. The Supreme Court returned to that issue seven years later in dealing with antitrust prosecution of John D. Rockefeller's Standard Oil trust.

The suit against Standard Oil of New Jersey (and some seventy other companies, as well as Rockefeller and seven other individuals) was brought on November 18, 1906, in the Circuit Court for the Eastern District of Missouri. The complaint was based on section 2 of the Sherman Act, charging a conspiracy to monopolize commerce in oil by means of acquisitions and agreements fixing prices and controlling petroleum. Predatory methods—such as price cutting, railroad rebates, abuse of the oil pipeline monopoly, bribery, and industrial espionage—were said to have led to control over 75 percent of the refining and marketing of petroleum in the United States, the marketing of more than four-fifths of all the illuminating oil sold in the country and exported abroad, and more than nine-tenths of all lubricating oil sold to railroads in the United States.[95] The government petitioned for dissolution of the holding company, Standard Oil of New Jersey, and for injunctions against all defendants to prevent them from any further anticompetitive actions.

The Standard Oil prosecution was an immense case. Evidence was taken for two years before the examiner appointed by the court. There were 444 witnesses, 11 million words of testimony, and 1,374 exhibits. The record ran to 12,000 printed pages fitting into twenty-three very thick printed volumes.[96]

The Circuit Court decided the case for the government in November 1909, although the bill was dismissed against thirty-three companies.[97] Judge Sanborn wrote for himself and Judges Van Devanter and Adams. The court found that the company controlled sixteen refineries and twelve transportation companies as well as six marketing companies with 3,574 "seller stations." It also found that Standard Oil of New Jersey, by means of its trust and its commanding volume of oil business, had exercised and was still exercising the power to fix the purchase price of crude oil, the rates for its transportation, and its selling price. The court held that the oil trust had prevented and was preventing any competition in interstate and international commerce in petroleum. When applying the second section of the Sherman Act, the Circuit Court's view of its reach was not as broad as that of Justice Harlan in *Northern Securities*. It held that section 2 barred only monopolies in which unlawful means were used to monopolize and continue an unlawful monopoly. Since the acts in restraint of the trade by Standard Oil had been achieved by illegal means, they could be enjoined.

Judge Sanborn approached the remedy carefully, stating that the court must forbid the performance of continuing and threatened illegal acts but not prohibit "all possible violations of the law; and thus put the whole conduct of the defendant's business at the peril of a summons for contempt." Standard Oil of New Jersey was directed to divest itself of its holdings in all the subsidiary companies and was forbidden any future exercise of control over the subsidiary companies. All individuals and companies were enjoined from any future conspiracies to restrain or monopolize trade.[98] Concurring, Judge Hook emphasized that neither monopoly alone nor an attempt to monopolize was itself sufficient to violate the Sherman Act; to violate the act, monopoly must have been secured by methods that were against public policy.[99]

Although the Circuit Court decision was handed down in November 1909, the Supreme Court did not decide the appeal until May 1911 because of illnesses, resignations, and deaths. By this time it had been joined on the Supreme Court docket by the *American Tobacco* prosecution, in which the Circuit Court for the Southern District of New York had enjoined the tobacco trust from doing business until reasonably competitive conditions had been restored to that market.[100]

The *Standard Oil* case came down on May 15, 1911. In *Standard Oil*, the Supreme Court affirmed the Court of Appeals in an opinion written by Chief Justice White for eight justices. The Supreme Court adopted the so-called rule of reason. According to the Court, the Sherman Act had been enacted in the light of the existing practical conception of the law against restraints of trade. Agreeing essentially with Sanborn's analysis, the High Court stated that the intent of Congress had not been to restrain the right to make and enforce contracts that did not unduly restrain interstate or foreign commerce. Businesses exercising the fundamental right of freedom of trade could still do so as long as interstate commerce was not unduly restrained. The Circuit Court decision was modified to the extent that only attempts at directly re-creating the former combination were enjoined. Justice Van Devanter, who had sat on the case in the Circuit Court, also did so in the Supreme Court and joined in White's opinion. Justice Harlan, although he agreed with the result, castigated the majority for cutting back the reach of the Sherman Act.[101]

The *American Tobacco* decision was decided harmoniously with *Standard Oil* but required a remand to the Circuit Court for the Southern

District of New York for a stronger remedy.[102] These two decisions generated support for passage of the Federal Trade Commission and Clayton Acts three years later, which strengthened the federal capacity to regulate business. Ironically, the stocks of the thirty-three companies divested from the holding company skyrocketed, and John D. Rockefeller became even richer as a result of the decision. The passage of time slowly dispersed ownership of the various companies. Monopoly gave way to oligarchy in the petroleum business.[103]

Railroad Litigation

Railroads were the principal private litigants in the Eighth Circuit and, as in the previous period, were involved in a rich variety of lawsuits. The most important railroad cases coming before the Court of Appeals for the Eighth Circuit involved state rate regulation. By 1891, the Supreme Court had moved a good distance away from the principle of the *Granger* cases, by which courts should defer to state regulation of businesses "affected by a public interest."[104] In 1886, the High Court, while not invalidating a Mississippi statute, had said that "under pretense of regulating fares and freights, the state cannot require a railroad corporation to carry persons or property without reward; neither can it do that which in law amounts to a taking of private property for public use without just compensation, or without due process of law."[105] Two years later, Circuit Judge Brewer temporarily enjoined Iowa's railroad rates, indicating that where the rates will not pay some compensation to the owners, then it is the duty of the courts to interfere and protect the companies from such rates.[106] After the Iowa Board of Commissioners issued a revised rate schedule, Brewer lifted his injunction. Finally, in 1890, in *Chicago, Milw. & St. P. R.R. Co. v. Minnesota,*[107] it became clear that the Supreme Court required judicial review of rates under the Due Process Clause, whether they had been set by a state railway commission or by the legislature. On the same day as the *Chicago, Milw. & St. P.R.R.* case, the Supreme Court affirmed *Chicago St. P., M. & O. v. Becker,*[108] where Judge Brewer, sitting in Minnesota, had followed his Iowa decision and held that it was not within the power of the state to put in force a schedule of rates when the rates prescribed would not pay the cost of service.

Lawsuits seeking to invalidate state-imposed rates multiplied rapidly.[109] The next major case originated in Nebraska, where the Populists gained control of the Nebraska legislature. That body passed the Newberry

Law in 1893, lowering maximum shipping rates on freight by 29.5 percent. Judge Elmer S. Dundy issued a temporary restraining order to prevent the law from going into effect. Although by then the justices had been "excused" from circuit riding, Justice David Brewer considered the matter so important that he traveled to Nebraska to hear the cases attacking the law. William Jennings Bryan, less than one year after his first unsuccessful run for the presidency, acted as co-counsel for the State of Nebraska.

In *Ames v. Union Pacific Ry. Co.,*[110] Brewer and Dundy upheld the Nebraska rate-setting process but also held that the rates themselves violated due process because they deprived the property owners of any chance to make a profit. Bryan argued for the state when the Supreme Court heard argument in the case in April 1987. When the cases came down almost a year later, the Circuit Court had been upheld. The railroads won a sweeping victory. *Smyth v. Ames* was a milestone, not only because it was the first case in which the Supreme Court held that particular rates violated due process but also because the Court used the case to attempt to explain to the lower courts how to make such determinations.[111] However, that explanation was not a masterpiece of clarity. The basis of all calculations as to the reasonableness of state rates had to be the fair value of "the property used for the convenience of the public." But it was when the Court attempted to state which elements were to determine "the property used for the convenience of the public" that its criteria were imprecise and confusing.[112] *Smyth v. Ames* had the effect of diminishing state legislative attempts to control rates by rate schedules. The states would in the future attempt to achieve the same goal through charters and contracts. However, it would be the competition from trucks and airplanes a generation later that would bring railway rates down.

About fifteen years later, several important rate-making cases from the Eighth Circuit reached the Supreme Court. The cases known as the Minnesota Rate cases evoked brilliant but opposite opinions at each level.[113] At issue was an order of the Minnesota Railway and Warehouse Commission that reduced the maximum rates for intrastate shipments of freight by 20 to 25 percent. Three railroads brought suit in the Circuit Court for the District of Minnesota. Sanborn, sitting as judge in that court, held that interstate commerce was burdened by Minnesota's intrastate rates. The rates would harm cities in neighboring states that were situated side by side with a Minnesota city, such as Fargo, North

Dakota, paired with Moorhead, Minnesota. If the non-Minnesota city had higher rates, its interstate trade would be devastated. Sanborn, relying on the findings of the special master, Charles E. Otis, also held the Minnesota rates to be "unreasonably low, unjust and confiscatory" because, to use the example of one of the railroads, the company's rate of annual return on its intrastate freight business would have been 1.94 percent. The companies, Sanborn thought, should be entitled to a net return of 7 percent.[114]

When the cases reached the Supreme Court, the Conference of [State] Governors filed an amicus curiae brief, as did the railroad commissions of seven states in the Eighth Circuit. The Supreme Court opinion reversing Sanborn, written by Charles Evans Hughes, is a tour de force, a brilliant analysis of state and federal power to regulate commerce.[115] Writing for a unanimous court, Hughes had no doubt about the state's authority to regulate rates for transportation that was wholly intrastate unless Congress had preempted state regulation by the Interstate Commerce Act (or by laws amending the act). Hughes refused to suppose that Congress had by indirection attempted to override the accustomed authority of the state without providing a substitute. Thus the Minnesota rates were constitutional, and if Congress was troubled about their effect on interstate commerce, it had the capacity to act. The Supreme Court also held that the rates for two of the railroads were constitutional, but the rates for the third were confiscatory and therefore unconstitutional.

Labor-Management Conflicts

Labor-management relations in the Eighth Circuit between 1921 and 1929 were most assuredly not free of the bitterness and violence that characterized labor-management relations in the United States between 1891 and 1929. Battles were waged over the mines of Arkansas and Colorado, in Minnesota's logging camps and its Iron Range, as well as on railroads throughout the circuit.

If the courts of the Eighth Circuit demonstrated that they were not friendly to big business, their attitude toward labor was cool at best. During these years, labor unions had few friends in the federal courts. As the number of injunctions issued to end strikes multiplied with each decade from 1890 to 1930,[116] the Supreme Court sanctioned the use of the Sherman Act as a weapon against labor by permitting private actions for treble damages against secondary boycotts and held that injunctions against picketing workers were not prohibited by the Clayton Act, even though the drafters of the Clayton Act had attempted to protect labor.[117]

The Circuit Court ruled in favor of the governor of Colorado in a lawsuit for violation of constitutional rights brought by Charles H. Moyer, president of the Western Federation of Miners, who had been held without trial for two and one-half months after bloody battles in Colorado mines during 1903–4. Yet the Court of Appeals sharply rebuked Governor Lynn J. Frazier, who had declared martial law and seized North Dakota's thirty-four lignite mines during a nationwide coal strike, when western North Dakotans depended absolutely on lignite for fuel during a brutally cold winter. Frazier had established maximum retail prices for coal that were much less that what the mine owners had been charging.[118]

In 1897, in an important case from Kansas involving a secondary boycott, the Circuit Court enjoined the Coopers' International Union by a 2–1 vote from making the boycott against the Oxley Stave Company effective. Judge Caldwell's dissenting opinion resounded with sympathy for laborers.[119]

At the end of the period, brutal conflict—shootings, arson, and dynamiting—that occurred over the ending of union shops in nine coal mines in far western Arkansas, near Frogtown, led to the lengthy Coronado Coal Company litigation. Affirming the district court, the Court of Appeals by a 2–1 vote held that the international union could be held for triple damages under the Sherman Act, even though mining itself had been held by the Supreme Court not to be interstate commerce.[120] The Supreme Court reversed and remanded for a trial as to whether the intention of the union leaders had been to keep the coal from entering interstate commerce. Once again, the Court of Appeals affirmed the district court, which had directed a verdict for the unions. The Supreme Court affirmed as to the international, but held against the local.[121] After the Supreme Court reversed and remanded for a trial as to whether the intention of the union leaders had been to keep the coal from entering interstate commerce, the district court directed a verdict for the unions. The Court of Appeals again affirmed. The Supreme Court then affirmed as to the international but held against the union.[122]

Native American Cases

The military battles between Native Americans and the U.S. Army were over (although the Chippewa were to fight once again on the east shore of Leech Lake in Minnesota in 1898).[123] No longer were Native Americans standing in the way of the settlement of the West. Yet the future of the states that constituted the Eighth Circuit remained intertwined with the fate of the Native Americans. Litigation by, for, or about Native Americans continued to be an important part of the work of the courts of the Eighth Circuit between 1891 and 1929 (and continues to the present day).

During these years, the federal government was committed to a policy of "civilizing" the Indian. This meant breaking down tribal structures and attempting to make yeoman farmers of Native Americans while educating their children into the white man's culture. It was believed that, by this means, Native Americans would be assimilated into the mainstream of American life.

The General Allotment Act of 1887 (or Dawes Act) was an important vehicle for achieving this policy.[124] Under the Dawes Act, tribal land was to be converted into land that would be owned individually. Each Native American household was entitled under the Dawes Act to claim 160 acres of land. Smaller tracts were allotted to women, children, and single men. To prevent the land from being "frittered away," the United States was to hold the land in trust for at least twenty-five years, and encumbrances or conveyances of the land during this period were to be void. Since Indian tribes owned far more land than was going in allotments to individual Indians, the Dawes Act provided that the surplus land could be sold to non-Indians, with the proceeds held by the United States in trust for the Indian tribes. It was largely by these means that North and South Dakota would be settled by white Americans. The Dawes Act also provided that all Native American allottees were to be granted American citizenship, as would Indians who voluntarily lived away from their tribes and adopted the habits of civilized life.[125]

In practice, the Dawes Act worked out differently from what some of its more well-meaning supporters had expected. The pressures for Indian land—from speculators, timber interests, railroads, and land-hungry Americans—were too great a force. The Dawes Act broke up the still huge amount of land owned by Native Americans, but the benefits went to non-Indians.[126] Over time, Congress would ease the restrictions on alienability after the death of allottees. After many allottees died, many heirs sold or leased their land. Twenty-seven million acres (two-thirds of the land allotted) passed from Indian allottees by sale between 1887 and 1934. Much was sold for a pittance. The Sioux, for example, who sold millions of acres to the United States, received an average of fifty-seven cents an acre. Between 1887 and 1934, Indian lands decreased from 138 million acres to 48 million (of which nearly 50 percent was desert).[127] In addition, real estate agents duped Indians into long-term leases and non-Indian occupiers then stripped the land of its natural resources, especially timber.[128]

In the Eighth Circuit, the effects of the failure of the policy of assimilation were to be seen primarily in South Dakota and Oklahoma. In South Dakota, under the agreement of March 2, 1889, between the United States and the Sioux, six separate reservations were created. Much land was allotted to Indians, but in a region not suited for farming on small parcels. In a little more than a quarter century, the Sioux made available some fifteen million acres for non-Indian homestead or purchase, plus the majority of six million acres to lease. As real estate holdings diminished, Indians became increasingly dependent on financial resources they had accumulated by selling, leasing, or working their land. The long-run result was an "Indian South Dakota," impoverished in wealth and culture.[129] A not dissimilar process occurred in Oklahoma, although it was politically far more complex.[130]

Many cases involving land allotted to Native Americans arose in the Eighth Circuit. After the discovery of oil on land allotted to Native Americans, there were widespread attempts—many of them successful— by non-Native Americans to get Native Americans to alienate their land. Between July 14, 1908, and October 12, 1909, in Oklahoma alone, the United States brought 301 bills in equity against some 16,000 defendants to cancel some 30,000 conveyances of allotted lands on the ground that the conveyances were in violation of existing restrictions on the power of alienation.[131] *United States v. Allen* was a mega-case, in which the United States brought suit to have 4,000 conveyances voided. Judge Ralph E. Campbell dismissed the bill.[132] The Court of Appeals sent it back for trial. Judge Amidon, writing for the Court of Appeals, thought that what was at issue was not a "simple real estate transaction." Rather, the government's plan for dissolving the five civilized nations and distributing their lands in severalty was "a great governmental project, having for its object the social and industrial elevation of the Indian." According to Amidon, the United States had standing, not just because the property rights of Native Americans were involved, but also because of the "governmental rights of the United States."[133] Judge Elmer B. Adams dissented, arguing that "such intervention in the way of institution of suits at wholesale as done in these cases without the request or consenting of the Indians is not only humiliating in itself, but tends to defeat the true national policy by discouraging self-reliance and independence of action."[134] Judge Amidon's position was upheld by the Supreme Court in *Heckman v. United States*.[135]

Talton v. Mayes was an important case involving a defendant indicted by a five-person grand jury and convicted for murder in a special Cherokee Nation Court. Habeas corpus was sought in the Circuit Court for the Western District of Arkansas on the ground that the Indian defendant's Fifth Amendment grand jury guarantee had been infringed on. The U.S. Supreme Court held that the tribes in many contexts were not limited by the same constitutional limits as were imposed on the state and federal governments.[136]

Nonpartisan League Cases

Political opponents of the Nonpartisan League used the courts to attempt to block parts of the league program or to harass its leaders. In April 1919, taxpayers from forty-two North Dakota counties brought suit in federal district court for an injunction to prevent the operation of state-owned grain elevators. The state could not have had a more sympathetic judge than Judge Amidon. Besides holding that he had no jurisdiction because the jurisdictional amount for a suit in equity had not been pleaded, Amidon noted that in the preceding ten years there had been a great extension of state authority throughout the nation into fields that formerly were private. He pointed out that

> as North Dakota has become more thickly settled and the means of intercourse have increased[,] the evils of the existing marketing system have been better understood. . . . The people here thus come to believe that the evils of the existing system consist, not merely in the grading of grain, its weighing, its discharge. . . . They believe that the evil goes deeper; that the whole system of shipping the raw materials of North Dakota to these foreign terminals is wasteful and hostile to the best interests of the state.[137]

These state-run businesses, Amidon thought, were the only effective means by which the farmers could escape economic injustices at the hands of the great combinations.

The Supreme Court coupled the appeal from Amidon's decision with an appeal from the North Dakota Supreme Court's decision in *Green v.*

Frazier, where that court had rejected a similar attempt to enjoin operation of the state enterprises.[138] Sensitive to the "peculiar conditions existing in North Dakota," the Supreme Court used the state court decision as the vehicle to uphold the North Dakota laws.[139]

Another challenge to the Nonpartisan League program came with an attack on a comprehensive state statute attempting to regulate the buying of grain. At this time, grain from North Dakota farms was stored for brief periods in the state before it was shipped out of state. (Ninety percent of that grain was ultimately purchased for shipment outside the state.) When so stored, it was vulnerable to fraudulent practices such as underweighing and undergrading. The state statute sought to protect farmers by establishing a system of state inspection, grading, and weighing; by licensing inspectors; and by empowering inspectors to absolutely establish the grades of the grain offered for sale or shipment, and therefore the respective prices that warehousemen, elevators, and mills were required to pay the grower. Thus the state grain inspector was able to determine the margin of profit which the buyer would realize.

The constitutionality of the North Dakota program was challenged in a test case brought by an elevator firm in Embden. Usually supportive of broad national power over commerce, Amidon this time took a broad view of the state police power and held that the purchase of grain in North Dakota for shipment out of state was not interstate commerce.[140]

The Court of Appeals, however, took a more modern approach to the Commerce Clause than that of Amidon. It ruled that the purchase of grain in North Dakota for shipment and sale at the terminal markets of Minneapolis and Duluth, taken in connection with the fact that the seller knew the grain was being sold for shipment out of the state, made the purchase and sale a unit in interstate commerce. Further, since the United States had a grain-licensing statute, the dual inspection and grading system of North Dakota was a direct and unreasonable burden on interstate commerce, as was the establishment by the inspectors of the reasonable margin to be paid by warehouses, elevators, and mills to the producers of grain.[141] The Supreme Court upheld the Court of Appeals over the dissents of Holmes, Brandeis, and Clarke.[142]

The bankruptcy of Arthur C. Townley, the leader of the Nonpartisan League, generated another Eighth Circuit case. Townley filed for bankruptcy after the failure of a flax speculation scheme. A creditor claimed that Townley had hidden assets, and the league's political opponents sought to look at their books. Amidon permitted a careful investigation, and nothing untoward was found. Amidon then granted the petition and discharged the bankrupt. The Court of Appeals affirmed.[143]

Cases from the Great War

When the United States finally entered World War I, "patriotic" citizens of the Eighth Circuit began to question the loyalty of immigrants, German Americans, and radicals. There was a large immigrant population in the north central states. In 1910, for example, 70 percent of North Dakota's population were immigrants or children of immigrants.[144] Many states in the circuit had relatively large, not yet fully assimilated German populations. In Nebraska, for example, where approximately 20 percent of the state's inhabitants were of German origin, there were forty German-language newspapers.[145] Before U.S. entry into the war, German-language papers throughout the nation had been strong supporters of Germany, bitterly condemned Great Britain, and interpreted interventionist agitation as propaganda inspired by Wall Street.[146] Furthermore, there was substantial opposition in the states of the Eighth Circuit (as in many parts of the United States) from radical and pacifist groups to America's entry into the war. Indeed, two months after war was declared, an antidraft rally in the little town of New Ulm, Minnesota, attracted a crowd of ten thousand.

If, at first, it was necessary to rally the public behind the war, that did not prove difficult to do, and in fact, it was done too well. In many states, chauvinism and intolerance were spurred, sometimes absurdly, by state councils of defense, to which the legislatures granted sweeping powers.[147] The Minnesota Council of Defense ordered saloons closed after 10 p.m. and declared them off-limits to women and girls. The Nebraska Council conducted an investigation of "conspicuous leaders" of the Lutheran churches, who were accused of utterances of a treasonable character, and the council took steps to cleanse the state's traveling library of German-language books. In South Dakota, where A. K. Gardner, later a member of the Court of Appeals for the Eighth Circuit, was attorney for the state council, actions were brought to dissolve the Hutterite and Mennonite colonies. Other political officials were not to be outdone. The superintendent of schools for the state of Missouri ruled that schools that offered instruction in German would not be certified. In Iowa, Governor William L. Harding decreed that only English could be spoken in public schools, on the telephone, in conversations on trains, and in any public place.[148]

But much anti-German activity involved spontaneous, mob-driven acts. In Yankton County, South Dakota, the Liberty Loan Committee, dissatisfied with the contributions made by the Hutterites in lieu of bond purchases (which they did not make for religious reasons), seized two hundred steers and one thousand sheep, sold them at auction, and turned the money over to the Red Cross or used it for the purchase of Liberty Bonds.[149] In Marysville, Nebraska, a mob broke into a school, removed all books and materials written in German or about Germany, including copies of the Bible in German, piled them outside, and burned them.[150] In Hawley, Minnesota, German texts were burned and citizens suspected of German leanings forced to kiss the American flag.[151] It would turn out that there was "an inverse relationship . . . between the degree of persecution evidenced by a German-American group and the threat it posed to American security."[152]

Little by little the campaign directed toward winning the war became redirected at radicals. Suppression of political dissent became transformed into suppression of nonconforming minorities.[153] The moment was seized by conservative groups to damage radical parties, unions, and, in the north central states, the Nonpartisan League.[154]

Two laws were the principal vehicles employed by the United States to limit criticism deleterious of the war effort. The Espionage Act of June 15, 1917, made it a felony to attempt to cause insubordination in the armed forces of the United States, to attempt to obstruct enlistment and recruiting services of the United States, or to convey false statements with intent to interfere with military operations.[155] The 1918 Amendments to the Espionage Act (Act of May 16, 1918), otherwise known as the Sedition Act, made it a felony

> to willfully cause or attempt to cause . . . or attempt to incite, insubordination, disloyalty, mutiny, or refusal of duty, in the military or naval forces of the United States, or shall willfully obstruct or attempt to obstruct the recruiting . . . service of the United States, and whoever, when the United States is at war, shall willfully utter, print, write, or publish any disloyal . . . language about the form of government of the United States, or the Constitution . . . or any language intended to bring the government of the United States into contempt . . . or shall willfully utter . . . or publish any language intended to promote the cause of its enemies.[156]

These laws were broad and vague, failing to draw a clear line at language that directly advised men to resist or violate laws. They made it possible for zealous or ambitious prosecutors to discourage dissent or discredit individuals or organizations or, as Judge Amidon, who saw as many Espionage and Sedition Act prosecutions as any judge in the United States, put it, converted "every United States Attorney into an angel of life and death, clothed with the power to walk up and down in his district, saying this one will I spare and that one will I smite."[157] Between 1917 and 1921, 2,168 prosecutions under the Espionage and Sedition Acts were brought in the United States. Four hundred seventy-six of them were brought in the Eighth Circuit—22 percent. Within the Eighth Circuit, only 12 were brought in both districts of Arkansas, 28 in South Dakota, 48 in Nebraska, but 103 in sparsely populated North Dakota.[158]

The latter was the work of U.S. Attorney Melvin A. Hildreth of the District of North Dakota. Many of his prosecutions were aimed at radicals or brought for the purpose of discrediting the Nonpartisan League. Amidon, more than any other U.S. judge, sought to narrow the scope of the Espionage Acts so that they would be applied only to clear-cut violations. He was able to persuade Hildreth to discontinue many prosecutions for lack of merit. He dismissed dozens of prosecutions and directed verdicts in still others.[159] At trial, Amidon cautioned jurors (many of whom had sons in the war) that there were many acts that might be suppressed by public sentiment but nevertheless were not crimes. As a matter of law, Amidon demanded that intent to interfere with recruiting or cause insubordination be demonstrated, that conduct be deliberate, and that the utterances have had a direct bearing on the forbidden results.

An Amidon jury charge in the trial of John Wishek served as a precedent throughout the nation for federal judges (and there were not many) who chose to employ a narrow interpretation of the Espionage Act. Wishek, an early settler and prosperous banker in McIntosh County, appears to have been greatly loved there but still fell victim to the calumnies of business rivals. He was charged under the Espionage Act with giving away a pamphlet, "German Achievements in America," allegedly remarking that banks having large holdings of Liberty Bonds were unsafe, and frequently stating that America would lose the war. Wishek had actually purchased $65,000 worth of war bonds, more than all his business rivals. At trial, Amidon excluded evidence of acts and speech that showed that Wishek lacked patriotism, as those things had not interfered with the success of the armed forces or been used to obstruct recruiting. In his charge, Amidon told the jury that three things were forbidden by the Espionage Act: false reports to interfere with the success of the armed forces, incitement to mutiny, and obstruction of recruiting. The jury was responsible for deciding whether Wishek's acts naturally tended to accomplish any of those things and also whether he had given away the pamphlet with such a deliberate purpose. The jury hung—it was deadlocked 9–3 for acquittal—and Amidon dismissed the case. For his handling of Espionage Act cases, Amidon was ostracized by the Fargo business community. People crossed the street to avoid meeting him and, at church, moved from the pew in which he sat.[160]

Many other judges in the Eighth Circuit and elsewhere were not as sensitive to the dangers of the wartime prosecutions or as courageous. When Rose Pastor Stokes, a socialist and nationally known critic of Wilson's war aims, was prosecuted for having written a letter to the editor of the *Kansas City Star*, in which she stated in part that "no government which is for the profiteer can also be for the people," Judge Arba S. Van Valkenburgh allowed into evidence in Stokes's prosecution such prejudicial matter as positive comments on the Soviet Union. Van Valkenburgh informed the jury that freedom of speech in wartime meant "criticism which is made friendly to the Government, friendly to the war, friendly to the policies of the Government." He then sentenced Stokes to ten years in prison. *After the war ended*, the Court of Appeals set aside the conviction.[161] When Amidon was away sitting with the Court of Appeals, Judge Martin Wade of the Southern District of Iowa tried Kate Richard O'Hare, a socialist and pacifist, in North Dakota. O'Hare was accused of obstructing enlistments by telling North Dakota mothers that they would be "no better than brood sows" if they "let the government send their sons to fight in France and become fertilizer." Wade sentenced O'Hare to five years. [162]

In times of public fervor, few judges go against the popular mood. Amid the hysteria of World War I, the federal courts (including the Supreme Court) did not distinguish themselves. There were only a few district judges like Amidon. However, the Court of Appeals for the Eighth Circuit was notably sensitive to individual rights, even overruling convictions secured when Amidon was the trial judge. One such case was the prosecution of Henry von Bank. Von Bank, president of a school district in Cass County, had been indicted for refusing to fly the flag over a school in his district and also for having stated (in the presence of a young man of draft age) that he "would as soon see a pair of old trousers flying over the school house as the American flag." Arguably, this was "obstruction" of the draft. Amidon let the case go to a jury. Von Bank was convicted, and Amidon sentenced him to sixty days. The Court of Appeals reversed Amidon for not having directed a verdict for the defendant.[163]

In *United States v. Fontana*, Amidon allowed the case of an Evangelical pastor to go to the jury, although he told the jury that the defendant had not committed a crime.[164] Amidon dismissed charges that Fontana had not purchased Liberty Bonds, supported the Red Cross, or displayed the flag in his church. However, Fontana was convicted for declaring that he was proud of the noble fight the Germans were making and that the United States had no reason to take up arms against Germany. After the jury verdict, Amidon sentenced Fontana to three years in prison. A Court of Appeals panel of Sanborn (writing), Stone, and Carland (concurring in the result) held that the indictment had lacked sufficient particularity—that Fontana had not been informed in the indictment as to what statements he had made, when, to whom, and in whose presence. They also held that there was insubstantial evidence to sustain the verdict. There had been no evidence of any public advocacy or suggestion or insinuation by the defendant of any of the evils the Espionage Act sought to prevent, or of any views tending to prove any of the evil intent required by the statute. In sum, at a time of public fervor that affected judges as it did others, both the U.S. Court of Appeals for the Eighth Circuit and the U.S. District Court for the District of North Dakota distinguished themselves for protection of individual rights.[165]

Federal Staples

In some of the traditional areas of federal law, such as admiralty and copyright, the Court of Appeals heard few cases during this period. In others, such as patent and taxation, a reasonable number of cases were decided, but they were of little significance other than to the parties. There were some criminal cases, however, about which brief mention is in order.

There were several important prosecutions for political corruption. Senator J. Ralph Burton of Kansas was convicted for mail fraud, and his conviction was affirmed by the Supreme Court.[166] There were also a number of successful prosecutions growing out of naturalization frauds perpetrated by Boss Edward Butler's Democratic machine in St. Louis. Those convictions, too, were affirmed.[167]

Hays v. United States,[168] an Eighth Circuit case, was one of three cases the Supreme Court consolidated and used to determine the reach of the Mann Act.[169] The issue was whether the act was limited only to those situations where a young woman was lured across state lines so the inducer could profit financially by her prostitution, or whether the act could be applied to situations where a couple simply crossed state lines and had sex. The plain language of the law suggests the latter interpretation; the title of the law, "White Slave Trade Act," suggests the former. In the *Hays* case, the Court of Appeals took the broader interpretation. So did the Supreme Court by a vote of five to three, using as the lead case not *Hays* but a Ninth Circuit case, *Caminetti v. United States*.[170] *Caminetti* has come to be a "much discussed object lesson in how not to discharge the function of statutory interpretation."[171]

From 1891 to 1929, the Court of Appeals for the Eighth Circuit was geographically the largest, as well as one of the busiest, circuits. Several of its judges—at least Caldwell, Sanborn, Van Devanter, and Hook—are entitled to an enduring reputation. As the principal object of the creation of the circuit courts of appeals was to relieve the Supreme Court of its more routine work, it should not be a surprise that much of what the Court of Appeals did attracted little public attention. Nevertheless, some of the great problems of the era found their way to the judges, when they were sitting either as court of appeals or circuit judges: what constituted a prohibited monopoly; which railroad rates violated due process; whether the United States owned the mineral rights in lands it had granted to the states; whether secondary boycotts violated the antitrust laws; how much dissent and disagreement was tolerable when a nation is mobilizing for total war. Often these questions made their way to the intermediate appellate court as narrow, technical, or intricate legal questions, which, when resolved, contributed in only a small way to resolving the greater questions. That, on the whole, was what the federal courts had been asked to do, and what they were asked to do, they did well. If a modern sensibility might resolve some of those questions differently, it nevertheless can be said from the perspective of almost a century that the federal courts contributed significantly to maintaining an atmosphere of constitutionalism, which would permit the United States to make the transition from a decentralized to a centralized nation and from a relatively laissez-faire state to a welfare state.

Here we leave the Eighth Circuit at its greatest expanse. No longer would it be concerned with legal problems arising in Colorado or

Wyoming, Kansas or Oklahoma, New Mexico or Utah. But if the jurisdiction of the Court of Appeals would in the future be less grand, it would nevertheless confront legal issues of equal, if not greater, importance—problems arising out of the Great Depression, mobilization for a second (and even greater) war, and the tensions of the Cold War. To those problems, the Eighth Circuit would bring an already distinguished tradition of judging.

CHAPTER 3

The Sanborn Court

1929–1959

*D*uring the three decades that followed the division of the Eighth Circuit, the United States was transformed from a laissez-faire, isolationist, and relatively weak federal government into a centralized welfare state and superpower.[1] The work of the federal government expanded as the nation passed through the Great Depression and the early years of the Cold War, accompanied by a growth of the jurisdiction of the federal courts. During this period, the lower federal courts increasingly applied centralizing policies generated by laws passed by Congress and decisions of the Supreme Court. The courts of appeals in particular contributed to the growing centralization of the American nation by oversight of the federal administrative agencies and its system of revenue collection, as well as by scrutiny of convictions for violation of the increased number of federal criminal laws. The courts of appeals also accommodated federal interests to state and local concerns by emphasizing principles of comity with state judiciaries and respect for state officials, laws, and the principles of federalism. While cases in the Eighth Circuit came increasingly to resemble those in other circuits, there were a few areas where distinctive regional problems and issues surfaced, including litigation connected with Mississippi River flood control projects and cases involving farming, Native Americans, and the instrumentalities of commerce. During these three decades of change, the U.S. Court of Appeals for the Eighth Circuit went about its business unobtrusively, making few waves while rendering relatively brief opinions.

Developments in the Nation and the Region

Although a deep agricultural depression began shortly after the end of World War I, the Great Depression as a national event commenced relatively few months after the division of the Eighth Circuit. The Wall Street crash led to a massive drop in consumer spending and the closings of shops, factories, and businesses, and greatly increased joblessness and homelessness and thousands of bank failures. Relying largely on private charity and local governments to meet the needs of the impoverished, President Hoover was unable to shake off the crisis. When Franklin Delano Roosevelt became president on March 4, 1933, industrial output was half what it had been in 1929. Fifteen million (out of a total population of 125 million) were out of work.

More significant social and economic legislation was enacted in the following year than in all previous American history. Although the New Deal was not successful in reducing long-term unemployment, popular confidence in the banking system was restored as the federal government created huge relief programs and government-financed jobs. The system for trading securities was reformed, the labor movement greatly strengthened, and a system of old-age pensions adopted. The extraordinary growth in the size and reach of the federal government posed profound challenges to the U.S. Constitution as it had previously been interpreted, constantly raised questions of statutory interpretation, and virtually created a new field of law—administrative law.

World War II led to unprecedented government control of the economy. From 1940 to 1944, federal spending grew from $9 billion to $95 billion. Output nearly doubled during the war, and net cash income increased by 400 percent.[2] The centralization of governmental power was not greatly reversed in the years following World War II. After the war, the government underwrote economic growth through the education of returning veterans, farm price supports, and subsidized housing construction. Government control of wages and prices ended after World War II, but resumed during the Korean War. Even when twenty years of Democratic leadership of the national government gave way to Republican rule, little was done to turn back the clock. In the meantime, a "long twilight struggle" with the Soviet Union commenced, which would last for two generations. Despite America's dominant military power, the years from 1945 to 1959 were dominated by a national crisis of self-confidence during which freedom of political expression was subjected to unprecedented legal restrictions and private pressures.

In the region of the Eighth Circuit, the onset of the Great Depression occurred much earlier than in the rest of the nation. It can be said that the Great Depression began on the farm in 1921. Fifty-four national banks and 402-state chartered banks failed in North Dakota alone during the 1920s.[3] The farm depression was accelerated by some of the worst weather in recorded history on the Great Plains and in the Mississippi Valley, especially the prolonged drought from 1928 to 1935. A huge area from Texas to the Dakotas turned into a dust bowl. "Black blizzards of dirt rolled across the landscape" of Nebraska.[4] In 1930 Arkansas produced only 66 percent of the cotton that it had the previous year. Iowa was virtually without crops from 1930 to 1932 because of drought, hail, and insect pests, and in 1934 the state was swept by fifteen major dust storms.[5] In North Dakota, grasshoppers ate the binder twine in the sheaves of grain, destroyed clothing, and gnawed wooden handles from farm tools.[6] Dust from the Great Plains fell on the Atlantic seaboard, almost blotting out the sun in Boston.[7] The devastating combination of low prices and poor crops caused thousands of foreclosures. Between 1932 and 1937, one-third of North Dakota's farmers lost their property by foreclosure.[8]

Desperation bred lawlessness. In 1931, three hundred farmers, half of them armed, stormed into England, Arkansas. In 1933, Iowa farmers with pitchforks stormed the state's General Assembly. During that same year, the Nebraska Farmer's Holiday Association briefly blocked roads, overturned milk trucks, dumped milk onto roads and ditches, halted trains, and burned bridges in order to draw attention to low farm prices. In 1935, a mob of farmers in Plattsburg, Missouri, held U.S. Marshal Henry Dellingham and three of his men hostage, preventing them from carrying out a mortgage sale. Merrill E. Otis, judge of the U.S. District Court for the Western District of Missouri, was threatened. In Iowa one hundred farmers demanded that a judge refuse to issue any more foreclosure orders, dragged him from his courtroom, smeared him with grease, and put a rope around his neck. In North Dakota, Governor William Langer tried a nonviolent approach of proclaiming a moratorium on foreclosures, employing the National Guard on at least thirty-one occasions to halt sheriff sales, and placing an embargo on the movement of wheat out of the state. Langer's actions were held unconstitutional by a federal judge.[9]

Away from the farm, the effects of the Depression in the region were also grim. Retail sales declined 23.8 percent in Nebraska between 1929 and 1939, and the number of manufacturing establishments dropped from 1,491 to 1,161 (22 percent).[10] Industrial employment in Missouri dropped from 371,000 (1930) to 142,000 (1933).[11] In Minnesota, the production of iron ore, which had averaged 33 million tons in the 1920s, plummeted to 2.2 million in 1932.[12]

The New Deal sought to address the problems of the region with a variety of programs. Its handiwork was everywhere. Works Progress Administration projects accounted for 11,417 miles of roads, 467 new schools, and 44 new parks in Arkansas. In North Dakota the WPA built 20,712 miles of streets and highways, 721 new bridges and viaducts, and 15,012 culverts. In South Dakota between 1933 and 1945, the Civilian Conservation Corps employed an average of 23,000 persons, who worked at reforestation, dam construction, and preventing soil erosion.[13]

The farm sector probably received the most direct and long-lasting benefits from the New Deal. Farmers received economic stability but paid the price of giving up genuinely free enterprise. Higher commodity prices followed the New Deal's produce contracts and price supports embodied in the Agricultural Adjustment Act. The Rural Electrification Administration distributed electricity to isolated rural areas. Efforts were made to save farms from bankruptcy, insure against natural disasters, and resettle impoverished farm families, as well as aid tenants and sharecroppers in purchasing their land.[14]

From 1933 to 1941, Nebraska farmers received $200 million in government payments, 19 percent of their income. In Nebraska, 73.6 percent of farms participated in government soil conservation programs.[15] If in 1930 only about 10 percent of South Dakota's farmers could use electric power in their farming and household operations, by 1950 69 percent of the state's farms had electric power.[16] There was also direct relief. South Dakota had the highest relief rate in the nation in 1934; North Dakota was in second place. By late 1936, half the population of North Dakota was receiving some kind of stipend from the government.[17]

It was not the New Deal, however, but World War II, which truly produced economic recovery. The farm sector benefited enormously from the war. The net cash income of the American farmer soared more than 400 percent from 1940 to 1945. In Iowa, for example, farm production was 50 percent higher than during World War I.[18] Wheat yield in North Dakota grew from 19.2 million bushels in 1936 to 156 million in 1944.[19]

Each of the states of the Eighth Circuit profited from more direct defense spending. Plants in St. Louis manufactured 95 percent of the military ammunition and explosives used by American forces. Bombers and gun stocks for rifles were manufactured in Kansas City. Defense contracts for Missouri industries, for example, amounted to $42 billion.[20] In Iowa, John Deere made tank transmissions, and Maytag manufactured fighter plane parts. Eleven army airfields were built in Nebraska. Army Air Corps installations of varying size and importance were located at Pierre, Mitchell, Rapid City, and Sioux Falls, South Dakota. There were fifteen POW camps in Nebraska and South Dakota. German prisoners of war worked on Iowa and Nebraska farms. Two of the ten permanent camps for Japanese Americans were located in Arkansas, one near Rohwer in Desha County, the other with a population of 17, 000 at Jerome in Chicot County.[21] Between 1940 and 1945, total personal income in North Dakota rose 145 percent. By the end of the war, North Dakota residents had accumulated the largest per capita bank deposits in the nation.[22]

The prosperity continued into the postwar years, which were marked by growing urbanization, industrial development, and, in some of the states of the Eighth Circuit, greater cultural pluralism. In 1930, Missouri was already less than 50 percent rural. By 1960, it was 66.6 percent urban. Arkansas became 50 percent urban in the 1940s. Not until 1950 did the urban population overtake the rural population in Minnesota. Between 1940 and 1960, Nebraska's urban population grew by about 50 percent.[23]

The farm sector declined during the 1950s, in some measure due to the Eisenhower farm program of flexible and lower price supports, restricted credit, and curtailed rural electrification (as well as a decline in the consumption of wheat). The average yields skyrocketed with growing mechanization, and the standard of living on the farm increased markedly. However, the number of farms dramatically decreased. Arkansas, for example, had 254,000 farms in 1933 and 74,000 in 1970. Between 1938 and 1988, the number of farms in Nebraska decreased by half. Yet most of the states of the Eighth Circuit had an enormously favorable fiscal relationship with the federal government as a result of farm subsidies, land and water reclamation projects, military bases, and interstate highway construction. Airports were developed, and interstate freeways were built, and the isolation of the region from the rest of the nation was further diminished by developments in communications.[24]

Transformation of the Land

Special mention must be made of the huge federal projects begun during this period damming the Mississippi, Missouri, and many smaller rivers in order to head off floods, create electric power, and supply water for irrigation. These efforts would produce an enormous amount of litigation that continues to this day.

After the greatest recorded flood of the Mississippi River in 1927, Congress passed the Mississippi Flood Control Act of May 15, 1928.[25] That act provided for a comprehensive ten-year program for the entire Mississippi Valley, embodying a general land protection scheme, channel stabilization, and river regulation. Further construction, authorized by the River and Harbor Act of July 3, 1930,[26] and continuing until 1963, created a nine-foot channel from Minneapolis to the mouth of the Missouri River by building a series of dams with locks, turning the Upper Mississippi into a chain of ponds, climbing like steps from St. Louis to Minneapolis.

The history of government involvement with the Missouri is more tortured than that of the Mississippi. The Missouri, the eighth longest river in the world, is of vital importance to all the states of the Eighth Circuit, except for Minnesota and Arkansas. The worst Missouri River floods in sixty years occurred in 1942, greatly affecting Omaha, Council Bluffs, Kansas City, and St. Louis, and established the atmosphere for a major federal program altering the course of the river. However, the needs of the upper and lower Missouri basin states were (and are) different. The lower Missouri basin states needed flood control and some irrigation. The inhabitants of the upper Missouri basin needed hydroelectric power and a great deal of irrigation.

Two apparently irreconcilable plans were presented to the Congress. That of the Corps of Engineers (the Pick Plan), aimed at taming the river, proposed a giant stairwell of dams to prevent ferocious spring runoffs and levees in the lower basin. However, the Bureau of Reclamation of the Department of the Interior pushed a plan (the Sloan Plan) that was aimed primarily at tapping the Upper Missouri for irrigation and hydroelectric power through a series of dams on its tributaries.[27]

Congress adopted both plans in the Flood Control Act of 1944. The result was to change the Missouri into a river far different from the one seen by Lewis and Clark.[28] A nine-foot channel was created below Sioux City, a stable channel for downstream navigation. Five large dams were built, four in South Dakota and one in North Dakota, which prevented flooding and provided cheap hydroelectric power. While the dams produced sites for excellent recreational activity, the expectations for irrigation have never been fulfilled. Further, well over a million acres were flooded in North and South Dakota, including historic sites, Indian bottomlands that provided water and shelter for Sioux livestock, and some of the best waterfowl habitation in the world.[29]

Judicial Administration

From 1925 to 1959, important changes occurred in the jurisdiction, caseload, management, and staffing of the U.S. courts of appeals. Because of the great expansion of the work of the federal government, the growth of jurisdiction of the federal courts generally, and the demonstrated success of the courts of appeals as the courts of last resort in most cases, the influence of those courts grew.

During the nineteenth century, the lower federal courts had been specialized courts. In addition to providing a forum for litigation between citizens of different states, the lower federal courts handled "federal question" cases, that is, cases resulting from jurisdiction allocated to the federal government or federal courts by the Constitution and amplified by laws passed by Congress. These areas essentially were admiralty, bankruptcy, patent, and copyright. There were a few areas of law that devolved on the federal courts from the common law or by statute, such as trademark, tax, and federal criminal law. As we have seen, between 1891 and 1929, the public law jurisdiction of the federal courts was greatly enlarged by legislation that occurred as a result of the Populist and Progressive movements. This included prosecutions for violating the antitrust laws brought against both business and labor and new federal criminal laws such as the Mann Act and the Harrison Anti-narcotic Act, as well as railroad regulation. More and more, the federal courts were called on to interpret federal statutes, apply federal criminal laws, and oversee federal regulation of business practices.

When the role of the federal government expanded in the years following 1929, the jurisdiction of the federal courts grew considerably. New Deal measures such as the National Labor Relations Act of 1935 provided for judicial oversight of the National Labor Relations Board, which regulated labor-management relations. Other statutes provided federal jurisdiction over price fixing (Robinson-Patman Amendments to the Clayton Act, 1936), over the securities markets (the Securities Exchange Act of 1934), and over minimum wages and maximum hours (Fair Labor Standards Act of 1938). After World War II, new business was brought to the federal courts as a result of passage of the 1946 Federal Tort Claims Act, the Taft-Hartley Act of 1947, and the 1952 McCarran-Walter Immigration Act. A few statutes spawned litigation evoking the special ambience of the region, especially laws regulating agriculture and farm bankruptcies, involving flood control projects on the Mississippi and the Missouri, as well as the Indian Reorganization Act of 1934. Finally, decisions of the Supreme Court in the 1930s and 1940s, evoking a new sensitivity to civil liberties, brought about a major new area of work for the lower federal courts.

In a few notable instances, important business was taken from the federal courts, namely the pre–New Deal Norris-LaGuardia Act of 1932, which denied the federal courts jurisdiction to issue injunctions in labor disputes except in strictly defined situations, and the repeal of Prohibition. In one important area, the business of the federal courts was largely unchanged, but the way they handled the business was. The Supreme Court's decision in *Erie Railroad Co. v. Tompkins* took from the federal courts the power to make general (federal) common law in diversity cases separate and apart from the common law of the states in which they sat.[30]

During this period, major developments enhanced the independence of the federal courts. Already in 1922, at the urging of Chief Justice William Howard Taft, the Conference of Senior Judges had been created. The senior circuit judges of each circuit met as a body semiannually with the Chief Justice to facilitate, when needed, the assignment of judges from outside their circuits and to be more effective in representing to Congress the need for larger appropriations, more judgeships, and better facilities.

The Administrative Office Act of August 7, 1939, ended two decades of tension between federal judges and the Justice Department over the department's handling of the budget of the lower federal courts, salaries of court employees, and disbursements.[31] Routine administrative housekeeping for the judicial branch was centralized in a newly created Administrative Office of the United States Courts (AO). Concurrently, Congress conferred responsibility for supervision of the dockets and performance of district courts on judicial councils for each circuit, which were composed of the judges of the court of appeals for the circuit. The AO would become a source of irritation for judges in the hinterland, but it freed them from dependence on the executive branch. The new judicial councils would, in most circuits, be paper tigers for generations but nevertheless brought home to many judges their responsibility for managing their docket.

Perhaps the most important development enhancing the stature of the federal courts during this era was the adoption of the Federal Rules of Civil Procedure. Before the rules were adopted in 1938, federal courts followed the procedural rules of the state in which they were located. As a result, federal procedures varied from state to state and often perpetuated the unnecessary forms and technicalities of the common law.

In 1934, Congress delegated to United States Supreme Court the power to draft rules of practice and procedure. The Federal Rules of Civil Procedure,[32] drafted by an advisory committee of practitioners and law professors (promulgated by the Supreme Court and ratified by Congress), was a single set of rules in civil cases for the federal courts. As a result of the adoption of the federal rules, federal practice became simpler, more precise, and more modern than state practice. Federal practice permitted the advancement of cases to decision on the merits with a minimum of procedural encumbrances. A pretrial discovery process was designed to eliminate surprise at trial and to uncover points of agreement between the parties. Federal Rules of Criminal Procedure, Appellate Procedure, and Evidence, created by similar processes, went into effect in 1946, 1968, and 1975. Barnacles would become attached to the federal rules over time, but of their value in enhancing the stature of federal courts there is no doubt.[33]

The 1930s also saw important changes in the staffing of the federal courts. Judges began to avail themselves of the procedure of retiring from active service at the age of seventy, whereby they could continue to sit as senior judges, but their court would benefit by a newly appointed judge on regular active service. In addition, in 1930 Congress authorized each court of appeals judge to appoint a law clerk. The use of law clerks soon became widespread.

Until 1948, the U.S. Court of Appeals for the Eighth Circuit held terms in St. Louis from September to Christmas. Until 1935, the Court of Appeals met in the Post Office and Federal Courts Building at Eighth and Olive, but in November 1935, it met in a new courthouse for the first time. When in St. Louis, the judges rented apartments near Forest Park. There was a May term in St. Paul, and the court sat occasionally in Kansas City and Omaha. After the retirement of Chief Judge Stone, whose chambers were in Kansas City, the court decided officially to sit regularly only in St. Louis. That city would be the exclusive site until the 1960s.

In 1932, the court established divisions: Stone, Booth, and Van Valkenburgh were in one; Kenyon, Gardner, and Sanborn in the other. District judges often made up the third seat on panels. The court heard argument in almost every case. Following argument, the judges met in conference. Each judge would then prepare a memorandum on each case, and the differences would be reconciled at a memorandum conference. When the judges were back in their home chambers, they communicated by mail.[34]

During these years, the Eighth Circuit was more removed from the centers of jurisprudential activity than a number of the other circuits. Its caseload grew erratically from 314 (1930) to a high of 353 (1936), then varied from a high of 328 cases docketed (1941) to a low of 189 (1948). From 1950 through 1959, the highest caseload was 259 (1955) and the lowest was 184 (1950). The proportion of Eighth Circuit cases to those of all other courts of appeals dropped appreciably during this period.[35]

During these thirty years—at least until the 1950s—the Court of Appeals was characterized by great intimacy, made even easier to achieve by the homogeneity of an aging, white, Protestant, Middle American bench. During the entire period, the court had only two chief judges, Kimbrough Stone and Archibald K. Gardner. Stone, who had already served twelve years when his senior associate judge (Gardner) for most of the 1930s and 1940s arrived, set a standard of gentility. Stone, Gardner, and John B. Sanborn sat together for fourteen years; Gardner, Sanborn, Joseph W. Woodrough, and Harvey M. Johnsen sat together for almost nineteen years. When the judges sat together, they usually stayed at the same hotel, dined together, worked together, and met together informally in the evening. Thus the work of the Eighth Circuit, unlike some of the other circuits, appears not to have been marked by interpersonal conflicts. Its rate of dissenting opinions was low.[36]

The Judges

During the years between the Act of February 28, 1929,[37] and June 30, 1959, when John Sanborn retired, the Court of Appeals was dominated by four judges—Kimbrough Stone, Archibald K. Gardner, John B. Sanborn, and Joseph W. Woodrough, who between them served 101 years on regular active service. Twelve other judges sat on the court during this period, but their years of regular active service during this period totaled to only eighty-two.

After division of the circuit in 1929, Kimbrough Stone of Missouri, William S. Kenyon of Iowa, Wilbur Booth of Minnesota, and Arba S. Van Valkenburgh of Missouri constituted the court, joined by Archibald Kenneth Gardner (1867–1962) of South Dakota. Gardner had been appointed by Herbert Hoover to the new seat created by the law dividing the court. Two of the judges, Stone and Gardner, would sit for many years. The three other judges would either take senior status or die within four years. Stone would sit as senior circuit judge (chief judge) until 1947, and thereafter on senior status. Gardner would remain on regular active service until 1960. Booth retired in 1932, although he would continue to sit until his death in 1944. Kenyon died in 1933, and Van Valkenburgh retired in the same year, although he would sit with senior status until 1944.

Kimbrough Stone (1875–1958), a member of the Eighth Circuit for forty-one years, could boast of a lineage that included a 1648 Maryland governor and a drafter of the Articles of Confederation. Born in Missouri, Stone attended that state's university and Harvard Law School. Joining his father in law practice in St. Louis, Stone moved to Kansas City when his father was elected U.S. senator. While a litigator in private practice, Stone served as clerk of the state legislative committee that revised Missouri's statutes and as a commissioner for the Missouri Supreme Court. For four years, Stone was judge of the Jackson County Circuit Court.

Woodrow Wilson appointed Stone to the Eighth Circuit in 1917 to succeed Elmer P. Adams. Stone's forty years of service (including his time with senior status from 1947 to 1958) spanned judges from Walter Sanborn, appointed in 1892, to Charles Vogel, who served until 1981. Stone sat on over 1,800 cases and wrote almost seven hundred opinions for the court, fifty-one dissenting opinions, and five concurring opinions. The U.S. Supreme Court reversed only twelve of his majority opinions, modified two, affirmed sixteen, and denied certiorari 125 times.[38]

If Sanborn was a much greater intellectual influence on the Court of Appeals, Stone, as senior circuit judge of the Eighth Circuit, was an excellent manager—effective and efficient, maintaining continuity and collegiality in a family-like atmosphere. As senior circuit judge from 1928 to 1947, Stone organized the first circuit conferences, which encouraged a close rapport among circuit and district judges in a far-flung circuit and proved a useful vehicle for communication with the (national) Conference of Senior Judges.

Stone also played an important role in the Conference of Senior Judges. For many years, he served as one of the five-person General Advisory Committee. Believing in separating the Department of Justice from housekeeping duties for the federal judiciary, Stone was a midwife in the creation of the Administrative Office of the United States Courts. Strongly believing in judicial independence, Stone was influential in restricting the powers of the director of the Administrative Office and in creating circuit judicial councils.[39]

Stone died in 1958 at the age of eighty-three. At his memorial service, Judge Harvey M. Johnsen spoke of Stone's "unfailing courtesy," "infinite patience," "calm dignity," "solid firmness," "exhaustive thoroughness," "conscientious responsibility," and the "enveloping legal and spiritual faith, with which every incident and element of his work were permeated."[40]

To the seat created at the time the Eighth Circuit was divided, President Hoover nominated Archibald Gardner (1867–1962), the first South Dakotan to sit on the Court of Appeals. Born in Canada, Gardner grew up in Iowa, attended Grinnell College and the University of Iowa, where he received both bachelor's and law degrees. Admitted to practice in Iowa, Gardner moved to Rapid City, South Dakota, then a center of gold mining and ranching. Later he moved to Huron.

Gardner was a remarkably versatile lawyer, appearing as counsel in the South Dakota Supreme Court some two hundred times. He handled cases involving water and mining rights, cattle litigation, condemnation proceedings, and criminal matters. He was city attorney, state attorney, and counsel to the Chicago and North Western Railroad. During World War I, Gardner was counsel for the State Council of Defense, representing the council in the unsuccessful attempt to dissolve the Hutterische (Russian) Colony Corporation. At the time of Gardner's appointment, District Judge James D. Elliott wrote that Gardner "has had more business in my Court than any other twelve lawyers in South Dakota."[41]

When the new seat on the Eighth Circuit was created in 1929, the two prime candidates were Gardner and Alfred Lee Wyman. Calvin Coolidge appointed Wyman to the district court and Gardner to the Court of Appeals. Gardner's appointment lapsed in the Senate when Coolidge's term ran out, but his name was resubmitted by Herbert Hoover, and he was confirmed. Three years later, Gardner was one of four persons considered for the vacancy on the U.S. Supreme Court created by the retirement of Oliver Wendell Holmes, but lost out to Benjamin Cardozo.[42]

During a tenure that lasted over thirty years, Gardner wrote 837 majority opinions, fourteen dissenting opinions, and two concurring opinions. Although he was seventy-nine, seven years older than Stone, Gardner succeeded Stone as senior circuit judge in 1947 and held the job until he was ninety-one. He was finally forced out by statute. Gardner retired from the court in 1961 and died the following year.[43]

John B. Sanborn Jr. (1883–1964) succeeded Judge Wilbur Booth in 1932. Sanborn, in regular active service until 1959 and then senior judge until the year of his death, was the most influential member of the Court of Appeals for the Eighth Circuit during his three-decade tenure. Sanborn's roots ran from seventeenth-century New Hampshire to pioneer Minnesota. Born in St. Paul on November 9, 1883, Sanborn was educated at the University of Minnesota and the St. Paul College of Law. He practiced from 1907 until 1922. For part of the time, he was associated with Butler and Mitchell, a firm that produced one Supreme Court Justice, Pierce Butler, and one U.S. Attorney General, William Mitchell. Sanborn was a member of the Minnesota House of Representatives (1913). His service as Minnesota's commissioner of insurance (1917–18, 1919–20) was interrupted by a stint as a private in the U.S. Army. Sanborn would also serve a short term on the Minnesota Tax Commission.

Sanborn's career on the bench began with three years on the Ramsey County District Court. In 1925, Calvin Coolidge appointed Sanborn to the U.S. District Court for the District of Minnesota. During eight years, he wrote more than one hundred opinions as a district judge and forty-eight for the Court of Appeals.[44] One-third of Sanborn's opinions while a district judge were in the area of bankruptcy law, an area in which he demonstrated a particularly keen grasp. Considered for the Court of Appeals in 1928 to replace his cousin, Walter Sanborn, and again in 1929, John Sanborn reached that court in 1932 by appointment of President Hoover. Sanborn sat on 2,400 cases in over thirty years, writing more than seven hundred opinions for the court, seventeen dissents, and seventeen concurring opinions.[45]

John Sanborn was a more conservative jurist than his cousin. He adhered to precedent, respected the legislative process, and never addressed questions of constitutionality unless it was absolutely necessary.[46] He never "thought it to be the business of the court to arouse the [conscience] of the people or seek to cause them to alter their institutions."[47] A former trial judge, Sanborn recognized and respected the role of federal district judges as fact finders, understood the pressures of conducting trials, and believed in deference to federal trial judges when interpreting open questions of state law. In criminal cases, Sanborn believed that criminal defendants were entitled to a fair, not a perfect, trial and almost always held in favor of the government.[48]

Sanborn was the intellectual leader of his court and may have had much to do with its amicable relations. Harry Blackmun, a Sanborn law clerk, suggested that perhaps it was Sanborn "who did the most to contribute to the balance and . . . to the team or family character" of the court, due to his "gentle, modest, and self-effacing character and to his ability to dispel tension . . . in the courtroom and in the conference room."[49] Blackmun spoke of Sanborn's profound concern for the court, his love of the law, fairness in assignments, his intimate and personal relationship and assistance to every member of his court, pithy opinions, absence of pride in authorship, absolute lack of pretence, sure-footedness, and intellectual modesty. Another Supreme Court justice, Charles Whittaker, singled out Sanborn's "disdain of display" and spoke of him as "a quiet and kind man of culture who has unwaveringly practiced the principles of honor, truth, integrity and fairness."[50] The Eighth Circuit, Blackmun concluded, was "a better court because John Benjamin Sanborn graced it with his character, strengthened it with his strength, lifted it with his wisdom, assured it with his judgment and his courage, made it cooperative and happier with his humor, and leveled it with his self-restraint."[51] When Sanborn took senior status in 1959, he was succeeded by Blackmun. Sanborn died at the age of eighty on March 7, 1964.

Franklin Delano Roosevelt made five appointments to the Eighth Circuit. His first, Joseph William Woodrough (1873–1977), succeeded Van Valkenburgh in 1933. Herbert Hoover's previous attempt to fill the vacancy with Assistant Attorney General Seth W. Richardson of North Dakota had failed when the nomination died in the Senate. Woodrough, who would live until the age of 104, was the first Nebraskan to sit on the Court of Appeals. Born in Cincinnati, Woodrough completed graduate work at Heidelberg. Woodrough practiced law in Texas and was elected county judge there in 1894. In 1897 he moved to Omaha, where he became a prominent member of the bar. Woodrow Wilson appointed Woodrough to the U.S. District Court for the District of

Nebraska, where he tried and sentenced the "Birdman of Alcatraz," Robert Stroud. Woodrough retired at the age of eighty-eight in 1961 after forty-five years judicial service. If not as much of a heavyweight as Sanborn, Woodrough was the court's most liberal member, willing to dissent in pithy prose.[52] He was a man of "plain, common sense," "simple, almost Spartan in the way he lived" and well loved by his colleagues.[53]

Roosevelt's second appointee, Charles B. Faris (1864–1938) was elevated from the Eastern District of Missouri in 1935 at the age of seventy-one to succeed Judge Kenyon. Faris had served for seven years on the Missouri Supreme Court and sixteen years as district judge. He accepted the position with an unusual understanding—that he would retire within a year and be succeeded by an appointee from Iowa.[54] Faris retired after nine months but continued to serve as senior judge until his death in 1938.

The Kenyon seat then went to Seth Thomas (1873–1962), who, as solicitor of the Department of Agriculture to Secretary Henry Wallace, was one of those charged with devising a New Deal agricultural program that would survive a constitutional test. Thomas was a member of the Court of Appeals for eighteen years. He retired from the court in 1954 and died in 1962.[55]

Congress created two more judgeships in 1940.[56] To the first, Roosevelt appointed Harvey M. Johnsen (1895–1976), who had served on the Nebraska Supreme Court from 1938 to 1940 but failed to win election in the latter year. Johnsen sat on regular active service until 1965. Chief Judge from 1959 to 1965, he served until his death as a senior judge.[57] In 1941, Roosevelt appointed Walter G. Riddick (1883–1953) to the second new judgeship. Riddick was a politically well-connected Little Rock practitioner, who became the first native Arkansan to sit on the Court of Appeals. He served for twelve years.[58]

To succeed Kimbrough Stone when he took senior status in 1947, Harry Truman appointed his good friend John Caskie Collet, then Missouri's "roving" district judge. While a district judge, Collet served as administrator of the Office of Economic Stabilization (where Professor Henry Hart of Harvard Law School was his deputy) and as consultant to the Office of War Mobilization and Conversion. It is not clear just how strong a grounding in wages and prices Collet had.[59] After elevation to the Court of Appeals, Collet continued as a White House consultant. Collet undertook his extrajudicial activities with the approbation of

Senior Judge Kimbrough Stone but broke under his double role, suffering heart attacks and dying at the age of fifty-seven.[60]

President Eisenhower made four appointments to the Eighth Circuit from his first inauguration until the retirement of John Sanborn on June 30, 1959. Three—Charles J. Vogel, Martin D. Van Oosterhout, and Marion C. Matthes—would be influential members of the Court of Appeals and are discussed in later chapters. Vogel (1898–1981), North Dakota's first member of the Court of Appeals, was elevated from the district court to replace Judge Riddick. Van Oosterhout (1901–79), an Iowa district judge, appointed on the same day as Vogel (August 20, 1954), filled the court's Iowa seat, left vacant when Thomas took senior status. Matthes (1906–80), appointed to the seat left open by the elevation of Charles Whittaker to the Supreme Court, was the first member of the court from St. Louis since Judge Faris. He had served in all three branches of Missouri state government—as president pro tem of the Senate, a member of the State Highway Commission, and judge of the St. Louis Court of Appeals. Matthes served as Chief Judge from 1970 to 1973. His most important opinion, in the Little Rock school desegregation case, is discussed in the following chapter.[61]

Charles E. Whittaker (1901–73)

A member of the Court of Appeals for only nine months, Charles Whittaker deserves separate treatment as one of four circuit judges of the Eighth Circuit to be elevated to the Supreme Court of the United States. Whittaker was born on a farm in northeastern Kansas on February 22, 1901. After he finished ninth grade, he dropped out of school to help support his family for the next two years by trapping small animals, hunting game, and farming. Entering the University of Kansas City Law School at night without having had a high school education, Whittaker was tutored on high school subjects while in law school, supporting himself as an office boy with a leading Kansas City law firm. Later he would become a partner in that firm, Watson, Gage, and Ess. Whittaker became an esteemed litigator and a leader of the Kansas City bar. He was elected president of the state bar of Missouri (1953–54).

Whittaker's career was advanced by Roy Roberts, owner of the *Kansas City Star,* a client of Whittaker's, who had been influential in persuading Eisenhower to run for president. Whittaker also had the strong recommendation of local political leaders, influential members of the bar, and Missouri's liberal Democratic senator Thomas C. Hennings, when Eisenhower appointed him judge of the Western District of Missouri in 1954. During two years on the district court, Whittaker was affirmed by the Court of Appeals in sixteen of twenty cases and proved efficient in managing his docket. In perhaps his most notable case, Whittaker rejected the claim of a tenured professor dismissed from a university faculty after refusing on constitutional grounds to answer whether he was a Communist.[62]

Whittaker's tenure on the Court of Appeals lasted only from June 5, 1956, until March 24, 1957, when he was elevated to the Supreme Court. In that short time, he wrote thirteen opinions in cases involving such areas as price fixing, bankruptcy, and eminent domain.[63] Whittaker's lower-court opinions are ably written and characterized by unusual clarity. Theodore Fetter has, however, suggested that Whittaker's "strong beliefs sometimes made it impossible to function smoothly as one of several members of an appellate bench."[64]

Elevated to the Supreme Court by a president determined to make prior judicial experience a precondition for appointment to that tribunal, Whittaker's career was disappointing. Superconscientious, he was a perfectionist who never was content until he had mastered the facts of the case and its record. At the same time, he was ill prepared to keep up intellectually with his brethren and lacked a true sense of the unusual policy-making role of the High Court. Agonizing over decisions, physically exhausted and mentally distressed by his work, Whittaker resigned in March 1962 after five years' service.[65]

While a member of the High Court, Whittaker was the swing vote in many cases. Most of the time, he voted against a claimed right or liberty—forty-one times in five-to-four decisions over five years. Whittaker's resignation, coupled with the almost simultaneous stroke that led to the retirement of Justice Frankfurter, made possible the formation of a liberal, activist majority on the Supreme Court.[66]

Whittaker returned to Kansas City. It took time to regain his health. He resigned his judicial commission in 1965 to accept a legal position with General Motors. His staunch criticism of the direction of the High Court led to Chief Justice Earl Warren's wry comment, "Charlie never could make up his mind about decisions until he left the court."[67] The most recent appraisal of Whittaker's career, by Judge Howard F. Sachs of the Western District of Missouri, agrees with virtually all observers: "Reconsideration of Whittaker's judicial career does not greatly enhance his reputation."[68]

Of the twelve judges appointed between 1929 and June 30, 1959, half were appointed by Democratic presidents and half by Republicans. Of the sixteen judges who served on active service during the era, six came from Missouri, two from Minnesota, three from Iowa, two from Nebraska, and one each from the Dakotas and Arkansas. Most of the judges had attended college and law school within their native state. Only three of the twelve held nonjudicial elective office. However, six held state elective judicial positions. Six of the twelve were elevated to the Court of Appeals from the federal district court. All were white, male, and Protestant.

Jurisprudence

The 1925 Judiciary Act, which made the Supreme Court a court of discretionary jurisdiction by greatly limiting the right of direct appeal to it, was a vote of confidence in the courts of appeals. Having succeeded in serving as a buffer for the Supreme Court, the potential of the courts of appeals for dealing with cases of great political salience was enhanced by the new law that extended their jurisdiction to questions involving the constitutionality of a U.S. law or treaty and to cases in which it was alleged that constitutional provisions or state laws violated the U.S. Constitution.[69] In addition, circuit judges ordinarily were members of the three-judge district courts, which dealt with cases under the antitrust and interstate commerce laws, where there was direct appeal to the Supreme Court.

If the major roles of the courts of appeals were still that of dispute settlers and buffer, during this period the role of those courts in applying centralizing policies generated by laws passed by the Congress and decisions of the Supreme Court became more important. This can be seen in the wholesale increase in opportunities for individuals and corporations to use the bankruptcy system and in the area of revenue collection where, as the tax system became more complex, the federal courts were called on to place a judicial imprimatur on a system that had profound centralizing effects. It also meant oversight of the district courts in increasing numbers of prosecutions of state and federal political leaders for corruption. Perhaps most important, the role of the courts of appeals in centralizing policies could be seen in cases where a court of appeals was petitioned to enforce or overturn decisions of federal administrative agencies.

Of course, not every case decided by the courts of appeals produced a centralizing result. Not infrequently, the court applied principles of comity in its relations with state judiciaries and deferred to state officials. Often it was called on to interpret and apply state laws in diversity of citizenship and other cases. Nevertheless, on the whole, the courts of appeals played a role in the great extension of the federal government into American life.

This is not to suggest that the years between the division of the Eighth Circuit and the Little Rock school desegregation case of 1957–58 (discussed in the following chapter) were for the U.S. Court of Appeals a period of great drama or brilliant fireworks. It is indeed difficult to point to individual cases of great significance decided by the Court of Appeals during this period (save the Little Rock school desegregation case). Not only were state courts still hearing on average cases of greater significance than the lower federal courts, but the docket of the Eighth Circuit presented fewer challenges than that of the distinguished Second Circuit of the Hands, Frank, and Clark with its securities, copyright, and immigration cases, or the District of Columbia Circuit of Edgerton, Rutledge, and Arnold with its local criminal caseload and great number of administrative agency cases. Rather, the Court of Appeals for the Eighth Circuit was constituted by a homogeneous group of judges, working together for many years, not seeking attention for themselves, who produced a solid body of work evidencing craftsmanship, but not scholarly exhaustiveness, quotabilility, or passion. The function of the Eighth Circuit Court of Appeals was, after all, primarily to settle disputes, and the disputes it settled arose in a region that had put the tumultuous years of settlement behind it and was not yet immersed in the dissonance of the 1960s.

Depression and War

The Great Depression and World War II did not produce many blockbuster cases in the Eighth Circuit but did lead to a greatly increased role of the federal courts in bankruptcy and administrative law. The only important Eighth Circuit cases reaching the Supreme Court that involved the constitutionality of New Deal legislation were two of the three Gold Clause cases, decided in the Supreme Court as *Norman v. B & O Railroad*.[70] The cases were decided in the Eastern District of Missouri. While the appeals were pending before the Court of Appeals, the Supreme Court granted certiorari.

The Gold Clause cases involved railroad bonds payable "in like gold coin semi-annually," a condition the bondholders sought to enforce after Congress abrogated the clauses in private contracts stipulating payment in gold. Judge Charles B. Faris upheld the act of Congress, holding that the power to say what shall be used as money lies with Congress alone, that everyone who enters into a contract is deemed to hold in contemplation Congress's power to alter and change the nature and volume of the medium of exchange, and therefore that payments for the bonds could be in U.S. currency.[71] The Supreme Court affirmed by a vote of five to four with Chief Justice Hughes's opinion tracing that of Faris. A different result might have, in FDR's words, returned the country to the "pre-existing chaos in foreign exchange and domestic currency."[72]

Bankruptcy

The Great Depression spurred reforms in the bankruptcy system, and the functions of the Bankruptcy Court grew greatly during the Depression. However, bankruptcy filings dropped precipitously during World War II, which led to the end of the fee system in 1946, when referees were put on salary.

The federal consent decree equity receivership, codified in a 1933 amendment to the 1898 Bankruptcy Act, remains to this day the source of modern corporate reorganization. The Act of June 22, 1938, changed the referee from a special master, who heard and reported, into a judicial officer, who exercised jurisdiction to make final adjudications subject to appeal in referred cases.[73] Under the 1938 law, bankruptcy procedures under Chapter 11 were made available to persons, partnerships, or corporations in financial distress, who could voluntarily petition for the settlement, satisfaction, or extension of time for payment of unsecured debtors so as to avoid liquidation. This had to be acceptable to a majority of creditors of each class affected.[74]

Bankruptcy appeals heard in the Eighth Circuit involved the reorganization of railroads (the most notable involved the Missouri-Pacific and the St. Louis–San Francisco Railway Companies), the Fox Rocky Mountain Theatre Company, the Cherokee Public Service Company, national banks, grocery store chains, a 160-acre farm just outside Omaha, rights to a rock crusher moved from Arkansas several months before bankruptcy intervened,[75] and a widow whose husband had pawned her jewelry.[76]

Bankruptcy cases involved such legal questions as the powers of trustees, the disinterestedness of receivers, the function of the Interstate Commerce Commission in railroad reorganizations, the role of the Federal Reserve, and the proof needed to establish a voidable preference. Many cases raised issues of federalism—when state statutes of limitations began to run,[77] whether the bankruptcy court had the power to hold a completely new hearing about the property value of a railroad in reorganization when a state taxing agency had already determined the value (it couldn't),[78] whether a federal bankruptcy could stay foreclosure proceedings in state court.[79] In the last case, the Court of Appeals, with Gardner writing, held that state judicial power is subject to control and regulation by Congress when acting pursuant to its constitutional power. However, in *Smith v. Chase National Bank,* with Sanborn writing, the Court of Appeals emphasized that the jurisdiction of the district court in bankruptcy proceedings is just that—jurisdiction over bankruptcy—and not jurisdiction to hear and determine controversies between adverse parties.[80]

The most important bankruptcy case was *Chicot County Drainage District v. Baxter State Bank,* which dealt with the problem of retroactivity in state law. The bank was suing to recover on fourteen government bonds that were in default. After the district had produced a plan of readjustment and a decree was issued, the Supreme Court, in a different case, held unconstitutional the statute on which the plan of readjustment had been based, on the ground that the bankruptcy power of Congress did not extend to the state or its political subdivisions. The question now became whether the earlier district court decree in the *Chicot County* case was res judicata. Judge Thomas C. Trimble of the Eastern District of Arkansas held that the bankruptcy decree now was void. The Court of Appeals, with Gardner writing, affirmed, holding that the decree that had been entered in the instant case was a nullity, while Judge Woodrough wrote a strong dissent. Chief Justice Hughes agreed with Woodrough, stating that the "actual existence of a statute, prior to such a determination [of unconstitutionality] is an operative fact and may have consequences which cannot justly be ignored."[81]

Administrative Law

Perhaps the most important development in American law between 1929 and 1959 was the enormous growth of federal administrative agencies. Among the most important challenges facing the federal courts was accommodating judicial review to administrative action.

The 1930s were the pivotal time for the growth of administrative law. The number of federal agencies and their involvement in private markets grew greatly during Roosevelt's first term. The agencies soon came under sharp criticism for deciding cases with careless procedures and inadequate evidence. As a result, President Roosevelt instructed the Attorney General to appoint a committee to report on the "need for procedural reform in the field of administrative law." After the war ended, this report served as the foundation for the drafting of the Administrative Procedure Act, which passed both houses of the Congress unanimously in 1946.[82] That act demanded due process in agency action in return for their power of wide-ranging intervention in the marketplace.

Before enactment of the Administrative Procedure Act, the agencies had a bumpy ride in the courts. Perhaps the most exhausting litigation in the administrative arena during the New Deal era involved the maximum rates set by the secretary of agriculture for market agencies buying and selling livestock in the Kansas City stockyard. Four times *Morgan v. United States* was decided by a three-judge district court of the Western District of Missouri—district judges Otis and Reeves and circuit judge Van Valkenburgh—and four times that court was reversed by the Supreme Court.

Under the Packers and Stockyards Act, the secretary of agriculture was authorized to set rates that were "just, reasonable, and nondiscriminatory," after a "full hearing."[83] The proceeding that originally took place was held before a hearing examiner, who took testimony from 1930 to 1931, compiling an 11,000-page record but making no decision. There were then oral arguments before an assistant secretary of agriculture. In 1932 the secretary of agriculture issued his findings and an order prescribing maximum rates. However, in view of changed economic conditions, the secretary vacated that order and granted a rehearing, which occurred in the fall of 1932. More hearings then took place, followed by brief and sketchy oral argument before the acting secretary of agriculture (for the new administration), Rexford Tugwell. Findings, prepared by the Bureau of Animal Industry of the Department of Agriculture, were signed by the secretary, who promulgated the rates on June 14, 1933.

As the case came up the first time on the government's motion to dismiss, it had not yet been proved that the secretary had read the briefs submitted by the companies and "dipped" into the record from time to time to get its drift. He had also conferred with the staff of the Bureau of Animal Industry, who had prepared the findings for the department. It was, however, known that he had not heard oral argument.

Fifty petitions for injunctions were brought in the district court. Although the litigation would focus on the decision-making process, the three-judge district court, with Merrill Otis writing, made short shrift of the argument that there had not been a full hearing. The court held that the findings were supported by the testimony and upheld the rates.[84]

The Supreme Court unanimously reversed. In the opinion by Chief Justice Hughes, the Court held that a rate-setting proceeding had special attributes that make it different from ordinary executive action. Congress had required the secretary to determine as a condition of the act that the rates set by the companies were or would be "unjust, unreasonable or discriminatory." This proceeding, Hughes wrote, had a "quasi-judicial character," which required a full hearing and evidence to support the findings. The weight ascribed by the law to the findings rested on the assumption that the officer who made the findings had addressed himself to the evidence and on that evidence had conscientiously reached the conclusions that he deemed it to justify.[85]

The Supreme Court decision in *Morgan I* seemed to allow the lower courts carte blanche to probe the mental processes of the decision maker. The case held that the one who decides "must hear," that there must be a hearing in a substantial sense.

In *Morgan II,* the three-judge court took evidence on the question of whether the secretary had issued the rate order without having heard or read the evidence or considered the arguments submitted. The secretary testified that he had read the briefs, dipped into the 11,000-page record (of which 1,000 pages were statistics) and transcript, and talked ex parte with those who had prepared the findings for his department before he signed the order. The lower court again ruled for the secretary, holding that the law did not demand that the secretary should have done more. Judge Van Valkenburgh dissented, believing that the approach of the secretary had been administrative rather than judicial.[86]

The Supreme Court again reversed, with Hughes writing. The Court believed the hearing fatally defective and the secretary's order invalid. The High Court thought that there had not been a "fair and open hearing" because the secretary had not accorded any reasonable opportunity to let the companies know the claims presented and to contest them. Hughes argued that there at least had to be "the rudimentary requirement of fair play." A fair and open hearing was an "inexorable safeguard," which embraced not only the right to prevent evidence, but also a reasonable opportunity to know the claims of the opposing party and to meet them.[87] The High Court, however, seemed to close some of the door it had opened in *Morgan I* by stating that "it was not the function of the Court to prove the mental processes of the Secretary in reaching his conclusions, if he gave the hearing which the law required."[88]

Morgan III involved what was to be done with the money ($586,000) derived from the higher rates, which the market agencies had paid into the court during the litigation. The district court held that because the secretary's order setting the rates been held invalid, the money had to be returned to the market agencies.[89] Again the Supreme Court reversed. The High Court held that since the secretary had sought to reopen the original proceedings, the money should be retained by the district court and added to the growing body of administrative law being made by this litigation while addressing the relationship between agency and court:

> In construing a statute setting up an administrative agency and providing for judicial review of its action, court and agency are not to be regarded as wholly independent and unrelated instrumentalities of justice, each acting in the performance of its prescribed statutory duty without regard to the appropriate functions of the other. . . . Neither can rightly be regarded by the other as an alien to be tolerated if must be, but never to be encouraged or aided by the other in the attainment of the common aim.[90]

The secretary of agriculture then determined that from 1933 to 1937, the period for which money had been paid into the court, the same rate schedule originally promulgated should be used. In *Morgan IV* the district court refused to apply the secretary's decision to the impounded funds. Its majority (Van Valkenburgh and Reeves) was influenced by a letter written by the secretary to the editor of the *New York Times* in May 1938, in which he indicated a desire that the money be returned to those who had originally paid it—the shippers of live stock. The majority thus thought that the secretary had a preconceived and fixed conception of the authority conferred and had denied the company a fair hearing. In his dissenting opinion, Judge Otis reflected on the controversy: "My colleagues, I think, have not been able to accept a certain new philosophy, nor do I accept it, although I recognize it, and I bow to it, when Congress incorporates into a valid statute—a philosophy that exalts the administrative agency and correspondingly lessens the powers of courts of justice."[91]

When the Supreme Court reversed for the fourth time, it reiterated that the courts should not have "probed the mental processes of the Secretary."[92] What emerges from the *Morgan* quartet is "the principle that those legally responsible for a decision must in fact make it, but . . . their method of doing so . . . is largely beyond judicial scrutiny."[93] Instead of questioning agency heads about their decision-making process, future courts have focused on the adequacy of the actual decision, particularly on findings of basic and ultimate facts, the extent to which findings are based on substantial evidence in the record, as well as on the agency's conclusions as to law.[94]

By far the largest number of administrative agency cases heard by the Eighth Circuit Court of Appeals during this period came from the National Labor Relations Board. After the National Labor Relations Act was upheld by the Supreme Court in 1937,[95] the profound tensions between labor and management of previous years gave way to a period of adjustment to the act and the board. Initial reception of the NLRB by the Eighth Circuit was positive, but judicial skepticism grew. By 1941, writing for the court, Judge Otis, discussing a decision of the board, wrote of "the hodge-podge of suspicions, far-fetched inferences and pure guesses."[96] During the 1950s, the Eighth Circuit was among the circuits most likely not to find "substantial evidence" to support a board decision,[97] although it did uphold the board in more than a majority of cases. The judges of the court most hospitable to the board were Woodrough and Sanborn, while Gardner was among the most inhospitable.

Cases from the other independent regulatory commissions were few and far between, although the Court of Appeals upheld the power of the Federal Trade Commission to enter a cease-and-desist order preventing the manufacture of lottery devices, upheld an order of the Federal Power Commission granting a public utility license to construct a hydroelectric project in the Cedar River in Iowa, and affirmed a conviction for perjury before the Securities and Exchange Commission.[98]

World War II and the Smith Act

Oversight of the immense powers wielded by the federal government during World War II in cases involving the draft, wage and price controls, and condemnation was no small matter for the federal courts. The Eighth Circuit had cases in each of these categories, as well as an appeal in an important case involving denaturalization.

On the whole, the Court of Appeals was not generous in permitting judicial review of the decisions of draft boards. In *Gibson v. United States*, for example, the court held that a conscientious objector, who contended that he was a regular or ordained "minister of religion" and thus exempt from the draft, could not contest his draft status by deserting from a Civilian Public Service Camp and applying for a writ of habeas corpus. Rather, he had submit to detention and then petition for habeas. The Supreme Court reversed after the war was over.[99]

Condemnation proceedings in the federal courts to acquire property for military purposes occurred with some frequency during the war. A case involving the plant of an Omaha laundry took seven years until final resolution by the Supreme Court. The laundry was used for three and one-half years by the Quartermaster Corps. In the condemnation proceedings, the company contended that the government, while ostensibly taking only the right to use and occupy the laundry, had in legal effect taken all of the company's physical assets and its business as well, including its trade routes and customers. The company argued that the government was obligated to pay the value in full (an estimated one million dollars), while the government asserted that just compensation was to be measured by the market value of the use of the laundry. The district court instructed the jury in conformity to the government's theory and awarded an annual rental of $70,000 plus some money for damages to the plant and machinery.

The Court of Appeals affirmed, holding that the government had taken "exactly what it purported to take, namely the temporary use and occupancy of the Company's laundry. The Government had not taken nor intended to take the Company's business, trade routes or customers."[100] The Supreme Court reversed, but by a five to four vote with a narrow concurring opinion. The Court held that as the government had, for all practical purposes, preempted the trade routes for the period of its occupancy, it had to pay compensation for whatever transferable value their temporary use may have had.[101]

Of the 1942 Emergency Price Control Act, Justice Wiley Rutledge wrote that "perhaps no other legislation in our history has equaled the Price Control Act in the wealth, detail, precision and completeness of its jurisdictional, procedural and remedial provisions."[102] *Porter v. Warner Holding Company,* an Eighth Circuit case, involved a major issue under the act. The administrator of the Office of Price Administration brought actions under the law to enjoin violations of it and to have restitution of rents collected in excess of the maximums established by regulations issued under the act. Judge Matthew M. Joyce of the District of Minnesota enjoined a landlord from collecting excess rents but refused to order him to return the money to his tenants.[103]

The Court of Appeals for the Eighth Circuit affirmed, holding that under the law, the administrator was not entitled to reparation orders.[104] After hearing the Eighth Circuit case along with a conflicting decision from the Sixth Circuit,[105] the Supreme Court announced its preference (by a vote of five to three) for the Sixth Circuit's approach. The majority held that all the inherent equitable powers of the district court were available to "do complete rather than truncated justice."[106]

Putting to one side the appalling treatment of Japanese Americans, civil liberties in the United States generally fared much better during World War II than during the earlier war. The most notable civil liberties case during the war in the Eighth Circuit involved the government's attempt to denaturalize Carl Wilhelm Baumgartner.

Baumgartner, born in Germany in 1895, had served in the German army during World War I and had been captured and taken to England as a POW. After the war, he returned to Germany but immigrated to the United States in 1927. He was employed by the Kansas City Power and Light Company. To cancel a certificate of naturalization, the government had to prove that at the time that Baumgartner was admitted to citizenship (1932), he had not truly and fully renounced his foreign allegiance and had not in fact intended to support the Constitution and laws of the United States. At trial in the Western District of Missouri, the government offered testimony and evidence from Baumgartner's diary that he was a Nazi sympathizer. Certainly he had indicated his respect for the Nazis, spoken better of Hitler than of Roosevelt, and was an anti-Semite. In November 1942, Judge Merrill E. Otis denaturalized Baumgartner on the ground that when he took the oath of citizenship, he "accepted as sound and believed to be righteous the principles then advocated and thereafter put in practice by Adolph Hitler."[107]

A divided Court of Appeals affirmed during the autumn of 1943, clearly impressed by the absence of any expression by Baumgartner of concern for the welfare of the United States, while he had consistently declared his sympathy for the German Reich. Writing for himself and Judge Sanborn, Judge Riddick stated:

> As a naturalized citizen appellant had the right to oppose the entry of this country into the war against Germany. He had the right to criticize the course pursued by the government of this country with reference to the war in Europe. . . . Naturalization did not require that appellant surrender his interest in the welfare of his native land, but it did demand that he hold the welfare of his adopted country first.[108]

In a passionate dissent, Judge Woodrough stated that "the grimness of war hardens us all and we lean to harshness." Woodrough attacked the notion that federal district judges have the power "to look into the utterances of foreign-born citizens arguing public questions" and "decide as 'fact' whether they are true believers in Americanism or tainted with heresy in that field."[109]

Six days after D-day, the Supreme Court unanimously reversed. The High Court's opinion was written by its only Jewish member, Felix Frankfurter. The High Court was unwilling to permit such grave punishment of a citizen to occur without the government marshaling the highest degree of proof. Frankfurter wrote that "citizenship once bestowed should not be in jeopardy nor in fear of exercising its American freedom through a too easy finding that citizenship was disloyally required." "One of the prerogatives of American citizenship," Frankfurter stated, "is the right to criticize public men and measures—and that means not only informed and responsible criticism but the freedom to speak foolishly and without moderation." The Court concluded that the evidence as to Baumgartner's attitude after 1932 "affords insufficient proof that in 1932 he had knowing reservations in forswearing his allegiance to the Weimar Republic and embracing allegiance to this country so as to warrant the infliction of the grave consequences involved in making an alien out of a man ten years after he was admitted to citizenship."[110]

The Smith Act, passed in 1940, made it a crime to overthrow the government of the United States by force or to advocate the overthrow of the government by force. The Eighth Circuit was the venue for the first major prosecution under the act. The defendants were leaders of the Socialist Workers Party, a Trotskyite party organized in 1937–38 with a national membership of about three thousand. The group had little significance except to its members and was constantly torn by factional strife. However, two of its leaders, Vincent (Ray) Dunne and Miles Dunne, had successfully engineered a series of dramatic strikes among Minneapolis Teamsters in 1934. The prosecution seems to have been inspired by factions of the Teamsters, who were opposed to the influence of the Socialist Workers within the union. Because after the invasion of the Soviet Union the Socialist Workers continued to oppose U.S. entry into the European war (in order not to strengthen Stalin), they were vulnerable to those who argued that if war came, it would be the Teamsters who would be responsible for delivering essential goods.[111]

In August 1941, twenty-eight Socialist Workers were indicted for conspiring to advocate the overthrow of the government through force and violence and for advocating insubordination in the armed forces. At the trial, the government did not introduce proof of overt acts by the Workers but argued that they constituted a clear and present danger to the government. The prosecution was authorized by the Attorney General Francis Biddle, who was anxious to avoid the loyalty hysteria that had occurred during World War I. He dispatched Henry Schweinhaut (later a judge in the U.S. District Court of the District of Columbia) to St. Paul to supervise the trial and see that the U.S. Attorney not be superpatriotic.[112] Although the trial, which began on October 27, 1941, became a forum for the defendants to explain their brand of Marxism to a far larger audience than they usually had, it seems to have been fair. Charges against five defendants were dropped. The jury convicted eighteen defendants of one charge and found five not guilty. The sentences imposed by Judge Matthew M. Joyce were light.

The Court of Appeals affirmed in an opinion by Judge Stone (joined by Judges Johnsen and Riddick),[113] which remained the leading interpretation of the Smith Act until the 1951 Supreme Court decision in *Dennis v. United States*.[114] The major issue was whether the Smith Act violated the First Amendment. Stone held that the act did not limit expressions of opinion or criticisms of the government or of its policies, officers, or actions, "so long as such expressions were not made with intent to bring about the unlawful things and situations covered by the section." Stone did not apply the "clear and present danger" test of *Schenck v. United States*[115] but relied instead on *Gitlow v. New York* for the key holding:[116] "That the Nation may protect the integrity of its armed forces and may prevent the overthrow of the Government by force and that it may, as a means to those ends, punish utterances which have a tendency to or are intended to produce the forbidden results is not open to question."[117]

To the surprise of the Attorney General, the Supreme Court denied certiorari.[118] Government repression, along with a lack of theoretical imagination, internal feuding, and the continued hostility of the Communist Party, kept the Socialist Workers marginalized during and after the war.

Enforcement of Other Centralizing Policies

In addition to its role in overseeing federal administrative agencies and the bankruptcy system, the Court of Appeals contributed to the growing centralization of the American nation by enforcement of the antitrust laws, oversight of the federal system of raising revenue, and oversight of prosecutions for violation of federal criminal laws brought in the U.S. district courts.

However, by no means did the Court of Appeals always decide cases in a manner favorable to centralizing policies. The American federal system is complex, and the Court of Appeals served to accommodate not only local and state interests to federal policy but federal interests to state and local concerns by emphasizing principles of comity with state judiciaries and by respecting state officials, laws, and the principles of federalism. There were, for example, many cases involving the relationship between state and federal courts. On the whole, proceedings in state courts could not be stayed in federal courts, except in a few areas such as bankruptcy, ship owners' liability, and cases where courts were in possession of a res.[119] As the Supreme Court put it, the federal courts were to "interfere with the administration of justice in the state courts only in rare cases where exceptional circumstances of peculiar urgency are shown to exist."[120]

Antitrust

There were two particularly notable antitrust cases. Three circuit judges—Stone (writing), Booth, and Gardner—held that a contemplated merger of the Standard Oil Company of New York (SOCONY) and the Vacuum Oil Company, two subsidiary corporations, would not violate section 6 of the decree in the original *Standard Oil* case.[121] The court held that the decree barred the subsidiary companies from entering into contracts that would restrain commerce or prolong the unlawful conspiracy, but that diminishing competition was not itself prevented by the decree. Only when the lessening of competition was with an unlawful purpose or by unlawful means, or when it proceeded to the point where it was or was threatening to become a menace to the public, would it be precluded by the decree.[122] The merger was thus upheld because the new company would not approach domination of the industry in the United States or in the Northeast and would meet keen and effective and continued competition in every substantial market throughout the country.

One day before Harry Truman, whose career had been made possible by the Pendergast machine, left the White House, the Department of Justice brought an antitrust action against the great enemy of the Kansas City machine, the *Kansas City Star,* and its chairman of the board and president Roy Λ. Roberts. The indictment was dismissed later as to Roberts. After a seven-week trial before Judge Richard M. Duncan of the Western District of Missouri, the newspaper would be found guilty of violating the Sherman Act. The Court of Appeals for the Eighth Circuit affirmed. A panel of Gardner, Woodrough, and Vogel (with Vogel writing) upheld the decision of the trial court, holding after examination of the "voluminous" record, which had been printed in its entirety, that it was "perfectly clear that the *Star*'s position in metropolitan Kansas City was of such dominance in the field in which it did business . . . that it could be found by the jury that it possessed monopoly power."[123]

Oversight of the Raising of Revenue

The role performed by the federal courts in tax cases is, in spite of its doctrinal obscurities, of great political significance, as it helps to legitimize one of the greatest weapons the federal government has in its arsenal—the capacity to raise revenue. The federal courts are part of a judicial subsystem that provides both for taxpayers to question assessments and for an efficacious sanctions process, whereby the Internal Revenue Service may bring suits for deficiency judgments and criminal prosecutions.

In no fewer than twenty-two cases between 1929 and 1959, the Supreme Court reviewed tax decisions of the Court of Appeals for the Eighth Circuit, rendering full opinions. The Eighth Circuit was affirmed nine times, reversed twelve times, and affirmed in part and reversed in part in one case. Among the issues in tax cases that reached the Supreme

Court from the Court of Appeals for the Eighth Circuit were the taxability of "alimony trusts";[124] the jurisdiction of the Board of Tax Appeals to determine and apply a tax overpayment for a particular year;[125] whether advertising and selling expenses were excludable from the selling price in computing the excise tax on toilet preparations;[126] in a case involving the merger of seventeen separate incorporated businesses, the meaning of the words "the taxpayer";[127] and whether the members of name dance bands, who play short-term engagements at public dance halls were, for purposes of the Social Security tax, employees of the band leaders or of the dance hall operators, notwithstanding contractual agreements (the Court of Appeals held that they were employees of the ballroom operators; the Supreme Court held that they were employees of the band leaders).[128]

In some of the many tax cases not reviewed by the Supreme Court, the Eighth Circuit dealt with the relationship for tax purposes between the Tunnel Railroad of St. Louis (which controlled the railroad tunnels under St. Louis), the St. Louis Bridge Co. (which owned the Eads Bridge), and the Terminal Railroad Association, the lessee of both;[129] whether ten- and twelve-volume hydrogen peroxide constituted "medicinal preparations" and were therefore not taxable as "toilet preparations" (they were taxable).[130]

Because of its implications for the federal system, the most important of the taxation opinions probably was that of the Supreme Court in *Willcuts v. Bunn*. There a panel of the Court of Appeals of Stone (writing), Booth, and Gardner held in a one-page opinion that the profits a taxpayer had made on the sale of municipal and county bonds in Minnesota could not be taxed because to do so was to unconstitutionally tax the instrumentalities of the state. The High Court reversed unanimously in an opinion by Chief Justice Charles Evans Hughes. What was exempt from federal taxation, the Court upheld, was the principal and interest of the obligation, not the profits derived from the sale of such bonds.[131]

Federal Criminal Law and Political Corruption

By the 1930s federal criminal appeals had become a significant portion of the docket of the Court of Appeals. While the "great experiment," Prohibition, begun in 1919 and ended in 1933, the number of federal criminal laws continued to increase. In particular, on May 18, 1934, Congress passed a package of laws making federal crimes out of assaulting or resisting federal agents performing their law enforcement duties, bank robbery, extortion, the transportation of stolen property across state lines, and flight to avoid prosecution. Kidnapping was made punishable by the death penalty.[132]

There were a number of celebrated prosecutions in the Eighth Circuit. One such was the celebrated prosecution of Wilbur B. Foshay and Henry M. Henley. Foshay and Henley had built a business selling securities and managing public utilities and other properties, a business that was national and international in scope. The two men had sold paper securities amounting to $60 million by making people believe that their company, which had 2,100 employees, controlled three banks, and owned a thirty-two-story office building, was a sound and conservative moneymaking investment, whose large dividends came from company earnings, when in fact they were paid out of capital.

Foshay and Henley's first trial ended in a hung jury. That hung jury of the first trial resulted from one holdout, Genevieve Clark, who would be convicted of contempt (by Judges Sanborn and Nordbye) for concealing the facts that she had briefly been employed by the Foshay Company and her husband was a friend of Foshay. Her conviction was affirmed by a divided Court of Appeals. Kenyon and Stone voted to affirm; Gardner dissented, concerned that the confidentiality of jury deliberations had been breached to prosecute Clark. The Supreme Court affirmed the Court of Appeals with an unusually passionate opinion by Justice Cardozo.[133]

Foshay and Henley's second trial took nine weeks. One thousand four hundred eighty-nine exhibits were entered into evidence. Appellants made five hundred assignments of error. Eleven volumes of condensed testimony had to be read on appeal. Judge Woodrough, joined by Judge Stone, wrote the opinion affirming the convictions. Judge Kenyon also voted to affirm but died before the opinion was written. The Supreme Court denied the petition for certiorari.[134]

During this period there also were several intriguing cases involving the Mann Act. One such case, *Mortensen v. United States,* reached the Supreme Court.[135] The case involved a married couple who operated a house of prostitution in Nebraska. They took two of their "employees" with them on what seems to have been an innocent "circle vacation trip"—a journey from Grand Island, Nebraska, to Salt Lake City by way of Yellowstone National Park and then back to Grand Island. A divided panel of the Court of Appeals (Johnsen and Thomas) affirmed the convictions, holding that at least the return trip from Salt Lake City to Grand Island, where the girls returned to their occupation, was transportation in interstate commerce for the purpose of prostitution. Johnsen and Thomas believed that Congress had made no distinction between the crossing of a state line with an immoral purpose or for a vacation. A divided Supreme Court agreed with Judge Woodrough, who had written in his dissent: "I am not convinced that their act of taking the named young women in the automobile on the vacation trip through the mountains and back was commerce."[136]

Appeals in Prohibition cases provided the first sustained encounters of the federal courts of appeal with the Fourth Amendment. In Eighth Circuit cases, federal agents had come upon "a strong order of mash" on a farm in Sarpy County, Nebraska; in a building in Branson, Missouri; on a street in Texarkana, Arkansas; and on an avenue in Kansas City. Opinions demonstrating considerable impatience with law enforcement officers were not infrequent. In *Day v. United States*, for example, Judge Kenyon wrote:

> It is carrying the doctrine of detection of crime by the process of smell-ing fermented mash entirely too far to conclude that every person within the range of the officer's olfactory nerves who may have something on his person or in an automobile under his control that might possibly be used in the unlawful making of intoxicating liquor is participating in a crime in the officer's presence.[137]

During the twentieth century, the federal courts have become an important forum for prosecutions of state and federal political figures for corruption. That the Eighth Circuit has had its share was suggested by the Teapot Dome prosecutions discussed in the previous chapter. During the period under consideration here, notable prosecutions took place in Missouri and North Dakota.

BOSS PENDERGAST   The most notable success occurred in Kansas City, where the federal courts took on the Pendergast political machine. The influence of that machine in Kansas City dated to the 1880s. Jim Pendergast won election to the Board of Aldermen in 1892. However, it was Jim Pendergast's brother, Thomas J. Pendergast (Boss Pendergast), described by Judge Albert L. Reeves of the Western District of Missouri as "squat, heavy set, thick necked, large jowled and porcine,"[138] who widened the machine's influence by providing services and favors to the middle class as well as to the poor. Soon, Kansas City became a wide-open town in which crime and vice thrived. The machine intimidated honest voters and profited from lucrative city contracts.[139] A 1933 massacre in the parking lot of Union Station focused national attention on Kansas City as a municipality controlled by the underworld. The following year, four people were killed at the polls on election day.

By 1932, Pendergast was a powerful force in Missouri and a player in national Democratic politics, perhaps "the most powerful American boss of his generation."[140] Judge Merrill Otis, also a judge of Missouri's Western District, described Pendergast's influence by writing that to Pendergast's "small monastic-like cubicle on the second floor of a two-story building . . . came he who would be governor, he who would be senator, he who would be judge, and he who was content to be only a keeper of the pound. Thither came alike great and little, craving audience and favors."[141] Harry Truman, personally honest, owed his career to the machine.

A series of vote-fraud cases, an insurance scandal, income tax evasion proceedings, and contempt actions in federal court led to Pendergast's downfall and the destruction of his machine. Among the most important contributors to bringing down Pendergast were District Judges Reeves and Otis, who, in the proceedings against Pendergast, demonstrated a confrontational style, considerable courage, and the ability to stay on course.[142]

The court proceedings began with a blue-ribbon grand jury impaneled by Reeves, called after the 1936 general elections to investigate irregularities. Reeves spoke of "individuals like worms in the nighttime in the dark places . . . boring into the pillars of the fabric of our government and digging into the heart of it" and likened a corrupt vote "to a loaded and cocked gun pointing at the very heart of America."[143] Two hundred seventy-eight persons would be accused of conspiracy to interfere with the right to vote, of whom 259 were convicted. The opinions of Judges Gardner, Sanborn, and Thomas affirming the convictions offer example after example of outrageous electoral fraud: stuffed ballot boxes, uncounted ballots, repeat voting, erased and changed ballots, and threats to poll watchers.[144]

The voting fraud cases caught only small-fry—women campaign workers and henchmen. However, as a result of the efforts, sixty thousand names were struck from the voting rolls, and Missouri enacted a new permanent registration act. For their work, the two district judges were accused by Senator Harry Truman of being "violently partisan" and of bribing the U.S. Attorney with bankruptcy fees. Truman stated that "a Jackson County, Missouri, Democrat has as much a chance of a fair trial in the Federal District Court of Western Missouri as a Jew would have in a Hitler court or a Trotzky follower before Stalin."[145] Reeves responded that Truman's denunciation of the court "was a speech of a man nominated by ghost votes, elected with ghost votes, and whose speeches are probably written by ghost writers."[146]

A compulsive gambler constantly strapped for funds, Boss Pendergast took a $500,000 bribe for working out a sham settlement of a dispute over fire insurance rates between 137 insurance companies and the Missouri Department of Insurance. The companies paid off Missouri's commissioner of insurance, Robert Emmet O'Malley, who agreed to a settlement that returned $10 million, most of which had been held in escrow in the courts, to the companies. Pendergast and O'Malley then were indicted for income tax evasion. Both men pleaded guilty, and the insurance companies were ordered to make restitution. Judge Otis sentenced Pendergast to fifteen months in prison, a $125,000 fine, and five years probation, during which he was prohibited from gambling or taking part in political activities. O'Malley was given one year in prison. Otis was sharply criticized for leniency but replied that "if one is charged with attempting to evade a tax and pleads guilty to that charge, he should not be punished for a score of other crimes with which he is not charged and as to which the law presumes his innocence."[147]

In the meantime, a three-judge district court made up of Otis, Reeves, and Kimbrough Stone directed the U.S. Attorney to secure indictments, if warranted, charging those who were involved with the insurance case with obstruction of justice and conspiracy to defraud the government. Judge A. Lee Wyman of the District of South Dakota threw those charges out, holding Otis's grand jury charge prejudicial.[148]

Otis had filed contempt proceedings against Pendergast and others relating to the disposition of the escrowed fire insurance money. He refused to disqualify himself from the ensuing proceedings of the three-judge court[149] that, rejecting a statute-of-limitations defense, sentenced Pendergast to two years in prison.[150] Whatever loyalty drove Truman's criticisms of the judges, reading Otis's opinion for the three-judge court leads one to conclude that Truman was not entirely off the mark. Otis wrote of the deception practiced on the court as "vicious behavior, committed and consummated in the presence of the Court," and of the continuing deception intended "to exert its deceiving, pernicious and poisonous influence indefinitely."[151] The Court of Appeals affirmed by a 2–1 vote. Writing for himself and Judge Thomas, Gardner referred to the settlement as "tainted with fraud and corruption . . . mere pretense and sham." Judge Riddick dissented.[152] The Supreme Court overturned the decision on statute-of-limitations grounds; Justice Jackson dissented.[153]

There was further litigation over the overpaid insurance premiums that had been escrowed. The three-judge district court ordered all the money returned to the policyholders because of the knowledge, actual or implied, of each of the companies.[154] Pendergast died in isolation in 1945. Harry Truman attended his funeral.

WILLIAM LANGER   If the prosecutions of Boss Pendergast were, to a degree, politically inspired, there was nevertheless fire underneath the smoke. That cannot be said with complete assurance about the prosecution of William Langer. In the 1930s, Langer was the dominant figure in North Dakota politics. Born in 1886, he was state attorney general before World War I, and his career in high office would end only with his death in 1959. A Republican progressive, Langer was a believer in activist government and a civil libertarian. He was also a colorful politician who made many enemies.

In 1934 a federal grand jury indicted Langer, then governor of North Dakota, and eight associates for conspiring to defraud the federal government by asking state employees paid with federal funds to contribute 5 percent of their salaries to a party newspaper, *The Leader*. Each person who contributed was given a one-year subscription to the newspaper for each dollar he contributed, but could get one dollar back for each subscription he sold. Some of this money reached Langer personally.

Langer and his associates stood trial before North Dakota's district judge, Andrew Miller.[155] Miller was a "lifelong, personal, professional and political opponent of Langer."[156] After a twenty-eight-day trial at which Langer admitted receiving $19,000 of the solicitations, Miller dismissed the charges against three minor defendants. After forty-eight hours of deliberation, the jury found Langer and five other defendants guilty. Miller told the jury that he was "delighted and pleased."[157] The same day, Langer won a sweeping victory in the Republican gubernatorial primary. Miller then sentenced Langer to eighteen months in prison and a $10,000 fine. Langer had to forfeit his office because, one day after he was sentenced, the North Dakota Supreme Court found him ineligible to serve as governor. In this wild political year, North Dakota had four governors within a seven-month period.

It appears that Langer's trial was unfair. The most informed current observer argues that Miller was biased and made many errors, including handling the selection of the jury, giving biased jury instructions, and refusing to allow testimony that the money Langer received for *The Leader* subscriptions was in repayment of a loan he made to his party. The Court of Appeals reversed all six convictions on the grounds of insufficient evidence.[158] After Langer's conviction, Miller required from Langer, then still governor of the state, a personal bond accompanied by cash or property so that he could stay out of jail pending appeal. Miller refused to disqualify himself for the second trial. The defendants then filed an affidavit of prejudice, and the Court of Appeals removed Miller from the case.

The second conspiracy trial occurred before Judge A. Lee Wyman of the District of South Dakota, who had dismissed the obstruction of justice charges against Pendergast. Wyman refused to allow Langer to show that he had not personally received large amounts of the *Leader* money. This time, a hung jury voted 10–2 for conviction. There was a taint to the second trial because of allegations that one of the jurors received $1,000 to vote not to convict. The third conspiracy trial resulted in Langer's acquittal. However, his ordeal was not over. He was tried for perjury on the basis of the affidavit of prejudice that had been filed against Miller. Wyman directed a not-guilty verdict, stating that "we cannot prosecute men for their opinions."[159]

The episode came back to haunt Langer after he won reelection to the Senate in 1940 over William Lemke and Charles Vogel. During hearings to determine whether Langer could take his seat in the Senate, Langer admitted that he had paid $500 to Judge Wyman's son and to former U.S. marshal Chet Leedom, to make sure that he had received an even break.[160] The Senate committee voted 13–3 against Langer, but the Senate seated him by a vote of 52–30.

Truman Administration Corruption

Harry Truman was personally honest, but as president, he "was strangely complacent and slow to offer presidential leadership to eliminate unethical conduct and expunge doubts about the probity of government agencies."[161] The last years of his administration were dogged by revelations that officials in his administration had accepted gifts from businessmen, granted favors, taken bribes, and fixed taxes.[162] Some of the most serious abuses occurred in the St. Louis Bureau of Internal Revenue and are traceable to the appointment of Robert E. Hannegan, a St. Louis ward healer, as its head while Truman was in the Senate. Further, an old friend of Truman, James P. Finnegan, accepted illegal fees while serving as collector of internal revenue in St. Louis. Indicted for accepting compensation while in public office, for assisting private parties in a matter before the Reconstruction Finance Corporation, and for accepting bribes as Collector of Revenue, Finnegan was acquitted of the two bribery counts but was convicted on two of the three counts relating to his assistance to private parties while in public office. Shortly after Truman left office, the Court of Appeals, with Gardner writing, affirmed the convictions in a matter-of-fact nine-page opinion.[163]

Truman's appointment's secretary and political lieutenant, Matthew J. Connelly, and T. Lamar Caudle, who was in charge of the Tax Division of the Department of Justice during the Truman administration, were convicted of conspiracy to defraud the United States through improper administration of the Internal Revenue laws and regulations. Connelly was indicted for having accepted, while in the White House, cash, clothing, and a $3,600 oil royalty for protecting from prosecution Irving Sachs, a St. Louis wholesale shoe dealer. It was alleged that Caudle received "substantial sums of money."[164] The Court of Appeals, with Gardner again writing, affirmed in an eleven-page opinion.[165]

Regional Cases

During this period, there were fewer cases evoking the ambience of the region. Among the few areas where distinctive regional problems and issues surfaced were those involving oversight of the district courts in cases involving determination of the value of land condemned for projects altering the circuit's waterways, cases involving the farm sector of the economy, and those involving Native Americans. There were also cases involving the instrumentalities of commerce, although these were less distinctive than those in previous periods involving steamboats and railroads.

CASES INVOLVING LAND AND WATER Litigation connected with the Mississippi River flood control projects occurred over property up and down the river. The most important case, *Sponenbarger v. United*

States, involved forty acres of land in Desha County, Arkansas, along the southern part of the river.[166] Sponenbarger's land lay in a part of the Boeuf Basin, which was contemplated as a diversion channel or floodway. In the event of excessive floods, two-thirds of the thirty thousand miles of the alluvial valley of the Mississippi was to be protected at the risk of potential damage to property in the floodways. Sponenbarger sued for compensation for the alleged taking of her property, claiming that its fair market value was reduced as a result of the Boeuf Floodway.

The Court of Appeals, reversing the Eastern District of Arkansas over Judge Woodrough's dissent, held that because under the plan for flood control it was intended and practically certain that the floodway would be used and serious destruction would occur, recovery against the government was appropriate. The Supreme Court unanimously reversed. The High Court considered it unwarranted to hold the government responsible for "conjectural major floods which may result from conjectural major flooding even though the same floods and the same damages would occur had the Government undertaken no work of any kind." In essence, governmental activities were not inflicting much damage on the land, and on the whole, the activities would certainly confer great benefit through flood control. The Fifth Amendment, Justice Black wrote, "does not make the Government an insurer that the evil of floods be stamped out universally before the evil can be attacked at all."[167]

CASES INVOLVING FARMING   Cases in the farm sector involved the Department of Agriculture, farmer cooperatives, dairies, seed companies, grain dealers, and exporters. There were disputes over ownership of a carload of wheat, actions in conversion for farm equipment, shareholder actions for repurchase of stock, litigation for breach of contract to sell soybeans, and prosecutions for activities such as purchasing a new variety of wheat in Canada and illegally importing it to the United States[168] or for fraud in administering the Frazier-Lemke farm bankruptcy program.[169] There also was trademark litigation over the use of the words "Mineral and Meal" in connection with the sale of hog seed[170] and the use of the names "Iowa Farmers Union" and "Iowa Union Farmer Association."[171]

CASES INVOLVING NATIVE AMERICANS   There was less litigation involving Native Americans during this period because the end of the allotment of Indian land to individual Native Americans was provided for in the Indian Reorganization Act of 1934,[172] one of the two major developments particular to Native Americans between 1929 and 1959. The Indian Reorganization Act, which blended assimilationist concerns with respect for Indian culture, attempted to encourage economic development, self-determination, and the revival of tribalism. Under the act, federal funds were offered for enlarging tribal land holdings. The secretary of the interior was authorized to create reservations for landless tribes and to restore to tribal ownership any lands that had been removed as "surplus" under the General Allotment Act and not as yet sold to non-Indians. Tribes were encouraged to adopt their own constitutions, become federally chartered corporations, and manage their own government and business affairs. Federal funds were found for on-reservation health facilities, roads, and irrigation.[173]

The Indian Reorganization Act did not bring about lasting prosperity or even self-sufficiency. Further progress was ended because of World War II, when more than one-half million acres of tribal lands were taken for military use by the United States, and by the Pick-Sloan Plan, which destroyed long-standing ties to the land.[174]

The second major development affecting Native Americans was the movement toward termination of reservations, which began in the late 1930s. In a narrow sense, termination was an experiment imposed on a small number of Indian tribes, which ended the special relationship between those tribes and the federal government. In addition, though, the assimilationist policies of the termination era subjected tribes not directly terminated to a series of laws transferring important areas of responsibility from the Bureau of Indian Affairs to other federal agencies and to the states.[175] By House Concurrent Resolution 108 of August 1, 1953,[176] Congress unanimously announced that its policy was to end the status of Indians as wards of the United States and to grant them all the rights and privileges of citizenship. Within a few years, Congress terminated tribes in Utah, Texas, Oregon, and Wisconsin. No Eighth Circuit tribe was affected during this period. However, by the Act of August 15, 1953,[177] Congress authorized state governments to take jurisdiction from Indian courts and federal employees on Indian reservations in five states, including Nebraska and Minnesota (save the Red Lake Reservation).[178] The termination legislation ended most aspects of the historical relationship between the federal government and the terminated tribes. Reservations were dissolved. Exemption from state taxation ended. Federal health, housing, and education programs were no longer available to the Indians affected. Criminal and civil cases were handled by state courts. Although termination directly affected only a small percentage of western tribes, it aroused intense fears and strident complaints by Indians, and during the termination era, many federal programs were transferred to the states.[179]

Several Eighth Circuit cases from the period are of interest. In *United States v. Minnesota*,[180] the state sought to condemn for a highway land in the Grand Portage Indian Reservation, held in trust for Native Americans by the United States. The Court of Appeals (and the U.S. Supreme Court) held that the United States was an indispensable party to the condemnation proceedings.

At issue in *Crow v. Ogallala Sioux Tribe*,[181] which arose in the District of South Dakota, was the jurisdiction of the Ogallala Sioux Tribal Court, which had been reorganized under a tribal constitution adopted under the Indian Reorganization Act. Marie Little Finger and David Black Cat, who had been tried and convicted of adultery in the tribal court, brought suit in federal court to enjoin the enforcement of their sentences. In an action joined to that of Little Finger and Black Cat, Thomas Crow contested the jurisdiction of the tribe to tax his land within the reservation—land that he had leased to nonmembers of the tribe. The trial judge found constitutional authority for the tribal court under the Indian Commerce Clause of the U.S. Constitution,[182] as well as authority derived from the continued sovereignty of the tribe. The Court of Appeals, with Judge Vogel writing, affirmed, holding that Indian tribes still possess their inherent sovereignty, except where it has specifically been taken away from them.[183]

CASES INVOLVING TRANSPORTATION   The channels and instrumentalities of commerce—railroads, trucking, air freight, and automobiles—continued to produce much litigation before the Court of Appeals, although these were less regionally distinctive than in earlier years. There were battles over seniority rights, litigation over personal injuries, issues of taxation, minor rate cases, litigation involving parsing the lines of authority between the Interstate Commerce Commission and the courts, and several attempts by railroads to enjoin the operation of full crew laws.[184]

During the almost four decades of the Sanborn era, the Court of Appeals for the Eighth Circuit decided cases unobtrusively. While nation and region were transformed by economic crisis and a great war, as well as by remarkable developments in transportation and communications, the Court of Appeals went about its business with dignity and gentle manner, making few waves with relatively brief opinions seemingly etched with little agony. If one finds few cases that are memorable, one must go a long way before finding an Eighth Circuit opinion that is poorly executed or evinces intracourt tension. Many decisions, to be sure, occurred in "ordinary" cases—diversity cases, bankruptcies, and conflicts over insurance policies—cases that once upon a time would have demanded review by the U.S. Supreme Court. Yet there also were many opinions that, if written in a matter-of-fact tone, reflected the changing role of the federal government and the necessity of accommodating state and local interests to federal policies. Bankruptcy, taxation, condemnations, and federal criminal cases played a much larger role in the work of the Court of Appeals than ever before. However, cases that in previous decades had given the court a regional distinctiveness—cases involving disputes over land, farming, railroads, and Native Americans—were in shorter supply.

Even before John Sanborn took senior status on June 30, 1959, the transition of the Eighth Circuit Court of Appeals into a tribunal that would persistently confront cases embodying important issues of public policy had begun. The Supreme Court of Earl Warren had already commenced its journey across stormy seas. The lower federal courts would follow in its wake. From the mid-1950s on, federal judges throughout the country would be asked with increasing frequency to wield judicial power to redress inequality in American society. For the Eighth Circuit, the events after which there would be no turning back occurred in Little Rock in 1957–58. Shortly thereafter, the dockets of both the district courts and the Court of Appeals for the Eighth Circuit would provide a remarkable contrast to the relatively quiet years when Sanborn and Stone, Gardner and Woodrough, had largely constituted the court.

CHAPTER 4

The Era of the Warren Court

1956–1969

*D*uring the late 1950s and throughout the 1960s, the most notable work of the Eighth Circuit occurred in litigation involving civil liberties, in which granting relief often required the strong assertion of judicial power. The Court of Appeals decided landmark cases involving African American children in Little Rock, secondary-school students in Des Moines wearing armbands to protest the Vietnam War, a popular college athlete who inexplicably killed three in a Nebraska bank robbery, a hoodlum crossing the Eads Bridge daily from East St. Louis to St Louis, and a young black couple in St. Louis attempting to buy a house. Members of the court, sitting as district judges, determined the size of electoral districts in six of the seven states of the Eighth Circuit. The Court of Appeals grappled with difficult issues such as whether the landmark decision in *Brown v. Board of Education* required desegregation or integration, whether a newly passed statute prohibiting destruction of draft cards violated the First Amendment, and the proper test for insanity in criminal cases.

Naturally, a large majority of the cases decided by the Eighth Circuit Appeals Court were not so highly charged. There was litigation involving the condemnation of land in North Dakota; the treatment of privately owned hogs trespassing in the Ozark National Forest by the U.S. Forest Service; whether the construction of a hydroelectric plant on the East Fork of the Black River in Missouri required a federal license; and whether gas produced, sold, and consumed in North Dakota could be regulated by the Federal Power Commission if the gas was transported in a pipeline and commingled in a common pipeline with gas destined for resale in interstate commerce.

The work of the Eighth Circuit during these years reflected the egalitarianism unleashed by the Supreme Court, the High Court's modification of traditional principles of federalism, and growing acceptance of the wielding of federal judicial power. The work of the Court of Appeals was also affected by a host of new laws passed by Congress, as well as by the litigating policies of the executive branch. The result was not only a significant increase in the number of cases involving sharp conflicts of political, social, or constitutional values but also a considerable increase in the total number of cases heard.

The Court of Appeals for the Eighth Circuit was a strong and harmonious court that came to grips with its somewhat changed judicial role with considerable courage. If the jurisprudence of the Fourth, Fifth, and District of Columbia Circuits attracted more attention, the Eighth Circuit's output was marked by greater agreement.

National and Regional Developments

The 1960s were a time of liberal reform and social tension over civil rights, the most important political issue of the time. The Warren Court had led the way with *Brown v. Board of Education* and other decisions dismantling constitutional apartheid. If the courts began the process, it was greatly accelerated by demonstrations. The sit-in movement, begun in Greensboro, North Carolina, on February 1, 1960, was followed by the freedom rides of 1961 and then by large and peaceful demonstrations that ultimately produced landmark legislation, vigorously enforced by the Justice Department. Later in the decade, black militancy grew, and rioting occurred in many cities.

During the Johnson administration, Congress passed a considerable number of important laws besides civil rights legislation. The role of the federal government grew considerably in elementary and secondary school education, water and air quality, housing, highways, and many other areas.[1] Some of the new laws substantially increased the role of the federal courts. Although its moral authority corroded appreciably during the Vietnam War, the power of the federal government increased considerably with respect to the states.

The isolation of the Great Plains from the rest of the nation and of farm dwellers from people living in towns and cities continued to erode, the result of better roads and other developments in transportation and communications. Within the Eighth Circuit, the migration from rural areas and small towns to urban areas continued. Farms continued to increase in size and decrease in number. Federal farm programs helped buffer the states against precipitous declines in agricultural prices, while the economic diversification occurring in most of the states of the Eighth Circuit also helped.[2]

Many visible cases of the Eighth Circuit during this period came from Arkansas, including the Little Rock high school desegregation case, capital cases, cases leading to recognition of the constitutional right of association, and litigation involving the state's prison system (discussed in the next chapter). In addition, Arkansas contributed condemnation cases growing out of the McClellan-Kerr Arkansas Navigation Project and a share of reapportionment litigation.

Overwhelmingly rural, Arkansas's law outlawing the teaching of evolution, on the books since the 1920s, was representative of the fear of modernity that many living in its countryside had. (The U.S. Supreme Court struck down the law, strongly criticizing the Arkansas Supreme Court.)[3] Arkansas's prisons may well have been the nation's worst. In the 1950s and early 1960s, race relations in Arkansas were not as bad as in Alabama and Mississippi, or several other states, but they would nevertheless lead to the greatest confrontation between the federal government and a state since Reconstruction. Arkansas state politics during the 1950s and 1960s were dominated by Orval Faubus, a demagogic but not stupid politician, who won six two-year terms as governor.[4] At the same time, the state was sending such able figures to Congress as J. William Fulbright, Wilbur Mills, John L. McClellan, Brooks Hays, and Oren Harris. By the latter part of the 1960s, there were signs of modernization in the state, the result, at least in part, of the work of the Arkansas Industrial Development Commission, headed by Winthrop Rockefeller, who in 1966 became the first Republican elected governor since Reconstruction. Industry was moving to Arkansas, attracted by its pool of unskilled and nonunionized labor. By 1980, Arkansas would have a greater percentage of its labor force in manufacturing than the nation as a whole.[5]

The Judges

During this period, the Court of Appeals was in transition, moving from what had been a middle-of-the-road, slightly right-of-center court to one that by the early 1970s would have a reputation as being fairly progressive. It was Lyndon Johnson's last three appointees to the court—Donald Lay, Gerald W. Heaney, and Myron Bright—who altered the balance of the court. Those three judges were more likely to vote for civil liberties claims and more willing to accept an activist judiciary (as well as more likely to publish dissents) than their predecessors.[6] Whatever the jurisprudential propensities of the members of the Court of Appeals, the court was well respected. As Harry Blackmun, who became a member of the Supreme Court in 1970, found out, his new colleagues regarded the Eighth Circuit as one of the strongest courts of appeals.[7]

Changes in membership slowly altered the customs of a hardworking, collegial court. At the beginning of this period, when the judges were hearing argument, they continued to stay at the Mayfair, walk two by two to the courthouse, lunch together on a bowl of soup and a piece of apple pie, and dine together at 5:30 p.m. The judges also partook en banc of a steam bath at the Missouri Athletic Club. However, the hotel deteriorated somewhat, and the judges started staying at other hotels.[8] The atmosphere was serene compared to many other courts. Relatively little dissent found its way into the *Federal Reporter,* and what did was composed in such a way as to minimize discord.

By the early 1960s, those judges who had been born during the early years of the circuit and had still been sitting at quite advanced ages had passed from the scene. However, throughout the 1960s a majority of the court—Chief Judge Harvey M. Johnsen, Charles Vogel, Martin D. Van Oosterhout, Marion C. Matthes, and Harry Blackmun—had received their initiation from the old-timers. When Johnsen relinquished the chief judgeship on July 17, 1965, to Vogel, the court was composed of six regular sitting judges, four nominated by Eisenhower (Vogel, Van Oosterhout, Matthes, and Blackmun), two by Kennedy (Albert A. Ridge, who served from June 1961 to April 1965, and J. Pat Mehaffy) and one by Lyndon Johnson (Floyd R. Gibson).

While Kennedy's two appointments and Johnson's first, Floyd R. Gibson, had not really affected the jurisprudential balance on the court, Johnson's later appointments changed the center of gravity. By the period's end, the court was composed of four moderately conservative judges (Van Oosterhout, Blackmun, Mehaffy, Gibson), three liberal judges (Donald Lay, Gerald Heaney, Myron Bright), and one judge who was closer to the moderate conservatives than the liberals (Matthes). However, the differences between these groups surfaced in relatively few cases.

Harvey M. Johnsen was chief judge for half of this period. Johnsen was appointed in 1940, served as chief judge from 1959 to 1965, took senior status in 1965, and continued to sit until his death in 1975. Johnsen was a Nebraskan, born in Hastings on July 16, 1895, the son of a railroad worker. He received his B.A. and LL.B. degrees from the University of Nebraska and worked as secretary to Chief Justice Andrew M. Morrisey of the Nebraska Supreme Court while in law school. Johnsen practiced in Omaha from 1920 to 1938 and was the first president of the integrated Nebraska bar. He was appointed as a justice of the Nebraska Supreme Court in 1938 but was defeated for election in 1939. In 1940, FDR appointed him to the Court of Appeals.

Upon his appointment, Johnsen, at the request of Chief Judge Stone, established chambers in Kansas City near the Chief Judge. Chief Justice Earl Warren had a high regard for Johnsen, whom he appointed to five committees of the U.S. Judicial Conference.[9] At Johnsen's memorial service, Harry Blackmun called him "a master of the adverb" and added: "He was impatient with the trivial and with the ostentatious and with the technical. He knew when the advocate was relying on words and technicalities rather than substance. He brought to the bench good judgment and a non-political attitude."[10]

In 1954, President Eisenhower appointed two men who would make important contributions to a seasoned but aging Court of Appeals— Charles J. Vogel and Martin D. Van Oosterhout. Vogel was the first judge from North Dakota to serve on the Court of Appeals. He would also be the first of four judges from what is now known as the Vogel Law Firm appointed to the Court of Appeals.[11] A relatively conservative New Dealer, Vogel was Democratic state chairman and ran unsuccessfully for the Senate in 1940 against William Langer. Langer defeated Vogel but respected him and supported his appointment as district judge in 1941.[12] Vogel seems to have been an excellent trial judge, controlling his courtroom, never raising his voice, and he was considered fair by attorneys. He tried many mail fraud cases, condemnations, and other land actions, and presided over the trial of a North Dakota attorney general for smuggling gambling equipment into the state.[13]

Vogel's elevation to the Court of Appeals resulted from a bitter battle fought by Langer, then a member of the Senate Judiciary Committee, to gain a Court of Appeals seat for North Dakota. To fill the seat, Langer favored Vernon D. Forbes, a Wahpeton attorney, whom the Justice Department opposed. North Dakota Republican leaders favored Chief

Justice James Morris of the North Dakota Supreme Court, whom Langer did not want. Part of Langer's tactics in this battle included delaying the confirmation of Earl Warren as Chief Justice to put pressure on the Eisenhower administration. In the end, Langer settled for Vogel, which permitted him to fill two vacancies on the district bench, the second being a newly created judgeship.

Serving on the Court of Appeals from 1954 to 1981 (as Chief Judge from 1965 to 1968), Vogel took senior status in 1968. He was generally a moderate judge, strong on civil rights and a supporter of other civil liberties.[14]

Appointed to succeed Seth Thomas on the same day as Vogel, Martin D. Van Oosterhout (1900–1979) was one of the powerful figures on the Court of Appeals until his death. "Judge Van" was a big man, six feet two inches and 250 pounds, whose massive appearance and deeply resonant voice were truly awesome. His colleagues spoke of him as "the Big Judge" or "Van."[15]

Born in 1900 in Orange City, Iowa, of Dutch ancestry, Van Oosterhout attended the University of Iowa, where he was a member of the football and track teams. After graduating from the University of Iowa Law School, he practiced law from 1924 to 1943. He then was a judge of the Iowa district court. In 1954 he was a prime candidate to replace an Iowan on the Court of Appeals, but Langer had to be placated with a North Dakotan.[16]

Van Oosterhout was a judge on regular service from 1954 to 1971, serving as Chief Judge from 1968 to 1970. After he took senior status, he continued to sit with the Eighth Circuit until his death in 1979. He also served by appointment of the Chief Justice as one of the nine judges of the Emergency Court of Appeals, which heard price control and energy regulation cases throughout the country.

In a twenty-five-year career, Van Oosterhout heard argument in over 1,500 cases but wrote only thirty-seven dissents.[17] More conservative than liberal, he saw the work of an appellate tribunal as that of correcting prejudicial error, but not substituting its judgment for that of the trier of fact. In school desegregation and employment discrimination cases, he was fully prepared to protect individuals who had been discriminated against, but reluctant to provide remedial relief to those who could not prove personal injury as a result of the discrimination.[18] Although he had a reputation as a law-and-order judge, Van Oosterhout several times wrote or joined important opinions insisting that the constitutional rights of defendants be respected.[19] In the Arkansas prison litigation discussed in the next chapter, he supported the use of judicial power to rectify unconstitutional abuses.[20]

Van Oosterhout was greatly respected and liked by his colleagues. Instead of a short memorial tribute, Judge Gerald Heaney wrote an extensive law review article about him, stating in part that "he was the essence of collegiality . . . always stating his views forthrightly . . . and never objected to you stating yours." Judge Pat Mehaffy said, "He was my favorite and everybody else's favorite on the court." Myron Bright said of him that "he was big in stature and big in brain power."[21]

Marion Charles Matthes (1906–80) is best known for having written the most celebrated court of appeals opinion of this period, that in the Little Rock school desegregation case. Growing up in rural Missouri, Matthes attended the Benton College of Law in St. Louis. A police court judge from 1928 to 1930, Matthes served with the State Finance Commission, then was a solo practitioner until 1955, when he was appointed to the St. Louis Court of Appeals. Matthes was active in state politics and a member of the Missouri State Senate from 1942 to 1950, serving as its president pro tem for two years. President Eisenhower appointed Matthes to the Court of Appeals in 1958.[22]

Although Matthes's formal legal education had been limited, he became one of the court's ablest members. He often wrote the most difficult and controversial opinions, volunteering to write when the judges were having trouble reaching a consensus.[23] No member of the court was anxious to write the opinion in the Little Rock school case, which occurred shortly after Matthes had been appointed to the court, so Matthes volunteered to take it on.[24] The opinion became so well known that Matthes was generally perceived as more liberal than he actually was. Chief Judge from 1970 to 1973, he left that position at the age of sixty-seven (when he also took senior status) so that Pat Mehaffy could serve as Chief Judge.[25]

Elevated to the Court of Appeals at the age of sixty-two, Albert Ridge served for less than four years. Born in Nevada, Missouri, in October 1898, Ridge left school when he was fourteen to help support his family. In 1918 he enlisted as a private in the 129th Field Artillery, Battery D, 35th Division, which was commanded for most of the war by Captain Harry Truman. After the war, Ridge obtained an appointment as a deputy clerk in the Jackson County Circuit Court through James Pendergast, another army buddy and the nephew of Boss Tom

Pendergast. In 1921, Ridge enrolled in the Kansas City School of Law and did some of his studying on the balcony of Truman's Kansas City haberdashery. While he was president, Truman signed his personal letters to Ridge "Captain Harry."

Ridge was associated in private practice with Jim Aylward, one of Kansas City's great trial lawyers. In 1934, Ridge was appointed a judge of the Jackson County Circuit Court. He was retained when Missouri adopted its pathbreaking nonpartisan court plan. Truman recommended Ridge for appointment to the Western District of Missouri, and FDR signed Ridge's commission only five days before his death.

As a district judge, Ridge tried antitrust cases against the movie industry and the *Kansas City Star*. He also handled the case that ended segregation in Kansas City's public swimming pools.[26] President John F. Kennedy elevated Ridge to the Court of Appeals in 1961. Ridge, a devout Catholic, was the first of his religion to serve on the Court of Appeals for the Eighth Circuit. An "ultra-perfectionist,"[27] he retired in April 1965 and died on February 2, 1967.[28]

Judge Pat Mehaffy (1904–81), who succeeded Woodrough in 1963, was the first native-born Arkansan to serve on the Court of Appeals. Mehaffy was born in Little Rock, the son of a justice of the Arkansas Supreme Court. He attended Hendrix College, the University of Arkansas, and the University of Arkansas Law School. Much of the early part of his career was spent as an assistant attorney general and prosecuting attorney. Entering private practice, Mehaffy in 1952 founded Mehaffy, Smith and Williams, one of the most prestigious law firms in Arkansas, which represented the Little Rock School District and the Missouri Pacific Railroad.

Active in Arkansas Democratic politics, Mehaffy served as Arkansas's national committeeman because, he wryly told Harry Blackmun, he "was the only person in the state who at the time could get along with the McClellan faction, the Fulbright faction and the Faubus faction."[29] When John F. Kennedy became president and Robert F. Kennedy became Attorney General, McClellan was close to both and a member of the Senate Judiciary Committee. Anxious that Arkansas have a seat on the Court of Appeals, McClellan saw to it that Mehaffy would be chosen over the seventy-three-year-old district judge John E. Miller.[30]

Mehaffy would be one of the more conservative members of the Court of Appeals, especially on criminal matters.[31] Yet Judge Donald Lay, certainly a judicial liberal, stated that "perhaps more than any other man that I have served with . . . [he] demonstrated human compassion and understanding for the individual."[32] Mehaffy was Chief Judge of the Court of Appeals in 1973–74, taking senior status in the latter year. An engaging conversationalist with a large fund of personal anecdotes, Mehaffy was very popular with his colleagues.[33]

Floyd Gibson (1910–2001) succeeded Ridge in 1965. Born in Prescott, Arizona, Gibson received his B.A. and LL.B. degrees from the University of Missouri. He practiced law in Independence and Kansas City. Like Ridge, Gibson was active in politics. He was a member of the Missouri House of Representatives (1940–46) and Senate (1947–61). Gibson served as majority leader and president pro tem of the Senate and, in 1960, was named the legislature's most valuable member by the *St. Louis Globe-Democrat*. In 1961 he was appointed to the U.S. District Court for the Western District of Missouri to succeed Judge Ridge. Lyndon Johnson elevated him to the Court of Appeals. Gibson can best be labeled a moderate conservative who was more conservative than moderate in criminal cases.[34] Gibson continued to sit until June 2000. He died on October 4, 2001.

The emergence of a "liberal wing" of the court was the result of a conjunction between a liberal Democratic president and the election of liberal Democratic senators from the northern part of the circuit. Donald P. Lay brought a liberal sensibility to the Court of Appeals, something it had not had since the early part of the century. Born in 1926 in Princeton, Illinois, Lay grew up in Iowa. He joined the navy in 1944. After the war, he attended the Naval Academy, where he suffered a serious football injury. He then transferred to the University of Iowa, where he received his B.A. and J.D. degrees. Lay practiced law successively in Omaha, in Milwaukee, and again in Omaha. When appointed to the Court of Appeals by Lyndon Johnson in July 1966, Lay, at thirty-nine, was the second youngest person ever appointed to a federal appellate court. Continuing to sit on the Court of Appeals, Lay wrote important opinions dealing with prisoners' rights, environmental law, gender discrimination, abortion, and the First Amendment.[35] The first member of the court in modern times to dissent frequently, Lay supported diversity jurisdiction, opposed sentencing guidelines, and believed that the government should "turn square corners in criminal cases."[36] Chief Judge of the Court of Appeals from 1980 to 1992, Lay, as a member of the U.S. Judicial Conference, strongly defended federal habeas corpus review of state criminal convictions.[37] A man of immense energy, Lay wrote over fifty articles and essays and delivered innumerable speeches, lectures, commencement addresses, and testimony at law schools, bar associations, judicial conferences, and legislative hearings.[38]

Gerald W. Heaney brought to the Court of Appeals extensive experience in Minnesota's liberal politics, strong grounding in labor law, and a powerful will tempered by compassion, forged at least in part by extraordinary wartime service. Heaney was born in 1918 in Goodhue in southeastern Minnesota, thirty miles north of Rochester. He attended the College of St. Thomas and received his bachelor's and law degrees from the University of Minnesota. Rejected by the marines because of color blindness, Heaney enlisted as a private in the army in the summer of 1942.[39]

Commissioned as second lieutenant, Heaney was one of the Rangers of the Second Rangers Infantry Battalion, who landed on Omaha Beach on D-day. Sixty percent of his unit took casualties as they tried to get to the top of the cliffs overlooking the Channel. Heaney went on to fight in the Brest Peninsula, in the Huergten and Ardennes forests with Patton, and in Bavaria and Czechoslovakia. He was one of only three of the original Rangers to make his way from the Normandy beaches to Czechoslovakia (and one of the seventy-seven Rangers who returned to France for the fiftieth anniversary of the Normandy landings).[40] After the war, Heaney was a labor relations officer for Bavaria, rewriting Bavaria's labor laws and helping to organize a free trade union movement.[41] During his military career, Heaney was awarded the Silver Star and Bronze Star and five battle stars as well as a presidential unit citation.

Back in the States, Heaney practiced labor law for Lewis Hammer Heaney Weyl & Halverson in Duluth. He entered politics and became one of the shrewdest politicians in Minnesota, defining the issues, twisting arms, organizing rallies, assessing the mood of the electorate, and calling elections with "uncanny accuracy."[42] In 1948, at Hubert Humphrey's request, Heaney helped wrest control of the Democratic Farmer-Labor Party away from alleged Communist sympathizers. Heaney was a close adviser to Governor Orville Freeman and also close to Eugene McCarthy and Walter Mondale.

Heaney is one of an impressive line of Minnesota politicians who have been able to harness their compassion to be of practical help to those less fortunate. He was chairman of the Duluth Inter-racial Council, a principal organizer of the Northeastern Minnesota Development Association and Natural Resources Research Institute, and active in establishing a branch of the University of Minnesota in Duluth. In 1967,

Heaney brought together nineteen Duluth women to rehabilitate an inner-city neighborhood. Building or renovating housing for 250 families, the group was given the National Volunteer of the Year Award by President Gerald Ford.[43]

Heaney was appointed to the Court of Appeals on November 30, 1966. He has written important opinions in desegregation cases dealing with the Little Rock, Kansas City, St. Louis, and Omaha schools. Heaney hired the first female clerk and the first African American clerk on the Court of Appeals for the Eighth Circuit.[44] Having taken senior status at the end of 1988, Heaney continued to sit with the court until 2006.

The last of Lyndon Johnson's appointees, Myron Bright, was born in Eveleth, Minnesota, on March 5, 1919, to Jewish parents who had emigrated from the Ukraine through Canada. Bright's father peddled merchandise, owned small stores, and worked in Duluth's shipyards. Bright grew up in the Minnesota Iron Range, a great melting pot of Slovenians, Serbs, Croats, Italians, Finns, Scots, Irish, and English.[45]

Bright received his B.A. from the University of Minnesota in 1941. He served in the India-Burma theater during the war. Bright attended the University of Minnesota School of Law and practiced law for twenty-one years with Wattam, Vogel and Vogel (later Vogel, Bright and Peterson) in Fargo. Bright was a good friend of Senator Quentin Burdick and Democratic county chairman for several years.

The seat on the Eighth Circuit that went to Bright was originally intended for Francis Dunn, a former South Dakota Supreme Court justice. However, after Dunn's sponsor, Senator George McGovern of South Dakota, announced his support for Robert Kennedy for president, Johnson was unwilling to appoint any South Dakotan and instead looked north. Although Senator Burdick's brother, a judge, also aspired to the vacant seat, Burdick recommended Bright.

Bright has always perceived the litigants before him not as abstractions but as actual people wrestling with life's difficulties. From the beginning of his tenure, he has identified with "underdogs."[46] His friend and ally Donald Lay wondered what made Bright "more caring and concerned about the rights and feelings of others" and answered:

> His early years provided first-hand observation of religious bias and prejudice. Myron became inculcated with tenets of fairness and justice by watching others practice unfairness and injustice. These experiences undoubtedly became affixed in his conscience and played a major role in developing his basic compassion for fair treatment of others.[47]

A deeply committed liberal, Bright has been able to hold to his strong convictions while maintaining warm personal and professional relationships with those with whom he disagrees.[48] Anyone meeting him is overwhelmed by his charm, warmth, vigor, creativity, and sense of humor.

Assuming senior status in 1985 only unleashed Bright's energy. Besides continuing to sit on the Eighth Circuit, Bright has been a visiting judge in six other circuits and a visiting district judge in five districts. He has traveled throughout the country giving continuing legal education classes for judges and attorneys, cajoling jurists such as Chief Justice William Rehnquist and Justices John Paul Stevens and Harry Blackmun to join him.

Harry Blackmun

The fourth Eighth Circuit judge to be elevated to the Supreme Court, Harry Blackmun (1908–99), was a member of the Court of Appeals for over a decade. Born in Nashville, Illinois, he grew up in St. Paul within a few miles of Warren Burger and Edward Devitt, Minnesota's distinguished district judge. Blackmun's father ran businesses; his mother was a talented musician. Blackmun attended Harvard College on a scholarship, working as janitor, postal worker, and painter to make ends meet. He graduated summa cum laude.

Graduating in 1932 from Harvard Law School, Blackmun was planning to work in Boston but returned to Minnesota because of the illness of his father. He landed a clerkship with Judge John B. Sanborn and entered practice, specializing in taxation, trusts, and civil litigation while teaching part-time at the St. Paul College of Law and the University of Minnesota Law School. In 1950, Blackmun left practice to become general counsel of the Mayo Clinic. Much less active in politics than his colleagues, Blackmun, a Republican, was a quiet supporter of Hubert Humphrey. Judge Sanborn seems to have engineered Blackmun's appointment to the Court of Appeals in 1959 with the support of Humphrey and Blackmun's old friend Warren Burger.[49]

From the beginning of his Eighth Circuit career, Blackmun was an unusually thorough and intellectual judge, seemingly finding it necessary in his opinions to dispose of all the contentions of losing counsel. Blackmun's opinions often were longer than those of his colleagues. Even his "flimsies" (bench memos) were so complete—sometimes running to twenty pages—that Mehaffy used to joke that he used them instead of writing opinions of his own.[50] At this point in a judicial career that lasted forty-five years, Blackmun's opinions were well, although not vividly, written. Though always attuned to the human element,[51] Blackmun's social vision during his Eighth Circuit years was fairly complacent. He believed that government worked well for most people most of the time without intervention from the federal judiciary.[52] Such views did not set him apart much from Van Oosterhout, Matthes, Mehaffy, and Vogel. Blackmun was definitely less sympathetic to civil liberties claims than Lay, Bright, and Heaney,[53] although on racial civil rights, Blackmun, like his colleagues, was an unwavering adherent of racial equality. In criminal cases he was essentially a law-and-order judge minus some of the rhetoric, although occasionally a very personal agony shows through, nowhere more than at the end of *Maxwell v. Bishop*, where he wrote for the Court of Appeals affirming a capital sentence.[54]

Blackmun enjoyed the craft of judging. He particularly liked writing tax cases and wrote many opinions involving jurisdiction and procedure. His most important opinions as an Eighth Circuit judge include *Pope v. United States*[55] and *Maxwell v. Bishop*, capital cases; *Jones v. Alfred H. Mayer Co.*,[56] a housing discrimination case; and *Jackson v. Bishop*,[57] involving the Arkansas prison farms. Although from time to time he irritated his colleagues by nitpicking over grammar and exhibited other kinds of perfectionism, Blackmun got along well with them. He was particularly close to Mehaffy and came to believe that Mehaffy had been an important force behind his appointment to the Supreme Court.[58]

Blackmun used to refer to himself as "old number three," because his elevation to the Supreme Court in 1970 to the vacant seat left by the resignation of Justice Abe Fortas occurred after bitter confirmation fights had prevented the confirmation of Clement Haynsworth and G. Harold Carswell of the Fourth and Fifth Circuits, respectively. At the time of his elevation, Blackmun was sixty-one years old and left the Court of Appeals regretfully. In the years ahead, Blackmun used to love to tell tales about his early days on the Court of Appeals and to speak about the court's unique traditions.[59] At an Eighth Circuit conference, Blackmun remarked poignantly, "It was happier here than it is there. It's a fast track and one feels lonely in his decision-making."[60]

Harry Blackmun's transformation while associate justice of the Supreme Court can only be sketched briefly here. In his early years on the High Court, he acquired a reputation for taking a long time to make up his mind and for being a slow writer,[61] and he appeared to be a sure conservative vote in criminal and civil liberties cases. But Blackmun was doing his own work and his own thinking. Alone among the justices, Blackmun could be seen working in the "judges' library" day after day, studying, checking his own citations by hand, agonizing.[62]

When he was more than sixty years old, Blackmun began to rethink his constitutional and philosophical views. His opinion in *Roe v. Wade* is an early example.[63] As he made a conscientious effort to reach out and understand people whose lives were different from his own, Blackmun's social vision and his views on the role of the federal courts changed profoundly.[64] Over the years, he came to see the Supreme Court as an essential voice for the vulnerable and powerless, and he moved to the center of the court and beyond.

With age, Blackmun, always modest, grew even more gentle and compassionate. Instead of pretense and pomposity, Blackmun had dignity and character,[65] although he also had an ornery streak. At Blackmun's retirement in 1994 in his eighty-seventh year, Chief Judge Richard Arnold wrote for his court: "All of us in the Eighth Circuit, especially the judges of the Court of Appeals, are proud of Justice Harry Blackmun today, as we have been for every day of his service on the federal bench."[66] Justice Blackmun died on March 5, 1999, at the age of ninety.

The Court of Appeals for the Eighth Circuit was, during the 1960s, a very able court. "Judge Van" may well have been both the intellectual and social leader of the court,[67] while Blackmun was an unusually thorough and scholarly colleague. Lay began to make his mark from the very beginning. But the work of Vogel, Johnsen, and Matthes was careful, solidly crafted, and well written, while toward the end of the period, Heaney and Bright began judicial careers of considerable distinction. Personal relations within the court continued to be very pleasant and published dissenting opinions were rare and decorous.

Jurisprudence

During the late 1950s and 1960s, the Court of Appeals for the Eighth Circuit, like the others courts of appeal, was constantly encountering cases involving value-laden issues. The most important of these cases involved racial discrimination, where the Supreme Court had forged the Equal Protection Clause into a powerful sword, which it then wielded in such other areas as legislative reapportionment. The Court of Appeals also heard capital and other significant criminal cases, as well as note-worthy First Amendment litigation.

While the increased role of the U.S. Supreme Court in the area of civil liberties dates to the 1930s, a new era began with the first Supreme Court decision in *Brown v. Board of Education*.[68] It was after *Brown* that civil liberties cases became an important part of the work of the lower federal courts; those courts became havens for those lacking po-litical clout. After *Brown,* the Supreme Court encountered resistance from state and local governments and almost every district judge in the Deep South. Soon the Supreme Court grew impatient with the manner in which principles of federalism, as well as other doctrines and legal fictions, were being used to protect state and local practices that, had they been undertaken by the federal government, would clearly have been held unconstitutional. One response of the Supreme Court was the incorporation of the Bill of Rights to protect individuals against un-constitutional actions of state and local officials.[69]

The number of cases testing the exercise of governmental powers also increased because the High Court began to sweep away technical doctrines impeding access to the courts. Rules regarding standing to sue in the federal courts, the right to intervene in administrative proceed-ings, and the ripeness of decisions for judicial review were greatly liberal-ized. In 1966 the judicial branch itself changed the Federal Rules of Civil Procedure to facilitate the bringing of class actions. Increased availability of counsel for the poor, the handiwork of all three branches, led to greater scrutiny of both federal and state criminal justice.

The Supreme Court also found remedies for individuals deprived of constitutional rights by state officials acting under color of state law by breathing life into the Civil Rights Act of 1871.[70] In addition, several Supreme Court decisions produced marked expansion of relief for state prisoners collaterally attacking the validity of their convictions.[71]

Laws passed by Congress in the 1950s and 1960s recognizing and creating rights added to the number of civil liberties cases in the fed-eral courts. The most important of the new laws was the omnibus Civil Rights Act of 1964, which prohibited discrimination in voting, employ-ment, housing, and public accommodations as well as authorizing the Department of Health, Education and Welfare to cut off funds to school districts continuing school segregation.

Taken together, greater access to the federal courts, willingness to modify traditional principles of federalism, and the generous reading of the Equal Protection Clause led to the assertion of judicial power in cases involving civil rights and liberties and the crafting of remedies permitting unprecedented oversight of state institutions.

Resistance by state officials (and district judges) made the role of the courts of appeals in enforcing national policies critical. This was especially true in the Fourth and Fifth Circuits, although quite possibly the greatest challenge occurred in the Eighth Circuit in the Little Rock school desegregation case, when a state governor directly flouted court orders. Challenges to federal court decisions by state and local officials had, of course, occurred since 1789, for example in the municipal bond cases in the Eighth Circuit after the Civil War. What was new in the 1950s and 1960s was the subject matter—civil rights and individual liberties—and the immediate visibility of the challenge throughout the nation (and the world).

If the encounters between the lower federal courts and state and local governments document the work of the courts of appeals as agents of centralization, the reader must not forget that, even during this period, the courts of appeals could be (and sometimes were) sensitive to local interests and political realities. In the reapportionment cases, for example, the three-judge courts tried to cut enough slack so that legislators and officials would devise their own apportionment plans, rather than having one thrust upon them by the courts. Nor had the courts of appeals completely abandoned traditional doctrines forged to avoid too much interference by the federal courts in state judicial proceedings.

In addition, the reader must not forget that a large number of cases decided by the courts of appeals were of interest only to the litigants themselves (and their attorneys). More and more, the courts of appeals were the final court for federal appeals, most especially for diversity cases and routine criminal prosecutions. In deciding the flotsam and jetsam of the docket, the intermediate tier provided an authoritative final solution to the dispute for the parties, oversaw the work of the district courts, and made it possible for the Supreme Court to avoid having a docket cluttered with insignificant cases. In such cases, when the Court of Appeals reviewed the trial record to determine if the district judge had made prejudicial errors in the handling of the trial or in rulings of law, reversals did not occur often and, in the Eighth Circuit (as in most circuits), were unmarked by asperity. [72] The judges of the Court of Appeals for the Eighth Circuit tended to write as if they understood the problems of trial judges (and no doubt much of the time they did). In *White v. United States*, for example, a panel of Mehaffy, Van Oosterhout, and Ridge affirmed a conviction for violating the drug laws following a trial before Judge James H. Meredith of the Eastern District of Missouri. Judge Mehaffy wrote for the appeals court:

> We would be indulging in legal gymnastics if we held that the District Judge, displaying the patience of Job and fairness of Solomon, by granting the defense two trial postponements, issuing subpoenas for defense witnesses at government expense, appointing a disinterested chemist, requiring a bill of particulars from the government, and subpoenaing defendant's military service records of achievement, deprived the defendant of due process of law in finally bringing the case to trial when all attempts at locating one recalcitrant witness became abortive.[73]

One role that does not describe the work of the Eighth Circuit from 1954 to 1969 is that of innovative policy maker. In constitutional matters, the Court of Appeals stayed close to Supreme Court precedent. The court was, as Learned Hand conceived a judge's prime duty, "an obedient court."[74] In addition to judicial modesty demonstrated in cases involving housing discrimination and capital punishment discussed later in this chapter, one example is offered here. *Ashe v. Swenson* involved the issue of double jeopardy. The defendant was one of three or four armed men who had allegedly robbed six poker players in one fell swoop. Charged with six separate counts for the robbery of each of the victims, the defendant went to trial on only one count and was acquitted. The government then sought to try him on a second count. It was argued that this would expose the defendant to double jeopardy. Under a ten-year-old Supreme Court case (decided 5–4), in a situation such as this, each robbery had to be viewed as a separate offense. Thus the defendant could be tried on the second count without producing double jeopardy. However, four members of the five-man majority had left the Supreme Court, while all four members of the minority remained on the court. Nevertheless, the Court of Appeals was "obedient" and followed precedent. Judge Blackmun wrote:

> This court is not the Supreme Court of the United States. We therefore are not free to disregard an existing fiat and still live holding of the Supreme Court even though that holding is one by a sharply divided tribunal and even though only one of the justices who participated in the majority decision remains active.[75]

Shortly before Judge Blackmun was elevated to the High Court, the Supreme Court reversed the Court of Appeals decision in *Ashe* by a vote of seven to one.[76]

Looking at the work of the Court of Appeals for the Eighth Circuit from 1954 to 1969, one can see, in the large number of ordinary disputes the court resolved, its role as overseer of the district courts and buffer for the Supreme Court. Then one is struck by the importance of its role in enforcing centralizing policies—especially in the civil rights and reapportionment cases, but also in the traditional federal specialties. However, if the full bench solidly supported school desegregation, its individual judges were more cautious in reapportionment cases, and a majority of the judges had little inclination to anticipate Warren Court jurisprudence in criminal and First Amendment cases.

The workload of the courts of appeals increased greatly in the 1960s, generally as a result of the developments just described, most particularly because of the increased number of federal criminal appeals and appeals from district court rulings on state habeas corpus petitions. While filings in the eleven courts of appeals tripled between 1960 (3,899) and 1970 (11,662), filings in the Court of Appeals for the Eighth Circuit increased from 237 to 589. Although Congress increased the number of court of appeals judgeships from sixty-eight to ninety-four during this period, the Eighth Circuit, with its relatively light caseload, was given only one new judgeship, that under the Act of March 18, 1966, to which Judge Heaney was appointed.[77] The court was now depending more than before on judges taking senior status around their seventieth birthday and continuing to sit in a large number of cases. Nevertheless the number of pending cases in the Eighth Circuit rose from 127 to 404 between 1960 and 1970.[78]

Civil Rights Litigation

The most important cases decided by the Eighth Circuit between 1957 and 1970 involved racial civil rights. At first, they were few in number, though great in significance. During the years 1957 to 1964, a little more than one-half of 1 percent of the docket involved civil rights cases (the Eighth Circuit ranking tenth out of eleven courts of appeals in this regard). However, from 1965 to 1972, civil rights cases rose to constitute 5 percent of the docket.[79] As one might anticipate, racial problems were far more salient in the two southernmost states of the Eighth

Circuit, Missouri and Arkansas. These two states have the largest African American populations in the circuit, were slave states before the Civil War, and had some kinds of formal segregation at the time of the *Brown* decision.[80]

Of the states of the Eighth Circuit, during the period between 1865 and 1954, race relations were worst in Arkansas. The state ranked sixth in the nation with 214 lynchings in the twenty-five years between 1889 and 1914.[81] While Jim Crow laws prevailed, a litcracy test, the poll tax, and a white primary law deprived most blacks in Arkansas of the vote. One of the bloodiest black-white encounters in American history took place in Elaine in 1919.[82] There was less state-sponsored segregation in Missouri, but there was also considerable private segregation.

Grave racial problems were not the sole property of Arkansas and Missouri. Omaha also had a horrible antiblack riot.[83] In the following year, a white mob lynched three circus hands on one of the main streets of Duluth.[84]

Several important civil rights cases arose in the Eighth Circuit before the era of *Brown v. Board of Education*.[85] *McCabe v. Atchison Topeka and Santa Fe Railway*, decided by the Supreme Court in 1914, involved an Oklahoma statute that provided for separate but equal railway cars for the races, except with regard to sleeping, dining, and parlor cars. Since it was expensive to provide such facilities and few African Americans could afford them, the legislature provided for only one set of those cars, which were to be for the exclusive use of either whites or blacks, but never both together. Five black plaintiffs sought an injunction to prevent the statute from going into effect. The Circuit Court for the Western District of Oklahoma denied relief.

The Court of Appeals affirmed by a vote of 2–1. Judge Adams, writing for himself and Judge Hook, chose practicality over equality. Equality of service did not necessarily mean "identity of service," for "practical considerations cannot be ignored,"[86] wrote Adams. Dissenting, Judge Walter Sanborn asked the pointed question: "Would one riding all night upon a train that carried a sleeping car, who was legally expelled from or forbidden by law to enter or occupy it, believe that he was provided with equality of service, or equal comforts and conveniences with the companions who were permitted to purchase berths and beds therein?" Indeed, in its brief before the U.S. Supreme Court, the state of Oklahoma contended that separation of the races was a "practical condition for Southerners" and pointed out that "from his environment" Sanborn had "come in contact only with the theoretical side of this extremely practical question." Sanborn was born in Epson, New Hampshire.[87]

The Supreme Court agreed with Sanborn. The Court, with Justice Charles Evans Hughes writing, held that if facilities are provided, substantial equality of treatment of persons traveling under like conditions cannot be refused. In *McCabe*, the Supreme Court appeared to be challenging the entire structure of Jim Crow laws by looking at the lack of equality in practice. In the short run, that was not to be, but later *McCabe* would become a major precedent for holding unconstitutional attempts to provide unequal facilities for African Americans based on a theory of differences in demand by whites and blacks. Ironically, while the substantive law of *McCabe* was favorable, the case did nothing directly for its plaintiffs, because the Court also held that they lacked standing.[88]

The Court of Appeals for the Eighth Circuit was a mere conduit for the important principle of law determined in *Guinn v. United States*. That case involved the constitutionality of Oklahoma's "grandfather clause," which provided that new property, literacy, or other voter qualifications would not apply to those whose ancestors had voted before 1867 or served in the military in the Civil War or earlier. After two state election officials who applied the grandfather clause were convicted of violations of federal civil rights for employing the grandfather clause to prevent African Americans from voting, their convictions were appealed to the Court of Appeals. That court, in turn, certified to the Supreme Court two questions involving the validity of the grandfather clause. Chief Justice White wrote the opinion for the unanimous High Court declaring the grandfather clause unconstitutional on its face.[89] Of *Guinn*, Benno C. Schmidt Jr. concluded that "in electing for the first time to use federal law to strike down a state law depriving blacks of the right to vote, the Court made a notable departure . . . not only from what went before, but from what came after."[90]

At the end of the 1940s, an employment discrimination case of national importance arose in the Eastern District of Missouri. *Howard v. St. Louis–San Francisco Railway Co.* was a personal and class action brought by "train porters" who performed braking work on the head end of Frisco's passenger trains. The train porters, who were black, had to have the same qualifications as the "brakemen," who were white. However, unlike the brakemen, the train porters spent 5 percent of their time sweeping aisles and assisting passengers, and they were paid less. For years, the Brotherhood of Railroad Trainmen (then an all-white union) had been attempting to eliminate the position of train porter to get those jobs for their own members. Finally, by threatening a strike, the Brotherhood succeeded in making an agreement with the Frisco, ousting the train porters from their jobs. The train porters sought a decree holding the contract void and petitioned for an injunction to save their jobs. Judge Richard M. Duncan of the Eastern District of Missouri refused to grant the injunction but continued a restraining order so that the railroad could not immediately take action to fire the train porters.[91]

The Court of Appeals reversed with a powerful opinion by Judge Johnsen (joined by Sanborn and Riddick), who described what he saw as "one of attempted predatory seizure and appropriation, by one railroad craft, of another's entire and forty year established positional field." The Court of Appeals directed the district court to enter a permanent injunction enjoining the railway and the brotherhood from using their agreement for any other purpose than accomplishing a consolidation of the positions and crafts of brakeman and train porter.[92] The Supreme Court affirmed. Nevertheless, the litigation continued into the 1960s.[93]

In the 1940s, conditions were better for African Americans in Arkansas than in the Deep South and improving. The Democratic primary was open to at least a small percentage of black voters. A few were elected to local political office. Later in the decade, Governor Sidney S. McMath repeatedly called for adherence to the Fourteenth Amendment, opposed the poll tax, and sponsored anti-lynching legislation. In 1948 Arkansas opened its law and medical schools to African Americans. Yet that there was an immense distance to be traveled to achieve racial equality may be seen from the case of Susie Morris. During the war, Morris and other black teachers sued to bring an end to the policy of paying African American teachers less than their white counterparts in Little Rock. Judge Thomas C. Trimble threw out the suit on the absurd ground that the plaintiffs had not been able to sustain their burden of proof by establishing the existence and maintenance of a policy, custom, and usage of paying "colored" teachers less than white teachers.[94]

Thurgood Marshall argued the appeal and won a reversal. The Court of Appeals—Judges Thomas (writing), Sanborn, and Woodrough—overturned the trial judge's finding that no policy, usage, or custom existing of paying "Negro" teachers less for comparable service than white teachers. It held that the teachers were entitled to a declaratory judgment but left a possible injunction for remand.[95]

None of this did Susie Morris any good. Like so many African Americans who came forward in the South to seek their rights during this era, she was fired.[96]

LITTLE ROCK Many of the important battles of the Second Reconstruction were fought in the federal courts. In the fifteen years following *Brown v. Board of Education,* the brunt of school desegregation cases was borne by the Fourth and Fifth Circuits, both of which were badly divided in dealing with them. The Eighth Circuit, which included two states where there had been formal segregation, Arkansas and Missouri, had many cases involving formal segregation but ordinarily gave the Supreme Court strong support. The schools of Missouri's two largest cities, St. Louis and Kansas City, were formally desegregated in the 1950s, but there was relatively little change in fact because of residential segregation. As the efforts to use the courts to desegregate the schools of the two cities in fact began in the 1970s and lasted decades, that experience is discussed in later chapters of this book.

Among the most important cases ever decided by the Court of Appeals for the Eighth Circuit were those connected with the desegregation of Central High School in Little Rock.[97] In *Aaron v. Cooper,* the Court of Appeal's strong adherence to *Brown v. Board of Education* and commitment to the primacy of the federal courts gave the Supreme Court support at a time it was receiving too little. After the *Brown* decision, it appeared that desegregation would occur peacefully in Arkansas. The state had been led for a generation by moderate white leadership and seemed as much a southwestern as a southern state. Soon after *Brown,* Fayetteville's schools were integrated without problems, except for a boycott of its football team by other Arkansas schools.[98]

In the mid-1950s, Little Rock appeared to be a moderate, middle-class city with an enlightened major newspaper, congressman, and mayor. Before 1954 the Little Rock public library had been desegregated, and all department stores had removed their segregated drinking fountains. In 1952 the Little Rock Council on Education had stated that only through integration could obstacles to real qualitative equality be overcome.[99] Yet the South was seething with resentment at the *Brown* decision. One hundred and one members of Congress, including both Arkansas senators, issued a Southern Manifesto which encouraged massive resistance to *Brown.* Local white citizens' councils had been formed throughout the South, encouraging lawlessness. For the optimists, the experience of

Hoxie might have been somewhat chastening. A town of two thousand in northeast Arkansas, 140 miles from Little Rock, Hoxie had attempted in good faith to desegregate its schools in 1955. After several peaceful weeks, segregationists, many from outside the town, began agitating against integration. Judge Thomas C. Trimble issued a temporary restraining order forbidding segregationist interference. Judge Albert L. Reeves made the injunction permanent, and the Court of Appeals affirmed, sustaining the board's right to sue and holding that attempted deprivation of constitutional rights could not be sheltered under the First Amendment. While schools were desegregated in Hoxie, its experience suggests just how vulnerable civic peace was in Arkansas.[100]

In May 1955, the Little Rock School Board committed itself to begin phased integration in the fall of 1957 with Central High School. It set May 1963 as the date for full compliance with *Brown*. In August 1956 Judge John E. Miller (who decades before had prosecuted African Americans for the Elaine riots) approved the school board's plan. Rejecting an attempt by the NAACP to speed up integration, Miller stated that he would not substitute his own judgment for that of the school board, whose plan, he thought, had been adopted after thorough and conscientious consideration. He did, however, retain jurisdiction of the case to deal with questions that might arise during implementation.[101]

The *Aaron v. Cooper* litigation (John Aaron was a black high school student, and William C. Cooper was a member of the Little Rock School Board) continued on appeal to the Court of Appeals, which affirmed in April 1957. Looking at places where the federal courts had used their injunctive powers to speed up or effectuate integration, Judge Vogel, for the court, wrote that those decisions served only "to demonstrate that local school problems are varied," and that a "reasonable amount of time to effect complete integration in the schools of Little Rock, Arkansas, may be unreasonable in St. Louis, Missouri, or Washington, D.C." Where Little Rock was concerned, the Court of Appeals found an "unqualified basis for the District Court's conclusions that the proposed plan constitutes a good-faith, prompt and reasonable start toward full compliance with the Supreme Court's mandate."[102] In the meantime, an interposition resolution and a state constitutional amendment aimed at blocking desegregation had been adopted by the state's voters at a referendum, while the state legislature had passed four laws aimed at preventing progress in civil rights.

By the late summer of 1957, the political environment had become increasingly tense. A state chancery court had issued an injunction ordering that desegregation not proceed. The governor, Orval Faubus, appeared to be encouraging disruption of desegregation, while President Eisenhower hesitated to act firmly. Then, on August 29, 1957, shortly before school was to begin, Judge Miller asked to be relieved of further involvement in the litigation. Chief Judge Archibald Gardner of the Court of Appeals temporarily assigned Ronald N. Davies, a district judge from North Dakota, to Little Rock to assist with the court calendar after the retirement of Judge Thomas Trimble, and to deal with the explosive case. Davies had no inkling that he would remain in Little Rock for thirty-nine days and play a central role in a drama that would command international attention.[103] He was fifty-three years old and a graduate of the University of North Dakota Law School. Five foot one and one-half inches tall, he was known in North Dakota as a delightful man in whose presence there rarely was a dull moment. He was quick in everything he did. When he took the bench, the door would pop open; he would go up three steps and leap into his chair.[104] In Little Rock, he would act firmly and courageously.

Davies first ruled that the state chancery court had no jurisdiction over the matter and ordered that desegregation proceed. On September 2, Faubus finally showed his true colors. Stating that there was uncertainty over whether the interposition statutes or the Supreme Court opinion in *Brown* was the law of the land, he said he would enforce the interposition amendment to the Arkansas Constitution, which had been adopted at referendum in November 1956, until "proper authority" determined its constitutionality. Faubus then ordered the Arkansas National Guard to surround the high school to "protect" the nine black students from possible violence. The following day, Davies repeated his order that integration be implemented "forthwith." On the fourth, the National Guard turned away the nine African American students. Davies then ordered the Justice Department to investigate the causes of disruption of desegregation and to enter the case and file for a preliminary injunction.

On September 14, Eisenhower met with Faubus in Newport, Rhode Island. Eisenhower would be proven wrong in his belief that those talks had ended the crisis. On September 20, when Davies issued a preliminary injunction against the governor, Faubus's attorneys walked out of the hearing, stating, "The Governor of the State of Arkansas cannot and will not concede that the United States in this court or anywhere else can question his discretion and judgment as chief executive of a sovereign state"[105] Faubus then removed the National Guard from Central High School.

On the twenty-third, the black students entered a high school surrounded by a screaming mob. When Elizabeth Eckford, one of the black students, appeared, there were cries of "The niggers are coming! Get her! Lynch her!"[106] The *New York Times* reported, "A mob of belligerent, shrieking and hysterical demonstrators forced the withdrawal of the students" from the high school. Two black newsmen were beaten, as well as a hapless passerby. Other reporters and photographers were manhandled. The next day, Little Rock's mayor asked for federal troops. The president was left with little choice but to order the 101st Airborne to Little Rock in battle array and to mobilize the National Guard. Faubus announced on television, "We are an occupied territory."[107] The troops would not be withdrawn for a year.

Neither Faubus nor Eisenhower emerged from the first phase of the crisis with his reputation enhanced—at least outside the South. Under intense pressure from the White Citizens Councils, segregationist southern governors, and political leaders in the plantation belt, Faubus was probably looking to force the federal executive branch to accept responsibility for the order of its courts and seeking a politically expedient accommodation. Although portrayed as a racist ideologue, Faubus was employing the time-tested formula for demagogues in Arkansas—rousing the backcountry against city folk, the *Arkansas Gazette*, and meddling Yankee outsiders.[108]

For his part, Eisenhower failed utterly at using the bully pulpit on behalf of civil rights, no doubt because he did not see desegregation as a moral imperative. At no point during or after his presidency, including during the Little Rock crisis, did Eisenhower endorse the *Brown* decision or even indicate awareness of the profound issues involved. His approach to the crisis was shaped by a genuine belief in the separation of powers and principles of federalism to which he adhered, but it also demonstrated a limited understanding of the judicial process.[109]

Black students did attend Central High School during the 1957–58 school year, while members of the armed forces patrolled the hallways. Black students were punched and kicked. Firecrackers were set off in their lockers, and food dumped in their laps. During the school year, there were forty-three bomb threats and numerous small fires. Three hundred students were suspended.[110]

There also was a great deal of litigation. The segregationist Mother's

League challenged the Little Rock School Board's phased desegregation and Eisenhower's use of federal troops. Governor Faubus appealed Davies's judgment against him for interference with federal court orders. The NAACP continued its lawsuits and initiated others.[111] Deciding the several appeals on April 18, 1958, the Court of Appeals held (1) against Governor Faubus's claim that the state's police power sanctioned obstruction of desegregation;[112] (2) that Davies had acted correctly in preventing enforcement of the state chancery court's decision enjoining School Board implementation of desegregation;[113] and (3) that a suit contesting the president's use of the military lacked jurisdiction.[114]

Already in February 1958, the school board, which was opposed by state officials, receiving relatively little backing from the federal government, and having exhausted its fount of courage, filed a petition with the district court requesting that further implementation of phased desegregation be postponed. On June 21, 1958, Judge Harry T. Lemley granted the petition as a "tactical delay" "in the public interest" because of the "very unfavorable" community attitude.[115]

Even before the Court of Appeals considered an application for a stay, the NAACP petitioned the Supreme Court, asking it to hear the case. The High Court refused to do so, stating on June 30, "We have no doubt that the Court of Appeals will recognize the vital importance of the time element."[116] On August 18, the Court of Appeals en banc reversed Lemley by a vote of six to one. With no member of the court anxious to write the opinion, Matthes, the court's junior judge, volunteered to write it and did so in two weeks. The Court of Appeals stated in its opinion:

> An impossible situation could well develop if the District Court's order were affirmed. Every school district in which integration is publicly opposed by overt acts would have "justifiable excuse" to petition the courts for delay and suspension in integration programs. An affirmance of "temporary delay" in Little Rock would amount to an open invitation to elements in other districts to overtly act out public opposition through violent and unlawful means. . . . The issue plainly comes down to the question of whether overt public resistance, including mob protest, constitutes sufficient cause to nullify an order of the federal court directing the Board to proceed with its integration plan.[117]

Matthes continued with a passage italicized in the original:

> We say the time has not yet come in these United States when an order of a Federal Court must be whittled away, watered down, or shame-

fully withdrawn in the face of violent and unlawful acts of individual citizens in opposition there to.[118]

Judge Gardner dissented alone, believing that Lemley had exercised his discretion wisely. Gardner thought that to be successful, changes to "long-established, cherished practice" are "usually accomplished by evolution rather than revolution, and time, patience, and forbearance are important elements in effecting all radical changes."[119]

Acting as Chief Judge, Gardner stayed immediate implementation of the order pending review by the Supreme Court. That court convened in special term to hear the case, one of the very few times it has done so in modern times. Briefs were filed by September 10, and oral argument occurred the following day. In the district court, the central issue in the case had been whether delay was justified in the light of severe disruptions of the judicial process. At the Supreme Court, the case was viewed in terms of state defiance of judicial authority.[120]

On September 12, the Supreme Court announced its per curiam unanimous judgment affirming the Court of Appeals.[121] The opinion in *Cooper v. Aaron*, handed down on September 29,[122] was, for the first time in the history of the Court, headed "Opinion of the Court by the Chief Justice," followed by the names of each of the associate justices.

The High Court began by stating that the case "raises serious questions of the highest importance to the maintenance of our federal system of government." All three branches of the Arkansas government had opposed the desegregation of the Little Rock schools by "enacting laws, calling out troops [and] making statements vilifying federal law and federal courts." The High Court was clear that constitutional rights were not to be "sacrificed or yielded to the violence and disorder which have followed upon the actions of the Governor and legislature." The federal judiciary, the High Court said (citing *Marbury v. Madison*), is supreme in the exposition of the Constitution.[123] If any doubt had survived the Civil War, *Cooper v. Aaron* settled the constitutional question that state officials have to obey the U.S. Constitution.

This was not the end of the crisis—only the beginning of the end. On September 27, 1958, the citizens of Little Rock voted at referendum to close their schools. Judge Miller, back with the case, had already declined to prevent the transfer of public educational facilities to a private school corporation, which was intending to operate segregated schools. In the spring of 1959, a three-judge district court held that the Arkansas laws closing the schools and establishing the private school corporation were unconstitutional.[124] Finally, in August 1959, the public schools opened on an integrated basis.

The battle over the integration of Central High School was reported in newspapers all over the world. Little Rock became the symbol of racist resistance to civil rights in the United States. Faubus lost the legal battle but won big from the conflict—four more terms as governor. Yet, paradoxically, the crisis also accelerated the achievement of equal rights in the South. The first all-out confrontation during the Second Reconstruction was a political drama; a conflict between the force of law and the force of the mob, in which the heroes and heroines were the black children, who, under assault, behaved bravely and with dignity. If Little Rock established the pattern of white resistance—southern officials at the barricades and a mob on the streets throwing bottles and yelling obscenities—it also set the precedent for strong enforcement of federal court orders by the executive branch. Resistance by the governments of the South would survive less than a decade longer.

The battle to desegregate Little Rock's schools was far from over. In 1966, in *Clark v. Board of Education of Little Rock School District,* the Court of Appeals upheld in principle a board "freedom of choice" plan but held Little Rock's plan deficient because it did not provide adequate notice for annual freedom of choice by students and because there was no definite plan for staff desegregation. Judge Floyd Gibson wrote of "delay, evasion, legislative and executive interference and disobedience to the law" but also stated that the board had evidenced a genuine desire to follow the commands of the *Brown* case.[125] Further skirmishes are briefly discussed in chapters 6 and 7.

DESEGREGATION OF OTHER ARKANSAS SCHOOLS   Between 1960 and 1964, the number of black children attending white schools in Arkansas, though small, had increased by 327 percent.[126] The gateway to southeastern Arkansas, Dollarway, was desegregated in 1960, and Pine Bluff followed two years later. In Fort Smith, desegregation occurred at the rate of one grade per year with a voluntary transfer provision and seemed to have worked well enough for the Court of Appeals to state that "desegregation of the Fort Smith public schools stands out in bold contrast to desegregation in some biracial districts where there was hard core opposition to any semblance of integration."[127] The Supreme Court, however, ordered faster desegregation in 1965.[128]

Desegregation of the El Dorado, Arkansas, School District came before the Eighth Circuit three times during this period. In *Kemp v. Beasley I*, the Court of Appeals, in an opinion by Judge Floyd Gibson, held that the mandate of *Brown* had not simply been to forbid segregation but to achieve integration. The court indicated that the time for delay had passed and that administrative problems shall not be used to deprive individuals of the right to attend nonsegregated schools.[129] In *Kemp II*, the court, in an opinion by Judge Lay, ordered complete faculty desegregation by the 1969–70 school year.[130] In *Kemp III*, the Court of Appeals, although remanding so that the district court could deal with five racially identifiable school districts, stated that "the District has come a long way. . . . It has a short distance yet to go. We have confidence that the distance which remains will be immediately and successfully traversed."[131] The court added praise for Judge Oren Harris of the Western District of Arkansas.

The experience in Jefferson County, Arkansas, was less happy. In *Kelly v. Altheimer, Arkansas Public School District No. 22*, the Court of Appeals firmly concluded that "the policies and practices of the appellee school district with respect to students, faculty, facilities, transportation and school expenditures, have been designed to discourage the desegregation of the school system, and have had that effect."[132] The Court of Appeals opinion included two pages devoted to the remedy.

Arkansas, to be sure, continued to be a battleground for some time after the great confrontation at Little Rock. The black sit-in movement spread there. Freedom Riders arrived. Civil rights workers from the North came to southern and eastern Arkansas in 1964. However, by the time Central High School opened for the 1976 school year, the *New York Times* was able to place on its front page the headline "Little Rock Now Integration Model."[133] In 1977, the U.S. Civil Rights Commission agreed, stating, "Although many problems still remain, the Little Rock School District has made good progress in desegregating its schools."[134] By 1981, having gone from 75 percent white to 75 percent black, Central High School was considered to be one of the best high schools in America. Over time, there was genuine progress in race relations in Arkansas. No better example of this can be seen than in the fact that, when Daisy Bates, the courageous leader of the Little Rock desegregation effort, died, her body lay in state on the second floor rotunda of the Arkansas State Capitol.[135]

OTHER CIVIL RIGHTS DECISIONS There were important Eighth Circuit decisions during this period dealing with other aspects of the struggle for racial equality. Arkansas's effort to drive the NAACP and the NAACP Legal Defense Fund out of the state led to a landmark case on freedom of association. In 1958 the legislature passed statutes requiring the disclosure of lists of supporters and financial contributors of certain organizations, statutes that were directed at the groups supporting racial equality. One law required schoolteachers to list all the organizations they had belonged to in the previous five years, while another made it unlawful for any NAACP member to be employed by the state or its subdivisions.

A three-judge district court, constituted of Circuit Judge Sanborn and two Arkansas district judges (Miller and J. Smith Henley), refused to abstain from considering the constitutionality of the statutes. The court upheld the statute requiring individuals to file affidavits listing the organizations they belonged to, but held unconstitutional the law making NAACP members ineligible for public employment: "Since the fact of membership also cannot be used to determine disloyalty or disqualification, it is obvious that mere membership in the NAACP cannot be made a bar to public employment."[136] However, the court refused injunctive relief.

The Supreme Court, dividing five to four, held on appeal in *Shelton v. Tucker* that while there was no question of the relevance of a state's inquiry into the fitness and competence of its teachers, to compel a teacher to disclose every associational tie over a five-year period was to impair that teacher's right of free association.[137] This was "an unlimited and indiscriminate sweep beyond what was necessary to achieve a legitimate public purpose." *Shelton* and contemporaneous cases from other jurisdictions rooted the right to association in the First Amendment.

Daniel v. Paul was an Arkansas case involving interpretation of the Public Accommodations title of the 1964 Civil Rights Act. At issue was whether the Lake Nixon Club, some miles west of Little Rock, was a "private club" rather than a "recreation facility." If the former, it was not covered under the 1964 law; if the latter, it was. The club was not selective as far as whites were concerned—any white who paid twenty-five cents was admitted—but it was quite selective where blacks were concerned, as no black had ever been admitted. The district judge, J. Smith Henley, held that the club was not covered by the statute because it was not involved in interstate commerce. It was not close to a public highway. It was not offering to serve interstate travelers. The food it sold was purchased locally. Thus, at most, the club had a minuscule effect on interstate commerce. The Court of Appeals affirmed. Judge Pat Mehaffy, an Arkansan, wrote the opinion for the court joined by Martin Van Oosterhout. Gerald Heaney dissented, arguing that the club did serve some interstate travelers and that its "membership" requirement was clearly a ruse to keep African Americans from using the club.[138]

Jones v. Alfred H.Mayer Co. was an important housing discrimination case involving interpretation of federal legislation dating back to Reconstruction. Joseph Lee Jones and Barbara Jones, both employees of the Veterans Administration, brought suit against a developer, who refused to sell a house to them in the Paddock Woods Subdivision of St. Louis County because of their race. The Joneses argued that the developer of a private subdivision was in a legally different position where racial discrimination was concerned than the ordinary individual selling his house. The Joneses contended that the developer's conduct violated the Civil Rights Act of 1866, which stated: "All citizens of the United States shall have the same right . . . as is enjoyed by white citizens thereof to inherit, purchase, lease, hold and convey real and personal property."[139]

At the time the Court of Appeals heard *Jones v. Alfred H. Mayer Co.*, the black-letter law was that the 1866 statute could not constitutionally reach beyond the language of the Fourteenth Amendment, which applied only to state action. Deciding the case in May 1966, Judge John K. Regan of the Eastern District of Missouri, relying heavily on some of the recent sit-in decisions of the Supreme Court, dismissed the complaint, holding that there must be some substantial involvement of the state or of one acting under color of its authority for the conduct of the developer to come within the ban. Regan saw no such involvement.[140]

In June 1967, the Court of Appeals affirmed in a thorough opinion written by Judge Blackmun.[141] Blackmun carefully reviewed the Reconstruction Amendments and statutes and considered the "possible incipient emergence from the shackles of the state action limitation." He looked at approaches put forward by Judge Jacob Trieber over sixty years before and the prescient dissenting opinion of Henry W. Edgerton of the District of Columbia Circuit in 1947.[142] While stating that "it would not be too surprising if the Supreme Court one day were to hold that a court errs when it dismisses a complaint of this kind," and even indicating how the High Court might do so, Blackmun believed "that each of these approaches at the present time, falls short of justification by us as an inferior tribunal." It was not "for our court, as an inferior one, to give full expression to any personal inclination any of us might have and to take the lead in expanding constitutional precepts when we are faced with a limiting Supreme Court decision which, so far as we are told directly, remains good law."[143] Relief would have to come either by Supreme Court decision or by legislation.

It came both ways. In this very case, the Supreme Court, by a vote of seven to two, held that the 1866 statute applied and had been a valid exercise of congressional power. The Fourteenth Amendment had not, Justice Potter Stewart wrote, been meant to limit the 1866 law to cases of state action. The drafters of the 1866 act would have relied on the Thirteenth Amendment, which authorized Congress to pass "all laws necessary and proper for abolishing all badges and incidents of slavery in the United States."[144] Further, several months before the Supreme Court decision, Congress had passed the Civil Rights Act of 1968 which prohibited housing discrimination.[145] Blackmun would say years later that he was pleased that he had been overruled in *Jones v. Alfred H. Mayer Co.*[146]

REAPPORTIONMENT   The reapportionment cases of the 1960s demonstrate the effective wielding of judicial power in a quintessentially political area. In the Eighth Circuit, this was accomplished by moving relatively slowly and carefully, but not fecklessly, to accustom legislatures to a new, bright-line Supreme Court rule. Federal courts were involved in the reapportionment process in six of the seven states of the Eighth Circuit. In those states, legislative redistricting took place either by court order or under the threat of court order employing guidelines established by the Supreme Court.[147] By law, such cases were to be heard by a three-judge district court constituted by the Chief Judge of the Court of Appeals. In the Eighth Circuit, this meant a Court of Appeals judge and two district judges from the state whose legislative apportionment was challenged. South Dakota was the exception because its legislature reapportioned both houses without the spur of an adverse court ruling.[148]

In *Baker v. Carr,* the Supreme Court held in 1962 that the federal courts had jurisdiction over claims of unconstitutional legislative districting, that voters had standing to bring such suits, and that allegations that the Equal Protection Clause was being violated were justiciable.[149] *Baker v. Carr* opened the way for judicial action to galvanize the political branches into more effective discharge of their political function of working out viable schemes of representation.[150] *Baker* did not, however, lay down a constitutional standard for legislative apportionment. Two years later, the High Court did so in *Wesberry v. Sanders*.[151] There it held that congressional districts must be substantially equal in population. Later in 1964, in *Reynolds v. Sims*,[152] as well as five other cases decided on the same day, the Supreme Court held that the Equal Protection Clause required that both houses of bicameral state legislatures be apportioned equally on a population basis. Space permits a description of the process in three states—Minnesota, where reapportionment occurred first under threat of court order before the Supreme Court decided *Baker v. Carr*; Nebraska, where the unicameral legislature was involved; and Iowa, where the issue affected the state's politics for over fifteen years—followed by much briefer descriptions of the process in Missouri, Arkansas, and North Dakota.

Minnesota was the first state in the circuit to be reapportioned in the era of *Baker v. Carr*.[153] Before 1959, state legislative districts varied in population from 11,730 to 107,000. In 1958 a suit was brought to reapportion the legislature. Judge Edward Devitt denied a motion to dismiss and referred the matter to a three-judge district court. That court stayed its hand, giving the 1959 legislature time to act. Under the threat of court action, the legislature acted that year. The plaintiff then moved to dismiss the suit as moot, which was granted.[154]

While the 1959 reapportionment did not favor or discriminate against any part of the state, it still contained gross disparities between districts. The senatorial districts ranged in population from 24,500 to 100,500; House districts varied from 8,500 to 56,000. This reapportionment was vulnerable under *Reynolds v. Sims* and was struck down on December 5, 1964, by a three-judge court made up of Circuit Judge Blackmun and District Judges Edward J. Devitt and Gunnar H. Nordbye. Blackmun wrote: "Discrimination against some urban areas is not justified because of the simultaneous discrimination against some rural areas. Discrimination is discrimination, wherever it exists and in whatever form it assumes."[155]

The court left the reapportionment to the 1965 legislative session with "every confidence that the Minnesota legislature will fulfill its constitutional obligations."[156] A tug-of-war ensued between Governor Karl Rolvaag and the legislature, resolved by a system that had the effect of shifting seats to metropolitan areas. After charges of gerrymandering and bad faith and the use of computer runs, a relatively fair apportionment ultimately was achieved.[157]

At the time of *Baker v. Carr,* Nebraska had not reapportioned its legislature since 1935. Based on the 1960 census, the most populous district in the Unicameral was more than five times greater in population than the least populous district (101,000 to 19,000). A three-judge district court, constituted of Circuit Judge Johnsen and District Judges Robert Van Pelt and Richard J. Robinson, had, before a 1962 referendum, refused to order at-large elections for either 1962 or 1964, reluctant to interfere with state elections "because of our desire and efforts to maintain a peaceful relationship within the federal system."[158] A state constitutional amendment, adopted in 1962, provided that representation based on population should be given primary emphasis but that some weight was still to be given to geographic area.

In 1963 the legislature reapportioned itself. The Unicameral increased its membership from forty-three to forty-nine and based 20 percent of its district lines on area. In July 1964, three months after the Supreme Court decided *Reynolds v. Sims,* the three-judge court held invalid the 1963 reapportionment, finding that it "did not provide for a substantially equal[ly] effective voice for voters throughout the state." It did, however, permit the 1964 election to be conducted pursuant to the invalidated legislation.[159]

The legislature tried again in 1965, but the court found this apportionment constitutionally defective because of the population deviation caused by the legislature's insistence on adhering to county lines and because the plan appeared to have been drafted with a view toward preventing incumbents from running against one another.[160] The court still refused to impose its own plan but indicated that if the legislature did not act during that current session, it would order an at-large election in 1966. This time, Circuit Judge Johnsen dissented because of his doubt that the reapportionment was "so lacking in rationality . . . as to require it to be held a constitutionally impermissible job and result."[161] Finally, on February 10, 1966, the reapportionment of the Unicameral on a straight population basis was upheld by both state and federal courts.[162]

In Iowa, reapportionment was a major political issue from the 1950s until the early 1970s, reflecting the state's transition from a rural to an urban society. At the beginning of the litigation, apportionment was largely based on a minimum representation for small political units. Rural legislators, who controlled the General Assembly, were unwilling to reapportion and disadvantage their communities.[163] In May 1963, a three-judge court in the Southern District of Iowa, constituted of Circuit Judge Van Oosterhout and District Judges Roy Stephenson and Edward J. McManus, dealt with constitutional attacks both on the existing apportionment and on a constitutional amendment affecting apportionment that was to be put before the voters (the Shaff Plan). The court stated that the Iowa legislature had made a conscientious effort to meet the requirements of the Fourteenth Amendment, but, as Judge Van Oosterhout wrote, the conclusion was "almost unavoidable" that the current apportionment of both houses "transgress the constitutional limits of equal protection."[164] The constitutional amendment (the Shaff Plan) appeared acceptable under the U.S. Constitution as to the state senate, but probably not as to the house of representatives. At this point, the court stayed its hand to avoid unnecessary conflict between federal and state instrumentalities. Judge McManus dissented.

The Shaff Plan was defeated at referendum. In January 1964, the three-judge court ruled that at least one house of the legislature had to be chosen on a strict population basis and the departure from equal population in the other house had to have a rational basis. The court left the matter to the legislature but reserved jurisdiction to consider prescribing an interim plan if no substantial progress was made.[165] In June 1964, after its *Reynolds* decision, the Supreme Court reaffirmed the district court's decisions of 1963 and January 1964 but remanded the case for further proceedings.[166] However, in the meantime, the district court had approved an interim plan of the legislature that materially reduced malapportionment.[167] After the remand, the district court (in 1965) held the formula for the senate invalid but did not decide on the validity of the house formula. By a divided vote (Judge McManus again dissenting), the court did not fix an exact date for legislative compliance, although it enjoined the use of the 1964 formula in 1966.[168]

Ultimate resolution of the problem turned out to be the job of the Iowa Supreme Court, which imposed its own plan in 1972. In the end, Iowa could boast of having the most equitably districted legislature in the nation.[169]

First Amendment Litigation

War, this time in Vietnam, brought First Amendment cases to the circuit again. Several involved claims of symbolic speech. In *United States v. Smith*, a twenty-year-old University of Iowa student was prosecuted for burning his draft card at an antiwar demonstration. Although the trial judge, Roy L. Stephenson (who would later serve on the Court of Appeals) of the Southern District of Iowa, "assumed" that the defendant's act was a form of communication, he held there had been no violation of the First Amendment because he had other, more normal forms of communication open to him. Anticipating the 1968 decision of the Supreme Court in *O'Brien v. United States*,[170] Stephenson refused to look beyond the express purpose of the statute that required Selective Service registrants to have their draft cards with them at all times—the effective and efficient operation of the selective service system. The Court of Appeals upheld the conviction, relying on the reasoning of a Second Circuit opinion by Judge Wilfred Feinberg.[171]

As a district judge, Stephenson also handled the most celebrated First Amendment case in the Eighth Circuit during this period, *Tinker v. Des Moines Independent Community School District*. Three students, two in high school and one in junior high, wore black armbands to school to mourn those who had died in Vietnam and to support indefinite extension of the 1965 Christmas Day truce. Aware of the forthcoming protest, school officials promulgated a regulation prohibiting the wearing of armbands in school. John and Mary Beth Tinker, ages fifteen and thirteen, and Chris Topler Eckhardt, age fifteen, wore armbands and were sent home by school officials for violating the regulation. Through their parents, the children sued for nominal damages and an injunction. Stephenson held that the wearing of armbands was symbolic speech, but that First Amendment rights were not absolute and that the regulation was a reasonable way to avoid classroom disturbances.[172] A Court of Appeals panel heard argument in April 1967 but then, in the same month, ordered reargument en banc, which occurred in October. On November 3, a one-paragraph per curium came down announcing that the judgment of the district court had been affirmed by an equally divided Court of Appeals. There was no Court of Appeals opinion. It seems likely that Judges Lay, Heaney, Van Oosterhout, and Vogel voted to reverse and Judges Blackmun, Mehaffy, Gibson, and Matthes to affirm.[173]

The U.S. Supreme Court, by a vote of 7–2 (Black and Harlan dissenting, Stewart and White concurring), held in a landmark decision that First Amendment rights are available to teachers and students subject to application in the light of the special characteristics of the school environment: "It can hardly be argued that either students or teachers shed their constitutional rights to freedom of speech or expression at the schoolhouse gate."[174] Justice Abe Fortas stated for the Court that a prohibition against expression of opinion without evidence that the rule is necessary to avoid substantial interference with school discipline or the rights of others is unconstitutional under the First and Fourteenth Amendments. "We do not," Fortas wrote, "confine the permissible exercise of First Amendment rights to a telephone booth or the four corners of a pamphlet, or to supervised and ordained discussion in a school classroom."[175] The district court had erred in *Tinker* because there had been no showing that engaging in the forbidden conduct would materially and substantially interfere with the work of the school or impinge on the rights of other students.

Between 1969 and the mid-1980s, *Tinker* served as a precedent in literally hundreds of students' rights cases concerning hair length, discipline, student publications, school elections, plays, and textbook selection.[176] *Tinker* then stood for the proposition that student expression is to be protected under the First Amendment unless it materially disrupts class work or involves substantial disorder or invasion of the rights of others.[177] Eventually the Burger and Rehnquist Courts cut back on *Tinker*, but it remains a landmark case on student rights and on symbolic speech.[178]

As opposition to the Vietnam War grew, many federal judges began to seek flyspecks to overturn convictions of those sincerely objecting to the war. Many years later, Judge Bright explained what he thought had happened:

> Regularly those offenders were brought before the federal courts and judges were giving out pretty stiff sentences. And I think judges on the courts of appeal recognized that here we're putting perfectly fine, intelligent, morally righteous, and religious people into jail. And that just didn't seem right. So, the judges started looking for loopholes in the Selective Service law and found loopholes and found ways to . . . set aside the convictions.[179]

In *Davis v. United States*, a panel of Van Oosterhout, Matthes, and Bright (writing) overturned a conviction of a conscientious objector for willfully refusing induction.[180] It held that Davis, a young community college teacher, had been deprived of his right to appear before his draft board to demonstrate the depth and quality of his beliefs as a conscientious objector. In *United States v. Pence*,[181] decided one day after *Davis*, a panel of Lay (writing), Gibson and Heaney overturned a conviction of a conscientious objector for not submitting to induction because he had been reclassified for punitive reasons. The Court of Appeals concluded that the defendant had been reclassified to I-A either because he had refused to volunteer for civilian work or because he had vocally protested the unfairness of the selective service laws. Neither reason was acceptable.

The Eighth Circuit has never had many cases involving arguably obscene materials. However, in 1968 it overturned convictions in the Northern District of Iowa for violating the federal obscenity statutes.[182] The *Luros* case dealt with nudist and "girlie" magazines (e.g., *Teenage Nudist, Urban Nudist*) and paperback novels primarily dealing with lesbians (*Lesbian Alley*, etc.). Writing for the Court of Appeals, Judge Lay held that the pictures in the nudist magazines were not prurient but "innocuous in their setting." As for the lesbian books, Lay wrote that "they produce high profits for appellants and can be described as distasteful, cheap and tawdry. Yet, these facts alone do not constitute a crime." Lay concluded that "it is far better there be a tight rein on authoritarian suppression ... than that we live in a stifled community of self-censorship."[183]

Criminal Cases

If, before the 1960s, difficult cases involving application of the Fourth, Fifth, and Sixth Amendments had been infrequent in the federal courts (save in the District of Columbia Circuit), that changed because of the increasing number of federal criminal laws and prosecutions, greater availability of defense counsel,[184] incorporation of those amendments to apply to state criminal justice, and, after 1963, the availability of relief in federal courts for state prisoners contending that their constitutional rights had been violated. Between 1957 and 1964, criminal cases occupied 32 percent of the docket of the Court of Appeals for the Eighth Circuit, the third highest among the circuits. That figure rose to 69 percent between 1965 and 1972 (fifth among the circuits). Habeas corpus cases constituted about 1 percent of the docket in the earlier period (the least of the circuits) and 11 percent in the later period (fourth among the circuits).[185] Some of the most important work of the Court of Appeals involved capital cases and cases involving application of the decisions of the Supreme Court dealing with searches and seizures.

One of the most notorious capital cases involved Duane Earl Pope, a twenty-two-year-old white male from Kansas with an apparently untroubled past. Pope had been a popular college athlete and had engaged in a wide range of artistic activities in high school. Seemingly out of the blue, Pope robbed a bank in Big Springs, Nebraska, ordered four bank employees to lie down on the floor, and shot and killed three of them. No clear motive for either the bank robbery or the homicides was uncovered. Pope was convicted before, and sentenced to death by, Judge Robert Van Pelt of the District of Nebraska.[186]

The Court of Appeals heard the case en banc. Judge Blackmun's thorough opinion for the unanimous court covers twenty-seven pages in the *Federal Reporter*. Among the questions discussed are several that would become major issues in forthcoming Supreme Court jurisprudence in capital cases: challenges to potential jurors who did not believe in capital punishment and whether a two-stage trial is constitutionally required in capital cases—one to determine guilt, and the second stage to determine the sentence. On the latter issue, the Eighth Circuit took a middle position. It neither required a two-stage trial nor forbade it.

Judge Blackmun also wrestled in *Pope* with the proper jury instruction on insanity. Perennially controversial, Judge David L. Bazelon's 1954 opinion in *Durham v. United States* for the D.C. Circuit had stimulated reconsideration of the appropriate test for insanity throughout the country.[187] The Eighth Circuit had previously rejected Bazelon's "product of mental disease or defect" standard,[188] but discussed it again in *Pope*. The Court of Appeals did not require that the trial judge use a specific formula, but did expect that three essential elements of sanity— knowledge (cognition), will (volition), and choice (capacity to control behavior)—would be emphasized in the charge.[189] The Eighth Circuit position was close to that of the Second, Third, and Tenth Circuits, all of which had abandoned the right-wrong test of the *M'Naghten* case.[190] When *Pope* was appealed to the Supreme Court, the solicitor general took the position that the death penalty in the statute Pope was prosecuted under, the Federal Bank Robbery Act, suffered from the same constitutional infirmity as that already found by the Supreme Court in the Federal Kidnapping Act. As a result, the Supreme Court vacated the sentence and remanded for new sentencing.[191]

Maxwell v. Bishop was an even harder capital case. Maxwell, an African American, was convicted for the rape of a thirty-five-year-old white woman. His death sentence had been affirmed by the Arkansas Supreme Court. Maxwell's first habeas corpus petition had been denied and the denial affirmed.[192] A second habeas petition was predicated on a statistical study by the noted criminologist Marvin Wolfgang. Wolfgang had attempted to demonstrate that the differential between the percentage of black men given capital sentences for raping white woman and the percentage of white or black men given capital sentences for raping black women could not simply be the result of the law of chance but rather was evidence of unconstitutional racial discrimination by Arkansas juries. The Court of Appeals—Judges Vogel, Matthes, and Blackmun—affirmed.[193] Writing for the court, Judge Blackmun was "not yet ready to condemn and upset the result reached in every case of a black raping a woman in the state of Arkansas on the basis of broad theories of social and statistical injustice." If "the death penalty for rape [was] to be nullified on constitutional grounds that step in the first instance is for the Supreme Court and not for this inferior federal court," said Blackmun.[194] Three years later, as a member of the Supreme Court, Blackmun refused to hold that capital punishment was unconstitutional. He finally abandoned that position in 1994, writing, "From this day forward I no longer shall tinker with the machinery of death."[195]

In *Spinelli v. United States,* a dissent in the Court of Appeals may have led the Supreme Court to grant certiorari and make important new constitutional law.[196] Three years earlier, the Supreme Court had decided *Aguilar v. State of Texas.*[197] In *Aguilar,* a search warrant had been issued on the basis of an affidavit by police officers, who had sworn that they had "reviewed reliable information from a credible person," who had told them that narcotics were being stored on the described premises. The Supreme Court held that probable cause could be satisfied by hearsay, but the affidavit filed by the law enforcement officer had to set forth the underlying circumstances in sufficient detail to enable the magistrate to independently judge the validity of the informant's conclusion. The officer in his affidavit thus had to support his claim that the informant was "credible" and his information "reliable." The case of William Spinelli involved the application of the *Aguilar* rule.

Spinelli had been convicted after trial in the Eastern District of Missouri of interstate travel in aid of racketeering and sentenced to three years' imprisonment and a $15,000 fine. A panel of Van Oosterhout, Heaney, and Gibson (dissenting) reversed the conviction because the evidence of involvement in gambling had been unconstitutionally seized. The Court of Appeals granted the petition of the United States for rehearing en banc and reversed by a vote of six to two.

After lengthy surveillance of Spinelli, the FBI sought arrest and search warrants. The warrants were granted on the basis of an FBI agent's affidavit that he had personal knowledge that Spinelli was a bookmaker, that he or other agents had observed Spinelli crossing the Mississippi River from East St. Louis to St. Louis four times (thus satisfying the interstate travel part of the offense), and that Spinelli had been observed entering a St. Louis apartment, which had two telephones listed under someone else's name. The agent added that the FBI had been told by a confidential, "reliable" informant that Spinelli was involved in wagering by use of the telephone. Using the warrants, the FBI arrested Spinelli and searched the apartment.

The central issue on appeal was the validity of the search warrant. The six-judge majority held that, viewing all the information in the affidavit, the search warrant had been issued with a substantial basis to conclude that gambling business was being conducted on the premises and that Spinelli had been engaged in interstate travel in connection with it. While each piece of information, if viewed in isolation, would probably not independently support a constitutional warrant, "when viewed in their totality, they together form a relatively composite picture of appellant visiting the described apartment for the purpose of conducting gambling activities."[198]

Dissenting, Judge Heaney argued that the "visits" the defendant made to the apartment, the telephones, and the agent's personal knowledge that defendant was a known gambler at most established "suspicion"; it was the informer's information that Spinelli was accepting wagers that ripened suspicion into probable cause. If the hearsay that was the basis for the search warrant was to be relied on, the magistrate had to be informed of the underlying circumstances supporting the affiant's conclusions, and his belief that any informant involved was credible or his information reliable. According to Heaney, what was missing from the affidavit in the Spinelli case was information from which the magistrate could have determined that the informant had furnished reliable information in the past. There also was no showing that the informer had spoken from his own personal knowledge.[199]

A closely divided eight-person Supreme Court reversed, holding that the "totality of the circumstances approach" taken by the Court of Appeals "paints with too broad a brush."[200] The informant's tip in *Spinelli* was not sufficient to provide a basis for a finding of probable cause. The Court emphasized that it was especially important that the tip describe the accused's criminal activity in sufficient detail so that the magistrate may know that he is relying on something more substantial than a casual rumor circulating in the underworld or an accusation based on an individual's general reputation.[201]

In his dissent, Justice Black said that "the Court of Appeals in this case took a sensible view of the Fourth Amendment and I would wholeheartedly affirm its decision.[202] A generation later, the Supreme Court would abandon what had been known as the *Aguilar-Spinelli* rule and turn to the "totality of the circumstances approach" used by the en banc Eighth Circuit majority in *Spinelli*.[203] The day after the *Spinelli* decision, one St. Louis paper ran the headline "Heaney Frees Mobster."[204]

Oversight of Other Federal Policies

During the 1960s, the older federal staples declined, not only as a percentage of the docket of the Court of Appeals but in the significance of the legal issues they presented.

Bankruptcy cases, for example, as a percentage of all cases on the Court of Appeals docket dropped from 5 percent (1949–56) to 2.22 percent (ninth of the eleven circuits) in the period 1957–64 and to 0.83 percent for the years 1967–72 (eighth of the circuits).[205] Tax appeals amounted to 13 percent of the docket from 1957 to 1964, dropping to 4.5 percent from 1965 to 1972.[206] The percentage of labor cases dropped from 13.3 percent (1949–56) to about 7.5 percent for the entire period from 1957 to 1972.[207] During this period, the Court of Appeals was more likely to hold for management (and for the NLRB, if it found against the union) than for unions (or for the labor board, if it had backed unions).

Antitrust cases were also a dwindling part of the docket. There were a few cases of interest. One involved the National Dairy Products Corporation, whose products were sold under Sealtest and Kraft trademarks, among others, indicted for price fixing under the Robinson-Patman Act and for elimination of competition under the Sherman Act. Unable to find prejudicial error, the Court of Appeals affirmed the convictions, which had been reached after a trial with ninety-seven witnesses and six hundred exhibits.[208] However, the Supreme Court reversed the Court of Appeals in a treble damage action against the *St. Louis Globe-Democrat*. The Eighth Circuit had held the newspaper's attempt to protect its policy that entrepreneur carriers charge no more than its suggested retail price "did not hinder, but fostered and actually created competition to the benefit of the public."[209] However, the Supreme Court saw the scheme as one that might "severely intrude upon the ability of buyers to compete and survive."[210]

In *Brown Shoe Co. v. Federal Trade Commission*, the FTC had issued a cease and desist order preventing the company from forcing its retail dealers to sell at noncompetitive resale prices and giving such favored treatment to the franchise stores as free signs, lower fire insurance, special below list prices on certain footwear, merchandising forms, retail sales training programs, and accounting system installation, while requiring that the stores refrain from stocking the shoes of competitors.[211] The Court of Appeals held that Brown Shoe's program was not an unfair method of competition or an unlawful "tying arrangement," or an exclusive dealing arrangement. The Supreme Court reversed.[212]

In several cases, the Court of Appeals curbed the power of federal administrative agencies on federalism grounds, only to be reversed by the Supreme Court. One such case was *Union Electric Company v. FPC*.[213] There the Court of Appeals reviewed an FPC order that had held that the construction by Union Electric of a hydroelectric power plant on the East Fork of the Black River in Reynolds County, Missouri, required a license from the commission because interstate commerce was affected. The Court of Appeals held that Congress had not intended to give the FPC jurisdiction over a project based on a nonnavigable tributary of a navigable river, which had no effect on navigation. For there to be FPC jurisdiction, there had to be an effect on downstream navigability or an irrigation development, flood control project, or planned use of water resources, in other words, matters that might affect water commerce. The project in Union Electric Company was local in character and intrastate in its operation. However, the Supreme Court disagreed, holding that, in passing the law, Congress had drawn on its full authority under the Commerce Clause to require a license for a water power project using the headwaters of a navigable river to generate energy for an interstate power system.[214]

While patent cases were a relatively insignificant portion of the court's work—patent, copyright, and trademark cases made up 3.33 percent of the docket in the years 1957–64 (tied for sixth among the circuits) and 1.25 percent in the years 1965–72 (tied for eighth)[215]—the Eighth Circuit approach to patent claims and several of its cases are worthy of discussion. Long before the 1960s, the U.S. Supreme Court and the Court of Appeals for the Eighth Circuit had been antipatent. From 1939 to 1966, the Supreme Court upheld only two patents, and the Eighth Circuit was hardly more positive.[216] When Congress redrafted the patent law in 1952, it sought with subtlety to reverse the approach of the Supreme Court (and the Eighth Circuit).

Two decisions of the Eighth Circuit interpreting the 1952 patent law—decisions that conflicted with each other—were the vehicles for the first Supreme Court decisions interpreting the statute: *John Deere Co. of Kansas City v. Graham*[217] and *Calmar, Inc. v. Cook Chemical Co.*[218] In the *John Deere* case, a panel of Matthes, Vogel, and Blackmun held a patent for a clamp for vibrating shank plows for chisel plowing invalid for lack of invention. The Eighth Circuit held that to be patentable, a combination of individually old elements must contribute something new and what this device offered was not new enough. In *Calmar*, a panel of Mehaffy, Van Oosterhout, and Ridge upheld the validity of a finger-operated sprayer for a "hold-down" cap for insecticides. The court found this a unique combination of old features in an assemblage that solved production, shipping, and operating problems that for years had beset the insecticide industry. It fulfilled an important need with an economical, utilitarian apparatus that achieved novel results and immediate commercial success.

The Supreme Court held neither patent valid, affirming in *John Deere* and reversing in *Calmar*.[219] For the first time, the High Court ruled that the standards of patentability were constitutional rather than statutory. It also held that the 1952 statute was merely a codification of earlier law and that the standards of invention had never changed. The result of these cases was to maintain the Supreme Court's continued commitment to a standard of invention far higher than that of the patent office.[220]

Regional Cases

In addition to the school desegregation and reapportionment cases, there were a few other areas where distinctively regional problems or fact patterns surfaced. These occurred in cases involving federal attempts to harness and restrain the rivers of the circuit, in cases involving federal farm programs, and in cases spawned by the increased number of military enclaves in the region.

The most regionally distinctive cases involving land and water were related to federal efforts to harness and restrain the rivers of the circuit. The Pick-Sloan Plan to channel and harness the Missouri began in 1946 and was completed in the late 1960s. Four major dams were constructed in South Dakota, and the Garrison Dam in North Dakota. The dams provided electric power, flood control, recreation, public water supplies, and much better nautical transportation at huge expense. Throughout the period battles were fought between the upper basin states (Montana and the Dakotas), where the great need was irrigation, and the more heavily populated states of the lower Mississippi basin (Nebraska, Iowa, and Missouri), where transportation intcrests dominated.[221]

A second major river projecl engendering a great deal of litigation was the McClellan-Kerr Arkansas Navigation Project, which was completed in 1970. With seventeen locks and dams raising water 429 feet, McClellan-Kerr cost $1.2 billion and allowed barge navigation from Tulsa to the Mississippi River, thus making much easier access to international markets for some Arkansas and Oklahoma products, while also providing flood prevention, electric power, and recreation.[222]

United States v. Birnbach involved the condemnation for the McClellan project of 156 acres of land five miles from Little Rock, with a frontage of 1,900 feet on the Arkansas River.[223] The lower court held that the enhancement in value flowing from a riparian location could not be recognized when the riparian character of the land was destroyed by the taking.

On appeal, litigation over condemnation may seem dry, but in the hands of the right judge, the feeling people have for land can be made eloquent. In *United States v. 3,698.63 Acres of Land in Burleigh . . . Counties*, Judge Bright was writing of 338 acres in central North Dakota condemned for the Oahe Dam. At trial, the landowner had testified as to its value and had won a generous award. The issue on appeal was whether the owner should have been allowed to testify to the value of land. The Court of Appeals affirmed. Judge Bright wrote in part:

> Alex Maclean, who had farmed the family land all of his life, described its topography, its many uses and its distinct attributes. He grew small grains and raised and fed cattle. River bottom farming produced high yields of wheat and barley. Timber acreage provided necessary and natural shelter for his cattle summer and winter. A natural spring flowed throughout the year.[224]

There were a few cases involving mines and mining. *Mothner v. Ozark Realty Co.* was a diversity case to establish ownership of the oil and gas underlying real estate in Johnson County, Arkansas.[225] *United*

States v. 339.77 Acres of Land . . . in Johnson and Logan Counties, Arkansas involved the value of an anthracite coal mine in a condemnation action growing out of the Dardanelle Lake and dam project on the Arkansas River.[226]

Cases involving farms and farmers increasingly involved federal programs. *Jones v. Hughes* involved an action by Arkansas cotton producers to review decisions of a market quota committee with respect to cotton allotment under the Agricultural Adjustment Act of 1938.[227] *Johnson v. United States* involved a fraudulent claim under the Soil Bank Conservation Reserve Program by a Missouri farmer.[228] *Jones v. Freeman* arose "out of efforts of the United States Forest Service to keep razorback hogs from foraging in the Ozark National Forest as they have been wont to do for decades."[229] The court held that by permitting the U.S. Forest Service to impound trespassing livestock, assess expenses for doing so to their owners (and, under certain circumstances, sell the animals and retain a portion of the proceeds to cover their expenses), all without a trial-type hearing, the secretary of agriculture had exceeded his delegated powers.

There were cases spawned by the increased number of military enclaves located in the circuit. *Holdridge v. United States* involved three young men who trespassed on the Mead Ordnance Depot in Nebraska, a missile site, to protest nuclear weapons.[230] In a careful opinion by Blackmun, the court rejected contentions that the building of nuclear facilities was a power reserved for the states because it did not promote the "general welfare." The court upheld the statute, one of absolute liability for which criminal intent was not necessary, and rejected a defense based on the First Amendment. Construction of facilities on military bases also led to lawsuits.[231]

Although this was not a period for significant opinions in Native American law, the court did decide cases involving water rights and taxation, criminal appeals, and cases related to the taking of reservation land for construction of the Oahe Dam. During these years, termination of reservations faded as a national policy, while the civil rights revolution sparked congressional interest in better treatment for Native Americans. The last tribe to be terminated was the northern Ponca of Nebraska by the Act of September 5, 1962. The Chippewa on the Turtle Mountain Reservation and the Pottawattamie of Nebraska and Kansas escaped termination. The important developments of the late 1960s—the passage of a number of laws, including the Indian Bill of Rights, and the creation by the Northern Plains Indians of the American Indian Movement (AIM), reflecting and spurring Native American militancy—will be addressed in the following chapter.

Confronting for the first time a docket with consistently visible cases involving civil liberties, the Court of Appeals for the Eighth Circuit did not shy away from the exercise of judicial power. Operating in a jurisprudential atmosphere where doctrines limiting access to the federal courts and traditional principles of deference to the states were being substantially modified and the reach of the Equal Protection Clause greatly enlarged, the Court of Appeals for the Eighth Circuit emerged as a strong supporter of the Supreme Court in civil rights cases and a politically cautious but firm follower of the High Court in reapportionment cases. In First Amendment cases and appeals in criminal cases, the majority of the Court of Appeals was somewhat more conservative than the Supreme Court. The Court of Appeals for the Eighth Circuit was during this period a strong court of able judges. Its work was well crafted and unmarred by internecine disputes.

In the next decade, a moderately liberal court would confront much more work in the area of civil rights, especially cases involving school desegregation and employment discrimination. There would be even more civil liberties cases than before and important institutional litigation requiring oversight of state governmental institutions. Like the other circuits, the Eighth Circuit would encounter important cases in other areas of law—abortion, gender discrimination, and the environment. In addition, one of the traditional regional concerns of the Eighth Circuit, Native American law, would offer important challenges.

Customhouse and Post Office in St. Louis, Missouri, which was completed in 1884. Courtesy of the U.S. Treasury Department, *A History of Public Buildings* (Washington, D.C.: Government Printing Office, 1901), 346–47.

The Honorable David J. Brewer of Kansas served on the U.S. Circuit Courts for the Eighth Circuit from 1884 until his appointment to the U.S. Supreme Court in 1889, where he served until his death in 1910. Courtesy of the Kansas State Historical Society.

The Honorable Willis Van Devanter of Wyoming served on the Eighth Circuit from 1903 until his appointment to the U.S. Supreme Court in 1910, where he served until taking senior status in 1937. Photograph by Underwood & Underwood (1929), Washington, D.C.; courtesy of the Minnesota Historical Society.

The Honorable Walter H. Sanborn, whom Justice Pierce Butler referred to as the "Dean of the Federal Judiciary of the West," served on the Eighth Circuit from the time of his appointment in 1892 until his death in 1928. Courtesy of the Minnesota Historical Society.

Eighth Circuit judges from 1925 to 1928: Wilbur F. Booth, William S. Kenyon, Kimbrough Stone, Walter H. Sanborn, Robert E. Lewis, and Arba S. Van Valkenburgh. Photograph courtesy of the U.S. Courts Library Eighth Circuit, Archives Collection.

St. Paul. Minn.

Post Office and Courthouse in St. Paul, Minnesota, which was completed in
1900. Courtesy of the National Archives, RG 121-C, Box 19, Folder D, Print 22.

Eighth Circuit judges with district judges (standing), circa 1941. Eighth Circuit judges are Seth Thomas, Joseph W. Woodrough, Archibald K. Gardner, Kimbrough Stone, John B. Sanborn, and Harvey M. Johnsen. Photograph courtesy of the U.S. Courts Library Eighth Circuit, Archives Collection.

The Honorable John B. Sanborn served as a federal district judge in Minnesota from 1925 until he was appointed to the Eighth Circuit in 1932, where he remained until his death in 1964. Photograph of oil portrait courtesy of Merry DeCourcy, artist.

The Honorable Charles E. Whittaker of Missouri served as a federal district judge and then on the Eighth Circuit until his appointment to the U.S. Supreme Court in 1957. Photograph courtesy of the U.S. Courts Library Eighth Circuit, Archives Collection.

U.S. Courthouse and Customhouse in St. Louis, Missouri, which was completed in 1935. Photograph courtesy of the National Archives, RG 121-BS, Box 54, Folder OO, Print 3.

Eighth Circuit judges Walter G. Riddick, John B. Sanborn, Seth Thomas, Archibald K. Gardner, Harvey M. Johnsen, Joseph W. Woodrough, and John Caskie Collet, circa 1948. Photograph courtesy of the U.S. Courts Library Eighth Circuit, Archives Collection.

Eighth Circuit judges Martin D. Van Oosterhout, Harvey M. Johnsen, John B. Sanborn, Archibald K. Gardner, Joseph W. Woodrough, Charles J. Vogel, and Marion C. Matthes, circa 1958. They were called the "Integration Court" in reference to their decision in *Faubus v. United States*. Photograph courtesy of the U.S. Courts Library Eighth Circuit, Archives Collection.

The Honorable Harry A. Blackmun works in his chambers in Rochester, Minnesota, circa 1967. He served on the Eighth Circuit from 1959 (when he was appointed to succeed his mentor, the Honorable John B. Sanborn Jr.) until 1970, when he was appointed to the U.S. Supreme Court. Photograph courtesy of the U.S. Courts Library Eighth Circuit, Archives Collection.

The Warren E. Burger Courthouse in St. Paul, Minnesota, which was completed in 1965. Photograph courtesy of the U.S. Courts Library Eighth Circuit, Archives Collection.

Former and current members of the Eighth Circuit, circa 1990. *Seated, left to right*: Theodore McMillian, Donald R. Ross, Myron H. Bright, Harry A. Blackmun, Donald P. Lay, William H. Webster, Floyd R. Gibson, and Gerald W. Heaney. *Standing*: Pasco M. Bowman II, Frank J. Magill, Roger L. Wollman, George G. Fagg, John R. Gibson, Richard S. Arnold, C. Arlen Beam, and J. Smith Henley. Photograph courtesy of the U.S. Courts Library Eighth Circuit, Archives Collection.

The Thomas F. Eagleton Courthouse in St. Louis, Missouri, which was completed in 2000. Photograph by Valerie Jaudon, "Filippine Garden" Collection, 2004; photograph copyright Jay Fram; courtesy of U.S. General Services Administration, Art and Architecture Program, Thomas Eagleton Courthouse, St. Louis, Missouri, and Visual Artists and Gallery Association, New York.

★ ★ ★ ★ ★ ★ ★

CHAPTER 5

The Moderately Liberal Court
of the 1970s

Confronting a docket shaped in many ways by the activism of the Warren and Burger courts as well as recent legislation, during the 1970s the U.S. Court of Appeals for the Eighth Circuit ruled on claims of individual liberty in a remarkable variety of situations. Coming before the court were black children from St. Louis seeking to be educated at desegregated schools, a Nebraska tribe of Native Americans and Iowa farmers each seeking clear title to land created by changes in the course of the Missouri River, thousands of employees of a Minnesota plant that had been dumping possibly deadly mineral wastes into Lake Superior, and the State of Missouri, seeking to end a boycott by the National Organization for Women. Tested before the court in one way or another was the right of a respected obstetrician from Minnesota to perform abortions; the behavior of Davenport, Iowa, police, who had shamed a child murderer into a confession; conditions in the Arkansas prisons; and the behavior of militant Native Americans and federal law enforcement personnel during the violent seventy-one-day takeover of Wounded Knee. While Richard Nixon's appointees to the Supreme Court were constraining High Court activism to a degree, lower federal court judges were, on the whole, more activist during this period than they had been in the 1960s, the result of Supreme Court precedents and appointments made during the Johnson, Nixon, Ford, and Carter administrations.

Such trends marked the work of the Eighth Circuit. Both its docket and the substance of its decisions were markedly different during the

1970s from what they had been when Harry Blackmun was appointed in 1959. New and controversial areas of law were encountered, such as environmental, abortion, and employment discrimination, while difficult new issues arose in more familiar areas of law, such as segregation in the schools of northern cities.

National and Regional Developments

During the 1970s, the United States, rich and powerful though it was, suffered what might be called a political nervous breakdown resulting from the military stalemate and withdrawal from Vietnam, revelations of constitutional abuses and corruption reaching to the presidency and vice presidency, and the belief that, because of dependence on sources of energy outside the country and environmental concerns, the era of rapid national growth was over. But, at least metaphorically, the 1960s were not yet over. The momentum of liberal reform continued as, along with African Americans, other groups pushed for change, among them women, gays, and Native Americans. Reforms were also brought about by the Congress. Responsive to concerns about water and air pollution, pesticides, acid rain, and toxic waste, Congress, in the late 1960s and early 1970s, passed a series of statutes extending federal power to prohibit practices viewed as destructive of the environment. Congress also enacted laws expanding federal power over campaign finance, voting, pensions, bankruptcy, and safety in the workplace.

During the 1970s, the U.S. Supreme Court was less sympathetic to racial civil rights claims than it had been when Earl Warren was Chief Justice, less generous about access to the federal courts, and tougher on the rights of criminal defendants. Yet the Burger Court upheld affirmative action programs, applied the Equal Protection Clause to claims of gender discrimination, and, in its most controversial decision, expanded a judicially created right to privacy to encompass the right of a woman to choose whether or not to have a child.

The major developments giving a regional flavor to the docket of the Court of Appeals for the Eighth Circuit during the 1970s were the environmental movement and Native American militancy. In addition, the state of Missouri began to reap the whirlwind of its racist past, while the antipathy of state legislatures to the newly recognized right of women to choose whether or not to bear a child spurred a series of laws attempting to constrain abortions, which, in turn, led to much visible litigation, especially in Missouri and Minnesota.

Among the other developments affecting the region was an agricultural boom spurred by the 1972 wheat deal between the United States and the Soviet Union. The effects of that agreement, coupled with federal tax policy, led to larger and larger farms worked on by fewer and fewer persons. While in states such as Iowa, agricultural modernization was spurred by agribusinesses,[1] as farmers left the farm, small businesses in nearby towns began to close. The Dakotas and Nebraska were becoming part of the "unpeopled west."[2] Even in North Dakota, though, greater productivity, farm consolidations, and electrification allowed farmers to close what had once been a massive gap between themselves and people living in towns. Great Plains states such as North Dakota also profited from an enormously favorable fiscal relationship with the federal government, the result of farm subsidies, tax breaks, and military bases. On the other hand, transportation became more of a problem in the 1970s as railroad lines were abandoned and airline service to many communities discontinued; during the wintertime there were shortages in boxcars and trucks on the Great Plains.[3] However, Mississippi valley states such as Minnesota and Missouri had successful, diverse economies, while the manufacturing sector continued to grow in Arkansas.[4]

Judicial Administration

During the 1970s, the press of cases on the federal courts was inexorable. Their number doubled between 1971 and 1981. In addition to the effects of Supreme Court jurisprudence of the 1950s and 1960s and litigation generated by its more recent jurisprudence involving gender discrimination, abortion, and capital cases (among others), year after year Congress passed legislation adding to federal jurisdiction. There was environmental legislation, consumer-oriented legislation, legislation affecting pensions, and new federal criminal laws. Some of this legislation, such as that affecting the environment, was highly complex. Congress also passed laws affecting the way the courts did business, laws such as the Speedy Trial Act, the Judicial Councils Reform and Judicial Conduct and Disability Act, and the Bankruptcy Reform Act.

The bottom line for the courts of appeals, the caseload, was that 12,788 appeals were docketed in the eleven courts of appeals in 1971, of which 713 were in the Eighth Circuit. In 1980, 23,200 appeals were docketed, 983 of them in the Eighth Circuit.[5] One way to keep up was to add new judgeships. One additional judgeship was created for the Eighth Circuit by statute on October 20, 1978. A second method was essentially to surround the judges with an ever-increasing bureaucracy: more law clerks, central legal staffs, and greater reliance by federal district judges on magistrate judges, assigned a wide variety of tasks, including hearing prisoner complaints and Social Security cases. Judges, circuit and district, spent more time managing staffs and less time deciding cases themselves.[6] A third response to mounting caseloads, one closely identified with Chief Justice Warren Burger, was to try to make the federal judiciary function more efficiently. The management of many courts was streamlined. All these methods coupled with hard judicial labor enabled the federal courts to stay abreast of their work.[7]

Much of the responsibility for management of the lower federal courts fell to the Chief Judges of the Courts of Appeals. During the 1970s, the Eighth Circuit had five Chief Judges: Martin D. Van Oosterhout, who had begun his chief judgeship in 1968 and completed it in 1970; Marion C. Matthes, from 1970 to 1973; Pat Mehaffy, for some months in 1973; Floyd Gibson, from 1974 to 1979; and Donald Lay, who began a twelve-year chief judgeship in 1980.

But even streamlined management required additional personnel. The Chief Judges were aided by circuit executives, a position created by Congress in 1971. The circuit executive was made responsible for "such duties as may be delegated to him by the Circuit Council."[8] Marion C. Matthes was Chief Judge when the first circuit executive, Robert J. Martineau, was appointed in 1972. Martineau, a graduate of the University of Chicago Law School, had been law clerk to the Chief Judge of the Maryland Court of Appeals, practiced law, and taught as a law professor of the University of Iowa. Martineau was succeeded by R. Hanson Lawton in 1975 and Lawton by Lester C. Goodchild in 1980. In the Eighth Circuit, the circuit executive became involved with matters of budget, personnel, accounting, record-keeping, and space management and served as liaison to the Judicial Council.[9]

Among the other staff positions created to assist the judges was the central legal staff, which evolved from funding approved by Congress in 1975 allowing the chief judge of each circuit to appoint a central law clerk. By 1991, the Eighth Circuit had a central legal staff of twenty-one responsible for motion practice, case screening, pro se cases, and rules committee work.[10] When Congress authorized the appointment of a senior staff attorney in 1980, Timothy E. Gammon was the first person named to that position in the Eighth Circuit.[11]

The Judges

Six judges were appointed to the Court of Appeals for the Eighth Circuit between 1971 and 1980. Even in 1971, a new, tentative majority of judges particularly sensitive to civil liberties concerns, Johnson and Nixon appointees, was developing. During the 1970s, it was, on the whole, the court's senior judges who were the more conservative judges, although the gap between the two groups was not large.

Donald Roe Ross (1922–) was appointed in 1971 by Richard Nixon to replace Harry Blackmun. Ross was born in Orleans, Nebraska, on June 8, 1922. He received his undergraduate and law degrees from the University of Nebraska. Serving in the U.S. Army Air Corps during the war, Ross flew forty-six missions and was twice awarded the Distinguished Flying Cross. He practiced law in Lexington (in southwestern Nebraska) with Cook & Ross from 1948 to 1953, and in Omaha with Swarr May from 1956 to 1970. He also served as vice president and general counsel of ConAgra (Nebraska Consolidated). At the age of thirty-one, Ross became mayor of Lexington, Nebraska, by winning a nonpartisan election. Ross served as U.S. Attorney for the District of Nebraska from 1953 to 1956, as general counsel to Nebraska's Republican Party (1956–58), and as a member of the Republican National Committee. After the rout of Barry Goldwater in the 1964 presidential election, Ross became vice chairman of the national Republican Party and played an important role in healing the party's wounds and making it viable again.[12]

While it might have been expected that the seat vacated by Harry Blackmun in 1970 would go to a Minnesotan, at the time of Blackmun's elevation, that state had no Republican senators. With the assistance of Nebraska Senator Roman Hruska, an influential member of the Senate Judiciary Committee, Ross received the appointment.[13]

Ross had been a moderate liberal jurist, sensitive to discrimination suffered by minorities and women. In many cases during the 1970s, Ross joined Judges Lay, Heaney, and Bright (the "liberal wing"), although in criminal cases and cases involving business interests he has been more conservative.[14] Ross took senior status in 1987.

Roy Stephenson (1917–82), the trial judge in the *Tinker* case, was named by Nixon to the Court of Appeals in 1971 to replace Judge Van Oosterhout. Born in Spirit Lake, Iowa, he earned his B.A. from Iowa State University and law degree from the University of Iowa. During World War II, Stephenson rose to the rank of captain in the infantry, serving in Tunisia and Italy. Remaining in the National Guard after the war, Stephenson ultimately held the rank of colonel. He practiced in Des Moines with Fountain, Bridges, Lundy & Stephenson (1946–53). From 1953 to 1960, Stephenson was U.S. Attorney for the Southern District of Iowa. President Eisenhower appointed Stephenson U.S. district judge for the Southern District of Iowa in 1960, a position he served in until his elevation to the Court of Appeals.

As a district judge, Stephenson was tough on criminal defendants and tax evaders and generally hostile to attempts to use the courts to reverse decisions affecting students made by school boards and colleges. As a judge of the Court of Appeals, Stephenson was a moderate, slightly less liberal than Judge Ross, but sympathetic to the rights of women and Native Americans, as well as to abortion rights. Stephenson took senior status in April 1982. Six months later, on the day a retirement dinner in his honor was scheduled, he died by his own hand after hearing that his wife had terminal cancer.[15]

William Webster (1924–), who served five years as a judge of the U.S. Court of Appeals, is better known for his tours of duty as director of the Federal Bureau of Investigation (1978–87) and Central Intelligence Agency (1987–91). Taking over both positions at critical times for the agencies, Webster helped restore the reputation and morale of each. Webster was born in St. Louis, attended Amherst College, and received his law degree from Washington University in 1949. He practiced law in St. Louis, where he was responsible for the development of the Master Charge system of nationwide bank credit.[16] Webster was U.S. Attorney for the Eastern District of Missouri for the years 1960–61. He was appointed to the U.S. District Court for the Eastern District of Missouri in 1971 by Richard Nixon, who elevated him to the Court of Appeals in 1973 to replace Judge Matthes. As a judge, Webster can properly be described as a moderate conservative.

J. Smith Henley (1917–97) was born in St. Joe, Arkansas, in 1917 into a family of attorneys. No model student, Henley never formally graduated from high school and seems to have been thrown out of college once.[17] He did, however, graduate from the University of Arkansas with a law degree in 1941. From 1941 to 1954, Henley practiced law in Harrison, Arkansas. He served as city clerk and referee in bankruptcy in the Western District of Arkansas briefly. An Eisenhower Republican, Henley came to Washington in 1954 to head the litigation division of the Federal Communications Commission. He left the FCC in 1956 to head the Office of Administrative Procedure of the Department of Justice (later the Administrative Conference of the United States). Henley was appointed to the U.S. District Court in February 1958. He served for eighteen months by recess appointments, as his confirmation was delayed because of the politics of the Little Rock crisis. In September 1959, he took the oath of office as a roving judge (judge of both the Eastern and Western Districts of Arkansas). For many years Chief Judge of the Eastern District of Arkansas, Henley at one point had a dozen or more school desegregation cases before him. He also "desegregated" housing at the University of Arkansas, public parks, and swimming pools.[18]

Because of a desire by segregationists for a more pliable district judge in civil rights cases, talk of elevating Henley to the Court of Appeals began as early as 1962. When Judge Mehaffy took senior status, Henley was slated as his successor, but the appointment was delayed by the resignation of President Nixon.[19] In 1975 he was elevated by President Ford.[20] Henley took senior status in 1982 and died in 1997 at the age of eighty.[21]

Although Henley probably will be most remembered as the overseer of Arkansas's prisons (discussed later in this chapter), he actually believed that "as far as the government in general is concerned, except for certain basic functions, I'm against it, always have been and still am," and that "the federal courts are being used to seek redress for grievances never intended by Congress."[22]

With the election of Jimmy Carter, the White House, rather than the home-state senator, became the dominant voice in the appointment of court of appeals judges.[23] Judge Theodore McMillian (1919–2006), the first African American to be a member of the Court of Appeals for the Eighth Circuit, was born in St. Louis, the son of a factory worker and the great-grandson of slaves. The eldest of ten children, McMillian attended a segregated St. Louis school, Stowe Teachers College, and Lincoln University, the only four-year institution of higher education in Missouri then open to African Americans. After McMillian graduated from Lincoln, Phi Beta Kappa with majors in mathematics and physics, he could find employment only as a dining-car waiter. After serving in the military during World War II, McMillian was unable to get into medical school because of his race. Instead he attended St. Louis University Law School, where he graduated at the top of his class. McMillian set up his practice but needed to supplement his income by work as busboy, movie projector operator, janitor, and adult-education teacher.

Appointed an assistant St. Louis circuit attorney, McMillian earned a reputation as a brilliant trial lawyer. When Governor Phil M. Donnelly appointed him to the Missouri Circuit Court in 1956, McMillian became the first African American judge in the history of Missouri. As juvenile court judge for six and one-half years, McMillian brought to his work a deep understanding of the problem of poverty. In 1972, Governor Warren E. Hearnes appointed McMillian to the Missouri Court of Appeals. In 1978, President Carter appointed him to the seat on the U.S. Court of Appeals left vacant by William H. Webster.[24] Deeply concerned with the First Amendment rights of students and constitutional protections for criminal defendants, McMillian was an ardent civil libertarian and the court's most frequent dissenter.[25]

Richard Sheppard Arnold was appointed to the Court of Appeals by President Carter in 1980. Arnold came from a family that has included Arkansas lawyers and judges dating back to 1880. The progenitor, William Hendrick Arnold of Texarkana, was president of the Arkansas bar and special associate justice of the Arkansas Supreme Court. Richard Arnold's brother, Morris "Buzz" Arnold, was appointed to the Court of Appeals for the Eighth Circuit in 1992 by President George Bush. Richard and Morris Arnold's mother, Janet Sheppard Arnold, was the daughter and stepdaughter of U.S. senators from Texas.

Born in 1936, Richard S. Arnold graduated from Yale College and Harvard Law School first in his class. After clerking for Justice William Brennan, Arnold practiced law in Washington before returning to an impressive small-town practice in Texarkana, defending corporations and representing civil rights plaintiffs. Arnold worked for Governor and Senator Dale Bumpers and ran unsuccessfully for Congress. In 1978 he was sworn in as judge of Arkansas's Eastern and Western Districts.[26] Serving as Chief Judge of the Court of Appeals for the Eighth Circuit from 1992 to 1998, Arnold rendered yeoman service to the federal judiciary as chairman of the Judicial Conference's Budget Committee (Senator Bumpers was a member of the Senate appropriations subcommittee that was handling the judiciary's budget) and as a member of the Conference's Executive Committee. At the time Arnold stepped down as Chief Judge (so that Pasco Bowman could serve in that position), the U.S. Judicial

Conference passed a resolution honoring him, which stated in part: "Recognized throughout the Judiciary for his gifted intellect, integrity and statesmanlike demeanor, Judge Arnold has contributed selflessly and immeasurably to the administration of the federal court system."[27]

As a member of the Court of Appeals, Arnold may be described as a moderate liberal. He is regarded throughout the nation as a superb jurist and appears to have been a serious contender for the vacancies on the U.S. Supreme Court that ultimately were filled by Ruth Bader Ginsburg and Stephen Breyer.[28]

By the end of the 1970s, the court's liberals and moderate liberals then included appointees of Johnson, Nixon, and Carter, while its somewhat more conservative judges were Van Oosterhout, Mehaffy, Floyd Gibson, and Henley. The court continued to be a good-humored, collegial court, although some of the collegiality had been lost as a result of the size of the court, more frequent turnover (in part, because of the attractions of senior status, and in part because of the need for more judges), because of the increased attention that was necessary to oversee larger staffs, and because the judges were not staying at the same hotel when they were in St. Louis. It should also be remembered that, as it had for much of its history, the Court of Appeals made ample use of district judges to constitute panels. Much less frequent was the use of judges from other circuits, although Judge Talbot Smith of the Eastern District of Michigan sat with the court quite frequently. Retired Supreme Court Justice Tom C. Clark also sat on a few cases during this period.

Jurisprudence

The most visible work of the Court of Appeals of the Eighth Circuit would not have been found on the court's docket twenty-five years before. There was a steady flow of cases embodying clashes of political and social values—school desegregation cases from large cities like St. Louis and Kansas City, review of laws passed to constrain abortions (enacted particularly in Missouri and Minnesota), difficult environmental cases, litigation over the First Amendment and due process rights of public school and university students, a first round of gender discrimination cases, civil and criminal cases involving claimed violations of the Fourth and Fifth Amendments, and a constant flow of cases involving Native Americans. In addition, the Court of Appeals was supervising the judge who was overseeing the management of the Arkansas prison system.

Some of these cases involved new areas of law, such as environmental issues, employment discrimination, and abortion, while others presented difficult new issues in more familiar areas of law, such as segregation in the unitary school systems of northern cities and affirmative action.

In addition to the large number of new federal statutes, there were many causes of the increase in the number of cases embodying clashes of social and political values: increased group militancy; recognition of new rights by the Warren Court in the sixties and Burger Court in the seventies, especially the nationalization of the Bill of Rights and invigoration of the Equal Protection Clause; liberalized access to the courts; the greater accessibility to counsel by criminal defendants and the poor; the growth of the public interest bar; the promise of attorneys' fees in civil rights and other cases. Furthermore, many liberal judges began to see themselves as protectors of those who received little protection in the political process.[29]

Fewer in number and generally raising less important questions were the federal staples of the past—admiralty, bankruptcy, patent, and taxation.[30] There were two antitrust actions of particular interest, however. *Pfizer v. Government of India* involved litigation brought by the governments of India and four other nations against six major drug companies. In an interlocutory appeal, the Court of Appeals in opinions by Judge Lay—written for the panel and adopted by en banc court—held that foreign countries were "persons," entitled to sue under the Clayton Act for treble damages. The Supreme Court affirmed by a 5–4 vote.[31]

Mackey v. National Football League involved the legality of professional football's "Rozelle Rule" (named for the NFL Commissioner, Alvin Ray "Pete" Rozelle) under the antitrust laws.[32] The Rozelle Rule essentially provided that when a player's contractual obligation to a team expired and he signed with a different club, the signing club had to provide compensation to the former team. If the two teams were unable to agree on the compensation, the commissioner had the authority to decide. The Rozelle Rule was an effective deterrent to the signing of free agents without negotiating a prior agreement on compensation with the previous owner. Sixteen football players were the plaintiffs; the NFL, the commissioner, and the twenty-six clubs were the defendants. The players argued that the practice was an illegal combination and conspiracy in restraint of trade, denying professional football players the right to freely contract for their services.

Judge Earl R. Larson of the District of Minnesota presided over a

fifty-day trial and held that the Rozelle Rule both constituted a con-
certed refusal to deal and a group boycott, and, therefore, was a per se
violation of the Sherman Act and also that it ran afoul of that statute's
rule-of-reason standard.[33] The Court of Appeals affirmed on the rule-of-
reason standard. Recognizing that the National Football League "has a
strong and unique interest in maintaining competitive balance among its
teams," the court rejected its argument that the labor exemption to the
antitrust laws immunized the Rozelle Rule from antitrust liability.[34]

While the docket of the Court of Appeals for the Eighth Circuit
now closely resembled that of the other circuits (save the District of
Columbia), there were some areas of law that were still primarily shared
(at least in quality) with only a few of the other circuits, most particularly litigation affecting Native Americans and resulting from large
waterway projects (discussed in the following chapter). There were also
cases reminding the court of the continued importance of agriculture
to the region, such as those involving companies accused of violating
the Packers and Stockyards Act by fraudulent weighing,[35] and the review of ICC orders approving tariff schedules by rail carriers of grain.[36]
Finally, while all circuits shared in the surfeit of environmental cases,
there were cases in the Eighth Circuit that vividly reminded the court of
some of the region's most attractive features.

While the Eighth Circuit continued to be an obedient court, faithful to Supreme Court precedent, in those areas where there was room
for choice among Supreme Court precedents or those not yet treated by
the High Court, the circuit demonstrated considerable sympathy for civil
liberties claims. This was particularly evident in gender discrimination
cases and cases involving the rights of students. Indeed, the Court of
Appeals for the Eighth Circuit was generally more sympathetic to claims
of constitutional or statutory rights than the district courts of the Eighth
Circuit or the U.S. Supreme Court under Chief Justice Warren Burger.
The court attacked segregation in northern cities as vigorously as it had
segregation in Arkansas; made major contributions to the developing
law of employment discrimination; stood solidly by the seminal precedent in the area of abortion, *Roe v. Wade*; and was sympathetic to judicial
oversight of prison conditions. The Court of Appeals was more liberal
than the Burger Supreme Court in criminal cases and, in cases involving procedural due process, caught up and forged ahead of the Supreme
Court. The court was also relatively sympathetic to the claims of Native Americans. In its most important environmental case, the Court

of Appeals made a conscious effort to balance environmental concerns with the protection of jobs.

During these years, collegiality continued to reign, although some of the old intimacy faded, and disagreements led to more dissents, more published dissenting opinions, more rehearings en banc, and more cases where two, three, or four members of the court dissented from denial of rehearing en banc. Nevertheless, in registering disagreement, the opinions of the judges continued to be unmarked by the querulousness demonstrated by many other courts.

Civil Rights

During the 1970s, the Court of Appeals continued to be a firm friend of racial equality. Important civil rights cases were concentrated in two areas—school desegregation and employment discrimination. In 1969, the U.S. Supreme Court finally held that "the obligation of every school district is to terminate dual systems at once and to operate now and hereafter only unitary schools."[37] School desegregation cases from Arkansas began to tail off as dual school systems were phased out among the holdouts of eastern Arkansas.[38] From 1971 to 1977, only nine cases came to the Court of Appeals from Arkansas. In many of the Arkansas cases, Judge Henley, who was tending to give the school boards too much time to desegregate, was reversed.[39]

The Little Rock schools case continued to drag on. In 1973, the school district and the minority community agreed to work together toward bringing about complete desegregation. Beginning with the 1973–74 school year, all grades in the Little Rock schools were desegregated.[40]

In the 1970s, the Supreme Court finally began to pay attention to the problem of segregated schools in the North and West, handing down three particularly significant decisions. In *Swann v. Charlotte-Mecklenburg Board of Education*, a Southern case, the Supreme Court permitted federal district judges considerable discretion in shaping remedies to end school segregation but pointedly confined racial quotas to use only as a starting point.[41] In *Milliken v. Bradley*, the Court held that suburban school systems could not be compelled to integrate with center city schools to alleviate center city school segregation, unless it was shown that the suburban districts had been affirmatively segregated.[42] Lastly, in *Dayton Board of Education v. Brinkman*, the Court held that there had been no formal desegregation, proof of intent to discriminate was essential.[43] If that was found, the segregation had to be eliminated root and branch. The Court also held that in a desegregation case, the court was not to prescribe a remedy broader than that required by the necessities of the case. Lower courts had to determine the incremental effect the constitutional violations had and what the racial distribution would have been in the absence of constitutional violations. Only where system-wide segregation existed would a system-wide remedy be justified. Finally, the High Court limited the obligation of school authorities in districts where mandatory racial segregation had long ceased to the elimination of the "incremental segregative effect."

Important desegregation cases were brought in Minneapolis and Omaha, while two blockbuster cases involved Missouri's two largest cities, St. Louis and Kansas City. When the Minneapolis case was brought in 1971, the Minneapolis School District had 56,000 white students, 6,000 black students and 2,225 Native American students. The minority school population was concentrated in a few schools. The trial judge, Earl R. Larson, found that, at least since 1954, the public schools of Minneapolis had been racially segregated. The segregation that continued had, in part, existed because of actions the school board had taken. Larson held that the segregation had to be eliminated.[44] He strengthened the desegregation/integration plan submitted by the school board and approved it. His decree established guidelines for percentages of minority students that might be enrolled in the schools of the district, forbade further school construction without judicial approval, and required the board to submit semiannual status reports to the court.[45]

In 1978, the board renewed a request for dissolution of the injunction. Larson refused the request, as well as another that would have permitted the school board to increase minority enrollments in individual schools, particularly in schools having a high concentration of Native American students.[46]

On appeal, the Eighth Circuit deferred to Judge Larson because of his "familiarity with this case and the problems that it presents." It noted that, before 1978, Larson had filed a total of at least fourteen opinions and orders in the case, none of which had been appealed by the school board. The Supreme Court denied certiorari.[47] Larson would retain control of the case for a total of twelve years to ensure compliance with the court's rulings.

In 1973, the United States sued the School District of Omaha, claiming that it was segregated and that the segregation had been created and maintained by the school board. Eighty percent of Nebraska's African Americans lived in Omaha, and 90 percent of them lived in the near north side of the city. Black unemployment in Omaha was ten times higher than the state's average. Looting, arson, and violence had occurred there in 1966, 1968, and 1969.[48]

Although the trial judge in the Omaha case, Albert G. Schatz of the District of Nebraska, found Omaha's schools to be racially imbalanced, he did not hold the school board accountable. Schatz found that the board had had no intent to segregate when it changed the boundaries of school districts and established junior high schools, as well as in its use of feeder schools and a special transfer system, in the maintenance of optional attendance zones, or even in hiring the small number of black faculty.[49]

The Court of Appeals was less ready to stand by Judge Schatz than Judge Larson. A panel of Heaney (writing), Bright, and Jones (of the Fifth Circuit) reversed, holding that once it had been established that school authorities had engaged in acts or omissions, the natural, probable, and foreseeable consequence of which was to bring about or maintain segregation, a presumption of "segregative intent" arose. The burden then shifted to the school board to establish that "segregative intent was not among the factors that motivated their actions."[50] The Court of Appeals found substantial evidence that the actions and inactions of Omaha's school board had the natural, probable, and foreseeable consequence of creating and maintaining segregation in such areas as faculty assignment, student transfers, optional attendance zones, and school construction, and that the board had been unable to establish that segregative intent was not one of the factors that had motivated its actions. The Court of Appeals held that racial discrimination in the Omaha public schools had to be eliminated root and branch. Certiorari was denied.[51]

Judge Schatz then promulgated an extensive desegregation plan, which included the system-wide transportation of pupils.[52] The plan was accepted in almost every respect by the en banc Court of Appeals.[53] However, the Supreme Court then remanded for the Court of Appeals to decide whether the systemic remedy was in compliance with the *Dayton* case.[54]

The Court of Appeals then reexamined its holding of intentional segregation and concluded unanimously that the evidence was clear that a discriminatory purpose had been a motivating factor behind the school board's actions. It remanded in turn to the district court to make sure that the remedial plan was not more extensive than was warranted by the incremental segregative effect.[55]

THE ST. LOUIS SCHOOL DESEGREGATION CASE   In the 1970s and 1980s, the major front in the battle for desegregated schools shifted from Arkansas to Missouri and was dominated by litigation involving the schools in the state's two largest cities, St. Louis and Kansas City. While Missouri generally escaped the determined and violent opposition to integration that occurred in the Deep South, the process in Missouri was far from easy.[56] In many respects, Missouri was a southern state and St. Louis a southern city. A state public accommodations law was not passed until 1965 and a fair housing law until 1972.[57]

Before the Civil War, Missouri, a slave state, had tried its utmost to discourage education for free African Americans. As Judge Gerald Heaney has written, "Not only would black students be barred from attending public schools, but efforts would be made to prevent them from receiving an education in homes or churches."[58] To evade state law, those trying to educate blacks during the antebellum period went so far as to hold classes on a steamship anchored in the Mississippi River.[59] By the end of Radical rule in Missouri after the Civil War, school segregation was firmly established. The state's 1875 constitution "elevated segregation to constitutional scripture."[60]

In the twentieth century, segregation was perpetuated by formal residential segregation and white flight from the center city.[61] When the U.S. Supreme Court held unconstitutional in 1938 Missouri's offer to pay an African American's tuition to an out-of-state law school instead of admitting him to the state's whites-only law school,[62] it took almost a decade for the University of Missouri to comply. From 1940 to 1970, the white population of St. Louis declined by 500,000, while the black population increased by 150,000. Although St. Louis's Catholic schools were effectively desegregated in 1947, attempts made to integrate the St. Louis public schools between 1950 and 1954 were unsuccessful.[63] As late as the mid-twentieth century, African American schools received less funding than white schools.[64] At the time *Brown* was pending in the Supreme Court, a facial challenge to Missouri's segregated schools was pending. The Court of Appeals heard oral argument on the appeal of a decision upholding the segregated schools but withheld judgment until *Brown* was decided.[65] After 1954, discriminatory practices affecting housing continued to exist—failure to enforce building codes, redlining, and separate colored advertisements in the newspapers.

As of 1970, Missouri had a population of 480,000 African Americans out of a total population of 4.7 million. Eighty-six percent of Missouri's blacks lived in the St. Louis and Kansas City areas. African Americans constituted 30 percent of the population of St. Louis and of Kansas City. In 1970 the income of an average black family in St. Louis was 25 percent lower than that of an average white family.[66]

In St. Louis, neighborhood schools were the basic method of assignment in a racially segregated city. As of June 1974, of the ten high schools in St. Louis, three were 100 percent black, and two were 90 percent black. Three were 90 percent white. Forty-eight elementary schools were 100 percent black, forty-four were 90 percent black, fifteen were 100 percent white, and twenty-four were equally divided.[67] (In Kansas City, 63 percent of the schools had at least 95 percent of the student body of one race).

Judge Gerald Heaney, who has been deeply involved in the St. Louis desegregation litigation, has written that "more than any other person Minnie Liddell was responsible for the integration of the St. Louis city and adjacent St. Louis County public schools."[68] It was Liddell who galvanized black parents to file the lawsuit in the Eastern District of Missouri against the city school board, individual board members, the school superintendent, and others, asking the court to order the school board to operate the schools within the requirements of the Fourteenth Amendment. Liddell not only initiated the litigation but pursued it until 1984, when a comprehensive plan to desegregate the city and county schools was approved by the federal courts.[69]

Based on the school board's denial that it had operated a segregated school system, but also on its recognition that there was racial imbalance in the school system, a consent decree was adopted in the *Liddell* case in 1975. The decree provided for neighborhood schools, enjoined discrimination, and required the board to take affirmative action to secure plaintiffs their right to attend racially nonsegregated and nondiscriminatory schools. It provided any new school facilities would be located with the objective of eradicating segregation in the public schools and committed the board to progressively increase the number of black teachers.[70] This would be, however, but the opening stage in litigation that would last a quarter century.

Judge James H. Meredith denied the NAACP's attempt in 1976 to intervene in the case for other plaintiffs. The Court of Appeals reversed and "suggested" to the district court that it also invite intervention by the Department of Justice and the Missouri Board of Education, and that the district court investigate whether school districts in St. Louis County would accept minority transfers.[71]

The St. Louis desegregation case was tried from November 1977 to May 1978. Mcredith's exhaustive opinion was released almost a year after the trial ended (April 12, 1979). He held that the plaintiffs had failed to meet their burden of demonstrating that there had been intentional segregation by the St. Louis School Board. Although Meredith did not object to the school board's receiving assistance from adjoining school districts, he opined that the only way desegregation could be achieved was by such quality education being offered within the City of St. Louis, which the County could not duplicate.[72]

In 1980, the Court of Appeals reversed in an en banc unanimous opinion specifically signed by every member of the court. It rejected Judge Meredith's finding that the city board had had no control over the factors that were substantially responsible for the segregation in St. Louis's schools. The court held that the board's neighborhood attendance policy had failed to fulfill its affirmative duty to take whatever steps were necessary to convert to a unitary system in which racial discrimination would be eliminated root and branch. The Court of Appeals rejected the school board's plan, remanded to the district court with instructions, and held that the city board had the principal responsibility for developing a comprehensive plan to integrate the school system by 1980–81.[73]

Two months later, Meredith approved a comprehensive desegregation plan that provided for an increase in the number of magnet schools and employed busing for integration and to deal with overcrowding. Holding that the state of Missouri had a responsibility to correct the effects of such discrimination, Meredith made the state responsible for funding half the costs of the desegregation plan up to a total of $11.1 million for the 1980–81 school year, and one-half the cost of desegregation thereafter, subject to such adjustments the court deemed necessary and proper.[74] Meredith recognized that the board plan, although conforming to the Court of Appeals mandate, would not provide a fully desegregated education for every black child in this school system, but held that it offered "the promise of providing the 'greatest possible degree of actual desegregation,' taking into account the practicalities of the situation."[75] Further, every possible effort was to be made to try to work out cooperative plans of pupil exchanges with other school districts in St. Louis County.

Meredith's last order before resigning from the case for reasons of health came in December 1980, when he ordered the state to submit another voluntary plan.[76] The next stages of the St. Louis case are discussed in the following chapter, as is the Kansas City school litigation brought in 1977.

EMPLOYMENT DISCRIMINATION The 1970s were the formative era for interpretation of Title VII of the 1964 Civil Rights Act, which banned discrimination in employment. The Court of Appeals heard sixty cases between 1971 and 1977 involving allegations of discrimination based on race and reversed the district courts about half the time.[77] Perhaps the two most important job discrimination opinions were written by Judge Bright—*Parham v. Southwestern Bell Telephone Co.*[78] and *Green v. McDonnell-Douglas Corp.*[79]

The *Parham* case involved a black applicant for a job as a lineman. While Southwestern Bell admitted that it had discriminated against African Americans in the past, it insisted that it was no longer doing so at the time Parham applied for the job. There were two important aspects to the *Parham* decision by the Court of Appeals. First, the court held as a matter of law that the failure of an individual's claim did not preclude granting relief to the class subject to discrimination. Second, the Court of Appeals accepted simple statistics as to the extremely small percentage of minorities employed by Southwestern Bell (most of whom were in menial positions) to establish past discrimination as a matter of law. Bright wrote that "statistics often tell much and Courts listen."[80] *Parham* is among the most frequently cited Title VII cases, especially for the use of statistics to establish that, as a matter of law, an employer was engaging in discriminatory employment practices. The legal principles articulated in the decision, while occasionally criticized and often distinguished, have generally had continuing legal significance.[81]

The Court of Appeals decision in *Green v. McDonnell-Douglas Corp.* had perhaps a greater influence on shaping the course of employment discrimination law in the United States. The Supreme Court not only affirmed the Eighth Circuit but adopted much of the reasoning of Judge Bright in what became the leading case in the field. As of September

1998, over eight thousand cases had cited the Supreme Court decision in *McDonnell-Douglas* for its holding establishing the shifting burden of proof in discrimination cases.[82] *McDonnell-Douglas* became the "paradigm for both plaintiffs and defendants in handling employment discrimination cases"—racial, gender, and age—setting out the basic requirements by which plaintiffs can make out a prima facie case of employment discrimination.[83]

The *McDonnell-Douglas* case involved a black employee who had been laid off during a general reduction in workforce. Green, a controversial civil rights activist, protested that his layoff had been racially motivated. The court held that when a black man demonstrates that he possesses the qualifications to fill a job opening and he was denied the job, a prima facie case of racial discrimination has been established. At that point, the burden of proof passes to the employer, who must demonstrate a substantial relationship between the reasons offered for denying employment and the requirements of the job. The original panel decision in *McDonnell-Douglas* was divided. Judge Lay had concurred, and Judge Johnsen delivered what for the Eighth Circuit was quite a vigorous dissent. To head off rehearing en banc, Judge Bright revised his opinion, modifying the test by employing language given to him by Judge Ross (possibly at the prompting of Judge Lay).[84] Rehearing en banc was denied by a division of 4–4. Mehaffy, Gibson, Stephenson, and Matthes voted to rehear en banc. Bright, Lay, Heaney, and Ross voted against.[85] The court also held in *McDonnell-Douglas* that an applicant's past participation in unlawful conduct directed at his prospective employer might indicate his lack of a responsible attitude toward performing work for that employer.[86] The Supreme Court affirmed the Eighth Circuit decision in part,[87] adopting the substance of its holding regarding the burden of proof.[88]

GENDER DISCRIMINATION   The Supreme Court entered the field of gender discrimination in 1971 when it held unconstitutional a provision of the Idaho Probate Code, which gave a mandatory preference to men over women as administrators of estates of persons dying intestate.[89] Although the Supreme Court never applied strict scrutiny to classifications based on gender, it nevertheless held a number of such laws unconstitutional as violating Equal Protection.[90]

The Eighth Circuit was not unaware of the great changes in the role of women that occurred during the 1960s and 1970s. In South Dakota alone, the National Organization for Women had chapters in Sioux Falls, Pierre, Vermillion, Rapid City, Aberdeen, and Brookings.[91] By the mid-1970s, women had been appointed to the Arkansas and Minnesota Supreme Courts. Between 1971 and 1977, the Eighth Circuit decided twenty-nine employment discrimination cases involving gender, reversing a little more than 40 percent of the time.[92] In *Gunther v. Iowa State Men's Reformatory,* for example, the Court of Appeals affirmed Judge McManus, who had held that employment practices preventing women from obtaining jobs in the Correctional Officer I level at the Men's Reformatory at Aramosa, Iowa, violated Title VII of the 1964 Civil Rights Act.[93]

Brenden v. Independent School District was a different kind of gender discrimination case.[94] It involved two excellent female tennis players who sought to participate on the boys' team at their high school because there was no girls' tennis team. Upholding their claim, the panel (Judge Heaney writing) held that the state was precluded from using assumptions about the nature of females as a class to deny to females an individualized determination of their qualifications for a benefit provided by the state.

One important case involved a boycott established by the National Association of Women (NOW) against the State of Missouri, which was one of two states in the Eighth Circuit that did not ratify the Equal Rights Amendment. (Arkansas also never ratified. South Dakota and Nebraska rescinded their ratification.) Alleging that it had lost at least $8.6 million in convention trade, the state sought an injunction against NOW for restraint of trade. Judge Elmo Hunter of the Western District of Missouri denied the injunction. The Court of Appeals affirmed. The issue was whether the antitrust laws might be used to limit the exercise of First Amendment rights. Writing for a divided panel, Judge Stephenson noted: "This is a unique case. It is different from any case in the law books anywhere. There simply has never been another one like it."[95] The court held that Congress had never intended to cover such activities when it passed the antitrust laws. To issue an injunction, the court thought, would be to infringe on the people's right to petition their government. Dissenting, Judge Floyd Gibson thought the majority had erred in balancing the important governmental interest in preserving free enterprise against the interest of using "this particular method of influencing legislation."[96]

Abortion Cases

The most controversial Supreme Court decisions of the 1970s involved abortion. The 1973 decisions in *Roe v. Wade*[97] and *Doe v. Bolton*[98] recognized the virtually unrestricted right of a woman during the first trimester of her pregnancy to choose in consultation with her physician whether or not to have an abortion. During the second trimester, the state could regulate abortion to protect a woman's health. Only in the third trimester was the state's interest in protecting the potential life of the fetus great enough to warrant severe restrictions on the woman's right to choose.

Before *Roe v. Wade*, abortion was legal in six of the states of the Eighth Circuit only if the life of the woman was endangered. In Arkansas, abortion was also permitted if the pregnancy was the result of rape or incest. In Minnesota, where 100 to 150 women were leaving the state weekly to get abortions,[99] a Minnesota woman, three years before *Roe v. Wade*, had brought an action for a declaration of the unconstitutionality of the Minnesota Anti-Abortion statute and for an injunction against its enforcement. The plaintiff, who already had three children, had an abortion performed at her request after she was exposed to German measles. She was joined in the action by Dr. Jane E. Hodgson, who would be involved in a number of abortion cases during the 1970s. Hodgson was no back-alley abortionist, but a founding fellow of the Minnesota Society of Obstetricians and Gynecologists. In thirty years' practice, she had delivered more than four thousand babies and performed fewer than a dozen abortions.[100] A three-judge district court dismissed the action for lack of an actual controversy and because the matter was one for a state court. Judge Vogel dissented without opinion.[101] On the petition for rehearing, the panel remained firm even though Dr. Hodgson was being prosecuted in state court for violating the state antiabortion law.[102] Supreme Court Justice Harry Blackmun also refused to stay Hodgson's trial. Hodgson was found guilty, given a suspended sentence, and praised by the judge.[103]

For the courts of the Eighth Circuit, *Roe v. Wade* marked not the end but the beginning of what has now been over a quarter century of litigation over abortion, as state legislatures, especially those of Missouri and Minnesota, have passed statute after statute attempting to constrain the exercise of that right. During the 1970s, the judges of the Court of

Appeals—whether sitting on appeals court panels or as members of three-judge district courts—would hold most of the restrictive provisions of the abortion laws that came before them unconstitutional.

Just two days after *Roe* was decided in January 1973, Justice Blackmun, the author of the Supreme Court's opinion, came to Iowa to address the Cedar Rapids–Marion Area Chamber of Commerce. He was met by around fifty antiabortion demonstrators. That night, he spoke with anguish about the case.[104] That year, Iowa's abortion law was challenged in the Southern District of Iowa. The three-judge court went to the merits, saw the statute as essentially identical to the one held unconstitutional in *Roe v. Wade*, and held it unconstitutional because it "sweeps too broadly in restricting legal abortions to those 'necessary to save her (mother's) life.'"[105]

Among the efforts to limit *Roe* to come before the Court of Appeals were (1) preventing abortions from being performed in public hospitals; (2) otherwise limiting the availability of abortion services available to the indigent; (3) staffing obstetrics-gynecology (ob-gyn) clinics with those opposed to abortion; (4) tying up abortion clinics in red tape; (5) prohibiting the use of the most effective methods of abortion; (6) tinkering with the definition of "viability"; (7) threatening physicians who performed abortions with suits for damages; requiring (8) spousal or (9) parental consent; and (10) mandating a waiting period between the time a woman gives informed consent and the performance of the abortion.

Soon after *Roe v. Wade*, a municipally owned hospital in Virginia, Minnesota, adopted a resolution that prohibited licensed physicians on its staff from using hospital facilities for the performance of abortions. Judge Philip Neville of the District of Minnesota enjoined enforcement of the resolution, holding that it "flies directly in the face of the holdings in *Roe v. Wade* and *Doe v. Bolton*." The Court of Appeals affirmed. Relying on *Roe*, the court held "that the abortion decision and its implementation is a fundamental right of personal liberty embraced within the Due Process Clause of the Fourteenth Amendment."[106] As there was no evidence to indicate that the performance of abortions would interfere with normal hospital routine or require further staff and facilities, a ban on nontherapeutic abortions was unconstitutional. The ban was also deemed overbroad because it did not take cognizance of the separate trimesters of pregnancy.

Disagreeing with the denial of rehearing en banc, Judge Heaney delivered the first of many dissents in abortion cases. Joined by Judge

Gibson, Heaney rejected the implication in the majority opinion that all public hospitals with adequate facilities permit abortions. The dissenters believed that "a decent regard for the deep-seated convictions of those in the community who favor abortions, as well as those who oppose abortions, can be recognized by determining whether the rights of pregnant women desiring abortions can be reasonably protected without requiring a municipal hospital to perform abortions against its will."[107] In 1982, the Virginia Hospital unsuccessfully attempted to vacate the injunction, arguing that there was support in recent Supreme Court decisions.[108]

John H. Poelker, who believed that abortion was murder, became mayor of St. Louis in 1973.[109] Poelker continually sought to ban the performance of abortions in the city-owned public hospitals (except for abortions to save the mother from physiological injury or death). In *Word v. Poelker*, a St. Louis ordinance aimed at tying up abortion providers in red tape was challenged.[110] The Court of Appeals held the abstention doctrine inapposite. It held that while the ordinance did not proscribe abortion, it imposed an unusually burdensome layer of regulations only on abortions. The ordinance was unconstitutional because the stringent requirements of the ordinance were not legitimately related to recognized state objectives and overbroad because it did not exclude the first trimester of pregnancy.

Doe v. Poelker was brought in the name of an indigent plaintiff to contest the policies, rules, regulations, and procedures of the two public hospitals in St. Louis. The plaintiff also questioned the staffing of the ob-gyn clinics because only faculty and students from the St. Louis School of Medicine, a Jesuit-operated institution, were employed. The clinics and the staff would not perform abortions. The Court of Appeals reversed Judge Roy W. Harper twice. In deciding the second appeal, Judge Ross stated that the municipal course of conduct at the least "reveals a wanton, callous disregard for the constitutional rights of indigent pregnant women in St. Louis."[111] Judge Ross got to the essence of the case:

> Stripped of all rhetoric, the city here, through its policy and staffing procedure, is simply telling indigent women, like Doe, that if they choose to carry their pregnancies to term the city will provide physicians and medical facilities for full maternity care, but if they choose to exercise their constitutionally protected right to determine that they wish to terminate their pregnancy, the city will not provide physicians and facilities for the abortion procedure.[112]

The Court of Appeals declared the policy of prohibiting all non-therapeutic abortions in publicly owned hospitals as well as the method of staffing their ob-gyn clinics unconstitutional, as an unwarranted infringement on a pregnant woman's right to privacy and a denial of equal protection to indigent pregnant women. Judge Van Oosterhout disagreed with the majority only regarding aspects of attorneys' fees.

However, by the time *Doe v. Poelker* had reached the U.S. Supreme Court, the High Court had decided *Maher v. Roe,* which held that even though a state may fund childbirth, it need not do so for abortion.[113] Thus, in *Poelker,* the Supreme Court found "no constitutional violation by the city of St. Louis in electing, as a policy choice, to provide publicly financed hospital services for childbirth without providing corresponding services for non-therapeutic abortions."[114] Three justices, including Justice Blackmun, dissented.

State legislative refusal to fund abortions gave the federal courts a great deal of trouble both before and after *Maher v. Doe.* In *Wolff v. Singleton,* the Court of Appeals held unconstitutional a Missouri statute that provided welfare payments if the pregnancy was carried to term or for therapeutic abortions, but none for nontherapeutic abortions.[115] The Supreme Court reversed and remanded on different grounds.[116] After *Poelker,* the Court of Appeals upheld the medical benefits plan of the University of Missouri, which reimbursed expenses for childbirth, but not for abortion.[117] In 1980, the Court of Appeals held that it was unconstitutional for Minnesota to grant funds for pre-pregnancy family planning to hospitals and HMOs, but not to other nonprofit organizations performing abortions.[118] On January 9, 1980, a panel of Stephenson, Ross, and McManus held that as a statutory matter, Minnesota need only finance abortions contemplated by the federal Hyde Amendment, but that Missouri's medical exclusion for non–Hyde Amendment abortions was invalid under the Equal Protection Clause.[119]

In 1974, Missouri enacted a comprehensive new law governing abortion. Planned Parenthood challenged the law's constitutionality three days after it became effective. A divided three-judge district court largely upheld the statute.[120] Concurring in part and dissenting in part, Judge Webster thought that the parts of the statutes requiring spousal consent and parental consent were unconstitutional, as was prohibiting the use of the saline amniocentesis method of abortion. He also stated that a section of the law terminating parental rights of a child born alive as a result of the abortion was unconstitutional. Webster did, however, agree with Missouri's two district judges who upheld a statutory definition of viability, record-keeping requirements, and a requirement that a woman give written consent to an abortion. All three judges held unconstitutional a provision placing the standard of care on the abortion provider without reference to any stage of pregnancy and providing for his or her civil and criminal liability.[121] The Supreme Court, affirming in part and reversing in part, agreed with Judge Webster's views on all challenged parts of the statute.[122]

In other abortion-related cases, the Court of Appeals refused to block the prosecution of a South Dakota physician for second-degree manslaughter in connection with the death of a patient on whom he had performed an abortion.[123] It enjoined the operation of an ordinance passed by the City Council of St. Paul over "clamorous public opposition," which imposed a six-month moratorium on the construction of abortion facilities in the city.[124] The court struck down a Nebraska law requiring a forty-eight hour waiting period from the time the physician obtained the patient's informed consent to the abortion to the performance of the abortion.[125] The Court of Appeals also struck down a Missouri law that provided in part that whenever an abortion of a potentially viable fetus results in a live birth, the child is to become a ward of the state, and a woman intending to have an abortion be so informed. In the district court, Judge Webster had labeled that particular section "the most offensive of the in terrorem clauses that were enacted by the Missouri legislature in 1974" and a "patently unconstitutional appendage totally lacking in due process."[126]

Criminal Cases

The criminal docket of the Eighth Circuit in the 1970s contained a large variety of cases. The Court of Appeals heard appeals in convictions for tax evasion, moonshining, contract fraud, and postal fraud, among others. It also heard a few Mann Act cases, one involving a pimp who brought prostitutes from Minnesota to ply their trade in Pierre, South Dakota, when the legislature was in session,[127] as well as appeals of convictions for political corruption. One of the most notable of these was the affirmance of the conviction for extortion and mail fraud of Kenneth O. Brown, building commissioner of St. Louis.[128]

The most notorious criminal case in the Eighth Circuit during this period involved Robert Anthony Williams, convicted by Iowa courts of murdering a ten-year-old girl, Pamela Powers. The child disappeared on December 24, 1968. The investigation rapidly focused on Williams, a part-time minister and organist in a small Des Moines church, who had a history of mental problems and an arrest record for molesting little girls. After kidnapping the child in Des Moines, Williams drove east on Interstate 80, stopped to put the body of the child in a ditch near Mitchellville, then drove on to Davenport. He spent the night in Rock Island, Illinois, from which he called his Des Moines attorney. The attorney advised Williams to surrender to the police in Davenport and not to talk about the case. The Davenport police warned Williams of his right to keep silent. Two Des Moines policemen picked up Williams in Davenport, gave him his *Miranda* warnings, and may have promised a Davenport attorney that they would not question Williams during his trip back to Des Moines. However, they refused to let the Davenport attorney ride along with them.

En route to Des Moines, one of the policemen, Detective Cleatus M. Leaming, delivered what became known as the "Christian burial speech." He reminded Williams that it was Christmas, that several inches of snow were predicted for that night, and that with snow covering the body, it might be impossible to find. The detective told Williams that "the parents of this little girl should be entitled to a Christian burial for the little girl who was snatched away from them on Christmas eve." Moved, Williams took the police to the body.

Williams was convicted of murder by the Polk County District Court and sentenced to life imprisonment. The statements he made in police custody, including those leading the police to the body, were used against him. The Iowa Supreme Court affirmed his conviction by a 5–4 vote. The majority, relying on the fact-finding of the trial court, held Williams's statement to be spontaneous and voluntary and held that he had waved his *Miranda* rights.[129] The dissenters expressed concern about "the obvious effort of the police officers to evade the good faith attempt of defendant's counsel to cooperate with the police department."[130]

Judge William C. Hanson of the U.S. District Court for the Southern District of Iowa granted Williams's petition for habeas corpus, holding that the state had not met "its heavy burden" of showing intelligent waiver of Fifth and Sixth Amendment rights and had failed to meet its burden of showing that his statement was made voluntarily.[131] The Court of Appeals affirmed—Vogel (writing) and Ross in the majority, Webster dissenting. The panel held that the "resolution of the waiver issue by the state court, although after fair consideration and following procedural due process, cannot be accepted as binding when it has misconceived a federal constitutional right," that is, the privilege against self-incrimination and right to have counsel present.[132] Webster, who four years later would become head of the FBI, wrote a careful, rational opinion, concluding:

> What transpired in the police automobile is clear. Williams understood his rights; he was promised nothing; he was not coerced. To say this much is not to approve of any techniques which involve misrepresentations to counsel. But, addressing myself to the findings of the state district judge, I believe they are supported by the record.[133]

The U.S. Supreme Court granted certiorari in the *Williams* case, possibly to use it as the vehicle for overturning *Miranda v. Arizona*.[134] Twenty-one state attorneys general joined in an amicus brief to that effect. However, Professor Robert D. Bartels of the University of Iowa Law School argued for Williams and was successful. The High Court upheld the Court of Appeals by a vote of 5–4 and did not reconsider *Miranda*. The majority rested its case on deprivation of the right to assistance of counsel. Writing for the Court, Justice Stewart stated:

> There can be no serious . . . doubt . . . that Detective Leaming deliberately and designedly set out to elicit information from Williams just as surely—and perhaps more effectively than—if he had formally interrogated him.[135]

Chief Justice Burger read his dissent angrily in open court:

> The result in this case ought to be intolerable in any society which purports to call itself an organized society. It continues the Court—by the narrowest margin—on the much criticized course of punishing the public for the mistakes and misdeeds of law enforcement officers. . . . It mechanically and blindly keeps reliable evidence from juries whether the claimed constitutional violation involves gross misconduct or honest human error.[136]

Williams was tried again. The Supreme Court had hinted that although Williams's incriminating statements and testimony describing his leading police to the body were inadmissible, "evidence of where the body was found and of its condition might well be admissible on the theory that the body would have been discovered in any event."[137] When retried, Williams was convicted on this basis and again sentenced to life imprisonment. Once again the Iowa Supreme Court affirmed, adopting a two-pronged inevitable discovery rule. Under their formulation of the rule, the prosecution had to demonstrate that the police had not acted in bad faith to accelerate the discovery of the evidence in question and prove that the evidence would have been found without the unlawful activity.[138]

Judge Harold Vietor of the Southern District of Iowa denied Williams new petition for habeas corpus.[139] However, the Court of Appeals reversed, refusing to accept the "inevitable discovery" or the "hypothetical independent source" exception to the exclusionary rule. It held that the state had not proved that the police had not acted in bad faith.[140] A petition to rehear the case en banc was denied by an equally divided court, Judges Bright, Ross, Gibson, and Fagg dissenting.[141]

More than fifteen years after the death of Pamela Powers, the U.S. Supreme Court finally upheld the conviction of her killer by a vote of 7–2. Chief Justice Burger wrote for the Court. He held that requiring the state to prove the absence of bad faith would "put the police in a worse position than they would have been if no unlawful conduct had transpired." "Nothing in the Court's prior holdings," Burger wrote, "supports any such formalistic, pointless, and punitive approach.[142]

Oversight of Prison Conditions

Until the mid-1960s, the federal courts refused to become involved in questions about the treatment of prisoners, employing a "hands-off" doctrine in dealing with complaints about correctional institutions. Because of the failure of state governments to improve institutions whose officials were protected from judicial oversight, such as prisons and jails, juvenile training schools, hospitals for the mentally ill, and institutions for the mentally retarded, and increasingly dubious about the expertise of specialists, federal judges began to play a more active role in their management.[143] One of the most important early examples of such institutional litigation took place in Arkansas, where, under the oversight of the Eighth Circuit Court of Appeals, District Judge J. Smith Henley played a major role running the Arkansas prisons.

The Arkansas prison system had been a disgrace at least since Arkansas had become a state, its history dominated by scandals caused by a mixture of corruption, mismanagement, and cruelty.[144] In the 1960s, most of the convicts in Arkansas lived on two farms where they were expected to produce their own food as well as cotton for sale on the open market. Prisoners were expected to work in the fields ten hours a day, six days a week, in rain or sun, heat or cold (so long as it was not below freezing), with no warm clothing or bad-weather gear.

The prisoners were even expected to guard each other. In Arkansas there was only one paid employee for fifty-eight prisoners, compared to one to four or five in Missouri.[145] As the Court of Appeals pointed out six years later, "inmate guards virtually ran the prison. They sold desirable jobs to other prisoners and trafficked in food, liquor or clothes. There was no way to protect prisoners from [the] assaults if the trusty guard permitted them."[146]

Prisoners slept in one large open space, packed solid with double-decker beds. It was "trusties" who guarded them, for there were only two state-employed guards available at night. Assaults, fights, and stabbings caused some inmates such fear that they came to the front of the barracks and clung to the bars all night. Theft, violence, and homosexual rape were endemic. And, as the U.S. Supreme Court recounted, inmates were lashed with a wooden-handled leather strap five feet long and four inches wide, and the "Tucker telephone" was used to administer electrical shocks to prisoners.[147]

In 1965, several petitions containing charges of corporal punishment in the Arkansas prisons came to Judge J. Smith Henley, then a district judge for seven years with a reputation as a relatively conservative jurist. Arkansas prison officials, mindful of the Little Rock school litigation, attempted to prevent a federal court "takeover" by redressing conditions for the complaining inmates and promising to generally improve the regulations governing inmate discipline. Seemingly satisfied with the improvements promised by Arkansas prison officials, Henley granted a substantial measure of relief by consent of the parties. The relief included an end to forcing prisoners to work beyond their physical capabilities, a prohibition against withholding reasonable medical attention, and a ban on inflicting corporal punishment without appropriate safeguards. In *Talley v. Stephens*, Henley entered judgment in only one contested matter, the interception of inmate communications to the court.[148] Neither side appealed.

During the next few years, there was trouble on the two prison farms as well as investigations by the state legislature, the state police, and Congress. There were documented reports of torture, near starvation diets, rampant violence, and widespread corruption.[149] Sitting together on another series of handwritten prisoner petitions, including one filed by William King Jackson, who was serving a five-year term for burglary, complaining of beatings, Judges Oren Harris and Gordon E. Young heard in *Jackson v. Bishop* of "brutal and sadistic atrocities," the crank telephone shocking apparatus, and the strapping of prisoners.[150] The judges enjoined the use of the Tucker telephone and similar instruments of torture but refused to hold corporal punishment per se unconstitutional.

In 1968, the Court of Appeals overturned the district court decision in *Jackson v. Bishop* as to corporal punishment.[151] However obedient Harry Blackmun was as an intermediate appellate court judge, however deep his belief in judicial restraint, however much he believed in federalism and the hands-off doctrine, this time his shock threshold had been passed. Reading the Eighth Amendment's ban on cruel and unusual punishment, Blackmun found in it an emphasis on man's basic dignity, on civilized precepts, and on flexibility and improvement in standards of decency as society progresses and matures. Blackmun wrote that the strap's use offended contemporary "standards of decency and human dignity and [those] precepts of civilization" that "we profess to possess," for "corporal punishment generates hate towards the keepers who punish and towards the system which permits it. It is degrading to the punisher and to the punished alike." *Jackson v. Bishop* was Blackmun's favorite opinion among those he wrote while a member of the Court of Appeals.[152]

In 1969, the Court of Appeals affirmed Judge Oren Harris's dismissal of a sweeping attack on conditions in the Arkansas prisons.[153] However, during the same year, Judge Henley consolidated another batch of prisoner petitions, certified them as a class action, and appointed excellent attorneys to represent the class. Henley decided the class action, *Holt v. Sarver*, in February 1970.[154] He held that the entire Arkansas prison system, "a brutal world run by brutal people," violated the Eighth Amendment, writing, "For the ordinary convict a sentence to the Arkansas penitentiary today amounts to a banishment from civilized society to a dark and evil world."[155] He condemned the prison for its profit-making policy, the use of inmate trusties as guards, and the absence of any program for training and rehabilitation. Henley held that the Eighth and Fourteenth Amendments had been violated by each of the valid complaints of the prisoners: lack of medical facilities, filthy bedding and clothing, widespread corruption, intimidation, and racial segregation. While he did not hold that inmates had a constitutional right to rehabilitation, he did hold that the absence of rehabilitation services and facilities was a "factor in the overall constitutional equation."[156] While ordering immediate, accelerated efforts to transform the corrections system, Henley did not lay out detailed steps. Rather, he commended state officials, including the governor, legislature, and commissioner of corrections, for their efforts and left it to them to deal with the problems.[157]

In May 1971, the Court of Appeals, stating that Henley's basic findings were supported by "overwhelming substantial evidence," affirmed the holding in *Holt v. Sarver* that the system as a whole constituted cruel and unusual punishment. It instructed Henley to retain supervision until he could be reasonably sure "that incarceration therein will not constitute cruel and inhuman punishment violative of the Eighth Amendment."[158] Henley then received the progress report he had demanded and, after six more days of hearings, issued a detailed decree urging State Corrections Commissioner Terrell Don Hutto to take more aggressive action.[159]

By now, Henley was involved in managing the Arkansas prisons. After a number of further complaints were consolidated in a new legal proceeding, Henley issued a supplemental decree on August 13, 1973, expanding the range of issues and pressing the department to establish a more precise timetable for their resolution.[160] Henley indicated that the inmate complaints encompassed practically the entire spectrum of prison life, and stated that in trying to resolve disputed factual issues, he had "encountered in full measure the credibility problems inherent in litigation of this kind." On the one hand, there already had been substantial change: the "trusty" system had been dismantled, a maximum-security unit had been created, and the prisons had law libraries and a full-time legal adviser. On the other, serious problems continued to exist in the areas of psychiatric services and sanitary and kitchen facilities.

Paradoxically, as prison facilities improved, Henley became more and more entangled in the administration of the prison system—overseeing hiring, training, and medical services. However, he was also becoming convinced that, at this point, his court was now dealing not so much with an unconstitutional prison system as with a poorly administered one.[161] After detailing a long list of problems the Department of Corrections still needed to resolve, Henley held that it was neither necessary nor desirable for the court to retain jurisdiction. While this order was being appealed, Henley personally visited the prisons for the first time, publicizing his continued concern about conditions.[162]

Fourteen months later, the Court of Appeals ordered Henley to retain jurisdiction of the litigation, holding that there was "a continuing failure by the correctional authorities to provide a constitutional and, in some respects, even a humane environment within their institutions." The court found a number of constitutional deficiencies, including arbitrary disciplinary procedures, abuse of mail regulations, and poor housing and medical care, and pointed to the total lack of rehabilitative programs. The court suggested that Henley use a special master or visiting committee to help gather facts, develop remedial plans, and monitor compliance.[163]

Henley was appointed to the Court of Appeals on March 24, 1975, but continued to act as the trial judge in the litigation. In *Finney v. Hutto,* he ordered the Department of Corrections to rectify a host of continuing deficiencies and urged the legislature and governor to better fund the prisons. He warned that if there was no improvement, the court was able to release inmates, but that if there was compliance with constitutionally mandated improvements, he could terminate the case.[164] *Finney I* was affirmed by the Court of Appeals on February 3, 1977, and by the Supreme Court the following year by a vote of 8–1.[165] Justice John Paul Stevens termed what had occurred in the Arkansas prisons "cruel and unusual punishment" and commended Henley's handling of the case.

Anxious to end the federal court takeover, Arkansas created the Arkansas Prison Study Commission, which found the department seriously deficient in virtually every area it examined. After Henley withdrew from the litigation in 1977 to concentrate on his work on the Court of Appeals, he was replaced by Judge G. Thomas Eisele. On October 5, 1978, the parties hammered out a consent decree with thirty-nine provisions. Eisele appointed Stephen C. LaPlante to the position of compliance coordinator under the decree. On August 20, 1982, seventeen years after the first complaint was filed, Eisele gave the department a clean bill of health. Not every issue—for example, crowding and inmate safety—had been resolved, but the Arkansas prison system was significantly different from the one that Henley had encountered at the beginning of the litigation. What once had been run by a small group of corrupt officials and a large number of inmates had become a modern bureaucratic institution governed by written rules and regulations, with strong central leadership and a staff of professionals.[166]

Miscellaneous Civil Liberties Cases

STUDENT RIGHTS   Between 1969 and 1977, the Court of Appeals decided fourteen cases that involved the rights of public school and university students. Nine times the Court of Appeals ruled for the student.[167] Three of those cases involved University of Missouri students. The first involved Barbara Susan Papish, a graduate student in journalism, who contested her expulsion for having distributed a radical newspaper, which had a political cartoon depicting policemen raping the Statue of Liberty and an article headlined "Mother F *** Acquitted."[168]

The panel divided. Judges Stephenson and Van Oosterhout believed that the federal courts should not cavalierly interfere in the internal affairs of the campus. Judge Ross, dissenting, saw the discipline as not for distribution but rather for the content of the publication. Rehearing en banc was denied by a vote of 4–4. The Supreme Court took the case and reversed, citing an intervening decision, *Healy v. James*,[169] which had held that dissemination of ideas—no matter how offensive to good taste—on a state university campus may not be shut off solely in the name of the conventions of decency.[170]

Horowitz v. Curators of the University of Missouri involved a medical student who did well academically but was dropped as a student for weakness in her clinical work—taking medical histories, performing physical examinations—and also because she was repeatedly late, poorly groomed, and unable to take criticism.[171] Horowitz brought a civil rights action, seeking to have her dismissal enjoined or, alternatively, for her reinstatement and damages. The District Court ruled for the university, believing it should have broad discretionary power to determine the fitness of a student to complete her studies. The Court of Appeals reversed. Judge Ross, writing, held that the Fourteenth Amendment applied and Horowitz had been denied the due process requisite of a hearing. Three members of the court (Gibson, Webster, and Henley) would have reheard the case en banc. The U.S. Supreme Court reversed, holding that hearings were not necessary when a student is dismissed for academic cause. The determination of whether to dismiss for academic reasons, the Court said, "is not readily adapted to the procedural tools of judicial or administrative decision-making."[172]

The University of Missouri's refusal to formally recognize a gay organization was contested in *Gay Lib v. University of Missouri*. Reversing Judge Elmo Hunter, who had upheld the university, Judge Lay stated that the argument that formal recognition would tend to perpetuate or expand homosexual behavior is "insufficient to justify a governmental prior restraint on the right of a group of students to associate for the purposes avowed in their statements."[173] Concurring, Judge Webster had no doubt "that the ancient halls of higher learning at Columbia will survive even the most offensive verbal assaults upon traditional moral values."[174] Judge John K. Regan of the Eastern District of Missouri dissented, believing that the university had the duty to protect latent or potential homosexuals from becoming overt homosexual students.[175] The Court of Appeals divided 4–4 on the petition for rehearing en banc. Three of the four judges who would have reheard the case were Gibson, Henley, and Stephenson, who dissented, stating that "this is yet another example of unwarranted judicial intrusion into the operations of an educational institution."[176]

Wood v. Strickland, a case involving public school students, led to an important U.S. Supreme Court decision on due process. The case involved two teenage girls in Mena, Arkansas, who spiked the punch at a school function and were expelled from school. The District Court for the Western District of Arkansas ruled against their suit for damages. A panel of Heaney (writing), Gibson, and Ross reversed, holding that if public school students are to be given lengthy suspensions for violating valid rules, they have to be accorded substantive and procedural due process. The court thought that procedural due process might have been denied because the students and their parents were not given notice of a school board meeting that considered the matter. However, the Court of Appeals rested on denial of substantive due process, holding that there had been no finding that the beverage the girls had put into the punch was intoxicating. Three judges (Mehaffy, Stephenson, and Webster) would have reheard the case en banc. Dividing 5–4, the U.S. Supreme Court reversed, holding that it was not the role of the federal courts to set aside decisions of school administrators just because the judges thought they were unwise or lacked compassion. However, the Supreme Court remanded on the procedural due process issue. The Court of Appeals then held that procedural due process had been violated.[177]

THE FIRST AMENDMENT   Among the First Amendment cases not involving students that reached the Eighth Circuit Court of Appeals in the 1970s were cases involving the First Amendment rights of government employees.[178] The court also upheld Judge Miles Lord's refusal to enjoin the operation of a St. Paul ordinance prohibiting nude dancing in establishments serving liquor,[179] and decided an appeal of a libel action brought by St. Louis mayor Alfonso J. Cervantes against *Life* magazine over an article that stated that Cervantes maintained "business and personal ties with the gangsters that operate in his city." Cervantes was unable to overcome the high barrier the Supreme Court set in *New York Times v. Sullivan*[180] for a public figure to prevail in a libel action.[181]

The Environment and Reserve Mining

Concern about foul air, dirty water, and toxic waste led to the passage of a number of important federal laws in the 1960s and early 1970s intended to reduce pollution and protect the environment. The Environmental Protection Agency (EPA), created in December 1970, was authorized to protect air and water and to control solid and hazardous wastes.[182] Although many of the major environmental lawsuits were litigated in the District of Columbia Circuit, the Eighth Circuit was the forum for several major cases, including litigation over the use of the Missouri River for flood control and irrigation projects (discussed in the following chapter), North Dakota lignite mining, and clear-cutting in Arkansas.

Minnesota's abundant natural resources include timber, rich soil, beautiful rivers and lakes, and vast wilderness in the north and northeast, which spawned mighty battles. There was litigation over logging in the Boundary Waters Canoe Area,[183] mining and snowmobiling in the Superior National Forest,[184] and duck hunting in Voyageurs National Park.[185] There is, however, little doubt that the most important Court of Appeals decision involved taconite mining on the shore of Lake Superior, litigation that seemed to pit public health and environmental concerns against the loss of thousands of jobs, and the Court of Appeals against a rambunctious and defiant trial judge. The Court of Appeals removed the trial judge from the case for intentional violation of the court's mandate and sought to strike a balance between unpredictable health effects and clearly predictable social and economic consequences.

After World War II, when Minnesota's rich iron ore was running out, the Reserve Mining Company undertook the risk of mining for taconite (low-grade iron ore). The construction of the first large plant on the shore of Lake Superior at Silver Bay began in 1946. The first taconite was produced at the plant in 1955. Disposal of the tailings, the finely crushed rock that is a by-product of the processing of taconite, presented a problem, which Reserve Mining solved by dumping the tailings into Lake Superior. Tests made at the time appeared to demonstrate that the tailings would sink to the bottom of the lake and do no harm. The state of Minnesota approved the dumping. Ultimately, 67,000 tons a day would be dumped into Lake Superior.

The production of taconite by Reserve Mining, which was owned by AMOCO Steel and Republic Steel, made no small contribution to the economy of northeastern Minnesota. By 1970, Reserve was producing ten million tons of taconite pellets annually and employing over 3,300 persons, while thousands more earned their livelihood through supporting the plant and its employees.[186] The time arrived, however, when effects of the taconite were seen in the lake. In front of the plant, the lake was filled with black mud. Patches of cloudy green water were seen for miles along the shore. Fishermen began to cry that the lake was dying. A Department of the Interior study (the Stoddard Report), leaked to the press in January 1969, raised serious questions about the effects of the tailings. The company disputed the study.[187]

After administrative and state court proceedings proved to be of no avail, the administrator of the Environmental Protection Agency notified Reserve Mining in April 1971 that it was in violation of federal-state water quality standards under the Water Pollution Control Act. The company was warned that, pursuant to statute, it had 180 days to achieve compliance. The EPA filed suit in the District of Minnesota on February 2, 1972, charging Reserve with violation of federal-state water quality standards, the Refuse Act of 1899, and common-law nuisance standards. The states of Wisconsin, Michigan, and Minnesota moved to intervene as plaintiffs (as did a variety of regional environmental groups). The Village of Silver Bay, the Duluth Area Chamber of Commerce, and the Northeast Development Association (among others) intervened on behalf of the company.

The case began as a water pollution abatement case but on the eve of trial, fifteen months later, was transformed into a public health case when tailings having the properties of asbestos were found in Duluth's water supply. In cities such as Duluth, whose drinking water came from Lake Superior, there was a run on stocks of bottled water.

The trial judge in the *Reserve Mining* case was Miles Lord, who had been attorney general of Minnesota and U.S. Attorney for the District of Minnesota before his appointment to the federal bench in 1966. As a judge, Lord was known for employing innovative methods to deal with his caseload. Lord, described by the *Minneapolis Star* as "an alley fighter, bell hop, cat skinner and fry cook," would sorely try the patience of the Court of Appeals in this case because of his populism, prejudice against the company, and defiance of the higher court.[188]

The acrimonious trial before Lord consumed 134 days, beginning on August 1, 1973, and ending on April 25, 1974. Over one hundred witnesses were heard. Testimony ran to 18,000 pages, and 1,600 exhibits were entered into the record.[189] The final order closing the record occurred on October 18, 1974.

On April 20, 1974, Lord issued an injunction ordering an end to the dumping of tailings (and emissions) by the next day. That meant closing the Silver Bay plant. Lord found that the fibers emitted into Lake Superior had the potential for causing great harm to the health of those exposed to them, that people relying on drinking water from the western arm of Lake Superior were endangered, and that discharges into the air substantially endangered the health of people as far away as Wisconsin's eastern shore. Lord held that Reserve had violated Minnesota's water and air pollution laws and the federal water pollution statute and had created a common-law nuisance.[190]

Within hours of Lord's injunction, Reserve sought a stay from the Court of Appeals. Chief Judge Mehaffy assigned Judges Bright, Ross, and Webster to hear the motion. Argument on the stay was held in a Springfield, Missouri, motel room, where the judges were attending a joint sentencing seminar with the Tenth Circuit. The panel granted a stay of the injunction pending a further hearing on May 15.[191]

After the May 15 argument, the court continued the stay for seventy days under certain conditions. Writing for the court, Bright thought it "painfully clear" that the decision to permit the discharge of tailings "amounted to a monumental environmental mistake." Yet the decision had been made in good faith to create jobs in a depressed area of northern Minnesota. There were, the court thought, "neither heroes nor villains among the present parties in the law suit nor among their predecessors in government, business and society."[192]

The court held that Reserve was unlikely to prevail as to the water or air pollution but that it would succeed on the public health issue because Reserve's dumping and pollution did not substantially endanger the health of residents in communities around Lake Superior, that "Judge Lord carried his analysis one step beyond the evidence."[193]

Attempting to maintain a balance between the potential loss of thousands of jobs and environmental risks, the court thought a further stay should be conditioned upon assurances that Reserve would promptly end its discharges into Lake Superior and control its emissions into the air. The seventy-day stay was conditioned on Reserve's filing plans with the states and the U.S. government as to how the company would deal with the environmental problems.[194]

On August 3, Lord rejected Reserve's plan as unreasonable and recommended against any further stay.[195] On August 9, the Court of Appeals remanded the case to Lord with a request that he expedite disposition of the unresolved issues. Holding a hearing on its own motion to consider the district court's recommendation against continuing the stay, the Court of Appeals, aware that significant progress had been made regarding an on-land disposal site and methods for abating the discharges into the lake, continued the stay.[196] The U.S. Supreme Court then denied an application to vacate the stay, although four justices stated that their denial was without prejudice to renewed application.[197]

On October 18, Lord issued a final order finding that Reserve had committed numerous violations of the law by its pollution.[198] An en banc court composed of five judges (Lay, Bright, Ross, Stephenson, and Webster) heard the appeal on December 9. The court's lengthy decision was again written by Judge Bright, whose background in the Iron Range made him well aware not only of the contributions the mining industry had made to that part of Minnesota but also how important it was for that industry to operate in an environmentally sound manner.[199]

Bright's opinion has become a staple of environmental law casebooks because of his sensitivity to environmental risks and realism about economic costs.[200] The Court of Appeals held that Reserve's discharges into the air and water violated federal and state law (thus justifying injunctive relief). Although no harm to the public health had been shown and the danger to public health was not imminent, the evidence called for preventive steps, as the potential threat to public health was so grave that it called for an abatement order with reasonable terms. Reserve was entitled to a reasonable time period to convert its taconite operations to on-land disposal or to close its Silver Bay operations, but it had to take reasonable, but immediate, steps to reduce its emissions.

However, the en banc court held that the district court had abused its discretion by immediately closing the plant. An immediate injunction was not justified in striking a balance between unpredictable health effects and clearly predictable social and economic consequences that would follow the plant closing. A remedy should be fashioned, the court said, "which will serve the ultimate public weal by ensuring clear air, clean water and continued jobs in an industry vital to the nation's welfare."[201]

By this time, Lord's behavior in the *Reserve Mining* case had become quite erratic. Although the Court of Appeals made clear that the resolution of the controversy over an on-land disposal site did not fall within the jurisdiction of the federal courts,[202] on the day after the Court of Appeals decision Lord summoned counsel and stated that he was not bound by the ruling. When he convened a hearing on the subject, he complained that the appeals court had tied his hands. After reading about that hearing in the newspapers, the Court of Appeals ordered a transcript and later branded the hearing "a complete nullity." Nevertheless, in November Lord convened another "irregular hearing."[203] Without giving notice of motion to Reserve or offering it the opportunity to be heard or to cross-examine witnesses, Lord ordered Reserve to pay Duluth $100,000 within two days to compensate the city for water filtration. Lord called witnesses and testified himself, announcing, "I have dispensed with the usual adversary procceding . . . because I simply don't have time to spend."[204]

The Court of Appeals sat en banc again on December 18, 1975, this time to hear Reserve's petition for mandamus, seeking to prevent Lord from interfering with state administrative proceedings. In open court, Reserve asked the Court of Appeals to recuse Lord from the case. Lord represented himself at the December 18 session. He testified for fifteen minutes without being interrupted for questions and asked the court for its "confidence [and] faith in me." The Court of Appeals removed Lord from the case, removing him not by Reserve's motion for removal (because it was oral) but on the court's own motion, *sua sponte*. The court saw "great bias against Reserve Mining" and "substantial disregard for the mandate of this court." "Lord seems to have shed the role of the judge and to have assumed the mantle of an advocate," the Court of Appeals said. It added, mincing no words:

> Disregard of this court's mandate by a lawyer would be contemptuous; it can hardly be excused when the reckless action emanates from a judicial officer. It is one thing for a district judge to disagree on a legal basis with the judgment of this court. It is quite another to openly challenge the court's ruling and attempt to discredit the integrity of the judgment in the eyes of the public.[205]

The Court of Appeals remanded the case to the Chief Judge of the District of Minnesota, Edward J. Devitt, who personally took over the case. Lord was the first judge taken off a case in the Eighth Circuit in twenty years.[206] No agreement was reached in finding a site for the on-land disposal of the tailings. Devitt then ordered that Reserve cease discharge of taconite tailings by July 7, 1977. On October 28, 1976, the en banc court, Bright writing, affirmed that order and affirmed fines against Reserve totaling $837,500.[207]

In 1978, Reserve reluctantly accepted an on-land disposal site, Milepost 7, on its railroad line, seven miles from the Silver Bay plant. In the 1980s, however, when taconite production dropped precipitously because of economic recession and foreign competition, Reserve Mining, having spent $370 million for Milepost 7 and air quality improvements, was ill prepared for such economic conditions. In 1986 it declared bankruptcy. Operations at Silver Bay were shut down until Cyprus Northshore resumed taconite pellet production four years later.[208]

Cases Involving Native Americans

Most of the Native Americans in the Eighth Circuit live in the Dakotas. Fourteen thousand Indians lived in North Dakota, most of whom belonged to the Three Affiliated Tribes (the Mandan, Gros Ventre, and Arikara). South Dakota had a Native American population of twenty-five thousand, many of whom lived on the Standing Rock, Pine Ridge, Rosebud, Cheyenne River, Lower Brule, and Crow Creek Indian reservations. In addition, there were thirty thousand Objiway in Minnesota, Omaha and Winnebago reservations in Nebraska, and a settlement for the Sac and Fox in Iowa.

Considerable progress was made nationally during the 1960s and 1970s on the road to Native American self-determination and self-government and in ameliorating conditions on the reservations, a result of efforts in Congress and the federal executive and the reassertion of Native American pride. In the 1960s, millions of dollars were pumped into reservations by New Frontier and Great Society programs. In 1968, Congress passed nine pieces of Indian legislation, the ninth being the Indian Civil Rights Act (or Indian Bill of Rights), which applied parts of the First, Fourth, Fifth, Sixth, Eighth, and Fourteenth Amendments to the reservation.[209]

Nevertheless, at the beginning of the 1970s, most Native Americans lived in deplorable conditions, suffering startling rates of tuberculosis, alcoholism, and infant mortality. Life expectancy was only forty-four years for Indians living on reservations. Unemployment was staggeringly high—in 1971, 70 percent of the available workforce on the Crow Creek reservation was unemployed. Only 35 percent of the homes on the Cheyenne River Sioux Reservation had electricity. Only 16 percent had running water.[210]

The early 1970s were marked by increased Indian militancy spurred by the American Indian Movement (AIM), organized in 1968 by urban Native Americans in Minneapolis. The activists in AIM, among them Dennis Banks (Chippewa), Russell Means (Sioux), and Clyde Warrior (Ponca), developed a program that targeted corrupt tribal governments, the Bureau of Indian Affairs, the FBI, police, and state courts.[211] With a sense of how to attract media attention, AIM occupied Alcatraz Island from November 1969 to 1971, the Bureau of Indian Affairs in November 1972, and, in 1973, two churches, a trading post, and seven homes at the site of the 1891 Wounded Knee Massacre on the Pine Ridge Reservation. A violent seventy-one-day standoff between the Indians and heavily armed federal agents ensued, followed by many trials in the district courts of the Eighth Circuit.[212]

While the performance of the federal government during Wounded Knee exemplified the dark side of the Nixon administration, that administration's approach in most Native American matters showed it at its most constructive. Its legacy includes enlightened laws such as the Indian Education Act of 1972 and the Indian Self-Determination and Educational Assistance Act of 1975. Underlying nearly all of this legislation were the dual but contradictory themes of government maintenance of trust responsibilities and assumption of administrative functions by the tribes. Probably the most important of the five statutes, the Indian Self-Determination and Educational Assistance Act, declared Congress's commitment

> to the maintenance of the Federal government's unique and continuing relationship with, and responsibility to, individual Indian tribes and the Indian people as a whole through the establishment of a meaningful Indian self-determination policy which will permit an orderly transition from Federal domination of programs for, and services to, Indians to effective and meaningful participation by the Indian people in the planning, conduct, and administration of those programs and issues.[213]

The law authorized agencies of the federal government to contract with and make grants directly to Indian tribal governments for the delivery of federal services. Both management and control of governmental service programs were vested in the tribal governments.[214]

Along with the laws of Congress and the programs of the executive, during the 1970s Native Americans were assisted by decisions of the lower federal courts, including the U.S. Court of Appeals for the Eighth Circuit. Native Americans are one of those small, vulnerable minorities with relatively little political clout that the Supreme Court has suggested are particularly deserving of special judicial protection.[215] The federal courts have evolved special doctrines and rules for Native American cases, which have been employed more sympathetically over the past forty years. Governmental agencies acting in their trust capacity for Indians are held to an exceedingly high level of conduct. Ambiguities in treaties are to be construed in favor of Native Americans; so, too, with statutes. As Charles F. Wilkinson has written: "[From treaties and treaty substitutes] emanate a kind of morality profoundly rare in our jurisprudence.... Somehow, these old negotiations ... are tremendously evocative. Real promises were made on these plains and the Senate of the United States approved them.... My sense is that judges cannot shake that."[216] Because Indian tribes are particularly vulnerable to arguments based on waiver, laches, statutes of limitations, adverse possession, and other doctrines premised on dilatory conduct, modern cases reflect the premise that tribes should be insulated against the passage of time. Further, the federal courts have come to offer tribal governments formidable protection against state intrusion. In considering whether states may extend their laws on to the reservation, the courts have moved away from their longtime reliance on the amorphous concept of tribal sovereignty, instead looking to see whether the applicable treaties and statutes constitute federal preemption—a formidable centralizing doctrine with a long history.[217]

As confrontations over land and cultural issues moved from the fields to the courtrooms, the amount of Native American cases decided by the U.S. Supreme Court rose from twelve in the 1960s to thirty-five in the 1970s, when tribes won an impressive number of victories reaffirming limited tribal sovereignty and exemptions from state taxes.[218] The U.S. Court of Appeals for the Eighth Circuit handled a wide variety of Native American cases during the 1970s, most of them coming from South Dakota and Nebraska. Those discussed here deal with land claims, the "diminishing" or "disestablishing" of reservations, the Indian Civil Rights Act, and cases growing out of the Wounded Knee uprising.

INDIAN LAND CLAIMS   During the 1970s and 1980s, the Omaha Indian tribe waged a lengthy court battle to regain possession of more than 11,000 acres of land that had originally been part of Nebraska but, because of a shift in the channel of the Missouri River, had come to be considered part of Iowa.[219] The Black Bird Bend litigation produced twelve federal court decisions, obtained for the tribe a small portion of the total acreage it claimed, and caused lingering discontent and resentment on the part both of the Omaha and of the white Iowa farmers who possessed the land before the litigation began.[220]

The dispute involved a treaty the United States had made with the Omaha Indian tribe on March 16, 1854, in which certain lands located in the Black Bird Bend area of the territory of Nebraska were reserved by the tribe. The Omaha ceded to the United States all other land west of the "centre of the main channel of said Missouri River." By 1923, the river had moved more than two miles to the west of the original boundary line, so that much of the land contained within the original Black Bird Bend area was situated on the east side of the river. From the 1940s until April 1975, white Iowans had occupied, cleared, and cultivated the land in dispute. That month, the Omaha, with the approval of the United States, seized possession of the land.

The central issue in the Black Bird Bend litigation was the location of the Missouri River a century before. After a lengthy trial, Judge Andrew Bogue of the District of South Dakota held for the Iowa farmers.[221] Bogue had placed the burden of proof on the Omaha and then determined that the tribe had failed to prove that the river movements were controlled by the doctrine of avulsion; rather, the river had changed by reason of erosion of the reservation land and accretion to Iowa riparian land.[222] The Court of Appeals reversed, holding that Bogue had erroneously placed the burden of proof on the wrong party, relying on a federal statute that stated that in trials about property rights in which an Indian is a party on one side and a white person on the other, the "burden of proof shall rest upon the white person, whenever the Indian shall make out a presumption of title in himself from the fact of previous possession or ownership."[223] The Omaha thus had the presumptive right of possession and title, while the Iowa landowners had the "onerous burden" of proving the "course of the river's movement occurring some 100 years after the event." In a dispute, the resolution of which would cause hardships to either side, the Court of Appeals stated that "the clear policy of the federal government mandates that the interests of the Omaha Indian Tribe be given their historical and statutory protection. Their important possessory land interests could not be taken away on proof that is basically speculative and conjectural."[224] The Supreme Court granted certiorari and upheld the Court of Appeals as to the burden of proof (with the exception of land claims against the State of Iowa) but vacated and remanded on choice of law issues.[225]

The Black Bird Bend litigation bounced between the district court and the Court of Appeals for twelve more years as the courts dealt with matters such as the application of Nebraska riparian law, the burden of proof regarding the land claims of the State of Iowa, whether the United States was responsible for reimbursing the landowners for the value of their improvements and the amount of the award to the Iowa landowners for those improvements, and whether the government had to pay simple rather than compound prejudgment interest on the amount owing to the Iowans.[226]

Meanwhile, relations between the Omaha, who were ultimately awarded title to approximately 1,900 of the 2,900 acres at issue, and the federal courts were deteriorating. When Judge Edward McManus of Iowa's Northern District issued an order awarding the remaining land to the state, members of the tribe physically barred surveyors from the land. McManus then held the entire tribal council in contempt and jailed them overnight.[227] In related litigation involving other (and larger) claims of the Omaha as the result of the wayward Missouri, Judge Warren Urbom of the District of Nebraska condemned the tribe's attorney, William H. Veeder, for his systematic pattern of failure to comply with court rules and dismissed all of the remaining claims of the Omaha. The Court of Appeals upheld the ruling and assessed a penalty against the tribe of double the costs for their "frivolous claims."[228] Finally, in 1995, the Eighth Circuit ruled finis to twenty-nine years of litigation.[229]

In still other cases dealing with the Omaha, Judges Robert V. Denney and Richard E. Robinson of the District of Nebraska both held Nebraska's retrocession of criminal jurisdiction over the Omaha valid.[230] Affirming on the basis of Judge Robinson's opinion, the Court of Appeals held that the retrocession acceptance procedures comported with a 1968 law and therefore that exclusive jurisdiction over offenses committed on the Omaha Reservation belonged to the federal government.[231]

RESERVATION DIMINISHING   Recognition as a reservation has important implications for criminal and civil jurisdiction involving Native Americans. Congress also has the power not only to terminate reservations but to "diminish" them, withdrawing land from the reservation, in which case the states may exercise jurisdiction over the land involved. The difficult cases arise when Congress does not speak clearly (or does not speak at all) as to whether it intends to diminish a reservation when, for example, it opens Indian reservations to non-Indian settlement through the homesteading of surplus land.[232]

During this period, the Court of Appeals decided several cases involving the diminishing of reservations. In *City of New Town, N.D. v. United States*, the Court of Appeals held that congressional intent rather than Native American title was the primary consideration in determining reservation boundaries.[233] It then held that a 1910 law reserving certain land for homesteading did not diminish the Fort Berthold reservation as established by an 1891 law. In *United States, ex rel Condon v. Erickson*, the Court of Appeals held that a 1908 law, which had opened certain portions of the Cheyenne Reservation to white settlement, had not diminished the boundaries of that reservation as established by acts passed in 1888 and 1889. "Where as here," the court said, "the question presented is close, we conclude that a holding favoring federal jurisdiction is required unless Congress has expressly or by clear implication diminished the boundaries of the reservation opened to settlement."[234]

In *Rosebud Sioux Tribe v. Kneip*, the Court of Appeals held that the Rosebud Sioux Reservation had been diminished by three "surplus" land statutes of 1904, 1907, and 1910, even though there had not been express disestablishment language.[235] The Supreme Court agreed with the Court of Appeals following a recent decision,[236] which had held that the Lake Traverse Reservation of the Sisseton-Wahpeton Sioux in South Dakota had been disestablished.[237]

THE INDIAN CIVIL RIGHTS ACT   The Indian Civil Rights Act (ICRA), passed in 1968, had twin and possibly conflicting goals: "to protect individual rights of Indians while fostering tribal self-government and cultural identity."[238] Before 1978, the judges of the Court of Appeals demonstrated their awareness of the ICRA's potential for creative lawmaking.

In a 1972 case, a panel of Bright, Ross, and Wangelin held that the federal courts could resolve intratribal controversies—in this case, whether a tribe had violated the rights of a member when it disqualified her from running for tribal council because of her employment at a Public Health Service Hospital.[239] In two other cases, the Court of Appeals held that under the Indian Civil Rights Act, the one-man, one-vote principle of *Baker v. Carr* applied to a tribal council and tribal elections. In one of those cases, the court also upheld a requirement of one-half Indian blood to sit on the tribal council.[240] Yet there were other cases in which the Court of Appeals invoked the doctrine of exhaustion of remedies and avoided ruling on clashes between the ICRA and tribal policy. In *Janis v. Wilson,* Judge Heaney commented that exhaustion is not an inflexible requirement but is "required as a matter of comity in furtherance of the federal policy to preserve the unique sovereign and cultural identity of the Indian people."[241] Sovereign immunity, too, was another doctrine that could be invoked to avoid too much interference with tribal matters.[242]

However, the decision of the U.S. Supreme Court in *Santa Clara Pueblo v. Martinez* cut off federal judicial activism in this area. There the High Court held that the Indian Civil Rights Act did not provide litigants with a list of civil remedies to challenge tribal policy in the federal courts; only a petition for habeas corpus might be used for that purpose and then only for unlawful detention. The ICRA had not limited the tribe's immunity from suit, so that it could not be enforced directly against a tribe, except in an equitable action; and there was no implied cause of action for equitable relief in the federal courts to enforce the ICRA. The Indian Civil Rights Act, thus, is primarily enforceable in tribal forums.[243]

WOUNDED KNEE   The most explosive confrontation in the twentieth century between Native Americans and the federal government occurred in 1973 at Wounded Knee on the Pine Ridge Reservation in South Dakota.[244] Following unrest on the Pine Ridge and Rosebud Reservations, members of the American Indian Movement, led by Dennis Banks and Russell Means, and supporters from the reservation occupied Wounded Knee on February 27, 1973.[245] After countless firefights, the deaths of four Indians and the wounding of seven, as well as the wounding of two federal agents, the standoff ended after seventy-one days with the surrender of the protesters. Approximately two hundred Native Americans were then prosecuted in the courts of the Eighth Circuit for offenses related to the confrontation at Wounded Knee.

The most visible trial was that of Banks and Means, who had been indicted for burglary, theft, assaulting a federal agent, interfering with federal law enforcement officers, possession of Molotov cocktails, auto theft, wounding two federal officers, and conspiracy to commit the previously mentioned crimes. Transferred to St. Paul, the trial was presided over by Judge Fred Nichol of the District of South Dakota. Taking more than eight months, it ended with Judge Nichol dismissing all charges.

The Banks-Means trial may properly be characterized a "political trial." The government made extraordinary and unseemly efforts to get convictions of the leaders of a dissident group that had led a small rebellion, while the defendants used the trial as a forum to dramatize the history of oppression of Native Americans and to draw attention to the abuses in their own prosecution. Both the attorneys and the defendants engaged in judge baiting. At one point, Judge Nichol had defense attorneys William Kunstler and Mark Lane jailed overnight. Visits to the trial from a succession of celebrities such as Marlon Brando and Harry Belafonte contributed to a circuslike atmosphere.

The behavior of the prosecution paralleled in an eerie way the Watergate scandal, which was unraveling at the time. A succession of government officials, for example, first denied any knowledge that phone calls had been monitored during the siege. Later they asserted that such monitoring had been unintentional. Still later they argued that listening in on an extension was not really eavesdropping.[246] The obvious misconduct of the prosecution during the trial came to trouble Nichol more and more. After the trial there were revelations that the defense had been infiltrated by an FBI informant.[247] Nichol had dismissed some charges before the beginning of the trial, and after the government's case-in-chief, he dismissed some more. Then one of the jurors became very ill while the jury was deliberating. After the government refused to allow an eleven-person jury to render the verdict, Nichol acquitted the defendants on the remaining counts. While Nichol was reading his decision on August 7, 1974, the White House was announcing that it would not respond to a subpoena for tapes about Wounded Knee. The president resigned from office the next day.[248]

The government appealed the dismissal, but the Court of Appeals dismissed the appeal, holding that Nichol had discretion to dismiss the case after jeopardy had attached. The Court of Appeals did say, however, that it was "concerned and ill at ease with the impact that this case has on the administration of justice. Presented with a civil rebellion, the government filed numerous charges; and now, after a protracted 8 ½ month trial no definitive result was achieved."[249] Even though ten of the sixteen jurors and alternates in the Banks-Means trial wrote the attorney general asking him to dismiss the remaining cases, many other Wounded Knee and Wounded Knee–related prosecutions followed.[250]

A number of trials occurred before Judge Warren Urbom of the District of Nebraska, whose reputation for fairness was such that the defendants opted for bench trials. Urbom handled his first trial so well that both sides agreed to remove the remaining trials to Lincoln to keep him on as presiding judge.[251] Judge Edward J. McManus of the Northern District of Iowa also proved effective. Although the Banks-Means trial took eight months, the trial of three defendants accused of conspiracy before McManus took just four days, although the judge, undoubtedly, was aided by the fact that the defendants chose not to put on a case. A jury found the defendants guilty. One hundred eighty-three of the 185 indictments had been disposed of by the fall of 1976. Only fifteen defendants had been convicted, and several of those convictions were still on appeal then.[252]

The most visible opinion of the Court of Appeals was its holding that the government had no right to appeal the dismissal of the Banks-Means case. The court also affirmed and adopted Judge Urbom's opinion on the politically controversial proposition that federal jurisdiction over crimes on the reservation was not precluded by treaty. The Court of Appeals upheld the conviction of Leonard Crow Dog against claims of selective prosecution, prosecutorial misconduct, unconstitutional delay, and violation of the right to counsel caused by the presence in the defense camp of an FBI informant.[253] In *United States v. Dodge*, the court found no prejudice resulting from such an informant but suggested that the result might have been different in the Banks-Means case, where it also allegedly occurred, because of the informant's proximity to their defense.[254] The Court of Appeals also upheld the dismissal of a suit against six FBI agents for the false arrest of persons trying to bring food to Wounded Knee in 1975.[255] In *Means v. Wilson*, where AIM attempted to set aside the Oglala Sioux tribal election by claiming that the winner's fraudulent and criminal acts, including the use of a "goon squad" to harass and threaten those who opposed his administration, violated their right to vote, the Court of Appeals held in a pre–*Santa Clara Pueblo* case that the right to vote was protected under the ICRA. However, that statute, the court said, should be used with great caution in applying traditional constitutional principles to Indian tribal governments.[256] The Court of Appeals also rendered several "housekeeping" opinions: affirming the refusal of a judge of the District of South Dakota to disqualify himself, rejecting a motion to hold all of the conspiracy trials together, and, in another case, limiting compensation of Indian defense lawyers.[257]

In the end, Wounded Knee probably cost Native Americans more than they gained. If they won sympathizers during the siege of Wounded Knee and because of the politicized trial achieved somewhat better public understanding of the history of the mistreatment of the Native Americans, AIM suffered by having to carry out its political program while trying to defend itself against criminal charges. By the end of 1975, the militant Indian movement had lost much of its momentum.[258]

During the 1970s, the Court of Appeals for the Eighth Circuit continued to be, first and foremost, faithful to the precedents of the U.S. Supreme Court. When, however, Supreme Court precedent was not clear or the case was one of first impression, the decisions of the Court of Appeals tended more often than not to favor civil liberties claims. The Court of Appeals strongly supported school desegregation and enforcement of the job discrimination provisions of the 1964 Civil Rights Act. It was unafraid to approve complex remedies where it found school segregation or cruel and inhuman prison conditions. Although its adherence to *Roe v. Wade* was consistently challenged, the court and its judges (for there were a number of three-judge district courts decisions) did not waver in its support. When, during the early 1970s, the Supreme Court began to carve out a new law of gender discrimination, the Eighth Circuit did not lag far behind. In cases involving the claims of public school and university students, the Eighth Circuit often refused to defer to university officials and school boards. In the most important environmental case, the court self-consciously attempted to balance environmental risks against economic damage. In the large number of cases involving Native Americans, the court generally was sympathetic to their claims.

In the decade that followed, the historically placid waters of the Court of Appeals for the Eighth Circuit would be roiled more than once. The new decade would bring important constitutional cases in areas of the law—church-state, separation of powers, and Commerce Clause— about which the court in the past had spoken little. Bankruptcy cases and cases involving the waterways of the circuit would once again become significant. As the court grew in size and judges took senior status, the new appointees of Ronald Reagan and George H. W. Bush would shift the balance of the court. Issues that had been dealt with tranquilly in the 1970s would in the 1980s engender divided panels and a remarkable number of rehearings en banc.

CHAPTER 6

"Debate, Differences, and a Robust Exchange of Ideas"

The Eighth Circuit during the 1980s

*T*he most significant characteristic of the work of the U.S. Court of Appeals for the Eighth Circuit during the 1980s was the strong intellectual differences among its judges, evidenced by the number of en banc proceedings overturning decisions made by panels, as well as by the number of dissents from the denial of en banc review. This occurred for several reasons. The docket of the Eighth Circuit continued to include large numbers of value-laden cases in areas such as abortion, school desegregation, the First Amendment (including, for the first time, a considerable number of church-state questions), criminal procedure, and matters of federalism. Then, too, the Reagan administration was unusually successful in appointing judges to the Court of Appeals who largely shared its legal outlook—an outlook different in many respects from those of other members of the court. Finally, the judges of the Eighth Circuit proved far more willing than ever before to depart from traditional norms limiting dissent and respecting panel decisions.

National, State, and Regional Developments

From 1981 on, conservative administrations controlled the executive branch of the federal government. The deregulation of formerly regulated industries, which began under the Carter administration, continued. Social welfare programs were cut; military spending dramatically increased; the federal deficit skyrocketed. The Reagan and Bush administrations had a discernible impact on questions of public law—greater respect for the power of the several states, restrictive of abortions, pro-government in criminal and First Amendment cases, pro-accommodation in church-state cases, favoring the reining in of judicial power. This "agenda" was advanced by four appointments to the Supreme Court and many to the lower federal courts.

On farms, a severe depression rivaling that of the 1930s in severity lasted until 1987. Farm income and land values declined sharply, causing an epidemic of forced auctions, foreclosures, and bankruptcies. Manufacturers and dealers of farm implements and many businesses in small towns also suffered greatly, while deregulation of the banking industry spawned dangerous practices causing the collapse or crippling of many banking institutions that loaned money to farmers or held their savings.[1]

During this period, Arkansas state politics was dominated by Governor Bill Clinton, who stood for pragmatic liberalism and an expanded role for women and minorities in public life.[2] Missouri's politics generally reflected national trends. For six years, John D. Ashcroft, a conservative Republican, was governor. In 1980, the Hancock Amendment, which provided that taxes could be raised only if approved at referendum, became law. By 1985 Missouri ranked last among the fifty states in per capita taxation. The needs of cities, schools, and prisons were not well attended.[3]

Iowa was particularly hard hit by the farm crisis. Its population declined by 100,000 between 1980 and 1990 (from 2.9 million to 2.8 million). During that period, 140,000 people left its farms. Iowa also lost hundreds of farm implement dealers and thousands of manufacturing jobs.[4] Nebraska and the Dakotas also suffered. More than one-third of Nebraska's farmers found themselves in financial distress during the 1980s. By 1990, farmers constituted only 6 percent of Nebraska's workforce, but manufacturing jobs did not, to any significant degree, make up for the flight from the farm. Eighty-three of the state's ninety-three counties lost population during the 1980s, so that by 1990, more than 60 percent of the state's population lived in the extreme eastern part of the state.[5]

South Dakota's farm population also dropped, and the average size of its farms grew. The state witnessed a significant migration from farms and small towns to cities over 2,500 in population. The growth of tourism, however, helped to some degree to lessen the impact of the farm recession. By 1989, tourism was bringing in six million visitors annually, who spent $576 million in the state.[6] Over the years, South Dakota, because of its low population density, limited commercial base, and relatively clean politics, had contributed fewer high-profile cases to the Court of Appeals than the other states of the Eighth Circuit. However, during the 1980s, important litigation involving dams and irrigation projects, church-state relations, Native American rights, libel, and federalism was spawned in the state.

North Dakota, afflicted by depression and drought, suffered a population decline of 2.1 percent. The exodus from the western counties was such that their population dropped to fewer than two persons per square mile, the indicator of the area's emergence from frontier status the Census Bureau had used a century before.[7]

Minnesota was much more fortunate. Its population increased by 7.3 percent and became more heterogeneous with the arrival of thousands of immigrants from Southeast Asia, Mexico, and Central America. By 1990, manufacturing was the largest single sector of Minnesota's economy. "Clean companies" and "brain" industries—electronics, insurance, medical technology, and computers—had by 1990 replaced the stockyards and flour mills of the past.[8]

Judicial Administration

Keeping up with greatly increased filings was the principal problem in the administration of justice confronting all the U.S. courts of appeals during the 1980s. In the Eighth Circuit, the number of filings grew from 1,147 (1980) to 2,792 (1990). To help handle the increased number of filings in the Eighth Circuit, one of the greatest percentage increases among the circuits,[9] Congress increased the size of the court to eleven judges. Staffs of individual judges and the central legal staff of the Court of Appeals also grew. A number of devices and techniques were adopted to deal with the case flow, but at bottom, keeping up with it took hard work on the part of the judges. However, the efficiency of the court was jeopardized by the marked increase in the number of cases reheard en banc.[10]

The number of judges, which had been increased to nine in 1978, was increased by one by the law of July 10, 1984. An eleventh judgeship would be added on December 1, 1990, as part of an omnibus judgeship bill that created eighty-four judgeships nationally.[11] The staffs of individual judges and the central legal staff of the Court of Appeals also grew. Senior and district judges made major contributions in assisting the court with its increased workload.

A number of new devices and techniques were adopted under the leadership of Donald Lay, Chief Judge from 1980 to 1992, with the important assistance of June L. Boadwine, acting circuit executive from 1985 to 1987 and circuit executive from 1987 to 1997. Following the lead of the Second Circuit, the Eighth established a Civil Appeals Mediation Plan in 1984. Cases were screened to lessen the number given oral argument. An appeals expediter worked with the various attorneys and court reporters to see that transcripts, records, and briefs reached the court in timely fashion and that oral argument was put in a proper logistical schedule for the court.[12] Senior staff counsel screened the pro se cases after briefs were filed. Staff counsel wrote drafts of memorandum and per curiam opinions and handled jurisdictional motions.[13] But nothing substituted for hard judicial work. By 1984, the court was sitting in three panels each month with twenty-five cases assigned to each panel. Decisions were being rendered in a median time of four to five months after the notice of appeal was filed.[14]

Other important innovations were implemented during the Lay chief judgeship. Each district set up federal practice committees to be the mechanism for attorneys to work with district courts to create new policies, modify court rules, deal with complaints, and foster continuing legal education. Federal advisory committees were established to provide input on appellate rules, the internal policies of the Court of Appeals, and the running of the Circuit Judicial Conference. The Judicial Council of the Eighth Circuit appointed a court management committee to deal with backlogs and encouraged scheduling conferences to control excesses of discovery. For these and other reasons, disposition time for trials and motions in the Eighth Circuit was shortened.[15]

Among the other administrative changes of the 1980s was the opening in 1983 of a division office in St. Paul, as an accommodation to lawyers of the northern states of the circuit. During his brief tenure on the court in 1998, Judge John D. Kelly successfully opposed the closing of that office because of its value to attorneys in North and South Dakota. The headquarters of the court, however, remained in St. Louis. In addition, the chief judge also scheduled oral arguments at every law school in the circuit on a regular basis.[16]

In 1981, the Judicial Conference of the Eighth Circuit was changed from a conference by invitation only to one open to any attorney who practiced before one of the federal courts of the circuit. As a result, the Eighth Circuit Judicial Conference became the most democratic and possibly the largest of the conferences in all the circuits.[17]

The administrative role of the chief judge continued to grow in the Eighth Circuit, as well as in the other circuits. The chief judge was responsible for oversight of the flow of cases, the court's budget, and decisions about the acquisition of new equipment. He was responsible for the coordination of the courts within the circuit and for administering the Judicial Discipline and Conduct Act. The chief judge chaired meetings of the Court of Appeals and of the Judicial Council and served as a member of the Judicial Conference of the United States. In addition, Chief Judge Lay served on the Judicial Conference Appellate Rules Committee and as a consultant to the Federal Judicial Center's Advisory Committees on State-Federal Relations and on Federal Rules.[18]

The Judges

It is fair to describe the Court of Appeals for the Eighth Circuit as a moderately liberal court when it entered the 1980s.[19] The court's most liberal members were the Lyndon Johnson appointees—Donald Lay, Gerald Heaney, and Myron Bright—and Jimmy Carter's appointee, Theodore McMillian. Three judges were more moderate than liberal— Richard Arnold, Donald Ross, and Roy Stephenson. There was also one judge who could be termed a moderate conservative, the Ford appointee, J. Smith Henley.

Between 1982 and 1987, President Reagan filled one preexisting vacancy, two newly created judgeships, and three vacancies created by judges taking senior status (Henley, Stephenson, and Bright). The Reagan administration screened appointments to the Court of Appeals more systematically for jurisprudential views than any administration since that of Franklin D. Roosevelt. Each of its appointees to the Eighth Circuit was at least moderately conservative.[20] Although the change in the court was relatively gradual, by the summer of 1990, its center of gravity was conservative. Excluding those on senior status, the court then consisted of two liberals (Lay and McMillian), one moderate liberal (Richard Arnold), one moderate conservative (J. R. Gibson), and five conservatives (Fagg, Bowman, Magill, Wollman, and Beam).[21] With time and new issues before the court, however, the Reagan judges by no means moved in lockstep.

The first of Reagan's nominees was John R. Gibson. He was appointed on March 9, 1982, to the seat left vacant when Floyd Gibson went senior in 1980. Born in 1925, Gibson served in the U.S. Army from 1944 to 1946. Attending the University of Missouri for both college and law school, Gibson practiced with Morrison, Hecker, Curtis, Kuder & Parrish in Kansas City. He served as vice president of the Board of Police Commissioners of that city from 1973 to 1977 and also had been president of the Missouri bar. In 1981, Reagan appointed Gibson as a judge of the U.S. District Court for the Western District of Missouri. He has been described as "'a conservative judge, who has gotten a little more liberal as he has gone along.'"[22] Indeed, he is not easy to pigeonhole. As an example, in his early years on the Court of Appeals, Gibson dissented over the broad relief in the St. Louis school desegregation case.[23] Yet he wrote several opinions for the Court of Appeals largely affirming the sweeping rulings issued by the lower court in the Kansas City school case.[24] Gibson has also been quite sympathetic to the claims of Native Americans but consistently voted to uphold criminal convictions and resisted broad use of Section 1983 to pursue civil rights claims.

George G. Fagg entered on duty on October 1, 1982. Fagg was born in Eldora, Iowa, in 1934. A graduate of Drake University and Drake Law School, Fagg practiced law from 1958 to 1972 with Cartwright, Druker, Ryden and Fagg in Marshalltown, Iowa. Fagg was a state district judge (for the Second Judicial District) for ten years before his appointment to the U.S. Court of Appeals. In Iowa, Fagg had chaired the state's Committee on Uniform Jury Instructions and served as a member of the Advisory Committee on Rules of Civil Procedure of the Iowa Supreme Court. He was also a faculty member of the National Judicial College. Even among his colleagues on the Court of Appeals, Fagg was known for extraordinarily long hours and hard work, arriving at the courthouse long before the sun rose. Fagg was described early in his tenure by Douglas O. Linder as a "swing judge in en banc cases," a judge who was "almost as likely to dissent over an arcane procedural issue as a sexy issue of constitutional law."[25] One of Fagg's most important opinions came in *South Dakota v. Dole*, where the Court of Appeals held that the secretary of transportation had the power to withhold a portion of federal highway funds to press the states to maintain a drinking age of twenty-one. The Supreme Court affirmed in a landmark interpretation of the scope of Congress's appropriations power.[26] If Fagg can fairly be typed as a conservative, he is one who reaches results not reflexively but after hard thought. He has, for example, supported the court's approach in the St. Louis school de-segregation case. Fagg took senior status in 1999.[27]

In 1983 Pasco Bowman, dean of the University of Missouri–Kansas City Law School, was appointed to the seat that had opened up when Judge J. Smith Henley took senior status. Born in 1933 in Harrisonburg, Virginia, Bowman graduated from Bridgewater College and New York University Law School, where he was managing editor of the law review. Then, as a Fulbright scholar, he attended the London School of Economics. Many years later Bowman received an LL.M. from the graduate program for judges of the University of Virginia Law School.

Bowman practiced law with the Wall Street firm Cravath Swaine & Moore (1958–64) before becoming a professor of law. He was a member of the faculties of the University of Georgia (1964–70), Wake Forest (1970–78), and the University of Missouri–Kansas City (1979–83), serving as dean at Wake Forest and Missouri–Kansas City.

Bowman entered on duty with the Court of Appeals on August 1, 1983. One of his earliest dissents occurred in the St. Louis desegregation case, where he wrote of "the singular inappropriateness in our Constitutional system of a federal court's ordering state and local taxing authorities to impose specific tax increases."[28] One of Bowman's strongest dissents in his early years occurred in *Bush v. Taylor*, a bankruptcy case discussed later in this chapter.[29]

Roger L. Wollman, appointed to the Court of Appeals by President Reagan, took the oath of office on September 6, 1985. The appointment had been facilitated by Senator Larry Pressler. Wollman was the first South Dakotan to be appointed to the court since A. K. Gardner in 1929. Born in 1934 on a farm in Frankfort, South Dakota, twenty-four miles north of Huron, Wollman attended Tabor College, a Mennonite institution, in Hillsboro, Kansas. After he served in the army from 1957 to 1959, Wollman earned a J.D. from the University of South Dakota. He clerked for Judge George T. Mickelson of the District of South Dakota, then studied for an LL.M. at Harvard Law School. Wollman confesses that the hardest day of his life was the day he told his father that he did not want to come back to the farm.[30] Instead he practiced law in Aberdeen, South Dakota, as part of a two-man firm that represented a small bank and insurance companies and also did some criminal defense work. From 1967 to 1971, he also served as state's attorney for Brown County.

In 1970, Wollman was elected without opposition to the South Dakota Supreme Court. When he took office in 1971, he was the youngest member of the court by twenty years. During his first year on the court, Wollman wrote over seventy-five opinions. In 1978 he was elected Chief Justice of South Dakota by his colleagues and presided for four years over a unified court system established in 1972. On July 24, 1978, he had the honor of swearing in his brother Harvey as governor of South Dakota, an office to which he had succeeded from the lieutenant governorship when Governor Richard F. Kneip left for an ambassadorship. It was a day of mixed emotions because Harvey had been defeated in a primary seeking a full term and knew that his political career was over. Wollman's own service as Chief Justice ended in 1982 when, after several changes in the membership of the court, he was defeated for reelection, depriving him of the opportunity to continue to work with the Conference of Chief Justices, a job he had greatly enjoyed.

Wollman served as Chief Judge of the Court of Appeals from 1999 until 2002. Judge Wollman describes himself as a conservative, coming from a fundamentalist background with a highly developed sense of morality and a pessimistic worldview, who does not believe that government can do much to make people better. Far from an ideologue, even where the criminal law is concerned, Wollman believes deeply in personal accountability yet is troubled by the death penalty, long sentences for crack, and disproportionate punishment of minorities. Wollman has evolved into a moderately conservative judge, close to the middle of his court. When he has time, Wollman continues to work on the family farm in Huron, running machinery and picking corn.[31]

Judge Frank J. Magill was appointed to the Court of Appeals in 1986 after Myron Bright took senior status. Born in 1927, the son of farmers, Magill was raised in southeast North Dakota. Magill served in naval intelligence from 1945 to 1947 and received his B.S.F.S. degree from Georgetown University School of Foreign Service in 1951, a master's degree from Columbia in 1953, and an LL.B. from Georgetown in 1955. From 1955 to 1986, Magill practiced law in Fargo with Nilles, Hansen, Magill and Davies. An able railroad defense lawyer, Magill also concentrated on public utility law and governmental relations. Magill was active in the North Dakota Bar Association, the American Bar Association, and was a fellow of the American College of Trial Lawyers. He was close to Senator Mark Andrews, who fought successfully to keep Bright's Court of Appeals seat in North Dakota. In his twenties, Magill was politically radical, but he has proved to be a conservative jurist. He handled the ungrateful assignment of heading the financial disclosure committee of the U.S. Judicial Conference from 1993 to 1998. In 1997, Magill took senior status.[32]

In 1987 President Reagan made his sixth and last appointment to the Court of Appeals, C. Arlen Beam, who had been a judge of the U.S. District Court for the District of Nebraska since 1982. Beam was born in Stapleton, Nebraska, in 1930. After graduating with a B.S. degree in agriculture from the University of Nebraska, Lincoln, Beam saw action with the U.S. Army in Korea. After his return to Nebraska, Beam worked in the agribusiness field for ten years. While attending the University of Nebraska College of Law (where he received his J.D. in 1965), Beam ran his own public relations firm. He then practiced law in Lincoln until his appointment to the district court. The seat on the Court of Appeals that Beam occupied almost went to Morris Arnold, who would reach the court several years later.[33] Since 1979, Beam has been Nebraska's commissioner on the Conference of Commissioners on Uniform State Laws. He was a member of the U.S. Judicial Conference Committee on Court Security from 1989 to 1993 and its chairman from 1992 to 1993. Beam has been classified as a moderate conservative, who is "both intellectual and practical."[34]

The number of dissenting opinions to Eighth Circuit decisions began to grow in the early 1980s. By the middle of the decade, the differences between the newer appointees and their more senior colleagues were evident in the number of cases reheard en banc. In the past, en bancing had primarily been used for cases of considerable moment or to reconcile differences between panels. By the mid-1980s, it was being employed to reverse panel decisions where the results were disliked by a majority of the court.[35] While this was occurring on most of the courts of appeals, the contrast with the past was particularly marked in the Eighth Circuit. Usually, the result of en bancing in the Eighth Circuit was almost the same as the vote to en banc the case. By the latter part of the decade, the Reagan appointees in many en banc cases lined up together, often joined by a colleague or two.[36] Justice Harry Blackmun expressed his concern about this development in his remarks at the 1988 Eighth Circuit Judicial Conference:

> When I see in en banc hearings all the appointees of the present administration voting one way and all the appointees of prior administrations, Democrat or Republican, voting the other way, I'm a little concerned. Maybe I'm more than a little bit concerned. Am I wrong in being concerned? I expect it on our court.[37]

Many of the Reagan appointees differed significantly from the more senior members of the court on questions involving the crafting of remedies in school desegregation cases, criminal cases (where they were more pro-government), some First Amendment cases (where they also were more pro-government), discharges in bankruptcy, as well as in their readings of laws that might be used to assist farmers facing bankruptcy.

There were some unseemly squabbles. In *Williams v. Armontrout*,[38] the majority denied permission to such respected litigating groups as the NAACP and the ACLU to file briefs in support of rehearing en banc in a criminal appeal. Judges Lay, Bright, Richard Arnold, and J. R. Gibson dissented. In *Walker v. City of Kansas City, Mo.*, a case involving the use of zoning to prevent the opening of a go-go girls establishment, three judges dissented from denial of rehearing en banc: Lay, McMillian, and J. R. Gibson. Lay wrote in dissent:

> We should grant a rehearing en banc in the present case because it is the first case in the history of the Eighth Circuit when we reverse a district court on grounds that were (1) not factually engaged in by the parties before the City Council; (2) not passed upon by the City Council; (3) not asserted in the district court, and (4) not briefed or argued before this court.[39]

In spite of the intellectual differences between the judges of the Eighth Circuit during the 1980s, the court remained a collegial body. Personal relations among newer and more senior judges alike continued to be amicable and constructive. Judge Wollman, for example, wrote that "the forcefulness of our rhetoric reflects deeply held beliefs and should not be interpreted as an expression of personal animosity or ill will."[40] Judge Beam stated:

> It should be pointed that the debate and differences evident from these and other opinions, enhance rather than diminish, the collegiality of the court. Each of us was in the past a practicing lawyer, familiar with the rough and tumble of the adversarial process. The robust exchange of ideas at conference and later, hones and strengthens our opinions and provides an enjoyable part of our nonjudicial lives.[41]

If the judges were socializing less than they once had, this was the result not of ideological tensions but of the enlarging of the court and other factors.

Indeed, the Court of Appeals of the 1980s was, for the most part, a court of warm, outgoing men who liked and respected one another.

There were the three "Hubert Humphrey liberals": Chief Judge Lay, a strong, competitive personality; Heaney of Duluth, with a deep humanitarian streak that asserted itself both on and off the bench, and who also was a fount of wisdom on practical politics; Bright of Fargo, indefatigable, extroverted, and warm, unabashedly admitting that the most important job of a judge was to do justice. The three were joined philosophically by McMillian of St. Louis, who had grown up in a segregated city and had by dint of enormous ability reached the top of his profession without forgetting those who were left behind.

There were the "moderate" judges: Ross of Nebraska, with his rich experience in Republican politics, conservative in criminal and business cases, but with views akin to Lay, Bright, and Heaney in civil rights cases; bow-tie wearing Richard Arnold of Arkansas, high powered intellectually with a prose style the envy of judges throughout the nation; Reagan appointee John R. Gibson, a strong and independent judge, difficult to characterize, but like Ross and Arnold often in the "middle" of the court. Stephenson of Iowa, whose tragic death occurred early in the decade, belonged in this group as well.

The conservative judges included Henley, the Arkansas prison reformer, with his paradoxical distrust of government. Five of the six Reagan appointees might be placed in this group during this period. There was Fagg, less extroverted than most of his colleagues, a man described as someone who "lives for the law, the Constitution, the Eighth Circuit Court of Appeals and everything that has to do with the law."[42] Bowman was a brilliant and charming academic. Wollman brought to his work a sensitive, thoughtful, inquisitive mind and a farm background. Magill's background included representing insurance companies and railroads, while Beam of Nebraska brought practical business experience.

Jurisprudence

The most important decisions of the Court of Appeals during the 1980s were drawn from areas that had been concerns for decades (racial civil rights, criminal law, Native Americans, and federalism); from heavily litigated areas that had become significant in the Eighth Circuit recently (the relationship between church and state); and areas that had become significant to the federal courts relatively recently (abortion and social security disability cases). In addition, there were a surprisingly large number of bankruptcy cases arising with striking clashes of values. In the 1980s, there were also more important regional cases than in many decades—cases involving farms and farmers, railroads, Native Americans, and litigation attempting to block major irrigation projects.

In the area of abortion, a more conservative Court of Appeals reflected the reservations the more conservative Supreme Court was having about *Roe v. Wade*. In the two major school desegregation cases involving large cities, the Court of Appeals proved willing to accept some, but not all, of the strong medicine ordered by the district judges. In cases involving the Establishment Clause of the Constitution, the court tended more to accommodate church and state than to erect a wall between them. In major federalism cases, the court tended to rule against the positions taken by the states. The court tended to rule for the government in the important cases involving efforts to block large irrigation projects, but the real outcome of the litigation was to slow or scale down the projects. In other areas, it is difficult to find a clear pattern.

While the Court of Appeals clearly continued to be an "obedient court," the Supreme Court heard more than its fair share of cases from the Eighth Circuit during this period and its reversal rate was not low. In 1987, for example, the circuit was ninth in the number of cases in which there were petitions for certiorari or jurisdictional statements, but fourth in the number of appeals noted and petitions granted. That year, eleven of its cases were reviewed and eight reversed.[43]

Abortion

Cases involving abortion arose in most of the states of the Eighth Circuit. With more conservative memberships of both the Court of Appeals and Supreme Court, there were fewer complete victories for pro-choice advocates in the Eighth Circuit.

In 1981, a panel of Heaney (writing), Henley, and McMillian struck down a North Dakota statute banning all public funds used for family planning by any agency encouraging or performing abortions. Unlike the district court, which had invalidated the statute on free speech grounds, the Court of Appeals held that the state statute conflicted with a federal statute and, therefore, was invalid under the Supremacy Clause.[44]

The following year, the Court of Appeals, employing strict scrutiny, struck down Nebraska's parental consent requirement and its requirement of a forty-eight hour waiting period between the expression of informed consent and the actual performance of the abortion. The Supreme Court vacated the decision after it decided *City of Akron Center for Reproductive Health* in 1983,[45] which struck down similar requirements.

Hodgson v. State of Minnesota involved the constitutionality of Minnesota's parental consent statute.[46] Passed in 1981, the law required a pregnant minor to notify both parents of her desire to obtain an abortion at least forty-eight hours before the abortion was to take place. Minnesota was the only state in the nation that required two-parent notification without an exception for divorce or separation. The statute was struck down by Chief Judge Donald D. Alsop of the District of Minnesota. Alsop's opinion was affirmed by a panel of the court (Rosenn-Lay-Heaney), but that decision was vacated, and rehearing en banc was granted. The *Hodgson* case was argued in the Court of Appeals (and in the U.S. Supreme Court) by Janet Benshoof, probably the leading pro-choice attorney in the United States. In the en banc decision, every judge appointed after 1979 voted to uphold the statute, while every one appointed earlier voted to strike it down.

Writing for the court, Judge John R. Gibson held that so long as there was a judicial bypass procedure, the two parent notification requirement was constitutional. The court also held that despite the district court's findings of fact concerning the general difficulties of obtaining an abortion in Minnesota and the emotionally traumatic effects of Minnesota's processes, that Minnesota's statute was constitutional because there were significant state interests justifying the statute. The court held that a statute requiring a minor seeking an abortion to give forty-eight hours' notice to both parents unless judicial waiver of the notice requirement was obtained was not unconstitutional.[47]

Dissenting, Judge Lay found "more than a little irony in the majority's assumption that the statute promotes 'family integrity'" by forcing minor children to locate and inform noncustodial parents of the decision to have an abortion, because 42 percent of all minors in Minnesota were not living with both parents.[48] Judge Heaney, often supportive of statutes constraining abortion, also dissented, finding that the statute "opens the door to creating intolerable tensions for the minor child at a time when he or she least needs additional stress."[49]

In a strange decision, a badly fractionated Supreme Court held that the forty-eight-hour waiting period between notification of the parents and performance of the abortion was constitutional; and that the two-parent notification provision was unconstitutional, but that two-parent notification with judicial bypass was constitutional, thus saving the statute as a whole.[50]

The Eighth Circuit was called on several times to determine the constitutionality of Missouri laws restricting abortions. The 1979 Missouri abortion law was tested in *Planned Parenthood v. [Attorney General] John Ashcroft*, decided in 1981.[51] In 1981 a panel upheld provisions requiring attending physicians to inform women as to the particular risks associated with the abortion techniques to be used and alternatives to abortion. The court narrowed the reach of a statute, which appeared to impose strict criminal liability on a physician for an erroneous, but good faith, determination of fetal nonviability, by holding that it might be used to punish only those physicians who knew the fetus was viable. However, it held unconstitutional a requirement of notice to parents of minors and of pathology reports for all abortions, a forty-eight-hour waiting period for abortions, and a requirement that a second doctor be present for second-trimester abortions. The Court of Appeals also held that the requirement that all second-trimester abortions be performed in hospitals was unconstitutional, but upheld record-keeping requirements for physicians.[52] A divided U.S. Supreme Court held the second-trimester hospitalization requirement unconstitutional but upheld the minor's consent and pathology report requirements and requiring a second physician to be present during abortions performed after viability.[53]

The most significant abortion case in the United States during this period was *Reproductive Health Service v. Webster*, which dealt with Missouri's 1986 abortion statute. When the Supreme Court granted certiorari in the case, it was widely expected that it would be the vehicle for overturning *Roe v. Wade*. In the end, the Supreme Court did not reconsider *Roe*, although it did modify and narrow it.

The preamble to the 1986 law contained "findings" that "the life of each human being begins at conception" and that "unborn children have protectable interests in life, health, and well-being." The law required that before performing an abortion on any woman whom a physician had reason to believe was more than twenty weeks pregnant, the physician had to make a finding as to whether the fetus was viable. The law prohibited the use of public facilities for abortions and public funds for encouraging or counseling a woman to have an abortion. It barred public employees from performing or assisting at abortions not necessary to save the life of the mother.

Judge Scott O. Wright of the Western District of Missouri held seven provisions of the statute unconstitutional.[54] The Eighth Circuit panel of Lay, McMillian, and Arnold affirmed the district court on virtually every holding. It held that the declaration in the preamble that life begins at conception was "simply an impermissible state adoption of a theory of when life begins to justify abortion regulation."[55] It invalidated viability testing, the prohibitions on public employees, and the ban on the use of public facilities. Judge Richard Arnold dissented as to the preamble, thinking it valid for subjects other than abortion.[56]

The Supreme Court ducked the issues connected with the preamble and the prohibition on the use of public funds for encouraging or counseling a woman to have non-therapeutic abortions. Reversing the Court of Appeals, the High Court upheld the provision making it unlawful for any public employee within the scope of his employment to perform or assist a nontherapeutic abortion. The Supreme Court narrowed but did not invalidate the viability testing. Most importantly, the plurality of the High Court thought that "the doubt cast upon the Missouri statute" was not so much "a flaw in the statute as it is a reflection of the fact that the rigid trimester analysis of the course of a pregnancy" had made "constitutional law in this area a virtual Procrustean bed."[57] Justice O'Connor, the swing vote, saw "no necessity to reexamine the constitutional validity of *Roe v. Wade*,"[58] resulting in what Justice Scalia called "the most stingy possible holding today."[59]

Three months before the Supreme Court decision in the *Webster* case, a somewhat differently constituted panel of the Court of Appeals upheld by a vote of 2–1 provisions of the Missouri abortion statute that required that physicians performing abortions maintain surgical privileges at hospitals providing ob-gyn care. The statement in the legislation that Missouri intended to regulate abortion to the extent permitted by the U.S. Constitution was an expression of the state's determination to exercise constitutional authority and not unconstitutional. Judge McMillian dissented.[60]

Civil Rights

The most important civil rights cases of this period in the Eighth Circuit involved employment discrimination, reapportionment, and school desegregation. One of the most important employment discrimination cases was *Moylan v. Maries County*, a case of first impression, in which the court recognized a cause of action for hostile environment sexual harassment without requiring the female plaintiff to prove that quid pro quo submission to her employer's advances was a condition of her employment.[61]

Two reapportionment cases generated important opinions by Judge Richard Arnold for three-judge district courts in Arkansas. In *Smith v. Clinton,* the court held that a multimember, all-white district in Crittenden County violated section 2 of the Voting Rights Act and ordered it split. The Supreme Court affirmed by an equally divided court.[62]

In *Jeffers v. Clinton,* Arnold wrote for a divided court, which held that the reapportionment of both the Arkansas Senate and House of Representatives violated the Voting Rights Act because although blacks made up 16 percent of Arkansas's population, the allocation of legislative district lines at issue would have made it very difficult to elect more than six black legislators out of a total of 135 in both houses.[63] The court concluded that section 2(b) of the Voting Rights Act had been violated.[64] Writing of *Jeffers v. Clinton,* Judge Patricia Wald of the U.S. Court of Appeals for the District of Columbia Circuit called it "a truly extraordinary voting rights opinion, calling into play virtually all the facets of his [Judge Arnold's] career."[65]

During these years, the Court of Appeals continued to wrestle with school desegregation cases from Little Rock, St. Louis, and Kansas City. In Little Rock, many whites had abandoned the city for the suburbs, and the entire school district was becoming unbalanced. Central High School's student body had become more than two-thirds black. In 1984, Judge Henry Woods granted the school district's suit to force consolidation with several contiguous districts in Pulaski County to restore a workable black-white ratio in the Little Rock schools. However, the Court of Appeals reversed, although it did expand the Little Rock School District boundaries to the city limits. In 1989, the three school districts, the African Americans and the state reached a settlement, but wealthier families increasingly placed their children in private schools. However, in 1990 the 1956 amendment committing the state to segregation was finally repealed by referendum.[66]

During the 1980s, the tortured history of school desegregation in St. Louis continued, while the desegregation suit involving Kansas City's schools developed into full-blown institutional litigation. In the St. Louis case, Judge William L. Hungate succeeded James H. Meredith as trial judge. As full integration could not be achieved because of the degree of racial imbalance in the St. Louis schools and the impossibility of compelling the participation of suburban schools, the judicial effort to desegregate and improve the St. Louis schools primarily involved voluntary exchanges between pupils in city schools and those in suburban districts, the creation of magnet schools in St. Louis, and large capital improvements for black schools expected to remain racially imbalanced. Most of the costs of the effort were borne by a not-very-willing state of Missouri.

In March 1981, the Court of Appeals, hearing the case for the third time, affirmed Judge Meredith's court-ordered desegregation plan, which (1) reassigned students to achieve the greatest possible number of desegregated schools, (2) established magnet schools designed to attract students of all races from throughout the St. Louis area, (3) initiated cooperative interdistrict desegregation programs, and (4) provided for integration of school personnel. The Court held that

> although the plan reflects the fact that it is not possible to fully integrate every school in the St. Louis system, the district court faithfully followed the directions of the Court by providing a variety of integrative experiences and continued educational opportunities for students remaining in the predominantly black schools.[67]

In 1982, the Court of Appeals, in what was known as *Liddell V,* disapproved of mandatory interdistrict transfers, holding the scope of interdistrict relief very narrow and requiring a trial on liability.[68] *Liddell V* did, however, establish a framework for consideration of a mandatory interdistrict desegregation plan and set the stage for settlement of the metropolitan area school desegregation case. The court implied in *Liddell V* that the state might be liable for the full costs of the voluntary segregation plan.

On the brink of trial to determine whether there was liability (which would have allowed a mandatory interdistrict remedy), twenty-two of twenty-three school districts and the other parties in the case came to a settlement agreement, which provided for voluntary interdistrict transfers, the establishment of magnet schools, and improvement of education in the city's schools. The trial judge approved the settlement, which was modified and affirmed by the en banc Court of Appeals in *Liddell VII.*[69] Under the settlement agreement, primary responsibility for funding the settlement plan rested with the State of Missouri and the Board of Education of the City of St. Louis. The court enjoined a scheduled property tax roll back in the City of St. Louis. The Court of Appeals made significant modifications in Judge Hungate's plan regarding the voluntary interdistrict transfers, magnet schools, and quality education components, which, in the aggregate, reduced the state's financial obligations. It also ordered creation of a budget review committee. Of the three Reagan appointees then on the court, George Fagg joined the majority, Pasco Bowman dissented, while John R. Gibson dissented in part. Within four years, eleven thousand city students were attending schools outside of their districts on a voluntary basis. However, only 724 white students from outside St. Louis were attending the St. Louis schools.

In 1986, the Court of Appeals ordered large increases in interdistrict magnet enrollment (Liddell IX).[70] In Liddell XII, the Court of Appeals ordered prompt completion of the magnet school master plan and its prompt implementation, ordered the Board of Education to achieve a 20:1 pupil-teacher ratio in the all-black city schools by the beginning of the 1988–89 school year, and indirectly held that the voluntary interdistrict transfer program was to continue.[71]

The Kansas City litigation had begun in 1977. At the time, while Kansas City, Missouri, was 30 percent African American, 63 percent of the city's schools had populations at least 95 percent of one race.[72] Before 1954, racially restrictive covenants and the practices of federal, state, and local housing agencies had made it almost impossible for African Americans to live anywhere in the Kansas City metropolitan area save in the southeast corridor. Furthermore, before 1954, many school districts provided no schools at all or inadequate ones for blacks.[73]

In 1977, the Kansas City, Missouri, School District (KCMSD), the Board of Education and Superintendent, and four children of members of the Board of Education filed suit against the state of Missouri, the Missouri State Board of Education, the State of Kansas, the Kansas City, Kansas School District, as well as a number of suburban school districts in both states, and against the secretaries of the U.S. Departments of Health, Welfare and Education, Housing and Urban Development, and Transportation. The plaintiffs sought a holding that the defendants had not eradicated segregation but actually contributed to it. The remedy sought was metropolitan-wide desegregation.

In the early stages of the litigation, the suit was dismissed against many of the defendants, including those from Kansas.[74] An amended complaint was filed in May 1979. The case was tried by Judge Russell G. Clark, a Democrat from rural Missouri. It began on October 21, 1983, and consumed sixty-four trial days with 140 witnesses and 10,000 pages of depositions. Clark found that the state of Missouri and the KCMSD had been maintaining a racially segregated dual school system in 1954 and had failed in their affirmative duty to dismantle that pre-1954 system. The state of Missouri was also liable, but not the eleven predominantly white suburban school districts, which were dropped from the suit, as was the U.S. Department of Housing and Urban Development.[75] As a result, there would be no forced transfers of students to and from the white suburbs. The Court of Appeals upheld the denial of interdistrict relief by a vote of 5–3. The majority was made up of all the judges appointed from 1979 onward and Judge Ross.[76]

In 1985, Clark ordered the state and the KCMSD to fund compensatory and remedial educational programs and necessary capital improvements for the KCMSD schools.[77] The following year, Clark ordered specialized academic programs in all of Kansas City's seventeen high schools and half of its fifty elementary schools in the hope of luring white students from the suburbs. Then, to improve the Kansas City schools and with the hope that it would attract children from the suburbs, Judge Clark approved a desegregation plan requiring huge expenditures. Every school in the district was "magnetized." New facilities were installed on a scale so immense that the district would never be able to maintain them on its own. In 1988, a panel of the Court of Appeals affirmed the scope of the remedy as to magnet schools and capital improvements with some slight modifications.[78]

Between 1987 and 1995, Kansas City received what most educators can only dream of—over $1.5 billion to improve its schools.[79] When he adopted the full-scale magnet plan in 1986, Clark had held the state and KCMSD jointly and severally liable and imposed 60 to 75 percent of the costs on the state. After Kansas City's voters had rejected proposed tax increases in four elections during the preceding fourteen months, Clark, holding that "a district court's broad equitable power to remedy the evils of segregation includes the power to order tax increases and bond issuances," ordered large increases in property and income taxes.[80]

The Court of Appeals dealt with the tax increases in the same opinion where it affirmed the scope of the remedy (magnet schools and capital improvements). It held that a judge could not order tax increases, but that he could order the school board to impose property taxes and enjoin state laws that might prevent the KCMSD from exercising that power. It did not approve an income tax surcharge because the "district court

[had] invaded the province of the legislature" and restructured "the state's schemes of school financing," creating "an entirely new form of taxing authority."[81] Judges Bowman and Wollman would have reheard the case en banc because they believed the remedy "without parallel in any other school district in the country." "In no other case," Bowman and Wollman wrote, "has federal judicial power been used to impose a tax increase in order to provide funding for a desegregation remedy."[82]

The Supreme Court of the United States held by a 5–4 vote that Judge Clark had gone too far but that the Court of Appeals' modification of Clark's order satisfied equitable and constitutional principles.[83]

First Amendment Jurisprudence

CHURCH–STATE CASES   The Court of Appeals had, for the first time, a number of significant cases raising questions of the relationship between church and state in the 1980s. Five were reviewed by the Supreme Court, which affirmed in four. On the whole, the Court of Appeals tilted toward accommodation of religion over strict separation of church and state, but less so than the Supreme Court.

Two cases, although involving religious groups, were decided based on free speech grounds. *Chess v. Widmar,* decided by the Court of Appeals in 1980,[84] involved University of Missouri rules prohibiting recognized student groups from using facilities for religious services and teaching. A panel of Heaney, Floyd Gibson, and Stephenson held that, once the University had created an open forum, it could not restrict access to it because of the contents of the speech. Judges Bright and McMillian dissented from the denial of rehearing en banc. The Supreme Court affirmed by a vote of 8–1 in the case retitled *Widmar v. Vincent.*

After the Supreme Court's *Widmar* decision, Congress passed the Equal Access Act of 1984, which banned public secondary schools that received federal financial assistance and had a limited open forum from denying access on the basis of religious, political, or other views.[85] When, several years later, the West Side High School in Omaha refused to permit a group of students to form a Christian Bible study club, Judge C. Arlen Beam, then of the District of Nebraska, believing that the Equal Access Act did not apply because the school maintained a closed forum, held that the formation of the club would violate the Establishment Clause. In *Mergens v. Board of Education of Westside Community Schools,*[86] the Court of Appeals held that the school had created a limited public forum and that, either by extending *Widmar* or by applying the Equal Access Act, the students were entitled to their club. The Supreme Court affirmed, using the decision to uphold the constitutionality of the Equal Access Act.

Two cases involved the tax deductibility of payments given to religious organizations or institutions. *Valente v. Larson* involved the constitutionality of Minnesota's Charitable Solicitation Act, which exempted from its requirements only religions that received less than one-half of their contributions from members.[87] The law was probably aimed at the fund-raising practices of the Unification Church. The Court of Appeals termed the statutory discrimination "religious gerrymandering," a departure from government neutrality between sects, and therefore unconstitutional. The court invalidated the 50 percent rule, upheld the statute as judicially limited, and remanded for proof of the religious status of the Unification Church. The Supreme Court also held the provision a violation of the Establishment Clause, but on different grounds.

Minnesota's tax deduction for school-related purposes, which included tuition paid to religious-oriented private schools, was upheld by the Court of Appeals "though not without difficulty." The panel of Lay (writing), Henley, and Arnold upheld the deductions for tuition as well as textbooks and transportation to schools, because "any benefit to religion or involvement between church and state . . . is so remote and incidental" that it did not violate the constitutional wall separating church and state. The Supreme Court agreed by a 5–4 vote.[88]

Chambers v. Marsh involved the constitutionality of the compensation paid by the Nebraska Unicameral to its chaplain, as well as the legislature's practice of publishing his prayers in book form. Writing for the Court, Judge Heaney, joined by Stephenson and John W. Oliver of the Western District of Missouri, referred to the Eighth Circuit's opinion in *Bogan v. Doty*,[89] a 1979 case that had upheld the constitutionality of invocations at public meetings of a county board, but warned the board of the "quagmire it [was] near" because everyone who had delivered the invocation had been a Christian. Heaney stated that Nebraska had "fallen into that quagmire" with its legislative prayer practice. While neither the invocations nor the paying of chaplains were per se unconstitutional, in this case the majority thought that the state had "placed its official seal of approval on one religious view for sixteen years."[90] The same Presbyterian minister had been paid over that period. The Supreme Court reversed by a vote of 5–4 because "the opening of sessions of legislative and other deliberative public bodies with prayer is deeply embedded in the history and tradition of this country."[91]

In cases that did not reach the Supreme Court, the Court of Appeals upheld the singing of Christmas carols and displays of religious symbols such as crosses and menorahs in Sioux Falls, South Dakota, kindergartens[92] and upheld the hiring of a chaplain paid by taxpayer money by an Iowa county hospital (in an opinion which was a model of careful Establishment Clause analysis written by John R. Gibson) because in situations of grave illness, insanity, and death, religious problems exist and have to be dealt with no matter how secular the hospital.[93] In *Quaring v. Peterson*,[94] the Court of Appeals upheld the free exercise claim of a woman who believed literally in the injunction of the Second Commandment: "Thou shalt not make unto thee any graven image or likeness of anything that is heaven above . . . ." She argued that she was entitled to a Nebraska driver's license without her photograph on it. Judges Bright (writing) and John R. Gibson ruled on her behalf, while Judge Fagg dissented, believing that this was "an instance where a religious belief must yield to the common good."[95]

Finally, in a lawsuit brought by students and parents against the school board of Purdy in southwestern Missouri, which had refused to allow student dances at the high school, allegedly because of religious beliefs, Judge Russell G. Clark held the policy unconstitutional, and the Court of Appeals granted a temporary restraining order against the policy. However, the appellate court ultimately ruled on behalf of the school board's right to control policy. Five Reagan appointees voted to deny rehearing en banc. Judges Lay, McMillian, Arnold, and John R. Gibson dissented.[96]

FREEDOM OF EXPRESSION   Among the number of cases involving freedom of speech and press during this period, about half of which were decided in favor of the rights of claimants, were decisions involving libel, student newspapers, antiabortion picketing, adult theaters, the public function doctrine, and freedom of association. In these cases, the Reagan appointees tended to support the government, while the more senior judges tended to support the claimants.

The doctrine based on *New York Times v. Sullivan* and its progeny continued to make it extremely difficult for public figures to succeed as plaintiffs in suits for defamation.[97] The trend may be illustrated by Eighth Circuit cases involving a state governor and a U.S. senator. Governor

William Janklow of South Dakota brought suit against *Newsweek* magazine, which had published a statement that Janklow had prosecuted the Native American leader, Dennis Banks, out of revenge because Banks had charged that Janklow had raped a fifteen-year-old girl. Granting summary judgment for *Newsweek*, the district court ruled that the characterization of Janklow's prosecution of Banks as revenge was a matter of opinion rather than fact and thus did not constitute libel.

A divided panel reversed, Bowman and Fagg in the majority.[98] The en banc Court of Appeals reversed the panel. Richard Arnold, who had delivered an opinion concurring and dissenting at the time of panel consideration, wrote for the en banc court, cautioning courts "against inquiring too closely into questions of editorial judgment such as the choice of specific words."[99] John R. Gibson, McMillian, and Wollman joined the majority. Dissenting with Judges Ross and Fagg, Judge Bowman lamented that the decision added "to the fortress of actual malice a virtually impenetrable outer barrier built on extremely broad and elastic definition of opinion."[100]

Secrist v. Harkin emerged out of a campaign for the United States Senate.[101] During Senator Tom Harkin's successful race for the Senate from Iowa against then-incumbent Senator Roger W. Jepson, Harkin's campaign committee had charged in a press release that Lieutenant Colonel James E. Secrist, who had been assigned to Jepson's personal staff while on active duty, had been put there to help enhance Jepson's campaign contributions. The Court of Appeals considered the alleged defamatory statement "opinion" rather than "fact" and held that summary judgment had been properly granted by the trial court for Harkin and the members of his staff.

The Court of Appeals continued to hear important student rights cases. *Kuhlmeier v. Hazelwood School District* involved the censorship of a school newspaper, published as part of a high school course in journalism.[102] The high school principal had refused to allow the publication of articles dealing with teenage pregnancy and divorce because he believed that the stories did not adequately disguise the identities of the students involved. The panel majority (Heaney and Arnold), following *Tinker v. Des Moines School District*, held that the newspaper was a public forum for the expression of student opinion and that, as neither of the articles could reasonably have been forecast to materially disrupt class work, give rise to substantial disorder, or involve the rights of others, the censorship was unconstitutional.[103] Dissenting, Judge Wollman stated that "it may be that the defendant school officials acted out of a too abundant sense of caution. We judges are not journalists, however, and even less school administrators."[104]

The Supreme Court reversed by a vote of 6–3, moving away from the spirit of *Tinker*. Writing for the Court, Justice Byron White saw not a public forum but a newspaper that was a part of the school curriculum. He saw "student sponsored expression," rather than the personal expressions of a student. The High Court held that the standard articulated in *Tinker* for determining when a school may punish student expression "need not also be the standard for determining when a school may refuse to lend its name and resources to the dissemination of student expression."[105] The First Amendment was not offended when educators exercised editorial control over the style and content of student-sponsored expressive activities, so long as their actions were reasonably related to legitimate pedagogical expression.[106] The Supreme Court's opinion in *Kuhlmeier* was taken as a signal that the expansive spirit of *Tinker* had been curtailed.[107]

The most important political speech case involved the annual open house at the Offutt Air Force Base near Bellevue, Nebraska, where SAC Headquarters is located. The annual open houses were attended by as many as a quarter million people. In 1981, a group calling themselves "Persons for Free Speech at SAC" sought to participate in the open house to express their views on nuclear proliferation, the conversion of weapons of war to instruments of peace, and the existence of the base in their community.[108] The air force denied the request.

In an en banc case heard before the first Reagan appointee took his seat on the court, the court held that, during its open house, the air force base was not a public forum.[109] The military could legitimately use its property to foster community relations and limit the groups participating in the open house to those activities consistent with the purpose of the open house. Judges Heaney, Lay, and McMillian forcefully dissented, arguing that the open house was conducted in a manner that created a public forum. Because the air force permitted defense contractors and other nonmilitary groups to assemble booths and distribute literature, by refusing permission to those wishing to distribute literature critical of defense policies, the air force had not been applying its regulation in a content-neutral manner.[110]

Pursley v. City of Fayetteville was an early abortion-picketing case in which the Reagan appointees on the panel were divided.[111] At issue was an ordinance that banned all pickets and demonstrations in front of residences and dwelling places. The ordinance had been prompted by the picketing of the home of a Fayetteville doctor, who performed abortions as part of his practice. The majority (Magill, writing, with Henley) held the ordinance overbroad. Dissenting, Judge John R. Gibson argued that the majority ignored the possibility and likelihood of a narrowing construction, concluding that "this court today delivers a thunderclap shattering the privacy and quiet of the home."[112] Gibson, Fagg, and Wollman would have had the court rehear the case en banc.

Avalon Cinema Corp. v. Thompson involved an attempt to prevent the opening of an adult theater.[113] The North Little Rock zoning ordinance, passed only after the city learned of the imminent opening of the city's first such theater, prohibited adult theaters from being within one hundred yards of a church, elementary school, or area restricted for residential use. A panel of McManus (writing), Floyd Gibson, and Richard Arnold (dissenting) upheld the ordinance, but the en banc Court of Appeals held unanimously that the ordinance was a content-based regulation of protected speech and therefore unconstitutional.

One of the most important First Amendment cases of the period involved the competing concerns of freedom of association and gender equality.[114] The United States Jaycees, a young men's civic and service organization, did not admit women to full membership. After the Minnesota Supreme Court interpreted the state statute forbidding discrimination on the basis of sex in "places of public accommodation" to include the Jaycees, the Minnesota Department of Human Rights ordered the Jaycees to admit women to its local chapters. The Jaycees then asked the federal district court to declare the statute unconstitutional as applied to them.

Judge Diana Murphy, then of the U.S. District Court for the District of Minnesota, denied relief. A panel of Arnold, Henley, and Lay (dissenting) reversed, ruling that the right of association was not rigidly limited to the context of political beliefs or expression. The court held the Minnesota public accommodations law invalid as to an organization's choice of its own members. For the court, Judge Arnold argued that while the Jaycees were not primarily a political organization, that part of their activities was the advocacy of political and public causes. Thus the effect of the government determining who would be eligible for membership in the Jaycees would change the basic purposes of the Jaycees. The court held the Minnesota public accommodations law invalid as to an organization's choice of its own members. In his strong opinion, Arnold wrote: "An organization of young people, as opposed to young men, may be more felicitous; more socially desirable, in view of the state legislature, or in the view of the judges of this court, but it will be substantially different from the Jaycees as it now exists."[115]

Rehearing en banc was denied by an equally divided court with Judge Heaney dissenting with Lay, Bright, and McMillian, while Arnold, Gibson, Henley, and Fagg voted not to rehear. The Supreme Court reversed in an opinion written by Justice William Brennan for whom Arnold had clerked many years before. Justice O'Connor's concurring opinion closely tracked that in which Judge Heaney argued for rehearing en banc.

Cases Involving Application of Federal Law

CRIMINAL LAW   A wide range of criminal cases came before the Eighth Circuit during the 1980s. Cases ran the gamut from prosecutions under the Racketeer Influenced and Corrupt Organization Act (RICO) to those involving moonshining, illegal timber cutting, and the Mann Act.[116] The war on drugs led to an increase in the number of appeals in federal criminal cases. The courts of the Eighth Circuit rendered notable decisions in capital cases, cases involving sentencing appeals, those raising contentions based on the Fourth Amendment, and in several cases where the "calls of justice" overrode technical legal considerations.

In 1984, as part of its revision of the federal criminal code, Congress established a U.S. Sentencing Commission and provided for appeals of sentences to achieve a uniform system of punishment.[117] The sentencing commission was authorized to create sentencing guidelines, which were to be used to ensure that sentencing judges selected terms of imprisonment from a discrete range of options provided for each criminal offense. The guidelines that were promulgated were sharply criticized for their harshness by many federal judges, particularly as they applied to nonviolent drug-related offenses.

The sentencing commission was established as an independent commission in the judicial branch. Seven members (at least three of whom had to be judges) were to be appointed by the president and confirmed by the Senate. They were subject to removal under limited circumstances. The authority of the Sentencing Commission was upheld on constitutional grounds by the U.S. Supreme Court in a case that came from the

Western District of Missouri, *United States v. Johnson,* in which four district judges out of five upheld the guidelines against claims that the commission violated the principle of separation of powers.[118] Both the defendant and the United States petitioned for certiorari before judgment in the Court of Appeals, which the Supreme Court granted. Over the solo dissent of Justice Antonin Scalia, the High Court upheld the guidelines.[119]

In 1972 the Supreme Court held all existing death penalty laws unconstitutional in *Furman v. Georgia.*[120] Many states—among them Arkansas, Missouri, Nebraska, and South Dakota—restored the death penalty, subject to guidelines established by the High Court. Many state cases in which the death penalty was imposed reached the federal courts via the writ of habeas corpus, even though the Supreme Court narrowed the use of the writ. While few convictions were overturned, the use of the writ slowed the pace of executions. For example, in January 1985, the Court of Appeals ruled by a vote of 5–4 that the rights of two Arkansas convicts scheduled for execution had been violated because they were tried before juries that excluded opponents of the death penalty. The first Arkansas execution since 1964 did not occur until 1990. Inmates in Nebraska, Missouri, and South Dakota also were affected by the decision.[121]

In 1989, a panel of Magill, Henley, and Arnold overturned a Missouri conviction in a capital case on several grounds, including prejudice caused by the prosecutor's closing argument.[122] The same year, a panel of Heaney, Floyd Gibson, and John R. Gibson (dissenting) overturned another Missouri conviction in a capital case on the ground of ineffectiveness of counsel. The public defender had neither interviewed nor called an eye witness and had sat mute at sentencing. The en banc court reached the same result. The swing vote was that of Judge Wollman. The five other Reagan appointees dissented.[123]

A number of other cases involved ineffective assistance of counsel. A first-degree murder conviction was overturned in *Hill v. Lockhart,* because the attorney had given the defendant, who had accepted a plea bargain, erroneous advice as to when he could be paroled.[124] The en banc court concurred with the panel by a vote of 5–4. This time Reagan appointees Fagg and Beam joined the majority.[125]

Whiteside v. Scurr has become a seminal case involving the ethics of defense counsel in a criminal case. There, an Eighth Circuit panel reversed a district court decision, denying habeas corpus to a petitioner convicted of homicide in state court. At the state trial, defense counsel had threatened to withdraw from the case because his client had signaled that he wished to testify falsely. Writing for the panel, Judge McMillian reminded counsel "that they are not triers of fact, but advocates." Counsel's "legitimate ethical concerns" were "inconsistent with the obligations of confidentiality and zealous advocacy."[126] The three Reagan appointees then on the Court of Appeals, Gibson, Fagg, and Bowman, along with Judge Ross, dissented from denial of a rehearing en banc.[127] The Supreme Court reversed. Chief Justice Burger wrote an unusual opinion for the Court, sounding more like a bar association ethics opinion than a Supreme Court decision, stating that "under no circumstance may a lawyer either advocate or passively tolerate a client's giving false testimony."[128]

Warren v. City of Lincoln was a Section 1983 action brought for false imprisonment on the allegations that Warren had been arrested without probable cause, falsely imprisoned, and subjected to harassing, crude, and lengthy interrogation without granting his request for counsel.[129] The panel of Heaney (writing), Wollman, and Larson reversed the verdict for the city on the grounds that the trial judge's charge to the jury should have submitted the issue of the arrest to the jury for the record was replete with evidence that the arrest for a traffic offense was but a pretext to get Warren into custody to question him for unsolved burglaries. Such an arrest was "unreasonable." The en banc majority vacated the panel decision by a vote of 6–4 because the majority thought probable cause had existed to arrest him for attempted burglary.[130] All six Reagan appointees voted to vacate the panel decision.

In *United States v. Childress*,[131] Judge McMillian presented a persuasive case for overturning *Swain v. Alabama*. *Swain* had held that evidence that the government had used its peremptory challenges to remove all prospective African American jurors from the jury panel in a single case would not support a claim of racial discrimination under the Equal Protection Clause.[132] However, the en banc court felt that Supreme Court jurisprudence did not permit them to deviate from *Swain*. After the Supreme Court overturned *Swain* in *Batson v. Kentucky*,[133] the Court of Appeals applied the later case.[134]

Two cases must be singled out as examples of the Court of Appeals "doing justice." In both, Judge Bright wrote the majority opinion. In *Helm v. Solem,* Bright was responsible for one of the rare times when the Supreme Court overturned a sentence on the grounds that it was not proportional to the crime. Pleading guilty to the charge of "uttering a no account [$100] check," a crime that ordinarily carried a maximum penalty of five years and a $5,000 fine, Jerry Helm, with six previous felony convictions (none for a violent crime), was sentenced under South Dakota's habitual offender statute, receiving life imprisonment without parole. Helm lost out in the South Dakota courts and the U.S. District Court. A staff attorney for the Eighth Circuit recommended summary affirmance. But Bright had the case placed on the calendar for oral argument and seized a small opening in the leading Supreme Court precedent, *Rummel v. Estelle*,[135] that Helm had been sentenced without the possibility of parole. As a result, the Court of Appeals reversed Helm's sentence. The Supreme Court affirmed by a 5–4 vote.[136]

To fully relate the saga of James Dean Walker and the Eighth Circuit Court of Appeals might require a small book.[137] In brief: Walker was convicted for a murder of a police officer in Little Rock in April 1963 and sentenced to death. His first conviction was reversed by the Arkansas Supreme Court. The prosecution used a different theory on retrial, but Walker was convicted again, although this time he was sentenced to life imprisonment. The Arkansas Supreme Court affirmed the second conviction.[138] A petition for habeas corpus to the U.S. District Court for the Eastern District of Arkansas was denied. In 1969, in its first take on the case, the U.S. Court of Appeals—Judges Mehaffy (writing), Heaney, and Floyd Gibson—affirmed, even though the original vote in conference had been to reverse.[139]

Twelve years later, Walker brought a second habeas petition, which the district court denied. The petition appeared to be based on four grounds identical to those in the first petition and three additional grounds that were insubstantial. Yet review of the record on appeal by Judge Bright and his law clerk, Patricia Maher, led to the conclusion that Walker had received an unfair trial because of the bias of the trial judge and government suppression of evidence. The panel of Bright, Ross, and Heaney (who had been on the panel in 1969) believed that Walker might be entitled to a new trial notwithstanding the Eighth Circuit's previous denial of habeas, but, since this would mean reversing the earlier Eighth Circuit panel, the matter had to be reviewed en banc. At conference, the en banc court ruled against Walker by a vote of 4–3. However, Judge McMillian changed his vote while opinions were being drafted, which seemed to mean Walker had won the new trial. However, it did not, because the appointment of Judges Fagg and Bowman to the Court of

Appeals after the conference caused a rehearing. Following the hearing, both of the new judges voted to deny habeas corpus relief. Judge Arnold was truly in the middle of the court. He stated that if he had been on the court at the time of the appeal of the first habeas corpus, he would have voted to grant the writ, but the standard for a successive habeas petition was higher, and he did not believe that Walker met it.[140]

However, the balance on the court would continue to shift. Walker filed a petition for recall of the court's mandate, asserting that new evidence had surfaced which warranted a successive habeas petition. Judge Arnold now concluded that the new information "sufficiently added to the uncertain[ties] of this case to justify additional proceedings."[141] Joining the four dissenters from the previous ruling, he helped to create a new majority to grant the motion to recall the mandate and remand the case to the district court for a hearing.

However, Walker lost once again in the district court, which held that the record contained no credible evidence meriting a new trial.[142] Finally, twenty-two years after the homicide had taken place, the Court of Appeals granted the petition for habeas corpus and ordered a new trial by a 5–4 vote.[143] Instead of a new trial, Walker and the government reached a plea bargain, whereby Walker pleaded guilty to a lesser offense that carried a maximum sentence less than the time he had already served. Later, Walker wrote to Judge Bright:

> I had no idea that a judge from Fargo, North Dakota would be the person to become so offended by an injustice that occurred in Arkansas 18 years earlier. . . . [My fine attorneys'] legal efforts would have been for naught had it not been for the fact that you were willing to uphold the integrity of your position and push to set right a very serious wrong.[144]

BANKRUPTCY AND ANTITRUST CASES   A number of bankruptcy cases with important policy ramifications were decided by the Court of Appeals in the 1980s. The raw number of bankruptcy filings and the number of difficult bankruptcy cases rose greatly during the 1980s and early 1990s. In the Eighth Circuit, bankruptcy filings and out-of-court restructurings were precipitated by fraud, high interest rates, overexpansion, decline in real estate values, poor management, and poor crop yields.

In the twentieth century, bankruptcy laws became a permanent feature of commercial law, developing into highly complex statutes designed not only to relieve consumers and small companies but also to assist corporate giants trying to survive any number of potentially catastrophic financial blows. From the late 1950s through 1990, an ever-increasing number of businesses of ever-increasing size required restructuring and resorted to reorganization proceedings.[145]

U.S. bankruptcy law underwent major substantive reform in 1978.[146] The jurisdiction of the bankruptcy court was enlarged by that statute, so it could function independently of the district court. Bankruptcy court jurisdiction now came to embrace all civil proceedings under Title 11 (or related to cases under Title 11) without regard to possession of property or consent by the defendant.

The major decision in which the Supreme Court restricted the involvement of the bankruptcy court to administrative duties in bankruptcy cases, holding unconstitutional the broad grant of jurisdiction to non–Article III judges (judges with limited tenure and reducible compensation) not subject to district court supervision and control, came in a case from the Eighth Circuit. In January 1980, the Northern Pipeline Construction Company filed a petition for reorganization in the District Court for the District of Minnesota. Pursuant to the law, Northern filed suit against the Marathon Pipeline Company for breach of contract. Marathon sought dismissal of the suit on constitutional grounds. The bankruptcy judge denied the motion to dismiss. On appeal to the district court, Judge Miles Lord held the delegation of authority to the bankruptcy judges unconstitutional.[147] The Supreme Court noted probable jurisdiction and held that the broad grant of jurisdiction to non–Article III judges not subject to district court supervision and control was unconstitutional.[148]

The bankruptcy system then worked under an "emergency rule" for several years until Congress revised the 1978 statute. Under the Bankruptcy Amendments and Federal Judgeship Act of 1984 (BAFJA), bankruptcy judges were once again adjuncts to district judges.[149] Bankruptcy judges were to be appointed by Courts of Appeals as judicial officers of district courts empowered to hear "noncore" bankruptcy matters in which final orders with judgments were entered by district judges or with the consent of the parties. The Judicial Councils were empowered to establish bankruptcy courts. A consenting district court majority could authorize referral of appeals from a bankruptcy judge to a Council-established bankruptcy appellate panel comprised of bankruptcy judges from districts within the circuit.[150] Toward the end of the 1980s, the Court of Appeals decided three bankruptcy cases of general interest. In addition, several cases involving farm bankruptcies are discussed as "regional cases" later in this chapter.

In 1989, a panel overturned a lower court decision discharging a judgment in a tort action, where the bankrupt had thrown a firecracker. The en banc court vacated the panel and held the debt nondischargeable by a vote of 5–5. Judges John R. Gibson, Bowman, Wollman, Magill, and Beam voted to affirm. Judges Lay, Henley, McMillian, Richard Arnold, and Fagg voted to reverse.[151]

The following year, the court grappled with the question of whether bankruptcy could free the bankrupt from a civil judgment that resulted from a criminal act. In *In re Lemaire,* the debtor had pumped five shots into his victim and nearly killed him. He served twenty-seven months of his sentence, then returned to graduate school at the University of Minnesota, where he received his doctorate in experimental behavioral pharmacology. Looking ahead to a career in research, the bankrupt sought to be discharged from the $50,000 civil judgment the victim had won. A divided panel of the Court of Appeals held the judgment dischargeable. The panel majority (Magill and McMillian) upheld the bankruptcy court's emphasis on the "principle of fresh start which is the cornerstone of bankruptcy law."[152] Dissenting, John R. Gibson argued that the panel had left "out of the equation the fact that the intentionally injured creditor has to live the rest of his life with the injuries inflicted."[153] The en banc majority, made up of five Reagan appointees and Arnold, held for the creditor, emphasizing the strong public policy reasons against the discharge of debts arising from crimes as heinous as Lemaire's. The dissenters were Magill, Lay, and McMillian.[154]

Bush v. Taylor raised the question of whether a husband was entitled to a discharge of his obligation under a state divorce decree to remit to his former wife one-half of the payments he received under his pension plan. A panel of Arnold (writing), Magill, and Bowman (dissenting) ruled for the husband, holding that a property settlement was "a species of debt Congress has not chosen to except from discharge."[155] Bowman considered the panel decision a manifest injustice:

> The Court's decision is indefensible. It permits a deadbeat husband to use the Bankruptcy Code's grace for honest debts as a slick scheme for euchring his former wife out of her "sole and separate" property in one-half of the benefits he received under a pension plan. . . . This result in unconscionable, we should not countenance it.[156]

On rehearing en banc, Bowman picked up the votes of three other Reagan appointees and Judge McMillian and won by a 5–4 vote. The court held that Congress had not intended that the former wife's interest in the pension be subservient to the goal of giving her debtor husband a fresh start.[157]

The most important antitrust case of the period once again involved the *Kansas City Star,* which attempted to change its system of delivery from having independent contract carriers to directly delivering and selling newspapers to subscribers. In 1984, the panel decision (in which Heaney and Bright formed the majority and Henley dissented) was overturned by the en banc court, in which three Reagan appointees joined Henley, McMillian, and Ross in holding that while there was monopoly power, no unreasonable anticompetitive effects would follow from the *Star*'s implementation of its new system. Judge Bright lamented that the majority "with some hesitation and a degree of uncertainty, permits a monopolist to destroy hundreds of businesses."[158]

SOCIAL SECURITY DISABILITY CASES   As was generally true of the lower federal courts during this period, the courts of the Eighth Circuit were skeptical of the performance of the Social Security Administration in disability cases. Congress, in 1980, had authorized a stepped up review of Social Security Disability beneficiaries to determine whether they remained eligible for benefits. The Social Security Administration interpreted that law as a directive to reduce the number of disability recipients and proceeded to terminate benefits of many. These decisions were reviewable by the federal courts, which time after time ordered benefits restored because the SSA had used improper standards.[159]

Like many other federal courts, the Eighth Circuit was disturbed by the nonacquiescence of the Social Security Administration to their decisions. In *Hillhouse v. Harris,* the Court of Appeals noted disapprovingly that the secretary "continues to operate under the belief that she is not bound by circuit court decisions." Concurring, Judge McMillian went so far as to threaten the secretary with contempt.[160] After hearing a case where the administrative law judge had treated a forty-two-year-old woman with a tenth-grade education rudely, offensively, and insensitively, Chief Judge Lay wrote to the secretary to suggest that the ALJ be reprimanded.[161]

The Court of Appeals for the Eighth Circuit was particularly concerned that the test used by the SSA allowed it to terminate benefits on the basis of evidence that was virtually identical to that used in making the initial award of eligibility.[162] Thus the secretary could remove benefits by simply interpreting differently the medical evidence upon which the original determination of eligibility was made. In 1984, the Court of Appeals for the Eighth Circuit explicitly established the medical improvement standard. Under it, the original disability determination had a res judicata effect that precluded the secretary from simply disregarding the earlier determination. To overcome the presumption of disability, the secretary had to come forward with evidence of improvement or some other acceptable proof. Congress then intervened by adopting the medical improvement standard, although it disallowed the presumption of continuing disability.[163]

MEGATORT CASES   The Circuit had a significant involvement in three megatort cases. The first involved the largest inoculation program in American history. Forty-five million Americans had been vaccinated against "swine flu." Twenty-three persons died from the vaccine and many others were badly injured by side effects. A panel majority of Chief Judge Lay and Floyd Gibson affirmed the lower court in the swine flu case, holding that recipients of the vaccine had not received adequate warning from the government to give informed consent.[164]

The second megatort case involved the collapse of two skywalks in the central lobby of the Hyatt Regency Hotel in Kansas City on July 17, 1981, killing 114 persons. The Court of Appeals held that the class action in federal court was barred by the Anti-injunction Act.[165]

The third megatort cases involved another run-in with Judge Miles Lord. At issue was litigation against the A. H. Robins Company over the misery caused by its IUD, the Dalkon Shield, which not only was less reliable as a birth control device than Robins claimed but caused pelvic inflammatory disease resulting in sudden, painful, acute infections of the fallopian tubes and ovaries, miscarriages, spontaneous septic abortions, babies born with cerebral palsy or mental retardation, and even death.

Lord's behavior at the court session on February 29, 1984, at which the settlement agreements were signed, was more Old Testament prophet than Article III judge. Lord compelled Robins's executives to read his speech, "The Church's Claim on the Corporate Conscience: Toward a Redefinition of Sin," seeking perhaps to ensure that the Robins executives would never again testify in court that they knew nothing about the dangers inherent in the Dalkon Shield. Lord then made a verbal appeal to the executives, one made, he stated, after months of reflection, study, and prayer. He stated that the three officials before him were not only guilty as part of the corporation, but that each bore personal guilt of a moral nature. Lord spoke of the corporate officers allowing "women, tens of thousands of them, to wear this device, a deadly depth charge in their wombs, ready to explode at any time." He stated, "You don't have to argue that I am prejudiced at this point. I am."[166]

Robins filed a complaint under the Judicial Conduct and Disability Act, accusing Lord of abusing his authority and exposing the Robins executives to public ridicule. As was his right, Lord asked for a public hearing. The hearing took place on July 9, 1984. Lord was represented by former attorney general Ramsey Clark, and Robins by former attorney general Griffin Bell. Lord brought his four children to the hearing, which was covered by reporters from the national news media.

The council dismissed the complaint on the theory that it arose out of ongoing litigation. But in the appeal of the case, the Court of Appeals struck Lord's moral appeal to the executives from the record and sharply rebuked Lord for crossing "the line separating permissible judicial comments from impermissible public accusations."[167] The brouhaha over Lord, however, led to more suits over the shield and higher verdicts for plaintiffs in Minnesota.[168]

It should be noted that during these years, the rate of reversal of district court decisions in the Eighth Circuit was relatively low. In 1983–84, for example, 15 percent of the cases disposed of by the Court of Appeals after hearing or submission resulted in reversals.[169]

Federalism

Between 1979 and 1989, there were five important Eighth Circuit cases involving important issues of federalism, which ultimately were determined by the Supreme Court. Most of them arose in North and South Dakota. The Court of Appeals rendered judgments against the states four times. It was affirmed by the Supreme Court in all five cases.

Consolidated Freightways Corp. v. Kasel involved the constitutionality of an Iowa law that limited the use of trucks longer than sixty feet on Iowa's interstate highways.[170] Battles over long trucks had divided the Iowa legislature for a generation. The statute involved in this case allowed exemptions for Iowa's border cities, the transportation of passenger vehicles and tractors, and the transportation of livestock in emergencies. The statute had the effect of preventing trucking companies from using a combination of a tractor and two trailers on interstate roads crossing Iowa, one of which is Interstate 80, a major route for the shipment of goods from the two coasts. The state contended that the law was a safety regulation and stressed that the Supreme Court had held that few subjects of state regulation involving interstate commerce are of such peculiarly local concern as highways. The plaintiff, Consolidated Freightways, at the time the nation's largest trucking firm, argued that the Iowa law was costing it $2 million annually.

The trial judge, William E. Stuart of the Southern District of Iowa, had voted for the statute when he had been a state senator. As a judge, he held that there was "a parochialism" about Iowa's approach to public health and safety and an "aura of protectionism."[171] Stuart held the statute unconstitutional. The Court of Appeals affirmed.[172] It held that the law violated the Commerce Clause because it placed "a substantial burden on interstate commerce and . . . cannot be said to make more than the most speculative contribution to highway safety." The court thought that the exceptions from the law reduced its "willingness to assume that the state's own political powers serves as a check on burdensome regulation."[173]

The Supreme Court affirmed by a 6–3 vote, but with only a plurality opinion. The justices were suspicious that Iowa's safety regulation was really intended to limit highway maintenance costs. The plurality said that "the incantation of a purpose to promote the public health or safety does not insulate a state law from Commerce Clause attack."[174]

Reeves v. Stake involved that unique institution, the South Dakota Cement Plant, created by the state in 1919, the survivor of the efforts of the Nonpartisan League. The state-owned plant, located in Rapid City, was created in response to regional cement shortages and cost $2 million. Using South Dakota's gypsum and its extensive hard limestone deposits, the plant always had made a profit. Over time, its capacity had increased enormously. South Dakota cement had been used for South Dakota bridges, runways, its university, dams, and hospitals. The plant was by far the major source of cement for the state and its wares were marketed to other Eighth Circuit states (all but Missouri and Arkansas), as well as Wyoming, Montana, and Colorado. However, in the 1970s, a sharp increase in demand for cement caused the plant to refuse to sell to out-of-state customers, provoking this litigation.[175]

The district court held that the cement plant's policy of not selling to out-of-state customers violated the Commerce Clause. The Court of Appeals, Lay writing, reversed. It held that the Commerce Clause was primarily intended to inhibit the power of the states to interfere with the natural functioning of the interstate market through burdensome regulations or prohibitions. However, in the case of the cement plant, South Dakota was simply acting in a proprietary capacity as a seller of cement within the interstate cement market. The Commerce Clause did not, the court said, "prohibit the state of South Dakota 'from participating in the market and exercising the right to favor its own citizens over others.'"[176] The Supreme Court remanded for consideration in light of a recent decision, but the Court of Appeals held to its original opinion.[177] The High Court then, Blackmun writing, affirmed by a vote of 5–4, rejecting the argument that the program was protectionist.

United States v. State of North Dakota raised once again in the Eighth Circuit competing federal and state policies over migratory birds. The principal breeding grounds for waterfowl in the continental United States are located in the Dakotas, Minnesota, and Montana. The case involved the acquisition of land for bird sanctuaries. The United States sought a declaration from the U.S. district court that the secretary of the interior could acquire land in North Dakota for breeding and nesting without obtaining additional consent from state officials. Judge Bruce M. Van Sickle of the District of North Dakota rendered judgment for the United States.

The Court of Appeals affirmed. It upheld the authority of the federal government, holding that state statutes limiting and placing conditions on any further acquisition of land by the federal government were invalid under the Supremacy Clause. The Supreme Court, Blackmun writing once again, affirmed.[178]

[State of] South Dakota v. Dole has become the leading case interpreting the extent to which Congress can condition the assistance it gives the states under its spending power. A 1984 federal statute directed the secretary of transportation to withhold a percentage of federal highway funds otherwise allocable from states that permitted purchase or public possession of an alcoholic beverage by persons under the age of twenty-one. As a result of the condition, South Dakota stood to lose $4 million

in 1987 and $8 million in 1988. The state brought suit for a declaratory judgment that the statute violated the constitutional limitations on congressional exercise of the spending power and also violated the Twenty-first Amendment to the U.S. Constitution.

Judge Andrew Bogue of the District Court for the District of South Dakota dismissed the complaint. The Court of Appeals, Fagg writing, affirmed, holding that in exercising its power under the Spending Clause, Congress must seek to further the well-being of the nation as a whole, that the statute be reasonably related to that national interest, and that it not violate any "independent constitutional bar." The court had no difficulty believing that Congress reasonably could have concluded that the problem of young adults drinking and driving was a concern of interstate and national proportions and that Congress properly could determine that a uniform minimum drinking age would lessen that problem. The court held that neither the Tenth nor the Twenty-first Amendments had been violated.[179]

The Supreme Court affirmed over the dissent of Justices Brennan and O'Connor, laying down a clear test for spending power cases, which resembled that of the Court of Appeals, although the High Court also held that Congress had to condition the funds unambiguously and that the financial inducement offered by Congress could not pass the point at which pressure turns to coercion.[180]

During the controversy over the use of American military power in Central America, several governors withheld or threatened to withhold their consent to federally ordered active duty missions by their states' National Guard, among them was Minnesota's governor Rudy Perpich. In response, Congress repealed the statutory requirement that had required the consent of a state governor or a declaration of national emergency when the president ordered members of the National Guard to active duty for purposes of training outside the United States during peacetime. Governor Perpich and the state of Minnesota challenged the law, arguing that it infringed Article I, Section 8, Clause 16 of the U.S. Constitution, which reserved to the states "the Authority of Training the Militia."

Chief Judge Donald Alsop of the District of Minnesota granted summary judgment for the United States. A panel majority of Heaney and Thomas E. Fairchild of the Seventh Circuit reversed over Magill's dissent, holding that an affirmative proclamation of a national emergency was required for the federal government to supercede the state's authority over its National Guard. Rehearing en banc was ordered and the full court upheld the district court by a vote of 7–2. All seven judges appointed since 1979 voted in the majority, while Judges Heaney and McMillian dissented. The majority held that the powers reserved to the states regarding the militia did not infringe on Congress's power to raise armies, which is plenary and exclusive. Judge Heaney began his dissent (in which he was joined by Judge McMillian) by stating that "in a few strikes of the word processor, the majority has written the Militia Clause out of the United States Constitution."[181] A unanimous Supreme Court affirmed the Court of Appeals with an opinion by Justice John Paul Stevens.[182]

Regional Cases

During the 1980s, the Court of Appeals once again encountered the kind of regional concerns that it dealt with in the early years of its history—disputes involving land, farms and farmers, regional reliance on railways for the shipping of goods, cases involving Native Americans, and those deriving from rivers and other waterways. There were other kinds of environmental cases as well; space precludes their discussion.[183]

FARMS, FARMERS, AND FARM BANKRUPTCIES Farm bankruptcies were an all-too-frequent occurrence of the 1980s. *In re Ahlers* was an activist decision, which, had it survived, would have helped farmers to retain possession of their farms during bankruptcy. James and Mary Ahlers, the owners of an 840-acre farm in southwestern Minnesota, owing one million dollars, defaulted on their loan to Norwest Bank in November 1984. Filing for bankruptcy in federal court, the Ahlerses first received an automatic stay of the bank's replevin action in state court, but later the bankruptcy court found the reorganization plan "utterly unfeasible" and granted relief from the stay.

The Court of Appeals held that the Ahlerses could retain their equity interest in the farm by their "yearly contributions of labor, experience and expertise." "Certainly," Judge Heaney (joined by Judge Wollman with his extensive background working on a farm) wrote, "a farmer's efforts in operating and managing his farm is essential to any successful farm reorganization, and the yearly contribution is measurable in money or money's worth."[184] Judge John R. Gibson dissented, thinking that the majority's sympathy for the farmers had produced the decision, the first in which a court supported the exchange of labor for equity participation. The tribunal had, Gibson believed, "unabashedly legislated a result which undermines reasonable commercial expectations and substantially reorders the risks of insolvency borne by farm debtors and their bankers."[185] The Supreme Court unanimously reversed.[186] However, the Court of Appeals decision spurred Congress to create by statute most of what the Court of Appeals had attempted to do with its decision. The Family Farmers Bankruptcy Act created a new Chapter 12 bankruptcy proceeding under which family farmers were able to retain an equity interest in their farm while making loan repayments under a reorganization plan.[187]

Attempting to assist farmers facing foreclosure in another case, *Zajac v. Federal Land Bank of St. Paul,* Judge Heaney read a private right of action into the Agriculture Credit Act of 1987. However, the panel result was overturned by the en banc court, in which the six Reagan appointees joined in the majority opinion. Judges Arnold and McMillian concurred in the judgment, agreeing with Lay and Heaney, who dissented, as to the private right of action.[188]

The courts of the Eighth Circuit made known their displeasure with the Farmers Home Administration (FmHA) in a number of cases. In *Arcoren v. Farmers Home Administration,*[189] the Court of Appeals panel held that where, pursuant to state law, the FmHA repossessed and sold cattle as essentially private creditors, without giving the farmer prior notice or opportunity to be heard, a private cause of action against federal officials was available. However, in a later phase of the case, the en banc court held that the government officials were entitled to qualified immunity because their conduct was not "clearly established" as violating the farmer's constitutional or statutory rights. Judges Lay and Heaney dissented. Heaney argued:

> It is unconscionable that the FmHA officials involved seized and immediately sold Arcoren's cattle without providing him notice, without providing him an opportunity to respond to accusations by third parties that he had abandoned the cattle, without engaging in any judicial proceeding, and without even making any effort to independently verify whether Arcoren has in fact abandoned the cattle.[190]

Class action litigation brought by farmers before Judge Bruce Van Sickle of the District of North Dakota led to an injunction prohibiting FmHA farm loan liquidation and foreclosure procedures.[191] By the

Agricultural Credit Act of 1987,[192] Congress sought to carry out the intent of Judge Van Sickle's decisions by making extensive changes in those statutory provisions which formed the background of the litigation. A panel of the Court of Appeals then held the case moot because it lacked the power to add to or subtract from the remedy enacted by Congress.[193]

TRANSPORTATION AND SHIPPING   Even in an age in which much was shipped by truck and by air, railroads continued to be important, necessary not only for the delivery of farm produce and the importation of manufactures, but also to ameliorate the geographic remoteness of the northern part of the circuit. From 1980 to 1986, South Dakota was threatened with the abandonment of more than half its total railroad mileage.[194] *Cartersville Elevator, Inc. v. ICC* involved the appropriate method for the Interstate Commerce Commission to employ when deciding whether to approve the abandonment of a railroad.[195] At issue were 35.6 miles between Mason City and Kelsey, Iowa, which the Chicago and North Western Railroad wanted to abandon. Shippers of grain fertilizer and agricultural supplies challenged the abandonment. A panel majority of Judges John R. Gibson and Myron Bright approved the ICC's consideration of opportunity costs as a factor in approving the abandonment. Judge Fagg dissented, expressing his belief that the solution to the problem of inadequate revenue was not the wholesale abandonment of branch lines that failed to earn a profit equal to the rail industry's cost of capital. The en banc decision affirmed the panel with only Judges Fagg and Heaney dissenting.

NATIVE AMERICAN CASES   While there were fewer important cases involving Native Americans during the 1980s than during the previous decade, there continued to be litigation triggered by Native American activism, as well as cases involving claims for land and natural resources. In a suit brought against former Nixon aide Alexander Haig and others over the use of the FBI, marshals, and military personnel at Wounded Knee for violation of the Posse Comitatus Act[196] and the Fourth, Fifth, and Eighth Amendments to the Constitution, an en banc Court of Appeals held that there was a valid Fourth Amendment claim and that the violation of the Posse Comitatus Act was relevant in determining the reasonableness of the government's conduct. Four of five Reagan appointees dissented.[197]

The conviction for homicide of Leonard Peltier, an AIM activist, became an international cause célèbre.[198] Peltier was convicted of the murder of two FBI agents in 1975 on the theory that he had used a high-velocity, small-caliber weapon and fired at point-blank range. The Court of Appeals had affirmed.[199] In 1982, Peltier filed a motion for a new trial, arguing on the basis of documents received under the Freedom of Information Act that the government had improperly withheld information, which would have tended to show that the agents had not been killed by the alleged murder weapon. The district judge denied the motion, and the Court of Appeals affirmed, holding that it was not reasonably probable that the jury would have acquitted Peltier had it been aware of the newly discovered evidence. Writing for the Court, Judge Heaney concluded:

> There is a possibility that the jury would have acquitted Leonard Peltier had the records and data improperly withheld from the defense been available to him in order to better exploit and reinforce the inconsistencies casting strong doubt [on the government's case]. [But, based on case law], the court was not convinced that had the data and records been made available, the jury probably would have reached a different result.[200]

The return of the Peltier case to the Eighth Circuit in 1992 is discussed in the following chapter.

Irving v. Clark was one of the cases involving Native American land. There the Court of Appeals dealt with a federal statute that provided that small amounts of land held by the United States in trust to individual members of the Oglala not pass at death by will or intestacy but instead revert to the tribe. The Court of Appeals held that the law was unconstitutional because it deprived individual Native Americans of their property without just compensation under the Fifth Amendment. There was an unconstitutional taking of property because the Native American individuals now only had a right to the land during their lifetimes.[201]

The Supreme Court upheld the Court of Appeals, although it took opinions by O'Connor, Brennan, Scalia, and Stevens to do so. Justice O'Connor emphasized that what had been destroyed was "one of the most essential sticks in the bundle of rights that are commonly characterized as property . . . the right to pass on a certain type of property to one's heirs."[202]

There were several cases involving the diminishing of reservations. In *Bartlett v. Solem*,[203] the Court of Appeals reaffirmed its holding in a 1979 case that the land on which a crime was committed was part of the Cheyenne River Reservation and that the reservation had not been diminished by an 1889 law. The Supreme Court affirmed.[204] In *United States v. South Dakota*,[205] the Court of Appeals held a housing project in Sisseton was a "dependent Indian community."

One of the most interesting Native American cases of the period involved the prosecution of a member of the Yankton Sioux Tribe for shooting four bald eagles on the Yankton Reservation. Under an 1858 treaty with the United States, the Yankton had the right to hunt bald and golden eagles within their reservation for noncommercial purposes. Dwight Dion Sr. was convicted under the Eagle Protection Act, the Migratory Bird Treaty Act, and the Endangered Species Act for offering bald eagle carcasses and parts for sale. His son, Lyle Dion, was convicted under the treaty and the Endangered Species Act after a trial in the District of South Dakota before Judge John B. Jones. Two other Native Americans were also convicted.

The defendants argued that they were protected by a 1974 Eighth Circuit decision, which had held that an enrolled member of the Red Lake Band of Chippewa who shot at a bald eagle within the confines of their reservation could not be convicted of "taking an eagle" in violation of the Eagle Protection Act because the right to hunt on the reservation was implicitly recognized in treaties.[206] The panel in the *Dion* case certified issues to the court en banc as to the effect of treaties that the Yankton Sioux had entered into. The full court then held that the Yankton would have understood the treaty as reserving in them the right to hunt eagles on their reservation, though not to hunt for commercial purposes. Relying on a principle of construction that statutory abrogation of treaty rights can only be accomplished by an express reference to treaty rights in the statute or legislative history, the court rejected the government's contentions that it should rely on the surrounding circumstances and the legislative history of the statute. Judges McMillian, Bright, and Fagg dissented.[207] A panel of Judges Heaney, John R. Gibson, and Fagg then upheld Dion Sr.'s conviction against contentions of religious freedom, selective prosecution, unconstitutional delegation of legislative authority, and equal protection, but reversed as to the son on grounds of entrapment.[208]

The Supreme Court reversed unanimously as to the convictions under the Endangered Species Act, holding that Congress actually had considered the conflict between its intended action, on the one hand, and Indian treaty rights, on the other, and had chosen to resolve that conflict by abrogating the treaty. The High Court refused to require an explicit statement by Congress as to abrogation of treaty rights, so long as there was clear evidence that Congress actually considered the conflict between its intended action and Indian treaty rights and had chosen to resolve that conflict by abrogating the treaty.[209] The High Court found such clear evidence regarding the Eagle Protection Act and would not recognize Dion's treaty defense regarding the Endangered Species Act.

DAMS AND IRRIGATION PROJECTS   The Missouri River has been instrumental to agriculture, industry, and transportation in the Eighth Circuit throughout its history. Of course, the days when one approached the river to hear "the wind blowing through the silver-lined leaves of a tall cottonwood" were long over.[210] Since 1832, the river has been "improved" by constant projects. Before World War II, the United States had gradually nationalized the Missouri River, assuming responsibility for flood control, power generation, and the improvement of irrigation and navigation. Yet as late as 1944, there was not a single dam on the Missouri between Fort Peck, Montana, and its confluence with the Mississippi 1800 miles away.

After Congress adopted the Pick-Sloan Plan for the Missouri Basin in 1944, a compromise between the need for irrigation in the northern basin states and the need for improved navigation desired by the southern basin states, it approved more than three hundred separate projects, including more than one hundred dams on the main channel and boundaries of the Missouri.[211]

The Missouri's shifting currents, side channels, sandbars, whirlpools, and rapids gave way in the Dakotas to a series of clear, cold deep lakes behind massive earthen dams and a narrowed and straightened river, a kind of dredged trench that provided a shipping lane for barges. Great benefits came from the dams for both city dwellers and those in rural areas. Agricultural and industrial growth transformed the former active erosion zone and meander belt areas. Power from the Garrison Dam made its way across North Dakota, bringing an end to the state's shortage of power. The Missouri came to be used not only for navigation, irrigation, flood control, and power generation but also for drinking water and recreation.

Yet a high price was paid. Thousands of acres of land perished—

backwater marshes, wood coulees, verdant forests. Five hundred thousand acres were flooded just for the Garrison Dam, completed in 1956. The construction of the six main stem dams resulted in the taking of Indian land of an area half the size of Rhode Island. The Oahe Reservoir in South Dakota alone took 160,000 acres of Sioux reservation. Natural habitat losses caused by construction of the main stem dams on the Missouri were estimated at over 1.2 million acres.[212]

Tensions caused by the conflicting desires to use the water for navigation or for electric power have continued for a half century. The Dakotas and Montana have been frustrated by the seemingly ironclad grasp the lower basin states have on Missouri River water, while the lower basin states have feared that because of proposed irrigation projects, the river flow would be reduced to a mere trickle. Overall, the lower basin states have profited much more from Pick-Sloan. Complicating the making of policy for the Missouri Basin is the fact that the governmental bodies concerned for the Missouri involve ten states, twenty-five tribes, numerous federal agencies, and the courts. Litigation has become an important part of the "policy-making" process for the Missouri.[213]

The Garrison Dam Diversion Project was a source of controversy for decades, pitting landholders against advocates of irrigation, environmentalists against farmers, rural residents against towns and cities. By 1976, the project was stalled by court challenges predicated on environmental impact, brought by, among others, the National Audubon Society and the Committee to Save North Dakota, which went to court to stop the seventy-three-mile-long McCluskey Canal. In 1986 a compromise was reached, and construction of a greatly reduced project was able to continue.[214]

The Oahe Irrigation Project, originally intended to irrigate 450,000 acres, was slowed by protests and court action and finally killed after becoming an important political issue in South Dakota. The United Family Farmers, a nonprofit corporation of one hundred members adversely affected by the project, brought suit to prevent construction of the first stage of the project, which was to irrigate 190,000 acres, provide water for municipal and industrial use in seventeen towns and cities, foster fish and wildlife development, and provide recreational uses. The organization contended that the planned pumping station and canal system for the Oahe Project would violate the National Environmental Protection Act, the Federal Water Pollution Control Act, and the Clean Water Act. Three district judges ruled against the environmentalists.

Judge Fred J. Nichol, after a trial, held the environmental impact statement adequate.[215] Only one of the United Family Farmers' nine claims was appealed, and the Court of Appeals affirmed.[216] However, if those opposing the dam lost the lawsuit, they still derived significant benefits from it. The Bureau of Reclamation was forced to produce data and documentation which confirmed the position of project skeptics and was used to recruit new opponents. In 1982, Oahe died in the Congress, the only federal reclamation project that ever was halted and terminated while under construction.[217]

Generally, the federal courts have recognized the broad authority of federal agencies and the federal government over the Missouri and have given sympathetic treatment to the contentions of the United States.[218] *Taylor v. United States* illustrates this phenomenon.[219] A farmer whose land was located midway between the Fort Peck and Garrison dams in western North Dakota brought suit against the United States. He claimed that after heavy rains in June 1975, the government negligently operated the Garrison Dam and Lake Sakakawea above the legally authorized water level, which caused water to back up on his property, destroying his crops and harming his pasture. Although Judge Bruce Van Sickle denied the government's request to dismiss, the Court of Appeals, with Stephenson writing, held that the government was not liable. Although Congress had provided for the absolute freedom of the government from flood damages, Taylor was claiming that his damage was the result of "backwater." The Court of Appeals saw "no rational distinction between floodwaters and backwaters" that would lead to a different result.

The federal government also emerged well from a suit brought by the State of North Dakota against the secretary of the interior. The state sought to quiet title to that part of the Little Missouri River which flowed through the state on its way from Wyoming to the Missouri River, to block the leasing of the river bed for oil and gas development. Judge Bruce Van Sickle ruled for the state. The Court of Appeals affirmed, holding that North Dakota acquired title at statehood because the stream had been navigable at the time. Secondly, it held that the statute of limitations in the Quiet Title Act did not apply to suits by states. However, the United States emerged victorious because the Supreme Court reversed on the ground that when legislation waiving sovereign immunity contains a statute of limitations, the limitation provision contains a condition on the waiver of sovereign immunity.[220]

In the 1980s, South Dakota, seeking to benefit from its excess of water, intended to sell water from the Oahe reservoir to Energy Transportation Systems Inc. (ETSI) for a coal-slurry pipeline to develop large deposits of coal, oil, and gas in Montana and Wyoming. ETSI planned to transport water by pipeline to Wyoming, where it would be mixed with locally mined coal to form a coal slurry. The slurry was then to be transported by pipeline for use in coal-fuel generated plants. Missouri, Iowa, Nebraska, and several railroads brought suit in the District of Nebraska to nullify the contract the secretary of the interior had signed with ETSI to allow them to use water from the reservoir. Judge Warren K. Urbom nullified the contract, holding that the federal statutes did not allow the Interior Department to furnish water for industrial purposes from a main stem reservoir. Instead the control of those reservoirs was committed to the Corps of Engineers of the U.S. Army.[221]

The Court of Appeals affirmed, holding that the secretary never had been given broad authority over irrigation storage in the army-controlled reservoirs, like Oahe. In dissent, Judge Bright lamented that "the irrigation water stored in the vast reservoir will sit unused and useless."[222] He then pointed out the real winners and losers from the decision:

> The Department of the Interior, representative of the irrigation interests of the upper basin states, will have no voice in the administration of the excess irrigation water. Instead, the Army Corps of Engineers, whose primary interests are in flood control and navigation, the same primary interests as the downstream states, will unilaterally regulate water in the largest federal reservoir in the Missouri Basin, a reservoir located in an upstream state and designed with the anticipation that its major consumptive use would be irrigation.[223]

Rehearing en banc was denied. The Supreme Court unanimously affirmed.[224] Finally, ETSI abandoned the project.

In related litigation, the Court of Appeals reversed a $600 million antitrust judgment (as well as a $244 million judgment for tortious interference) won by South Dakota in the federal district court of that state in a suit against the Kansas City Southern Railroad. The railroad had staunchly opposed the ETSI project. The court held that the coal slurry pipeline project had ended because of the decline in the price of oil, railroad deregulation, because there were a number of government authorizations still to secure, and because of the opposition of the railroad. That opposition, the court held, was privileged under the Noerr-Pennington Doctrine as the right to petition the government.[225]

The frustrations of the upper basin state were pithily expressed by Governor William Janklow of South Dakota, "[We're the lower valley's] water tower and that's all we are,"[226] and triggered a suit brought in the District of North Dakota in 1990 by both Dakotas and Montana against the Army Corps of Engineers. The plaintiffs charged that the huge releases of water from behind the Missouri River reservoirs to aid downstream navigation posed a dire threat to their water supplies, would affect their boat and recreation industry, and, potentially, their wildlife; and that if the water level continued to drop, fish could not spawn. The corps argued that its decision was not reviewable by the courts except for bad faith or unconstitutionality. The District Court for North Dakota enjoined the corps from releasing water at a rate greater than that at which water was flowing into the reservoir. At first, the Court of Appeals granted a stay. Ultimately, though, it dismissed the case as moot after the fish spawn was completed, pointing to efforts by all the states to discuss and advance their needs as they related to the Oahe.[227]

During the 1980s, a divided but collegial Court of Appeals, confronting a great quantitative increase in its docket, was asked to decide a remarkable number of value-laden cases. While a docket of difficult civil rights, abortion, criminal, federalism, and First Amendment cases would not have been surprising, more so were the number of bankruptcy cases with broad policy implications, the revival of the court's "regional" docket, and, for the first time, the presence of important cases raising problems of the relationship between church and state. Matching a great number of new judges with a value-laden docket contributed to producing a great number of cases reheard en banc.

For a more conservative Eighth Circuit, the 1990s would prove to be a somewhat calmer period, although the docket would be quantitatively heavier than before. The Court of Appeals continued to field difficult cases involving civil rights, abortion, and criminal prosecutions, which arose in both federal and state court. Traditional federal concerns—taxation and bankruptcy—would challenge the court. There would continue to be important regional cases involving Native Americans, farmers, and dams and irrigation projects. Finally, there would be high-profile litigation involving the conduct of the president of the United States.

CHAPTER 7

★ ★ ★ ★ ★ ★ ★

Leaving the Old Century
and Entering the New

*I*n the final years of the twentieth century, the work of the U.S. Court
of Appeals for the Eighth Circuit attracted more attention than ever
before. The Eighth Circuit continued to be an important forum in which
state attempts to restrict abortion were contested as well as the First
Amendment rights of those protesting abortion. Last-minute attempts
to prevent executions in Missouri, Arkansas, and Nebraska also placed
the court in the spotlight, as did the decades-old school desegregation
cases in Kansas City and St. Louis sputtering to a close. Efforts seeking
the freedom of, or a new trial for, Leonard Peltier, the Native American
convicted in the killing of two FBI agents in the 1970s, came not only
from all over the United States but from as far away as South Africa and
Australia. Nevertheless, the litigation evoking the greatest public interest was that involving the president of the United States, Bill Clinton:
cases spawned by investigations of a failed real estate investment in
Arkansas and a lawsuit against the president for sexual harassment.

National, Regional, and State Developments

The United States stood unopposed as the world's single superpower of
the 1990s and enjoyed the longest economic boom of the century. Yet
what should have been a halcyon period was one in which government
was conducted over a yawning gulf caused by differences over social issues. Such divisions, fanned by political partisanship, yielded, among
other things, the second trial of an impeached president in the nation's

history. Though a less obvious target than Clinton, the federal courts were far from immune from the political atmosphere. The process of appointing federal judges became an important battleground for the political branches. Further, while its position on the international stage was unrivaled, the United Sates remained vulnerable to terrorism, something brought home sharply by bombs in the garage of the World Trade Center, the federal building in Oklahoma City, and in Kenya and Tanzania.

During this period, the Eighth Circuit in many respects shared the prosperity of the nation. For most of the period, farm prices were high and unemployment relatively low. Even on the reservation, life was easier. In 1998, for example, ten years after the enactment of the Indian Gaming Regulatory Act,[1] Native American tribes were doing seven billion dollars of gambling business. In Minnesota alone there were eighteen casinos. Many Native Americans returned to the reservations as a result of new jobs created by casinos and by businesses created from their profits. Profits from the casinos were also used to improve infrastructure, to increase opportunities for education, and for health care. Yet unemployment, inadequate educational opportunities, and discrimination were not yet limited to memories of the past.

Although the Native American population on the plains grew rapidly—more than 20 percent in the Dakotas and Nebraska—white farmers continued their exodus. Of the three Great Plains states of the Eighth Circuit, between 1990 and 2000, Nebraska and South Dakota grew in population by about 8.5 percent, but North Dakota only by .5 percent. Empty homesteads and schools and padlocked city halls gave the state a ghostly look.[2]

The four eastern states of the Eighth Circuit fared better. Minnesota prospered and its population grew 12.4 percent to 4.9 million. However, with the election of Jesse Ventura as governor in 1998, Minnesota seemed to be abandoning its vibrant civic culture for a view of government as inconsequential, irrelevant, and entertaining.[3]

Iowa grew 5.4 percent in population but was hard hit by floods, especially in 1993, the worst disaster in its history; by a collapse in the price of hogs; and, in the later years of the decade, by lower prices for corn, soybeans, and grain.

Missouri was also devastated by the 1993 floods, but its population grew 9 percent. The state contributed fewer significant abortion cases to the Court of Appeals than in the previous two decades but provided the circuit with many capital cases, important litigation over laws governing campaign contributions and expenditures, as well as the two most important school desegregation cases.

Bill Clinton continued to be the dominant figure in Arkansas political life. After serving five terms as governor, he moved on to the White House. A master of the perpetual populist campaign necessary to overcome the weak, formal powers of Arkansas's governor, Clinton continued the interracial cooperation that prevailed in Arkansas public life for most of the last quarter of the twentieth century. From 1990 to 2000, Arkansas's population grew 13.7 percent.[4]

Judicial Administration

For much of Clinton's presidency, a Congress controlled by conservatives caused protracted delays in the confirmation of federal judges. In 1998, the Senate confirmed only seventeen judges, the lowest election year total in forty years. Although control of the political branches was reversed, after the election of George W. Bush in 2000 the partisanship continued.

Congress also kept a tight leash on funding for the judiciary. Federal judges were hard hit by Congress's unwillingness to raise judicial salaries at a time when the salaries of blue chip attorneys were skyrocketing. As of January 1, 2003, for example, the salary of a Court of Appeals judge was $164,000. With only three cost-of-living increases since 1993, the purchasing power of the salaries of federal judges declined 13.4 percent between 1993 and 2000. Forty-two federal judges left the bench during that period.[5] In addition, both legislators and the press flayed the judiciary over wasted money (especially in the construction of courthouses, with which judges had relatively little to do) and over arguable conflicts of interest by judges, who attended conferences sponsored by groups with possible axes to grind.[6]

While legislation aimed at overturning by statute or constitutional amendment abortion, school prayer, desegregation,[7] and term limits decisions did not pass, Congress was able to arrest the direction of the federal courts in several areas. The Antiterrorism and Effective Death Penalty Act of 1996 streamlined habeas corpus procedures, making it far more difficult for federal prisoners to overturn state convictions on federal constitutional grounds. The 1996 Prison Litigation Reform Act provided that consent decrees in prison litigation would expire in two years unless the judge held a new trial and made findings of constitutional or statutory violations. A third statute, the Illegal Immigration Reform and Immigrant Responsibility Act of 1996, eliminated class actions to challenge practices of the Immigration and Naturalization Service and judicial review of some discretionary decisions of the attorney general.[8]

Congress also created new federal causes of action, which cumulatively added quite considerably to the already crowded dockets. Congress continued to turn what were essentially local offenses into federal crimes, including car-jacking (Anti-Car Theft Act of 1992; later held unconstitutional by the Supreme Court), nonpayment of child support (Child Support Recovery Act of 1992) and violence against women (Violence against Women Act of 1994; also held unconstitutional). There was even an Animal Enterprise Protection Act, which made it a federal offense to travel interstate to disrupt zoos or circuses.[9] Congress also expanded the number of crimes for which the death penalty could be imposed from two to sixty.

There were also important new civil statutes to be enforced in the federal courts, including the Worker Adjustment and Retraining Notification Act of 1990, the Family and Medical Leave Act of 1993, the Access to Abortion Act of 1994 (protecting access to abortion clinics), and the 1996 Privacy Protection Act.[10]

Finally, during this period, the federal courts reaped a harvest of cases from antidiscrimination laws passed in previous decades, including Title VII of the 1964 Civil Rights Act, the Age Discrimination Acts of 1975 and 1986, and the Americans with Disabilities Act of 1990.[11]

The result of this was many more cases, additional judges and larger court staffs. Of the workload, Judge George Fagg said early in the decade: "Each day is sort of like running down a rocky slope with an avalanche right behind you."[12] The caseload of the U.S. Court of Appeals for the Eighth Circuit increased almost every year from 1990 to 1999. In 1990, there were 2,726 filings; the peak, 3,393, was reached in 1997. There were 3,356 filings in 1999. Terminations largely kept up with filings, although the number of pending cases crept upward from 1,684 (1990) to 1,930 (1999). Criminal appeals generally constituted about 20 percent of the docket. However, there were 641 criminal appeals in 1999. Most of the rest of the docket was made up of civil cases brought by the United States and civil cases brought by private parties. Bankruptcy appeals, original actions (largely habeas corpus), prisoner suits and administrative agency cases ranged from 75 cases (1991) to 127 (1997).[13]

The Eastern and Western Districts of Missouri were the main feeders of cases to the Court of Appeals during the 1990s, together contributing about 30 percent of the cases every year. The District of Minnesota and the Eastern District of Arkansas always placed either third or fourth, together contributing between 400 and 500 appeals each year. The Southern District of Iowa and the Districts of South Dakota and Nebraska each contributed about half of that. Appeals from the Northern District of Iowa and the Western District of Arkansas never exceeded 175 in the 1990s, while the District of North Dakota generated between 57 and 105 appeals each year.

During the 1990s, oral argument was afforded in between 37.5 percent and 44.9 percent of the cases. The bulk of the work of the court was undertaken by its regular active judges, but important contributions were made by senior and district judges. Participation by judges from outside the circuit was comparatively rare, although retired Supreme Court Justice Byron White, Daniel Friedman of the Federal Circuit, and John Peck of the Third Circuit, as well as a few others, did sit with the court.

One of the ways to make their dockets more manageable, employed by all the courts of appeals, was to render brief, unpublished opinions in "routine" cases. The Eighth Circuit has been doing so in about half the cases it decides. In 1999, for example, there were 737 published opinions (665 signed) and 671 unpublished. Under Eighth Circuit rules, unpublished opinions did not have precedential effect.

In the summer of 2000, in a decision which received wide publicity, *Anastasoff v. United States*,[14] a panel of the Eighth Circuit (Richard Arnold, Gerald Heaney, and the Chief Judge of the District of Minnesota, Paul Magnuson) held in an opinion by Arnold that it was unconstitutional for a court not to follow a prior opinion—whether published or unpublished—unless overruled by the court. The issue of ignoring unpublished opinions had not been briefed by the parties but was raised at oral argument by Arnold, who had written an article on the subject in 1999. The court panel struck down the portion of the court's rule 28A (i) that declares that an unpublished opinion is not precedent.

Anastasoff involved the issue of whether a retired teacher was to be denied a refund of $6,000 for overpaying her taxes because her claim had been received and filed a day after the three-year limitation period had expired. The panel held against the taxpayer, stating that the only way she could prevail was if the en banc court overturned the unpublished opinion. However, in a filing made two months later, the government announced it would acquiesce in a taxpayer-friendly interpretation of the law. Thus, in December 2000, the full court vacated the panel decision as moot.[15]

Whatever may happen regarding the precedential value of unpublished opinions, the "appeal of right" in the Courts of Appeals throughout the nation now only guarantees review by staff working under judicial supervision. Traditional appellate review occurs only with a select portion of the entire caseload.[16]

For most of this period, Richard Arnold was Chief Judge of the Court of Appeals. Lay described the position this way: "To paraphrase Casey Stengel, my main job is to keep five guys who hate me away from the five guys who are undecided."[17] Arnold succeeded Donald Lay on January 7, 1992, and served until April 17, 1998, when he stepped down eight months before he had to in order to allow Pasco Bowman to serve.[18] Arnold's retirement as Chief Judge would have permitted George Fagg to hold the position before Bowman, but Fagg declined. For his part, Bowman stepped down five years early so that the position could be held by Roger Wollman, who became Chief Judge on April 23, 1999.[19] Although Arnold spoke of the position as "simply the person you call when you need a new rug or lamp,"[20] his tenure was greatly admired by his colleagues on the Court of Appeals and those on the Judicial Conference of the United States.

In August 1997, June Boadwine retired as circuit executive after a decade and was succeeded by Millie Adams. Boadwine's activities reflected the range of activities circuit executives are now involved in, including the annual budget request, space discovery and allocation, plans for compliance with the Speedy Trial Act, collection and analysis of statistics, security, and "her biggest headache, automation." Among Boadwine's most important activities were her involvement in the creation of the Eighth Circuit Historical Society and with the "parent" federal advisory committee and the federal practice committees in each district, the opening up of the Judicial Conference, and putting together an immense Manual for Operation of the Court.[21]

The 1990s were a period of courthouse construction and renovation throughout the United States. In the Eighth Circuit, new courthouses were built in Minneapolis, Kansas City, and Omaha and a new courthouse annex in Fargo. Restoration, remodeling, or renovation occurred in the courthouses in Sioux Falls, Little Rock, and Des Moines. Members of the Courts of Appeals now maintain chambers in new and renovated buildings everywhere except in St. Paul.

After a long and frustrating process, in 2000 the Court of Appeals for the Eighth Circuit moved into a new facility in St. Louis, the Thomas P. Eagleton Courthouse,[22] built for $200 million. There had been a pro- tracted dispute over the cost of the five and one-half acre site in St. Louis ($10.3 million), which was selected in 1991. Six stories were lopped from the original design to save money. Groundbreaking took place in 1994. During construction, the same general contractor was fired twice and walked off the job once. Even truncated, the building is the fourth tall- est structure in St. Louis. Its dome, built of stainless steel, follows the same curve as the Gateway Arch, the tallest structure in St. Louis. The main courtroom for the Court of Appeals is in a horseshoe shape and sixty-five-feet long with a curving bench broad enough to accommodate twenty judges. The Court of Appeals had already moved into the top six floors of the building by the time it was dedicated on September 11, 2000. At the dedication, Chief Judge Wollman said that the building "signifies the fact that St. Louis, the birthplace of our circuit, will remain forever our home."[23] The building also houses the federal district court, the mag- istrate judges, bankruptcy judges, and the U.S. Attorney's Office.

The Court of Appeals, however, continues to use St. Paul as a second home and to "ride circuit." During this period, it sat for brief sessions in Grand Forks, Fargo, Omaha, Lincoln, and Sioux Falls, as well as at a number of law schools.

The Judges

Six judges were appointed to the Court of Appeals during the 1990s to fill one newly created judgeship (the court's eleventh); four judgeships opened as the result of judges taking senior status and one resulted from death. These nominations, three by George H. W. Bush and two by Bill Clinton, were confirmed without much delay. Bill Clinton made an ad- ditional nomination—Bonnie Campbell of Iowa—to the vacancy cre- ated when George Fagg took senior status, but that nomination died in Congress after the 2000 election. As of July 1, 2001, President George W. Bush had made three appointments, of which one has already been con- firmed. The court sustained two deaths during this period: senior Judge

J. Smith Henley on October 18, 1997,[24] and John Kelly, on October 23, 1998, only two months after he had taken the oath of office.

James B. Loken

The first of President George H. W. Bush's appointees, James B. Loken, was appointed to fill the seat left vacant by Gerald Heaney's taking senior status. When Loken took the oath of office in January 1991, he was fifty years old. Born in Madison, Wisconsin, in 1940, he undertook his undergraduate work at the University of Wisconsin, then attended the Harvard Law School, where he was a member of the *Harvard Law Review* and graduated magna cum laude. Loken served as a law clerk to Chief Judge J. Edward Lumbard of the U.S. Court of Appeals for the Second Circuit and Justice Byron White. He then began practice in Minneapolis with the law firm Faegre and Benson but soon left to become general counsel to the President's Committee on Consumer Interests. That same year (1970), Loken became staff assistant to the president. Loken returned to Faegre and Benson in 1973 and continued to practice with the firm until he was sworn in as judge of the Court of Appeals. A specialist in antitrust litigation, as a practicing attorney Loken handled cases for Minnesota corporations such as Norwest Bank and out-of-state corporations such as Union Carbide.

Loken's appointment to the Court of Appeals was delayed by a tug-of-war between Minnesota's Republican senators David Durenberger and Rudy Boschwitz (who supported Judge Paul Magnuson of the District of Minnesota) and the Bush administration.[25] Chief Judge Donald Lay has written that he was able to assist what proved to be an expeditious confirmation.[26] Loken's formal investiture occurred on February 12, 1991. One of a moderately conservative court's more conservative members, Judge Loken was a member of the panel that heard the major appeals in the case of *Clinton v. Jones*.[27]

David R. Hansen

Senator Charles Grassley of Iowa, a member of the Senate Judiciary Committee, strongly advanced Iowa's claim to the new seat Congress had created by the Act of December 1, 1990,[28] arguing that his state had fewer judges per capita than any other state in the Eighth Circuit. Grassley's credentials as a Republican senator on the Judiciary Committee secured the appointment to the Court of Appeals for David R. Hansen over Morris Arnold, who was supported by Arkansas's only Republican member of Congress, John Paul Hammerschmidt.[29] For that seat, Grassley recommended Charles Brooke, a Davenport lawyer, Linda K. Neuman, the first woman on the Iowa Supreme Court, and Hansen, U.S. district judge for the Northern District of Iowa. The president nominated Hansen.

David Hansen was born in Exira, in southwestern Iowa, on March 16, 1938. After graduating from Northwest Missouri State University, Hansen served for three years as an aide to a member of Congress. He attended George Washington University School of Law and began practice with Jones, Cambridge & Carl in Atlantic, Iowa. After four years on active duty with the U.S. Army Judge Advocate General Corps, Hansen returned to Iowa to practice with Barker, Hansen & McNeal in Iowa Falls. During this period, he was Hardin County Republican chairman and chaired the Hardin County Congressional campaign of Charles Grassley.

From 1969 to 1973, Hansen served as a police court judge in Iowa Falls. In 1976 he was appointed to the Iowa district court by Governor Robert Ray. While president-elect of the Iowa Judges Association in 1986, Hansen was nominated to be a federal district judge by President Reagan. He came to the bench with the reputation of being very able, tireless, politically conservative, and tough on criminals.[30] A relatively conservative member of the Court of Appeals, Hansen authored the most important Eighth Circuit securities case of the 1990s, *United States v. O'Hagan*.[31]

Morris Sheppard Arnold

Morris Arnold had been seriously considered several times for the Court of Appeals before his appointment in 1992. Born in Texarkana, Texas, in 1941, Arnold attended Yale University, received his bachelor's degree from the University of Arkansas, and graduated first in his class from the University of Arkansas Law School. After attending the University of London, Arnold received an S.J.D. from Harvard. He then taught in succession at the law schools of the University of Indiana, the University of Pennsylvania (where he was vice president of the university), and the University of Arkansas, Little Rock.[32] Arnold is an important legal historian and probably the most important scholar of the history of Arkansas before the Louisiana Purchase. A precise and elegant pen characterizes such works as *Colonial Arkansas, 1686–1804: A Social and Cultural History* (1991) and *Unequal Laws unto a Savage Race: European Legal Conditions in Arkansas, 1686–1836* (1985).

In addition to his scholarly activities, Morris Arnold was also involved in Republican Party politics, serving as party chairman for Arkansas. He was appointed U.S. district judge for the Western District of Arkansas by President Reagan in 1985. While a district judge, Arnold was seriously considered for the seats on the Eighth Circuit that went to Judges Beam, Loken, and Hansen. It also appears that he was considered for a seat on the D.C. Circuit and possibly even as a successor to William Brennan and Thurgood Marshall. Arnold was appointed to the Eighth Circuit on June 1, 1992.[33]

While Morris Arnold was a district judge, Richard Arnold did not participate in the review of his decisions. The two men are the first pair of brothers to sit together on a Court of Appeals and may prove to be the only such pair because, in 1998, Congress provided that no one "'related by affinity or consanguinity within the degree of first cousin to a current judge can be appointed to the same court.'"[34] Richard Arnold administered the oath of office to his brother. At that ceremony, Morris Arnold stated: "Let us simply say that you have here a fierce votary of the Bill of Rights and of the rule of law and one who knows where to find the books to back up and add substance to his views."[35] Morris Arnold has proven to be a moderate conservative member of the Court of Appeals on some issues, but has been a strong advocate of First Amendment rights. In *Miller v. Moore*,[36] Arnold wrote for the court holding that an amendment to the Nebraska constitution, which required state officials to work for a U.S. constitutional amendment to impose term limits on elected federal officials, violated the U.S. Constitution.[37]

Diana Murphy

While he was chief judge, Donald Lay made no secret of his concern that the Eighth Circuit was one of the few circuits without a female judge. In 1994, Diana E. Murphy, the first woman judge of the District of Minnesota and the first woman to serve as a chief district judge in the Eighth Circuit, was elevated to the Court of Appeals to fill the vacancy created by John R. Gibson's assumption of senior status.[38]

Born in Faribault, Minnesota, Murphy received her bachelor's degree and J.D. magna cum laude from the University of Minnesota and its Law School, where she was a member of the editorial board of the *Minnesota Law Review*. Murphy also undertook graduate work in history at the university and as a Fulbright scholar at Johannes Gutenberg University in Mainz.

Briefly practicing in Minneapolis with Lindquist & Vennum, Murphy served in quick succession on the Hennepin County Municipal Court and the Minnesota District Court. President Carter appointed her a U.S. district judge in 1980. Active in civic affairs, Murphy had served as president of the League of Woman Voters, a member of the Minneapolis Urban Commission, and chair of the Minneapolis Charter Commission. She has been equally active as a judge, serving on committees of the U.S. Judicial Conference and on the board of the Federal Judicial Center, and in 1999 she was appointed the chair of the U.S. Sentencing Commission.[39] She is a recipient of the Devitt Award.

Among Murphy's decisions as a district judge was the *U.S. Jaycees* case[40] discussed earlier and *Mille Lacs Band of Chippewa Indians v. Minnesota*,[41] an important decision dealing with Native American hunting and fishing rights discussed later. As Chief Judge of the District of Minnesota, Murphy helped to draw together the Minnesota congressional delegation, the City of Minneapolis, the General Services Administration, and the Administrative Office of the United States Courts in the successful effort to build a new U.S. courthouse in Minneapolis.[42]

John Kelly

In 1999, John Kelly was appointed to succeed Frank Magill, who had taken senior status on April 19, 1997. Descended on his mother's side from a pioneer North Dakota family, Kelly attended St. John's University in Minnesota and the University of Michigan Law School. He practiced with the Vogel firm for thirty-five years and acted as its president for twenty. A past president of the North Dakota Bar Association, Kelly had argued over forty cases before the North Dakota Supreme Court and about a dozen before the Eighth Circuit.

Although Kelly was a lifelong Democrat, his political involvements had not been substantial. However, his wife, Patricia, had been a member of the North Dakota state legislature for twenty years and Speaker of the North Dakota House of Representatives in 1983.

Among the serious candidates from North Dakota to succeed

Magill—there were also candidates from South Dakota and Missouri—the strongest possibilities in addition to Kelly were Kermit E. Bye, also of the Vogel Law Firm, North Dakota Justice William Neumann, former North Dakota Agriculture Commissioner Sarah Vogel, and U.S. Magistrate Judge Karen Kline. Kelly's only serious weakness was his age—sixty-two when Magill took senior status.

Late in October 1997, President Clinton selected Kelly. With the strong support of Senators Byron Dorgan and Kent Conrad, confirmation was not a serious problem. Kelly was confirmed by unanimous consent of the Senate on July 31, 1998. He was commissioned in August and took the oath of office privately on August 25.[43] Kelly did not live to attend what would have been the public ceremony commemorating his ascent to the bench.

After attending one sitting in St. Louis and producing several opinions,[44] Kelly died on October 21, 1998, a few days before his scheduled formal investiture. He was sixty-four years old. The cause of death was a severe bodily infection, which led to multiple organ failure. Kelly was mourned as "a man of sparkling wit, keen intelligence and superior legal skills" and as someone who "never lost his identification with loyalty to or empathy for the underprivileged and the underpowered."[45] Having spent a little more than an hour alone with Kelly, and that when he clearly was seriously ill, I was greatly impressed by his courtesy, decency, and nobility of spirit.

Kermit Bye

Kelly was replaced by Kermit Bye, the fifth attorney from the Vogel firm to be nominated to the Court of Appeals. Bye, born in 1937, undertook his undergraduate work and legal studies at the University of North Dakota. After service as assistant U.S. Attorney, special assistant to the North Dakota attorney general, and deputy state securities commissioner, Bye began a career that lasted over thirty years at the Vogel firm. He was president of the North Dakota State Bar Association in 1983–84 and North Dakota delegate to the ABA House of Delegates from 1986 to 1995. Clinton nominated Bye to the Court of Appeals in April 1999. He was confirmed in late February 2000 and was sworn in in June.[46]

The Court of Appeals for the Eighth Circuit during the 1990s can properly be characterized as a conservative, but by no means uniformly conservative, court. Excluding those on senior status, no member of the court was a judicial liberal of the school of Lay, Heaney, or Bright. Indeed, only Richard Arnold and Diana Murphy could be characterized as moderate liberals. With a reasonable consensus on many issues and with the smooth leadership of Richard Arnold, differences on the court were much harder to spot in the 1990s than during the previous decade.

William J. Riley, Michael Melloy, and Lavenski R. Smith

Toward the end of the period covered in this chapter, George Fagg, C. Arlen Beam, and Richard Arnold took senior status. Jockeying between the states of the Eighth Circuit, political partisanship in Washington, and the 2000 election affected who would be their successors. To succeed Fagg, President Clinton nominated Bonnie Campbell, former Iowa attorney general and unsuccessful candidate for governor in 1994, who was serving as director of the Federal Violence against Women office in the U.S. Department of Justice. Opposed by Christian conservatives and other Republicans, Campbell's nomination did not come to a vote before Clinton's tenure ended.[47]

By August 1, 2001, President George W. Bush had made three nominations to seats on the Court of Appeals, all of whom were confirmed without great difficulty. The first to be confirmed, William J. Riley, was a fifty-four-year-old Nebraskan, appointed to Beam's seat. Riley had attended college and law school at the University of Nebraska, Lincoln (where he was editor of the law review). He had clerked for Donald Lay, practiced in Omaha for twenty-eight years with Fitzgerald, Schorr, Barmettler and Brennan, taught as an adjunct professor at Creighton Law School, and served as president of the Omaha Bar. Riley was selected for the Court of Appeals over such candidates as Nebraska's Attorney General Donald Stenberg, then Speaker of the Unicameral; Doug Kristensen; and U.S. District Judge Richard G. Kopf. Riley was confirmed on August 2 by a vote of 97–0.[48]

Although Missouri Senator Christopher "Kit" Bond had been pushing for another judge from Missouri, Michael J. Melloy, judge of the Northern District of Iowa, was named to succeed Fagg.[49] Melloy, fifty-three years old, had served as a U.S. Bankruptcy Court judge from 1986 until 1992, when George Bush was nominated him to the district court. Melloy served as chief judge of that court from 1993 to 2000.[50] Melloy was confirmed by a vote of 91–0 on February 11, 2002.

Lavenski R. Smith was appointed to succeed Richard Arnold. A forty-two-year-old African American, Smith had been in private practice and a member of the Arkansas Supreme Court. At the time of his appointment to the Eighth Circuit, he was serving on the Arkansas Public Service Commission. He was confirmed on July 15, 2002 by a vote of 97–3.[51]

In recent years, the senior judges of the Eighth Circuit have received many honors and celebrated many milestones. Judge Floyd Gibson sat with the court almost until his ninetieth birthday, which was commemorated by a special session of the court.[52] Gibson died on October 4, 2001. Donald Lay received a Life Fellowship to the American Bar Foundation. A residence hall of the University of Minnesota, Duluth, was named for Gerald Heaney. Myron Bright received the Herbert Harley award, given by the American Judicature Society for outstanding contributions to improve the administration of justice.[53] Donald Ross received an honorary doctor of laws degree from the University of Nebraska, Lincoln. Theodore McMillian, honored repeatedly by bar associations in Missouri, was chosen for the Hall of Fame of the National Bar Association. Both Richard Arnold and Diana Murphy received the Edward J. Devitt Distinguished Service to Justice Award, a national award given for an exemplary career in which significant contributions to the administration of justice, rule of law, and improvement of society have been made. John R. Gibson received the Citation of Merit Award of the University of Missouri at Kansas City Law School.[54]

Harry Blackmun

Harry Blackmun's Indian summer came to an end on March 4, 1999, in his ninety-first year. Remaining on the Supreme Court until 1994, at his retirement Blackmun was the third oldest man ever to sit on that court. In spite of years of effort to overturn *Roe v. Wade* and of anticipation that it would be overturned, the decision was reaffirmed by the Supreme Court in *Planned Parenthood v. Casey* in 1992, although somewhat eroded.[55] A descendant of Joseph Story, Blackmun played Story in Steven Spielberg's film *Amistad*.[56] Blackmun's ninetieth birthday was celebrated over an entire weekend in November 1998. A fitting epitaph was written by Blackmun himself in his farewell response to his colleagues: "Let us hope that, in the years far down the line, where history places us in such perspective as we deserve, it at least will be able to say: 'They did their best and did it acceptably well.'"[57] In July 2001, the Blackmun Rotunda on the twenty-seventh floor of the Eagleton Courthouse was dedicated.[58]

Jurisprudence

During the 1990s, a less-divided Court of Appeals dealt with a diverse and growing docket. That its decisions proved to be more conservative than the court of the 1970s and 1980s was a factor of both the dominance of the Reagan and Bush appointees on the court and the growing conservatism of the U.S. Supreme Court. In cases involving state restrictions on abortion, the Court of Appeals continued to hold unconstitutional many, but by no means all, sections of statutes. In the most important cases, involving bans on partial-birth abortion, the court held the laws of three states unconstitutional and was vindicated by the Supreme Court. In the meantime, laws passed to limit anti-abortion protests in residential areas posed a difficult conflict between protecting the right to choose and that of freedom of speech, a conflict that closely divided the Court of Appeals.

While lawsuits over job discrimination swamped the courts of the Eighth Circuit, the most important civil rights cases were those involving desegregation of the Kansas City and St. Louis schools. Although more divided than before, the Court of Appeals continued to support the strong desegregation medicine prescribed by the district courts, but was limited by the desire of a majority of the Supreme Court to bring lengthy desegregation litigation to an end.

Although litigation involving church and state was far less significant than during the 1980s, the Court of Appeals continued to hear a rich variety of cases involving free speech, to which it generally was a friend, save when adult theaters and bookstores and other sexually suggestive activities were involved.

The traditional federal specialties, especially federal criminal, antitrust, bankruptcy, tax, and trademark law, continued to produce interesting and important cases, which are difficult to generalize about with the exception of antitrust, where the Court of Appeals was consistently pro-defendant.

The most important "regional" cases involved Native Americans and environmental law. In probably the most important Native American cases—involving hunting and fishing rights—the Eighth Circuit held for Native Americans, while the results in environmental appeals produced no clear pattern. However, in cases involving questions of federalism, the Court of Appeals consistently invalidated state laws on Dormant Commerce Clause and preemption grounds.

Most visible were the cases connected with scandals that, fairly or unfairly, surrounded President Bill Clinton. In the most important of these cases, the Court of Appeals held that a sexual harassment suit against the president for conduct unrelated to his conduct in office could move forward, so long as the trial judge handling the case was sensitive to the demands on the president's time. The Court of Appeals also heard an appeal from the dismissal of that lawsuit on a motion for summary judgment, but the case settled before its decision was released.

Abortion

After years of vulnerability, the core of *Roe v. Wade* was reaffirmed, if somewhat eroded, by the Supreme Court in *Planned Parenthood v. Casey*, decided in 1992.[59] In that case, the High Court held that laws which constituted an "undue burden" on the woman's right to choose were unconstitutional. During the 1990s, the Court of Appeals for the Eighth Circuit continued to hear the "common garden variety" of statutes attempting to regulate abortion that were characteristic of the 1970s and 1980s (laws barring public funding of abortion; those requiring the consent of husbands or of parents of minors, etc.). The Court of Appeals also considered the constitutionality of statutes banning partial birth abortion and attempts by the states to restrict funding of abortions Congress was willing to fund through the Medicaid program, and wrestled with restrictions on the picketing of abortion providers.

The 1991 amendments to the North Dakota Abortion Control Act provided for a twenty-four-hour waiting period for an abortion after information had been provided to patients about fetal development and alternatives to abortion. This was similar to the law of Pennsylvania, which the Supreme Court sustained in *Planned Parenthood v. Casey*. However, those seeking abortions confronted a different situation in North Dakota, a state that was large in area yet had only a single abortion provider, the Fargo Women's Health Organization. The twenty-four-hour waiting period appeared likely to add to the cost and inconvenience of women coming to Fargo from other parts of the state. What might not have been an "undue burden" in Pennsylvania might have been one in North Dakota.

The matter turned out to be resolved relatively painlessly by a ruling of the state attorney general that the abortion provider could give the information over the telephone. Believing thus that the statute did not require women to pay two visits to Fargo, the Court of Appeals upheld the law in an opinion by Judge John R. Gibson over the dissent of Judge McMillian.[60] Toward the end of the period, the Court of Appeals considered the constitutionality of the statutes of Nebraska, Arkansas, and Iowa banning partial-birth abortion. Partial-birth abortion, the most common method of second-trimester abortion, called dilation and evacuation, involves extraction from the uterus and into the vagina of all of the body of a fetus except the head, following which the fetus is killed by extracting the contents of the skull.[61]

On September 24, 1999, a panel of Richard Arnold (writing), Roger Wollman, and Paul Magnuson held the laws of the three states unconstitutional. The leading opinion was written in the Nebraska case by Chief Judge Arnold, who stated that the partial-birth abortion bans imposed an undue burden on the woman's right to choose to have an abortion.[62] That case involved Dr. LeRoy H. Carhart, one of only three doctors known to perform abortions in Nebraska and the only one to perform them after the sixteenth week.

The Supreme Court granted certiorari and heard argument in the Nebraska case, the first time it had heard an abortion case on the merits since *Casey*. The Eighth Circuit was affirmed, but with eight opinions and by an unexpectedly close vote, 5–4.[63]

During some years in the 1990s, Congress used a less restrictive standard for funding abortions under Medicaid (abortions would be funded when a woman's life was in danger or in cases of rape or incest) than that of many states, which only permitted public funding if a woman's life was in danger. District judges in Arkansas and Nebraska voided these provisions of state law or of the state constitution. Consolidating the two cases, the Court of Appeals held that the federal statute preempted the provisions of the state laws and that states participating in the Medicaid program were barred from denying funding to Medicaid-eligible women for abortions in cases of rape or incest. Judge Pasco Bowman concurred reluctantly.[64]

While the Supreme Court did not review the principal issue in the Arkansas case, it agreed with Judge Bowman's view that the Court of Appeals decision was too broad, holding that it was not necessary to completely invalidate Amendment 68 of the Arkansas Constitution, which includes the statement of Arkansas policy "to protect the life of every unborn child from conception until birth, to the extent permitted by the Federal Government."[65]

During the 1990s, the federal courts were called on to judge the constitutionality of local ordinances limiting picketing of abortion providers and clinics. The Supreme Court had dealt with the problem in major decisions in 1988 and 1994,[66] but the lower court had to apply those rules to jerry-built ordinances reflecting a variety of circumstances. The Court of Appeals heard cases involving municipalities in North Dakota, Iowa, and Nebraska.

In *Kirkeby v. Furness,* a panel held over the dissent of John R. Gibson that antiabortion demonstrators were entitled to an injunction preventing the application of a Fargo ordinance, revised in 1993, which prohibited all "targeted residential picketing" within 200 feet of a residential dwelling, if there were written material identifying occupants of the dwelling by name. The court thought the statute "probably unconstitutional" and remanded the case to the district court.[67] After the district court held the statute unconstitutional, the same panel held that the ordinance violated the First Amendment on its face and that the restricted picketing zone established pursuant to the ordinance also violated the Amendment. Judge Gibson dissented once again.[68]

In separate litigation, the Court of Appeals, in February 2001, upheld by a 6–5 vote Fargo's 1985 ordinance on the ground that it had not targeted specific groups. The decision came in a Section 1983 action brought by Chris Veneklase and four other anti-abortion protestors who had picketed the home of the administrator of the city's only abortion clinic in October 1991.[69] The Court of Appeals also upheld the residential picketing ordinance of Clive, Iowa, but struck down Clive's parade ordinance as overbroad.[70] In 2000, the court upheld Lincoln, Nebraska's, "focused picketing" ordinance.[71]

The Court of Appeals was the first circuit to uphold the constitutionality of the 1994 Federal Access to Clinics Act (FACE) in a case arising in the Western District of Missouri involving an abortion protestor. Based on Congress's commerce power, the statute provides criminal and civil penalties for someone who by force intimidates or interferes with any person obtaining or providing reproductive health services.[72] The court held in an opinion by Richard Arnold that interstate commerce was involved because many patients and members of the staff of Planned Parenthood's Kansas City clinic resided in states other than

Missouri and because Congress had found that the blockading of clinics and the use of violence and threats of violence against patients and staff depressed interstate commerce in reproductive health services. The court did not believe that the statute violated the First Amendment, but finding the injunction in the case before it overbroad, the court limited it.[73]

Civil Rights

SCHOOL DESEGREGATION   The Kansas City, St. Louis, and Little Rock desegregation cases moved glacierlike toward the end of judicial supervision. While this finally occurred with St. Louis, the Kansas City and Little Rock cases were still in the courts as the new century began.

Throughout the years, the Eighth Circuit Court of Appeals panels had supported the strong medicine that Judge Russell G. Clark had forced on the State of Missouri and the (more willing) School District. This included the magnetizing of all of Kansas City's schools and new facilities which cost over one billion dollars through the year 1995. Although the Court of Appeals had not allowed Clark to order tax increases directly, it had permitted him to order the school board to impose property taxes. However, when the Court of Appeals went en banc in the Kansas City litigation, divisions became apparent.

In a trio of cases, beginning in 1991 with Oklahoma City and concluding with the Kansas City case in 1995, the Supreme Court signaled that the patience of the majority of the Rehnquist Court had run out on court-supervised school desegregation.[74] The three cases spelled out procedures for court approval of the dismantling of judicial responsibility for school systems. According to the Supreme Court, once racial imbalance traceable to the constitutional violation had been remedied, a school district was under no duty to remedy imbalance brought about by demographic factors. The effect of the three decisions was to replace the goal of rooting out the vestiges of school segregation with that of returning responsibility for schools to localities.

The Court of Appeals had been unsympathetic to the State of Missouri's attempt to end its responsibility for educational improvement programs and for salary increases for teachers and other school system employees. Judge John R. Gibson wrote in 1991: "There is a unique irony in this situation in which one of the parties substantially contributing to the protracted litigation presents an argument that because there has not been immediate success, the plan should be scrapped."[75]

The Court of Appeals had held in the Kansas City case that it was permissible for the district court to order a different cost formula than that employed in the St. Louis case.[76] In late 1993, it held (J. R. Gibson writing, with McMillian and Heaney) that the court-ordered desegregation plan and the state financing of it had to last until the vestiges of Missouri's old dual-race school system—reduced student achievement and white flight—were eliminated. The success of a desegregation remedy, the Court of Appeals held, could not be measured solely by the funding of programs required by the remedy. The school district could not be released from judicial supervision if student test scores were low. The Court of Appeals held that the KCMSD had not attained unitary status; only a start had been made in eliminating the vestiges of past discrimination. It also held that the district court had the power to order salary increases for employees of the district.[77] Reagan and Bush appointees were on both sides of the 6–5 denial of rehearing en banc.[78]

Between 1986 and 1994, property taxes in Kansas City doubled. By 1995, when the Supreme Court decided the *Jenkins* case, desegregation in the schools of Kansas City had already cost $1.3 billion. Furthermore, evidence was accumulating that the goal for which these immense expenditures were made was not being achieved.[79] In the Supreme Court, the State of Missouri, which had shouldered most of the cost, argued for an end to "a remedy of unprecedented breadth and unparalleled expense."[80]

In deciding *Jenkins v. State of Missouri*, the Supreme Court limited the extent of judicially ordered educational reform in the Kansas City schools and authorized the end of state funding.[81] The High Court held that Judge Clark's attempt to transform the KCMSD into a magnet district to draw white students from the surrounding suburbs had been improper absent evidence that the suburban districts had done anything to cause the school segregation. The Court also held that it was inappropriate to require that student test scores rise before recognizing the unitary status of the school district because the district judge had failed to specify how past discrimination had caused the lower scores. The order requiring salary increases was also held invalid for the district's lower relative salaries could not be traced to intentional segregation. The majority opinion in the case, decided 5–4, emphasized that the duty of the lower court was to restore control of the school system to local authorities as soon as possible.

Dissenting, Justice Ruth Bader Ginsburg wrote: "Given the deep, inglorious history of segregation in Missouri, to curtail desegregation at this time and in this manner is an action at once too swift and too soon."[82]

In 1996, the school board announced an agreement with the attorney general of Missouri to end state desegregation payments in 1999 pending judicial approval.[83] In January 1997, after a three-week hearing, Judge Clark rejected as "grossly premature" Missouri's argument that the Supreme Court considered the state's work done. He ruled that in deciding whether to release the state, he had to balance three interests: the degree of segregation, restoring the victims of segregation to a position as near as possible to the position they would have been in without segregation, and the importance of state and local autonomy. Clark also announced that after he issued his next court order, he would withdraw from the case he had handled for more than nineteen years.[84]

Clark issued his last order in the case, ending state responsibility for Kansas City school desegregation, in March 1997. He approved a settlement calling for an end to the lawsuit by 2000 and an end to state support by 1999. He asked school officials to come up with a plan by August 15, 1999, to deal with the loss of nearly $100 million in annual state moneys. However, Clark also indicated his deep disappointment with the results of the Kansas City experiment—"Dismal at best"—and issued a scathing indictment of the district's ability to manage its educational and financial affairs.[85] In the same year, the Court of Appeals ruled that the Kansas City schools remained segregated, but approved a plan by which the state could end its involvement after three more years of payments.[86]

In June 1998, the school board approved a plan to wean the district from state payments, while Governor Mel Carnahan signed a bill to help the Kansas City School District avoid bankruptcy once the state payments ended. Those monies were, however, contingent on settlement of the St. Louis litigation.[87]

In January 1999, Judge Dean Whipple, who had succeeded Clark with the case, held that the state of Missouri had met its obligations under the 1996 settlement agreement and was entitled to be dismissed as a defendant. Two months later, State Attorney General Jay Nixon delivered the paperwork to the state capitol ending the state's involvement in the Kansas City lawsuit.[88] After twenty-two years of litigation and fourteen years of "desegregation," the expenditure of $2 billion, and a school population that had risen from 74 percent African American (1984) to 80 percent (1998), the lawsuit appeared to be ending.[89]

In November 1999, without a hearing, Judge Whipple dismissed the desegregation case subject to resolution of pending motions and future motions for litigation-related costs and fees. He ordered that the Desegregation Monitoring Committee remain in place until all issues were resolved. Whipple also refused to overrule the state's decision to strip the Kansas City School District of its accreditation.[90]

Yet all was not over. In February 2000, the Court of Appeals panel ruled that the school district should remain under federal court control, holding that Judge Whipple had erred when he dismissed the desegregation case without allowing the parties to present evidence. The panel ordered that the case be given to a different judge.[91]

A little less than four months later, the court en banc held by a vote of 9–3 that there should have been a hearing before deciding that the district had been desegregated to the extent possible, but returned the case to Whipple. There were six opinions. Among them were John R. Gibson's for the en banc court and Judge Beam's dissenting opinion stating that the educational program of the school district was in shambles.[92] Bearing this out, the KCMSD School Board fired the superintendent of schools in 2001 and hired a new one, the twentieth in thirty years.[93] Judicial oversight of the Kansas City Missouri School District was still alive in 2001.

The situation in St. Louis was somewhat happier. The Supreme Court decision in the Kansas City case spurred resolution of the St. Louis desegregation case. While St. Louis had a far more modest magnet program than Kansas City, it did have a voluntary interdistrict transfer program—the largest in the country—so that African American students could attend white suburban school districts. African American students attending suburban school districts—13,000 in 1999—proved to be nearly twice as likely to graduate from high school as students who remained in city schools. On the other hand, only 1,300 white suburban children were attending magnet schools in the St. Louis area. There were successes within the St. Louis school system. The percentage of black students in integrated classrooms had tripled. The pupil-teacher ratio had been cut to 20:1. Black students attending the city's twenty-five magnet schools performed better on standardized tests than transfer students. But the cost was high—by 1995, the state of Missouri had spent $1.2 billion on schools in the St. Louis area. Four of ten black children remained in all-black schools. If on standardized tests black students attending the city's twenty-five magnet schools performed even better than transfer students, black students in traditional schools lagged behind.[94]

After the Supreme Court decision in *Jenkins,* there was a trial before Judge George F. Gunn to determine if and how state funding of the voluntary transfer program in St. Louis would end. Gunn asked the former chancellor of Washington University, William H. Danforth, to serve as settlement coordinator. His role would prove to be crucial.

In January 1997, the Court of Appeals refused to put a deadline on settlement negotiations.[95] In September of that year, the court denied Attorney General Jay Nixon's request for an end to recruitment of students from the suburbs and repeated its position that a negotiated settlement was preferable to a court order for an end to the suit.[96] Early in 1998, Gunn, the fourth judge to have overseen the St. Louis desegregation case, died of cancer. Stephen L. Limbaugh, who had the responsibility for the case once before, took it on again.[97]

On June 23, 1998, Governor Mel Carnahan signed the bill under which the St. Louis desegregation case was able to come to an end. Under that law, the state provided for a school board elected by districts. The St. Louis public schools were to receive more than forty million of the seventy million dollars it was then receiving annually from the state. The voluntary transfer program with the suburbs was to continue and the suburban school districts involved were also to receive state funding.[98] The *St. Louis Post Dispatch,* a not uncritical observer, editorialized: "The Missouri legislature accomplished the impossible last week. Now St. Louis must merely accomplish the improbable."[99]

What was meant by the latter sentence was that, for the suit really to end, the parties had to reach a final settlement and the residents of St. Louis had to approve a tax increase, property or sales, through a referendum. The settlement was reached on January 6, 1999. Minnie Lidell, who had started the battle one-quarter of a century before and that year had three grandchildren in the St. Louis schools, was present as Danforth announced a settlement agreement that ran to more than one hundred pages. Among the details: the settlement agreement provided that the city would receive $180 million over ten years to build new school facilities. The transfer program was to continue for at least three years, after which the suburban districts could opt out (though, even if they did, participating districts had to continue to accept city students for at least six years). The city school board was to be responsible for trying to change the balance at magnet schools from 60 percent black to 55 percent and was to reduce by a minimum of 3 percent a year the number of students in the bottom two achievement levels of the Missouri Assessment Program test.[100]

The "improbable" was accomplished. At the referendum, 63 percent of the voters of St. Louis supported a sales tax increase. A final settlement agreement of 140 pages was filed with the court in late February 1999. On March 13, Judge Limbaugh signed a twenty-page order marking the end of the case. Two days later, Attorney General Jay Nixon personally delivered the papers to notify state officials that the St. Louis desegregation case was over.[101]

In October 1999, state officials announced, not unexpectedly, that both St. Louis and Kansas City had failed to meet four of eleven minimum academic standards for school systems and would both lose their state accreditation. St. Louis, spared the bickering and animosity that occurred in Kansas City, moved quickly to produce a comprehensive plan involving teacher incentives, parent mentoring, and summer classes and regained provisional accreditation in October 2000.[102]

Space does not permit detailed discussion of the desegregation action brought in 1982 by the Little Rock School Board against Pulaski County to consolidate the districts. White flight had left an unstable balance in many of the Little Rock schools, which were becoming resegregated. The litigation would not be free of acrimony between the district judges, Henry Woods and (then) Susan Webber Wright, and the Court of Appeals.[103]

On December 15, 1997, reversing a 1996 order of Judge Wright, the Court of Appeals held that the Little Rock School District was entitled to be dismissed from its desegregation lawsuit (the state had already been dismissed from the case),[104] but that it still should be subject to federal court monitoring. Judge Wollman wrote the opinion for a panel that included Richard Arnold and Heaney. In January 2001, the Little Rock School Board adopted a covenant promising to stay the desegregation course when the district would be released from federal court supervision.[105] However, the School District had not been released from desegregation monitoring by the summer of 2001.[106]

Perhaps the most important event involving the Little Rock schools in the 1990s was historical. The fortieth anniversary of the desegregation of Central High School was commemorated in 1997. By that time, the high school, one of the most visited sites in Arkansas, was multiracial—40 percent white. Its principal was African American—the third in the school's history. The school had been attended by children of high Clinton administration officials and by the daughter of Governor Mike Huckabee.[107] President Bill Clinton attended the fortieth anniversary commemoration in Little Rock and later, at the White House, presented the nine students who had desegregated the school in 1957–58 with the nation's highest award for civilians, the Congressional Gold Medal.[108]

EMPLOYMENT DISCRIMINATION   One observer commented in 1997 that it might be said that employment litigation was "swamping the federal courts of the Eighth Circuit."[109] The Court of Appeals heard many cases involving claims of racial and gender discrimination under the Civil Rights Act of 1964, of age discrimination under the Age Discrimination Act of 1986, and of discrimination against the disabled under the Americans with Disabilities Act of 1990 (ADA)[110] and the Individuals with Disabilities Education Act (IDEA).

Some examples suggest the variety: The Court of Appeals held that a woman with epilepsy was protected by the Americans with Disabilities Act,[111] but also held that nearsightedness was not a condition covered by the act.[112] A divided panel held in an Arkansas case that a two-year-old with a severe allergy to peanuts was not "disabled" within the meaning of IDEA and could be refused day care services.[113] On the other hand, the U.S. Supreme Court agreed with the Eighth Circuit when it held, under the same law, that public schools were responsible for one-on-one nursing care for some disabled students.[114] The Court of Appeals upheld an $800,000 verdict against Doctors Hospital in Little Rock in an age discrimination case, as well as a judgment against Farmers Insurance Company, although it reduced the punitive damages in that case from $4 million to $700,000.[115]

Several important cases dealt with the abrogation of the Eleventh Amendment immunity of the states by antidiscrimination legislation. Reversing its panels, the en banc court held that Congress had acted unconstitutionally in abrogating Eleventh Amendment immunity under the IDEA[116] and under the Americans with Disabilities Act.[117] A panel took the same approach to the Age Discrimination in Employment Act,[118] placing the Eighth Circuit in the minority of the circuits that had dealt with the issue. The Supreme Court, however, vindicated the Eighth Circuit's position.[119]

In cases involving claims of racial discrimination in employment under Title VII of the 1964 Civil Rights Act, the Court of Appeals upheld a $152,000 award to a black corrections officer in Douglas County, Nebraska, for racial epithets made by a deputy warden.[120] By overturning a summary judgment, the court held that six black firefighters could attempt to prove at trial that the St. Paul Fire Department permitted racial discrimination creating a hostile work environment.[121]

While many job discrimination holdings were fact specific, there were several cases of much broader interest. In a strong opinion by Judge Lay, the court sought to allay the trends toward summary judgment for employers in the district court.[122] The court also held, over the dissent of Judge Heaney, that a professional corporation with fewer than fifteen associates and support staff could not be sued for sexual harassment.[123] The Eighth Circuit was the first circuit to rule that actionable sexual harassment could occur between persons of the same sex.[124]

Claims of gender discrimination in the work place were frequent. Under Title VII, sexual harassment had traditionally been found only if there were a quid pro quo, such as having to provide sex as a condition for one's job. However, a second theory, that of a "hostile work environment," was later accepted by the Supreme Court. This typically involved a woman employee complaining of an abusive environment created by men. Much of the upswing in the number of sexual harassment cases in the Eighth Circuit during the 1990s were hostile environment cases. In *Carter v. Chrysler Corp.*, the court, in an opinion by Judge Murphy, clarified the elements that had to be established in order to state a claim for a hostile work environment.[125] In another Murphy opinion, the court held that a hostile work environment claim had to be evaluated by considering whether there was a pattern of abusive conduct rather than by considering each incident of alleged abuse in isolation.[126]

In some cases, the fact patterns were vivid. One case involved an Iowan woman who had posed nude for two magazines. Her boss at McGregor Electric Industries had not only made every effort to date her but also had made lewd gestures, asked her to watch pornography, and to pose nude. Other employees made sexual comments and engaged in obscene name-calling. The district court ruled against her, but a "conservative" panel of Wollman (writing), Henley, and Fagg reversed. Once again, the district court held for the company. A different panel of the

Court of Appeals (Lay writing, with McMillian and Bowman) then reversed and directed that judgment be entered for the plaintiff.[127]

One of the most appalling, if not the most appalling, of these cases also made important law. It involved harassment of female miners at the Eveleth Mines in Eveleth, Minnesota. The case, certified as a class action in 1993, was the first certified class action, hostile work environment, sexual harassment suit.

Women miners, employed in the mid-1970s, had become the daily target of relentless dirty jokes, propositions, and rumor-mongering about their sex lives. The women were groped and fondled. Nearly every work area was covered with pornographic pictures and obscene graffiti. During the trial, the women plaintiffs were cross-examined about domestic abuse, illegitimate children, abortions and, in one case, a rape.

In December 1997, the Court of Appeals harshly overruled the special master who had tried the case, which had ended with awards of $11,000 each to the plaintiffs. Judge Donald Lay, writing for a panel that included Floyd Gibson and Theodore McMillian, described the effect of the harassment:

> The callous pattern and practice of sexual harassment engaged in by Eveleth Mines inevitably destroyed the self-esteem of the working women opposed to it. The emotional harm, brought about by this record of human indecency, sought to destroy the human psyche, as well as the human spirit of each plaintiff.[128]

The case was remanded but then was settled with each woman apparently getting several hundred thousand dollars.[129]

First Amendment Cases

CASES INVOLVING RELIGION   In contrast to the 1980s, no decision of the Court of Appeals in the area of church-state led to an important Supreme Court decision. Nevertheless, knotty problems continued to arise, and during this period, the Court of Appeals was reaching "accomodationist" results. The court upheld a governmental remedial mathematics and reading program, which served two thousand educationally deprived children in 128 Missouri parochial schools. It also held, although by a divided panel, that the Wabasso School District in southwestern Minnesota could continue to operate a small village school in a building owned by a religious group (the Brethren), even though all of the students were the children of members of the religious group. The Brethren did not want their children to be exposed to computers, films, videos, and other forms of technology. Presumably they were not, although computers and electronic devices were available for students who wanted them.[130] In a holiday display case, the Court of Appeals held that the city of Florissant, Missouri, could display a crèche at its civic center because the display also included a snowman, a Christmas tree, and candy canes.[131]

Probably the most important church-state case came out of a bankruptcy matter. An amount of $13,450 had been tithed to the Crystal Evangelical Free Church of New Hope, Minnesota, the year before the bankruptcy filing. The issue was whether the tithed money could be reclaimed by a bankruptcy trustee. The bankruptcy court ordered the church to return the money; a ruling upheld on appeal by the district judge, who held that the church's free exercise claim failed because the bankruptcy code was a neutral law of general applicability, which had only an incidental effect on religion. Although the U.S. government had been expected to appear in support of the trustee, the federal lawyer did not show up when the case was argued for the first time before the Court of Appeals. Minutes before argument, President Clinton had changed the government's position. Of the missing lawyer, Judge McMillian commented at the time, "I suppose he was spoken to by God on High."[132]

While the appeal was pending, the Religious Freedom Restoration Act (RFRA) became law. Intended to reverse the effect of a Supreme Court decision, the law provided that the government may substantially burden a person's exercise of religion only if it can demonstrate that application of the burden to the person is in furtherance of a compelling governmental interest and is the least restrictive means of furthering that interest.[133]

The Court of Appeals first determined that the contribution to the church was not an exchange for services and therefore constituted an avoidable transfer that ought to have been recoverable by the trustee. However, the panel then held that to require the church to return the contributions would violate the RFRA because, on the one hand, tithing was an important expression of religious belief but, on the other, protecting the interests of creditors was not a compelling governmental interest.[134] When rehearing en banc was denied, Judge Beam specially concurred in the denial to emphasize that "the court's decision cannot mean that all religious contributions by a bankruptcy debtor constitute a preferential transfer under the Bankruptcy code."[135]

The Supreme Court granted certiorari but then remanded the case to the Court of Appeals to consider in light of a High Court's ruling that the RFRA was unconstitutional at least as far as it touched on state action.[136] On remand, the court again ruled for the couple, holding that to force the church to return the money to a bankruptcy trustee would "substantially burden" the couple's free exercise of religion.[137] The court also held the RFRA constitutional as applied to federal matters. Congress cemented the matter by passing the Religious Liberty and Charitable Donation Protection Act of 1998, which prevents bankruptcy trustees from voiding pre-bankruptcy petition transfers to "a qualified religious or charitable entity," if the transfer does not exceed 15 percent of the debtor's gross annual income in the year it was made.[138] The Crystal Free Church spent hundreds of thousands of dollars in litigation to keep a $13,450 donation but, by winning its case, may have provided a bonanza for religious institutions generally.[139]

FREE SPEECH CASES   The Court of Appeals continued to hear a rich variety of First Amendment speech cases in addition to those involving abortion protestors which have already been discussed. Some of them were classic, garden variety free speech cases involving the distribution of fliers on government property, an arrest for carrying a wooden cross through the streets on Good Friday, and cases involving adult theaters and bookstores. Others raised newer questions, such as the constitutionality of laws limiting campaign contributions and expenditures.

Gilleo v. City of Ladue involved a wealthy suburb of St. Louis, graced by winding roads lined with trees and shrubbery, which banned signs of almost every variety.[140] The city argued that this would preserve natural beauty, maintain real estate values, and promote safety. However, Ladue allowed the distribution of handbills and permitted residents to hang flags with messages on them, so long as the flags were rectangular. Further, the ordinance permitted commercial establishments, churches, and nonprofit organizations to erect certain signs that were not allowed at residences, and permitted homeowners to place "for sale" and "for rent" signs.

The plaintiff in this case, Margaret Gilleo, was informed that the 8 ½ by 11 inch sign with the words "For Peace in the Gulf" taped to a window of her home violated a city ordinance. She filed a complaint in district court to test its constitutionality. The city then passed another ordinance to the same effect, which Gilleo amended her complaint to challenge. Judge Jean C. Hamilton of the Eastern District of Missouri held the ordinance unconstitutional.[141]

The Court of Appeals affirmed on the theory that the ordinance was content based, discriminating in favor of commercial speech, and that it failed strict scrutiny because the suburb's interests were not "compelling" and the ordinance not the least restrictive alternative to achieve its goal.[142]

At oral argument before the Supreme Court, the justices appeared to have been intrigued and even amused by the case. When Justice Stevens learned that the city permitted residents to distribute leaflets, he seemed incredulous, but Justice Scalia interjected in a stage whisper that leaflets were acceptable so long as they were distributed by people in colonial costumes.[143] The High Court ruled unanimously for Gilleo, but surprised observers with a holding that was more broadly protective of free speech than that of the Court of Appeals. Assuming the regulation was content neutral, the High Court ruled that cities may not bar residents from posting signs on their own property. The law of Ladue had simply suppressed too much speech.[144]

In a case involving the First Amendment right of an organization seeking changes in welfare policy to distribute fliers and discuss public policy issues with recipients in a Nebraska welfare office, a panel upheld the First Amendment contention, but then was overturned by the full court.[145] On the other hand, the court also held that a man arrested on Good Friday carrying a wooden cross through Moorhead, Minnesota, might pursue his Section 1983 action against the city and police officers because the arrest had violated his right to convey religious messages in a public forum.[146]

In a long and colorful battle beginning in 1994, the Court of Appeals upheld the right of the Ku Klux Klan to participate in Missouri's Adopt-a-Highway program. Under that program, one that most states have, in return for picking up trash, planting flowers, and mowing a one-mile stretch of road, a business or other organization is entitled to a sign indicating its participation. In March 2000, a panel of Bowman (writing), Wollman, and Hansen held that Missouri's denial of the Klan's application to participate in the program was unconstitutional viewpoint discrimination. Although twenty-seven states filed an amicus brief on behalf of Missouri, the Supreme Court denied certiorari.

After that, the Urban League, the Anti-Defamation League, and other groups sponsored a 672-foot billboard to be placed on the same part of the highway (one mile of Interstate 55 in south St. Louis County), which read: "Freedom of Speech Protects All People, Even When They're Wrong," and the state named that particular stretch of road the "Rosa Parks Highway." In April 2001, the state dropped the Klan from the program after it failed to pick up any trash, but at the time of this writing, the organization was attempting to obtain a different spot, on Highway 21 north of Potosi, and was back in court.[147]

It is hardly unknown for high school students to push the limits of freedom of speech and for the results of their handiwork to end up in federal court. In *Henerey v. St. Charles School*, a student candidate who had used the slogan "The Safe Choice" and handed out condoms to student voters was disqualified from an election by the school principal.[148] The Court of Appeals upheld that decision because it was a school-sponsored activity that took place in a nonpublic forum.

During the 1980s, the Eighth Circuit was not friendly to claims of protected speech made by adult theaters and bookstores and those connected with other sexually suggestive activities. In 1991 the Court of Appeals upheld obscenity convictions of an adult theater and bookstore in Lincoln, Nebraska.[149] In 1993 it upheld Iowa prison regulations that barred inmates from receiving many sexually explicit publications and in 1999 a prison ban on possession of music cassettes bearing the warning "parental advisory—explicit lyrics."[150] In 1994 it rejected an attempt to invalidate Ramsey, Minnesota's, zoning ordinance directed at sex-oriented shops.[151] In 1998, the court upheld the constitutionality of another Kansas City ordinance that prohibited doors on video booths in adult bookstores.[152] In a case in which the Court of Appeals upheld a zoning ordinance under which a southeast Kansas City bar owner had been prohibited from presenting "exotic dancers," Judge Bowman wrote: "Even those who hold such conduct protected speech make no pretension that near-naked girls jiggling for the titillation of the boozing clientele at a bar have any 'serious literary, artistic, political or scientific values.'"[153]

The most important of these cases was the prosecution under the Racketeer Influenced and Corrupt Organizations Act (RICO) of Ferris J. Alexander, the owner of a chain of places for "adult entertainment." Although he had gone to considerable lengths to conceal his identity as owner and operator of his various businesses, Alexander had been in the adult entertainment business for more than thirty years, selling magazines, showing movies, and leasing videocassettes. After a four-month trial, he was convicted of twenty-four counts of a forty-one-count indictment. He was sentenced to a prison term of from thirty-six to seventy-two months, to a $100,000 fine, and had to pay the cost of his incarceration. In addition, after a jury decided that seven of his books and tapes were obscene, the court ordered the forfeit to the government of ten pieces of commercial real estate owned by Alexander, his interest in fourteen businesses, and almost nine million dollars. More than one hundred thousand books and tapes would eventually be destroyed.

The Court of Appeals rejected Alexander's argument that the forfeitures constituted a prior restraint on the press and had an unconstitutionally chilling effect on his First Amendment rights.[154] The Supreme Court also upheld the convictions and the forfeitures, rejecting the prior restraint and chilling effect contentions. Three justices—Anthony M. Kennedy, Blackmun, and Stevens—dissented, while Justice Souter dissented in part. However, on the same day, in another forfeiture case discussed in this chapter, the Supreme Court held that such forfeitures connected with the prosecution of crimes are limited by the "excessive fine" clause of the Eighth Amendment and remanded both cases to the Court of Appeals to determine whether the amount of property forfeited constituted an "excessive fine."

The line between speech and action was at issue in the appeal of a Minnesota man who constructed and burned a cross on a hill adjacent to an apartment complex in which a number of black families resided. A panel affirmed the conviction for conspiracy to intimidate others in the exercise of their federally guaranteed rights (in this case, the right to be free from racial discrimination in housing).[155]

Rehearing en banc was granted. Before the full Court of Appeals decided the case, a fractured Supreme Court rendered decisions in two cases involving hate crime statutes.[156] The en banc Court of Appeals was also fractured, although it held that cross burning might be protected by the First Amendment. Writing the plurality opinion for five judges, Judge John R. Gibson held that cross burning was expression and that the government was limited to punishing expression directed towards inciting or producing lawless action. However, the case was remanded for a jury to determine if the expression had been done with the intent to advocate the use of force or violence and was likely to produce such action, or if the defendant had intended to cause the residents of the apartments to reasonably fear the use of imminent force or violence.

Three judges, Lay writing, agreed as to reversal of the conviction but argued that there was insufficient evidence to sustain a retrial because the conduct had not been directed to inciting lawless action. The dissenting opinion, written by Judge McMillian for four judges, held that the defendant was being prosecuted not for expressing ideas but rather for conspiring to threaten African Americans in the exercise of their federally guaranteed housing rights.[157]

FIRST AMENDMENT AND REGULATION OF CAMPAIGN ACTIVITIES

With each passing decade since the 1962 *Baker v. Carr* decision, the lower federal courts throughout the nation have become involved with more and more aspects of the political system. In the 1990s the Court of Appeals heard few "classic" reapportionment cases,[158] but considered a number of cases involving the rights of third parties and third-party candidates, limitations on political contributions and expenditures, and ground rules for initiatives. These cases presented unusual trade-offs for limits on speech. Here it is possible only to sketch briefly several of these complex cases.

In an Arkansas case, the Court of Appeals held that a minor-party candidate had a constitutional right to participate in a debate on the state's public television station. The Supreme Court, however, disagreed. Although the Court of Appeals first dealt with the case in 1992,[159] the principal Court of Appeals decisions were rendered by the court en banc in 1994 and 1996. In 1994, Chief Judge Richard Arnold wrote for six members of the court, holding that the First Amendment was violated when the Arkansas Educational Television Network (AETN), a state actor, denied Ralph Forbes, a former American Nazi Party member and Christian supremacist, access to a debate for candidates for Congress. Judge Theodore McMillian wrote for five judges, who would have dismissed the entire suit, holding that the FCC had exclusive jurisdiction of the litigation.[160]

On remand, the jury expressly found that AETN's decision to exclude Forbes had not been influenced by political pressure or disagreement with his views. The Court of Appeals, Arnold once again writing, held that the decision to exclude Forbes was made in good faith, yet by opening its facilities to Third District Congressional candidates, AETN had created a public forum to which all candidates had a presumptive right of access. Applying strict scrutiny, Forbes's exclusion was held unconstitutional. The Supreme Court, however, reversed by a vote of 6–3, holding that although the debate was subject to constitutional constraints applicable to nonpublic forums, the decision to exclude the candidate was a reasonable viewpoint exercise of journalistic discretion. The record demonstrated that Forbes had been excluded not because of his viewpoint but because he had not generated appreciable public interest.[161]

The Court of Appeals struck down a Minnesota law that prevented candidates from appearing on the ballot as the nominee of both a major and a minor party. Judge Fagg, writing for the court, held the statute overbroad and violative of the freedom of association. The Supreme Court reversed by a 6–3 vote, holding the burden Minnesota's fusion ban imposed on the New Party's associational rights was justified by correspondingly weighty and valid state interests in ballot integrity and political stability.[162]

In cases arising in Minnesota and Missouri, the Court of Appeals demonstrated a distinct lack of enthusiasm for laws capping political contributions and expenditures. In 1994, the Court of Appeals struck down several provisions of Minnesota's campaign finance laws, among them a law preventing the acceptance of contributions for a particular candidate of more than $100 a year from individuals, political committees, and political funds. The court held that an annual $100 limit on contributions to or by political funds and committees was too low to allow meaningful participation in protected political speech and association. It also held that denial of an exemption from prohibition against independent expenditures by corporations was unconstitutional as applied to a nonprofit corporation. Finally, it struck down a statute providing an increase in a candidate's expenditure limit and public subsidies based on the amount of independent expenditures as violating the First Amendment rights of those making independent expenditures.[163]

Beginning in 1994, the Court of Appeals three times struck down Missouri laws—twice in 1995 invalidating laws limiting contributions and expenditures, as well as in 2000. The Supreme Court reversed the second of these decisions. Following the Supreme Court decision, the Court of Appeals, with Judge Bowman writing, unenthusiastically discarded its earlier decision.[164] In 2000, a divided Court of Appeals struck down Missouri's limits on contributions given by political parties to candidates. The Supreme Court granted certiorari in the case, vacated it, and remanded it to the Court of Appeals for consideration in light of its decision in a Colorado case.[165]

There were several important cases related to the national drive for term limits for elected officials. In 1999, the Court of Appeals struck down a voter-initiated amendment to the Missouri constitution, which directed the state's congressional delegation and candidates for such offices to support a constitutional amendment providing term limits for federal officeholders. Under the law, the ballot would have to indicate whether those instructions had been disregarded by incumbents or went unsupported by nonincumbent candidates. The Court of Appeals decision was affirmed by the Supreme Court.[166] Earlier the same year, a different panel held unconstitutional a voter-initiated constitutional amendment in Nebraska, which provided that incumbents who failed to support term limits would be so labeled on election ballots.[167]

President Clinton and the Eighth Circuit

Highly visible litigation connected with the scandals involving President Bill Clinton occurred both in the Eighth and in the District of Columbia Circuits. The Whitewater scandal began in 1978, while Clinton was Arkansas attorney general, with the purchase of a little more than two hundred acres of undeveloped land in the Ozarks (at the juncture of Crooked Creek and White River) by James and Susan McDougal and Bill and Hillary Rodham Clinton. The Whitewater Development Corporation was then formed. In 1979, Clinton began serving the first of his five terms as governor. Three years later, James McDougal took control of Madison Guaranty, a savings and loan association, which closed in 1989, costing taxpayers tens of millions of dollars. Serious questions as to the mingling of friendships, business, and politics by the Clintons were raised by these events, including the possibility that they had profited from illegal loans.

After Clinton became president, the suicide of White House Deputy Counsel Vincent Foster, Hillary Radham Clinton's former law partner who had been looking after some Whitewater matters, raised further questions. Attorney General Janet Reno, under considerable pressure, selected Robert B. Fiske Jr. as special counsel to investigate the Whitewater affair. Months later, the independent counsel mechanism was triggered, and Kenneth Starr, a former judge of the U.S. Court of Appeals for the District of Columbia Circuit and former solicitor general, was selected to replace Fiske. Starr moved aggressively, taking a broad view of his authority, and opened investigations into a number of matters that were not closely related to Whitewater.

In several years during which the Clinton scandals were constantly on the front pages, the Court of Appeals for the Eighth Circuit dealt with a number of matters, including whether the president could stand trial in a civil suit while in office (or at least be required to comply with pretrial discovery); whether the notes of interviews White House lawyers had taken during their interviews of Hillary Rodham Clinton were protected by the attorney-client privilege; the scope of the authority of the independent counsel and his possible conflicts of interest; the possible disqualification of district judges from presiding over criminal prosecutions; and the appeals of those convicted of crimes. The Court of Appeals also heard argument on the appeal of the district court decision dismissing the sexual harassment case brought by Paula Corbin Jones, but that matter was settled before a decision was issued.

United States v. Tucker involved an indictment brought against Arkansas governor Jim Guy Tucker and two others for tax fraud, bankruptcy fraud, making false material statements, and conspiracy.[168] The indictment was dismissed by Judge Henry Woods on the ground that the independent counsel did not have jurisdiction to prosecute the case. A panel of Judges Bowman (writing), Beam, and Loken held that the attorney general's referral to the office of independent counsel was not reviewable. The court went on to indicate that the independent counsel's original jurisdiction to investigate the relationship of the Clintons to the Whitewater Development Corporation and Madison Guaranty was sufficiently related to the Tucker prosecution.

At the request of the independent counsel, the panel went further, instructing the Chief Judge of the Eastern District of Arkansas to see that further stages of the case were assigned to a judge other than Woods in order to "preserve the appearance of impartiality." The panel was troubled by the fact that Woods was generally seen as a personal friend of the Clintons. Woods had, for example, spent election night in 1994 in the White House. In turn, the Clintons had steadfastly supported Tucker since his indictment by the grand jury. The Court of Appeals panel stated that "the risk of a perception of judicial bias is sufficiently great so that our proper course is to order reassignment on remand."[169] Judge McMillian wrote a very strong opinion (in which he was joined by

Judge Murphy) dissenting from the decision not to rehear the case en banc and objecting to the treatment of Judge Woods.[170]

In 1998, the Court of Appeals dismissed the appeal of a Connecticut lawyer, Francis Mandanici, who had complained to the district court that Starr had a conflict of interest because of his ties to the Republican Party as well as other associations. The Court of Appeals held that the Connecticut attorney lacked standing, but differed as to what the district court should have done when the complaint was brought to it. Judge McMillian wrote for the court and Judges Beam and Loken each wrote a concurring opinion.[171]

When the McDougals and Jim Guy Tucker stood trial on fraud and conspiracy charges, Clinton gave videotaped testimony, after which the defense rested. The tactic did not work. On May 28, 1996, a jury convicted Jim McDougal on eighteen of nineteen counts, Susan McDougal of all four she was charged with, and Governor Tucker of two of seven.[172] Tucker resigned his office after he was convicted.

The main event in the Arkansas phase of the Clinton investigations was Paula Corbin Jones's lawsuit. In May 1991, Jones, a clerk in the Arkansas Rural Development Commission, allegedly was crudely propositioned by then-governor Clinton in a hotel room he was using during a conference. The incident became public knowledge in December 1993 with the publication of an article in the *American Spectator.* After settlement negotiations broke down, Jones brought suit in May 1994, just before the statute of limitations expired. She alleged that Clinton had engaged in sexual harassment and assault and conspired with a state trooper to entice her into a sexual liaison. She also contended that her character had been defamed.

The case was assigned to Judge Susan Webber Wright of the Eastern District of Arkansas, who had been a student of Clinton's at the University of Arkansas Law School. In December 1994, Wright declined to dismiss Jones's lawsuit. She held that the case could not go to trial until Clinton left office, but that, in the meantime, discovery could proceed.[173] Clinton appealed, seeking reversal of the district court's rejection of his motion to dismiss the complaint on the ground of presidential immunity. In the alternative, he asked for a reversal of the decision denying his motion to stay discovery.

The Court of Appeals rendered judgment on January 9, 1996. Judge Bowman wrote the opinion for the court rejecting both of Clinton's requests. The court held that the president was not entitled to immunity during the years of his presidency from civil suits alleging actionable behavior by him in his private capacity. In his official capacity as president, he would have been entitled to absolute immunity.[174]

The court believed that for purposes of the separation of powers, what was needed was not immunity for the president but rather "judicial case management sensitive to the burdens of the Presidency and the demands of the President's schedule."[175] The court reversed that part of Judge Wright's order staying the trial for duration of the Clinton presidency but affirmed the part that permitted discovery to proceed.

In his concurring opinion, Judge Beam directed attention to the fact that Paula Jones, too, had constitutional rights. A lengthy stay of proceedings quite possibly might prejudice her case for a witness might die or become incompetent, while her defamation claims would be totally extinguished, if either party died.[176]

Dissenting, Judge Ross thought that the separation of powers doctrine required that private civil actions against a sitting president for unofficial acts be stayed during the president's term office. The president should not ordinarily be required to defend himself against civil actions while in office unless there were exigent circumstances. Only if the plaintiff could demonstrate that she would suffer irreparable injury without immediate relief, and that immediate adjudication would not significantly impair the president's duty to attend to the duties of his office, would legal proceedings be justified during the president's term of office. Judge Ross argued that "the burdens and demands of civil litigation can be expected to impinge on the President's discharge of his constitutional office by forcing him to divert his energy and attention from the rigorous demands of his office to the task of protecting himself against personal liability."[177]

The *St. Louis Post-Dispatch* applauded the decision as "persuasive"; the law protected "equally the great and the small."[178] Judge McMillian did not. Dissenting from the decision not to rehear the case en banc, McMillian wrote that "the majority opinion not only has put short pants on President William Jefferson Clinton, but has succeeded in demeaning the office of the President of the United States."[179]

The Supreme Court unanimously affirmed in an opinion by Justice John Paul Stevens. (Justice Breyer concurred.) The justices held that neither the Constitution nor public policy justified giving the president a delay of the pretrial proceeding or of the trial itself.[180] The Court of Appeals majority and the Supreme Court, thus, were relatively sanguine about the possibility that litigation might seriously distract the president from his official duties. Some years later, Judge Patricia Wald, who had been involved in "Bill Clinton litigation" in the District of Columbia Circuit, writing of the legacy of Whitewater, commented that "perhaps the most humbling lesson for the judiciary is our proven inability to predict the unintended consequences of our decisions."[181]

Clinton did testify a number of times in Whitewater investigations and trials. In the trial of the McDougals, he repeatedly denied that he had asked for an improper loan or ever traded patronage for contributions. He was also questioned in the trial of two Arkansas bankers accused of concealing cash withdrawn from banks and reimbursing themselves for making campaign contributions. It was, however, Clinton's deposition before the Washington, D.C., grand jury in August 1998, when he admitted "inappropriate intimate contact" with Monica Lewinsky, contradicting his deposition testimony in the *Jones* case, given in January 1998, which led to his impeachment by the House of Representatives and to being held in contempt by Judge Wright.

Whether White House attorneys could quash Starr's subpoena of notes they had taken in meetings with Hillary Rodham Clinton on either the ground of lawyer-client privilege or under the attorney work product doctrine was the second major issue to come before the Court of Appeals. At issue were two sets of notes—the first from 1995 concerning Mrs. Clinton's activities after the death of Vincent Foster; the second, her debriefing by the attorneys about her tesimony before a Washington grand jury in 1996.

The Court of Appeals (Bowman writing, joined by Wollman with Richard G. Kopf of Nebraska dissenting) held that the White House had to turn over the subpoenaed notes, stating that "to allow any part of the Federal Government to use its in-house attorneys as a shield against the production of information relevant to a criminal investigation would represent a gross misuse of public assets."[182] A petition for certiorari was denied.[183]

Paula Jones's lawsuit was dismissed on April 1, 1998. Judge Wright ruled that while Clinton's alleged behavior had been "boorish," Jones had failed to prove that she endured a hostile work environment or suffered professionally. What Jones experienced, Wright said, was "a mere sexual proposition or encounter, albeit an odious one, that was relatively brief in duration and was abandoned as soon as plaintiff made clear that the advances were not welcome."[184]

The case was appealed. The sixty-five-minute argument took place in St. Paul on October 20, 1998, before the panel that heard the appeal on the presidential immunity issue: Bowman, Beam, and Ross. With home state pride, the *Lincoln Journal Star* headlined "Nebraskans to decide fate of Jones Suit."[185] Ten sound trucks were parked outside the courthouse. The courtroom was crowded with an estimated 145 spectators, and sound was piped into two other rooms, each with one hundred seats.[186]

Paula Jones's attorney, James Fisher, asked the court to send the message that President Clinton "cannot commit perjury again and again." He told the judges that Mr. Clinton "split hairs, dodged questions and lied" in his January 1997 deposition.[187] Amy Sabrin argued for President Clinton. During argument, Chief Judge Bowman was dismissive of suggestions that Clinton's conduct did not amount to legal sexual harassment.[188]

It has been suggested that the comments of the judges at oral argument convinced White House officials that the case would go to trial and led them to advise settlement.[189] Whether or not that was so, the case was settled without Clinton apologizing, but paying Paula Corbin Jones $850,000 to drop her suit. The Court of Appeals dismissed the suit subject to the terms of the settlement. It is, of course, not known what they would have decided. Much of the settlement went to Jones's various sets of lawyers.[190] That was not, however, quite the end of the saga of the Eighth Circuit and *Jones v. Clinton.* On April 12, 1999, Judge Susan Webber Wright held Clinton in civil contempt, imposing financial penalties and referring the matter to the Arkansas Supreme Court for disciplinary action.[191] Wright wrote: "The record demonstrates by clear and convincing evidence that the President responded to (Paula Jones' lawyers) questions by giving false, misleading and evasive answers that were designed to obstruct the judicial process."[192]

The Court of Appeals heard appeals of over a dozen individuals caught up in the Whitewater scandal. In the appeals that captured the widest attention, the convictions on eighteen felony counts of Jim McDougal and the convictions of Susan McDougal were upheld.[193] In a separate appeal, a panel of Bowman, Loken, and Hansen held that Susan McDougal could not refuse to testify before the grand jury investigating Clinton's business dealings. Just before Clinton left office, he pardoned Susan McDougal.[194]

Criminal Cases

The federal War on Drugs was by far the most influential factor shaping the criminal docket of the Court of Appeals. However, in addition to drug cases, the Court of Appeals heard many sentencing appeals, appeals involving convictions for political corruption, appeals attempting to prevent executions, as well as an important case involving entrapment.

DRUG CRIMES   Before the 1980s, prosecutions for possession of drugs had almost completely been left to state courts. Beginning with the Reagan administration, federal prosecutions were stepped up. Once the sentencing guidelines were promulgated, sentences were fixed according to the type and the amount of drugs charged and proved by the prosecution. As a result, sentencing discretion, which had once belonged to district judges, passed to prosecutors. Judges of virtually every persuasion were strongly critical of the role of the federal courts in drug cases, arguing that such cases trivialized and distorted federal justice and, when combined with the sentencing guidelines, made the courts parties to profound inequities.[195]

Under the sentencing guidelines, extremely harsh sentences had to be meted out to individuals possessing drugs for their personal use, small-time dealers, and drug couriers; and yet it was possible for those higher up in the drug business to considerably reduce their sentences by giving the government the names of small dealers and couriers. The guidelines also led to severe racial inequities in drug cases, for a small amount of crack cocaine (smoked largely by African Americans) was treated as equal to one hundred times the same amount of powdered cocaine (snorted generally by whites). In 1988–89, for example, crack sentences in the Western District of Missouri averaged 180 months; noncrack cocaine sentences only seventy-nine months.[196] Neither the Court of Appeals for the Eighth Circuit nor any other court of appeals held such disparities to violate the Equal Protection Clause. Judge Lyle Strom of the District of Nebraska attempted to give African American crack dealers significantly shorter sentences than those required by the sentencing guidelines but was rebuffed by the Court of Appeals.[197]

Judge Myron Bright was a particularly strong critic of the rigidity of guidelines sentencing, believing that "sentencing in many federal drug cases [was] unworthy of American justice."[198] In 1998, for example, Bright dissented strongly from a thirty-year sentence for drug conspiracy given to a man with the mental level of an eight-year-old. The sentence was seven years longer than that given to the chief supplier in the conspiracy.[199]

Although the states of the Eighth Circuit were far from the Mexican border and the circuit lacked a major port for drugs to enter into the United States, it did not lack for drug cases. I-80, which crosses Iowa and Nebraska, was a major east–west route, and the circuit also was a pathway for drugs being transported from Mexico to Canada.[200] Drug cases in federal courts mounted, although the war against drugs was being lost. Between 1994 and 1997, drug cases climbed 21 percent nationally.[201] The number of felony cases doubled in the District of Nebraska between 1995 and 2000. Almost three-quarters of those felony cases were drug offenses.[202]

Judge Scott O. Wright of the Western District of Missouri spoke of the "cascading exceptions to the Fourth Amendment,"[203] as the War on Drugs, like Prohibition before it, led law enforcement personnel to take actions going to the edge or beyond constitutionality. Courts then stretched to uphold such actions. In a Section 1983 action, *Thompson v. Carthage School District*,[204] the Court of Appeals (Judge Loken writing) held that, even if the search of a high school student's coat pocket was improper, the fruits of the search could be used as evidence in the student's expulsion hearing. By a 6–5 vote in *United States v. Bloomfield*, the court upheld an extensive search which turned up 797 pounds of marijuana found after an automobile had been stopped (and eventually searched) on the grounds that it "abruptly changed lanes without signaling."[205]

On the other hand, the Court of Appeals also held that a warrant to search a suspected drug runner did not empower law officers to have a doctor search his stomach with a tube after he was apprehended at Minneapolis–St. Paul International Airport.[206] It also ruled that a Nebraska State Patrol trooper illegally stopped and arrested two men near Gibben because they were Hispanic.[207]

More troublesome was the use made by the government to the power of forfeiture, revitalized in the 1980s as a tool to fight organized crime. Judge C. Arlen Beam, a Reagan appointee, became a strong critic of forfeiture, pointing to "the mischief to which our eagerness to employ forfeiture as a weapon in the war against drugs can lead."[208] Beam deplored the statutory scheme under which the government could declare the forfeiture of up to $500,000 administratively:

> The war on drugs has brought us to the point where the government may seize up to $500,000 of a citizen's property, without any showing of cause, and put the onus on the citizen to perfectly navigate the bureaucratic labyrinth in order to liberate what is presumptively his or hers in the first place. . . . Should the citizen prove inept, the government may keep the property, without ever having to justify or explain its actions.[209]

Yet, in 1998, the Court of Appeals upheld a police seizure of $142,000 in suspect drug money during a traffic stop near Grand Island, Nebraska, although the driver was never charged with a crime. The court ruled that prosecutors were right to assume the money confiscated in the traffic stop was linked to drug trafficking, in part because California was "a state of drug origin" and the defendant was known to have traveled to Illinois and Wisconsin, "drug destination states."[210]

Two Eighth Circuit cases, considered together by the Supreme Court in 1993, led the U.S. Supreme Court to place some limits on forfeiture. One, briefly discussed in the First Amendment section of this chapter, involved Ferris J. Alexander, the owner of adult entertainment businesses. The second case involved the seizure of the shop and mobile home of a Garretson, South Dakota, man, Richard Lyle Austin, who had distributed between one and two grams of cocaine to a police informer. Austin had pleaded guilty to one count of possessing cocaine with the intent to sell and served a year in prison. The Court of Appeals upheld that seizure, but the Supreme Court reversed, holding that forfeitures were subject to the Excessive Fines Clause of the Eighth Amendment. The case was remanded for a determination as to whether the clause had been violated.[211] The High Court upheld the forfeiture of Alexander's $25 million pornography business (after a jury had found seven books and tapes obscene) but remanded for a determination as to whether this was an "excessive fine."[212]

CHILD PORNOGRAPHY   During the 1980s, the federal government gave considerable attention to preventing commerce in child pornography. The most important case in the nation involved a retired member of the armed forces, Keith Jacobson, who at the age of fifty-six was living in Newman Grove, Nebraska, supporting his elderly father. Before this encounter with the law, his record had been clean.

When doing so was still legal, Jacobson had ordered from an "adult bookstore" two magazines containing photographs of young boys. Several months later, Congress made purchasing such depictions through the mail illegal. After the government discovered his name on the mailing list of the bookstore, Jacobson was made a target of an extraordinarily persistent government sting operation. For over two and one-half years, the government, using the mails repeatedly, attempted to get Jacobson to make another purchase. It mailed him seven letters, two catalogs, and two sexual attitude surveys. Finally Jacobson ordered a publication and became one of five Nebraskans indicted for receiving child pornography through the mail.

A panel majority of Heaney (writing) and Lay reversed the conviction, holding that for the government to target an individual for an undercover sting operation, there must be "reasonable suspicion based on articulable facts," and there were no such facts here.[213] Judge Fagg disagreed, arguing that "the panel had declared war on the government's power to initiate undercover investigations."[214]

The panel decision was vacated. After rehearing the case en banc, the full court affirmed the conviction by a vote of 8–2 (Heaney and Lay were alone in dissent). The court held that the Constitution "does not require reasonable suspicion of wrongdoing before the government can begin an undercover investigation." It held that Jacobson had not, as a matter of law, been entrapped and also refused to invalidate the government's conduct on due process grounds because the government's conduct had not been "outrageous."[215]

In one of the few cases in which the Supreme Court has ever invalidated a conviction on entrapment or closely related grounds, it held by a vote of 5–4 in this case that the government had gone too far. The High Court held that the prosecution had failed, as a matter of law, to support the jury verdict that Jacobson had been predisposed, independently of the government's acts and beyond a reasonable doubt, to violate the law by receiving child pornography through the mail.[216]

POLITICAL CORRUPTION During this period, the federal courts continued to be the forum for many prosecutions of state and local officials for political corruption. Putting aside the prosecutions related to the Whitewater scandal, most of the cases came from Missouri. While the biggest fish to be netted was probably Bob Griffin, former Speaker of the Missouri House of Representatives, one-third of the members of the Kansas City Council elected in 1991 either pleaded guilty or were charged with crimes related to their public lives.[217] Griffin himself was acquitted of three counts of bribery, while the jury deadlocked on six other charges involving racketeering, bribery, and fraud. However, he pleaded guilty to two federal felony charges of bribery and mail fraud.

The role of the Court of Appeals in the Missouri political corruption cases was not very important. It held that Griffin was not entitled to a reduction of his four-year prison sentence.[218] Reversing the district court, the Court of Appeals reinstated the conviction of former Missouri state representative E. J. "Lucky" Cantrell on charges he embezzled $10,000 in union money. In addition, after former St. Louis Comptroller Virvus Jones pleaded guilty to income tax fraud, the Court of Appeals upheld the conviction of a close ally of Jones for taking part in a scheme to "steal" the 1993 city comptroller election.[219] The Court of Appeals (Magill and Hansen; McMillian dissenting) also upheld the extortion conviction and prison sentence of a former Sarpy County, Nebraska, commissioner, Dean Loftus, for taking a bribe in a zoning case involving a shopping center.[220]

CRIMINAL MISCELLANY Except for the prosecutions connected with the Whitewater scandal, the most visible criminal appeals handled by the Court of Appeals during the 1990s were capital cases coming from Missouri and Arkansas. In particular, there were many appeals from Missouri, which trailed only Texas, Florida, Virginia, and Louisiana in the number of executions. Between 1989 and 2002, Missouri executed fifty-seven persons. An intervention by Pope John Paul II during his visit to St. Louis in January 1999 did save the life of one Missouri death row inmate as Governor Mel Carnahan gave executive clemency to triple murderer Darrell Mease.[221]

However, because of legislation and Supreme Court decisions limiting the use of the writ of habeas corpus, the role of the lower federal courts in capital cases was limited.[222] Stays of execution did occur. In 1997, the Court of Appeals denied a stay by a 5–4 vote at three in the afternoon of one of the three men Arkansas would execute in a single night. That man would remain strapped to the gurney for thirty-eight minutes after he was scheduled to die as the Supreme Court considered one last appeal.[223] But decisions favorable to the condemned were exceedingly rare. The parade of last-minute filings slowed but nevertheless continued.

Of course, not every case was a capital case or a drug case or involved political corruption. Among the appeals heard and convictions affirmed were those of a man who murdered his wife by letting her freeze to death in Lake Superior,[224] five men convicted and sentenced to life for their involvement in an explosion that killed six Kansas City firefighters,[225] and an Arkansan convicted of illegal duck hunting.[226] The court also affirmed the conviction of Stephen Blumberg, who purloined rare books worth millions of dollars from libraries all over the United States, not for financial gain, but just for their possession. From all over the country, librarians came to a federal warehouse in Omaha housing Blumberg's "collection," hoping to find missing books.[227]

When the judges disagreed in criminal cases, those most likely to vote to affirm the position of the government were Judges Magill, Fagg, Bowman, Loken, and Hansen. Those most likely to vote to uphold the position taken by the defendant were Judges Bright, Heaney, McMillian, and Lay. Somewhere in between were John R. Gibson, Richard Arnold, Murphy, Wollman, Morris Arnold, and Beam. Participating in too few cases during this period to be classified were Floyd Gibson, Ross, Henley, Kelly, and Bye.

Federal Specialties: Bankruptcy, Antitrust, Tax, Copyright, Admiralty

Many of the traditional federal specialties, especially antitrust, bankruptcy and tax and trademark law, continued to bring significant cases to the Court of Appeals. During this period, the Court of Appeals tended to support the defendant in antitrust cases. By a vote of 6–5, the full court upheld the dismissal of a massive suit brought by fertilizer distributors and other direct buyers that accused major Canadian and U.S. potash producers of price fixing.[228] The Court of Appeals also reversed a $133 million verdict against the Brunswick Corporation, a manufacturer of small boats.[229] It overturned two jury verdicts in a case brought against the Nebraska Heart Institute and the three doctors who owned it on the grounds that the trial judge's view of the geographic market was too restrictive.[230] It also ruled that a Sioux Falls radiology group had not monopolized the x-ray business in that city, throwing out a $1.8 million judgment.[231] The Court of Appeals also upheld the dismissals of lawsuits brought in Nebraska accusing Casey's General Stores of cutting gasoline prices to run small-town gas stations out of business and in North Dakota alleging that WDAY Radio and the Forum Publishing Co. operated an illegal monopoly.[232] It also upheld dismissal of a claim that milk processors had conspired to fix their wholesale prices.[233] Finally, the Court of Appeals upheld the decision of Judge Jean Hamilton of the Eastern District of Missouri, who had thrown out an antitrust case brought by the St. Louis Convention and Visitors Commission against the National Football League over the amount of money St. Louis had to pay to lure the Los Angeles Rams to the city in 1995, seven years after they had lost their professional football team.[234]

On the other hand, the Court of Appeals affirmed a district court decision that voided on antitrust grounds the sale of the *Northwest Arkansas Times* to a company controlled by Little Rock financier Jackson T. Stephens and members of his family[235] and reinstated an antitrust lawsuit brought against Northwest Airlines for overcharging ticket buyers after its 1986 merger with Republic.[236]

The most lucrative tax cases involved the Ordway family, whose money came primarily from the Minnesota Mining and Manufacturing Company and were well known in Minnesota for their philanthropy. Six hundred million dollars was at stake over resolution of the issue of whether the Internal Revenue Service could levy gift taxes on certain transfers from trusts that had been created in 1917, before the creation of the federal gift tax. There was no question that such transfers would have been taxable once that tax was adopted. By a vote of 7–4, the full court ruled that the transfer could have been taxable only if there had been an applicable tax in existence when the transfer was made in 1917.[237] However, the Supreme Court reversed, holding that a disclaimer made after enactment of the gift tax statute of an interest created before its enactment is not necessarily free of any consequent federal gift taxation.[238]

There were interesting trademark cases involving Anheuser-Busch, the Missouri brewery. In a case demonstrating the tension between the protection afforded to trademark owners and the First Amendment rights of parodists, the Court of Appeals ruled that *Snicker,* a humor magazine, had gone too far in a parody advertisement for "Michelob Oily beer" and had infringed on Anheuser-Busch's trademark. The Court of Appeals held that the parody was likely to cause confusion among the public—confusion wholly unnecessary to the purpose of the parody.[239] Having been vindicated, Anheuser-Busch, which had been seeking one dollar in damages and an injunction, settled by buying all the remaining copies of the magazine for $10,000.[240] In a trademark case brought against the brewery, the Court of Appeals ruled that its "ice beer" had not infringed on the trademark of Labatt's "Molson Ice."[241]

During the latter part of the 1990s, there was a considerable increase in personal bankruptcies, the result of an overabundance of credit, gambling losses, advertising by bankruptcy lawyers as well as because of a change in attitude toward bankruptcy. The Eighth Circuit led the nation in the greatest percentage increase in bankruptcy filings.[242] However, while heavy use was being made of the bankruptcy system, the Court of Appeals rendered relatively few important bankruptcy opinions during the period.

In addition to deciding that money tithed to a church before filing for bankruptcy could be not be reclaimed by a trustee, the Court of Appeals decided three important bankruptcy cases. It held that individuals, not just businesses, could file for bankruptcy under Chapter 11, but the Supreme Court reversed.[243] The Court of Appeals held in a bankruptcy fraud case that creditors claiming fraud had to convince a jury or judge by a high standard, "clear and convincing evidence." However, the Supreme Court ruled that the standard was lower—"preponderance of the evidence."[244] Finally, by a vote of 6–5, the full court held that where a company had extended credit without security to a debtor during a Chapter 11 reorganization, it could not make a claim—in the subsequent Chapter 7 liquidation—against property that had been pledged to secure a bank loan. The Supreme Court affirmed.[245]

CASES INVOLVING FEDERALISM   In cases involving preemption of state law by federal legislation and the Dormant Commerce Clause, the Court of Appeals continued to take positions supportive of federal authority and against state parochialism.

In 1999, the Court of Appeals held that parts of Iowa's electronic funds transfer law were preempted by federal law. The Iowa law regulated automatic teller machines, prohibiting surcharges and providing other consumer protections. After Bank One, a national bank, opened ATMs at twenty-four retail store locations in Iowa, the state division of banking took the position that the machines were illegal. A district judge denied Bank One a temporary injunction but was overruled by a panel of Wollman (writing), Richard Arnold, and Bright (dissenting), which held that Bank One could operate ATMs without Iowa branches. The

Court of Appeals also struck down a provision on ATM advertising and a requirement that banks file an application or informational statement with Iowa banking officials. Rehearing en banc was denied. Although twenty states filed an amicus brief on behalf of Iowa, the Supreme Court let the Eighth Circuit ruling stand. In the spring of 2001, five national banks filed another suit to have Iowa's ban on ATM surcharges held unconstitutional.[246]

In other preemption cases, the Court of Appeals preempted an Arkansas law that had been designed to guarantee patients the right to see the doctors of their choice,[247] and held that the Missouri sales tax on motor fuels was preempted by the federal Rail Reorganization Act.[248]

In a number of cases, the Court of Appeals, applying the Commerce Clause, invalidated state and local protectionist legislation involving the disposal of garbage. In 1992, it held in an opinion by Richard Arnold that Arkansas could not ban landfill operators from bringing in out-of-state garbage.[249] A few months later, it rendered a similar ruling in a case involving two southern Minnesota counties.[250] In 1995, it held that the result of a South Dakota referendum, in which the building of a garbage facility in the southwest part of the state was rejected, violated the Commerce Clause.[251] In a Nebraska case, the court ruled unconstitutional a municipal ordinance that required that all garbage collected within the city limits, except garbage destined for out-of-state disposal, be processed at the city-owned transfer station.[252] The court also held in 1996 that Hennepin County could charge high fees for garbage from in-state haulers, but not those from out of state.[253]

The Court of Appeals also wrestled with laws requiring all meat-packers to pay the same price for meat of the same quality, thus attempting to level the playing field for smaller, independent beef producers. In 1999, it struck down a South Dakota law that required that packers must pay uniform prices for equal-quality livestock, including that paid outside of South Dakota. However, in 2001 the Court of Appeals upheld a Missouri law that regulated the prices only of livestock sold on Missouri soil.[254]

Regional Cases

NATIVE AMERICANS   The most important Native American litigation during the 1990s involved hunting and fishing rights and other aspects of tribal authority over non-Indians; reservation diminishing;

whether land acquired for Native American tribes to start businesses was free from state taxation; gambling; the First Amendment; and criminal cases, including the latest developments in the saga of Leonard Peltier.

The most important hunting and fishing case involved the rights of the Mille Lacs Band of Chippewa (Ojibwe) to fish, gillnet, hunt, and gather without state regulation on a wide area of east central Minnesota, thirteen million acres of land outside of their reservation. The area included Lake Mille Lacs, Minnesota's prime site for walleye, and land that also offered excellent hunting for animals such as deer, bear, and ruffled grouse. In 1993, after a heated debate, Minnesota turned down a settlement proposal that offered better terms for the state than what it ultimately received from litigation, which evoked bitter resentment of Native Americans by many non-Native Americans, especially anglers, resort owners, and taxing authorities.

In the *Mille Lacs* litigation, the primary issue was whether the special hunting and fishing rights guaranteed to the Chippewa by treaty in 1837, twenty-one years before Minnesota became a state, had been nullified by later executive orders and legislation. In August 1994, then district judge Diana Murphy ruled for the Chippewa. In June 1997, a panel of Lay, McMillian, and John R. Gibson heard eighty minutes of oral argument. In August, the court affirmed in a sixty-three-page opinion by Judge Lay that the treaty rights of the Native Americans had not been taken away by the executive order of President Zachary Taylor in 1850 or by any other government actions. A petition to rehear the case en banc was denied by a 7–2 vote.[255]

The Supreme Court granted certiorari. Because the High Court in recent years had been less sympathetic to Native American contentions than in the recent past, there was concern not only that the Chippewa might lose the case, but that the decision might jeopardize the interpretation of dozens of treaties and weaken long-held principles of Indian law. The Chippewa sponsored a sixteen-day run from Lac du Flambeau, Wisconsin, to Washington before the oral argument, during which a spiritual treaty staff was carried and which concluded with a sacred fire. The tribe won by a 5–4 vote. The High Court held that the Chippewa were entitled to harvest up to half the fish and game on public land in east central Minnesota.[256]

A second important case involved the rights of the Cheyenne River Sioux to regulate hunting and fishing by non-Native Americans on tribal land that had been taken when Lake Oahe was constructed. After the tribe indicated in 1998 that it would no longer honor state permits issued for hunting on that land, the State of South Dakota sued and won in district court. The Court of Appeals reversed with an opinion by Judge Bowman, ruling that, when Congress passed the Cheyenne River Act authorizing the U.S. Army and Department of the Interior to negotiate a contract with the Cheyenne River Sioux, it was not intending to destroy tribal self-government, or to eliminate tribal regulatory rights, but only to acquire the property rights necessary to operate the Oahe Dam and Reservoir. Bowman wrote: "As the purpose of the Act was simply to enable the United States to acquire the land needed for the construction of the Oahe Dam and Reservoir and to do so with as little disruption as possible to the life of the tribe, the tribe must be given the benefit of the doubt."[257]

Reversing by a 7–2 vote, the Supreme Court held that in the Cheyenne River Act and in a prior statute, Congress had taken the land and opened it for recreational use by the general public. Congress had thus abrogated the tribe's treaty rights within the taking area of the Oahe Dam project.[258] On remand, the Court of Appeals held that the tribe could not regulate hunting and fishing on land and water taken to form the reservoir.[259]

An important case involved the diminishing of the Yankton Sioux Reservation. Former senator James Abourezk, who represented the tribe in the case, said of it that the Yankton Sioux had narrowly escaped judicial annihilation. In a scholarly opinion by Judge Murphy, the Court of Appeals ruled that the Yankton Sioux Reservation had not been diminished by an 1894 act in which Congress provided that the tribe would sell its surplus land to the United States. Judge Magill dissented. The Supreme Court, however, held that the land sold under the 1894 act was no longer part of the reservation.[260]

State of South Dakota v. U.S. Department of Interior raised the issue of whether the United States was able to acquire land and place it in trust for an Indian tribe, thereby removing from state and local taxation land intended for commercial development.[261] To create an industrial park, the Lower Brule Tribe of Sioux Indians sought a ninety-one-acre piece of land in central South Dakota, seven miles from the reservation, partially within the city of Tacoma and bordering on the Missouri River near Chamberlain and Interstate 90. The panel majority, Judges Loken and Magill, recognized the broad inherent power of the United States but held that the Nondelegation Doctrine required that Congress provide standards for the acquisition of land in trust for Native Americans. The court saw no such standards in the statute. Judge Murphy dissented. The Supreme Court reversed by a 7–2 vote without plenary argument.

There was also litigation over gambling. Unlike other states, the state of Nebraska, which banned gambling within the state, was unwilling to negotiate gambling compacts under the Indian Gaming Act. Thus the small casino run by the Santee Sioux on their reservation near the South Dakota border, no larger than a grocery store, had not been authorized by the state. On a reservation where unemployment was 74 percent, the casino provided twenty-three jobs. The U.S. District Court for the District of Nebraska dismissed a suit brought by the Santee against the state and its governor. A divided panel of the Court of Appeals affirmed. Three years later, the Court of Appeals ruled that the tribe had been in contempt of court and stated that the government could seize funds from tribal accounts to satisfy the court-ordered fine.[262] In separate litigation, the Court of Appeals, in a case of first impression in the federal appellate courts, held that the Indian Gaming Act completely preempted state law.[263]

Several First Amendment cases were brought by Native American prisoners. The Court of Appeals held (with some reluctance and over Judge Heaney's dissent) that a Missouri prison regulation banning long hair did not violate free exercise of religion of a Standing Rock Sioux, even though to a member of the tribe hair is a gift from the Great Spirit, the cutting of which is an offense to the Creator.[264] Although the Court of Appeals held that a Native American prisoner was entitled to a trial over the issue of the constitutionality of regulations banning sweat lodges—small, tentlike structures in which Native Americans perform a ceremony cleansing and purifying their body and spirit—in a later stage of the litigation, it held that those regulations violated neither the Religious Freedom Restoration Act of 1993 nor the Constitution.[265]

During the 1990s, the Court of Appeals upheld the convictions for political corruption of several Native American leaders, including Darrell "Chip" Wadena, leader of the White Earth Band of Chippewa, who was convicted of embezzlement, bribery, conspiracy, and money laundering. The Court of Appeals also affirmed the conviction of Minnesota

State Senator Harold "Skip" Finn for cheating his Leech Lake Band of Chippewa out of one million dollars.[266]

United States v. Rouse involved the prosecution of four Native Americans for child abuse of their nieces and raised the issue whether the trial court should have allowed an expert witness appointed by the court to testify that the testimony of the children (ages seven, six, five, and four years and twenty months at the time of the alleged abuse) might have been tainted by suggestion. A panel of Bright and McMillian held that the trial judge had erred by not allowing the expert testimony; Bright compared the case to the mass delusions in the Salem witch trials. Judge Loken strongly dissented.[267] The full court vacated the panel opinion, and the panel reheard the case. This time, the convictions were upheld, with Judge McMillian joining Judge Loken.[268]

The Leonard Peltier case continued to be an international cause célèbre. Judge J. Smith Henley, who received "letters from Russia, from Holland, from all over," noted that Peltier had become "a folk hero, an international symbol."[269] Books (most notably Peter Matthiessen's *In the Spirit of Crazy Horse*) were written about Peltier and films made (such as Robert Redford's documentary, *Incident at Oglala*). Amnesty International recognized Peltier as a political prisoner.

The most important development in the judicial system involving Peltier during this period was his appeal, the second since the 1981 release of 12,000 pages of FBI documents through the Freedom of Information Act, of the denial of his motion for a new trial. A panel of McMillian, Morris Arnold, and Daniel Friedman of the U.S. Court of Appeals for the Federal Circuit heard argument on November 9, 1992, in a courtroom jammed with media and Peltier supporters. The St. Paul courthouse was surrounded by cars with licenses from as far away as Florida and California. Peltier's attorneys included Ramsay Clark, who argued the case, William Kunstler, and a Canadian representing fifty-five members of the Canadian Parliament.[270] The appeal was once again unsuccessful.[271]

After that, efforts, vigorously opposed by the FBI and former FBI agents, were made to get Peltier parole or clemency. Gerald W. Heaney, who served twice on panels rejecting Peltier appeals, urged "favorable action" on executive clemency in a 1991 letter to Senator Daniel Inouye.[272] Support for Peltier's parole also came from Nelson Mandela, the Dalai Lama, and Kurt Vonnegut Jr. However, Peltier was denied parole in 2000, and his best opportunity for executive clemency passed with the end of Bill Clinton's presidency.[273]

Environmental Cases

The Court of Appeals heard a rich variety of environmental cases from every state in the circuit. The Court of Appeals was called on to oversee the cleanup of the Vertac Chemical Corporation plant in Jacksonville, Arkansas, a hazardous waste site from which 30,000 drums of dioxin had to be removed. Several times the Court of Appeals stayed orders shutting down the incinerator. That case was still alive on the issue of liability in 2001.[274] The Court of Appeals also upheld logging in the Buffalo National River watershed under the authority of the U.S. Forest Service.[275]

In Missouri, the Ford Motor Company saved $54 million by winning a major air pollution case involving a plant making Ford Tempos in the Kansas City area.[276] The Court of Appeals also upheld the positive FAA review of a $2.66 billion expansion of Lambert Airport in the St. Louis metropolitan area, a project expected to displace two thousand families.[277] A decision of the Court of Appeals opened the way for development of a 6.2-mile trail for bicycles and hikers along the Missouri Pacific Railroad right-of-way in southern St. Louis County under the National Trails Systems Act.[278] In probably the most publicized Missouri environmental litigation, the Court of Appeals, over the dissent of Judge Loken, gave permission to the United States to corral a small herd of wild horses that were trampling meadows in the Ozark National Scenic Riverway.[279]

The most important Nebraska litigation involved a battle between Nebraska and the four other states of the Central Interstate Low-Level Radioactive Waste Compact. Under a 1986 law that made each state responsible for storing its low-level nuclear waste (encompassing items such as contaminated tools and clothing from nuclear power plants, hospitals, and research centers) but permitted them to work with other states, Nebraska had joined with Arkansas, Oklahoma, Louisiana, and Kansas in an interstate compact. The commission created under the compact chose Boyd County, Nebraska, close to the South Dakota border, as the place for storing the low-level nuclear waste. Community resistance and political opportunism led Nebraska's governor to use a variety of stratagems to stall construction.

In the lengthy litigation involving the Central Interstate Low-Level Radioactive Waste Compact, Judge Richard Kopf of the District of Nebraska invariably ruled against Nebraska and the Court of Appeals consistently supported Kopf. In 1999, Nebraska sought to withdraw from the compact, while lawyers for waste-generating companies sued the state to recover some of the $95 million already spent on the project.[280] In 2001, Nebraska asked for a rehearing en banc after a Court of Appeals panel held that Nebraska could be sued by the other compact states for trying to block the waste dump.[281]

From the Dakotas came cases involving the Black Hills and the Badlands. In 1995 the Court of Appeals upheld the decision of the National Forest Service to allow logging in a 17,000-acre portion of the Black Hills National Forest west of Rapid City.[282] In a case dealing with the location of a road in the Badlands, the Court of Appeals held that the Forest Service had limited authority to regulate drilling and road development on its land.[283] In another North Dakota environmental case, the Court of Appeals dismissed the appeal of the United States in the largest wetland protection lawsuit in the history of the Clean Water Act, a case involving the Sargent Water Resource District, which had been working on a county dam without securing a permit from the Corps of Engineers.[284]

The struggle between preservationists and utilizers continued in litigation involving Voyageurs National Park and the Boundary Waters Canoe Area. In 1992, the Court of Appeals held that Congress had expressly authorized snowmobiling on the Kabetogama Peninsula, the central land mass of the Voyageurs Park.[285] After Judge James Rosenbaum of the District of Minnesota lifted the ban on snowmobiles on 6,500 acres of bays and lake shores in the 218,000-acre park, he was reversed by the Court of Appeals, which held that the National Park Service had the power to ban snowmobiles in part of the park to protect Voyageurs' thirty-five timber wolves.[286] In a case involving the BWCA, a panel of McMillian, John R. Gibson, and Magill (dissenting) ruled that the use of trucks to haul motorboats across three portages in the BWCA had to end. The Supreme Court let the decision stand.[287]

Several important cases were also connected with government regulation of agriculture. In August 1998, the Court of Appeals (Loken writing) upheld the sixty-year-old federal pricing scheme for fluid milk under which the further away dairy products are produced from Eau Claire, Wisconsin, the higher is the part of their price within the discretionary power of the secretary of agriculture (20 percent), a policy that favored sunbelt over upper Midwestern producers.[288]

Because of its more conservative membership and its sensitivity to a more conservative Supreme Court, the U.S. Court of Appeals for the Eighth Circuit chartered a more conservative course between 1990 and 2001 with less apparent discord than it had in the 1980s. As it had been throughout its history, the Court of Appeals was obedient to the Supreme Court, sensitive to the norm of collegiality, and maintained a high professional standard.

Here we must leave the Court of Appeals for the Eighth Circuit, an unheralded tribunal, but nevertheless a court that has made significant contributions to the economy, institutions, and people of its region and to American constitutionalism.

Four additional judges have been appointed to the Eighth Circuit by President George W. Bush. The contributions and impact that these individuals will make in the years to come I will leave for another author to describe in a future study.

The Honorable Steven M. Colloton received his commission on September 10, 2003. Judge Colloton is a native Iowan who attended Princeton University and subsequently received his law degree from Yale Law School. Judge Colloton served as law clerk for the Honorable Laurence H. Silberman of the D.C. Circuit, and then for Chief Justice William H. Rehnquist on the United States Supreme Court. Before his appointment to the Eighth Circuit, Judge Colloton was a federal prosecutor and served as U.S. Attorney for the Southern District of Iowa.

The Honorable Raymond W. Gruender is a native of St. Louis, Missouri, who received his commission on June 5, 2004. Judge Gruender received his bachelor's degree, MBA, and law degree from Washington University in St. Louis. He was engaged in private practice and worked as a federal prosecutor in St. Louis. Judge Gruender was serving as U.S. Attorney for the Eastern District of Missouri at the time of his appointment.

The Honorable W. Duane Benton, also a native of Missouri, received his commission on July 2, 2004. He received his undergraduate degree from Northwestern University and his law degree from Yale Law School. He also earned an MBA and an LL.M. Judge Benton engaged in private practice and worked in state government before his appointment to the Missouri Supreme Court in 1991, where he served until his appointment to the Eighth Circuit.

The Honorable Bobby E. Shepherd, a native of Arkansas, received his commission on October 10, 2006. Judge Shepherd was in private practice for fifteen years following his graduation from the University of Arkansas in 1975. He served as an Arkansas circuit-chancery judge from 1991 to 1993 and was a U.S. Magistrate in the Western District of Arkansas from 1993 until his appointment to the Eighth Circuit.

At the time of this publication in 2007, the Eighth Circuit is at full strength with all eleven active circuit judgeships filled, and enjoys significant contributions by a number of senior circuit judges who continue to render great assistance with the court's workload.

NOTES

★ ★ ★ ★ ★ ★ ★

Abbreviations

In the notes to chapter 7, NSW refers to *Newswatch*, a weekly compilation of newspaper articles of interest to judges in the Eighth Circuit prepared by the U.S. Courts Library Eighth Circuit and available in that library.

In later chapters, when there were more divisions on the court, the record of votes in a decision is often given parenthetically at the end of the case citation in the notes (if not specified in the text). In citations of cases to the court of appeals (and three-judge district courts on which members of the court of appeals sat), the names of the participating judges are either given in full or abbreviated as follows. The names of district court judges and visiting judges from other circuits are always spelled in full. The majority and minority are separated by a solidus, and judges issuing written opinions are italicized. The symbol (c) indicates a concurring opinion, and (c/d) means concurring in part and dissenting in part.

ABBREVIATIONS	JUDGES
Bmun	Harry Blackmun
Br	Myron H. Bright
Bow	Pasco Bowman
Fgib	Floyd Gibson
JRGib	John R. Gibson
John	Harvey M. Johnsen
K. Stone	Kimbrough Stone
MArn	Morris S. Arnold
Matt	Marion C. Matthes
McM	Theodore McMillian
Meh	Pat Mehaffy
Mur	Diana E. Murphy
RArn	Richard S. Arnold
Sanb	John B. Sanborn
Steph	Roy L. Stephenson
Van	Martin D. Van Oosterhout
Web	William H. Webster
Woll	Roger L. Wollman
Wood	Joseph W. Woodrough

Introduction

1. Omitted from this description of the land of the states that make up the modern Eighth Circuit are the Dakotas, the least well favored by nature, but reserved for discussion in the following chapter.

2. Among the histories on which this section is based are Berta L. Heilbron, *The Thirty-second State: A Pictorial History of Minnesota*, 2nd ed. (1966), 32–33; William E. Parrish et al., *Missouri: The Heart of the Nation*, 2nd ed. (1992); Charles Phillips, *Missouri: Mother of the American West* (1988), 11; Gerald T. Dunne, *The Missouri Supreme Court* (1993), x; Herbert S. Schell, *History of South Dakota*, 3rd rev. ed. (1975), 14; Geoffrey C. Ward, *The West: An Illustrated History*; Leland L. Sage, *A History of Iowa* (1974), 9, 11; James C. Olson and Ronald C. Naugle, *History of Nebraska* 3rd. ed. (1997), 10–11; Frederick C. Luebke, *Nebraska: An Illustrated History* (1995), 6; Frederick C. Luebke, "Time, Place, and Culture in Nebraska History," *Neb. L. Rev.* 69 (1988): 150, 152; E. E. Dale, "Arkansas: The Myth and the State," *Ark. Hist. Q.* 12 (1953): 8–29. See also Michael B. Dougan et al., *Arkansas History: An Annotated Bibliography* (1984), xiii.

3. Save for part of Minnesota between Lake Superior and the Lake of the Woods, which was defined as the nation's northwest border by the Treaty of Paris of 1783, but which was poorly enough defined that it would require further negotiation by England and the United States.

4. On the Lewis and Clark expedition, see Stephen E. Ambrose, *Undaunted Courage: Meriwether Lewis, Thomas Jefferson, and the Opening of the American West* (1996); and Stephen E. Ambrose, *Lewis and Clark: Voyage of Discovery* (1988).

5. John Milton, *South Dakota: A Bicentennial History* (1977), 46.

6. Parrish et al., *Missouri*, 157.

7. Parrish et al., *Missouri*, 156, 157, 159; Olson and Naugle, *History of Nebraska*, 102; Linda Hasselstrom, *Roadside History of South Dakota* (1994), 201; Paul C. Nagel, *Missouri: A Bicentennial History* (1977), 64; Roman W. Paul, *The Far West and the Great Plains in Transition, 1859–1900* (1988), 50–51; Dorothy Schweider, *Iowa: The Middle Land* (1996), 64.

8. Dorothy Schweider et al., *Iowa Past to Present: The People and the Prairie*, 2nd ed. (1991), 78.

9. Olson and Naugle, *History of Nebraska*, 111; Allan Nevins, *The Emergence of Modern America, 1865–1878* (1927), 52.

10. Parrish et al., *Missouri*, 44–45.

11. Michael B. Dougan, *Arkansas Odyssey: The Saga of Arkansas from Prehistoric Times to Present* (1994), 59.

12. Dorothy Schweider, *Iowa: The Middle Land*, 2nd ed. (1991), 30, 35; William E. Lass, *Minnesota: A History*, 2nd ed. (1998), 136–37.

13. See, e.g., Suzanne Winckler, *The Smithsonian Guides to Historic America: The Plains States*, rev. ed. (1998), 12; Parrish et al., *Missouri*, 40–41; Dougan, *Arkansas Odyssey*, 80–82.

14. Robert Cook, "The Political Culture of Antebellum Iowa: An Overview," in *Iowa History Reader*, ed. Marvin Bergman (1996), 86, 87–88.

15. The Timber Culture Act of 1873 would grant settlers an additional 160 acres if one quarter was planted with trees within a four-year period.

16. Nevins, *The Emergence of Modern America*, 118.

17. Alvin M. Josephy Jr., *500 Nations: An Illustrated History of North American Indians* (1994), 376; Geoffrey C. Ward, *The West: An Illustrated History* (1890), 236; James O. Gump, *The Dust That Rose like Smoke* (1994), 102, 134; Schell, *History of South Dakota*, 321; Luebke, *Nebraska: An Illustrated History*, 143, 145.

18. Parrish et al., *Missouri*, 223; Heilbron, *The Thirty-second State*, 156, 159; Dale, "Arkansas: The Myth and the State," 20–21.

19. Olson and Naugle, *History of Nebraska*, 161–62.

20. Act of March 25, 1867, 15 Stat. 5.

21. Act of July 23, 1866, 14 Stat. 209.

22. *World Book Encyclopedia*, vol. 11 (1998), 216.

23. See John J. Kane Jr., "Colorado: The Territorial and District Courts," in *The Federal Courts of the Tenth Circuit: A History*, ed. James K. Logan (1992), 37, 40, 43, 45–50.

24. Shelton Stromquist, "Town Development, Social Structure, and Industrial Conflict," in *Iowa History Reader*, ed. Marvin Bergman (1996), 159, 160; George Mills and Richard W. Peterson, *No One Is above the Law* (n.d.), 4.

25. William J. Petersen, *Story of Iowa*, vol. 1 (1952), 559.

26. Charles Fairman, *Reconstruction and Reunion, 1864–88*, Oliver Wendell Holmes Devise History of the United States, vol. 6, ed. Paul A. Freund (1971), 1668; Richard W. Peterson, *The Court Moves West* (1988), 12.

27. Dougan, *Arkansas Odyssey*, 180.

28. Parrish et al., *Missouri*, 218; Rhonda R. Gilman, *The Story of Minnesota's Past* (1989), 137; Nevins, *The Emergence of Modern America*, 115; Dougan, *Arkansas Odyssey*, 282.

29. Joseph Frazier Wall, *Iowa: A Bicentennial History*, 26–27; see, however, Schweider, *Iowa*, 54, which states that in 1880 Iowa officials could boast that no one in the state was ever more than eight miles from a railroad.

30. Ward, *The West*, 222; Luebke, "Time, Place and Culture in Nebraska History," 154, 157; Olson and Naugle, *History of Nebraska*, 199.

31. *The Wild West* (Time-Life Books, n.d.), 86–87; Nevins, *The Emergence of Modern America*, 65; Ambrose, *Lewis and Clark*, 57; Alan Wexler, *Atlas of Westward Expansion* (1995), 190.

32. Allan G. Bogue, "Farming in the Prairie Peninsula, 1830–1890," in *Iowa History Reader*, ed. Marvin Bergman (1996), 61, 75; Nevins, *The Emergence of Modern America*, 234; Paul, *The Far West and the Great Plains in Transition, 1859–1900*, 234; Luebke, *Nebraska: An Illustrated History*, 117; Walter Prescott Webb, *The Great Plains* (1931), 205; *The Wild West*, 51.

33. Nevins, *The Emergence of Modern America*, 369–71; D. Jerome Tweton and Theodore B. Jelliff, *North Dakota: The Heritage of a People* (1976), 21; Schell, *History of South Dakota*, 223; Webb, *The Great Plains*, 503.

1. "An Empire in Itself"

1. Jeffrey B. Morris, *Federal Justice in the Second Circuit* (1987), xi, 6–7.

2. Richard J. Richardson and Kenneth N. Vines, *The Politics of Federal Courts* (1970), 18.

3. The Judiciary Act of February 13, 1801, greatly altered the federal judiciary by expanding federal jurisdiction and creating five circuit courts staffed by sixteen newly created circuit judges. However, the revised jurisdiction was caught up in party bitterness, and the new judiciary act was repealed a little more than a year later by acts of March 8 and April 1, 1802. Essentially the system created in 1789 was then reestablished.

4. Morris, *Federal Justice*, 11. See also Peter Graham Fish, *The Politics of Federal Judicial Administration* (1973), 1–14.

5. Except for the short period of the Judiciary Act of 1801. See note 3, *infra*.

6. Act of March 16, 1822, Sect. 2, 3 Stat. 653.

7. Act of June 15, 1836, 5 Stat. 50.

8. 2 Cong. Deb. 13 (1825).

9. 5 Stat. 176.

10. By that statute, the district court for the District of Arkansas was given criminal jurisdiction of the Indian Territory west of the Mississippi. In 1851, Arkansas was divided into two districts presided over by the same judge. Six years later, Congress established two districts in Missouri, each with a district judge. Iowa would be divided into two districts, each staffed by a different judge, in 1882.

11. S. Doc. No. 50, 25th Cong., 3rd Sess. 39 (1838).

12. Charles Fairman, *Mr. Justice Miller and the Supreme Court, 1862–1890* (1939), 44; Leland L. Sage, *A History of Iowa* (1974), 163; David M. Silver, *Lincoln's Supreme Court*, Illinois Studies in the Social Sciences, vol. 38 (1956), 48; William Gillette, "Samuel Miller," in *The Justices of the Supreme Court, 1789–1969: Their Lives and Major Opinions*, vol. 2, ed. Leon Friedman and Fred L. Israel (1969), 1011.

13. 12 Stat. 572.

14. Act of January 23, 1863, 12 Stat. 637.

15. Act of July 23, 1863, 12 Stat. 637.

16. Act of March 25, 1867, 15 Stat. 5.

17. David J. Brewer, "Growth of the Judicial Function," in *Report of the Organization and First Annual Meeting of the Colorado Bar Association* (1898), 82, 93.

18. 16 Stat. 44.

19. 26 Stat. 826.

20. Letter from Samuel Miller to William Pitt Ballinger, May 6, 1877, quoted in Fairman, *Mr. Justice Miller*, 355, 356.

21. Letter from Samuel F. Miller to William P. Ballinger, October 3, 1879, quoted in Fairman, *Mr. Justice Miller*, 411, 412.

22. Clyde Jacobs, *Law Writers and the Courts* (1954), 111.

23. Unpublished article by Richard S. Arnold on Henry C. Caldwell, 39–40 (in possession of the author).

24. Letter from Samuel F. Miller to William P. Ballinger, July 1, 1874, quoted in Fairman, *Mr. Justice Miller*, 414–15.

25. Michael J. Brodhead, *David J. Brewer: The Life of a Supreme Court Justice, 1837–1920* (1994), 53–54.

26. Dorothy Schweider, "Iowa: The Middle Land," in *Iowa History Reader*, ed. Marvin Bergman (1996), 1, 5.

27. Sage, *A History of Iowa*, 127; Robert R. Dykstra, "Iowans and the Politics of Race in America," in *Iowa History Reader*, ed. Marvin Bergman (1996), 129, 131.

28. Keokuk Gate City, July 18, 1862, quoted in Richard W. Peterson, "Samuel Freeman Miller Remembered," address presented at the Miller Commemoration Observance, Lee County (Iowa) Historical Society, October 14, 1990 (in possession of the author).

29. Gillette, "Samuel Miller," 1015.

30. 69 U.S. (2 Bl.) 635 (1863).

31. 83 U.S. (16 Wall.) 36 (1873).

32. Letter from Samuel F. Miller to William P. Ballinger, April 28, 1878, quoted in Fairman, *Mr. Justice Miller*, 301, 302.

33. Quoted in Richard W. Peterson, "Samuel Freeman Miller Remembered," address presented at the Miller Commemoration Observance, Lee County (Iowa) Historical Society, (October 14, 1990).

34. Gillette, "Samuel Miller," 1014.

35. Fairman, *Mr. Justice Miller*, 431; Peterson, "Samuel Freeman Miller Remembered," 12.

36. *A Treatise on the Constitutional Limitations Which Rest upon the Legislative Power of the States of the American Union*, 1st ed. (1868).

37. Harold M. Hyman and William M. Wiecek, *Equal Justice under Law: Constitutional Developments, 1835–1875* (1982), 351–52; Harold M. Hyman, *A More Perfect Union: The Impact of the Civil War and Reconstruction on the Constitution* (1973), 232, 376, 516–17.

38. *City of Clinton v. Cedar Rapids & Missouri Railroad Co.*, 24 Iowa 455 (1868).

39. 27 Iowa 28 (1869).

40. See Clyde E. Jacobs, *Law Writers and the Courts*, 112–15.

41. *Stewart v. Supervisors of Polk County*, 30 Iowa 9 (1870).

42. Jacobs, *Law Writers and the Courts*, 120–21; Hyman and Wiecek, *Equal Justice under Law*, 356–57.

43. Arnold M. Paul, *Conservative Crisis and the Rule of Law* (1960), 78, 164.

44. Felix Frankfurter and James M. Landis, *The Business of the Supreme Court* (1928), 78–79.

45. *Cases Argued and Determined in the Circuit Courts of the United States for the Eighth Judicial Circuit (1873–1883)* (1881–84). McCrary also wrote *A Treatise on the American Law of Elections* (1875).

46. On McCrary, see *Bicentennial Committee of the Judicial Conference of the United States, Judges of the United States*, 2nd ed. (1983), 325; *Biographical Dictionary of the Federal Judiciary*, ed. Harold Chase et al. (1976), 184; *Who Was Who in America, Historical Volume, 1607–1896*, Marquis-Who's Who (1963), 345; Theodore F. Fetter, *A History of the United States Court of Appeals for the Eighth Circuit* (1977), 6–7. On McCrary's involvement with the electoral commission, see

Charles Fairman, *Five Justices and the Electoral Commission of 1877,* Oliver Wendell Holmes Devise History of the United States, vol. 7, ed. Paul A. Freund and Stanley N. Katz (1988), 47–50, 63–77.

47. Brodhead, *David J. Brewer,* 186, 187.

48. Ibid., 9.

49. Ibid., 27.

50. *Wright v. Noell,* 16 Kan. 601 (1876); *Board of Education v. Tinnon,* 26 Kan. 1, 19 (1881).

51. 29 Kan. 252 (1883), *rev'd sub nom Mugler v. Kansas,* 123 U.S. 623 (1887).

52. *State v. Waldruff,* 25 Fed. 178 (C.C.D.Kans.1886).

53. Arnold M. Paul, "David J. Brewer," in *The Justices of the Supreme Court, 1789–1969: Their Lives and Major Opinions,* vol. 2, ed. Leon Friedman and Fred L. Israel (1969), 1515, 1520.

54. Brodhead, *David J. Brewer,* 75.

55. 153 U.S. 391, 408, 410 (1894).

56. David J. Brewer and Charles H. Butler, *International Law* (1910).

57. Frankfurter and Landis, *The Business of the Supreme Court,* 65. On the growth of federal jurisdiction, see Erwin C. Surrency, *History of the Federal Courts* (1987), 95.

58. On the role and functions of federal courts, see Jeffrey B. Morris, "The Second Most Important Court: The United States Court of Appeals for the District of Columbia Circuit" (Ph.D. diss., Columbia University, 1972), 25–85.

59. *United States v. Maxwell Land Grant Co.,* 26 F. 118 (C.C.D.Colo.1886).

60. *Id.; United States v. Maxwell Land Grant Co.,* 21 F. 19 (C.C.D.Colo.1884); *Interstate Land Co. v. Maxwell Land Grant Co.,* 41 F. 275 (C.C.D.Colo.1889).

61. Act of August 8, 1846, 9 Stat. 77. See Richard W. Peterson, *The Court Moves West* (1988), 31–33.

62. Peterson, *The Court Moves West,* 33–34. See, e.g., *Emigrant Co. v. Adams Co.,* 100 U.S 61 (1879).

63. Paul C. Nagel, *Missouri: A Bicentennial History* (1977), 65; Lawrence H. Larsen, *Federal Justice in Western Missouri* (1994), 40.

64. *Mississippi & Missouri Railroad Co. v. Ward,* 67 U.S. 485 (1962). See also George Mills and Richard W. Peterson, *No One Is above the Law: The Story of Southern Iowa's Federal Court* (n.d.), 18–19.

65. *In re Clinton Bridge,* 5 F. Cas. 1060 (C.C.D.Iowa 1867) (No.2900), *aff'd* 77 U.S. (10 Wall.) 454 (1870). See Charles Fairman, *Reconstruction and Reunion, 1864–1888,* vol. 1, Oliver Wendell Holmes Devise History of the United States, vol. 6, ed. Paul A. Freund (1971), 1407–10; Mills and Peterson, *No One Is above the Law,* 133; Peterson, *The Court Moves West,* 35–37.

66. *The Driven Well Cases, Andrews and Others v. Hovey,* 16 F. 387 (C.C.S.D.Iowa 1883). See also Mills and Peterson, *No One Is above the Law,* 22.

67. *Deering v. McCormick Harvesting Machine Co.,* 40 F. 236 (C.C.D.Minn.1889).

68. Walter Prescott Webb, *The Great Plains* (1931), 270, 282, 309, 312–13.

69. *Washburn & Moen Manufacturing Co. v. Grinnell Wire Co.,* 24 F. 23, 24, 25 (C.C.E.D.Ark.1884).

70. 24 F. 667 (C.C.E.D.Ark.1884).

71. 14 Stat. 517. See, e.g., *In re Clemens*, 5 F. Cas. 1013 (E.D.Mo.1873) (Case no. 2877), *rev'g*, 5 F. Cas. 1011 (C.C.E.D.Mo.1873) (No. 2878), a case of first impression for a federal appellate court, involving the effect of an accommodation endorsement.

72. *Trade-Mark Cases*, 100 U.S. 82 (1879).

73. *United States v. Roche*, 27 F.Cas. 875 (C.C.D.Colo.1879) (No.16,180).

74. *United States v. Koch*, 40 F. 250, 252 (C.C.E.D.Mo.1889).

75. 78 U.S. (11 Wall.) 652 (1870).

76. 99 U.S. 225 (1878).

77. 96 U.S. 395, 396 (1877).

78. Surrency, *History of the Federal Courts*, 111; Larsen, *Federal Justice in Western Missouri*, 66–67, 85.

79. See Leonard D. White, *The Republican Era, 1869–1901* (1958), 372-74; Allan Nevins, *The Emergence of Modern America, 1865–1878* (1927), 311.

80. Act of March 3, 1879, 20 Stat. 354.

81. Act of January 25, 1889, 25 Stat. 1889; Act of February 6, 1990, 25 Stat. 656.

82. Glenn Shirley, *Law West of Fort Smith: A History of Frontier Justice in the Indian Territory* (1957), 30.

83. Fred Harvey Harrington, *Hanging Judge* (1951), 191, quoting Attorney General Philander Knox; Shirley, *Law West of Fort Smith*, 63, 41. See also Paul E. Wilson, "The Early Days," in *The Federal Courts of the Tenth Circuit: A History*, ed. James K. Logan (1992), 1, 6; Mary M. Stolberg, "Politician, Populist, Reformer: A Reexamination of 'Hanging Judge' Isaac Parker," *Ark. Hist. Q.* 47 (1988): 3, 17.

84. William C. Kellough, "Oklahoma: The Territorial and District Courts," in *The Federal Courts of the Tenth Circuit: A History*, ed. James K. Logan (1992), 173, 207.

85. Shirley, *Law West of Fort Smith*, 181, 190, 318n25; Harrington, *Hanging Judge*, 185–86; Brodhead, *David J. Brewer*, 111.

86. Stolberg, "Politician, Populist, Reformer," 4; Harrington, *Hanging Judge*, 56. But c.f. Shirley, *Law West of Fort Smith*, 198.

87. Harrington, *Hanging Judge*, 55, 58.

88. Harrington, *Hanging Judge*, 171, 178; see also Shirley, *Law West of Fort Smith*, 75.

89. Kellough, "Oklahoma," 179–86; Alan Wexler, *Atlas of Westward Expansion* (1995), 210; Stolberg, "Politician, Populist, Reformer," 25.

90. 25 F.Cas. 695 (C.C.D.Neb.1879) (No. 14,891).

91. *Id.* at 695.

92. Dee Brown, *Bury My Heart at Wounded Knee* (1972), 344. On the trial, see p. 334; James C. Olson and Ronald C. Naugle, *History of Nebraska*, 3rd ed. (1997), 119-20.

93. *United States ex rel Standing Bear v. Crook*, 25 F.Cas. 695, 701 (C.C.D.Neb.1879) (No. 14,891).

94. *United States v. Kan-Gi-Sun-Ca (in English, Crow Dog)*, 3 Dak. 104, 14 N.W. 437 (1882).

95. *Ex Parte Crow Dog*, 109 U.S. 556, 571 (1883).

96. Herbert S. Schell, *History of South Dakota*, 3rd rev. ed. (1975), 324.

97. *Civil Rights Cases*, 109 U.S. 3 (1883); *Plessy v. Ferguson*, 163 U.S. 537 (1896).

98. *Elk v. Wilkins*, 112 U.S. 94, 110, 120, 122–23 (1884). See also Vine Deloria Jr., *Of Utmost Good Faith* (1971), 128.

99. John Forrest Dillon, *Commentaries on the Law of Municipal Corporations*, 4th ed. (1890), 580.

100. Charles Warren, *The Supreme Court in United States History*, vol. 2, rev. ed. (1926), 529, 530–33. John F. Dillon, *The Law of Municipal Bonds* (1876), 7; Fairman, *Reconstruction*, 1:919; Schell, *History of South Dakota*, 114.

101. *State ex rel Burlington & Missouri R.R. v. County of Wapello*, 13 Iowa 388 (1862).

102. 68 U.S. (1 Wall.) 175 (1864).

103. *Mercer County v. Hacket*, 68 U.S. (1 Wall.) 83 (1864).

104. 75 U.S. (8 Wall.) 575 (1869).

105. *Id.* at 582.

106. *Id.* at 585, 586.

107. Fairman, *Reconstruction*, 1:951. See, e.g., *Benshow v. Iowa City*, 74 U.S. (7 Wall.) 310 (1869). See also *Rusch v. Des Moines County*, 21 F. Cas. 16 (C.C.D.Iowa 1868) (No. 12,142), holding that the circuit itself could not levy a tax.

108. *Riggs v. Johnson County*, 75 U.S. (8 Wall.) 575 (1869).

109. *Durant v. Washington County*, 8 F.Cas. 128 (C.C.D.Iowa 1869) (No. 4191). See also Fairman, *Reconstruction*, 1:956.

110. Fairman, *Reconstruction*, 1:956.

111. Ibid., 981. The case was *United States v. Treasurer of Muscatine County*, 28 F.Cas. 213 (No. 16,538) (C.C.D.Iowa 1870).

112. Fairman, *Reconstruction*, 1:984–85.

113. On the battles in Missouri, see Larsen, *Federal Justice in Western Missouri*, 67–69; and Fairman, *Reconstruction*, 1:1050–51, 1069. See also *Foot v. Pike County*, 101 U.S. 688 (1881).

114. See *Chamberlain v. St. Paul & Sioux City Railroad Co.*, 92 U.S. 299 (1879). See also William Watts Folwell, *A History of Minnesota*, vol. 3 (1869), 428.

115. *Hanauer v. Woodruff*, 82 U.S. (15 Wall.) 439 (1872).

116. Letter from Samuel F. Miller to William P. Ballinger, January 13, 1878, quoted in Fairman, *Reconstruction*, 1:1068–69. See also Miller's dissenting opinion in *Butz v. City of Muscatine*, 75 U.S. (8 Wall.) 575, 587 (1869).

117. 27 Iowa 28 (1869).

118. *King v. Wilson*, 14 F.Cas 562 (C.C.D.Iowa 1871) (No.7810).

119. *Chicago, B.C.Q.R.R. v. County of Otoe*, 5 F.Cas. 598 (C.C.D.Neb.1871) (No. 2,667), 83 U.S. 668 (1873).

120. 6 F.Cas. 737 (C.C.D.Kan.1874) (No. 2,734).

121. *Id.* at 223, 225.

122. 5 F.Cas. 737 (C.C.D.Kan.1874) (No. 2,734), *aff'd* 87 U.S. (20 Wall.) 655 (1875).

123. Jacobs, *Law Writers and the Courts*, 134.

124. Dorothy Schweider, *Iowa: The Middle Land* (1996), 62.

125. William E. Parrish, et al., *Missouri: Heart of the Nation*, 2nd ed. (1992), 213–17; Charles Phillips, *Missouri: Mother of the American West* (1988), 64–65.

126. Ellwyn B. Robinson, *History of North Dakota* (1966), 241.

127. Sage, *A History of Iowa*, 189; Phillips, *Missouri*, 189.

128. George H. Miller, *"Chicago, Burlington & Quincy Railroad Company v. Iowa," Iowa J. Hist.* 54 (1956): 289.

129. Charles Fairman, *Reconstruction and Reunion, 1864–1888,* vol. 2, Oliver Wendell Holmes Devise History of the United States, vol. 7, ed. Paul A. Freund and Stanley N. Katz (1987), 332–33; *In re McElrath,* 16 F.Cas. 72 (C.C.D.Minn.1873) (No. 8780).

130. Fairman, *Reconstruction,* 2:339–41.

131. Ibid. *Chicago, Burlington & Quincy R.R. v. Attorney General,* 5 F. Cas. 594 (C.C.D.Iowa 1875)(No. 2666). On this case, see Fairman, *Reconstruction,* 2:339–41; Sage, *A History of Iowa,* 192; Mills and Peterson, *No One Is above the Law,* 25–26; Richard, Lord Acton, and Patricia Nassif Acton, *To Go Free: A Treasury of Iowa's Legal Heritage* (1995), 159–60.

132. George H. Miller, *"Chicago, Burlington & Quincy Railroad Company v. Iowa," Iowa J. Hist.* 54 (1956): 289, 305.

133. C. Peter Magrath, *Morrison R. Waite* (1963), 189.

134. 94 U.S. 113 (1877).

135. 94 U.S. 113, 161 (1877).

136. Warren, *The Supreme Court,* 2:76–77; Magrath, *Morrison R. Waite,* 192.

137. The lengthy litigation is described in William Watts Folwell, *A History of Minnesota,* vol. 3 (1969), 441.

138. Peterson, *The Court Moves West,* 38–39.

139. *Barton v. Barbour,* 104 U.S. 126 (1881). See also *Fosdick v. Schall,* 99 U.S. 235 (1879).

140. *Barton v. Barbour,* 104 U.S. 126, 134–35 (1881).

141. *Id.* at 136, 137.

142. *Dow v. Memphis & L.R.R.Co.,* 20 F. 260 (C.C.E.D.Ark.1884), *rev'd* 20 F. 768 (C.C.E.D.Ark.1884). See also Richard S. Arnold's unpublished article on Henry C. Caldwell, 33; Fairman, *Mr. Justice Miller,* 245–46.

143. *Fosdick v. Schall,* 99 U.S. 235 (1878); *Burnham v. Bowen,* 111 U.S. 776 (1884).

144. See Brodhead, *David J. Brewer,* 62; Fairman, *Mr. Justice Miller,* 245–47.

145. See Ari Hoogenbaum, *The Presidency of Rutherford B. Hayes* (1988), 74.

146. 25 F. 544 (C.C.E.D.Mo.1885).

147. Brodhead, *David J. Brewer,* 62–63.

2. The Early Years, 1891–1929

1. Elwyn B. Robinson, "The Themes of North Dakota History," *N.D. Hist.* (Winter 1959): 5, 6.

2. Daniel J. Elazar, "Political Culture on the Plains," *West. Hist.* 11 (July 1980): 261, 269.

3. Those courts succeeded to the jurisdiction that Judge Isaac Parker had once been responsible for as judge of the Western District of Arkansas as well as to the jurisdiction that had been parceled out to the District of Kansas, the Northern District of Texas, and a United States Court for the Indian Territory at Muskogee.

4. William C. Kellough, "Oklahoma: The Territorial and District Courts," in *The Federal Courts of the Tenth Circuit: A History*, ed. James K. Logan (1992), 173, 199 (cited hereafter as *Tenth Circuit History*).

5. U.S. Department of Commerce, Bureau of the Census, *Historical Statistics of the United States, Colonial Times to 1970*, vol. 1 (1975), 24.

6. William E. Parrish et al., *Missouri: The Heart of the Nation*, 2nd ed. (1992), 297; Charles Phillips, *Missouri: Mother of the American West* (1988), 192; C. Fred Williams et al., eds., *A Documentary History of Arkansas* (1984), 185.

7. Donald J. Pisani, "The Irrigation District and the Federal Relationship," in *The Twentieth Century West*, ed. Gerald W. Nash and Richard E. Etulain (1989), 257, 262.

8. James C. Olson and Ronald C. Naugle, *History of Nebraska*, 3rd ed. (1997), 286, 305.

9. Herbert S. Schell, *History of South Dakota*, 3rd rev. ed. (1975), 277, 283.

10. William E. Lass, *Minnesota: A History* (1998), 164.

11. Leland L. Sage, *A History of Iowa* (1974), 216.

12. Olson and Naugle, *History of Nebraska*, 253.

13. Phillips, *Missouri*, 109.

14. Elazar, "Political Culture on the Plains," 261, 263; David B. Danbom, "North Dakota: The Most Midwestern State," in *Heartland*, ed. James H. Madison (1988), 107, 119.

15. Howard R. Lamar, "Perspectives on Statehood: South Dakota's First Quarter-Century, 1889–1914," *S.D. Hist.* 19 (1989): 2, 11–12; Eric Monkkonen, "Can Nebraska or Any State Regulate Railroads?" *Neb. Hist.* 54 (1973): 365, 374.

16. See William D. Rowley, "The West as a Laboratory and Mirror of Reform," in *The Twentieth Century West: Historical Interpretations*, ed. Gerald D. Nash and Richard W. Etulain (1989), 339, 342; Carl H. Moneyhon, *Arkansas and the New South* (1997), 101.

17. Kenneth Smemo, *Against the Tide: The Life and Times of Federal Judge Charles F. Amidon, North Dakota Progressive* (1986), 115.

18. Elwyn B. Robinson, *History of North Dakota* (1966), 327, 342, 388; Smemo, *Against the Tide*, 115; D. Jerome Tweton, "The Anti-League Movement: The IVA," in *The North Dakota Political Tradition*, ed. Thomas W. Howard (1981), 93, 120.

19. Phillips, *Missouri*, 101; Parrish et al., Missouri, 293.

20. Parrish et al., *Missouri*, 293; Shelby Lee, "Traveling the Sunshine State," *S.D. Hist.* 19 (1989): 194, 209–10.

21. Michael B. Dougan, *Arkansas Odyssey* (1994), 299–300.

22. Joey McCarty, "The Red Scare in Arkansas: A Southern State and National Hysteria," *Ark. Hist.* 37 (Autumn 1978): 264, 268.

23. Dougan, *Arkansas Odyssey*, 313.

24. Ibid., 320.

25. Orville D. Menard, "Tom Dennison, the *Omaha Bee*, and the 1919 Omaha Race Riot," *Neb. Hist.* 69 (1987): 152, 159; Michael L. Lawson, "Omaha, a City in Ferment: Summer 1919," *Neb. Hist.* 58 (1977): 395. The following year, a white mob lynched three circus hands on one of the main streets of Duluth. Annette Atkins,

"Minnesota Left of Center and Out of Place," in *Heartland,* ed. James H. Madison (1988), 9, 23.

26. See Michael L. Tate, *Nebraska History: An Annotated Bibliography* (1991), xxi; Linda Hasselstrom, *Roadside History of South Dakota* (1994), 49.

27. 26 Stat. 826.

28. Act of February 13, 1925, 43 Stat. 936.

29. The statistics on the workload of the Eighth Circuit and those of all nine courts of appeals are taken from Theodore J. Fetter, *A History of the United States Court of Appeals for the Eighth Circuit* (1977), 14, 20 (cited hereafter as *Eighth Circuit History*).

30. Act of June 23, 1894, 26 Stat. 826.

31. Act of January 31, 1903, 32 Stat. 791.

32. Act of March 3, 1925, 43 Stat. 1116.

33. Arthur J. Stanley Jr. and Irma S. Russell, "The Political and Administrative History of United States Court of Appeals for the Tenth Circuit," in *Tenth Circuit History,* 291, 294.

34. Denise Bonn, *The Geographical Division of the Eighth Circuit Court of Appeals* (Federal Judicial Center Report, 1974), 8.

35. 45 Stat. 1346.

36. Richard S. Arnold, untitled draft article on Henry Clay Caldwell (n.d.), 6 (unpublished manuscript in possession of the author).

37. *Osborn v. Nicholson,* 18 F. Cas. 847 (C.C.E.D.Ark.1870), *rev'd* 13 Wall. (8 U.S.) 654 (1871).

38. Letter of Samuel F. Miller to William P. Ballinger, July 30, 1869, quoted in Charles Fairman, *Mr. Justice Miller and the Supreme Court, 1862-1890* (1939), 340, 342, 343.

39. Arnold manuscript, 56-58.

40. Ibid., 22.

41. Ibid., 33, 60.

42. Ibid., 39.

43. Ibid., 23, 30, 33, 35; *Eighth Circuit History,* 15-16.

44. Thomas H. Boyd, "Walter Henry Sanborn and the Development of the Law in the Northwest" (n.d.), 1 (unpublished manuscript in possession of the author).

45. See, e.g., Dee Brown, *Bury My Heart at Wounded Knee* (1971), 97, 152-53.

46. Thomas H. Boyd, "Walter Sanborn and the Eighth Circuit Court," *Ramsey County Hist.* (Summer 1991), 22, 23.

47. This apt description was suggested to me by Gerald T. Dunne.

48. Van Devanter wrote caustically of Sanborn's "change of views" about the Commerce Clause, while Sanborn may have been the author of an anonymous memorandum that reached William Howard Taft that gave the figures for the number of opinions written by every circuit judge. Sanborn came out first in the nation, doubling the productivity of Van Devanter. Alexander M. Bickel and Benno C. Schmidt Jr., *The Judiciary and Responsible Government, 1910-21,* Oliver Wendell Holmes Devise History of the Supreme Court of the United States, vol. 9, ed. Paul A. Freund and Stanley N. Katz (1984), 49-54.

49. Ibid., 48–49, 58–59.

50. Quoted in Boyd, "Walter Henry Sanborn," 32.

51. On Walter Sanborn, see also *Eighth Circuit History*, 16–17, 34–35.

52. *Eighth Circuit History*, 17–18.

53. Bickel and Schmidt, *The Judiciary and Responsible Government*, 45.

54. 187 U.S. 553 (1903).

55. Bickel and Schmidt, *The Judiciary and Responsible Government*, 51.

56. On Van Devanter see David Burner, "Willis Van Devanter," in *The Justices of the Supreme Court, 1789–1919: Their Lives and Major Opinions*, vol. 3, ed. Leon Friedman and Fred L. Israel (1969), 1945. See also Rebecca Thompson, "Wyoming: The Territorial and District Courts," in *Tenth Circuit History*, 79, 97–99, 285–86; *Eighth Circuit History*, 21–22; Drew Pearson and Robert S. Allen, *The Nine Old Men* (1937), 186.

57. J. H. Atwood, William Cather Hook, 7 A.B.A.J. 552, 555 (1921), quoted in Bickel and Schmidt, *The Judiciary and Responsible Government*, 325. On Hook generally, see Bickel and Schmidt, 54, 318; *Eighth Circuit History*, 24–25; *Bicentennial Committee of the Judicial Conference of the United States, Judges of the United States*, 2nd ed. (1983), 229 (cited hereafter as *Judges of the United States*); *Biographical Dictionary of the Federal Judiciary*, ed. Harold Chase et al. (1976), 128 (cited hereafter as *Biographical Dictionary*).

58. *Eighth Circuit History*, 15–16; *Judges of the United States*, 2.

59. On Smith, see *Eighth Circuit History*, 25; *Judges of the United States*, 460; *Biographical Dictionary*, 257–58.

60. On Carland, see Peggy J. Teslow, *History of the United States District Court for the District of South Dakota*, 17; *Eighth Circuit History*, 23–25. On the assignment of judges of the U.S. Commerce Court, see Staff of Senate Comm. on the Judiciary, 92d Cong., 2d Sess, *Legislative History of the United States Circuit Courts of Appeals and the Judges Who Served during the Period 1801 through May 1972*, comp. Richard F. Wambach (1972), 161–62.

61. By the Act of June 18, 1910, 36 Stat. 539, Congress created the Commerce Court and authorized the president to appoint five additional circuit court of appeals judges. The Chief Justice, Edward Douglas White, pursuant to the statute, assigned Judge Carland to the Eighth Circuit. When Congress abolished the Commerce Court on October 22, 1913, 38 Stat. 208, it provided that its judges be continued on assignment. These judgeships were not filled after their incumbents died.

62. On Kimbrough Stone, see U.S. Court of Appeals for the Eighth Judicial Circuit, Memorial Service for Kimbrough Stone, 255 F2d 3 (May 6, 1958); *Eighth Circuit History*, 25–27, 47.

63. On Lewis, see John L. Kane Jr. and Sharon Marks Elfenbein, "Colorado: The Territorial and District Courts," in *Tenth Circuit History*, 37, 54–56; Harry F. Tepker, "The Judges of the Court of Appeals," in *Tenth Circuit History*, 54–56, 323–26; *Eighth Circuit History*, 27–28.

64. On Kenyon, see Elizabeth T. Putnam, "An Investigation of the Judicial Appointment of Senator William Squire Kenyon" (M.A. thesis, University of Iowa, 1968); *Eighth Circuit History*, 28–30; Sage, *A History of Iowa*, 160–61.

65. On Booth, see Bicentennial of the Constitution Committee for the District of Minnesota, *History of the United States District Court for the District of Minnesota* (1989), 11; *Eighth Circuit History*, 30–33; *Biographical Dictionary*, 26.

66. On Van Valkenburgh, see Larsen, *Federal Justice in Western Missouri*, 98; *Eighth Circuit History*, 31; *Biographical Dictionary*, 284.

67. On Cotterall, see William C. Kellough, "Oklahoma: The Territorial and District Courts," in *Tenth Circuit History*, 173, 200–201; Tepker, "The Judges of the Court of Appeals," 319, 326–30; *Eighth Circuit History*, 32. The sources seem evenly divided as to whether the judge's name is spelled "Cotteral" or "Cotterall."

68. See Smemo, *Against the Tide*, esp. 53, 56, 57, 71; Robinson, *History of North Dakota*, 260.

69. Gerald W. Heaney, "Jacob Trieber: Lawyer, Politician, Judge," *U.Ark.LittleRockL.Rev.* 8 (1985–86): 421, 437.

70. *United States v. Midwest Oil Co.*, 206 F. 141 (D.Wyo.1913).

71. *United States v. Midwest Oil Co.*, 236 U.S. 459 (1915).

72. *United States v. Midwest Oil Co.*, 236 U.S. 459, 472–73 (1915).

73. *United States v. Midwest Oil Co.*, 236 U.S. 459, 484, 511 (1915).

74. Another case often used as a precedent for the exercise of presidential power, *Missouri v. Holland,* 252 U.S. 416 (1920), had its genesis in the Eighth Circuit during this period. After congressional legislation to protect migratory birds from promiscuous hunting was held unconstitutional by district judges in Arkansas and Kansas, the United States negotiated a treaty with Great Britain. Pursuant to that treaty, Congress passed the Migratory Bird Act to achieve the same end as the previous statute. The state of Missouri then brought suit in the U.S. District Court for the Western District of Missouri to enjoin enforcement of the act. That court upheld the law, and the Supreme Court affirmed in a landmark opinion by Justice Oliver Wendell Holmes. See *United States v. Shauver,* 214 F. 154 (E.D.Ark.1914), and *United States v. McCullagh,* 221 F. 288 (D.Kan.1915), *writ of error dismissed United States v. Shauver,* 248 U.S. 594 (1919). *United States v. Samples,* 258 F. 479 (W.D.Mo.1919), *aff'd Missouri v. Holland,* 246 U.S. 416 (1920). See also *United States v. Thompson,* 258 F. 257 (E.D.Ark.1919).

75. 14 F2d 705 (1926: *Kenyon*–Van Val–Cant), *aff'd* 275 U.S. 13 (1927).

76. See Frederick Lewis Allen, *Only Yesterday* (1946), 96.

77. David C. Frederick, *Rugged Justice* (1994), 164–65.

78. *United States v. Mammoth Oil Co.*, 5 F2d 330 (D.Wyo.1925).

79. Rebecca W. Thompson, "Wyoming: The Territorial and District Courts," in *Tenth Circuit History*, 79, 111.

80. *United States v. Mammoth Oil Co.*, 14 F2d 705, 729 (1926).

81. *Id.* at 729, 731.

82. *Mammoth Oil v. United States,* 275 U.S. 13, 53 (1927). The Teapot Dome oil reserve remained free of private drilling until 1976, when Congress authorized "emergency pumping" during the energy crisis. Frederick, *Rugged Justice,* 167.

83. See John L. Kane and Sharon Marks Elfenbein, "Colorado: The Territorial and District Courts," in *The Federal Courts of the Tenth Circuit*, 37, 46.

84. 245 U.S. 563 (1918).

85. 41 Stat. 437.

86. See Nancy J. Taniguchi, "The Shifting Significance of *United States v. Sweet*," *West. Hist.* 9 (1996): 131.

87. Bayard H. Paine, "Decisions Which Have Changed Nebraska History," *Neb. Hist.* 16 (1935): 203–7.

88. Under the Act of February 11, 1903, 32 Stat. 823.

89. 26 Stat. 209.

90. *United States v. E. C. Knight Co.*, 156 U.S. 1 (1895).

91. *United States v. Trans-Missouri Freight Ass'n*, 166 U.S. 290 (1897); *United States v. Joint Traffic Ass'n*, 171 U.S. 505 (1898); *Addyston Pipe & Steel Co. v. United States*, 175 U.S. 211 (1899). See Owen F. Fiss, *Troubled Beginnings of the Modern State, 1888–1910*, Oliver Wendell Holmes Devise History of the Supreme Court of the United States, vol. 8, ed. Stanley N. Katz (1993), 260.

92. *Minnesota v. Northern Securities Co.*, 184 U.S. 199 (1902). See also William Watts Folwell, *A History of Minnesota*, vol. 3 (1969).

93. *United States v. Northern Securities Co.*, 120 F. 721, 724 (8th C.: *Thayer-Caldwell-Sanborn–Van Devanter*, 1903). Judge Van Devanter is listed with the judges joining in the opinion, but his name is omitted from those joining in the decree. No explanation is given. In 1911 the Eighth Circuit dismissed a Sherman Act prosecution brought to prevent the merger of the Union Pacific and the Southern Pacific Railroads. The court (Judge Elmer Adams writing) held that the two merged railroad systems had not been in competition, and therefore that no competition was eliminated by the merger. Judge William Hook sharply dissented. The Supreme Court unanimously reversed, holding that the two lines had been in "sharp well-defined and vigorous competition." *United States v. Union Pacific R.R.*, 188 F. 102 (1911), *rev'd* 226 U.S. 61 (1912). For the decree in the case, see 226 U.S. 470 (1913).

94. *Northern Securities Co. v. United States*, 193 U.S. 197 (1904), *aff'g* 120 F. 721 (D.Minn.1903).

95. Boyd, "Walter Henry Sanborn," 23.

96. On the case, see Rod Chernow, *Titan: The Life of John D. Rockefeller, Sr.* (1998), 545. Sixty-seven-year-old John D. Rockefeller was examined in November 1908 and, reminiscent of a recent American president, came off as an "amiable old gent" with sudden memory lapses and fuzzy logic (547). Rockefeller had been involved earlier in a colossal Eighth Circuit case involving the profits from land mined in the Mesabi. The backwoods Merritt family—four brothers and three nephews—were pioneers in mining Mesabi ore. They purchased vast tracts of land and launched construction of a railroad to carry ore to Lake Superior. Faced with a severe cash shortage, however, they needed Rockefeller to bail them out. Rockefeller advanced nearly two million dollars in what to many was a harebrained scheme. While advancing the money, Rockefeller created a holding company for the properties, a company in which as he lent more and more money, he took more and more shares. After steel men found ways to adapt their furnaces to Mesabi ore, stock in the holding company rose to stratospheric heights. The Merritts then brought suit against Rockefeller in the Circuit Court for the District of Minnesota. Concerned about local prejudice, Rockefeller retained a Minnesota newspaperman and even stepped up charitable donations in the area. Nevertheless a Duluth jury brought in

a verdict for the Merritts, which was overturned on appeal. Ultimately the Merritts settled for a paltry $525,000 (383–85).

97. *United States v. Standard Oil Company of New Jersey*, 173 F. 177 (C.C.E.D.Mo.Nov. 20, 1909).

98. *Id.* at 182–83, 192.

99. *Id.* at 193, 195.

100. See Jeffrey B. Morris, *Federal Justice in the Second Circuit* (1987), 104.

101. Standard *Oil Company of New Jersey v. United States*, 221 U.S. 1 (1911).

102. *United States v. American Tobacco*, 221 U.S. 106 (1911).

103. In the late 1990s, the wheel turned. Exxon, which had been created by the merger of Standard Oil of New Jersey and Anglo-American Oil, merged with Mobil (originally Standard Oil of New York), while Amoco (formed by the Standard Oil companies of Kansas, Indiana, and Nebraska) agreed to be purchased by British Petroleum (the former Standard Oil of Ohio). *U.S. News and World Report,* December 14, 1998, 26–28.

104. *Munn v. Illinois,* 134 U.S. 418 (1877).

105. *Stone v. Farmer's Loan & Trust Co.,* 116 U.S. 307 (1886).

106. *Chicago & N.W. Ry. Co. v. Dey,* 35 F. 866, 879 (C.C.S.D. Iowa 1888).

107. 134 U.S. 418 (1890).

108. 35 F. 883 (C.C.D.Minn.1888).

109. James W. Ely Jr., "The Railroad Question Revisited: *Chicago, Milwaukee & St. Paul Railway v. Minnesota* and Constitutional Limits on State Regulation," in *Law and the Great Plains,* ed. John R. Wunder (1996), 73, 82.

110. 64 F. 165 (C.C.D.Neb.1894).

111. 169 U.S. 466 (1898).

112. One example of this occurred in South Dakota. After the decision in *Smyth v. Ames,* Judge J. Emmett Carland personally reviewed that state's schedule of railroad fares. The Supreme Court, Brewer writing, reversed Carland on his findings and required him to remand the case to a master. In an unusually personal opinion, Justice Brewer wrote: "The questions are difficult, the interests are vast, therefore, the aid of the trial court should be had. The writer of the opinion appreciates the difficulties which attend a trial court in a case like this. In *Smyth v. Ames* . . . , a similar case, he, as Circuit Judge, presiding in the Circuit Court of Nebraska, undertook the work of examining the testimony, making computations and finding the facts. It was very laborious and took several weeks. It was a work which really ought to have been done by a master." *Chicago, M. & St. P. Ry. Co. v. Tompkins,* 176 U.S. 167, 179 (1900), *rev'g* 90 F. 362 (C.C.S.D.1898).

113. *Minnesota Rate Cases,* 230 U.S. 352 (1913).

114. *Shepard v. Northern Pac. Ry. Co.,* 184 F. 765 (C.C.D.Minn.1911).

115. *Minnesota Rate Cases,* 230 U.S. 352 (1913).

116. William E. Forbath and Craig Becker, "Labor," in *The Oxford Companion to the Supreme Court of the United States,* ed. Kermit L. Hall (1992), 565, 566.

117. See *Loewe v. Lawlor,* 208 U.S. 274 (1908); *Duplex Printing Press v. Deering,* 254 U.S. 443 (1921); *American Steel Foundries v. Tri-City Trades Council,* 257 U.S. 184 (1921).

118. *Moyer v. Peabody,* 212 U.S. 78, 85 (1909), *aff'g* 148 F. 870 (C.C.D. Colo.1906);

Dakota Coal Co. v. Fraser, 213 F. 415, 418 (D.N.D.Amidon1919), *rev'd Dakota Coal v. Fraser,* 267 F. 130 (1920: *Johnson*-Sanborn-Stone).

119. *Hopkins v. Oxley Stave Co.,* 83 F. 912 (1897). Judge Caldwell's opinion is in *id.* at 921, 929, 935, 934, 938.

120. *United Mine Workers v. Coronado Coal Co.,* 258 F. 828 (1919: *Trieber*-Sanborn/*Hook*). The original complaint was filed in September 1914. The district court sustained a demurrer, but the court of appeals reversed, holding that the unions might be sued under the Sherman Act. *Down v. United Mine Workers,* 235 F. 1 (1914).

121. *United Mine Workers v. Coronado Coal Co.,* 259 U.S. 344, 407, 410–11 (1922). The case had been argued for the union in the court of appeals by Alton B. Parker, a former judge and the Democratic Party's presidential nominee in 1904. In the U.S. Supreme Court, the union was represented by another former presidential candidate and judge, Charles Evans Hughes.

122. *Coronado Coal Co. v. United Mine Workers,* 268 U.S. 295 (1925), *aff'g/rev'g* 300 F. 972 (8th Cir.: *Kenyon*-Sanborn-Lewis, 1924). On the Coronado Coal Cases, see Alexander Bickel, *The Unpublished Opinions of the Mr. Justice Brandeis,* 99, 254n30; Dougan, *Arkansas Odyssey,* 322; Charles O. Gregory, *Labor and the Law,* 2nd rev. ed. (1961); 211–22; Alpheus T. Mason, *William Howard Taft: Chief Justice* (1964), 202–3.

123. See Bertha L. Heilbron, *The Thirty-second State: A Pictorial History of Minnesota,* 2nd ed. (1966), 146.

124. 24 Stat. 388. On the Dawes Act, see F. Cohen, *Handbook of Federal Indian Law* (1982), 130.

125. By 1924, all Native Americans had been granted U.S. citizenship, although citizenship did not guarantee the right to vote, which both North Dakota and Minnesota still denied. See Vine Deloria Jr. and Clifford M. Lytle, *American Indians, American Justice* (1983), 222–26.

126. John R. Wunder, *Retained by the People: A History of American Indians and the Bill of Rights* (1974), 33.

127. Ibid.

128. F. Cohen, *Handbook of Federal Indian Law,* 135, 138; Herbert T. Hoover, "The Sioux Agreement of 1889 and Its Aftermath," *S.D. Hist.* 19 (Spring 1989): 56, 70; James O. Gump, *The Dust Rose like Smoke* (1994) 139; Wunder, *Retained by the People,* 33, 45.

129. Hoover, "The Sioux Agreement of 1889," 56, 82, 93.

130. See Wunder, *Retained by the People,* 34.

131. Kellough, "Oklahoma," 173, 201.

132. 171 F. 907 (C.C.E.D.OK.1909).

133. *United States v. Allen,* 179 F. 13, 16 (8th Cir.: *Amidon*-Hook/*Adams,* 1910).

134. *United States v. Allen,* 179 F. 13, 23, 25 (1910).

135. *United States v. Allen,* 179 F. 13, 16 (1910), *aff'd & modified sub nom. Heckman v. United States,* 224 U.S. 12 (1912). Two other cases that were part of the *Allen* litigation were decided by the Supreme Court at the same time. See *Goat v. United States,* 224 U.S. 458 (1912), modifying and affirming the result below; and *Mullen v. United States,* 224 U.S. 448 (1912), reversing the result below.

136. *Tarleton v. Mayes,* 163 U.S. 376 (1896). See F. Cohen, *Handbook of Federal Indian Law,* 664–65.

137. *Scott v. Frazier,* 258 F. 669, 678–79 (D.N.D.1919), *aff'd* 253 U.S. 243 (1920).

138. 176 N.W. 11 (1920) *aff'd* 253 U.S. 233 (1920).

139. *Green v. Frazier,* 253 U.S. 233, 242–43 (1920).

140. Amidon's opinion sustaining the scheme against Commerce Clause attack is unreported. The case was *Farmers' Grain Co. of Embden v. Langer.* See Smemo, *Against the Tide,* 167.

141. *Farmers' Grain Co. of Embden v. Langer,* 273 F. 635 (8th Cir.: *Carland*-Lewis-Cotterall, 1921).

142. *Lemke v. Farmers' Grain Co. of Embden,* 58 U.S. 50, 58 (1922).

143. *McCutcheon v. Townley,* 266 F. 985 (1920).

144. David B. Danbom, "North Dakota: The Most Midwestern State," in *Heartland,* ed. James H. Madison (1988), 107, 126; Robinson, *History of North Dakota,* 538.

145. Jack W. Rogers, "The Foreign Language Issue in Nebraska, 1918–1923," *Neb. Hist.* 39 (1958): 1, 5; Frederick C. Luebke, "The German-American Alliance in Nebraska, 1910–1917," *Neb Hist.* 49 (1968): 165.

146. Carl H. Chrislock, *The Progressive Era in Minnesota, 1899–1918* (1971), 139.

147. Frederick C. Luebke, *Bonds of Loyalty: German-Americans and World War I* (1974), 214.

148. Carl H. Chrislock, *Watchdog of Loyalty* (1991), 107; Luebke, *Bonds of Loyalty,* 237, 251; Donald W. Grebin, "The South Dakota Council of Defense, 1917–1919" (M.A. thesis, University of South Dakota, 1967), 21, 85; Luebke, *Bonds of Loyalty,* 289; Robert F. Karolevitz, *Challenge: The South Dakota Story* (1978), 243; Parrish et al., *Missouri,* 280–82; Joseph Frazier Wall, *Iowa: A Bicentennial History* (1978), 188–90.

149. Luebke, *Bonds of Loyaly,* 245, 277.

150. Paul L. Murphy, *World War I and the Origin of Civil Liberties in the United States* (1979), 129.

151. Carl Wittke, *German Americans and the World War* (1936), 188–90.

152. Luebke, *Bonds of Loyalty,* 311–12.

153. Jeffrey B. Morris, "Reds, Reverends, Resisters and Robes: The Second Circuit and Free Expression, 1917–1920," Second Circuit History Lecture, June 16, 1988, 4 (manuscript in possession of the author).

154. See Chrislock, *Watchdog of Loyalty,* 161; Grebin, "South Dakota Council," 68; Douglas Bakken, "NPL in Nebraska, 1917–1920," *N.D. Hist.* 39 (1972): 26, 30.

155. 40 Stat. 217, sec. 3.

156. 40 Stat. 553, sec. 3.

157. Smemo, *Against the Tide,* 104.

158. Harry V. Scheiber, *The Wilson Administration and Civil Liberties, 1917–21* (1960), 47.

159. Smemo, *Against the Tide,* 108, 110, 118–19.

160. Ibid., 142; Robinson, *History of North Dakota,* 366.

161. Larsen, *Federal Justice in Western Missouri,* 123, 125. See also Zechariah Chafee Jr., *Free Speech in the United States* (1941), 52–53, 79, 193, 461; *United States v. Stokes,* 264 F. 18 (8th Cir.: *Sanborn*-Stone-*Carland,* 1920).

162. Smemo, *Against the Tide*, 131; Robinson, *History of North Dakota*, 364.

163. *United States v. von Bank*, 253 F. 641 (8th Cir.: *Carland*-Stone-Elliott, 1918); Smemo, *Against the Tide*, 134; Robinson, *History of North Dakota*, 367.

164. 262 F. 283 (1919).

165. Among the other decisions of the court of appeals are *Stenzel v. United States*, 261 F. 161 (8th Cir.: *Stone*-Carland-Sanborn, 1919); *Bentall v. United States*, 262 F. 744 (8th Cir.: *Stone*-Sanborn/*Carland*, 1919); *Grubl v. United States*, 264 F. 44 (8th Cir.: *Sanborn*-Munger/Stone), 1920).

166. *Burton v. United States*, 202 U.S. 344 (1906).

167. *Dolan v. United States*, 133 F. 440 (8th cir.: *Amidon*–Van Devanter–Hook, 1904).

168. *Hays v. United States*, 231 F. 106, 109 (8th Cir.: *Amidon*-Carland-Van Valkenburgh, 1916), *aff'd sub nom. Caminetti v. United States*, 242 U.S. 470 (1917). On Mann Act cases, see generally David J. Langum, *Crossing over the Line: Legislating Morality and the Mann Act* (1944).

169. 36 Stat. 825.

170. Hays and a friend had persuaded an unmarried woman under eighteen to travel from Oklahoma City to Wichita. Although the woman was paid, Hays's motivation was not to make a profit but rather to procure the woman's sexual services for himself. Caminetti, the son of the Democratic leader of San Francisco, and a friend of his had taken two girls from Sacramento to Reno and had sex with them. No money was involved.

171. Bickel and Schmidt, *The Judiciary and Responsible Government* 434.

3. The Sanborn Court, 1919–1959

1. This section is based on William E. Leuchtenburg and the editors of *Life, New Deal and Global War* (1964); William E. Leuchtenburg and the editors of *Life, The Great Act of Change* (1964); James MacGregor Burns, *The Workshop of Democracy* (1985), 539; James MacGregor Burns, *The Crosswinds of Freedom* (1989), 3; Jeffrey B. Morris, *Federal Justice in the Second Circuit* (1987), 123–24.

2. Leuchtenburg, *New Deal and Global War*, 107, 102, 116.

3. Robert P. Wilkins and Wynona Huchette Wilkins, *North Dakota: A Bicentennial History* (1977), 87.

4. Frederick C. Luebke, *Nebraska: An Illustrated History* (1995), 279.

5. Allan Carpenter and Randy Lyon, *Between Two Rivers: Iowa Year by Year, 1846–1996*, 3rd ed. (1996), 181; Joseph Frazier Wall, *Iowa: A Bicentennial History* (1978), 207.

6. Wilkins and Wilkins, *North Dakota*, 12–13; Elwyn B. Robinson, *History of North Dakota* (1995), 10, 397–98.

7. Leuchtenburg, *New Deal and Global War*, 33–34; Ian Frazier, *Great Plains* (1989), 96–97.

8. Wilkins and Wilkins, *North Dakota*, 103.

9. *Arkansas Gazette*, January 4, 1931, reprinted in *A Documentary History of Arkansas*, ed. C. Fred Williams et al. (1984), 204 (cited hereafter as *Arkansas Documentary History*); Carpenter and Lyon, *Between Two Rivers*, 176–79; Leland L.

Sage, *A History of Iowa* (1974), 290; Michael L. Tate, *Nebraska History: An Annotated Bibliography* (1991), xxii; Luebke, *Nebraska*, 280; James C. Olson and Ronald C. Naugle, *History of Nebraska*, 3rd ed. (1997), 312; Dorothy Schweider, *Iowa: The Middle Land* (1996), 257; Lawrence H. Larsen, *Federal Justice in Western Missouri* (1994), 156; Wilkins and Wilkins, *North Dakota*, 116; Glenn H. Smith, "William Langer and the Art of Personal Politics," in *The North Dakota Political Reader*, ed. Thomas W. Howard (1981), 123, 134; Robinson, *History of North Dakota*, 405.

10. Olson and Naugle, *History of Nebraska*, 311.

11. William E. Parrish et al., *Missouri: The Heart of the Nation*, 2nd ed. (1992), 304, 306.

12. William E. Lass, *Minnesota: A History* (1998), 256.

13. See Dougan, *Arkansas Odyssey* (1994), 452; Robinson, *History of North Dakota*, 408; Herbert S. Schell, *History of South Dakota*, 3rd rev. ed. (1975).

14. See Dorothy Schweider and Joseph W. Wall, "Rural Iowa in the 1920s and 1930s," in *Iowa History Reader*, ed. Marvin Bergman (1996), 343.

15. Olson and Naugle, *History of Nebraska*, 321.

16. Gilbert C. Fite, "The Transformation of South Dakota Agriculture: The Effects of Mechanization," *S.D. Hist.* 19 (1989): 278, 288; Deborah Fink, "World War II and Rural Women," in *Iowa History Reader*, ed. Marvin Bergman (1996), 347.

17. Schell, *History of South Dakota*, 292; David B. Danbom, "Postscript," in Robinson, *History of North Dakota*, 583.

18. Leuchtenburg, *New Deal and Global War*, 117; Schweider, *Iowa*, 277.

19. Elwyn B. Robinson, "The Themes of North Dakota History," *N.D. Hist.* 26 (Winter 1959): 5.

20. Charles Phillips, *Missouri: Mother of the American West* (1988), 118; Parrish et al., *Missouri*, 221.

21. Schweider, Iowa, 28; Dougan, *Arkansas Odyssey*, 461; Luebke, *Nebraska*, 279, 299; Robert E. Karolevitz, *Challenge: The South Dakota Story* (1978), 279; Warren A. Beck and Ynez D. Haase, *Historical Atlas of the American West* (1989), maps, 74–78; Russell Bearden, "The False Rumor of Tuesday: Arkansas's Internment of Japanese-Americans," *Ark. Hist. Q.* 41 (1982): 322; Dougan, *Arkansas Odyssey*, 467.

22. Robinson, *History of North Dakota*, 424.

23. Parrish et al., *Missouri*, 297, 346; *Arkansas Documentary History*, 213; Lass, *Minnesota*, 232; Olson and Naugle, *History of Nebraska*, 352.

24. Dougan, *Arkansas Odyssey*, 476; Frederick C. Luebke, "Time, Place, and Culture in Nebraska," *Neb. Hist.* 69 (1988): 150, 166.

25. 45 Stat. 534. See also *United States v. Sponenbarger*, 308 U.S. 256, 262 (1939).

26. 46 Stat. 927. See also Rhonda R. Gilman, *Northern Lights: The Story of Minnesota's Past* (1989), 201. And see also *United States v. Chicago, M.,St.P. & P.R.Co.*, 113 F2d 919, 920 (1940).

27. See Schell, *History of South Dakota*, 305; Mark Harvey, "North Dakota, the Northern Plains, and the Missouri Valley Authority," in *The Centennial Anthology of North Dakota History*, ed. Janet Daley Lysengen and Ann M. Rathke (1996), 376;

John Ferrell, "Developing the Missouri: South Dakota and the Pick-Sloan Plan," *S.D. Hist.* 19 (1989): 306; Vine Deloria Jr., *Of Utmost Good Faith* (1971), 310.

28. Today the parts of the river closest to what the explorers saw, with its "snags, sandbars, islands, eroding banks and . . . merrily meandering channel," are the sixty miles northwest of Sioux City to the Gavins Point Dam and the river from the mouth of the Niobrara River to Fort Randall." See Julie Fanselow, *The Traveler's Guide to the Lewis and Clark Trail* (1994), 32.

29. Marc Reisner, *Cadillac Desert* (1996), 191; Karolevitz, *Challenge*, 284; Wilkins and Wilkins, *North Dakota*, 96; Linda Hasselstrom, *Roadside History of South Dakota* (1990), 131; Ferrell, "Developing the Missouri," 351.

30. 304 U.S. 64 (1938).

31. 53 Stat. 1223.

32. 304 U.S. 64 (1938).

33. On the Conference of Senior Judges, Administrative Office, Judicial Councils, and Federal Rules of Civil Procedure, see Jeffrey Brandon Morris, "The Changing Federal Courts," *Proc. Acad. Pol. Sci.* 34, no. 2 (1981): 90.

34. Theodore J. Fetter, *A History of the United States Court of Appeals for the Eighth Circuit* (1977), 63, 86 (cited hereafter as *Eighth Circuit History*).

35. Ibid., 48–49, 66.

36. Long service also characterized the careers of the court officers. John D. Jordan, the first clerk, served until 1920. His successor, E. E. Koch, served until 1957.

37. 45 Stat. 1346.

38. *Eighth Circuit History*, 26–27.

39. Peter Graham Fish, *The Politics of Federal Judicial Administration*, 130–31, 147, 149–50; *Eighth Circuit History*, 64.

40. "In Memoriam: Kimbrough Stone, 1875–1958," May 6, 1958, St. Louis, 255 F2d 3, 39, 40.

41. See "Archibald K. Gardner: Senior Circuit Judge—Eighth Circuit," A.B.A.J. 33:1103, 1104; Peggy J. Teslow, *History of the United States District Court for the District of South Dakota* (1991), 109–10.

42. Teslow, *History of the United States District Court*, 110.

43. In addition to the foregoing references on Gardner, see *Eighth Circuit History*, 50–52; *Bicentennial Committee of the Judicial Conference of the United States, Judges of the United States*, 2nd ed. (1983), 176 (cited hereafter as *Judges of the United States*); *Biographical Dictionary of the Federal Judiciary*, ed. Harold Chase et al. (1976), 98 (cited hereafter as *Biographical Dictionary*); O. W. Coursey, "A Leader of the State Bar," in *Who's Who in South Dakota*, vol. 3 (1920), 87.

44. Thomas H. Boyd, "The Life and Career of John B. Sanborn, Jr.," *Wm. Mitchell L.Rev.* 23 (1997):203, 226, 242n, 268.

45. Ibid., 255.

46. Ibid., 253, 248n293, 258.

47. Charles E. Whittaker, "A Tribute to Judge John B. Sanborn," *Minn.L.Rev.* 44 (1959): 197, 199.

48. Boyd, "Life and Career," 267–68, 270, 276.

49. United States Court of Appeals for the Eighth Circuit, Memorial Proceed-

ings for Judge John Sanborn, St. Louis, September 11, 1964, 358 F2d 3, 15 at 16 (cited hereafter as Sanborn Memorial Proceedings).

50. Whittaker, *Tribute*, 197, 198.

51. Sanborn Memorial Proceedings, 18.

52. See, e.g., his decision as a district judge in *United States v. Cunningham*, 37 F2d 349 (1929), opposing the use of equity power to place violators of Prohibition in jail.

53. On Woodrough, see Memorial Proceedings for the Honorable Joseph W. Woodrough, St. Paul, May 17, 1978, 583 F2d 1, 14, 20, 28. See also *Eighth Circuit History*, 64–66; *Judges of the United States*, 546; *Biographical Dictionary*, 308. Woodrough was a party in *O'Malley v. Woodrough*, 307 U.S. 277 (1939), the test case that sustained the constitutionality of the federal income tax as applied to the salaries of federal judges. In their joint tax return for 1936, Woodrough and his wife disclosed his judicial salary of $12,500 but claimed that it was constitutionally immune from taxation. A deficiency of $631.60 was assessed. Woodrough paid the tax under protest and filed a claim for a refund, which was denied. He then brought suit in the U.S. District Court for the District of Nebraska to recover the amount of the tax. In the Revenue Act of 1932, 49 Stat. 1648, 1657, Congress taxed the salaries of all judges appointed after the date of its enactment. The district court held unconstitutional the application of that tax to Woodrough. The Supreme Court of the United States reversed. *O'Malley v. Woodrough*, 307 U.S. 268, 282 (1939).

54. *Eighth Circuit History*, 56–57. On Faris, see also *Biographical Dictionary*, 88–89; *Judges of the United States*, 158.

55. See Memorial Proceedings, Henry Seth Thomas, September 12, 1962, 314 F2d 3. See also *Eighth Circuit History*, 57–58; *Biographical Dictionary*, 88–89; *Judges of the United States*, 158.

56. Act of May 24, 1940, 54 Stat. 219.

57. See especially Memorial Proceedings for the Honorable Harvey M. Johnsen, St. Louis, March 10, 1976, 527 F2d 7, 20; and C. Arlen Beam, "Chief Justice Harvey M. Johnsen: A Prophet with Honor," *Creight.L.Rev.* 20 (1987): 949, 956. See also *Eighth Circuit History*, 58–59; *Judges of the United States*, 248.

58. See *Eighth Circuit History*, 59–60; *Biographical Dictionary*, 234.

59. See Robert J. Donovan, *Conflict and Crisis: The Presidency of Harry S. Truman, 1945–1948* (1977), 112.

60. See especially Larsen, *Federal Justice in Western Missouri*, 161–63, 208–10. See also *Eighth Circuit History*, 67; *Biographical Dictionary*, 54–55.

61. On Matthes, see Ceremony for Unveiling of Portrait of Chief Judge Marion C. Matthes, St. Louis, January 12, 1987, 822 F2d xciii; *Eighth Circuit History*, 70–71; *Biographical Dictionary*, 179.

62. *Davis v. University of Kansas City*, 129 F. Supp. 716 (W.D.Mo.1955).

63. *Moog Industries v. Federal Trade Commission*, 238 F2d 43 (1956); *Hartman v. Lauchli*, 238 F2d 881 (1956); *United States v. Mills*, 237 F2d 401 (1956).

64. *Eighth Circuit History*, 70.

65. William F. Swindler, *Court and Constitution in the Twentieth Century: The New Legality, 1932–1969* (1970), 286.

66. Leon Friedman, "Charles Whittaker," in *Justices of the Supreme Court*,

1789–1969: Their Lives and Major Opinions, vol. 3, ed. Leon Friedman and Fred L. Israel (1969), 2899–3000.

67. Bernard Schwartz, *Super Chief* (1983), 428.

68. Howard F. Sachs, "Thinking about the Justice," (October 1994), 1 (unpublished manuscript in possession of the author). On Whittaker, in addition to what has already been cited, see Larsen, *Federal Justice in Western Missouri,* 228–34; "In Memoriam: Charles Evans Whittaker," 94 S.Ct. 1 (1975); Schwartz, *Super Chief,* 215–17, 427–28; Clare Cushman, ed., *The Supreme Court Justices: Illustrated Biographies, 1789–1983* (1993), 451. But see Craig Alan Smith, *Failing Justice: Charles Evans Whittaker on the Supreme Court* (2005).

69. Act of February 13, 1925, 43 Stat. 936. See David A. Frederick, *Rugged Justice* (1994), 99.

70. 294 U.S. 240 (1935).

71. *In re Missouri Pacific R. Co.,* 7 F. Supp. 1 (E.D.Mo.1934).

72. Alpheus Thomas Mason, *Harlan Fiske Stone* (1956), 392.

73. 52 Stat. 840.

74. United States Courts for the Second Circuit, Committee on History and Commemorative Events, *The Development of Bankruptcy Law in the Courts of the Second Circuit of the United States* (1995), 13.

75. *Robbins v. Bostian,* 138 F2d 622 (8thC.1943).

76. See the sympathetic opinion of Judge Woodrough in *Ashby v. Francis,* 119 F2d 142 (8thC.1941).

77. *Rawlings v. Ray,* 312 U.S. 97 (1941), *rev'g* 111 F2d 695 (8thC.1940).

78. *Arkansas Corp. Comm. v. Thompson,* 313 U.S. 132 (1941), *rev'g* 116 F2d 179 (8thC.1941).

79. *U.S. National Bank of Omaha v. Pamp,* 77 F2d 9 (8thC.1935).

80. 54 F2d 608 (8thC.1936).

81. *Chicot County Drainage District v. Baxter State Bank,* 308 U.S. 371, 374 (1940).

82. 7 U.S.C.A. 1 et seq.

83. 42 Stat. 163.

84. *Morgan v. United States,* 8 F. Supp. 766 (W.D.Mo.1934).

85. *Morgan v. United States,* 298 U.S. 468 (1936).

86. *Morgan v. United States,* 23 F. Supp. 380, 384 (W.D.Mo.1937).

87. *Morgan v. United States,* 304 U.S. 1, 14–15 (1938).

88. *Id.* at 18.

89. *Morgan v. United States,* 24 F. Supp. 214 (W,D.Mo.1938).

90. *Morgan v. United States,* 307 U.S. 183, 191 (1938).

91. *Morgan v. United States,* 32 F. Supp. 546, 556, 557 (W.D.Mo.1940).

92. *Morgan v. United States,* 313 U.S. 400, 422 (1941).

93. See *KFC v. Nat. Management Corp. v. N.L.R.B.,* 497 F2d 298, 304 (8thC.1974).

94. Florence A. Heffron and Neil McFeeley, *The Administrative Regulatory Process* (1983), 281.

95. *N.L.R.B. v. Jones & Laughlin Steel Co.,* 301 U.S. 1 (1937).

96. *N.L.R.B. v. International Shoe Co.,* 116 F2d 31, 38 (8thC.1941).

97. Frank E. Cooper, "Administrative Law: The 'Substantial Evidence' Rule," *A.B.A.J.* 44 (1958): 470.

98. *Zitserman v. Federal Trade Commission*, 200 F2d 519 (8thC.1952); *State of Iowa v. Federal Power Commission*, 178 F2d 421 (8thC.1949); *Boehm v. United States*, 123 F2d 791 (8thC.1941).

99. *Gibson v. United States*, 149 F2d 751 (8thC.1945), *rev'd* 329 U.S. 388 (1946).

100. *Kimbull Laundry v. United States*, 166 F. 856, 860 (8thC.1948).

101. *Kimball Laundry v. United States*, 228 U.S. 1 (1948).

102. *Porter v. Warner Holding Co.*, 328 U.S. 395, 403, 408 (1946).

103. *Brut v. Warner Holding Co.*, 50 F. Supp. 593 (D.Minn.1943).

104. *Bowles v. Warner Holding Co.*, 151 F2d 529 (8thC.1945).

105. *Bowles v. Skaggs*, 151 F2d 817 (6thC.1945).

106. *Porter v. Warner Holding Co.*, 328 U.S. 395, 398 (1946).

107. *United States v. Baumgartner*, 47 F. Supp. 622 (W.D.Mo.1942).

108. *Baumgartner v. United States*, 138 F2d 29, 35 (8thC.1943).

109. *Id.* at 35, 36.

110. *Baumgartner v. United States*, 322 U.S. 665, 674, 676 (1944).

111. Elizabeth Raasch-Gilman, "Sisterhood in the Revolution: The Holmes Sisters and the Socialist Workers Party," *Minn.Hist.* 56 (Fall 1999): 358.

112. Francis Biddle, *In Brief Authority* (1962), 151–52.

113. *Dunne v. United States*, 138 F2d 137 (8thC.1943).

114. 341 U.S. 494 (1951).

115. 249 U.S. 47 (1919).

116. 268 U.S. 652 (1925).

117. *Dunne v. United States*, 138 F2d 137, 145 (1943).

118. 341 U.S. 494 (1951). See Biddle, *In Brief Authority*, 151–52.

119. See *Toucey v. New York Life Ins. Co.*, 314 U.S. 118, 132, 134 (1941).

120. *Ex Parte Hawk*, 321 U.S. 114, 117 (1944). See also *In re Anderson*, 117 F2d 939, 940 (9thC.1941).

121. 221 U.S. 1 (1911).

122. *United States v. Standard Oil Company of New Jersey*, 47 F2d 288, 297, 310–11 (1931).

123. *Kansas City Star Company v. United States*, 240 F2d 643, 661 (1957). See also Larsen, *Federal Justice in Western Missouri*, 226–28.

124. *Helvering v. Fitch*, 309 U.S. 149 (1940), *rev'g Fitch v. Commissioner of Internal Revenue*, 103 F2d 702 (8thC.1939).

125. *Commissioner v. Gooch*, 320 U.S. 418 (1943), *rev'g* 133 F2d 131 (1943).

126. *F. W. Fitch Co. v. United States*, 323 U.S. 582 (1945), *aff'g* 141 F2d 380 (1944).

127. *Libson Shops v. Koehler*, 353 U.S. 382, 385 (1957), *aff'g* 229 F2d 220 (1956).

128. *Bartels v. Birmingham*, 322 U.S. 126 (1947), *rev'g* 157 F2d 295 (1946).

129. *Tunnel R.R. of St. Louis v. C.I.R.*, 61 F2d 166 (1932).

130. *Peroxide Chemical Co. v. Sheehan*, 108 F2d 306 (1939).

131. *Willcuts v. Bunn*, 282 U.S. 216 (1931), *rev'g* 35 F2d 29 (1929).

132. Lawrence M. Friedman, *Crime and Punishment in American History* (1993), 266; Richard B. Morris and Jeffrey B. Morris, eds., *Encyclopedia of American History*, 7th ed. (1996), 387.

133. *United States v. Clark*, 1 F. Supp. 747 (D.Minn.1931), *aff'd Clark v. United States*, 62 F2d 695 (1932), *aff'd* 289 U.S. 1 (1933).

134. *Foshay v. United States*, 68 F2d 205 (8thC.1933), *cert. den'd* 54 S.Ct. 531 (1933).

135. 139 F2d 967 (1943), *rev'd* 322 U.S. 369 (1944).

136. *Mortensen v. United States*, 139 F2d 967, 969 (1943). See also *Ellis v. United States*, 138 F2d 612 (1943), *rev'd* 322 U.S. 369 (1944).

137. 37 F2d 80, 83 (1929). See also Judge Woodrough's strong opinion as a district judge, holding the use of equity to ban the defendant's bootlegging as violating the right of a jury trial. *United States v. Cunningham*, 37 F2d 349 (1929). And see Judge Gardner in *Perkins v. United States*, 35 F2d 849 (1929).

138. Larsen, *Federal Justice in Western Missouri*, 180.

139. Parrish et al., *Missouri*, 388; Phillips, *Missouri*, 110; Larsen, *Federal Justice in Western Missouri*, 165.

140. John Gunther, *Inside USA* (1947), 346.

141. *United States v. Pendergast*, 28 F. Supp. 601, 602 (Aug. 19, 1939). See also Larsen, *Federal Justice in Western Missouri*, 165.

142. Larsen, *Federal Justice in Western Missouri*, 190.

143. *Walker v. United States*, 93 F2d 383, 389 (1937).

144. See *Walker v. United States*, 93 F2d 383, 393 (8thC.1937); *Luteran v. United States*, 93 F2d 395 (8thC.1937); cf. *Little v. United States*, 93 F2d 401 (8thC.1937).

145. Larsen, *Federal Justice in Western Missouri*, 175.

146. Duane Mayer, *The Heritage of Missouri* (1963), 652–53.

147. *United States v. Pendergast*, 28 F. Supp. 601, 609 (W.D.Mo.1939).

148. Larsen, *Federal Justice in Western Missouri*, 189.

149. *United States v. Pendergast*, 34 F. Supp. 269 (W.D.Mo.1940).

150. *United States v. Pendergast*, 35 F. Supp. 593 (W.D.Mo.1940).

151. *United States v. Pendergast*, 39 F. Supp. 189, 191 (W.D.Mo.1941).

152. *O'Malley v. United States*, 128 F2d 676 (8thC.1942).

153. *O'Malley v. United States*, 317 U.S. 412 (1943).

154. *American Insurance Co. v. Lucas*, 38 F. Supp. 896 (W.D.Mo.1940). See also 38 F. Supp. 826 (W.D.Mo.1941).

155. On the Langer prosecution, see Dan Rylance, "Fred G. Aandahl and the ROC Movement," in *The North Dakota Political Reader*, ed. Thomas W. Howard (1981), 151, 166; Glenn H. Smith, "William Langer and the Art of Personal Politics," in Howard, *The North Dakota Political Reader*, 123, 125; Charles M. Barber, "A Diamond in the Rough: William Langer Examined," *N.D. Hist.* 65 (Fall 1998): 2, 15. Lawrence H. Larsen, "*United States v. Langer, et al.*: The U.S. District of Attorney Files," in *The Centennial Anthology of North Dakota History*, ed. Janet Daley Lysengen and Ann M. Rathke (1996), 329; Wilkins and Wilkins, *North Dakota*, 134; Robinson, *History of North Dakota*, 410; D. Jerome Tweton and Theodore B. Jeliff, *North Dakota: The Heritage of a People* (1976), 158.

156. Robert Vogel, "So I Made a Lot of Enemies of Bill Langer and His Enemies, an Unequal Contest," paper delivered at the Great Plains Historical Conference, Sioux Falls, October 2, 1998, 5 (manuscript in possession of the author). See also Smith, "William Langer and the Art of Personal Politics," 136.

157. Robert Vogel, "The First Conspiracy," 54 (unpublished, undated manuscript in possession of the author).

158. *Langer v. United States,* 76 F2d 817 (1935).

159. Vogel, "So I Made a Lot of Enemies," 7.

160. Smith, "William Langer and the Art of Personal Politics," 136.

161. Robert J. Donovan, *Tumultuous Years: The Presidency of Harry Truman, 1949–1953* (1982), 334.

162. Ibid., 372–81.

163. *Finnegan v. United States,* 204 F2d 105 (8thC.1953).

164. *Connelly v. United States,* 249 F2d 576, 585 (8thC.1957).

165. *Connelly v. United States,* 249 F2d 576 (8thC.1957).

166. 101 F2d 506 (8thC.1939).

167. *Sponenbarger v. United States,* 308 U.S. 256, 265, 266 (1939). Actually, the government never commenced work on the Boeuf Floodway, substituting a different one for it. The work that had already been done afforded Sponenbarger greater, rather than lesser, protection.

168. See *Kleven v. United States,* 240 F2d 270 (8thC.1957).

169. *Joyce v. United States,* 153 F2d 364 (8thC.1946).

170. *Sargent & Co. v. Welco Feed Mfg. Co.,* 195 F2d 929 (8thC.1952).

171. *Stover v. Farmers' Educational and Cooperative Union of America,* 250 F2d 809 (8thC.1958).

172. 48 Stat. 984.

173. F. Cohen, *Handbook of Federal Indian Law* (1982), 146–47; Richman L. Claw, "Tribal Populations in Transition: Sioux Reservations and Federal Policy, 1934–65," *S.D. Hist.* 19 (Fall 1989): 362, 370; Donald L. Parman, "Indians of the Modern West," in *The Twentieth Century West,* ed. Gerald O. Nash and Richard W. Etulain (1989), 155; Stephen L. Pevar, *The Rights of Indians and Tribes* (1983), 5–6.

174. John R. Wunder, *Retained by the People: A History of American Indians and the Bill of Rights* (1974), 79; Cohen, *Handbook of Federal Indian Law,* 165; Parman, "Indians of the Modern West," 161; Deloria, *Of Utmost Good Faith,* 301.

175. Cohen, *Handbook of Federal Indian Law,* 152–53, 156, 157.

176. 67 Stat. B132.

177. P.L.280, 67 Stat. 588.

178. Wunder, *Retained by the People,* 107.

179. Cohen, *Handbook of Federal Indian Law,* 174–75; Pevar, *The Rights of Indians and Tribes,* 6; Wunder, *Retained by the People,* 104–5; Parman, "Indians of the Modern West," 163.

180. 95 F2d 468 (8thC.1938), *aff'd Minnesota v. United States,* 305 U.S. 1939.

181. 129 F. Supp. 15 (1955).

182. Article I, Section 8, Clause 3.

183. *Crow v. Oglala [sic] Sioux Tribe of Pine River Reservation,* 231 F2d 89 (1956).

184. *Missouri Pacific Railroad Co. v. Norwood,* 42 F2d 765 (1930).

4. The Era of the Warren Court, 1956–1969

1. Daniel J. Elazar, *American Federalism: A View from the States* (1972), 233.

2. David B. Danbom, "North Dakota, the Most Midwestern State," in *Heartland,* ed. James H. Madison (1988), 107, 115–16.

3. Cal Ledbetter Jr., "The Antievolution Law: Church and State in Arkansas," *Ark. Hist. Q.* (1979): 299, 302. See also *Epperson v. Arkansas,* 393 U.S. 97 (1968).

4. See, e.g., Roy Reed, *Faubus: The Life and Times of an American Prodigal* (1997), 159.

5. C. Fred Williams et al., eds., *A Documentary History of Arkansas* (1984) (cited hereafter as *Arkansas Documentary History*). Joey McCarty, "The Red Scare in Arkansas: A Southern State and National Hysteria," *Ark. Hist.Q.,* 37 (Autumn 1978): 264, 266–67; Michael B. Dougan, *Arkansas Odyssey* (1994), 515–16, 528, 577. See also Harry S. Ashmore, *Arkansas: A Bicentennial History* (1978), 158.

6. "Unveiling of the Portrait of Judge Gerald W. Heaney, St. Paul, May 11, 1989," lxxxv at xciii (hereafter cited as Heaney Portrait Ceremony); "A Conversation with Justice Blackmun [with Ted Gest]" (n.d.), 10, 24 (hereafter cited as Conversation with Blackmun); Charles E. Lundberg, "Chief Judge Donald P. Lay: Reflections on Appellate Judging after Twenty Years on the Eighth Circuit Court of Appeals," *Minn. Defense* 20 (Fall 1986): 6; Gerald W. Heaney, interview by Jeffrey B. Morris.

7. Handwritten notes taken by Theodore J. Fetter on his interview with Harry Blackmun, in possession of the author.

8. Conversation with Blackmun, 7–8; Myron H. Bright, "Justice Harry Blackmun—Some Personal Recollections," *N.D. L.Rev.* 71 (1995): 7, 10; Memorial Proceedings for the Honorable Pat Mehaffy, St. Louis, September 15, 1991, lxxxi at lxxxiv (hereafter cited as Mehaffy Memorial Proceedings).

9. Conversation with Blackmun, 23.

10. See Memorial Proceedings for the Honorable Harry M. Johnsen, St. Louis, March 10, 1976, 527 F2d 20. Judge C. Arlen Beam has said that Johnsen was so "immersed in the law and his responsibilities as a judge," that he could forget about cashing his paycheck. After he died, the funeral director called in some perplexity when he found some $30,000 in uncashed paychecks in the pocket of the suit Johnsen was to be buried in. C. Arlen Beam, "Chief Justice Harvey M. Johnsen: A Prophet with Honor," *Creight.L.Rev.* 20 (1987): 949, 950–51.

11. Vogel, Myron Bright, John Kelly, and Kermit Bye sat as commissioned judges. Seth W. Richardson, nominated to the Court of Appeals by Herbert Hoover in 1932, but not confirmed, also came from the firm.

12. "Vogel Named Federal Judge," *Fargo Forum,* July 15, 1941, 1.

13. Interview with Robert Vogel [no relative] by Jeffrey B. Morris, October 3, 1998.

14. Memorial Service for the Honorable Charles J. Vogel, St. Paul, June 17, 1981, 648 F2d lxiii, lxvvii, lxxviii–lxxix (response of Myron Bright). In addition to what has already been cited on Judge Vogel, see Harold Chase et al., eds., *Biographical Dictionary of the Federal Judiciary* (1976), 509; Jeffrey B. Morris interview with Mart Vogel, September 25, 1998; Daniel Vogel, September 30, 1998.

15. Letters of William Webster and Marion C. Matthes, quoted in Memorial

Proceedings for the Honorable Martin D. Van Oosterhout, St. Paul, May 15, 1979, 602 F2d 5,7,9 (remarks of Floyd Gibson) (hereafter cited as Van Oosterhout Memorial Proceedings).

16. Gerald W. Heaney, "Judge Martin Donald Van Oosterhout: The Big Judge from Orange City, Iowa," *Iowa L.Rev.* 79 (1979): 1, 13. On Van Oosterhout's appointment, I also relied on handwritten notes taken by Theodore J. Fetter for his history of the Eighth Circuit. Copies of the notes are in my possession.

17. Heaney, "Judge Martin Donald Van Oosterhout," 16.

18. Ibid., 20–21.

19. See, e.g., *Spinelli v. United States*, 382 F2d 871 (en banc, 1967), *rev'd* 393 U.S. 410 (1969); *Parker v. Sigler*, 413 F2d 459 (1969), *vacated Sigler v. Parker*, 396 U.S. 482 (1970).

20. *Holt v. Sarver*, 442 F2d 304 (1971).

21. Heaney, "Judge Martin Donald Van Oosterhout," 1; Walter Nunn, *Arkansas' Judge Pat Hehaffy* (1977), 153; letter of Marion C. Matthes quoted in Van Oosterhout Memorial Proceedings, 9; "A Conversation with the Honorable Myron H. Bright, Senior Circuit Judge, U.S. Court of Appeals for the Eighth Circuit," August 18, 1987, 6 (hereafter cited as Conversation with Bright).

22. Theodore J. Fetter, *A History of the United States Court of Appeals for the Eighth Circuit* (1997), 70–71 (cited hereafter as *Eighth Circuit History*).

23. Ceremony for Unveiling of Portrait of Chief Judge Marion C. Matthes, St. Louis, January 12, 1987, 822 F2d xcii at ci (remarks of Gerald W. Heaney). See also interview of Myron Bright by Jeffrey B. Morris, September 30, 1998.

24. *Aaron v. Cooper*, 257 F2d 33 (1958).

25. Walter Nunn, *Arkansas Judge: Pat Mehaffey* (1977), 158.

26. *Williams v. Kansas City*, 104 F. Supp. 848 (W.D.Mo.1952). See Lorenzo J. Greene, Gary R. Kremer, and Antonio F. Holland, *Missouri's Black Heritage*, revised and updated by Gary R. Kremer and Antonio Holland (1993), 165, 167.

27. In Memoriam: Honorable Albert A. Ridge, 1898–1967, St. Louis, October 13, 1967, 383 F2d 3 at 12 (hereafter cited as Ridge Memorial Ceremony).

28. Ibid., 6–8, 24–26 (remarks of Floyd Gibson). On Ridge, see also Lawrence H. Larsen, *Federal Justice in Western Missouri* (1994), 215.

29. Mehaffy Memorial Proceedings, lxxi.

30. Nunn, *Arkansas Judge*, 140.

31. Ibid., 154–55.

32. Mehaffy Memorial Proceedings, lxxi (remarks of Chief Judge Harry Lay).

33. Ibid., lxxxiv (remarks of Floyd Gibson).

34. *Almanac of the Federal Judiciary*, vol 2. (1997), 19; *Biographical Dictionary of the Federal Judiciary*, 101.

35. "Donald P. Lay," in *Almanac of the Federal Judiciary*, vol. 2 (1997), 25, 27; Douglas O. Linder, "How Judges Judge: A Study of Disagreement on the United States Court of Appeals for the Eighth Circuit," *Ark. L.Rev.* 38 (1985): 479, 542–43.

36. Linder, "How Judges Judge," 541–42.

37. Presentation of the Portrait of the Honorable Donald P. Lay, St. Paul, October 15, 1992, 979 F2d, xci at xcvi (remarks of Theodore McMillian).

38. Ibid., cxii (remarks of Dean Robert Stein). On Donald Lay, see also Amy

Lindgren, "Judge Donald Lay: Absolute Passion for the Law," *Wm. Mitchell*, Summer 1996, 8.

39. Unpublished interview with Judge Gerald Heaney [by Dick Peterson], July 8, 1994, 2 (in possession of the author).

40. Heaney Portrait Ceremony, lxxxviii.

41. Unpublished interview with Judge Gerald Heaney [by Dick Peterson] July 8, 1994, 4 (in possession of the author).

42. Larry Oakes, "Power outside the Spotlight," *Minneapolis Star Tribune*, December 26, 1995, A1.

43. Ibid., A17.

44. Heaney Portrait Ceremony, xci (remarks of Rebecca A. Knittle).

45. Gerald W. Heaney, "A Tribute to Myron H. Bright," *Minn. L.Rev.* 83 (1998): 223; Conversation with Bright, 77.

46. Jo Lee Adamich, Nick Chase, Jennifer Nestle, and Evan Rice, "The Select Cases of Myron H. Bright: Thirty Years of His Jurisprudence," *Minn. L.Rev.* 83 (1998): 239, 240; interview of Myron H. Bright by Jeffrey B. Morris, September 28–29, 1998.

47. Donald P. Lay, "Judge Myron Bright," *Minn. L.Rev.* 83 (1998): 225, 228.

48. Heaney, "Tribute," 223.

49. Conversation with Blackmun, 6; Linda Greenhouse, "Justice Blackmun, Author of Abortion Right, Dies," *New York Times*, March 5, 1999, A1, A18.

50. Nunn, *Arkansas Judge*, 149.

51. See, e.g., *Peterson v. Peterson*, 400 F2d 336, 344 (1969: *Bmun*-Gib-Heaney).

52. Greenhouse, "Justice Blackman," A18.

53. See, e.g., *Esteban v. Central Missouri State College*, 415 F2d 1077 (1968: *Bmun*-Mehaffy/*Lay*).

54. *Maxwell v. Bishop*, 398 F2d 138, 153–54 (1968: *Bmun*-Vogel-Matt). While Blackmun wrote the opinion of the court, his two colleagues did not go along with him when he indicated that he was not personally convinced of the rightness of capital punishment and questioned it as an effective deterrent.

55. 372 F2d 710 (1967).

56. 379 F2d 33 (1967: *Bmun*-Meh-Lay).

57. 404 F2d 571 (1969: *Bmun*-Van–Van Pelt).

58. Interviews by Jeffrey B. Morris of judges of the Court of Appeals for the Eighth Circuit; Nunn, *Arkansas Judge*, 152.

59. Myron H. Bright, "Justice Harry Blackmun: Some Personal Recollections," *N.D.L.Rev.* 71 (1995): 1, 10.

60. Justice Blackmun's Comments before the Judicial Conference on July 15, 1988, 22.

61. Greenhouse, "Justice Blackmun," A1, A18.

62. Each member of the Supreme Court has a miniature library in chambers. The "Judges' Library" is housed on the second floor of the Supreme Court building one floor beneath the main reading room. The main library is open to members of the bar of the Court. By tradition, the "Judges'" is for the use of the justices. When the justices are using that library, other building employees do not.

63. 410 U.S. 113 (1973).

64. Greenhouse, "Justice Blackmun"; Stephen G. Breyer, "Remarks at Memorial Service for Harry Blackmun," Washington, D.C., March 4, 1999, 20 *Sup.Ct.Hist. Soc.* 20, no. 1 (1999): 6–7 (cited hereafter as Blackmun Memorial Service). And see Linda Greenhouse, *Becoming Justice Blackmun* (2005), published after this manuscript was completed.

65. Remarks of William Alden McDaniel Jr. at Blackmun Memorial Service, 19.

66. Quoted in Bright, "Justice Harry Blackmun," 1.

67. David J. Danelski, "The Influence of the Chief Justice in the Decisional Process of the Supreme Court," in *The Federal Judicial System*, ed. Sheldon Goldman and Thomas P. Jahnige (1968), 147–60.

68. 347 U.S. 483 (1954).

69. See, e.g., *Mapp v. Ohio*, 367 U.S. 643 (1961).

70. 42 U.S.C. 1983; *Monroe v. Pape*, 365 U.S. 167 (1961).

71. *Fay v. Noia*, 372 U.S. 391 (1963); *Townsend v. Sain*, 372 U.S. 293 (1963).

72. There is a sharp contrast with the District of Columbia Circuit. See Jeffrey Brandon Morris, *Calmly to Poise the Scales of Justice: A History of the Courts of the District of Columbia Circuit* (2001), 212–13.

73. *White v. United States*, 330 F2d 811, 814 (1964).

74. See Marvin Schick, *Learned Hand's Court* (1970), 167 .

75. *Ashe v. Swenson*, 399 F2d 40, 45 (1968: *Bmun*-Van–Van Pelt).

76. *Ashe v. Swenson*, 397 U.S. 436 (1970).

77. See *Eighth Circuit History*, 66; Act of March 18, 1966, 82 Stat. 183.

78. *Eighth Circuit History*, 86–87.

79. Erin B. Kaheny, "Agenda Change in the U.S. Courts of Appeals, 1925–1988," *Justice System J.* 20 (1999):275, 283.

80. Before the division of the circuit, it contained two other states in which there was state-sponsored segregation, Kansas and Oklahoma.

81. Joel McCarty, "The Red Scare in Arkansas," 264, 278.

82. Dougan, *Arkansas Odyssey*, 371–73.

83. Orville D. Menard, "Tom Dennison, the *Omaha Bee* and the 1919 Omaha Race Riot," *Neb. Hist.* 69 (1987): 152, 159; Michael L. Lawson, "Omaha, a City in Ferment: Summer 1919," *Neb. Hist.* 58 (1977): 395.

84. Annette Atkins, "Minnesota Left of Center and Out of Place," in *Heartland*, ed. James H. Madison (1998), 9, 23.

85. During this period, one of the district judges in the Eighth Circuit, Jacob Trieber, was among the most advanced thinkers on racial civil rights in the federal judiciary. Judge Trieber took guilty pleas in peonage cases, struck down the Arkansas poll tax, and denied demurrers in cases involving indictments against members of the Ku Klux Klan for forcing African Americans to give up their farms and for intimidating a small company into discharging African Americans. See, generally, Gerald W. Heaney, "Jacob Trieber: Lawyer, Politician, Judge," *Univ.Ark.L.Rock L.J.* 8 (1985–86): 421, 439–55.

86. *McCabe v. Atchison, T & S.F. Ry. Co.*, 186 F. 966, 970, 971 (1911).

87. *Id.* at 977, 978. See also Alexander M. Bickel and Benno C. Schmidt Jr., *The*

Judiciary and Responsible Government, 1910–21, Oliver Wendell Holmes Devise History of the Supreme Court of the United States, vol. 9, ed. Paul A. Freund and Stanley N. Katz (1984), 777–78.

88. *McCabe v. Atchison, T & S.F, Ry. Co.,* 235 U.S. 151, 161 (1914). See Bickel and Schmidt, *The Judiciary and Responsible Government,* 775–84. See also *Missouri ex rel Gaines v. Canada,* 305 U.S. 337 (1938).

89. *Guinn v. United States,* 228 F. 103 (8th Cir. Smith-Sanborn, 1915); 238 U.S. 347 (1915); Bickel and Schmidt, *The Judiciary and Responsible Government,* 933–34n95.

90. Bickel and Schmidt, *The Judiciary and Responsible Government,* 958.

91. *Howard v. Thompson,* 72 F. Supp. 695 (W.D.Mo.1947).

92. *Howard v. St. Louis–San Francisco Ry. Co.,* 191 F2d 442, 446 (8thC.1951), *aff'd Brotherhood of R. Trainmen v. Howard,* 343 U.S. 768 (1952).

93. See *Howard v. St. Louis–San Francisco Railway Co.,* 215 F2d 690 (1954); *Howard v. St. Louis–San Francisco Railway Co.,* 244 F.Supp. 1008 (E.D.Mo.1965), *aff'd* 361 F2d 905 (1966). See also *Beal v. Missouri Railroad Co.,* 108 F2d 897 (1940), *rev'd* 312 U.S. 45 (1941).

94. *Morris v. Williams.* 59 F. Supp. 508 (E.D.Ark.1944).

95. *Morris v. Williams,* 149 F2d 703, 707 (8th C.1945).

96. Dougan, *Arkansas Odyssey,* 465–66.

97. On the Little Rock crisis, see Harry S. Ashmore, *Civil Rights and Wrongs* (1994), 133; Roy Reed, *Faubus: The Life and Times of an American Prodigal* (1997); Tony Freyer, *The Little Rock Crisis: A Constitutional Crisis* (1984); David Halberstam, *The Fifties* (1993), 668–69; Herbert Brownell, *Advising Ike* (1993), 198–216, 365–84; Jack Greenberg, *Crusaders in the Courts* (1994), 228.

98. Dougan, *Arkansas Odyssey,* 495.

99. *Arkansas Documentary History,* 238.

100. *Hoxie v. Brewer,* 1 RRLR 43 (E.D.Ark.1955), 1 RRLR 299 (E.D.Ark.1956), *aff'd* 1 RRLR 1027 (8thC.1956). See also Reed, *Faubus,* 182; Ashmore, *Civil Rights and Wrongs,* 113–14; Anthony Lewis and the *New York Times, Portrait of a Decade* (1964), 30.

101. *Aaron v. Cooper,* 143 F. Supp. 855 (E.D.Ark.1956).

102. *Cooper v. Aaron,* 243 F2d 361, 363–64 (1957: *Vogel*-Wood-Van).

103. Years later, Judge Axel John Beck of the District of South Dakota would preside over school desegregation litigation in Arkansas. Peggy J. Teslow, *History of the United States District Court for the District of South Dakota* (1991), 68.

104. Interview of Robert Vogel by Jeffrey B. Morris, October 3, 1998. Davies died at the age of ninety-two in April 1996. *Fargo Forum,* April 19, 1996.

105. Ashmore, *Civil Rights and Wrongs,* 129.

106. Quoted in Dougan, *Arkansas Odyssey,* 500.

107. Frederick S. Calhoun, *The Lawmen* (1989), 262.

108. Freyer, *The Little Rock Crisis,* 109, 111. See also Ashmore, *Civil Rights and Wrongs,* 150, 153; Reed, *Faubus,* 132, 198; Halberstam, *The Fifties,* 672.

109. Ashmore, *Civil Rights and Wrongs,* 121–22; Halberstam, *The Fifties,* 685; Brownell, *Advising Ike,* 56, 119. See also James C. Duram, *A Moderate among Extremists: Dwight D. Eisenhower and the School Desegregation Crisis* (1981).

110. Reed, *Faubus,* 232.

111. See also Freyer, *The Little Rock Crisis,* 108–9.

112. *Faubus v. United States,* 254 F2d 797 (1958: *Sanb*-Wood-John).

113. *Thomason v. Cooper,* 254 F2d 808 (1958: *Sanb*-Wood-John).

114. *Jackson v. Kuhn,* 254 F.2d 555 (1958).

115. *Aaron v. Cooper,* 163 F. Supp. 13 (E.D.Ark.1958).

116. *Aaron v. Cooper,* 357 U.S. 567 (1958).

117. *Aaron v. Cooper,* 257 F2d 33, 40 (1958).

118. *Id.*

119. *Id.* at 40, 41.

120. Freyer, *The Little Rock Crisis,* 152; Ashmore, *Civil Rights and Wrongs,* 132–33.

121. *Aaron v. Cooper,* 358 U.S. 5 (September 12, 1958).

122. 358 U.S. 1 (September 29, 1958).

123. *Id.* at 15, 16, 18.

124. *Aaron v. McKinley,* 173 F. Supp. 944 (W.D.Ark.1959:PC:Sanb-Miller-Beck)

125. *Clark v. Board of Education of Little Rock School District,* 369 F2d 662, 666 (1966: *Fgib*-Vogel-Register).

126. Greenberg, *Crusaders in the Courts,* 255; Anthony Lewis and the *New York Times, Portrait Of A Decade,* 25.

127. *Rogers v. Paul,* 345 F2d 117, 123 (1965: *Matt-Vogel-Meh*).

128. *Rogers v. Paul,* 382 U.S. 198 (1965).

129. *Kemp v. Beasley,* 352 F2d 14, 21 (1965).

130. *Kemp v. Beasley,* 389 F2d 78 (1968).

131. *Kemp v. Beasley,* 423 F2d 851, 858 (1970: *Bmun*-Fgib-Lay).

132. 378 F2d 483, 498 (1967: *Heaney*-Mat-Lay).

133. Ashmore, *Arkansas,* 184.

134. United States Commission on Civil Rights, "School Desegregation at Little Rock, Arkansas," in *Arkansas Documentary History,* 305.

135. "Daisy Bates, Civil Rights Leader, Dies at 84," *New York Times,* November 5, 1999, B11.

136. *Shelton v. McKinley,* 174 F. Supp. 351, 360 (*PC*: Sanb-Miller-Henley).

137. 364 U.S. 479 (1960).

138. *Kyles v. Paul,* 263 F. Supp. 412 (E.D.Ark.Henley1967), *aff'd Daniel v. Paul,* 395 F2d 118 (1968: *Meh*-Van/*Heaney*).

139. 42 U.S.C. 1982.

140. 255 F. Supp. 115 (E.D.Mo.1966).

141. *Jones v. Alfred H. Mayer Co.,* 397 F2d 33 (1967: *Bmun*-Meh-Lay).

142. *United States v. Morris,* 125 F. 322 (E.D.Ark.1903); *Hurd v. Hodge,* 162 F2d 233, 235, 240–41 (1947).

143. *Jones v. Alfred H. Mayer Co.,* 397 F2d 33, 44–45 (1967).

144. *Jones v. Alfred H. Mayer Co.,* 392 U.S. 409 (1968).

145. 82 Stat. 73.

146. Conversation with Blackmun, 16.

147. See, generally, Robert B. Mckay, *Reapportionment: The Law and Politics of Equal Representation* (1965), 422–24. See also 283–85, 323–27, 351–54, 358–63, 365–68, 393–97.

148. Ibid., 422–24.

149. 369 U.S. 186 (1962).

150. Robert G. Dixon Jr., *Democratic Representation: Reapportionment in Law and Politics* (1968), vii–viii, 12.

151. 376 U.S. 1 (1964).

152. 377 U.S. 533 (1964).

153. Indeed, litigation over Minnesota's congressional districting had reached the U.S. Supreme Court as long ago as 1932, when a taxpayer challenged the legality of a legislative attempt to avoid the governor's veto of districting by depositing the law with the secretary of state on the theory that the U.S. Constitution, Article I, Section 4, designated the legislature as a mere agency to carry out the particular duty. The U.S. Supreme Court held that the Legislature's act could not be sustained by virtue of any authority conferred by the federal Constitution on the legislature of Minnesota to create congressional districts independently of the governor. *Smiley v. Holm*, 285 U.S. 355 (1932).

154. *Magraw v. Donovan*, 159 F. Supp. 901, 903 (D.Minn.Devitt1958); 163 F. Supp. 184 (D.Minn.PC: Sanb-Bell-Devitt 1958); 177 F. Supp. 803 (D.Minn.Bell 1959).

155. *Honsey v. Donovan*, 236 F. Supp. 8, 20 (D.Minn.1964).

156. *Id.* at 21.

157. *Honsey v. Donovan*, 249 F. Supp. 987 (D.Minn.1966). See William E. Lass, *Minnesota: A History*, 2nd. ed. (1988), 271; Dixon, *Democratic Representation*, 346–49.

158. *League of Nebraska Municipalities v. Marsh*, 209 F. Supp. 189, 196 (1962).

159. *League of Nebraska Municipalities v. Marsh*, 232 F. Supp. 411, 413 (D.Neb.1964).

160. *League of Nebraska Municipalities v. Marsh*, 242 F. Supp. 357 (D.Neb.1965).

161. *Id.* at 361, 362.

162. *Carpenter v. State*, 139 N.W.2d 541 (1966); *League of Nebraska Municipalities v. Marsh*, 253 F. Supp. 27 (D.Neb.1966).

163. Dorothy Schweider, *Iowa: The Middle Land* (1996), 293–94, 297–301.

164. *Davis v. Synhorst*, 217 F. Supp. 492, 501 (1963).

165. *Davis v. Synhorst*, 225 F. Supp. 689 (S.D.Iowa.1964).

166. *Hill v. Davis*, 378 U.S. 565 (1964).

167. *Davis v. Synhorst*, 231 F. Supp. 540 (S.D.Iowa 1964).

168. *Davis v. Cameron*, 238 F. Supp. 462 (S.D.Iowa 1965).

169. *Kruidenier v. McCulloch*, 142 N.W.2d 355 (1966), *cert. den'd* 385 U.S. 851 (1966). Schweider, *Iowa*, 300–301. In Missouri, after *Reynolds v. Sims*, a three-judge court held unconstitutional the apportionment of each house of the legislature in 1964 but ultimately upheld plans submitted by commission. Congressional districting was struck down several times, before an acceptable districting was upheld. In Arkansas, both state legislative and congressional lines were struck down by a three-judge court before ultimately being approved. In North Dakota, there had been a challenge to legislative apportionment before *Baker v. Carr*. The federal court stayed its hand to allow the Supreme Court of North Dakota to pass on questions of state law. The three-judge court struck down a proposal put forward by

a commission constituted of members representing all three branches of the state government. After considerable delay in order to permit the legislature to act, the district court twice struck down legislative plans and then ordered its own plan, which divided the state into thirty-nine legislative districts, none of which varied as much as 15 percent from the population ratio. During this process, Judge Ronald N. Davies dissented consistently from the decisions of Circuit Judge Vogel and District Judge George S. Register. Robert B. Mckay, *Reapportionment: The Law and Politics of Equal Representation* (1965), 283–85, 358–63, 393–97, 611.

170. 391 U.S. 367 (1968).

171. *Smith v. United States*, 249 F. Supp. 515 (S.D.Iowa 1966), *aff'd* 368 F2d 529 (1966: *PC*: Vogel-Matt-Duncan). See also *United States v. Miller*, 367 F2d 72 (2ndC.1966).

172. 258 F. Supp. 971 (S.D.Iowa 1966).

173. On Van Oosterhout's vote, see Heaney, "Judge Martin Donald Van Oosterhout," 1, 23.

174. *Tinker v. Des Moines Independent Community School District*, 393 U.S. 503, 506 (1969).

175. *Id*. at 513.

176. For example, in *Turley v. Adel Community School District*, 322 F. Supp. 403 (S.D.Iowa 1971), Judge William C. Hanson held unconstitutional a public-school hair-length regulation, stating that the individual right to govern one's appearance is constitutionally protected.

177. John W. Johnson, *The Struggle for Student Rights* (1997), 207.

178. Ibid., 212. See *New Jersey v. T.L.O.*, 469 U.S. 325 (1985); *Fraser v. Bethel S.D. No. 403*, 478 U.S. 675 (1986); *Hazelwood School District v. Kuhlmeier*, 484 U.S. 260 (1988). *Hazelwood*, an Eighth Circuit case, is discussed in chapter 6.

179. Conversation with Bright, 8.

180. 410 F2d 89 (1969), *rev'g* 284 F. Supp. 93 (S.D.Iowa Stephenson).

181. 410 F2d 557 (1969).

182. *Luros v. United States*, 389 F2d 200 (1968: *Lay*-Vogel-Fgib), *aff'g* 260 F. Supp. 697 (N.D.Iowa Hanson1966).

183. The first two quotations are at *id*. at 204; the third is *id*. at 206.

184. Within twenty-four months of *Gideon v. Wainwright*, 372 U.S. 335 (1963), the landmark case requiring counsel in felony cases, Minnesota, Missouri, Nebraska, and North Dakota all expanded or improved their systems of assigned counsel. In *Bosler v. Swenson*, 363 F2d 154 (1967), the Court of Appeals, applying a Supreme Court decision retroactively, held that defendants in Missouri had to be assigned counsel on appeal. The Supreme Court affirmed. *Swenson v. Bosler*, 386 U.S. 996 (1967).

185. Kaheny, "Agenda Change," 280–82.

186. *United States v. Pope*, 251 F. Supp. 234 (D.Neb.1966).

187. 214 F2d 862 (1954).

188. *Voss v. United States*, 259 F2d 699, 703 (1958); *Dusky v. United States*, 271 F2d 385, 395, 401 (1959), and 295 F2d 743, 759 (1961). See also *Feguer v. United States*, 302 F2d 214, 243 (1962: *Bmun*-Vogel-Van).

189. *Pope v. United States*, 372 F2d 710, 735 (1967).

190. The 1843 decision of the Court of King's Bench in *M'Naghten's Case*, 10 Clark & F 200 (1943), formulated what became the standard rule for the issue of criminal insanity. Under *M'Naghten*, the trial judge charged: "Whether the accused was labouring under such a defect of reason from disease of the mind as not to know the nature and quality of the act he was doing, or, if he did know it, that he did not know right from wrong."

191. *Pope v. United States*, 392 U.S. 651 (1968).

192. *Maxwell v. Stephens*, 229 F. Supp. 205 (E.D.Ark.1964), *aff'd* 348 F2d 325 (1965), *cert. den'd* 382 U.S. 994 (1965).

193. *Maxwell v. Bishop*, 250 F. Supp. 710 (E.D.Ark.Henley1966), *aff'd* 398 F2d 138 (1968: *Bmun*-Vogel-Matt), *vac. & rem.* 398 U.S. 262 (1970).

194. *Maxwell v. Bishop*, 398 F2d 138, 147 (1968).

195. *Furman v. Georgia*, 408 U.S. 238, 406 (1972); *Callins v. Collins*, 510 U.S. 1141, 1143, 1145 (1994).

196. 382 F2d 871 (1967: *Fgib*-Vogel-Matt-Bmun-Meh-Lay/*Heaney*-Van), *rev'd* 393 U.S. 410 (1969).

197. 378 U.S. 108 (1964).

198. *Spinelli v. United States*, 382 F2d 871, 880 (1967).

199. *Id.* at 898 (1967).

200. *Spinelli v. United States*, 393 U.S. 410, 415 (1969).

201. *Id.* at 416.

202. *Spinelli* at 429, 433.

203. *Illinois v. Gates*, 462 U.S. 213 (1983).

204. Heaney Portrait Ceremony, cv.

205. Kaheny, "Agenda Change," 291. *Poolman v. Poolman*, 289 F2d 332 (1961: *Sanborn*-Van-Matt), was among the more interesting bankruptcy cases.

206. Kaheny, "Agenda Change," 291. *Nordstrom v. United States*, 360 F2d 734 (1966: *Fgib*-Matt-Meh), was among the more interesting tax cases.

207. Kaheny, "Agenda Change," 285.

208. *National Dairy Products Corp. v. United States*, 350 F2d 321, 338 (1965: *Matt*-John-Vogel).

209. *Albrecht v. Herald Company*, 367 F2d 517, 522 (1966: *Meh*-Matt-Fgib).

210. *Albrecht v. Herald Company*, 390 U.S. 145, 152 (1968). See also 389 U.S. 805 (1967), 389 U.S. 910 (1967), in which the newspaper sought to convince the Supreme Court not to hear the case. See also *Herald Co. v. Harper*, 293 F. Supp. 1101 (E.D.Mo.Duncan1969), *aff'd* 410 F2d 125 (1969: Matt-Meh-Lay), a suit against three judges of the Eastern District of Missouri to prevent them from complying with the Supreme Court mandate and to convene a three-judge court to consider the constitutionality of the treble damage provision of the antitrust law.

211. 339 F2d 45 (1964: *Vogel*-Matt-Ridge).

212. 384 U.S. 316 (1966).

213. 326 F2d 535 (1964: *Fgib*-Matt-John), *rev'd F.P.C. v. Union Electric Co.*, 381 U.S. 90 (1965).

214. For similar cases, see *Travelers Health Association v. F.T.C.*, 262 F2d 241 (1959: *Sanb*-John/*Vogel*), *rev'd* 362 U.S. 293 (1960); *Amerada Petroleum v. F.P.C.*, 334 F2d 404 (1964: *Meh*-Van-Ridge), *rev'd* 379 U.S. 687 (1965).

215. Kaheny, "Agenda Change," 286.

216. Martin Shapiro, *The Supreme Court and Administrative Agencies* (1968), 177–78.

217. 333 F2d 529 (1964: *Matt*-Vogel-Bmun) reversing Floyd Gibson, 216 F. Supp. 272 (W.D.Mo.1963).

218. 336 F2d 110 (1964: *Mehaffy*-Van-Ridge).

219. The two cases were consolidated by the Supreme Court and reported as *Graham v. John Deere Company of Kansas City*, 383 U.S. 1 (1966).

220. Shapiro, *The Supreme Court*, 221.

221. Mark W. T. Harvey, "The Northern Plains and the Missouri Valley Authority," in *The Centennial Anthology of North Dakota History*, ed. Janet Daley Lysengen and Ann M. Rathke (1996), 376, 377; Donald J. Pisani, "The Irrigation District and the Federal Relationship: Neglected Aspects of Water History," in *The Twentieth Century West*, ed. Gerald O. Nash and Richard W. Etulain (1989), 257, 264.

222. *Arkansas Documentary History*, 272, 278; Dougan, *Arkansas Odyssey*, 512.

223. 400 F2d 378 (1968: *Vogel*-Bmun-Lay).

224. 416 F2d 65, 66 (1965: *Bright*-Matt-Fgib).

225. 300 F2d 617 (1962: *Matt*-Sanb-Ridge).

226. 420 F2d 324 (1970: *Lay*-Bmun-Meh).

227. 400 F2d 585 (1968: *Heaney*-Van-Register).

228. 410 F2d 38 (1969: *Heaney*-Bmun-Meh).

229. 400 F2d 383, 385 (1968: *Heaney*-Meh-Fgib).

230. 282 F2d 302 (1960: *Bmun*-Sanborn-Matt).

231. See *Joseph A. Bass Co. v. United States*, 340 F2d 842 (1965: *Matt*-Vogel-Ridge).

5. The Moderately Liberal Court of the 1970s

1. Mark Friedberger, "The Modernization of Iowa's Agricultural Structure," in *Iowa History Reader*, ed. Marvin Bergman (1996), 375, 380; Dorothy Schweider, *Iowa: The Middle Land* (1996), 316.

2. Walter Nugent, *Into the West* (1999), 335–37. See also Robert P. Wilkins and Wynona Huchette Wilkins, *North Dakota: A Bicentennial History* (1977), 129; D. Jerome Tweton, "The Future of North Dakota: An Overview," *N.D.Hist.* 56 (1989): 7, 8.

3. David B. Danbom, "Postscript," in Elwyn B. Robinson, *History of North Dakota* (1995), 588; David B. Danbom, "North Dakota: The Most Midwestern State," in *Heartland* ed. James H. Madison (1988), 115–16; D. Jerome Tweton and Theodore B. Jelliff, *North Dakota: The Heritage of a People* (1976), 176–77; Warren A. Beck and Ynez D. Haaze, *Historical Atlas of the American West* (1989), 59.

4. Mark Friedberger, "The Modernization of Iowa's Agricultural Structure," in *Iowa History Reader*, ed. Marvin Bergman (1996), 375, 380; David B. Danbom, "The Future of Agriculture in North Dakota," *N.D.Hist.* 56 (Winter 1989): 31, 32, 37; Schweider, *Iowa*, 316.

5. Theodore J. Fetter, *A History of the United States Court of Appeals for the Eighth Circuit* (1977), 66 (cited hereafter as *Eighth Circuit History*).

6. Omnibus Judgeship Act, P.L. 95–486, 92 Stat. 1629. See also Edward A. Tamm

and Paul C. Reardon, "Warren E. Burger and the Administration of Justice," *B.Y.U. L. Rev.* (1981): 447; Alvin B. Rubin, "Bureaucratization of the Federal Courts: Tension between Justice and Efficiency," *Notre Dame L. Rev.* 55 (1980): 648.

7. Jeffrey B. Morris, *Federal Justice in the Second Circuit* (1987), 168.

8. 28 U.S.C. 332 (e) (1971).

9. Unpublished, unattributed memorandum entitled "Circuit Executive's Office" (c. 1997) (in possession of the author).

10. Timothy E. Gannon, "The Central Staff Attorney's Office in the United States Court of Appeals, Eighth Circuit: A Five Year Report," *S.D.L.Rev.* 29 (1984): 457; memoranda from Kim P. Jones to Gerald W. Heaney, January 8, 1999, and December 13, 1990, in the possession of the author.

11. The first professionally trained librarian in the history of the Eighth Circuit, Patricia Rodi (later Patricia Rodi Monk), was hired in 1971. The Eighth Circuit was the first authorized by Congress to hire someone to perform the functions of a librarian. In 1896, Congress authorized it to hire someone to perform the duties of librarian, crier, and messenger. Congress did not provide this authority for all the circuits until 1948. From 1938 to 1964, (Colonel) Allen Rothwell served as "court crier and librarian" and also assisted the judges in robing. Ann T. Fessenden, "U.S. Court of Appeals for the Eighth Circuit Library," *Show Me Libraries* 38 (September 1989): 13.

12. Oral History of the Honorable Donald R. Ross, 14 (by Richard Shugrue, n.d.) (unpublished copy in the possession of the author).

13. Ibid., 16–17.

14. Ceremonial Session, United States Court of Appeals for the Eighth Circuit, Presentation of the Portrait of the Honorable Donald R. Ross, Omaha, October 30, 1987, 843 F2d xcii–iii, ciii (hereafter cited as Ross Portrait Presentation); Douglas O. Linder, "How Judges Judge: A Study of Disagreement on the United States Court of Appeals for the Eighth Circuit," *Ark. L.Rev.* 38 (1985): 479.

15. George Mills and Richard W. Peterson, *No One Is above the Law: The Story of Southern Iowa's Federal Court* (n.d.), 67; John W. Johnson, *The Struggle for Student Rights*, 79–80, 99–100; U.S. Court of Appeals Eighth Circuit, Special Ceremonial Session in Commemoration of the Honorable Roy L. Stephenson, Des Moines, November 17, 1982, 696 F2d lxxxv.

16. *Eighth Circuit History*, 78.

17. Oral History of Judge H. Smith Henley (by Francis M. Ross, March 23–24, 1987), 1:8, 16 (hereafter cited as Henley Oral History).

18. Henley Oral History, 2:27.

19. He also appears to have been considered for the vacancy Ross filled in 1971.

20. Henley Oral History, 2:19, 26.

21. See Unveiling of the Portrait of Judge J. Smith Henley, [St. Louis], January 17, 1985, 783 F2d lxxv; "Judge Who Reformed Prison System Dies," *Arkansas Democrat-Gazette*, October 20, 1997, A2.

22. Henley Oral History, 2:3, 7; Linder, "How Judges Judge," 538.

23. Interview of Judge Myron Bright by Jeffrey B. Morris, September 28–29, 1998.

24. Lorenzo J. Greene, Gary Kremer, and Antonio F. Holland, *Missouri's Black*

Heritage, ed. G. Kremer and A. Holland (1993), 22; Norman S. London, "Tribute to Judge Theodore McMillian," *Wash.U. J. Urb. & Contemp. L.* 52 (1979): 35.

25. On McMillian, see Richard S. Arnold, "Tribute to Judge Theodore McMillian," *J. U. J. Urb & Contemp. L.* 52 (1997): 23, 25; Karen L. Tokarz, "Tribute to Judge Theodore McMillian," *Wash. U. L. J. Urb & Contemp L.* 52 (1997): 5, 13. See also Terry Winkelman, "Profile of the Times: Judge Theodore McMillian," *St. Louis Times,* February 1996.

26. Morris S. "Buzz" Arnold, "The Arnolds of Southwest Arkansas," *Ark. Law.,* July 1984, 136.

27. *The Third Branch* 30, no. 3 (March 1998).

28. Stuart Taylor Jr., "Taking Issue: Arnold, Class of the Field," *Legal Times,* April 25, 1994, 23; "Arnold to Step Down as Chief Judge for U.S. Appeals Court," *Arkansas Democrat-Gazette,* January 29, 1998. On Arnold, see also Donald Lay, "My Colleague Richard S. Arnold," *Minn. L. Rev.* 78 (1993): 25; Phyllis D. Brandon, "High Profile: Richard Sheppard Arnold," *Arkansas Democrat-Gazette,* March 23, 1997.

29. "Judge Alfred T. Goodwin: An Oral History" (by Rick Harmon, 1985–86), *W.LegalHist.* 4 (1991): 27, 32–35; see also Robert A. Kagan, "The Political Constructing of American Adversarial Legalism," in *Courts and the Political Process,* ed. Austin Ranney (1996), 19, 35.

30. Erin B. Kaheny, "Agenda Change in the U.S. Court of Appeals, 1925–1988," *Just. Sys. J.* 20 (1999): 275, 279.

31. *Pfizer, Inc. v. Lord,* 550 F2d 396, 400 (1976), *aff'd* 434 U.S. 308 (1978). The original panel was Judges Lay, Ross (concurring), and Stephenson. In the en banc Judges Webster and Floyd Gibson joined Judge Lay's majority and Judge Ross's concurring opinion, while Judges Heaney and Stephenson just joined Lay. Judges Bright and Henley dissented. In another opinion in the litigation, *Pfizer, Inc. v. Lord,* 522 F2d 612 (1975: *Lay*-Fgib-Ross), the court of appeals panel held that the plaintiff governments could not sue *parens patriae* on behalf of their citizens, but left open the possibility of a class action.

32. 543 F2d 606 (1976: *Lay*-Fgib-Webster).

33. *Mackey v. National Football League,* 407 F. Supp. 1000 (D.Minn.Larson 1975).

34. In another "sports page" case, the court of appeals in *Kansas City Baseball Corp. v. Major League Baseball Players Ass'n.,* 532 F2d 615 (1976: *Heaney*-Fgib-Steph), upheld an arbitration award freeing pitchers Andy Messersmith and Dave McNally (of the Los Angeles Dodgers and Montreal Expos respectively) of their obligations under the Reserve Clause and making them free agents, who could contract with any major-league team.

35. *Butz v. Glover Livestock Commission, Inc.,* 411 U.S. 182 (1973), rev'g *Glover Livestock Commission v. Hardin,* 454 F2d 109 (1972: *Steph*-Lay-Heaney).

36. *North Dakota State Wheat Commission v. United States,* 565 F2d 621 (1977: Henley-Fgib-Heaney).

37. *Alexander v. Holmes County Board of Education,* 396 U.S. 19, 20 (1969).

38. Michael B. Dougan, *Arkansas Odyssey* (1994), 615.

39. Henley Oral History, 1:132.

40. United States Commission on Civil Rights, "School Desegregation in Little Rock, Arkansas" (1977), reprinted in *A Documentary History of Arkansas,* vol. 1, ed. C. Fred Williams et al. (1994), 302, 305.

41. *Swann v. Charlotte-Mecklenburg Board of Education,* 402 U.S. 1 (1971).

42. 418 U.S. 717 (1974).

43. 433 U.S. 406 (1977).

44. *Booker v. School District No. 1, Minneapolis, Minn.,* 351 F. Supp. 799 (D.Minn. Larson 1972).

45. *Id.* The description is based on Judge Henley's opinion in *Booker v. Special School District No. 1,* 585 F2d 347 (1978: Henley-Fgib-Ross).

46. *Booker v. Special School District No. 1, Minneapolis,* 451 F. Supp. 659 (D.Minn. Larson 1978).

47. *Special School District No. 1, Minneapolis v. Booker,* 443 U.S. 915 (1979).

48. Frederick C. Luebke, *Nebraska: An Illustrated History* (1995), 333.

49. *United States v. School District of Omaha,* 389 F. Supp. 293 (D.Neb. Schatz 1974).

50. *United States v. School District of Omaha,* 521 F2d at 530, 536 (1975), *cert. den'd* 423 U.S. 946 (1975).

51. *United States v. School District of Omaha,* 521 F2d at 530, 535–37, 546 (1975).

52. *United States v. School District of Omaha,* 418 F. Supp. 22 (D.Neb. Schatz 1976).

53. *United States v. School District of Omaha,* 541 F2d 708 (1976: PC: Fgib-Lay-Heaney-Br-Ross-Steph-Web-Henley).

54. *School District of Omaha v. United States,* 433 U.S. 667, 668 (1977).

55. *United States v. School District of Omaha,* 565 F2d 127 (1977).

56. Greene, Kremer, and Holland, *Missouri's Black Heritage,* 174.

57. Ibid., 180, 219.

58. Gerald W. Heaney, untitled draft manuscript about St. Louis school desegregation (2000), chap. 1, p. 11 (copy in possession of the author) (hereafter cited as Heaney Manuscript).

59. Ibid., 25.

60. Ibid., 33–34.

61. Paul C. Nagel, *Missouri: A Bicentennial History* (1977), 172; Marc Carnes and John A. Garraty, *Mapping America's Past* (1996), 205.

62. *Missouri ex rel Gaines v. Canada,* 305 U.S. 337 (1938); Richard Kluger, *Simple Justice* (1976), 289.

63. William E. Parrish et al., *Missouri: The Heart of the Nation,* 336; Greene, Kremer, and Holland, *Missouri's Black Heritage,* 168, 175.

64. On school segregation in Missouri, see Linda Brown-Kubisch and Christine Montgomery, "Show Me Missouri History: Celebrating the Century (Part I)," *Mo. Hist. Rev.* 114 (2000): 176, 195.

65. Greene, Kremer, and Holland, *Missouri's Black Heritage,* 169.

66. Ibid., 213; Parrish et al., *Missouri,* 355.

67. Heaney Manuscript, chap. 5, p. 14 (based on the written stipulation of facts

filed by the parties on June 7, 1974, in *Liddell v. Caldwell,* 469 F. Supp. 1304, 1312 [1979]).

68. Heaney Manuscript, chap. 5, p. 1.

69. Ibid.

70. *Liddell v. Board of Education,* 469 F. Supp. 1304, 1387 (E.D.Mo.1979).

71. *Liddell v. Caldwell,* 546 F2d 768 (1976: *Lay*-Br-T.Smith), stay denied 430 U.S. 906 (1977).

72. *Liddell v. Board of Education,* 469 F. Supp. 1304 (E.D.Mo.1979).

73. *Adams v. United States,* 620 F2d 1277 (1980 EB).

74. *Liddell v. Board of Education,* 491 F. Supp. 351 (E.D.Mo.1980).

75. *Id.* at 358.

76. *Liddell v. Board of Education,* 508 F. Supp. 101 (E.D.Mo.1980).

77. American Civil Liberties Union of Eastern Missouri, "A Study of the Civil Rights and Liberties Decisions of the United States Court of Appeals of the Eighth Circuit, 1965–77" (September 1979), 14–15, (hereafter cited as ACLU Study).

78. 433 F2d 421 (1970: Br-Vogel-Lay).

79. 463 F2d 337 (1972: Br-Lay[c]/John), *aff'd* 411 U.S. 792 (1973).

80. *Parham v. Southwestern Bell Telephone Co.,* 433 F2d 421, 426 (1970).

81. Jo Lee Adamich et al., "The Selected Cases of Myron H. Bright: Thirty Years of His Jurisprudence," *Minn. L. Rev.* 83 (1973): 239, 287.

82. Ibid., 289.

83. Donald P. Lay, "Judge Myron Bright," *Minn. L.Rev.* 83 (1998): 225, 227.

84. *Green v. McDonnell Douglas,* 463 F2d 337, 353 (1972).

85. Adamich et al., "Selected Cases," 294n274.

86. *Green v. McDonnell-Douglas,* 463 F2d 337, 353 (1972).

87. *Green v. McDonnell-Douglas Corp.,* 411 U.S. 792, 802 (1973).

88. During this period, the Eighth Circuit also handled important cases dealing with the remedy for longtime discrimination against minority firefighters in Minneapolis and St. Louis. See *Carter v. Gallagher,* 452 F2d 315 (1971); *Firefighters Institute for Racial Equality v. City of Minneapolis,* 616 F2d 350 (1980).

89. *Reed v. Reed,* 404 U.S. 71 (1971). See also *Phillips v. Martin Marietta Corp.,* 400 U.S. 542 (1971), a statutory case.

90. Compare *Frontiero v. Richardson,* 411 U.S. 677 (1973), with *Craig v. Boren,* 429 U.S. 57 (1975).

91. Ruth Ann Alexander, "A Federalist Memoir, 1964–1989," *S.D.Hist.* 19 (1989): 539, 543.

92. ACLU Study, 19.

93. 612 F2d 1079 (1980: *Steph*-Fgib-Henley), *aff'g* 462 F. Supp. 952 (N.D.Iowa McManus 1979).

94. 477 F2d 1292 (1973: *Heaney*-Lay-Steph), *aff'g* 342 F. Supp. 1224 (D. Minn. Lord 1972).

95. *State of Missouri v. National Organization for Women, Inc.,* 467 F. Supp. 289 (W.D.Mo.1979), *aff'd.* 620 F2d 1301, 1304 (1980: *Steph*-Henley/Fgib), *cert. denied* 449 U.S. 842 (1980).

96. *State of Missouri v. National Organization for Women, Inc.,* 620 F2d 1301,

1319, 1324. But see *Junior Chamber of Commerce of Kansas City v. Missouri State Junior Chamber of Commerce*, 508 F2d 1031 (1975: *Ross*-Fgib/Heaney).

97. 410 U.S. 183 (1973).

98. 410 U.S. 179 (1973).

99. Peter Irons, *The Courage of her Convictions* (1990), 271.

100. Ibid., 256.

101. *Doe v. Randall*, 314 F. Supp. 32 (D.Minn.1970: *Devitt*-Neville/Vogel[d]).

102. *Doe v. Randall*, 314 F. Supp. 32, 36 (D.Minn.1970: *Devitt*-Neville[c]-Vogel[c]).

103. Irons, *Courage*, 258, 261. After *Roe v. Wade*, Hodgson, then working in Washington, went to see Blackmun to congratulate him (271).

104. James C. Mohr, "Iowa's Abortion Battles of the Late 1960s and Early 1970s: Long-Term Perspectives and Short-Term Analyses," in *Iowa History Reader*, ed. Marvin Bergman (1996), 411, 430.

105. *Doe v. Turner*, 361 F. Supp. 1288 (1973: *Hanson*-Lay-Stuart), appeal dismissed *Doe v. Turner*, 488 F2d 1134 (1973: *PC*: Meh-Gib-Steph).

106. *Nyberg v. City of Virginia*, 495 F2d 1342, 1344–45 (February 19, 1974: *Steph*-Br-Stuart), *aff'g* 361 F. Supp. 932 (D. Minn. Neville Aug. 10, 1973). The Supreme Court dismissed the appeal in the case at 419 U.S. 891 (1974).

107. *Nyberg v. City of Virginia*, 495 F2d 1342, 1347, 1348 (1973).

108. *Nyberg v. City of Virginia*, 667 F2d 754 (1982: *Lay*-Hunter/*Heaney*).

109. *Doe v. Poelker*, 515 F2d 541, 547 (1975).

110. 495 F2d 1349 (February 20, 1974: *Steph*-Br-Stuart).

111. *Doe v. Poelker*, 515 F2d 541, 548 (1975: *Ross*-T.Smith/Van [c/d]). See also 497 F2d 1063 (1974: *Ross*-Br-T.Smith).

112. *Doe v. Poelker*, 515 F2d 541, 544 (1975).

113. 432 U.S. 464 (1977).

114. *Poelker v. Doe*, 432 U.S. 519, 521 (1977).

115. 508 F2d 1211 (1974: *Steph*-Matt-Ross).

116. *Singleton v. Wulff*, 428 U.S. 106 (1976).

117. *Lehocky v. Curators of the University of Missouri*, 558 F2d 887 (1997: PC: Heaney-Ross-Steph), *aff'g* 422 F. Supp. 124 (E.D.Mo.1976).

118. *Planned Parenthood of Minnesota v. State of Minnesota*, 612 F2d 359 (1980: *Lay*-Br-Henley).

119. *Hodgson v. Board of County Commissioners, County of Hennepin*, 614 F2d 601 (1980: Steph-Ross/*McManus*); *Reproductive Health Services v. Freeman*, 614 F2d 585 (1980: *Steph*-Ross-McManus[c]).

120. *Planned Parenthood of Central Missouri v. Danforth*, 392 F. Supp. 1362 (E.D.Mo.: Harper-Wangelin/Web[c/d] 1974), *aff'd/rev'd/rem* 428 U.S. 53 (1976). See also *Rodgers v. Danforth*, printed as an addendum to *Wulff v. State Board of Registration*, 380 F. Supp. 1137 at 1145 (1973: Fgib-Hunter-Collinson), *aff'd Rodgers v. Danforth*, 414 U.S. 1035 (1973). And see *Wulff v. State Board of Registration for the Healing Arts*, 380 F. Supp. 1137 (1974: PC: Harper-Meredith-Web), *rev'd Wulff v. Singleton*, 508 F2d 1211 (1974: *Steph*-Matt-Ross), *rev'd rem. Singleton v. Wulff*, 428 U.S. 106 (1976).

121. *Planned Parenthood of Central Missouri v. Danforth*, 392 F. Supp. 1362, 1374 (1976).

122. *Planned Parenthood v. Danforth*, 428 U.S. 52 (1976).

123. *Munson v. Janklow*, 563 F2d 933 (1976: *Devitt*-Fgib-Heaney[c]), *aff'g* 421 F. Supp. 544 (D.S.D.1976).

124. *Planned Parenthood of Minnesota, Inc. v. Citizens for Community Action*, 558 F2d 861, 864 (1977: *Fgib*-Web-Henley).

125. See *Women's Services, P.C. v. Thone*, 636 F2d 206 (1980: PC: Ross-Fgib-Sachs), *aff'g* 483 F. Supp. 1022 (D.Neb. Urbom 1979), *vacated & rem'd* 452 U.S. 911 (1981), 690 F2d 606 (1982: PC: Ross-McM-RArn).

126. *Freiman v. Ashcroft*, 440 F. Supp. 1193, 1194–95 (1977: PC: Wangelin-Nangle/Web[c]), *aff'd* 584 F2d 247, 252 (1978: *Steph*-Henley-Ingraham).

127. *United States v. Drury*, 582 F2d 1181 (1978: *Ingraham[5th C.]*-Bright-Steph).

128. *United States v. Brown*, 540 F2d 364 (1976: *Web*-Fgib-Heaney).

129. *State v. Williams*, 182 N.W.2d 396 (1970).

130. *Id.* at 406, 408.

131. *Williams v. Brewer*, 375 F. Supp. 170, 183 (1974).

132. *Williams v. Brewer*, 509 F2d 227, 233 (1974).

133. *Id.* at 236.

134. 384 U.S. 436 (1976).

135. *Brewer v. Williams*, 430 U.S. 387, 398 (1977).

136. *Id.* at 416, 416–17.

137. *Brewer v. Williams*, 430 U.S. 387 at 407 n. 12.

138. *State v. Williams,* 285 N.W.2d 248, 258 (Iowa 1979).

139. *Williams v. Nix*, 528 F. Supp. 664 (S.D.Iowa 1981).

140. *Williams v. Nix*, 700 F2d 1164 (1983: *RArn*-Heaney-Henley).

141. Judges Lay, McMillian, Arnold, and Henley voted not to rehear. *Williams v. Nix*, 700 F2d 1164, 1175 (1983).

142. *Nix v. Williams*, 467 U.S. 431, 445 (1984). Williams had been permitted to represent in federal court a state prisoner, Jasper Falkner, who had been beaten by jailers at Council Bluffs in 1978. Falkner was awarded damages of $1,000. Mills and Peterson, *No One Is above the Law*, 94–5.

143. Jeffrey B. Morris, *Federal Justice in the Second Circuit* (1987), 185–86.

144. Malcolm M. Feeley and Edward L. Rubin, *Judicial Policy Making and the Modern State: How the Courts Reformed America's Prisons* (1998), 51. On the Arkansas prisons, see also *Arkansas Documentary History*, 142, 167; Carl H. Moneyhorn, *Arkansas and the New South*, 125; Calvin R. Ledbetter Jr., "The Long Struggle to End Convict Leasing in Arkansas," *Ark. Hist. Q.* 52 (1993): 1, 3, 6–7, 22; Gerald E. Bayliss, "The Arkansas State Prisons under Democratic Control, 1874–1896," *Ark. Hist. Q.* 34 (1975): 195.

145. *Jackson v. Bishop*, 268 F. Supp. 804, 814 (1967).

146. *Finney v. Arkansas Board of Corrections*, 505 F2d 194, 204 (1974: *Lay*-Heaney-Devitt).

147. Feeley and Rubin, *Judicial Policy Making*, 53–55; *Hutto v. Finney*, 437 U.S. 678 (1978).

148. *Talley v. Stephens*, 247 F. Supp. 683 (E.D.Ark.1965); Feeley and Rubin, *Judicial Policy Making*, 55–56.

149. Feeley and Rubin, *Judicial Policy Making,* 58–59.

150. 268 F. Supp. 804, 815 (E.D.Ark.1967).

151. 404 F2d 571 (1968: *Bmun*-Van-Van Pelt).

152. *Id.* at 578, 579, 580; Greenhouse, "Justice Blockmun," A18.

153. *Courtney v. Bishop,* 409 F2d 1185 (1969).

154. 309 F. Supp. 362 (E.D.Ark.1970).

155. *Id.* at 381 (1970).

156. *Id.* at 382.

157. Feeley and Rubin, *Judicial Policy Making,* 65.

158. *Holt v. Sarver,* 442 F2d 304, 307–8, 309 (1971: *Van*-Matt-Lay[c]).

159. Feeley & Rubin, *Judicial Policy Making,* 67.

160. *Holt v. Hutto,* 363 F. Supp. 194 (1973).

161. *Holt v. Hutto,* 363 F. Supp. 194, 198–99 (1973). See also Feeley and Rubin, *Judicial Policy Making,* 68–69.

162. *Holt v. Hutto,* 363 F. Supp. 194, 216–17 (1973).

163. *Finney v. Arkansas Board of Corrections,* 505 F2d 194, 200 (1975: Lay-Heaney-Devitt).

164. *Finney v. Hutto,* 410 F. Supp. 257 (E.D.Ark.1976).

165. *Hutto v. Finney,* 548 F2d 740 (1977: *Ross*-Heaney–Van Pelt); *aff'd* 437 U.S. 678 (1978).

166. Feeney and Rubin, *Judicial Policy Making,* 73; Malcolm Feeley, "Federal Courts in the Political Process: Assessing the Consequences of Prison Conditions Litigation," in *Courts and the Political Process,* ed. Austin Ranney (1996), 64–65.

167. ACLU Study, 16.

168. *Papish v. Board of Curators of the University of Missouri,* 410 U.S. 667 (1973), *rev'g* 464 F2d 136 (1972: *Steph*-Van/*Ross*), *aff'g* 331 F. Supp. 1321 (W.D.Mo.1971).

169. 408 U.S. 169 (1972).

170. *Papish v. Board of Curators of the University of Missouri,* 410 U.S. 667, 670 (1972).

171. 447 F. Supp. 1102 (W.D.Mo. Juergens 1975), *rev'd* 538 F2d 1317 (1976: *Ross*-Heaney-Steph), reh'g *en banc* denied 542 F2d 1335 (1976), *rev'd* 435 U.S. 78 (1978).

172. *Board of Curators of University of Missouri v. Horowitz,* 435 U.S. 78, 90 (1978). In 1975 the Court of Appeals had held that a student dismissed from medical school was entitled to an informal hearing. *Greenhill v. Bailey,* 519 F2d 5 (1975: *Web*-Steph-Br).

173. 558 F2d 848, 854 (1977: Lay-Web[c]/Regan), *rev'g* 416 F. Supp. 1350 (W.D.Mo.1976).

174. *Id.* at 857.

175. *Id.* at 858, 859.

176. *Id.* at 860, 861.

177. *Wood v. Strickland,* 420 U.S. 308, 326 (1975), *rev'g sub nom. Strickland v. Inlow,* 485 F2d 186 (1973), *rev'g* 348 F. Supp. 244 (W.D.Ark. Williams 1972), *on remand* 519 F2d 744 (1975: *Heaney*-Ross/*JRGib*).

178. *Atcherson v. Siebenmann,* 605 F2d 1058 (1979: *Br*-Steph-Larson).

179. *Frejlach v. Butler,* 573 F2d 1026 (1978: PC: Br-Henley-T.Smith).

180. 376 U.S. 254 (1964).

181. *Cervantes v. Time, Inc.*, 464 F2d 986 (1972: *Steph*-Van-Meh), *aff'g* 330 F. Supp. 936 (W.D.Mo.1970). See also Mills and Peterson, *No One Is above the Law*, 65–66.

182. If environmental law as a distinct field of law was new, lawsuits to enjoin pollution and other nuisances were not. In 1932, for example, when the sewage system of Harrisonville, Missouri, was discharging putrescent matter into a creek, rendering its water unfit for drinking by cattle and causing offensive odors, the W. S. Dickey Manufacturing Company sought an injunction and damages. The company was successful in district court, but the court of appeals reduced the damages quite considerably, and the U.S. Supreme Court (Brandeis writing) overturned the injunction. *City of Harrisonville, Mo. v. Dickey Clay Mfg. Co.*, 61 F2d 210 (1932: *Cant*-Stone-Kenyon) *rev'd sub nom. Harrisonville v. Dickey Clay Mfg. Co.*, 289 U.S. 334 (1933).

183. The logging case brought about a rare Democrat/Republican split in an Eighth Circuit en banc decision. A majority of Floyd Gibson (writing), Mehaffy, Lay, Heaney, and Bright held that the National Environmental Protection Act applied to pre-NEPA U.S. Forest Service timber sales. Judges Ross, Stephenson, and Webster dissented. *Minnesota Public Interest Research Group v. Butz*, 498 F2d 1314 (1974).

184. *State of Minnesota by Alexander v. Block*, 660 F2d 1240 (1981), *aff'g* 499 F. Supp. 1223 (D.Minn.Lord 1980).

185. *United States v. Brown*, 552 F2d 816 (1977), *cert. denied* 431 U.S. 949 (1977).

186. Annette Atkins, "Minnesota: Left of Center and Out of Place," in *Heartland*, ed. James H. Madison (1989), 9, 16. See also *Reserve Mining Co. v. E.P.A.*, 514 F2d 492 (1975).

187. Frank D. Schaumburg, *Judgment Reserved: A Landmark Environmental Case* (1976), 64; Rhoda Gilman, *Northern Lights: The Story of Minnesota's Past* (1989), 212–14.

188. *Minneapolis Star*, December 8, 1974, quoted in *History of the United States District Court for the District of Minnesota*, updated by Diana Murphy (1989), 19. See also *History of the United States District Court for the District of Minnesota*, prepared by Kenneth G. Owens and Jacob Dinn (May 5, 1976), 18.

189. Schaumburg, *Judgment Reserved*, 158.

190. *United States v. Reserve Mining Co.*, 380 F. Supp. 11, 20 (D.Minn.Lord 1974). See also Schaumburg, *Judgment Reserved*, 107–8.

191. *Reserve Mining Co. v. United States*, 498 F2d 1073, 1075 n. 3 (1974).

192. *Reserve Mining Co. v. United States*, 498 F2d 1073, 1085 (1974).

193. *Id.* at 1084.

194. *Reserve Mining Co. v. United States*, 498 F2d 1073 (1974).

195. *United States v. Reserve Mining Co.*, 380 F. Supp. 91 n. 6 (1974).

196. *Reserve Mining Co. v. United States*, No. 74-1291 (1974).

197. *United States v. Reserve Mining Co.*, 419 U.S. 802 (1974).

198. Judge Lord's unpublished opinion is discussed in *Reserve Mining Co. v. United States*, 514 F2d 492, 505 (1975).

199. *Reserve Mining Co. v. United States*, 514 F2d 492 (1975). See also Gerald W. Heaney, "A Tribute to Judge Myron H. Bright," *Minn. L. Rev. 83* (1998): 223–24.

200. Daniel A. Farber, "The Legacy of Reserve Mining," *Minn. L. Rev.* 83 (1998): 299, 302 .

201. *Reserve Mining Co. v. United States,* 514 F2d 492, 537 (1975).

202. *Id.* at 539 n. 87.

203. Vena C. Corgan, *Controversy, Courts and Community: The Rhetoric of Judge Miles Welton Lord* (1995), 103n49, 229.

204. *Reserve Mining Co. v. Lord,* 529 F2d 181, 185 (1976).

205. *Id.* at 188. See also Corgan, *Controversy,* 97.

206. *Reserve Mining Co. v. Lord,* 529 F2d 181, 188 (1976). See Corgan, *Controversy,* 87.

207. *United States v. Reserve Mining Co.,* 543 F2d 1210 (1976).

208. William E. Lass, *Minnesota: A History,* 2d ed. (1998), 263.

209. P.L. 90–284; 82 Stat.55; 25 U.S.C.A. Sect. 1302–03 (1968). See, generally, Michael L. Lawson, *Damned Indians* (1994), 174; Vine Deloria Jr. and Clifford M. Lytle, *American Indians, American Justice* (1983), 103; John R. Wunder, *Retained by the People: A History of American Indians and the Bill of Rights* (1974), 121–22.

210. See Wunder, *Retained by the People,* 157; Lawson, *Damned Indians,* 175–76; Mary Jane Schneider, "North Dakota Society in the Second Century," *N.D. Hist.* 56 (Winter 1989): 39, 46; Alvin M. Josephy Jr., *500 Nations* (1994), 444.

211. Wunder, *Retained by the People,* 145.

212. Robert V. Hine and John Mack Farragher, *The American West* (2000), 539.

213. Act of January 4, 1975; P.L. 93–368; 88 Stat. 2203-4. And see John Fredericks III, "American's First Nations: The Origins, History, and Future of American Indian Sovereignty," *J. L. & Policy* 7 (1999): 347, 380–81; Donald L. Parman, "Indians of the Modern West," in *The Twentieth Century West,* ed. Gerald O. Nash and Richard W. Etulain (1989), 147, 165.

214. Deloria and Lytle, *American Indians, American Justice,* 103, 107; Hine and Farragher, *The American West,* 538.

215. See *United States v. Carolene Products, Co.* 304 U.S. 144, 152 n.4 (1938).

216. Wilkerson, *American Indians, Time, and the Law* (1988), 121.

217. *McClanahan v. Arizona Tax Commission,* 441 U.S. 164 (1973). See Deloria and Lytle, *American Indians, American Justice,* 39, 46, 57; Wilkerson, *American Indians,* 32, 52, 105. See also "Judge Alfred T. Goodwin: An Oral History" (by Rick Harmon, 1985–86), *W. Legal Hist.* 4 (1976): 27, 36.

218. Wunder, *Retained by the People,* 148; Wilkerson, *American Indians,* 2; Hine and Farragher, *The American West,* 540.

219. In 1969 the Court of Appeals had upheld a decision by Judge Richard E. Robinson of the District of Nebraska awarding land created by the movement of the Missouri River after 1867 to collateral descendants of Logan Fontanelle, famed mid-nineteenth-century leader of the Omaha. *Fontanelle v. Omaha Tribe of Nebraska,* 430 F2d 143 (1970: *Heaney*-Meh-Br).

220. The litigation is described in Mark. R. Scherer, *Imperfect Victories: The Legal Tenacity of the Omaha Tribe* (1991), 89–91.

221. Because of their involvement in the politics of their home states before appointment to the bench, Judge Edward J. McManus of the Northern District of Iowa

and Bogue "traded" cases. Bogue took over the Black Bend trial while McManus presided over several of the most sensitive Wounded Knee cases.

222. *United States v. Wilson*, 433 F. Supp. 67 (N.D.Iowa 1977). See also *United States v. Wilson*, 433 F. Supp. 57 (N.D.Iowa 1977).

223. 25 U.S.C. 194.

224. *Omaha Indian Tribe, Treaty of 1854 v. Wilson*, 575 F2d 620, 631, 651 (1978: *Lay*-Henley-Stcph).

225. *Wilson v. Omaha Indian Tribe*, 442 U.S. 653 (1979).

226. *Omaha Indian Tribe, Treaty of 1854 v. Wilson*, 614 F2d 1153, 1159 (1980: *Lay*-Steph-Henley); *United States v. Wilson*, 707 F2d 304, 311 (1982: PC: Lay-Henley-RArn); *United States v. Wilson*, 578 F. Supp. 1191 (N.D.Iowa 1984); *Omaha Indian Tribe v. Jackson*, 854 F2d 1089 (1988: *Lay*-Fagg-Doty), *cert. denied*, 490 U.S. 1090 (1989); *United States v. Wilson*, 926 F2d 725 (1991: PC:Lay-Magill-Loken).

227. Scherer, *Imperfect Victories*, 109.

228. *Omaha Indian Tribe v. Tract I—Blackbird Bend Area*, 933 F2d 1462 (1991: PC: Lay-Magill-Loken), *cert. den'd sub. nom. Omaha Indian Tribe v. Agricultural & Industrial Inv. Co.*, 502 U.S. 942 (1991).

229. *Rupp v. Omaha Indian Tribe*, 45 F3d 1241 (1991: *Magill*-Heaney-Loken).

230. *United States v. Brown*, 334 F. Supp. 536 (D.Neb. Denney 1971); *Omaha Tribe of Nebraska v. Village of Walthill*, 334 F. Supp. 823 (D.Neb. Robinson 1971). See also *Tyndall v. Gunter*, 681 F. Supp. 641 (D.Neb. Urbom 1987).

231. *Omaha Tribe of Nebraska v. Village of Walthill, Nebraska*, 460 F. 2d. 1327 (1972: PC: Matt-Heaney-Steph), *cert. denied* 409 U.S. 898 (1973).

232. F. Cohen, *Handbook of Indian Law* (1982), 44; Deloria and Lytle, *American Indians, American Justice*, 77.

233. 454 F2d 121 (1972: *Fgib*-Br-Ross). See especially the discussion in Deloria and Lytle, *American Indians, American Justice*, 76–77.

234. 478 F2d 684, 689 (1973: *Steph*-Lay-Heaney).

235. 521 F2d 87 (1975: *T.Smith*-Fgib-Br).

236. See *DeCoteau v. District County Court*, 420 U.S. 425 (1975).

237. See also *Weddell v. Meierheanry*, 636 F2d 211 (1980: *Ross*-Henley-Renner), refusing to expand the definition of a "local Indian community"; and *United States v. South Dakota*, 665 F2d 837 (1981: *McM*-Henley-Collinson), holding that a housing project located in Sisseton was a "dependent Indian community."

238. *Wounded Head v. Tribal Council of Oglala Sioux Tribe*, 507 F2d 1079, 1982 (1975).

239. *Luxon v. Rosebud Sioux Tribe of South Dakota*, 455 F2d 698 (1972: PC: Br-Ross-Wangelin).

240. *White Eagle v. One Feather*, 478 F2d 1311 (1973: PC: Lay-Steph-T.Smith); *Daly v. United States*, 483 F2d 700 (1973: *Heaney*-Br-T.Clark). See also *Brown v. United States*, 486 F2d 658 (1973: *Heaney*-Steph-Web).

241. 521 F2d 724, 726 (1975: *Heaney*-Van-Lay). See also *O'Neal v. Cheyenne River Sioux Tribe*, 482 F2d 1140 (1973: *Ross*-Van-Matt); *Necklace v. Tribal Court of Three Affiliated Tribes*, 554 F2d 845 (1977: PC: Matt-Lay-Henley).

242. See *United States v. United States Fidelity Co.*, 309 U.S. 506 (1940). But

compare with *Namekagon Dev. Co. v. Bois Fort Res Hous Au.*, 395 F. Supp. 23 (D.Minn.1974), *aff'd* 517 F2d 508 (1975: *Lay*-Ross-Web).

243. *Santa Clara Pueblo v. Martinez*, 436 U.S. 39 (1978).

244. On Wounded Knee, see John William Sayer, *Ghost Dancing the Law: The Wounded Knee Trials* (1977); Wunder, *Retained by the People*, 145; Gilman, *Northern Lights*, 201; Peggy J. Teslow, *History of the United States District Court for the District of South Dakota* (1991), 82; T. D. Griffith, *South Dakota* (1998), 182; Herbert S. Schell, *History of South Dakota*, 3d rev. ed. (1975), 340; Linda Hasselstrom, *Roadside History of South Dakota* (1994), 263; Ronald J. Bacigal, *May It Please the Court: A Biography of Judge Robert R. Merhige* (1992), 121.

245. How premeditated the occupation was is not clear. Akim D. Reinhardt, "Spontaneous Combustion: Prelude to Wounded Knee 1973," *S.D. Hist.* 29 (1999): 229–30.

246. Sayer, *Ghost Dancing the Law*, 114, 117.

247. Ibid., 207.

248. *United States v. Banks*, 383 F. Supp. 368 (D.S.D.Nichol August 20, 1974). See also Sayer, *Ghost Dancing the Law*, 147, 194.

249. *United States v. Means*, 513 F2d 1329, 1336 (1975: *Fgib*-Lay-T.Clark).

250. Sayer, *Ghost Dancing the Law*, 201.

251. Perhaps the most impressive opinion written in the Wounded Knee cases was Urbom's on jurisdiction, holding that the 1868 treaty with the Sioux did not preclude federal jurisdiction over certain crimes committed on the reservation. See *United States v. Consolidated Wounded Knee Cases*, 389 F. Supp. 235 (D.Neb.1975), which was adopted by the Court of Appeals, *United States v. Dodge*, 538 F2d 770 (1976: *Heaney*-Br/Web[c/d]).

252. Sayer, *Ghost Dancing the Law*, 128, 133, 210, 228. On the trials before Judge Urbom, see also James C. Olson and Ronald C. Naugle, *History of Nebraska*, 3rd ed. (1997), 382–83.

253. *United States v. Leonard Crow Dog*, 532 F2d 1182 (1976: *Steph*-Fgib-Lay[c]).

254. *United States v. Dodge*, 538 F2d 770, 778 (1976: *Heaney*-Br/Web [c/d]). On the possible informer during the Banks-Means trial, see Sayer, *Ghost Dancing the Law*, 207.

255. Sayer, *Ghost Dancing the Law*, 214.

256. *Means v. Wilson*, 383 F. Supp. 378 (D.S.D.Bogue1974), *rev'd & rem'd*, 522 F2d 833 (1975: *Ross*-Lay/Web[c/d]).

257. Sayer, *Ghost Dancing the Law*, 57, 248n64, 72, 249n73.

258. Ibid., 5, 12, 50, 225.

6. "Debate, Differences, and a Robust Exchange of Ideas"

1. Mark Friedberger, "The Modernization of Iowa's Agricultural Structure in the Twentieth Century," in *Iowa History Reader*, ed. Marvin Bergman (1996), 383; Walter Nugent, *Into the West* (1999), 339; Frederick C. Luebke, *Nebraska: An Illustrated History* (1995), 344; Annette Atkins, "Minnesota: Left of Center and Out of Place," in *Heartland*, ed. James H. Madison (1988), 19.

2. Michael B. Dougan, *Arkansas Odyssey* (1994), 577, 584, 592, 596, 626.

3. Lawrence O. Christensen, "Missouri: The Heart of the Nation," in *Heartland*, ed. James H. Madison (1988), 105; William E. Parrish et al., *Missouri: The Heart of the Nation*, 2nd ed. (1992), 346, 348–49, 386.

4. Dorothy Schweider, *Iowa: The Middle Land* (1996), 315, 318, 322; Dorothy Schweider, Thomas Morain, and Lynn Nielsen, *Iowa Past to Present*, 2nd ed. (1991); Friedberger, "Modernization," 375, 379, 392–94; Allan Carpenter and Randy Lyon, *Between Two Rivers: Iowa Year by Year, 1846–1996*, 3rd ed. (1996), 345.

5. Frederick C. Luebke, *Nebraska: An Illustrated History* (1995), 344, 354, 363.

6. On South Dakota during this period, see Herbert T. Hoover, "South Dakota: An Expression of Regional Heritage," in *Heartland*, ed. James H. Madison (1988), 202–4; James D. McLair, "From Bib Overalls to Cowboy Boots: East River/West River Differences in South Dakota," *S.D. Hist.* 19, no. 4 (Winter 1989): 454; Herbert T. Hoover and Karen P. Zimmerman, *South Dakota History: An Annotated Bibliography* (1993), ix; George S. Mickelson, "South Dakota's First Century: Legacies Past and Future," *S.D. Hist.* 19, no. 4 (Winter 1989): 557, 568; South Dakota History Chronology (comp. South Dakota State Historical Society), http://www.state.s.d.us/state/executive/deca/cultural/soc_hist.htm, 6. See also John Milton, *South Dakota: A Bicentennial History* (1977), 81, 160, 195; Gilbert C. Fite, "The Transformation of South Dakota Agriculture: The Effects of Mechanization, 1939–1964," *S.D. Hist.* 19, no. 3 (Fall 1989): 278, 305; Shebby Lee, "Traveling the Sunshine State: The Growth of Tourism in South Dakota, 1914–1939," *S.D. Hist.* 19, no. 2 (Summer 1989): 194.

7. David B. Danbom, "Postscript," in Elwyn B. Robinson, *History of North Dakota*, 2nd ed. (1995), 589; David B. Danbom, "North Dakota: The Most Midwestern State," in *Heartland*, ed. James H. Madison (1988), 107, 121; D. Jerome Tweton and Theodore Jeliff, *North Dakota: The Heritage of a People* (1976), 216; D. Jerome Tweton, "The Future of North Dakota: An Overview," *N.D. Hist.* 56, no. 1 (Winter 1989): 8; Curt Eriksmoen and Larry Remele, North Dakota Chronology, State Historical Society of North Dakota Web site, http://www.state.nd.us/hist/chrono.htm.

8. Rhoda R. Gilman, *The Story of Minnesota's Past* (1989), 198, 208; Atkins, "Minnesota," 21; William E. Lass, *Minnesota: A History*, 2nd ed. (1998), 270.

9. Donald P. Lay, "A Blueprint for Judicial Machinery," *Creighton L.Rev.* 17 (1984): 1047, 1066.

10. See Robert Oliphant, "En Banc Polarization in the Eighth Circuit," *Wm. Mitch.L.Rev.* 17 (1991): 701.

11. 98 Stat. 333, 346; 104 Stat. 5089, 5099.

12. Lay, "A Blueprint for Judicial Machinery," 1062.

13. Timothy E. Gammon, "The Central Staff Attorneys' Office in the United States Court of Appeals, Eighth Circuit: A Five Year Report," *S.D.L.Rev.* 29 (1984): 457, 459.

14. Lay, "A Blueprint for Judicial Machinery," 1062, 1067.

15. Ibid., 1055; A. Leo Levin, "A Tribute to Judge Donald P. Lay," *Wm. Mitch. L.Rev.* 18 (1992): 581–82.

16. Charles E. Lundberg, "Chief Judge Donald P. Lay: Reflections on Appellate Judging after Twenty Years on the Eighth Circuit Court of Appeals," *Minn. Def.* 20

(Fall 1986): 6; United States Court of Appeals Eighth Circuit, Presentation of the Portrait of the Honorable Donald P. Lay, St. Paul, October 15, 1982, 979 F2d xci, xcii–xciii.

17. Lay, "A Blueprint for Judicial Machinery," 1047, 1056; Gerald W. Heaney, "A Tribute to Judge Donald P. Lay," *Wm. Mitch.L.Rev.* 18 (1992): 571, 576.

18. Donald P. Lay, "My Colleague—Richard S. Arnold," *Minn. L.Rev.* 78 (1993): 25, 28; Donald P. Lay, "Observations of Twenty-five Years as a United States Circuit Judge," *Wm. Mitch. L. Rev.* 18 (1992): 595, 625–31, 635–38.

19. There are, to be sure, hazards in relying too much on the liberal/conservative labels. *Martin v. White*, a section 1983 action, engendered one of the strongest "liberal" opinions of the court even though the panel—Ross (writing), Henley, and Bowman—was a conservative one. Its subject matter and tone may be suggested by the opening paragraph: "In this case we deal with a subject matter which has become a national disgrace . . . the inability or unwillingness of some prison administrators to take the necessary steps to protect their prisoners from sexual and physical assaults by other inmates." *Martin v. White*, 742 F2d 469, 470 (1984).

20. Christopher E. Smith, "Polarization and Change in the Federal Courts: En Banc Decisions in the U.S. Court of Appeals," *Judicature* 74 (1990): 133.

21. President George Bush appointed James B. Loken to the court of appeals, but Loken was not officially sworn in until February 1991 and thus is left for consideration in the following chapter.

22. *Almanac Fed. Jud.* 2 (2001): 23.

23. *Liddell v. State*, 731 F2d 1294, 1331 (1984), *cert. denied* 103 S.Ct. 82 (1984).

24. *Jenkins v. Missouri*, 855 F2d 1295 (1988), *rev'd in part* 495 U.S. 33 (1990); 13 F3d 1170 and 11 F.3d 755 (1994), *rev'd* 115 S.Ct. 2038 (1995); 122 F3d 588 (1997).

25. Douglas O. Linder, "How Judges Judge: A Study of Disagreement on the United States Court of Appeals for the Eighth Circuit," *Ark. L. Rev.* 38 (1985): 479, 530–31.

26. 791 F2d 628 (1986), *aff'd* 483 U.S. 203 (1987).

27. On Judge Fagg, see *Almanac Fed. Jud.* 2 (2001): 20–21; "Judge George G. Fagg," *Creighton L. Rev.* 17, no. 4 (1983–84): xviii; Linder, "How Judges Judge," 529–32; *Creighton L.Rev.* 20, no. 4 (1986–87): xviii.

28. *Liddell v. State*, 731 F2d 1294, 1333 (1984), *cert. denied sub nom. Leffett v. Liddell*, 469 U.S. 816 (1984).

29. *Bush v. Taylor*, 893 F2d 962, 967 (1990: R*Arn*-Magill/*Bow*); 912 F2d 989, 993–94 (1990: *Bow*-McM-Fagg-Woll-Beam/R*Arn*-Lay-JRGib-Magill). On Bowman, see "Judge Pasco M. Bowman," *Creighton L.Rev.* 17, no. 4 (1983–84): xxxv; *Creighton L.Rev.* 20, no. 4, (1987): xix.

30. Morris interview of Roger L. Wollman, October 1, 1998.

31. The discussion of Judge Wollman is based on my interview with him, October 1, 1998; *Almanac Fed. Judic.* 2 (2001): 3–4; *Sioux Empire*, March 23, 1998; "Justice Roger L. Wollman," *Creighton L. Rev.* 20, no. 4 (1987): xxxv; *South Dakota Justice: The Justices and the System* (1989); Peggy J. Teslow, *History of the United States District Court for the District of South Dakota* (1991), 121–22; *Sioux Falls Argus-Leader*, March 23, 1998.

32. Morris interviews with Frank J. Magill, Myron Bright, Bruce M. Van Sickle, and Ardell Thoraldson; Morris interview with Daniel Vogel, September 30, 1998;

"Frank J. Magill," *Creighton L.Rev.* 20, no. 4 (1987): xxix; Almanac Fed. Jud. 2 (2001): 31–32.

33. Interview of Judge J. Smith Henley by Frances M. Ross, April 24, 1987 (copy available from Historical Society of the U.S. Courts in the Eighth Circuit, St. Paul, MN), 109–10 (hereafter cited as Henley Oral History).

34. "The Honorable Clarence Arlen Beam," *Creighton L.Rev.* 21, no. 4 (1987–88): xii; "Clarence Arlen Beam," *Almanac Fed. Jud.* 2 (2001): 8–9. The quotation comes from the latter profile.

35. However, it was not unknown for the liberal members of the court to resort to it to overturn a panel decision they viewed as conservative.

36. Linder, "How Judges Judge," 499–500; Smith, "Polarization," 135; Donald P. Lay, "The Federal Appeal Process: Whither We Goest? The Next Fifty Years," *Wm. Mitch.L.Rev.* 15 (1989): 515, 531.

37. Harry Blackmun, Remarks at Eighth Circuit Judicial Conference, July 15, 1988, 23. See, for example, *Williams v. Butler,* 762 F2d 73 (1985), where the district court's decision was affirmed by an equally divided court. Judges Lay, Floyd Gibson, Heaney, Bright, and Richard Arnold voted to affirm; Judges Ross, McMillian, J. R. Gibson, Fagg, and Bowman to reverse. All but McMillian fillowed the "party line." See also *Ozark Airlines v. Airlines Pilot Association,* 761 F2d 1259 (1985).

38. 891 F2d 656 (1989: *Br-McM/Fagg*), *reh en banc* 912 F2d 924 (1990: *Fagg-Bow-Woll-Magill-Beam/Lay-RArn/Br-McM/JRGib*).

39. 911 F2d 80 (1990: *Bow-Dumbauld[c]/Lay*); 919 F2d 1339, 1341–42 (1990), *cert. denied,* 500 U.S. 941 (1941). Arnold, Fagg, Bowman, Wollman, Magill, and Beam voted not to rehear *en banc.*

40. Roger L. Wollman, "Foreword," *Wm.Mitch.L.Rev.* 16 (1990): 607, 609.

41. C. Arlen Beam, "Foreword," *Wm.Mitch.L.Rev.* 17 (1991): 697, 699.

42. Linder, "How Judges Judge," 529.

43. Blackmun, Remarks, 10, 11.

44. *Valley Family Planning v. State of North Dakota,* 661 F2d 99 (1981), *aff'g* 489 F. Supp. 238 (D.N.D.Benson1981).

45. *Women's Services, P.C. v. Thone,* 483 F. Supp. 1022 (D.Neb.Urbom1979), *aff'd* 636 F2d 206 (1980: *PC*: Ross-Fgib-Sachs), *vac/rem* 452 U.S. 911 (1981), 690 F2d 667 (1982: *PC*: Ross-McM-RArn), *vac. sub nom. Kerrey v. Women's Services,* 462 U.S. 1126 (1983). See also *City of Akron v. Akron Center for Reproductive Health,* 462 U.S. 416 (1983).

46. 648 F. Supp. 756 (D.Minn.Alsop1986), *aff'd* 827 F2d 1191 (1987), *reh. gr.op. vac.,* 835 F2d 1545 (1987), *rev'd* 853 F2d 1452 (1988: *JRGib-RArn-Fagg-Bow-Woll-Magill-Beam/Lay-Heaney-McM*), *aff'd* 497 U.S. 417 (1988).

47. *Hodgson v. Minnesota,* 853 F2d 1452, 1459ff (1988).

48. *Id.* at 1466, 1470.

49. *Id.* at 1472.

50. 497 U.S. 717. In 1990, a court of appeals panel upheld a Minnesota law that required "dignified and sanitary disposition of fetal remains resulting from abortions and miscarriages." *Planned Parenthood of Minnesota v. State of Minnesota,* 910 F2d 479 (1990: *Lay*-Bow-Stuart).

51. 483 F. Supp. 679 (W.D.Mo.Hunter 1980), *aff'd sub nom. Planned Parenthood v. Kasar*, 655 F2d 848 (1980: *Lay*-Henley-Harris).

52. *Planned Parenthood Association of Kansas City, Mo. v. Kasar*, 664 F2d 687 (1981: *Lay*-Henley-Harris).

53. *Planned Parenthood Association of Kansas City, Mo. v. Ashcroft*, 462 U.S. 476 (1983).

54. *Reproductive Health Services v. Webster*, 662 F. Supp. 407 (W.D.Mo. Wright1987).

55. *Reproductive Health Service v. Webster*, 851 F2d 1071, 1076 (1988: *Lay*-McM/*RArn* [c/d]).

56. *Id.* at 1084, 1085.

57. *Webster v. Reproductive Health Service*, 492 U.S. 490, 517 (1989).

58. *Id.* at 521, 525.

59. *Id.* at 531, 534.

60. *Women's Health Center v. Webster*, 871 F2d 1377 (1989: *Bow*-Henley/*McM*). During this period, the court also decided a case dealing with the procedures for female minors seeking an abortion. *T.L.J. v. Webster*, 792 F2d 734, 739 (1986: *RArn*-Bow-Woll). One other case involving abortion, *Pursley v. City of Fayetteville*, 850 F2d 951 (1987), is discussed later in this chapter in connection with First Amendment cases.

61. 792 F2d 746 (1986: *McM*-Hen-*JRGib* [c]).

62. *Smith v. Clinton*, 687 F. Supp. 1310, 1311 (E.D.Ark: *RArn*-Harris-Woods1988) *aff'd* 488 U.S. 988 (1988). See Dougan, *Arkansas Odyssey*, 618.

63. 730 F. Supp. 196 (E.D.Ark.:*RArn*-Howard/*Eisele* 1989), *aff'd* 498 U.S. 1019 (1991).

64. *Jeffers v. Clinton*, 740 F. Supp. 585 (E.D.Ark.1990), *appl. dism.*, 498 U.S. 1019 (1991).

65. Patricia M. Wald, "Judge Arnold and Individual Rights," *Minn.L.Rev.* 78 (1993): 35, 43, 47n76. The first *Jeffers* opinion, which focused on interpreting the Voting Rights Act, was followed by a second, which held that violations of the Fourteenth Amendment had been committed. *Jeffers v. Clinton*, 756 F. Supp. 585 (E.D.Ark.1990).

66. Harry S. Ashmore, *Civil Rights and Wrongs* (1994), 279; Dougan, *Arkansas Odyssey*, 616–17; Mark C. Carnes and John A. Garraty, *Mapping America's Past: A Historical Atlas* (1996), 218–19.

67. *Liddell v. Board of Education*, 667 F2d 643, 648 (1981: *Heaney*-Br-Steph), *aff'g* 491 F. Supp. 351 (E.D.Mo.Meredith1980).

68. 677 F2d 626 (1982: *Heaney*-Br-Steph), *cert. denied* 559 U.S. 877 (1982).

69. *Liddell v. Board of Education*, 567 F. Supp. 1037 (E.D.Mo.Hungate1983), *aff'd as mod.* 731 F2d 1294 (1984: EB: Lay-Heaney-Br-Ross-McM-RArn-Fagg/*JRGib*[c/d]/*Bow*[d]), *cert. denied* 469 U.S. 816 (1984). No single judge was credited with the court's opinion, which was designated "Opinion of the Court En Banc."

70. *Liddell v. Board of Education [Liddell-IX]*, 801 F2d 278 (1986). See also *Lidell v. Board of Education [Liddell-XI]*, 804 F2d 500 (1986).

71. *Liddell v. Board of Education*, 823 F2d 1252 (1987: PC: Heaney-McM-Fagg). See also D. Bruce La Pierre, "Voluntary Inter-district School Desegregation

in St. Louis: The Special Master's Tale," in *Justice and School: The Role of the Courts in Education Litigation*, ed. Barbara Flicker (1990), 233; Gary Orfield, "Unexpected Costs and Uncertain Gains of Dismantling Desegregation," in *Dismantling Desegregation*, ed. Gary Orfield, Susan E. Eaton, and the Harvard Project on School Desegregation (1996), 73, 89–90, 95–96; Parrish et al., *Missouri*, 392–93.

72. Lorenzo J. Greene, Gary Kremer, and Antonio F. Holland, *Missouri's Black Heritage*, rev. ed. (1993), 34; Parrish ct al., *Missouri*, 355.

73. *Jenkins v. Missouri*, 807 F2d 657, 695, 701–2 (1986).

74. *School District of Kansas City, Missouri v. State of Missouri*, 460 F. Supp. 421 (W.D.Mo.Clark1978), *app. dism.* 592 F2d 493 (1979: PC: Fgib-Heaney-Steph).

75. *Jenkins v. Missouri*, 593 F. Supp. 1485 (W.D.Mo.Clark1984).

76. *Jenkins v. State of Missouri*, 807 F2d 657 (1986: *JRGib*-Ross-Fagg-Woll/ R*Arn*[c]/*Lay*-Heaney-McM). The lower court was upheld on other issues by an equally divided court (JRGib-Ross-Fagg-Woll/*RArn*-Lay-Heaney-McM).

77. *Jenkins v. Missouri*, 639 F. Supp. 19 (W.D.Mo.1985).

78. *Jenkins v. State of Missouri*, 672 F. Supp. 400 (W.D.Mo.1987), *aff'd* 855 F2d 1295, 1305 (1988: *JRGib*-Heaney/*Lay*[c/d]), *cert. denied sub nom. Clark v. Jenkins*, 490 U.S. 1034 (1989).

79. Parrish et al., *Missouri*, 293; Alison Morantz, "Money and Choice in Kansas City," in *Dismantling Desegregation*, ed. Gary Orfield, Susan E. Eaton, and the Harvard Project on School Desegregation (1996), 241, 242, 247–48.

80. *Jenkins v. State of Missouri*, 672 F. Supp. 400, 411–12 (W.D.Mo.1987).

81. *Jenkins v. State of Missouri*, 855 F2d 1295, 1299, 1315 (1988: *JRGib*-Heaney/ *Lay*). Judge Lay would not have approved the property tax levy by the KCSMD but instead would have billed the state. *Id.* at 1317, 1318.

82. *Id.* at 1317, 1318.

83. *Missouri v. Jenkins*, 495 U.S. 33 (1990).

84. *Chess v. Widmar*, 635 F2d 1310 (1980: *Heaney*-Fgib-Steph), *aff'd sub nom. Widmar v. Vincent*, 454 U.S. 263 (1981).

85. 20 U.S.C. 4077 (a) (1984).

86. 867 F2d 1076 (1989: *McM*-Lay-Fgib), *aff'd Board of Education of the Westside Community Schools (Dist. 66) v. Mergens*, 496 U.S. 226 (1990).

87. 637 F2d 562 (1981: *Sachs*-Ross-Fgib), *aff'd Larson v. Valente*, 456 U.S. 228 (1982).

88. *Mueller v. Allen*, 676 F2d 1195, 1204, 1205–6 (1982), *aff'd* 464 U.S. 388 (1983).

89. *Bogan v. Doty*, 598 F2d 1110, 1114 (1979: *Fgib*-Henley-Hanson).

90. *Marsh v. Chambers*, 675 F2d 228, 233–35 (1982).

91. *Marsh v. Chambers*, 463 U.S. 783, 786 (1983).

92. *Florey v. Sioux Falls School District 49-5*, 619 F2d 1311 (1980: *Heaney*-Ross/*McM*).

93. *Carter v. Broadlawns Medical Center*, 857 F2d 448, 452 (1988: *JRGib*-Heaney-Harper).

94. 728 F2d 1121 (1984: *Br*-JRGib/*Fagg*).

95. *Id.* at 1128.

96. *Clayton v. Place*, 90 F. Supp. 850 (W.D.Mo.1988), *rev'd* 884 F2d 376 (1989:

Fagg-Fgib-Timbers), *reh. denied* 889 F2d 192 (1989: Fagg-Bow-Woll-Magill-Beam/*Lay*-RArn-McM-JRGib), *cert. denied* 410 U.S. 1081 (1990). See also Parrish et al., *Missouri,* 394.

97. 376 U.S. 254 (1964).

98. *Janklow v. Newsweek, Inc.,* 759 F2d 644 (1985: *Bow*-Fagg/*RArn*[c/d]).

99. *Janklow v. Newsweek, Inc.,* 788 F2d 1300, 1304 (1986: *RArn*-Lay-Heaney-McM-JRGib-Woll/*Bow*-Ross-Fagg).

100. *Id.* at 1306, 1307.

101. 874 F2d 1244 (1989: *Larson*-Woll-Magill).

102. 795 F2d 1368 (1986: *Heaney*-RArn/*Woll*).

103. See chapter 4.

104. *Kuhlmeier v. Hazelwood School District,* 795 F2d 1368, 1378 at 1379.

105. *Hazelwood School District v. Kuhlmeier,* 484 U.S. 260, 272–73 (1988).

106. *Id.* at 273.

107. John W. Johnson, *The Struggle for Student Rights* (1997), 209–12. See also *Bystrom v. Fridley High School, Independent School District No. 14,* 822 F2d 747 (1987: *RArn*-Henley/*McM*[c/d]*),* involving the censorship of an underground newspaper in Minnesota.

108. *Persons for Free Speech v. U.S. Air Force,* 675 F2d 1010 (1982: *Ross*-RArn-Steph-Henley-Br/*Lay*-Heaney-McM), *cert. denied* 459 U.S. 1092 (1982).

109. *Persons v. Free Speech,* 675 F2d 1010 at 1022 (1982). The panel opinion is excerpted in *id.* at 1010.

110. *Id.* at 1023, 1025.

111. 820 F2d 951 (1987: *Magill*-Hen/*JRGib*).

112. *Id.* at 957, 959.

113. 506 F. Supp. 526 (W.D.Ark.Roy1981), *aff'd* 658 F2d 655 (1981: *McManus*-Fgib/*RArn*), *on reh en banc rev/rem* 667 F2d 659 (1981: *RArn*-Lay-Br-Ross-Steph-Henley-McM-*Heaney*[c]). Compare with *Young v. American Mini Theatres,* 427 U.S. 50 (1976).

114. *United States Jaycees v. McClure,* 534 F. Supp. 766 (D.Minn.Murphy1982), *rev'd* 709 F2d 1560 (1983: *RArn*-Henley/*Lay*), *reh eb denied by equally divided court* 709 F2d 1560 (1983), *rev'd sub nom. Roberts v. United States Jaycees,* 464 U.S. 1037 (1984). See also *United States Jaycees v. McClure,* 305 N.W.2d 764 (Minn.1981). Judges Richard Arnold, John R. Gibson, Henley, and Fagg voted to deny rehearing *en banc.* Chief Judge Lay and Judges Heaney, Bright, and McMillian voted to rehear *en banc.* And see Wald, "Judge Arnold," 35, 55n138.

115. *United States Jaycees v. McClure,* 709 F2d 1560, 1583 (1983).

116. See, e.g., *United States v. Le Amous,* 754 F2d 795 (1985: *Fgib*-Lay-Br); *United States v. Clark,* 646 F2d 1259 (1981: *McM*-Ross-Henley).

117. Sentencing Reform Act of 1984, P.L. No. 98–473, 98 Stat. 1987, 18 U.S.C. 3551ff; 28 U.S.C. 991ff.

118. *United States v. Johnson,* 682 F. Supp. 1033 (1988: W.D.Mo.: *Sachs*-Hunter-Bartlett-Whittle/*Wright*).

119. *Mistretta v. United States,* 488 U.S. 361 (1989).

120. 408 U.S. 238 (1972).

121. *Omaha World-Herald,* August 8, 1985, 23. See Michael Dougan et al., *Arkansas History: An Annotated Bibliography* (n.d.), xxiii.

122. *Newton v. Armontrout,* 885 F2d 1328 (1989: *Magill*-Henley-RArn).

123. *Chambers v. Armontrout,* 907 F2d 825 (1990: *Heaney*-McM-RArn-Lay-Woll-Fgib/*JRGib*-Fagg-Bow-Magill-Beam).

124. 877 F2d 698 (1989: *RArn*-McM/*Bow*).

125. *Hill v. Lockhart,* 894 F2d 1009 (1990: *RArn*-Lay-McM-Fagg-Bean/*JRGib*-Bow-Woll-Magill).

126. 744 F2d 1323, 1328, 1329 (1984: *McM*-RArn-Bennett).

127. *Whiteside v. Scurr,* 750 F2d 713 (1984).

128. *Nix v. Whiteside,* 475 U.S. 157, 170 (1985).

129. 816 F2d 1254 (1987: *Heaney*-Woll-Larsen).

130. *Warren v. City of Lincoln,* 864 F2d 1436 (1989: *Woll*-Fagg-Bow-JRGib-Bean-Magill/*Lay*-Heaney-RArn-McM). See also *United States v. Williams,* 714 F2d 777 (1983: *Heaney*-RArn/*McM*).

131. 721 F2d 1148 (1982: *McM*-Lay-Heaney), *on reh.* 715 F2d 1313 (1983: *McM*-Lay-Heaney-Br-RArn-Fagg-*Ross*[c]/*JRGib*[c/d]), *cert. denied* 464 U.S. 1063 (1984).

132. Karen L. Tokarz, "Tribute to Judge Theodore M. McMillian," *Wash. U. Urb. & Contemp. L.* 52 (1997): 5, 16; 380 U.S. 79 (1986).

133. 476 U.S. 79 (1986).

134. *United States v. Wilson,* 884 F2d 1121 (1989: *Br*-Lay-Heaney-McM-RArn-Magill/*Bow*-JRGib-*Beam*-Fagg-Woll).

135. 445 U.S. 263 (1980).

136. *Helm v. Solem,* 684 F2d 582 (1982: *Br*-Lay-Ross), *aff'd Solem v. Helm,* 463 U.S. 277, 284 (1983). See also *State of South Dakota v. Helm,* 287 N.W. 2d 497, 499 (1980), for then South Dakota Chief Justice Roger Wollman's special concurrence. See also Jo Lee Adamich, Nick Chase, et al., "The Selected Cases of Myron H. Bright: Thirty Years of His Jurisprudence," *Minn. L.Rev.* 83:239, 258 (observations of Michael J. Schaffer).

137. The story is told at greater length in Adamich et al., "Selected Cases," 240–54.

138. *Walker v. State,* 408 S.W.2d 905 (Ark.1966).

139. *Walker v. Bishop,* 408 F2d 1378 (1969), *aff'g* 295 F. Supp. 767 (E.D.Ark. Henley1969). See also Adamich et al., "Selected Cases," 245n43.

140. *Walker v. Lockhart,* 726 F2d 1238, 1249ff (1984: *JRGib*-Ross-Fagg-Bow-RArn[c]/*Br-Lay*-Heaney-McM), *cert. denied* 478 U.S. 1020 (1986).

141. *Id.* at 1267.

142. *Walker v. Lockhart,* 598 F. Supp. 1410, 1431 (E.D.Ark.Woods1984).

143. *Walker v. Lockhart,* 763 F2d 942 (1985: *Br*-Lay-Henley-McM-*RArn*[c]/*JRGib*-Fagg-Bow-Ross), *cert. denied* 478 U.S. 1020 (1986).

144. Adamich et al., "Selected Cases," 253–54.

145. Frank R. Kennedy, "The Bankruptcy Court," in *The Development of Bankruptcy and Reorganization Law in the Courts of the United States (United States Courts for the Second Circuit, Committee on History and Commemorative Events)* (hereafter cited as *The Development of Bankruptcy Law*), 1, 34; and in the same volume, Elizabeth Warren, "Evaluate the Present and Shape the Future," 257;

Harvey R. Miller and Erica M. Ryland, "The Role of Major Cases in the Development of Bankruptcy Law," 191, 192.

146. 92 Stat. 2668, 28 U.S.C. 1471 (Supp.1971).

147. *Marathon Pipeline Co. v. Northern Pipeline Construction Co.*, 12 B.R. 946, 955 (1981).

148. *Northern Pipeline Construction Co. v. Marathon Pipeline Co.*, 458 U.S. 50 (1982). See also Kennedy, "The Bankruptcy Court," 21–24.

149. P.L. 98–353; 98 Stat. 333 (1984); 28 U.S.C. 1334 (1988).

150. Kennedy, "The Bankruptcy Court," 1, 3, 4, 20.

151. *In re Hartley*, 869 F2d 394 (1989: *McM*-Henley/*Barnes*), *vac.* 874 F2d 1254 (1989).

152. 883 F2d 1373, 1380 (1989: *Magill*-McM/*JRGib*).

153. *Id.* at 1382.

154. *In re LeMaire*, 898 F2d 1346 (1990: *JRGib*-RArn-Fagg-Bow-Woll-Beam/*Magill*-Lay-McM).

155. *Bush v. Taylor*, 893 F2d 962, 963 (1990).

156. *Id.* at 967.

157. *Bush v. Taylor*, 912 F2d 989, 994 (1990: *Bow*-McM-Fagg-Woll-Beam/*RArn*-Lay-JRGib-Magill). See also *In re NYFX, Inc.*, 881 F2d 530 (1989: *Fgib*-Fagg/*Timbers*), *vac. and aff'd* 904 F2d 469 (1990), involving the bankruptcy of NWYX, a firm that had sold money orders nationwide through grocery stores. The case involved whether a grocery store chain could refund money orders to its customers rather than turn the money over to the bankrupt's estate. The *en banc* court vacated the panel and held that the money belonged to the bankrupt estate by a vote of 5–5. Lay, Henley, McMillian, Arnold, and Magill voted against the turnover; four Reagan appointees and Floyd Gibson voted the opposite way.

158. *Paschall v. Kansas City Star Co.*, 695 F2d 322 (1982: *Heaney*-Br/*Henley*), *rev'd and vac. Paschal v. Kansas City Star*, 727 F2d 692, 706 (1984: *McM*-Henley-RArn-JRGib-Fagg-Ross/*Heaney-Br*-Lay). See also 605 F2d 403 (1979: *Steph*-Ross-Henley).

159. Susan Gluck Mezey, *No Longer Disabled: The Federal Courts and the Politics of Social Security Disability* (1988), 1.

160. 715 F2d 428, 430 (1983: *PC*: Ross-Collinson-*McM*[c]). See also Mezey, *No Longer Disabled*, 135–36.

161. *Etis v. Bowen*, No. 88-539 (1989). See Mary E. Shearon, "A Tribute to Judge Donald P. Lay," *Wm.Mitch. L.Rev.* 18 (1992): 590.

162. *Rush v. Sec'y of Health and Human Resources*, 738 F2d 909 (1984: *RArn*-Heaney-Fgib); *Weber v. Harris*, 640 F2d 176 (1981: *Steph*-Br-McM).

163. Mezey, *No Longer Disabled*, 110–13, 147. See also *United States v. Brown*, 786 F2d 870 (1986: *Heaney*-Hanson/*Bow*[c/d]), involving the invalidation of the second step of the sequential evaluation process.

164. *Petty v. United States*, 740 F2d 1428 (1984: *Lay*-Fgib/*Br*), *aff'g Petty v. United States*, 592 F. Supp. 687 (N.D.Iowa 1983). See also *Petty v. United States*, 536 F. Supp. 860 (N.D.Iowa 1980), *rem.* 679 F2d 719 (1982: *Br*-Heaney-Ross). And see George Mills and Richard W. Peterson, *No One Is above the Law: The Story of Southern Iowa's Federal Court* (n.d.), 94.

165. *In re Federal Skywalk Cases,* 93 F.R.D. 415 (W.D.Mo.Wright1982), *vac.* 680 F2d 1175 (1982: *McM*-RArn/*Heaney*), *cert. denied* 459 U.S. 998 (1982).

166. Verna C. Corgan, *Controversy, Courts, and Community: The Rhetoric of Miles Lord* (1995), 121, 127.

167. *Gardiner v. A. H. Robins Co.,* 747 F2d 1180, 1192 (1984). The opinion was credited as having been written by all three judges on the panel, Lay, Bright, and Arnold.

168. Corgan, *Controversy,* 131.

169. Linder, "How Judges Judge," 507, 507n102.

170. 475 F. Supp. 544 (S.D.Iowa Stuart1979).

171. *Id.* at 551.

172. *Consolidated Freightways Corp. v. Kassel,* 612 F2d 1064 (1979: *Heaney-Henley*[c]-Lay).

173. *Id.* at 1067, 1070.

174. *Kassell v. Consolidated Freightways,* 450 U.S. 662, 669 (1981).

175. See V. E. Montgomery, "The South Dakota Cement Plant," Bulletin no. 62 of Business Research Bureau, School of Business, State University of South Dakota (May 1959). See also Herbert S. Schell, *History of South Dakota,* 3rd ed. (1975), 383; Robert F. Karolevitz, *Challenge: The South Dakota Story* (1975), 249.

176. *Reeves, Inc. v. Kelley,* 586 F2d 1230, 1232, 1233 (1978: *Lay*-Ross-McM).

177. *Reeves, Inc. v. Kelley,* 441 U.S. 39 (1979), *on remand* 603 F2d 736 (1979: *Lay*-Ross-McM), *aff'd* 447 U.S. 429 (1980).

178. 650 F2d 911 (1981: *Robinson*-Ross-Lay), *aff'd sub nom. North Dakota v. United States,* 460 U.S. 300 (1983).

179. *South Dakota v. Dole,* 791 F2d 628 (1986: *Fagg*-RArn-Timbers).

180. *South Dakota v. Dole,* 483 U.S. 203 (1987).

181. *Perpich v. U.S. Department of Defense,* 880 F2d 11, 16, 39 (1989: *Magill*-RArn-JRGib-Fagg-Bow-Woll-Bean/*Heaney*-McM), *aff'd* 666 F. Supp. 1319 (D.Minn.Alsop1987). The citation for the unpublished panel opinion is *Perpich v. United States Department of Defense,* 1988 U.S.App. LEXIS 16494, No. 87-5345 (December 6, 1988).

182. *Perpich v. Department of Defense,* 496 U.S. 33 (1990). One further important case involving issues of federalism was decided by the Eighth Circuit and overturned by the Supreme Court, *United States v. State of North Dakota,* 675 F. Supp. 555 (D.N.D.1987), *rev'd* 856 F2d 1107 (1988: *Henley*-JRGib/*Lay*), *rev'd North Dakota v. United States,* 495 U.S. 423 (1990). In this case, the court of appeals once again rendered judgment against the state by holding that the Twenty-first Amendment did not provide a basis for the state to regulate the military's purchase of liquor from out-of-state suppliers for its Grand Forks and Minot air force bases. However, this time the Supreme Court reversed by a 5–4 vote.

183. Among the many environmental cases was a challenge to the Boundary Waters Canoe Area Wilderness Act of 1978 over a ban on snowmobiling mentioned in the previous chapter. *State of Minnesota by Alexander v. Block,* 660 F2d 1240 (1981: Br-Steph-Lay). See also *Continental Insurance Companies v. Northeastern Pharmaceutical and Chemical Co.,* 811 F2d 1180 (1987), which involved the cleanup of dioxin waste on a farm near Verona, Missouri.

184. *In re Ahlers,* 794 F2d 388, 402 (1986: *Heaney*-Woll/*JRGib*).

185. *Id.* at 404.

186. *Norwest Bank Worthington v. Ahlers,* 485 U.S. 197 (1988).

187. Morris interview with Judge Gerald Heaney. See P.L. 99–544, 100 Stat. 3105ff; 11 U.S.C. 1201 et seq. On the difference between the Eighth Circuit's decision in *Ahlers* and the new Chapter 12, see *Norwest Bank Worthington v. Ahlers,* 485 U.S. 197, 210–11 (1988).

188. 887 F2d 844 (1989: *Heaney*-Hansen/*Fagg*); 909 F2d 1181 (1990: *Fagg*-Bow-JRGib-Beam-Woll-Magill/*RArn*-*McM*[c]/Lay-Heaney).

189. 770 F2d 137 (1985: *Lay*-JRGib-Phillips).

190. *Arcoren v. Peters,* 829 F2d 671, 678, 683 (1987: *Ross*-McM-RArn-JRGib-Fagg-Bow-Woll-Magill/*Lay-Heaney*).

191. *Coleman v. Block,* 580 F. Supp. 194 (D.N.D.1984). See also 663 F. Supp. 1315 (D.N.D.1987).

192. P.L. 100–233, 101 Stat. 1568.

193. *Coleman v. Lyng,* 864 F2d, 604 (1988: *RArn*-Lay-Henley).

194. *South Dakota History Chronology,* comp. South Dakota Historical Society, http://www.state.sd.us/state/executive/deca/cultural/soc_hist.htm.

195. *Cartersville Elevator, Inc. v. I.C.C.,* 724 F2d 668, 676 (1984: *JRGib*-Br/*Fagg*); 735 F2d 1059 (1984: *JRGib*-Lay-Br-Ross-McM-RArn-Bow/*Fagg*-Heaney).

196. 18 U.S.C. 1355.

197. *Bissonette v. Haig,* 776 F2d 1384 (1985: *RArn*-JRGib-Phillips); 800 F2d 812 (1986: *RArn*-Lay-Heaney-McM-JRGib/*Fagg*-Bow-Woll-Magill).

198. Henley Oral History, 55.

199. *United States v. Peltier,* 585 F2d 314 (1978: *Ross*-Fgib-Steph), *cert. denied* 440 U.S. 945 (1979).

200. *United States v. Peltier,* 800 F2d 772, 779–80 (1986: *Heaney*-Ross-JRGib).

201. *Irving v. Clark,* 758 F2d 1260 (1985: *JRGib*-Heaney-Henley).

202. *Hodel v. Irving,* 481 U.S. 704, 716 (1986).

203. 691 F2d 420 (1982: *Heaney*-Lay-Br-Ross-JRGib/*McM*-RArn).

204. 465 U.S. 463 (1984).

205. 665 F2d 836 (1981: *McM*-Henley-Collinson).

206. *United States v. White,* 508 F2d 453 (1974: *Ross*-Web/*Lay*).

207. *United States v. Dion, Jr.,* 752 F2d 1261 (1985: *Ross*-Heaney-RArn-JRGib-Bow/*McM*-Br-Fagg).

208. *United States v. Dion,* 762 F2d 674 (1985: *Heaney*-JRGib-Fagg).

209. 476 U.S. 734, 740 (1986).

210. Robert Kelly Schneiders, *Unruly River: Two Centuries of Change along the Missouri* (1999), 10.

211. Mark Harvey, "North Dakota, the Northern Plains, and the Missouri Valley Authority," in *The Centennial Anthology of North Dakota History,* ed. Janet Daley Lysengen and Ann M. Rathke (1996), 376; Schneiders, *Unruly River,* 35–36, 54, 148; John E. Thorson, *River of Promise, River of Peril: The Politics of Managing the Missouri River* (1994), 1, 6, 114. See also Priya Kurian and Robert V. Bartlett, "The Garrison Diversion Dream and the Politics of Landscape Engineering," *N.D. Hist.* 59, no. 3 (Summer 1992): 40, 42; Peter Carrels, *Uphill against Water: The*

Great Dakota Water War (1999), 14; Donald J. Pisani, "The Irrigation District and the Federal Relationship," in *The Twentieth Century West,* ed. Gerald W. Nash and Richard E. Etulain (1989), 257, 264, 279.

212. Carrels, *Uphill against Water,* 31; Schneiders, *Unruly River,* 20, 212, 235; Harvey, "North Dakota," 38; Thorson, *River of Promise,* 83, 84. See also Michael Lawson, *Dammed Indians: The Pick-Sloan Plan and the Missouri River Sioux, 1944–1980,* (1994), 75, and also xxviii, xxix, 55–56; Kurian and Bartlett, "The Garrison Diversion Dream," 43.

213. John Ferrell, "Developing the Missouri: South Dakota and the Pick-Sloan Plan," *S.D. Hist.* 19, no. 3 (Fall 1989): 306, 336–37; Harvey, "North Dakota," 29; Carrels, *Uphill against Water,* 40–41; Thorson, *River of Promise,* 3–4, 195.

214. Kurian and Bartlett, "The Garrison Diversion Dream," 45n17; Tweton and Jeliff, *North Dakota,* 184.

215. *United Family Farmers v. Kleppe,* 418 F. Supp. 591, 601 (D.S.D.Nichol 1976).

216. *United Family Farmers v. Kleppe,* 552 F2d 823 (1977: *Lay*-Ross-Wangelin).

217. Carrels, *Uphill against Water,* 99, 200–204.

218. Thorson, *River of Promise,* 116.

219. 590 F2d 263, 267 (1979: *Steph*-F.Gib-Br).

220. *State of North Dakota v. Andrus,* 506 F. Supp. 619 (D.N.D.1981), *aff'd. sub nom. State of North Dakota v. Lands,* 671 F2d 271 (1982: *Larson*-Fgib-Br), *rev. and rem. sub nom. Block v. North Dakota ex rel. Board of University and School Lands,* 461 U.S. 273 (1983).

221. *State of Missouri v. Andrews,* 586 F. Supp. 1268 (D.Neb.Urbom1984).

222. *State of Missouri v. Andrews,* 787 F2d 270, 287 at 291 (1986: *JRGib*-Fagg/*Br*).

223. *Id.*

224. *ETSI Pipeline Project v. Missouri,* 484 U.S. 495 (1988).

225. *State of South Dakota v. Kansas City Southern Industries, Inc.,* 880 F2d 40 (1989: *Lay*-Heaney-Fagg). The Noerr-Pennington doctrine states that it cannot be a violation of the federal antitrust laws for competitors to lobby the government to change the law in a way that would reduce competition.

226. Schneiders, *Unruly River,* 249.

227. *State of South Dakota v. Hazen,* 914 F2d 147 (1990: *Bow*-Fagg-Woll). See also Harvey, "North Dakota," 276.

7. Leaving the Old Century and Entering the New

1. Act of October 17, 1988, 102 Stat. 2467.

2. Robert V. Vine and John Mack Farragher, *The American West: A New Interpretive History* (2000), 542; Thomas D. Peacock and Donald R. Day, "Nations within a Nation: The Dakota and Objiway of Minnesota," in *Minnesota, Real and Imagined,* ed. Stephen R. Grabaud (2000), 116, 128; Timothy Egan, "As Others Abandon Plains, Indians and Bison Come Back," *New York Times,* May 27, 2001, 1; Peter T. Kilborn, "Boom in Economy Skips Towns on the Plains," *New York Times,* July 2, 2000, 1; Frederick C. Luebke, *Nebraska: An Illustrated History* (1995), 308.

3. John E. Brandl, "Policy and Politics in Minnesota," in Grabaud, *Minnesota, Real and Imagined,* 171.

4. All state census figures come from Steven A. Holmes, "After Standing Up to Be Counted, Americans Number 281,421,906," *New York Times,* December 29, 2000, A1, A17.

5. Rhonda McMillan, "Troubled Verdict on Judicial Pay," *A.B.A.J.* (March 2000): 38, 2000 NSW No. 13, 38; *Legal Times,* July 18, 2000, 2000 NSW No. 35, 29–30.

6. See, e.g., *Kansas City Star,* July 19, 1998, 1998B NSW No. 11, 1–3.

7. Senator John Danforth of Missouri sponsored a constitutional amendment inspired by the Kansas City desegregation case, which would have barred federal judges from increasing state and local taxes. It did not get out of Congress.

8. 110 Stat. 3009-546. See *New York Times,* October 27, 1996, 1996 NSW No. 31, 52.

9. *New York Times,* October 27, 1996, 1996 NSW No. 31, 52.

10. See, e.g., Chief Justice William Rehnquist's 1998 end-of-the-year report, discussed in the *Los Angeles Times,* January 1, 1999, 1999 NSW No. 1, 1.

11. 80 Stat. 728.

12. *Des Moines Register,* February 16, 1992, 1992 NSW No. 7, 4.

13. All caseload figures come from the annual reports of the U.S. Court of Appeals for the Eighth Circuit, 1990 to 1999.

14. 223 F2d 898 (2000: *RArn*-Heaney–Paul Magnuson).

15. *Anastasoff v. United States,* 235 F3d 1054 (2000). See *St. Louis Daily Record,* December 19, 2000, 2000 NSW No. 44, 3. On *Anastasoff,* see, e.g., Tony Mauro, "Stealth Decisions under Fire," *Legal Times,* September 4, 2000, 2000 NSW No. 32, 18; Kenneth C. Jones, "'Unpublished Opinion' Rule Struck Down in 8th Circuit," *Mo. Lawyers Weekly,* August 28, 2000, 2000 NSW No. 32, 10; 69 U.S.L.W. No. 15, 2267 (October 24, 2000); Bennette Kramer, "Constitutional Issues: Unpublished Decisions," *Fed.B.Coun.News* 7, no. 5 (December 2000): 19–20; John Borger and Chad Oldfather, "The Uncertain Status of Unpublished Opinions," *Minn. Bench & Bar,* December 2000, 2001 NSW No. 1, 1. See also symposium in *J.App.Prac.* 3, no. 1 (2001): 175–451.

16. William Richman and William L. Reynolds, "Appellate Justice Bureaucracy and Scholarship," *U.Mich.J.L.Ref.* 21 (1988): 623, 642.

17. *Omaha Daily-Record,* May 7, 1991, 1991 NSW No. 15, 1.

18. *Arkansas Democrat-Gazette,* April 18, 1998, 1998A NSW No. 16, 1.

19. *St. Louis Daily Record,* October 16, 1991; *Sioux Falls Argus-Leader,* October 11, 1995; *St. Louis Daily Record,* April 22, 1999, 1999 NSW No. 15, 10. Wollman stepped down as Chief Judge on February 1, 2002, in accordance with an agreement with Judge James B. Loken, who, senior in commission to Judge David R. Hansen, agreed to step aside until March 2003, so that Hansen could serve as chief judge. *St. Louis Daily Record,* February 13, 2002, 2000 NSW No. 7, 8.

20. *Arkansas Democrat-Gazette,* October 11, 1995.

21. June L. Boadwine, interview by the author.

22. Thomas Eagleton was U.S. senator from Missouri from 1971 to 1987.

23. *St. Louis Daily Record,* September 12, 2000.

24. See *Arkansas Democrat-Gazette,* October 20, 1997, 1–2.

25. See *Minneapolis Star Tribune,* July 27, 1990, 1990 NSW No. 24, 5; *St. Paul Pioneer Press,* September 12, 1990, 1990 NSW No. 31, 4.

26. Donald P. Lay, "Observations of Twenty-five Years as a United States Circuit Judge," *Wm. Mitch. L. Rev.* 18 (1992): 595, 632–33.

27. On Judge Loken, see *Almanac of the Federal Judiciary* 2 (2001): 13–14.

28. 104 Stat. 5089.

29. *Cedar Rapids Gazette,* July 31, 1991, and *Des Moines Register,* July 31, 1991, 1991 NSW No. 25, 1–4.

30. Frank J. Margolin and Edward J. Mcmanus, *History of the United States District Court for the Northern District of Iowa, 1882–1987* (1987), 33–34.

31. 92 F3d 612 (1995), *rev'd* 521 U.S. 642 (1997), *on remand* 139 F3d 641 (1998). On Hansen, see also *Almanac Fed. Judiciary* 2 (2001): 11–12.

32. Morris Arnold was also dean of the University of Indiana Law School for a brief time and a member of the faculty of law at Cambridge University.

33. On Morris Arnold, see the *Arkansas Democrat* on the following dates: July 25, 1990; April 11, 1991, 1991 NSW No. 12, 4; October 21, 1991, 1991 NSW No. 32, 3; November 6, 1991, 1991 NSW No. 34, 2. See also "Oral History of Judge J. Smith Henley," by Francis M. Moss, vol. 2 (April 24, 1987), 110.

34. *Legal Times,* March 12, 2001, 2001 NSW No. 10, 44, 45.

35. *Arkansas Democrat-Gazette,* June 30, 1992, 1992 NSW No. 23, 1.

36. 67 U.S.L.W. 1535 (1999).

37. On Morris Arnold, see also *St. Louis Post-Dispatch,* November 6, 1991, 1991 NSW No. 33, 3; *Omaha News-Herald,* October 16, 1991, 1991 NSW No. 31, 4.

38. On the appointment process, see *St. Louis Post-Dispatch,* January 24, 1994, 1994 NSW No. 3, 11; *Minneapolis Star Tribune,* March 4, 1994, 1994 NSW No. 11, 3. Murphy has also been mentioned for a slot on the U.S. Supreme Court. See *Washington Post,* January 19, 1996, 1996 NSW No. 34.

39. Michael W. Unger, "U.S. Circuit Judge," *Fed. Law.* (November–December 1997); See also *History of the United States District Court for the District of Minnesota* (1989), 21–22.

40. *U.S. Jaycees v. McClure,* 534 F. Supp. 766 (D.Minn.1982).

41. 853 F. Supp. 1118 (D.Minn.1994).

42. See *Minneapolis Star Tribune,* October 8, 1994, and October 12, 1994, 1994 NSW No. 43, 1–2.

43. The main source for Kelly's appointment was the author's interview with Kelly on September 9, 1998. See also the following articles from the *Fargo Forum*: July 25, 1997, 1997 NSW No. 31, 14; October 30, 1997, 1997 NSW No. 46; August 1, 1998, 1998B NSW No. 2, 4–5.

44. *Qualls v. Affel,* 158 F3d 425 (1998: *Kelly*-Bow-Woll) (social security); *United States v. Geralds,* 158 F3d 977 (1998: *Kelly*-Bow-Woll) (sentencing); *Nesser v. TWA,* 160 F3d 442 (1998: *Kelly*-Bow-Loken) (Americans with Disabilities Act). See also Presentation of Portrait, Honorable John D. Kelly, Fargo, June 29, 1999, 218 F3d xxxvii.

45. *Fargo Forum,* October 23, 1998, 1998B NSW No. 23, 3.

46. *Fargo Forum,* April 23, 1999, 1999 NSW No. 15, 11; February 25, 2000, 2000 NSW No. 7, 4; June 3, 2000, 2000 NSW No. 22, 3.

47. On Campbell's appointment, see *Des Moines Register*, April 26, 1999, 1999 NSW No. 17, 2; June 11, 2000, 2000 NSW No. 23, 27; September 29, 2000, 2000 NSW No. 35, 5; February 5, 2001, 2001 NSW No. 7, 1. On Harkin's preference, see *Des Moines Register*, June 21, 1999, 1999 NSW No. 23, 2.

48. *Lincoln Journal Star*, April 20, 2001; May 24, 2001, 2001 NSW No. 18, 6; August 3, 2001, 2001 NSW No. 26, 1.

49. On Senator Bond's efforts, see *Des Moines Register*, March 8, 2001, 2001 NSW No. 9, 7–8;*St. Louis Post Dispatch*, March 4, 2001, 2001 NSW No. 8, 4.

50. On Melloy, see *Des Moines Register*, April 11, 2001, 2001 NSW No. 13, 3; July 11, 2001, 2001 NSW No. 23, 6; *Almanac of the Federal Judiciary* (2001), 20–21.

51. On Smith, see *Arkansas Democrat-Gazette*, April 12, 2001, 2001 NSW No. 13, 5; May 23, 2001, 2001 NSW No. 18, 3; *St. Louis Post Dispatch*, May 23, 2001, 2001 NSW No. 17, 6; May 24, 2001, 2001 NSW No. 18, 8. See also Doug Smith, "Ascending the Bench, under the Radar," *Arkansas Times*, July 6, 2001, 2001 NSW No. 22, 3.

52. *Kansas City Star*, March 4, 2000, 2000 NSW No. 11, 2.

53. *Fargo Forum*, May 19, 2000, 2000 NSW No. 20, 1.

54. See *Fargo Forum*, May 19, 2000, 2000 NSW No. 20, 1.

55. 505 U.S. 833 (1992).

56. On the *Amistad* case, see, e.g., Jeffrey Morris, *Federal Justice in the Second Circuit* (1987), 57–60.

57. Quoted in *Des Moines Register*, July 1, 1994. On Blackmun's final years and career, see *Legal Times*, November 23, 1998, 1998B NSW No. 28, 1; *New York Times*, March 5, 1999, 1999 NSW No. 9, 6. There are a number of other newspaper obituaries in 1999 NSW Nos. 9 and 10.

58. After Blackmun's retirement, Justice Clarence Thomas succeeded him as circuit justice for the Eighth Circuit.

59. 505 U.S. 833 (1992).

60. *Fargo Women's Health Organization v. Schafer*, 18 F3d 526 (1994: *JRGib-*Woll/*McM*). See also *Fargo Forum*, March 26, 1993, and March 31, 1993, 1993 NSW No. 12, 4–5. See also *Planned Parenthood v. Miller*, 63 F3d 1452 (1995: *RArn*-JRGib-Fagg), *cert. denied sub nom Janklow v. Planned Parenthood, Sioux Falls Clinic*, 517 U.S. 1174 (1996), dealing with mandatory information and other requirements of a South Dakota abortion statute.

61. See *Carhart v. Stenberg*, 192 F3d 1142, 1145 (1999: *RArn*-Woll-Magnuson).

62. *Carhart v. Stenberg*, 192 F3d 1142 (1999: *RArn*-Woll-Magnuson); *Little Rock Family Planning Services v. Jegley*, 192 F3d 794 (1999: *RArn*-Woll-Magnuson); *Planned Parenthood of Greater Iowa v. Miller*, 195 F3d 386 (1999: *RArn*-Woll-Magnuson). On the argument, see *Arkansas Democrat-Gazette*, April 20, 1999, 1999 NSW No. 15, 6, 7.

63. *Carhart v. Stenberg*, 192 F3d 1142 (1999), *aff'd* 530 U.S. 914 (2000). See also *New York Times*, June 20, 2000, 2000 NSW No. 25, 2.

64. *Little Rock Family Planning Services, P.A. v. Dalton*, 60 F3d 497, 503 at 504 (1995: *McM*-JRGib-*Bow*[c]). See also *Arkansas Democrat-Gazette*, October 28, 1994; July 26, 1995, 1995 NSW No. 24, 1; March 19, 1996, 1996 NSW No. 12, 1.

65. *Dalton v. Little Rock Family Planning Services*, 516 U.S. 474 (1996).

66. *Frisby v. Schultz,* 487 U.S. 474 (1988); *Madsen v. Women's Health Center, Inc.,* 514 U.S. 753 (1994).

67. 52 F3d 772 (1995: *MArn*-Magill/*JRGib*). See also *Fargo Forum,* April 21, 1995.

68. *Kirkeby v. Furness,* 92 F3d 655 (1996: *MArn*-Magill/*JRGib*).

69. *Veneklase v. City of Fargo,* 248 F3d 738 (2001: PC: McM-Loken-Hansen-Mur-Bye-Br/*RArn*-Woll-Bow-Beam-MArn), *cert. denied* 534 U.S. 815 (2001). The history of the lengthy litigation can be found in *Veneklase v. City of Fargo,* 200 F3d 111 (1999). See also *Fargo Forum,* February 15, 2001, 2001 NSW No. 7, 1; May 22, 2001, 2001 NSW No. 18, 2. And see Judge Bye's opinion refusing to excuse himself from the case in 236 F3d 899 (2000).

70. *Douglas v. Brownell,* 88 F3d 1511, 1521, 1523–24 (1996: *JRGib*-McM-Beam). See also *Des Moines Register,* July 17, 1996, 1996 NSW No. 23.

71. *Lincoln Journal Star,* October 20, 2000, 2000 NSW No. 38, 3.

72. 18 U.S.C. 248.

73. *United States v. Dinwiddie,* 76 F3d 913 (1996: *RArn*-Br-Fagg), *cert. denied,* 519 U.S. 1043 (1996). See also *Kansas City Star,* February 17, 1996, 1996 NSW No. 8, 2.

74. *Board of Education of Oklahoma City v. Dowell,* 498 U.S. 237 (1991); *Freeman v. Pitts,* 503 U.S. 467 (1992); *Jenkins v. State of Missouri,* 515 U.S. 70 (1995).

75. *Jenkins v. State of Missouri,* 942 F2d 487, 492–93 (1991: *JRGib*-Heaney-McM).

76. *Jenkins v. State of Missouri,* 965 F2d 654 (1992: *JRGib*-McM-Heaney).

77. *Jenkins v. State of Missouri,* 11 F3d 755 (1993: *JRGib*-McM-Heaney). See also *Jenkins v. State of Missouri,* 13 F3d 1170 (1993: *JRGib*-McM.-Heaney)

78. *Jenkins v. State of Missouri,* 19 F3d 393 (1994: *JRGib*-McM-Magill-Rarn-Fagg-Hansen/*Beam*-Bow-Woll-Loken-MArn).

79. *St. Paul Pioneer Press,* May 9, 1995; *Kansas City Star,* September 23, 1992, 1992 NSW No. 33, 1–2; January 14, 1996, 1996 NSW No. 4, 7.

80. *St. Louis Post Dispatch,* January 12, 1995, 1995A NSW No. 1, 38.

81. *Jenkins v. State of Missouri,* 515 U.S. 70 (1995).

82. *Id.* at 175, 176.

83. *Kansas City Star,* May 23, 1996, 1996 NSW No. 19, 46.

84. *Kansas City Star,* January 11, 1997, 1997 NSW No. 3, 26; January 28, 1997, 1997 NSW No. 5, 26.

85. *Kansas City Star,* March 26, 1997, 1997 NSW No. 14, 29–30; *St. Louis Post Dispatch,* March 27, 1997, 1997 NSW No. 13, 14; *Kansas City Star,* March 29, 1997, 1997 NSW No. 14, 33–34.

86. *St. Louis Post Dispatch,* August 13, 1997, 1997 NSW No. 33, 20.

87. See *Kansas City Star,* June 6, 1998, 1998B NSW No. 5, 31–32.

88. *Kansas City Star,* January 29, 1999, 1999 NSW No. 5, 23.

89. *Kansas City Star,* December 15, 1998, 1998A NSW No. 8.

90. *Kansas City Star,* November 18, 1999, 1999 NSW No. 43, 22, 23.

91. 205 F3d 361 (2000). See also *Kansas City Star,* March 1, 2000, 2000 NSW No. 9, 33.

92. 216 F3d 720 (2000: *JRGib*-RArn-Hansen-Mur-Bye/*Woll*[c]-MArn/

Heaney[c]-McM-*JRGib*[c]/*Beam*[d]-Bow-*Loken*[d]). Judge Gibson wrote the opinion for the en banc court as well as a concurring opinion joined by Judges Heaney and McMillian. See also *Kansas City Star*, June 16, 2000, 2000 NSW No. 25, 26.

93. On recent developments, see *Kansas City Star*, April 20, 2001, 2001 NSW No. 14, 38; April 21, 2001, 2001 NSW No. 14, 42; April 28, 2001, 2001 NSW No. 16, 40.

94. *St. Louis Post Dispatch*, March 19, 1995, 1995 NSW No. 9; Joan Little, "Across Color Lines," May 12, 1997, 1997 NSW No. 20, 39; William H. Freivogel, "Decades of Conflict Cut a Path to Current Case," March 3, 1996, 1996 NSW No. 10, 45.

95. *St. Louis Post Dispatch*, January 29, 1997, 1997 NSW No. 5, 25.

96. *St. Louis Post Dispatch*, September 26, 1997, 1997 NSW No. 40, 38–39.

97. The district judges who handled the St. Louis desegregation cases were Judges James Meredith, William Hungate, George Gunn, and Stephen N. Limbaugh.

98. *St. Louis Post Dispatch*, July 15, 1998, 1998B NSW No. 8, 30, 32.

99. *St. Louis Post Dispatch*, July 19, 1998, 1998B NSW No. 2, 21.

100. *St. Louis Post-Dispatch*, January 7, 1999, 1999 NSW No. 1, 30–34; January 21, 1999, 1999 NSW No. 5, 24–27.

101. *St. Louis Post Dispatch*, February 3, 1999, 1999 NSW No. 5, 34; March 13, 1999, 1999 NSW No. 10, 53; March 16, 1999, 1999 NSW No. 10, 54.

102. *Kansas City Star*, January 12, 2001, 2001 NSW No. 3, 28–29.

103. The milestones of this litigation include *Little Rock Sch. Dist. v. Pulaski Cty. Special Sch.*, 778 F2d 404 (1985: *Heaney*-Lay-Br-Ross-McM/*RArn* [c/d]/*Bow*[c/d]/ *JRGib*-Fagg); *Little Rock School District v. Pulaski County Sp.S.D.No. 1*, 921 F2d 1371, 1383 (1990: *RArn*-Woll-Heaney); appeal of *Little Rock School District*, 949 F2d 253 (1991: *RArn*-Heaney-*Woll*[c]); *Little Rock School District v. Pulaski County Special School District*, 971 F2d 161 (1992: *Heaney*-RArn-Woll).

104. *Arkansas Democrat-Gazette*, December 16, 1997, 1997 NSW No. 51, 30.

105. *Arkansas Democrat-Gazette*, January 12, 2001, 2001 NSW No. 3, 29.

106. *Arkansas Democrat-Gazette*, July 10, 2001, 2001 NSW No. 23, 29.

107. *St. Paul Pioneer Press*, September 10, 1996, 1996 NSW No. 27.

108. *St. Louis Post Dispatch*, October 1, 1997, 1997 NSW No. 40, 43; *St. Louis Post Dispatch*, November 10, 1999, 1999 NSW No. 40, 36.

109. Ellen F. Harris, "'Non-specialists' Join in Discrimination Boom," *Mo.Law Wkly*, July 21, 1997, 1997 NSW No. 30, 7.

110. 104 Stat. 327.

111. See *Otting v. J.C. Penney*, 223 F3d 704 (2000). The panel was Floyd Gibson (writing), McMillian, and Morris Arnold.

112. See *Sioux Falls Argus-Leader*, May 31, 2000, 2000 NSW No. 22, 1.

113. *Land v. Baptist Medical Center*, 164 F3d 423 (January 6, 1999: *Fagg*– Cynthia Holcomb Hall/*RArn*).

114. *Cedar Rapids Community School District v. Garret F.*, reported in *St. Louis Post Dispatch*, March 4, 1999, 1999 NSW No. 8, 4.

115. *St. Paul Pioneer Press*, March 7, 1997, 1997 NSW No. 11, 12; *Arkansas Democrat-Gazette*, March 21, 1996, 1996 NSW No. 12. *Denesha v. Farmers Ins. Co.*, 161 F3d 491 (1998: *Heaney*-McM-Fagg), *cert. denied* 526 U.S. 1115 (1999).

116. *Alsbrook v. Maumelle, Ark.*, 156 F3d 825 (1998: McM-*RArn*/*Beam*), *vac.*

184 F3d 999 (1999: *Beam*-Bow-Woll-Loken-Hansen-MArn/*McM*-RArn-Fagg-Mur), *cert. gr.* 528 U.S. 1146 (2000); *cert. dism.* 529 U.S. 1001 (2000).

117. *Bradley v. Arkansas Dept. of Education*, 189 F3d 745 (1999: *Bow*-Loken), *vac. & reh e b gr. Jim C. v. Arkansas Department of Education*, 197 F3d 958 (1999); *different resuit on rehearing en banc*, 235 F3d 1079 (1999: *RArn*-Woll-McM-Hansen-MArn-Mur/*Bow*-Beam-Loken-Bye), *cert. denied* 533 U.S. 949 (2001).

118. *Humenansky v. Regents of the University of Minnesota*, 152 F3d 822 (1998: *Loken*-Woll/*Bataillon*). Judges McMillian, Richard Arnold, and Fagg would have reheard en banc.

119. See *Kimel v. Florida Board of Regents*, 528 U.S. 62 (2000); *St. Louis Daily Record*, January 14, 2000, 2000 NSW No. 3, 1.

120. *Omaha World-Herald*, December 12, 2000, 2000 NSW No. 44, 1.

121. *St. Paul Pioneer Press*, August 4, 2000, 2000 NSW No. 3, 2.

122. *Bassett v. Minneapolis*, in *St. Louis Daily Record*, April 14, 2000, 5. The panel was Lay, Beam, and John R. Gibson.

123. *Devine v. Stone, Leyton & Gershman, Mo. Lawyers Weekly*, 100 F3d 78 (1996: *Murphy*-Beam/*Heaney*), *cert. denied* 520 U.S. 1211 (1997).

124. *Quick v. Donaldson Co.*, 90 F3d 1372 (1996: *Murphy*-Bean/*Nangle*); *Missouri Lawyers Weekly*, August 5, 1996, 1996 NSW No. 24.

125. See *St. Louis Post Dispatch*, April 23, 2999, 1999 NSW No. 5, 12–33. The panel was constituted of Judges Murphy (writing), Bowman, and Vietor.

126. See *Hathaway v. Runyon*, 132 F3d 1214 (1997: *Murphy*-McM-Hansen).

127. *Burns v. McGregor Electric Industries*, 955 F2d 959 (1992: *Woll*-Henley-Fagg), on remand 807 F.Supp. 506 (S.D.Ia 1992), *rev'd* (1993: *Lay*-McM-Bow). See *Des Moines Register*, April 2, 1993, 1993 NSW No. 12, 6.

128. *Jenson v. Eveleth Taconite Co.*, 130 F3d 1287, 1304 (1997: *Lay*-McM-Fgib), *cert. denied sub nom. Ogleby Norton Co. v. Jenson*, 524 U.S. 953 (1998).

129. See, generally, John Tevlin, "What Price Pain," *Minneapolis Star-Tribune*, November 29, 1998, 1998 NSW No. 28, 11; January 4, 1999, 1999 NSW No. 2, 13.

130. Gravette: *Arkansas Gazette*, March 19, 1991, 1991 NSW No. 19. Missouri parochial schools: *Kansas City Star*, 1991 NSW No. 17. Wabasso: *Saint Paul Pioneer Press*, August 8, 1997, 1997 NSW No. 35, 1. The panel was Wollman, Beam, and Murphy (dissenting).

131. *Kansas City Star*, August 17, 1999, 1999 NSW No. 30, 2; *St. Louis Post Dispatch* (editorial), August 19, 1999, 1999 NSW No. 30, 3.

132. *St. Paul Pioneer Press*, September 16, 1994, 1994 NSW No. 40, 5.

133. 42 U.S.C. 2000(bb).

134. *United States v. Crystal Evangelical Free Church (In re Young)*, 82 F3d 1407 (1996: *McM*-Magill/*Bogue*).

135. *United States v. Crystal Evangelical Free Church (In re Young)*, 89 F3d 494 (1996).

136. *Christians v. Crystal Evangelical Free Church*, 521 U.S. 114 (1997). The intervening case was *City of Bourne v. Flores*, 521 U.S. 507 (1997).

137. *Fargo Forum*, April 15, 1998, 1998 NSW No. 16, 1.

138. *St. Paul Pioneer Press*, October 16, 1998, 1998 NSW No. 21, 1–2; *Kan.City Bus. J.* 19, No. 27, 1999 NSW No. 10, 37.

139. *St. Louis Post Dispatch*, September 16, 1994, 1990 NSW No. 40, 4.

140. *St. Louis Post Dispatch*, October 5, 1993, 1993 NSW No. 32, 4.

141. *Gilleo v. City of Ladue*, 774 F. Supp. 1559 (E.D.Mo.1991).

142. *Gilleo v. City of Ladue*, 986 F2d 1180 (1993: *Reavley*-MArn-Fgib). The opinion was written by Judge Thomas M. Reavely of the Court of Appeals for the Fifth Circuit.

143. *New York Times*, February 28, 1994, 1994 NSW No. 8, 5.

144. *City of Ladue v. Gilleo*, 512 U.S. 43 (1994). See also *Kansas City Star*, June 14, 1994, 1994 NSW No. 26, 1. Later in the decade, the court of appeals held unconstitutional a Fort Smith ban (also used in three other Arkansas cities) prohibiting putting leaflets on parked cars unless someone in the car was willing to receive them. *Arkansas Democrat-Gazette*, June 25, 1999, 1999 NSW No. 23, 1.

145. *Families Achieving Independence v. Nebraska Department of Social Services*, 111 F3d 1308 (1997: *Magill*-RArn-Fagg-Bow-Woll-Beam-Loken-Hansen/ *Heaney*-McM-MArn-Mur) vac. 91 F3d 1076 (1996: *Heaney*-Mur/*Magill*).

146. *Fargo Forum*, June 10, 1992.

147. *Cuffley v. Mickes*, 208 F3d 702 (2000: *Bow*-Woll-Hansen), *cert. denied sub nom Yarnell v. Cuffley*, 532 U.S. 903 (2000). See also *Missouri ex rel. Missouri Highway & Transp. Comm'n v. Cuffley*, 112 F3d 1332 (1997: *Woll*-Bow-Hansen). See *St. Louis Post-Dispatch*, December 1, 1999, 1999 NSW No. 43, 3; January 2, 2000, 2000 NSW No. 2, 19; November 3, 2000, 2000 NSW No. 39, 14; April 5, 2001, 2001 NSW No. 12, 13. And see *Lincoln Star Journal*, October 31, 2000, 2000 NSW No. 38, 2; *Des Moines Register*, March 6, 2001, 2001 NSW No. 8, 2. In a case in court since the 1980s, the Court of Appeals in 2001 ordered the state of Missouri to issue Mary E. Lewis the license plate "ARYAN-1." To do otherwise, said the court, would be viewpoint discrimination. *Lewis v. Wilson* (2001: *MArn*-Heaney-Battey), *St. Louis Daily Record*, June 15, 2001, 6.

148. See *St. Louis Daily Record*, December 31, 1999, 2000 NSW No. 1, 1. The panel was Wollman (writing), Richard Arnold, and Charles R. Wolle (dissenting).

149. *Omaha World Herald*, May 1, 1991, 1991 NSW No. 14, 2. The panel was Heaney (writing), Lay, and Wollman.

150. *Dawson v. Scurr*, 986 F2d 257 (1993: *Lay*-RArn-Loken); *Herlein v. Higgins* 172 F3d 1089 (1999: *MArn*-Woll-Loken), *St. Louis Daily Record*, April 24, 1999, 1999 NSW No. 15, 15–16.

151. *St. Paul Pioneer Press*, January 6, 1994, 1994 NSW No. 1, 2.

152. *Kansas City Star*, April 21, 1998, 1998A NSW No. 16, 2.

153. Quoted in *Kansas City Star*, August 8, 1990, 1990 NSW No. 28, n.p.

154. *Alexander v. Thornburgh*, 943 F2d 825 (1991: *JRGib*-Woll-Fgib).

155. *United States v. Lee*, 935 F2d 952 (1991: *Benson*-Magill/*RArn*).

156. *R.A.V. v. City of St. Paul, Minn.*, 505 U.S. 377 (1992); *Wisconsin v. Mitchell*, 508 U.S. 476 (1993). See also *United States V. J.H.H.*, 22 F3d 821 (1994: *Bow*-Lay-Campbell).

157. *United States v. Lee*, 6 F3d 1297 (1993 : *JRGib*-RArn-Bow-Woll-Hansen/ *Lay*-Loken-MArn[c/d]/*McM*-Fagg-Magill-Beam).

158. One complex redistricting case the court of appeals was involved with pitted the Minnesota Democratic-Farmer-Labor Party and state courts against the

Independent-Republicans and the federal courts. In 1993 the Supreme Court threw out the federal court's districting plan, the work of Judges Lay, McLaughlin, and Paul A. Magnuson. *St. Paul Pioneer Press*, January 11, 1992, 1992 NSW No. 3, 1.

159. *Forbes v. Arkansas Educational Television Communication Network Foundation*, 982 F2d 289 (1992: *PC*: RArn-McM-JRGib), dismissing appeal on issue of preliminary injunctive relief as moot.

160. 22 F3d 1423 (1994: *RArn*-Bow-Woll-Beam-Loken-MArn/*McM*-JRGib-Fagg-Magill-Hansen[c/d]), *cert. denied* 513 U.S. 995 (1995). See also *Arkansas Times*, November 22, 1996; *Arkansas Democrat-Gazette*, June 6, 1995, 1995 NSW No. 19, 7.

161. *Forbes v. Arkansas Educational Television Communications*, 93 F3d 497 (1996: *RArn*-McM-JRGib), *rev'd* 523 U.S. 666 (1998). See *St. Paul Pioneer Press*, October 7, 1997, 1997 NSW No. 42, 3; *New York Times*, May 19, 1998, 1998B NSW No. 2, 1; *Arkansas Democrat-Gazette*, October 6, 1997, 1997 NSW No. 42, 1. See also 145 F3d 1017 (1998: PC: McM-JRGib-RArn). After the *Forbes* decision, the court of appeals upheld Judge Charles Wolle's ruling in the Southern District of Iowa that allowed Iowa Public Television to exclude a group of third-party candidates from a weekly news program. *Des Moines Register*, July 31, 1998, 1998B NSW No. 12, 4.

162. *Twin Cities Area New Party v McKenna*, 73 F3d 196 (1996: *Fagg*-RArn-Woods) *rev'd Twin Cities Area New Party v. Timmons*, 520 U.S. 350, 377 (1997). See also *Minneapolis Star-Tribune*, January 6, 1996, 1996 NSW No. 3, 1.

163. *Day v. Holahan*, 34 F3d 1356, 1366 (1994: *Bow*-Loken-Stevens).

164. *Springfield News-Leader*, Dec. 20, 1995, 1996 NSW No. 1; *Kansas City Star*, December 20, 1995, 1996 NSW No. 1; *Nixon v. Shrink Missouri Government PAC*, 528 U.S. 377 (2000), *rev'g* 161 F3d 519 (1998: *Bow*-Ross[c]/*JRGib*). See also *New York Times*, January 25, 2000, 2000 NSW No. 4, 6. See, e.g., Linda Greenhouse, *After 23 Years, Justices will Revisit Campaign Limits, New York Times*, January 28, 1999, 1999 NSW No. 4, 4. See also *Kansas City Star*, January 26, 1999, 1999 NSW No. 4, 2. See also *New York Times*, January 28, 1999, 1999 NSW No. 4, 4; *St. Louis Post-Dispatch*, March 1, 2000, 2000 NSW No. 10, 4.

165. *Missouri Republican Party v. Lamb*, 227 F3d 1070 (2000: *MArn*-Bow/*JRGib*). See also *St. Louis Daily Record*, September 13, 2000, 2000 NSW No. 33, 8; *Kansas City Star*, September 12, 2000, 2000 NSW No. 33, 4.; *Nixon v. Missouri Republican Party*, 533 U.S. 945 (2001). In mid-1998, a panel of Beam, Wollman, and Morris Arnold held unconstitutional an Arkansas law passed through initiative, which imposed a $300 contribution limit for state constitutional offices and $100 for other state and local offices. The Supreme Court denied certiorari. See *Arkansas Democrat-Gazette*, June 5, 1998, 1998B NSW No. 5, 4.

166. *Gralike v. Cook*, 191 F3d 911 (1999: *McM*-Fgib/*Hansen*[in part]), *aff'd Cook v. Gralike*, 531 U.S. 510 (2001). See also *St. Louis Daily Record*, September 3, 1999, 1999 NSW No. 32, 3.

167. *Miller v. Moore*, 169 F3d 1120 (1999: *MArn*-Magill-*Beam* [c/d]). See also *St. Louis Daily Record*, March 4, 1999, 1999 NSW No. 8.

168. 78 F3d 1313 (1996: *Bow*-Beam-Loken).

169. *Id.* at 1324, 1325.

170. *United States v. Tucker*, 82 F3d 1423, 1424 (1996: *McM*-Mur).

171. *In re: Independent Counsel v. Mandanici, St. Louis Daily Record,* June 26, 1998, 1998B NSW No. 7, 26–27.

172. *St. Louis Post Dispatch,* May 29, 1996, 1996 NSW No. 19, 14–15.

173. *Jones v. Clinton,* 869 F. Supp. 690 (E.D.Ark.1994); 879 F.Supp. 86 (1995).

174. *Jones v. Clinton,* 72 F3d 1354, 1357ff. (1996).

175. *Id.* at 1361.

176. *Id.* at 1363, 1365.

177. *Id.* at 1367. See also *Id.* at 1368–70.

178. *St. Louis Post-Dispatch,* January 11, 1996, 1996 NSW No. 2, 8.

179. *Jones v. Clinton,* 81 F3d 78 (1996: *McM*), dissenting from denial of rehearing *en banc.*

180. *Clinton v. Jones,* 520 U.S. 681 (1997).

181. Patricia M. Wald, "A Whitewater Legacy: Running the Rapids of Constitutional Law," *Rec. Ass'n. B. City N.Y.,* no. 1 (January-February 2000), 22, 41.

182. *In re Grand Jury Subpoena Duces Tecum,* 112 F3d 910, 921 (1997: *Bow-Woll/Richard G. Kopf*).

183. *Office of the President v. Office of Independent Counsel,* 521 U.S. 1105 (1997).

184. *National Law Journal,* April 13, 1998, 1998A NSW No. 14, 25.

185. *Lincoln Journal Star,* October 23, 1998, 1998B NSW No. 23, 33.

186. Including the seventy-eight-year-old Miles Lord. *Minneapolis Star-Tribune,* October 22, 1998, 1998B NSW No. 22.

187. *Kansas City Star,* October 21, 1998, 1998B NSW No. 23, 31–32.

188. *New York Times,* October 21, 1998, 1998B NSW No. 22, 30–31. See also *USA Today,* October 21, 1998, 1998B NSW No. 22, 29.

189. *St. Louis Post Dispatch,* 1998B NSW No. 26, 28.

190. *U.S.A. Today,* November 18, 1998, 1998B NSW No. 26, 29.

191. *Wall Street Journal,* April 13, 1999, 1999B NSW No. 13, 25–26.

192. Ibid., 20.

193. Jim McDougal: *Arkansas Democrat-Gazette,* January 17, 1998, 1998A NSW 4, 7. The panel was Fagg (writing), Hansen, and Magill. Susan McDougal: *St. Louis Post-Dispatch,* February 24, 1998, 1998A NSW No. 8, 8. The panel was John R. Gibson, McMillian, and Beam.

194. *Minneapolis Star-Tribune,* January 21, 2001, 2001 NSW No. 4, 16.

195. See, e.g., the analysis of Judge Scott O. Wright of the Western District of Missouri of the failure of the war on drugs, *Kansas City Star,* November 13, 2000, 2000 NSW No. 41, 20.

196. *St. Louis Post-Dispatch,* September 15, 1991 (editorial), 1991 NSW No. 29, 4; May 28, 1997, 1997 NSW No. 23, 63–64.

197. See, e.g., *United States v. Maxwell,* 25 F3d 1389 (1994: *Woll*-McM-Magill) *aff'g in part, vac'g in part, rem'd United States v. Majied,* 1993 U.S. Dist. LEXIS 15126 (D. Neb. 1993).

198. *United States v. Weekly,* 128 F3d 1198, *mod.* 118 F3d 576, 582, 584 (1997: *JRGib*-Bow/*Br*), *cert. denied sub nom Romero v. United States* 522 U.S. 945 (1997). See also Judge Bright's opinion in *United States v. Hively,* 61 F3d 1358 (1995: *PC*: Beam-Mur-*Br*[c]).

199. *United States v. Jones,* 97–1344, discussed in *St. Louis Post-Dispatch,*

May 29, 1998, 1998B NSW No. 3, 2–3; and *St. Louis Daily Record,* May 29, 1998, 1998B NSW No. 3, 2. See also Bright's opinions in *United States v. Alatorre,* 207 F3d 1078 (2000); and *United States v. Chavez, St. Louis Daily Record,* October 25, 2000, 2000 NSW No. 37, 8.

200. *Omaha World-Herald,* August 26, 1994, 1994 NSW No. 36, 2.

201. *National Law Journal,* October 26, 1998, 1998B NSW No. 24, 21.

202. *Omaha World-Herald,* September 11, 2000, 2000 NSW No. 33, 22.

203. See *Kansas City Star,* November 13, 2000, 2000 NSW No. 41, 20.

204. *Missouri Lawyers Weekly,* July 15, 1996, 1996 NSW No. 22, 4.

205. 40 F3d 910 (1994: *Magill*-Fagg-Bow-Beam-Loken-Hansen/*McM-Br-Marn*[diss]/*RArn-Woll* [diss. in part]). See, however, Judge Wollman's careful, balanced opinion in *United States v. Lucht,* 16 F3d 541 (1994: *Woll*-Henley-MArn).

206. *Minneapolis Star-Tribune,* September 30, 1994, 1994 NSW No. 42, 4.

207. *Lincoln Journal Star,* May 5, 1994, 1994 NSW No. 18, 5.

208. *Muhammed v. Drug Enforcement Agency,* 92 F3d 648, 650 (1996: *Beam*-Loken/*MArn*).

209. *Id.* at 654.

210. *United States v. $141,700 in United States Currency,* 157 F3d 600 (1998: *Hansen*-Loken-*Davis*), *St. Louis Daily Record,* October 9, 1998, 1999B NSW No. 21, 8. However, see *United States v. Beck,* 140 F3d 1129 (April 6, 1998: *Bennett*-McM-Fagg).

211. See *Sioux Falls Argus-Leader,* June 29, 1993, 1993 NSW No. 22, 3.

212. *Minneapolis Star-Tribune,* June 29, 1993, 1993 NSW No. 22, 3.

213. *United States v. Jacobson,* 893 F2d 999, 1002 (1990: *Heaney*-Lay/*Fagg*).

214. *Id.* at 1002.

215. *United States v. Jacobson,* 916 F2d 467, 469, 470 (1990: *Fagg*-McM-RArn-JRGib-Bow-Woll-Magill-Beam/*Lay-Heaney*).

216. *United States v. Jacobson,* 503 U.S. 540, 554 (1992).

217. *Kansas City Star,* July 20, 1996, 1996 NSW No. 24, 32–33.

218. See *St. Louis Post Dispatch,* June 30, 1997, 1997 NSW No. 24, 42; August 18, 1998, 1998 NSW No. 14, 5–6. In 2000, President Bill Clinton granted clemency to Griffin, whose wife apparently was seriously ill. *Kansas City Star,* December 23, 2000, 2001 NSW No. 1, 9.

219. *St. Louis Post Dispatch,* December 13, 1991, 1991 NSW No. 35, 3; October 4, 1996, 1996 NSW No. 28, 7.

220. See *Lincoln Journal Star,* May 10, 1993, 1993 NSW No. 17, 2.

221. *St. Louis Post Dispatch,* August 15, 2002, 2002 NSW No. 29, 27, 28.

222. In 1990 seven Chief Judges of the courts of appeals including Donald Lay were successful in engineering a rejection by the U.S. Judicial Conference of a recommendation of a committee headed by former justice Lewis Powell Jr. that would have placed new limits on *habeas corpus* by prisoners on death row. *New York Times,* March 15, 1990, A1. This, however, only delayed the inevitable, the enactment of the Antiterrorism and Effective Death Penalty Act of 1996.

223. *Arkansas Democrat-Gazette,* January 10, 1997, 1997 NSW No. 3, 27.

224. *Saint Paul Pioneer Press,* July 6, 1990, 1990 NSW No. 21, 2.

225. *Kansas City Star,* October 31, 1998, 1998B NSW No. 25, 3.

226. *Arkansas Democrat-Gazette*, November 13, 1991, 1991 NSW No. 34, 3.

227. *Des Moines Register*, February 16, 1992, 1992 NSW No. 7, 1–3; *Des Moines Register*, April 14, 1992, 1992 NSW No. 13, 1; *Des Moines Register*, February 22, 1992, 1992 NSW No. 8, 1; *Blumberg v. United States*, 961 F2d 787 (1992: *Fagg*-Bow-Hansen).

228. *Blomkest Fertilizer, Inc. v. Potash Corp. of Sask Inc.*, 203 F3d 1028 (2000: *Beam*-Bow-Woll-Loken-Hansen-MArn/*JRGib*-Heaney-McM-RArn-Mur), vacating a panel decision in which Judges J. R. Gibson and Heaney were in the majority and Judge Beam dissented. See *St. Louis Daily Record*, 1999 NSW No. 18, 1–2.

229. *St. Paul Pioneer Press*, July 25, 2000, 2000 NSW No. 29, 2.

230. *Omaha World-Herald*, July 21, 1994, 1994 NSW No. 32, 2.

231. *Sioux Falls Argus-Leader*, April 3, 1997, 1997 NSW No. 16, 3.

232. *Omaha World-Herald*, August 16, 1995, 1995 NSW No. 27, 1; *Fargo Forum*, August 30, 1991, 1991 NSW No. 27, 2.

233. *Minneapolis Star-Tribune*, November 16, 1999.

234. The panel was Murphy (writing), Wollman, and Kyle. See *St. Louis Daily Record*, September 5, 1998, 1998B NSW No. 17, 4.

235. *Arkansas Democrat-Gazette*, March 26, 1998, 1998A NSW No. 12, 2.

236. *Minneapolis Star-Tribune*, April 20, 1999, 1999 NSW No. 15, 9; *Sioux Falls Argus-Leader*, February 3, 1999, 1999 NSW No. 6, 1.

237. *Irvine v. United States*, 936 F2d 343 (1991: *McM-Br*[c]/*Bow*), rev'd *Irvine v. United States*, 981 F2d 991, 998 (1992: *Bow*-Fagg-Woll-Beam-Hansen/*Loken*[c]/*McM*-Br-Lay-JRGib).

238. *United States v. Irvine*, 511 U.S. 224 (1994).

239. *Anheuser-Busch, Inc. v. Balducci Publications*, 28 F3d 769 (1994: *JRGib*-McM-Bow).

240. *St. Louis Post-Dispatch*, July 1, 1994, 1994 NSW No. 29, 4; January 18, 1995, 1995 NSW No. 2, 1.

241. *St. Louis Post-Dispatch*, February 19, 1997, 1997 NSW No. 8, 1.

242. See *St. Paul Pioneer Press*, March 5, 1997, 1997 NSW No. 11, 20; *Des Moines Register*, March 12, 1997, 1997 NSW No. 11, 27; July 27, 1999, 1999 NSW No. 28, 43, 44; *Lincoln Journal Star*, September 8, 1996, 1996 NSW No. 27; *Saint Louis Post-Dispatch*, January 8, 1997, 1997 NSW No. 2, 23–24.

243. *Saint Louis Post-Dispatch*, June 14, 1991, 1991 NSW No. 19, 2.

244. *Kansas City Star*, October 27, 1990, 1990 NSW No. 33, 1; *Kansas City Star*, January 16, 1991, 1991 NSW No. 1, 1.

245. *Hartford Underwriters Insurance Co. v. Magna Bank, N.A.*, 177 F3d 719 (1999: *Bow*-Fagg-Woll-Loken-Hansen-MArn/*Heaney*-McM-RArn-Beam-Mur), aff'd sub nom. *Hartford Underwriters Ins. Co. v. Planters Bank, N.A.*, 530 U.S. 1 (2000).

246. *Bank One v. Guttau*, 190 F3d 844 (1999). See *Des Moines Register*, September 8, 1999, 1999 NSW No. 34, 1; November 11, 1999, 1999 NSW No. 42, 3; April 6, 2000, 2000 NSW No. 15, 1. See also *Des Moines Register*, April 14, 2001, 2001 NSW No. 16, 20.

247. The law banned higher copayment charges for patients who visit a health

care provider of their choosing, so long as the provider would be willing to adopt the insurance company's schedule of fees. *Arkansas Democrat-Gazette*, September 3, 1998, 1998B NSW No. 17, 1–2.

248. *St. Louis Post-Dispatch*, October 23, 1998, 1999 NSW No. 38, 6.

249. *Arkansas Democrat-Gazette*, December 27, 1992, 1993 NSW No. 1, 2.

250. Paul Gustafson, "Court Rules against Laws Dictating Deliveries to Waste Plant," *St. Paul Pioneer Press*, February 19, 1993.

251. *SDDS, Inc. v. State of South Dakota*, 47 F3d 263 (1995: *Magill*-JRGib-Beam).

252. *U & I Sanitation v. Columbus, Neb.*, 205 F3d 1063 (2000: *JRGib*-Mur-Lay).

253. *Minneapolis Star-Tribune*, December 16, 1997, 1997 NSW No. 51, 1.

254. *Des Moines Register*, July 3, 1999, 1999 NSW No. 25, 36; *Omaha World-Herald*, May 15, 2001, 2001 NSW No. 17, 1–2.

255. *Mille Lacs v. State of Minnesota*, 124 F3d 904 (1997: *Lay*-McM-JRGib), *aff'g Mille Lacs Band of Chippewa Indians v. Minnesota*, 861 F. Supp. 784 (D.Minn. Murphy1994). Judges Wollman and Loken would have reheard the case. See also *St. Paul Pioneer Press*, August 27, 1997, 1997 NSW No. 36, 1.

256. 526 U.S. 172 (1994).

257. *State of South Dakota v. Bourland*, 949 F2d 984, 994 (1991: *Bow*-Heaney-Br).

258. *South Dakota v. Bourland*, 508 U.S. 679 (1993). See also *Fargo Forum*, June 15, 1993, 1993 NSW No. 21, 3.

259. *Fargo Forum*, November 8, 1994, 1994 NSW No. 44, 2. Judge Bowman wrote the opinion of the court, joined by Judge Bright; Judge Heaney dissented.

260. *Yankton Sioux Tribe v. Southern Missouri Waste Management District*, 99 F3d 1439 (1997: *Murphy*-RArn/*Magill*), *rev'd* 522 U.S. 329 (1998). See also *Sioux Falls Argus-Leader*, March 21, 1998, 1998A NSW No. 12, 22; and *Fargo Forum*, January 27, 1998, 1998A NSW No. 5, 1–2.

261. 69 F3d 878 (1995: *Loken*-Magill/*Murphy*), *rev'd* 519 U.S. 919 (1996).

262. *Lincoln Journal Star*, August 14, 1997, 1997 NSW No. 34, 1; October 10, 1998, 1998B NSW No. 21, 3; November 25, 1998, 1998B NSW No. 28, 30; *Lincoln Journal Star*, July 8, 2001, 2001 NSW No. 22, 20. See also *Omaha World-Herald*, January 7, 1997, 1997 NSW No. 4, 25–26. The court of appeals opinions were *Santee Sioux Tribe v. Nebraska*, 121 F3d 427 (1997: *Hansen*-Fgib-McM); *United States v. Santee Sioux Tribe*, 135 F3d 558 (1998: *Bow*-Br-Mun); *United States v. Santee Sioux Tribe*, 254 F3d 728 (2001: *Beam*-Bow-Mun).

263. *Gaming Corp. of America v. Dorsey & Whitney*, 88 F3d 536 (1996: *Mur*-Loken-Hansen).

264. *Iron Eyes v. Henry*, 907 F2d 819 (1990: *JRGib*-Magill/*Heaney*).

265. *Omaha World-Herald*, August 12, 1994, 1994 NSW No. 33, 7; *St. Louis Post-Dispatch*, January 13, 1996, 1996 NSW No. 3, 9; *Kansas City Star*, January 13, 1996, 1996 NSW No. 4, 2.

266. On Wadena, see *Fargo Forum*, June 11, 1998, 1998B NSW No. 4, 7; November 22, 1996, 1996 NSW No. 34; January 23, 2000, 2000 NSW No. 5, 12. The

panel was McMillian, Lay and Bean, who dissented in part. On Finn, see *Fargo Forum*, August 2, 1997, 1997 NSW No. 3.

267. *United States v. Rouse*, 100 F3d 560 (*Br*-McM/*Loken*).

268. *United States v. Rouse*, 111 F3d 591 (*Loken*-McM/*Br*).

269. See, e.g., *National L.J.*, January 25, 1990; *St. Paul Pioneer Press*, September 25, 1996, 1996 NSW No. 27; *Kansas City Star*, June 24, 1995, 1995 NSW No. 22, 35–37; 2 Henley O.H. 55.

270. See *St. Paul Pioneer Press*, November 10, 1992, 1992 NSW No. 39, 5; *New York Times*, November 10, 1992, 1992 NSW No. 39, 3; *Minneapolis Star Tribune*, November 10, 1992, 1992 NSW No. 39, 1; *National Law Journal*, November 30, 1992, 1992 NSW No. 40, 1.

271. *Sioux Falls Argus-Leader*, July 8, 1993, 1993 NSW No. 23, 1.

272. Dennis McAuliffe Jr., "Last Stand for Leonard Peltier," *Washington Post*, July 4, 1995, 1995 NSW No. 22, 35–37.

273. See letter from Peter Matthiessen et al., *United States v. Leonard Peltier*, *New York Review of Books*, July 20, 1999, 56.

274. See articles in *Arkansas Democrat-Gazette*, February 27, 1993, 1993 NSW No. 10, 1; April 3, 1993, 1993 NSW No. 14, 3; October 13, 1994, 1994 NSW No. 43, 3; April 11, 2001, 2001 NSW No. 13, 1.

275. *Arkansas Democrat-Gazette*, May 7, 1997, 1997 NSW No. 20, 6.

276. *Kansas City Star*, April 10, 1996.

277. *St. Louis Post-Dispatch*, April 8, 2000, 2000 NSW No. 15, 7. The panel was made up of Judges Loken, Floyd Gibson, and Richard Arnold (dissenting).

278. *St. Louis Post-Dispatch*, September 10, 1996, 1996 NSW No. 27, 3.

279. *St. Louis Post-Dispatch*, June 16, 1993, 1993 NSW No. 21, 5. Judge McMillian wrote the opinion for the court.

280. See *St. Paul Pioneer Press*, January 31, 1997, 1997 NSW No. 6; *Sioux Falls Argus-Leader*, February 25, 1995, 1995 NSW No. 7, 3; April 17, 1999, 1999 NSW No. 15, 31; *Omaha World-Herald*, August 17, 1999, 1999 NSW No. 31, 23; December 12, 1999, 1999 NSW No. 45, 19; April 5, 2000, 2000 NSW No. 14, 8.

281. *Lincoln Journal Star*, March 24, 2001, 2001 No. 11, 3.

282. *Sioux Falls Argus-Leader*, February 3, 1995, 1995 NSW No. 4, 3.

283. *Fargo Forum*, April 14, 1995, 1995 NSW No. 12, 3.

284. *Fargo Forum*, July 18, 1995, 1995 NSW No. 23, 2.

285. *Minneapolis Star Tribune*, June 11, 1992, 1992 NSW No. 20, 3.

286. *St. Paul Pioneer Press*, December 13, 1996; *Minneapolis Star Tribune*, September 25, 1997, 1997 NSW No. 41, 2. See also *Mausolf v. Babbitt*, 93 F3d 1295 (1996: *RArn-Woll*[c/d]/*Marn*).

287. *Friends of Boundary Waters Wilderness v. Robertson*, 978 F2d 1484 (1992: *JRGib*-McM/*Magill*), cert. denied sub nom *City of Ely v. Friends of the Boundary Waters Wilderness*, 508 U.S. 972 (1993).

288. See *Fargo Forum*, August 14, 1998, 1998B NSW No. 1–2. See also *St. Louis Post-Dispatch*, August 14, 1998, 1998B NSW No. 14, 3.

INDEX

★ ★ ★ ★ ★ ★ ★

Jeffrey Brandon Morris has been a professor of political science at City College of the City University of New York and the University of Pennsylvania, as well as a visiting professor at Brooklyn Law School and professor of law at Touro Law Center in New York. He was chief research associate to Chief Justice Warren Burger on the U.S. Supreme Court in his role as head of the federal court system. He is the author or editor of fifteen other books, including the histories of four federal courts.

The Honorable William H. Webster was appointed to the Eighth Circuit in 1973 after having served the United States as a naval officer, federal prosecutor, and federal district judge. He left the court to become director of the Federal Bureau of Investigation in 1978 and subsequently served as director of the Central Intelligence Agency from 1987 to 1991. In 1991 he was awarded the Presidential Medal of Freedom by President George H. W. Bush.